LOCATION OF VIDEONOTES IN THE TEXT

(continued on the next page)

LOCATION OF VIDEONOTES IN THE TEXT (continued)

STARTING OUT WITH

JAVA™

From Control Structures through Objects

FOURTH EDITION

STARTING OUT WITH

JAVA™

From Control Structures through Objects

FOURTH EDITION

Tony Gaddis

Haywood Community College

Addison-Wesley

Boston   San Francisco   New York
London   Toronto   Sydney   Tokyo   Singapore   Madrid
Mexico City   Munich   Paris   Cape Town   Hong Kong   Montreal

Executive Editor	Michael Hirsch
Editorial Assistant	Stephanie Sellinger
Managing Editor	Jeffrey Holcomb
Production Supervisor	Heather McNally
Marketing Manager	Erin Davis
Marketing Coordinator	Kathryn Ferranti
Online Product Manager	Bethany Tidd
Senior Manufacturing Buyer	Carol Melville
Production Coordination	Kelly Ricci/Aptara®, Inc.
Composition, and Illustrations	Aptara®, Inc.
Copyeditor	Helen Greenberg
Proofreader	Sandy Bishop
Art Director	Linda Knowles
Cover Design	Joyce Consentino Wells
Cover Image	© ShutterStock

Access the latest information about Addison-Wesley Computer Science titles from our World Wide Web site: http://www.pearsonhighered.com/cs

Many of the designations used by manufacturers and sellers to distinguish their products are claimed as trademarks. Where those designations appear in this book, and Addison-Wesley was aware of a trademark claim, the designations have been printed in initial caps or all caps.

The programs and applications presented in this book have been included for their instructional value. They have been tested with care, but are not guaranteed for any particular purpose. The publisher does not offer any warranties or representations, nor does it accept any liabilities with respect to the programs or applications.

The interior of this book was composed in Adobe InDesign CS2. The basal text font is set in Sabon; the chapter titles, headings, running heads, and folios are all set in Stone Sans; the programming code is set in Courier 10 Pitch.

Library of Congress Cataloging-in-Publication Data

Gaddis, Tony.
 Starting out with Java: from control structures through objects/Tony Gaddis.—4th ed.
   p. cm.
 Includes index.
 ISBN-13: 978-0-13-608020-6
 ISBN-10: 0-13-608020-0
 1. Java (Computer program language) 2. Data structures (Computer science) 3. Object-oriented
programming (Computer science) I. Title.
 QA76.73.J38G333 2008b
 005.1'17—dc22

                                                                                    2008052703

Addison-Wesley
is an imprint of

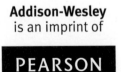

www.pearsonhighered.com

ISBN-13: 978-0-13-608020-6
ISBN-10:   0-13-608020-0

6 7 8 9 10—EB—13 12 11

Contents in Brief

Contents

Chapter 9   A Second Look at Classes and Objects   539

Chapter 10   Text Processing and More about Wrapper Classes   603

Chapter 11   Inheritance   659

Student CD-ROM:

Preface

Welcome to *Starting Out with Java: From Control Structures through Objects,* Fourth Edition. This book is intended for a one-semester or a two-quarter CS1 course. Although it is written for students with no prior programming background, even experienced students will benefit from its depth of detail.

Control Structures First, Then Objects

This text first introduces the student to the fundamentals of data types, input and output, control structures, methods, and objects created from standard library classes. Then the student learns to write his or her own classes and develop simple GUI applications.

Next, the student learns to use arrays of primitive types and reference types. After this, the student progresses through more advanced topics, such as inheritance, polymorphism, the creation and management of packages, advanced GUI applications, and recursion. From early in the book, applications are documented with `javadoc` comments. As the student progresses through the text, new `javadoc` tags are covered and demonstrated.

As with all the books in the *Starting Out with* series, the hallmark of this text is its clear, friendly, and easy-to-understand writing. In addition, it is rich in example programs that are concise and practical.

Changes in This Edition

This book's pedagogy, organization, and clear writing style remain the same as in the previous edition. Many improvements have been made, which are summarized here:

- **Improved Organization in Chapter 3** The section covering the `if-else-if` statement has been simplified and now appears immediately following the section on nested `if` statements. These sections have been rewritten to highlight the similarities between an `if-else-if` statement and a nested `if` statement.
- **New** *In the Spotlight* **Sections** Many of the chapters have new sections titled *In the Spotlight*. Each of these provides a programming problem and a detailed, step-by-step analysis showing the student how to solve it.
- **VideoNotes** An extensive series of videos have been developed to accompany this text. Throughout the book, VideoNote icons alert the student to the availability of videos on specific topics. Further, one Programming Challenge at the end of each chapter now has an accompanying VideoNote explaining how to develop the problem's solution. VideoNotes are available at www.aw.com/gaddis. In addition, VideoNotes are

available on CD if adopted for a course using a special ISBN. Contact your Pearson Education representative for details.

- **Additional Programming Problems** Additional Programming Challenge problems have been added to most chapters. Several of these are simple games that will challenge and motivate students.

Organization of the Text

The text teaches Java step-by-step. Each chapter covers a major set of topics and builds knowledge as students progress through the book. Although the chapters can be easily taught in their existing sequence, there is some flexibility. Figure P-1 shows chapter dependencies. Each box represents a chapter or a group of chapters. An arrow points from a chapter to the chapter that must be previously covered.

Figure P-1 Chapter Dependencies

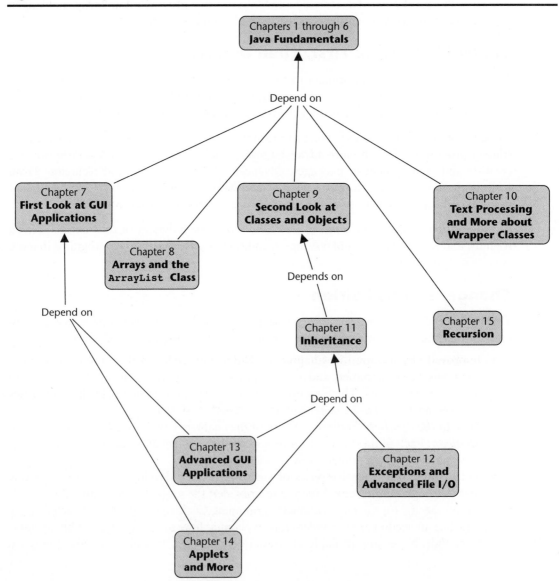

Brief Overview of Each Chapter

Chapter 1: Introduction to Computers and Java. This chapter provides an introduction to the field of computer science and covers the fundamentals of hardware, software, and programming languages. The elements of a program, such as key words, variables, operators, and punctuation, are discussed by examining a simple program. An overview of entering source code, compiling, and executing a program is presented. A brief history of Java is also given.

Chapter 2: Java Fundamentals. This chapter gets students started in Java by introducing data types, identifiers, variable declarations, constants, comments, program output, and simple arithmetic operations. The conventions of programming style are also introduced. Students learn to read console input with the Scanner class and with dialog boxes using JOptionPane.

Chapter 3: Decision Structures. In this chapter students explore relational operators and relational expressions and are shown how to control the flow of a program with the if, if-else, and if-else-if statements. Nested if statements, logical operators, the conditional operator, and the switch statement are also covered. The chapter discusses how to compare String objects with the equals, compareTo, equalsIgnoreCase, and compareToIgnoreCase methods. Formatting numeric output with the DecimalFormat class is covered, and the System.out.printf method is introduced.

Chapter 4: Loops and Files. This chapter covers Java's repetition control structures. The while loop, do-while loop, and for loop are taught, along with common uses for these devices. Counters, accumulators, running totals, sentinels, and other application-related topics are discussed. Simple file operations for reading and writing text files are included.

Chapter 5: Methods. In this chapter students learn how to write void methods, value-returning methods, and methods that do and do not accept arguments. The concept of functional decomposition is discussed.

Chapter 6: A First Look at Classes. This chapter introduces students to designing classes for the purpose of instantiating objects. Students learn about class fields and methods, and UML diagrams are introduced as a design tool. Then constructors and overloading are discussed. A BankAccount class is presented as a case study, and a section on object-oriented design is included. This section leads the students through the process of identifying classes and their responsibilities within a problem domain. There is also a section that briefly explains packages and the import statement.

Chapter 7: A First Look at GUI Applications. This chapter presents the basics of developing GUI applications with Swing. Fundamental Swing components and the basic concepts of event-driven programming are covered.

Chapter 8: Arrays and the ArrayList Class. In this chapter students learn to create and work with single and multi-dimensional arrays. Numerous array-processing techniques are demonstrated, such as summing the elements in an array, finding the highest and lowest values, and sequentially searching an array, are also discussed. Other topics, including ragged arrays and variable-length arguments (varargs), are also discussed. The ArrayList class is introduced, and Java's generic types are briefly discussed and demonstrated.

Chapter 9: A Second Look at Classes and Objects. This chapter shows students how to write classes with added capabilities. Static methods and fields, interaction between objects, passing objects as arguments, and returning objects from methods are discussed. Aggregation and the "has a" relationship is covered, as well as enumerated types. A section on object-oriented design shows how to use CRC cards to determine the collaborations among classes.

Chapter 10: Text Processing and More about Wrapper Classes. This chapter discusses the numeric and `Character` wrapper classes. Methods for converting numbers to strings, testing the case of characters, and converting the case of characters are covered. Autoboxing and unboxing are also discussed. More `String` class methods are covered, including using the `split` method to tokenize strings. The chapter also covers the `StringBuilder` and `StringTokenizer` classes.

Chapter 11: Inheritance. The study of classes continues in this chapter with the subjects of inheritance and polymorphism. The topics covered include superclasses, subclasses, how constructors work in inheritance, method overriding, polymorphism and dynamic binding, protected and package access, class hierarchies, abstract classes, abstract methods, and interfaces.

Chapter 12: Exceptions and Advanced File I/O. In this chapter students learn to develop enhanced error trapping techniques using exceptions. Handling exceptions is covered, as well as developing and throwing custom exceptions. The chapter discusses advanced techniques for working with sequential access, random access, text, and binary files.

Chapter 13: Advanced GUI Applications. This chapter continues the study of GUI application development. More advanced components, menu systems, and look-and-feel are covered.

Chapter 14: Applets and More. In this chapter students apply their knowledge of GUI development to the creation of applets. In addition to using Swing applet classes, AWT classes are discussed for portability. Drawing simple graphical shapes is discussed.

Chapter 15: Recursion. This chapter presents recursion as a problem-solving technique. Numerous examples of recursive methods are demonstrated.

Features of the Text

Concept Statements. Each major section of the text starts with a concept statement that concisely summarizes the focus of the section.

Example Programs. The text has an abundant number of complete and partial example programs, each designed to highlight the current topic. In most cases the programs are practical, real-world examples.

Program Output. Each example program is followed by a sample of its output, which shows students how the program functions.

Checkpoints. Checkpoints, highlighted by the checkmark icon, appear at intervals throughout each chapter. They are designed to check students' knowledge soon after learning a new topic.

NOTE: Notes appear at several places throughout the text. They are short explanations of interesting or often misunderstood points relevant to the topic at hand.

TIP: Tips advise the student on the best techniques for approaching different programming problems and appear regularly throughout the text.

WARNING! Warnings caution students about certain Java features, programming techniques, or practices that can lead to malfunctioning programs or lost data.

In the Spotlight. Many of the chapters provide an *In the Spotlight* section that presents a programming problem, along with detailed, step-by-step analysis showing the student how to solve it.

VideoNotes. A series of videos, developed specifically for this book, are available at www.aw.com/gaddis or on CD. Icons appear throughout the text alerting the student to videos about specific topics.

Case Studies. Case studies that simulate real-world business applications are introduced throughout the text and are provided on the accompanying Student CD.

Common Errors to Avoid. Each chapter provides a list of common errors and explanations of how to avoid them.

Review Questions and Exercises. Each chapter presents a thorough and diverse set of review questions and exercises. They include Multiple Choice and True/False, Find the Error, Algorithm Workbench, and Short Answer.

Programming Challenges. Each chapter offers a pool of programming challenges designed to solidify students' knowledge of topics at hand. In most cases the assignments present real-world problems to be solved.

Supplements

Student CD-ROM

Throughout the text, references to the Student CD are indicated with the CD icon. Resources located on the CD include:

- The source code for each example program in the book
- Appendixes A–L (listed in the Contents)
- A collection of seven valuable Case Studies (listed in the Contents)
- The Java™ Standard Edition Development Kit
- Numerous programming environments including jGRASP™, Eclipse™, TextPad™, NetBeans™, and DrJava

Many of these resources on the Student CD are also available at www.aw.com/cssupport

VideoNotes: See inside front of this book for a specific list of VideoNotes to accompany this book. The VideoNotes are available at www.aw.com/gaddis or in a special package with the book. Contact your Pearson Education sales representative for more details.

myCodeMate—Your Own T.A. Just a Click Away

Addison-Wesley's *MyCodeMate* is a book-specific Web resource that provides tutorial help and evaluation of student programs. Selected Programming Challenges throughout the book have been integrated into *MyCodeMate* (indicated by the *MyCodeMate* icon). Using this tool, students are able to write and compile programs from any computer with Internet access and receive guidance and feedback on how to proceed and on how to address compiler error messages. Instructors can track each student's progress on Programming Challenges from the text or can develop projects of their own. **A complimentary subscription to *MyCodeMate* is included when an access code is ordered packaged with a new copy of this text.** Subscriptions can also be purchased online. For more information about *MyCodeMate*, visit www.mycodemate.com, or contact your campus Pearson Education representative.

Instructor Resources

The following supplements are available to qualified instructors:

- Answers to all of the Review Questions
- Solutions for the Programming Challenges
- PowerPoint Presentation slides for each chapter
- Computerized Test Banks
- Source Code
- Lab Manual
- Student Files for the Lab Manual
- Solutions to the Lab Manual

Visit the Addison-Wesley Instructor Resource Center (www.pearsonhighered.com/irc) or send an e-mail to computing@aw.com for information on how to access these resources.

Acknowledgments

There have been many helping hands in the development and publication of this book. We would like to thank the following faculty reviewers for their helpful suggestions and expertise:

Ahmad Abuhejleh
University of Wisconsin, River Falls

Colin Archibald
Valencia Community College

Ijaz Awani
Savannah State University

Bill Bane
Tarleton State University

N. Dwight Barnette
Virginia Tech

Asoke Bhattacharyya
Saint Xavier University, Chicago

Marvin Bishop
Manhattan College

Heather Booth
University of Tennessee, Knoxville

David Boyd
Valdosta University

Julius Brandstatter
Golden Gate University

Kim Cannon
Greenville Tech

James Chegwidden
Tarrant County College

Kay Chen
Bucks County Community College

Brad Chilton
Tarleton State University

Diane Christie
University of Wisconsin, Stout

Cara Cocking
Marquette University

Walter C. Daugherity
Texas A & M University

Michael Doherty
University of the Pacific

Jeanne M. Douglas
University of Vermont

Sander Eller
California Polytechnic University, Pomona

Brooke Estabrook-Fishinghawk
Mesa Community College

Mike Fry
Lebanon Valley College

Georgia R. Grant
College of San Mateo

Chris Haynes
Indiana University

Ric Heishman
Northern Virginia Community College

Deedee Herrera
Dodge City Community College

Mary Hovik
Lehigh Carbon Community College

Brian Howard
DePauw University

Norm Jacobson
University of California, Irvine

Stephen Judd
University of Pennsylvania

Harry Lichtbach
Evergreen Valley College

Michael A. Long
California State University, Chico

Tim Margush
University of Akron

Blayne E. Mayfield
Oklahoma State University

Scott McLeod
Riverside Community College

Dean Mellas
Cerritos College

Georges Merx
San Diego Mesa College

Martin Meyers
California State University, Sacramento

Pati Milligan
Baylor University

Steve Newberry
Tarleton State University

Lynne O'Hanlon
Los Angeles Pierce College

Merrill Parker
Chattanooga State Technical Community College

Bryson R. Payne
North Georgia College and State University

Rodney Pearson
Mississippi State University

Daniel Spiegel
Kutztown University

Peter John Polito
Springfield College

Caroline St. Clair
North Central College

Charles Robert Putnam
California State University, Northridge

Karen Stanton
Los Medanos College

Y. B. Reddy
Grambling State University

Peter van der Goes
Rose State College

Carolyn Schauble
Colorado State University

Tuan A Vo
Mt. San Antonio College

Bonnie Smith
Fresno City College

Xiaoying Wang
University of Mississippi

I would like to thank my family for all the patience, love, and support they have shown me throughout this project. I would also like to thank everyone at Addison-Wesley for making the *Starting Out with* series so successful. I am extremely fortunate to have had Michael Hirsch as my editor and Erin Davis as marketing manager. I had a great team working on this book with me at Addison-Wesley, including Stephanie Sellinger, Jeff Holcomb, Heather McNally, Bethany Tidd, Carol Melville, and Linda Knowles. Thanks to you all!

About the Author

Tony Gaddis is the principal author of the *Starting Out with* series of textbooks. He has nearly two decades of experience teaching computer science courses, primarily at Haywood Community College. Tony is a highly acclaimed instructor who was previously selected as the North Carolina Community College "Teacher of the Year" and has received the Teaching Excellence award from the National Institute for Staff and Organizational Development. The *Starting Out with* series includes introductory textbooks covering programming logic and design, Alice, C++, Java™, Microsoft® Visual Basic®, and Python, all published by Addison-Wesley.

STARTING OUT WITH

JAVA™

From Control Structures through Objects

FOURTH EDITION

1 Introduction to Computers and Java

1.1 Introduction

This book teaches programming using Java. Java is a powerful language that runs on practically every type of computer. It can be used to create large applications or small programs, known as applets, that are part of a Web site. Before plunging right into learning Java, however, this chapter will review the fundamentals of computer hardware and software, and then take a broad look at computer programming in general.

1.2 Why Program?

CONCEPT: Computers can do many different jobs because they are programmable.

Every profession has tools that make the job easier to do. Carpenters use hammers, saws, and measuring tapes. Mechanics use wrenches, screwdrivers, and ratchets. Electronics technicians use probes, scopes, and meters. Some tools are unique and can be categorized as belonging to a single profession. For example, surgeons have certain tools that are designed specifically for surgical operations. Those tools probably aren't used by anyone other than surgeons. There are some tools, however, that are used in several professions. Screwdrivers, for instance, are used by mechanics, carpenters, and many others.

The computer is a tool used by so many professions that it cannot be easily categorized. It can perform so many different jobs that it is perhaps the most versatile tool ever made. To the accountant, computers balance books, analyze profits and losses, and prepare tax reports. To the factory worker, computers control manufacturing machines and track production. To the mechanic, computers analyze the various systems in an automobile and pinpoint hard-to-find problems. The computer can do such a wide variety of tasks because it can be *programmed*. It is a machine specifically designed to follow instructions. Because of the computer's programmability, it doesn't belong to any single profession. Computers are designed to do whatever job their programs, or *software*, tell them to do.

Computer programmers do a very important job. They create software that transforms computers into the specialized tools of many trades. Without programmers, the users of computers would have no software, and without software, computers would not be able to do anything.

Computer programming is both an art and a science. It is an art because every aspect of a program should be carefully designed. Here are a few of the things that must be designed for any real-world computer program:

- The logical flow of the instructions
- The mathematical procedures
- The layout of the programming statements
- The appearance of the screens
- The way information is presented to the user
- The program's "user friendliness"
- Manuals, help systems, and/or other forms of written documentation

There is also a science to programming. Because programs rarely work right the first time they are written, a lot of analyzing, experimenting, correcting, and redesigning is required. This demands patience and persistence of the programmer. Writing software demands discipline as well. Programmers must learn special languages such as Java because computers do not understand English or other human languages. Programming languages have strict rules that must be carefully followed.

Both the artistic and scientific nature of programming makes writing computer software like designing a car: Both cars and programs should be functional, efficient, powerful, easy to use, and pleasing to look at.

1.3   Computer Systems: Hardware and Software

CONCEPT: All computer systems consist of similar hardware devices and software components.

Hardware

Hardware refers to the physical components that a computer is made of. A computer, as we generally think of it, is not an individual device, but a system of devices. Like the instruments in a symphony orchestra, each device plays its own part. A typical computer system consists of the following major components:

- The central processing unit (CPU)
- Main memory
- Secondary storage devices
- Input devices
- Output devices

The organization of a computer system is shown in Figure 1-1.

Figure 1-1   The organization of a computer system

Let's take a closer look at each of these devices.

The CPU

At the heart of a computer is its *central processing unit*, or *CPU*. The CPU's job is to fetch instructions, follow the instructions, and produce some resulting data. Internally, the central processing unit consists of two parts: the *control unit* and the *arithmetic and logic unit (ALU)*. The control unit coordinates all of the computer's operations. It is responsible for determining where to get the next instruction and regulating the other major components of the computer with control signals. The arithmetic and logic unit, as its name suggests, is designed to perform mathematical operations. The organization of the CPU is shown in Figure 1-2.

Figure 1-2   The organization of the CPU

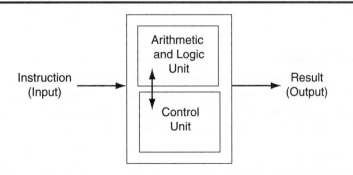

A program is a sequence of instructions stored in the computer's memory. When a computer is running a program, the CPU is engaged in a process known formally as the *fetch/decode/execute cycle*. The steps in the fetch/decode/execute cycle are as follows:

Fetch   The CPU's control unit fetches, from main memory, the next instruction in the sequence of program instructions.

Decode   The instruction is encoded in the form of a number. The control unit decodes the instruction and generates an electronic signal.

Execute The signal is routed to the appropriate component of the computer (such as the ALU, a disk drive, or some other device). The signal causes the component to perform an operation.

These steps are repeated as long as there are instructions to perform.

Main Memory

Commonly known as *random-access memory*, or *RAM*, the computer's main memory is a device that holds information. Specifically, RAM holds the sequences of instructions in the programs that are running and the data those programs are using.

Memory is divided into sections that hold an equal amount of data. Each section is made of eight "switches" that may be either on or off. A switch in the on position usually represents the number 1, while a switch in the off position usually represents the number 0. The computer stores data by setting the switches in a memory location to a pattern that represents a character or a number. Each of these switches is known as a *bit*, which stands for *binary digit*. Each section of memory, which is a collection of eight bits, is known as a *byte*. Each byte is assigned a unique number known as an *address*. The addresses are ordered from lowest to highest. A byte is identified by its address in much the same way a post office box is identified by an address. Figure 1-3 shows a series of bytes with their addresses. In the illustration, sample data is stored in memory. The number 149 is stored in the byte at address 16, and the number 72 is stored in the byte at address 23.

RAM is usually a volatile type of memory, used only for temporary storage. When the computer is turned off, the contents of RAM are erased.

Figure 1-3   Memory bytes and their addresses

0	1	2	3	4	5	6	7	8	9
10	11	12	13	14	15	16 149	17	18	19
20	21	22	23 72	24	25	26	27	28	29

Secondary Storage

Secondary storage is a type of memory that can hold data for long periods of time—even when there is no power to the computer. Frequently used programs are stored in secondary memory and loaded into main memory as needed. Important data, such as word processing documents, payroll data, and inventory figures, is saved to secondary storage as well.

The most common type of secondary storage device is the disk drive. A *disk drive* stores data by magnetically encoding it onto a circular disk. *Hard drives*, which are the most common type of disk drives, are capable of storing very large amounts of data and can access data quickly. Most computers have a hard drive mounted inside their case. External hard drives are also available which connect to one of the computer's communication ports.

External hard drives can be used to create backup copies of important data or to move data to another computer.

In addition to external hard drives, many types of devices have been created for copying data, and for moving it to other computers. For many years floppy disk drives were popular. A *floppy disk drive* records data onto a small floppy disk which can be removed from the drive. Floppy disks have many disadvantages, however. They hold only a small amount of data, are slow to access data, and are sometimes unreliable. The use of floppy disk drives has declined dramatically in recent years, in favor of superior devices such as USB drives. *USB drives* are small devices that plug into the computer's USB (Universal Serial Bus) port, and appear to the system as a disk drive. These drives do not actually contain a disk, however. They store data in a special type of memory known as *flash memory*. USB drives are inexpensive, reliable, and small enough to be carried in your pocket.

Optical devices such as the *CD* (compact disc) and the *DVD* (digital versatile disc) are also popular for data storage. Data is not recorded magnetically on an optical disc, but is encoded as a series of pits on the disc surface. CD and DVD drives use a laser to detect the pits and thus read the encoded data. Optical discs hold large amounts of data, and because recordable CD and DVD drives are now commonplace, they make a good medium for creating backup copies of data.

Input Devices

Input is any data the computer collects from the outside world. The device that collects the data and sends it to the computer is called an *input device*. Common input devices are the keyboard, mouse, scanner, and digital camera. Disk drives, optical drives, and USB drives can also be considered input devices because programs and data are retrieved from them and loaded into the computer's memory.

Output Devices

Output is any data the computer sends to the outside world. It might be a sales report, a list of names, or a graphic image. The data is sent to an output device, which formats and presents it. Common output devices are monitors and printers. Disk drives, USB drives, and CD recorders can also be considered output devices because the CPU sends data to them in order to be saved.

Software

As previously mentioned, software refers to the programs that run on a computer. There are two general categories of software: operating systems and application software. An operating system is a set of programs that manages the computer's hardware devices and controls their processes. Most all modern operating systems are multitasking, which means they are capable of running multiple programs at once. Through a technique called time sharing, a multitasking system divides the allocation of hardware resources and the attention of the CPU among all the executing programs. UNIX, Linux, Mac OS X and Windows are multitasking operating systems.

Application software refers to programs that make the computer useful to the user. These programs solve specific problems or perform general operations that satisfy the needs of the user. Word processing, spreadsheet, and database packages are all examples of application software.

Checkpoint

1.1   Why is the computer used by so many different people, in so many different professions?

1.2   List the five major hardware components of a computer system.

1.3   Internally, the CPU consists of what two units?

1.4   Describe the steps in the fetch/decode/execute cycle.

1.5   What is a memory address? What is its purpose?

1.6   Explain why computers have both main memory and secondary storage.

1.7   What does the term "multitasking" mean?

1.4 Programming Languages

CONCEPT: A program is a set of instructions a computer follows in order to perform a task. A programming language is a special language used to write computer programs.

What Is a Program?

Computers are designed to follow instructions. A computer program is a set of instructions that enable the computer to solve a problem or perform a task. For example, suppose we want the computer to calculate someone's gross pay. The following is a list of things the computer should do to perform this task.

1. Display a message on the screen: "How many hours did you work?"
2. Allow the user to enter the number of hours worked.
3. Once the user enters a number, store it in memory.
4. Display a message on the screen: "How much do you get paid per hour?"
5. Allow the user to enter an hourly pay rate.
6. Once the user enters a number, store it in memory.
7. Once both the number of hours worked and the hourly pay rate are entered, multiply the two numbers and store the result in memory.
8. Display a message on the screen that shows the amount of money earned. The message must include the result of the calculation performed in Step 7.

Collectively, these instructions are called an *algorithm*. An algorithm is a set of well-defined steps for performing a task or solving a problem. Notice that these steps are sequentially ordered. Step 1 should be performed before Step 2, and so forth. It is important that these instructions be performed in their proper sequence.

Although you and I might easily understand the instructions in the pay-calculating algorithm, it is not ready to be executed on a computer. A computer's CPU can only process instructions that are written in *machine language*. If you were to look at a machine language program, you would see a stream of binary numbers (numbers consisting of only 1s and 0s). The binary numbers form machine language instructions, which the CPU interprets as commands. Here is an example of what a machine language instruction might look like:

1011010000000101

As you can imagine, the process of encoding an algorithm in machine language is very tedious and difficult. In addition, each different type of CPU has its own machine language. If you wrote a machine language program for computer A and then wanted to run it on computer B, which has a different type of CPU, you would have to rewrite the program in computer B's machine language.

Programming languages, which use words instead of numbers, were invented to ease the task of programming. A program can be written in a programming language, which is much easier to understand than machine language, and then translated into machine language. Programmers use software to perform this translation. Many programming languages have been created. Table 1-1 lists a few of the well-known ones.

Table 1-1   Programming languages

Language	Description
BASIC	Beginners All-purpose Symbolic Instruction Code is a general-purpose, procedural programming language. It was originally designed to be simple enough for beginners to learn.
FORTRAN	FORmula TRANslator is a procedural language designed for programming complex mathematical algorithms.
COBOL	Common Business-Oriented Language is a procedural language designed for business applications.
Pascal	Pascal is a structured, general-purpose, procedural language designed primarily for teaching programming.
C	C is a structured, general-purpose, procedural language developed at Bell Laboratories.
C++	Based on the C language, C++ offers object-oriented features not found in C. C++ was also invented at Bell Laboratories.
C#	Pronounced "C sharp." It is a language invented by Microsoft for developing applications based on the Microsoft .NET platform.
Java	Java is an object-oriented language invented at Sun Microsystems. It may be used to develop stand-alone applications that operate on a single computer, applications that run over the Internet from a Web server, and applets that run in a Web browser.
JavaScript	JavaScript is a programming language that can be used in a Web site to perform simple operations. Despite its name, JavaScript is not related to Java.
Perl	A general-purpose programming language used widely on Internet servers.
PHP	A programming language used primarily for developing Web server applications and dynamic Web pages.
Python	Python is an object-oriented programming language used in both business and academia. Many popular Web sites contain features developed in Python.
Ruby	Ruby is a simple but powerful object-oriented programming language. It can be used for a variety of purposes, from small utility programs to large Web applications.
Visual Basic	Visual Basic is a Microsoft programming language and software development environment that allows programmers to create Windows-based applications quickly.

A History of Java

In 1991 a team was formed at Sun Microsystems to speculate about the important technological trends that might emerge in the near future. The team, which was named the Green Team, concluded that computers would merge with consumer appliances. Their first project was to develop a hand-held device named *7 (pronounced star seven) that could be used to control a variety of home entertainment devices. In order for the unit to work, it had to use a programming language that could be processed by all the devices it controlled. This presented a problem because different brands of consumer devices use different processors, each with its own machine language.

Because no such universal language existed, James Gosling, the team's lead engineer, created one. Programs written in this language, which was originally named Oak, were not translated into the machine language of a specific processor, but were translated into an intermediate language known as *byte code*. Another program would then translate the byte code into machine language that could be executed by the processor in a specific consumer device.

Unfortunately, the technology developed by the Green Team was ahead of its time. No customers could be found, mostly because the computer-controlled consumer appliance industry was just beginning. But rather than abandoning their hard work and moving on to other projects, the team saw another opportunity: the Internet. The Internet is a perfect environment for a universal programming language such as Oak. It consists of numerous different computer platforms connected together in a single network.

To demonstrate the effectiveness of their language, which was renamed Java, the team used it to develop a Web browser. The browser, named HotJava, was able to download and run small Java programs known as applets. This gave the browser the capability to display animation and interact with the user. HotJava was demonstrated at the 1995 SunWorld conference before a wowed audience. Later the announcement was made that Netscape would incorporate Java technology into its Navigator browser. Other Internet companies rapidly followed, increasing the acceptance and the influence of the Java language. Today, Java is very popular for developing not only applets for the Internet, but also stand-alone applications.

Java Applications and Applets

There are two types of programs that may be created with Java: applications and applets. An application is a stand-alone program that runs on your computer. You have probably used several applications already, such as word processors, spreadsheets, database managers, and graphics programs. Although Java may be used to write these types of applications, other languages such as C, C++, and Visual Basic are also used.

In the previous section you learned that Java may also be used to create applets. The term "applet" refers to a small application, in the same way that the term "piglet" refers to a small pig. Unlike applications, an applet is designed to be transmitted over the Internet from a Web server, and then executed in a Web browser. Applets are important because they can be used to extend the capabilities of a Web page significantly.

Web pages are normally written in Hypertext Markup Language (HTML). HTML is limited, however, because it merely describes the content and layout of a Web page. HTML does not have sophisticated abilities such as performing math calculations and interacting with the user. A Web designer can write a Java applet to perform operations that are normally performed by an application, and embed it in a Web site. When someone visits the Web site, the applet is downloaded to the visitor's browser and executed.

Security

Any time content is downloaded from a Web server to a visitor's computer, security is an important concern. Because Java is a full-featured programming language, at first you might be suspicious of any Web site that transmits an applet to your computer. After all, couldn't a Java applet do harmful things, such as deleting the contents of the hard drive or transmitting private information to another computer? Fortunately, the answer is no. Web browsers run Java applets in a secure environment within your computer's memory and do not allow them to access resources, such as a disk drive, that are outside that environment.

1.5 What Is a Program Made of?

CONCEPT: There are certain elements that are common to all programming languages.

Language Elements

All programming languages have some things in common. Table 1-2 lists the common elements you will find in almost every language.

Table 1-2 The common elements of a programming language

Language Element	Description
Key Words	These are words that have a special meaning in the programming language. They may be used for their intended purpose only. Key words are also known as *reserved words*.
Operators	Operators are symbols or words that perform operations on one or more operands. An operand is usually an item of data, such as a number.
Punctuation	Most programming languages require the use of punctuation characters. These characters serve specific purposes, such as marking the beginning or ending of a statement, or separating items in a list.
Programmer-Defined Names	Unlike key words, which are part of the programming language, these are words or names that are defined by the programmer. They are used to identify storage locations in memory and parts of the program that are created by the programmer. Programmer-defined names are often called *identifiers*.
Syntax	These are rules that must be followed when writing a program. Syntax dictates how key words and operators may be used, and where punctuation symbols must appear.

Let's look at an example Java program and identify an instance of each of these elements. Code Listing 1-1 shows the code listing with each line numbered.

> **NOTE:** The line numbers are not part of the program. They are included to help point out specific parts of the program.

Code Listing 1-1   `Payroll.java`

```
 1  public class Payroll
 2  {
 3      public static void main(String[] args)
 4      {
 5          int hours = 40;
 6          double grossPay, payRate = 25.0;
 7
 8          grossPay = hours * payRate;
 9          System.out.println("Your gross pay is $" + grossPay);
10      }
11  }
```

Key Words (Reserved Words)

Two of Java's key words appear in line 1: `public` and `class`. In line 3 the words `public`, `static`, and `void` are all key words. The word `int` in line 5 and `double` in line 6 are also key words. These words, which are always written in lowercase, each have a special meaning in Java and can only be used for their intended purpose. As you will see, the programmer is allowed to make up his or her own names for certain things in a program. Key words, however, are reserved and cannot be used for anything other than their designated purpose. Part of learning a programming language is learning the commonly used key words, what they mean, and how to use them.

Table 1-3 shows a list of the Java key words.

Table 1-3   The Java key words

abstract	const	final	int	public	throw
assert	continue	finally	interface	return	throws
boolean	default	float	long	short	transient
break	do	for	native	static	true
byte	double	goto	new	strictfp	try
case	else	if	null	super	void
catch	enum	implements	package	switch	volatile
char	extends	import	private	synchronized	while
class	false	instanceof	protected	this	

Programmer-Defined Names

The words `hours`, `payRate`, and `grossPay` that appear in the program in lines 5, 6, 8, and 9 are programmer-defined names. They are not part of the Java language but are names made up by the programmer. In this particular program, these are the names of variables. As you will learn later in this chapter, variables are the names of memory locations that may hold data.

Operators

In line 8 the following line appears:

```
grossPay = hours * payRate;
```

The = and * symbols are both operators. They perform operations on items of data, known as operands. The * operator multiplies its two operands, which in this example are the variables `hours` and `payRate`. The = symbol is called the assignment operator. It takes the value of the expression that appears at its right and stores it in the variable whose name appears at its left. In this example, the = operator stores in the `grossPay` variable the result of the `hours` variable multiplied by the `payRate` variable. In other words, the statement says, "the `grossPay` variable is assigned the value of `hours` times `payRate`."

Punctuation

Notice that lines 5, 6, 8, and 9 end with a semicolon. A semicolon in Java is similar to a period in English: It marks the end of a complete sentence (or statement, as it is called in programming jargon). Semicolons do not appear at the end of every line in a Java program, however. There are rules that govern where semicolons are required and where they are not. Part of learning Java is learning where to place semicolons and other punctuation symbols.

Lines and Statements

Often, the contents of a program are thought of in terms of lines and statements. A *line* is just that—a single line as it appears in the body of a program. Code Listing 1-1 is shown with each of its lines numbered. Most of the lines contain something meaningful; however, line 7 is empty. Blank lines are only used to make a program more readable.

A statement is a complete instruction that causes the computer to perform some action. Here is the statement that appears in line 9 of Code Listing 1-1:

```
System.out.println("Your gross pay is $" + grossPay);
```

This statement causes the computer to display a message on the screen. Statements can be a combination of key words, operators, and programmer-defined names. Statements often occupy only one line in a program, but sometimes they are spread out over more than one line.

Variables

The most fundamental way that a Java program stores an item of data in memory is with a variable. A *variable* is a named storage location in the computer's memory. The data stored in a variable may change while the program is running (hence the name "variable"). Notice that in Code Listing 1-1 the programmer-defined names `hours`, `payRate`, and `grossPay` appear in several places. All three of these are the names of variables. The hours variable is used to store the number of hours the user has worked. The payRate variable stores the user's hourly pay rate. The grossPay variable holds the result of hours multiplied by payRate, which is the user's gross pay.

Variables are symbolic names made up by the programmer that represent locations in the computer's random-access memory (RAM). When data is stored in a variable, it is actually stored in RAM. Assume that a program has a variable named length. Figure 1-4 illustrates the way the variable name represents a memory location.

In Figure 1-4, the variable length is holding the value 72. The number 72 is actually stored in RAM at address 23, but the name length symbolically represents this storage location. If it helps, you can think of a variable as a box that holds data. In Figure 1-4, the number 72 is stored in the box named length. Only one item may be stored in the box at any given time. If the program stores another value in the box, it will take the place of the number 72.

Figure 1-4   A variable name represents a location in memory

The Compiler and the Java Virtual Machine

When a Java program is written, it must be typed into the computer and saved to a file. A *text editor*, which is similar to a word processing program, is used for this task. The Java programming statements written by the programmer are called *source code*, and the file they are saved in is called a *source file*. Java source files end with the *.java* extension.

After the programmer saves the source code to a file, he or she runs the Java compiler. A *compiler* is a program that translates source code into an executable form. During the translation process, the compiler uncovers any syntax errors that may be in the program. *Syntax errors* are mistakes that the programmer has made that violate the rules of the programming language. These errors must be corrected before the compiler can translate the source code. Once the program is free of syntax errors, the compiler creates another file that holds the translated instructions.

Most programming language compilers translate source code directly into files that contain machine language instructions. These files are called *executable files* because they may be executed directly by the computer's CPU. The Java compiler, however, translates a Java source file into a file that contains byte code instructions. Byte code instructions are not machine language, and therefore cannot be directly executed by the CPU. Instead, they are executed by the Java Virtual Machine. The *Java Virtual Machine* (JVM) is a program that reads Java byte code instructions and executes them as they are read. For this reason, the JVM is often called an interpreter, and Java is often referred to as an interpreted language. Figure 1-5 illustrates the process of writing a Java program, compiling it to byte code, and running it.

Although Java byte code is not machine language for a CPU, it can be considered as machine language for the JVM. You can think of the JVM as a program that simulates a computer whose machine language is Java byte code.

Portability

The term *portable* means that a program may be written on one type of computer and then run on a wide variety of computers, with little or no modification necessary. Because Java byte code is the same on all computers, compiled Java programs are highly portable. In fact, a compiled Java program may be run on any computer that has a Java Virtual Machine. Figure 1-6 illustrates the concept of a compiled Java program running on Windows, Linux, Mac, and UNIX computers.

With most other programming languages, portability is achieved by the creation of a compiler for each type of computer that the language is to run on. For example, in order for the C++ language to be supported by Windows, Linux, and Mac computers, a separate C++ compiler must be created for each of those environments. Compilers are very complex programs, and more difficult to develop than interpreters. For this reason, a Java Virtual Machine has been developed for many types of computers.

Figure 1-5
Program development process

1. The programmer uses a text editor to create a Java source code file.

Text Editor

→

Source File

2. The programmer runs the compiler, which translates the source code file into a byte code file.

Java Compiler

→

Byte Code File

3. The Java Virtual Machine reads and executes each byte code instruction.

Java Virtual Machine

Figure 1-6 Java byte code may be run on any computer with a Java Virtual Machine

Source File

→

Java Compiler

→

Byte Code File

Java Virtual Machine for Windows

Java Virtual Machine for Linux

Java Virtual Machine for Mac

Java Virtual Machine for UNIX

Java Software Editions

The software that you use to create Java programs is referred to as the *JDK* (Java Development Kit) or the *SDK* (Software Development Kit). There are the following different editions of the JDK available from Sun Microsystems:

- *Java SE*—The Java Standard Edition provides all the essential software tools necessary for writing Java applications and applets.
- *Java EE*—The Java Enterprise Edition provides tools for creating large business applications that employ servers and provide services over the Web.
- *Java ME*—The Java Micro Edition provides a small, highly optimized runtime environment for consumer products such as cell phones, pagers, and appliances.

These editions of Java may be downloaded from Sun Microsystems at:

> http://java.sun.com

Compiling and Running a Java Program

Compiling a Java program is a simple process. Using the Sun JDK, which is included on the Student CD that accompanies this book, go to your operating system's command prompt.

> **TIP:** In Windows click Start, go to All Programs, and then go to Accessories. Click Command Prompt on the Accessories menu. A command prompt window should open.

VideoNote
Compiling and Running a Java Program

At the operating system command prompt, make sure you are in the same directory or folder where the Java program that you want to compile is located. Then, use the `javac` command, in the following form:

```
javac Filename
```

`Filename` is the name of a file that contains the Java source code. As mentioned earlier, this file has the *.java* extension. For example, if you want to compile the *Payroll.java* file, you would execute the following command:

```
javac Payroll.java
```

This command runs the compiler. If the file contains any syntax errors, you will see one or more error messages and the compiler will not translate the file to byte code. When this happens you must open the source file in a text editor and fix the error. Then you can run the compiler again. If the file has no syntax errors, the compiler will translate it to byte code. Byte code is stored in a file with the *.class* extension, so the byte code for the *Payroll.java* file will be stored in *Payroll.class*, which will be in the same directory or folder as the source file.

To run the Java program, you use the `java` command in the following form:

```
java ClassFilename
```

`ClassFilename` is the name of the *.class* file that you wish to execute. However, you do not type the *.class* extension. For example, to run the program that is stored in the *Payroll.class* file, you would enter the following command:

```
java Payroll
```

This command runs the Java interpreter (the JVM) and executes the program.

Integrated Development Environments

VideoNote
Using an IDE

In addition to the command prompt programs, there are also several Java integrated development environments (IDEs). These environments consist of a text editor, compiler, debugger, and other utilities integrated into a package with a single set of menus. A program is compiled and executed with a single click of a button, or by selecting a single item from a menu. Figure 1-7 shows a screen from the jGRASP IDE.

Figure 1-7 An integrated development environment (IDE)

 Checkpoint

1.8 Describe the difference between a key word and a programmer-defined symbol.

1.9 Describe the difference between operators and punctuation symbols.

1.10 Describe the difference between a program line and a statement.

1.11 Why are variables called "variable"?

1.12 What happens to a variable's current contents when a new value is stored there?

1.13 What is a compiler?

1.14 What is a syntax error?

1.15 What is byte code?

1.16 What is the JVM?

1.6 The Programming Process

CONCEPT: The programming process consists of several steps, which include design, creation, testing, and debugging activities.

Now that you have been introduced to what a program is, it's time to consider the process of creating a program. Quite often when inexperienced students are given programming assignments, they have trouble getting started because they don't know what to do first. If you find yourself in this dilemma, the following steps may help.

1. Clearly define what the program is to do.
2. Visualize the program running on the computer.
3. Use design tools to create a model of the program.
4. Check the model for logical errors.
5. Enter the code and compile it.
6. Correct any errors found during compilation. Repeat Steps 5 and 6 as many times as necessary.
7. Run the program with test data for input.
8. Correct any runtime errors found while running the program. Repeat Steps 5 through 8 as many times as necessary.
9. Validate the results of the program.

These steps emphasize the importance of planning. Just as there are good ways and bad ways to paint a house, there are good ways and bad ways to create a program. A good program always begins with planning. With the pay-calculating algorithm that was presented earlier in this chapter serving as our example, let's look at each of the steps in more detail.

1. Clearly define what the program is to do

This step commonly requires you to identify the purpose of the program, the data that is to be input, the processing that is to take place, and the desired output. Let's examine each of these requirements for the pay-calculating algorithm.

Purpose   To calculate the user's gross pay.

Input   Number of hours worked, hourly pay rate.

Process   Multiply number of hours worked by hourly pay rate. The result is the user's gross pay.

Output   Display a message indicating the user's gross pay.

2. Visualize the program running on the computer

Before you create a program on the computer, you should first create it in your mind. Try to imagine what the computer screen will look like while the program is running. If it helps, draw pictures of the screen, with sample input and output, at various points in the program. For instance, Figure 1-8 shows the screen we might want produced by a program that implements the pay-calculating algorithm.

Figure 1-8   Screen produced by the pay-calculating algorithm

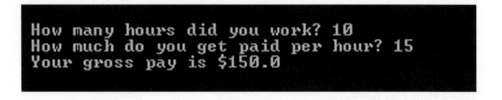

```
How many hours did you work? 10
How much do you get paid per hour? 15
Your gross pay is $150.0
```

In this step, you must put yourself in the shoes of the user. What messages should the program display? What questions should it ask? By addressing these concerns, you can determine most of the program's output.

3. Use design tools to create a model of the program

While planning a program, the programmer uses one or more design tools to create a model of the program. For example, *pseudocode* is a cross between human language and a programming language and is especially helpful when designing an algorithm. Although the computer can't understand pseudocode, programmers often find it helpful to write an algorithm in a language that's "almost" a programming language, but still very similar to natural language. For example, here is pseudocode that describes the pay-calculating algorithm:

> *Get payroll data.*
> *Calculate gross pay.*
> *Display gross pay.*

Although this pseudocode gives a broad view of the program, it doesn't reveal all the program's details. A more detailed version of the pseudocode follows:

> *Display "How many hours did you work?".*
> *Input hours.*
> *Display "How much do you get paid per hour?".*
> *Input rate.*
> *Store the value of hours times rate in the pay variable.*
> *Display the value in the pay variable.*

Notice that the pseudocode uses statements that look more like commands than the English statements that describe the algorithm in Section 1.4. The pseudocode even names variables and describes mathematical operations.

4. Check the model for logical errors

Logical errors are mistakes that cause the program to produce erroneous results. Once a model of the program is assembled, it should be checked for these errors. For example, if pseudocode is used, the programmer should trace through it, checking the logic of each step. If an error is found, the model can be corrected before the next step is attempted.

5. Enter the code and compile it

Once a model of the program has been created, checked, and corrected, the programmer is ready to write source code on the computer. The programmer saves the source code to a file and begins the process of compiling it. During this step the compiler will find any syntax errors that may exist in the program.

6. Correct any errors found during compilation. Repeat Steps 5 and 6 as many times as necessary

If the compiler reports any errors, they must be corrected. Steps 5 and 6 must be repeated until the program is free of compile-time errors.

7. Run the program with test data for input

Once an executable file is generated, the program is ready to be tested for runtime errors. A runtime error is an error that occurs while the program is running. These are usually logical errors, such as mathematical mistakes.

Testing for runtime errors requires that the program be executed with sample data or sample input. The sample data should be such that the correct output can be predicted. If the program does not produce the correct output, a logical error is present in the program.

8. Correct any runtime errors found while running the program. Repeat Steps 5 through 8 as many times as necessary

When runtime errors are found in a program, they must be corrected. You must identify the step where the error occurred and determine the cause. If an error is a result of incorrect logic (such as an improperly stated math formula), you must correct the statement or statements involved in the logic. If an error is due to an incomplete understanding of the program requirements, then you must restate the program purpose and modify the program model and source code. The program must then be saved, recompiled, and retested. This means Steps 5 though 8 must be repeated until the program reliably produces satisfactory results.

9. Validate the results of the program

When you believe you have corrected all the runtime errors, enter test data and determine if the program solves the original problem.

Software Engineering

The field of software engineering encompasses the whole process of crafting computer software. It includes designing, writing, testing, debugging, documenting, modifying, and maintaining complex software development projects. Like traditional engineers, software engineers use a number of tools in their craft. Here are a few examples:

- Program specifications
- Diagrams of screen output
- Diagrams representing the program components and the flow of data
- Pseudocode
- Examples of expected input and desired output
- Special software designed for testing programs

Most commercial software applications are large and complex. Usually a team of programmers, not a single individual, develops them. It is important that the program requirements be thoroughly analyzed and divided into subtasks that are handled by individual teams, or individuals within a team.

Checkpoint

1.17 What four items should you identify when defining what a program is to do?

1.18 What does it mean to "visualize a program running"? What is the value of such an activity?

1.19 What is pseudocode?

1.20 Describe what a compiler does with a program's source code.

1.21 What is a runtime error?

1.22 Is a syntax error (such as misspelling a key word) found by the compiler or when the program is running?

1.23 What is the purpose of testing a program with sample data or input?

1.7 Object-Oriented Programming

CONCEPT: Java is an object-oriented programming (OOP) language. OOP is a method of software development that has its own practices, concepts, and vocabulary.

There are primarily two methods of programming in use today: procedural and object-oriented. The earliest programming languages were procedural, meaning a program was made of one or more procedures. A *procedure* is a set of programming statements that, together, perform a specific task. The statements might gather input from the user, manipulate data stored in the computer's memory, and perform calculations or any other operation necessary to complete its task.

Procedures typically operate on data items that are separate from the procedures. In a procedural program, the data items are commonly passed from one procedure to another, as shown in Figure 1-9.

Figure 1-9 Data is passed among procedures

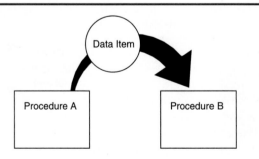

As you might imagine, the focus of procedural programming is on the creation of procedures that operate on the program's data. The separation of data and the code that operates on the data often leads to problems, however. For example, the data is stored in a particular format, which consists of variables and more complex structures that are created from variables. The procedures that operate on the data must be designed with that format in mind. But, what happens if the format of the data is altered? Quite often, a program's specifications change, resulting in a redesigned data format. When the structure of the data changes, the code that operates on the data must also be changed to accept the new format. This results in added work for programmers and a greater opportunity for bugs to appear in the code.

This has helped influence the shift from procedural programming to object-oriented programming (OOP). Whereas procedural programming is centered on creating procedures, object-oriented programming is centered on creating objects. An object is a software entity that contains data and procedures. The data contained in an object is known as the object's *attributes*. The procedures, or behaviors, that an object performs are known as the object's *methods*. The object is, conceptually, a self-contained unit consisting of data (attributes) and procedures (methods). This is illustrated in Figure 1-10.

OOP addresses the problem of code/data separation through encapsulation and data hiding. *Encapsulation* refers to the combining of data and code into a single object. *Data hiding* refers to an object's ability to hide its data from code that is outside the object. Only the object's methods may then directly access and make changes to the object's data. An object typically hides its data, but allows outside code to access the methods that operate on the data. As shown in Figure 1-11, the object's methods provide programming statements outside the object indirect access to the object's data.

When an object's internal data is hidden from outside code and access to that data is restricted to the object's methods, the data is protected from accidental corruption. In addition, the programming code outside the object does not need to know about the format

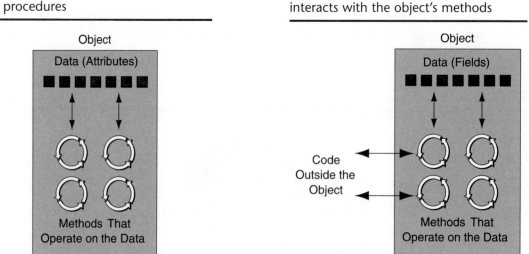

Figure 1-10   An object contains data and procedures

Figure 1-11   Code outside the object interacts with the object's methods or internal structure of the object's data. The code only needs to interact with the object's methods. When a programmer changes the structure of an object's internal data, he or she also modifies the object's methods so they may properly operate on the data. The way in which outside code interacts with the methods, however, does not change.

These are just a few of the benefits of object-oriented programming. Because Java is fully object-oriented, you will learn much more about OOP practices, concepts, and terms as you progress through this book.

Checkpoint

1.24   In procedural programming, what two parts of a program are typically separated?

1.25   What are an object's attributes?

1.26   What are an object's methods?

1.27   What is encapsulation?

1.28   What is data hiding?

Review Questions and Exercises

Multiple Choice

1.   This part of the computer fetches instructions, carries out the operations commanded by the instructions, and produces some outcome or resultant information.
     a. memory
     b. CPU
     c. secondary storage
     d. input device

2.   A byte is made up of eight
     a. CPUs
     b. addresses
     c. variables
     d. bits

3.   Each byte is assigned a unique
     a. address
     b. CPU
     c. bit
     d. variable

4.   This type of memory can hold data for long periods of time—even when there is no power to the computer.
     a. RAM
     b. primary storage
     c. secondary storage
     d. CPU storage

5. If you were to look at a machine language program, you would see _____.
   a. Java source code
   b. a stream of binary numbers
   c. English words
   d. circuits

6. This type of program is designed to be transmitted over the Internet and run in a Web browser.
   a. application
   b. applet
   c. machine language
   d. source code

7. These are words that have a special meaning in the programming language.
   a. punctuation
   b. programmer-defined names
   c. key words
   d. operators

8. These are symbols or words that perform operations on one or more operands.
   a. punctuation
   b. programmer-defined names
   c. key words
   d. operators

9. These characters serve specific purposes, such as marking the beginning or ending of a statement, or separating items in a list.
   a. punctuation
   b. programmer-defined names
   c. key words
   d. operators

10. These are words or names that are used to identify storage locations in memory and parts of the program that are created by the programmer.
    a. punctuation
    b. programmer-defined names
    c. key words
    d. operators

11. These are the rules that must be followed when writing a program.
    a. syntax
    b. punctuation
    c. key words
    d. operators

12. This is a named storage location in the computer's memory.
    a. class
    b. key word
    c. variable
    d. operator

13. The Java compiler generates _____.
    a. machine code
    b. byte code
    c. source code
    d. HTML

14. JVM stands for _____.
    a. Java Variable Machine
    b. Java Variable Method
    c. Java Virtual Method
    d. Java Virtual Machine

Find the Error

1. The following pseudocode algorithm has an error. The program is supposed to ask the user for the length and width of a rectangular room, and then display the room's area. The program must multiply the width by the length in order to determine the area. Find the error.

   area = width × length.
   Display "What is the room's width?".
   Input width.
   Display "What is the room's length?".
   Input length.
   Display area.

Algorithm Workbench

Write pseudocode algorithms for the programs described as follows:

1. **Available Credit**

   A program that calculates a customer's available credit should ask the user for the following:

   - The customer's maximum amount of credit
   - The amount of credit used by the customer

   Once these items have been entered, the program should calculate and display the customer's available credit. You can calculate available credit by subtracting the amount of credit used from the maximum amount of credit.

2. **Sales Tax**

   A program that calculates the total of a retail sale should ask the user for the following:

   - The retail price of the item being purchased
   - The sales tax rate

   Once these items have been entered, the program should calculate and display the following:

   - The sales tax for the purchase
   - The total of the sale

3. **Account Balance**

    A program that calculates the current balance in a savings account must ask the user for the following:

    - The starting balance
    - The total dollar amount of deposits made
    - The total dollar amount of withdrawals made
    - The monthly interest rate

    Once the program calculates the current balance, it should be displayed on the screen.

Predict the Result

The following are programs expressed as English statements. What would each display on the screen if they were actual programs?

1. The variable x starts with the value 0.
    The variable y starts with the value 5.
    Add 1 to x.
    Add 1 to y.
    Add x and y, and store the result in y.
    Display the value in y on the screen.

2. The variable a starts with the value 10.
    The variable b starts with the value 2.
    The variable c starts with the value 4.
    Store the value of a times b in a.
    Store the value of b times c in c.
    Add a and c, and store the result in b.
    Display the value in b on the screen.

Short Answer

1. Both main memory and secondary storage are types of memory. Describe the difference between the two.
2. What type of memory is usually volatile?
3. What is the difference between operating system software and application software?
4. Why must programs written in a high-level language be translated into machine language before they can be run?
5. Why is it easier to write a program in a high-level language than in machine language?
6. What is a source file?
7. What is the difference between a syntax error and a logical error?
8. What is an algorithm?
9. What is a compiler?
10. What is the difference between an application and an applet?

11. Why are Java applets safe to download and execute?

12. What must a computer have in order for it to execute Java programs?

13. What is the difference between machine language code and byte code?

14. Why does byte code make Java a portable language?

15. Is encapsulation a characteristic of procedural or object-oriented programming?

16. Why should an object hide its data?

17. What part of an object forms an interface through which outside code may access the object's data?

18. What type of program do you use to write Java source code?

19. Will the Java compiler translate a source file that contains syntax errors?

20. What does the Java compiler translate Java source code to?

21. Assuming you are using the Sun JDK, what command would you type at the operating system command prompt to compile the program `LabAssignment.java`?

22. Assuming there are no syntax errors in the *LabAssignment.java* program when it is compiled, answer the following questions.

     a. What file will be produced?
     b. What will the file contain?
     c. What command would you type at the operating system command prompt to run the program?

Programming Challenge

myCodeMate

1. Your First Java Program

This assignment will help you get acquainted with your Java development software. Here is the Java program you will enter:

```java
// This is my first Java program.
public class MyFirstProgram
{
    public static void main(String[] args)
    {
        System.out.println("Hello World!");
    }
}
```

VideoNote
Your First
Java Program

If You Are Using the Sun JDK:

1. Use a text editor to type the source code exactly as it is shown. Be sure to place all the punctuation characters and be careful to match the case of the letters as they are shown. Save it to a file named *MyFirstProgram.java*.

2. After saving the program, go to your operating system's command prompt and change your current directory or folder to the one that contains the Java program you just created. Then use the following command to compile the program:

```
javac MyFirstProgram.java
```

If you typed the contents of the file exactly as shown, you shouldn't have any syntax errors. If you see error messages, open the file in the editor and compare your code to that shown. Correct any mistakes you have made, save the file, and run the compiler again. If you see no error messages, the file was successfully compiled.

3. Next, enter the following command to run the program:

    `java MyFirstProgram`

    Be sure to use the capitalization of `MyFirstProgram` exactly as it is shown here. You should see the message "Hello World!" displayed on the screen.

If You Are Using an IDE:

Because there are many Java IDEs, we cannot include specific instructions for all of these. The following are general steps that should apply to most of them. You will need to consult your IDE's documentation for specific instructions.

1. Start your Java IDE and perform any necessary setup operations, such as starting a new project and creating a new Java source file.

2. Use the IDE's text editor to type the source code exactly as it is shown. Be sure to place all the punctuation characters and be careful to match the case of the letters as they are shown. Save it to a file named *MyFirstProgram.java*.

3. After saving the program, use your IDE's command to compile the program. If you typed the contents of the file exactly as shown, you shouldn't have any syntax errors. If you see error messages, compare your code to that shown. Correct any mistakes you have made, save the file, and run the compiler again. If you see no error messages, the file was successfully compiled.

    Use your IDE's command to run the program. You should see the message "Hello World!" displayed.

CHAPTER 2

2 Java Fundamentals

2.1 The Parts of a Java Program

CONCEPT: A Java program has parts that serve specific purposes.

Java programs are made up of different parts. Your first step in learning Java is to learn what the parts are. We will begin by looking at a simple example, shown in Code Listing 2-1.

Code Listing 2-1 (`Simple.java`)

```
1  // This is a simple Java program.
2
3  public class Simple
4  {
5     public static void main(String[] args)
6     {
7        System.out.println("Programming is great fun!");
8     }
9  }
```

> **TIP:** Remember, the line numbers shown in the program listings are not part of the program. The numbers are shown so we can refer to specific lines in the programs.

As mentioned in Chapter 1, the names of Java source code files end with *.java*. The program shown in Code Listing 2-1 is named *Simple.java*. Using the Sun Java compiler, this program may be compiled with the following command:

```
javac Simple.java
```

The compiler will create another file named *Simple.class*, which contains the translated Java byte code. This file can be executed with the following command:

```
java Simple
```

> **TIP:** Remember, you do not type the *.class* extension when using the `java` command.

The output of the program is as follows. This is what appears on the screen when the program runs.

Program Output

```
Programming is great fun!
```

Let's examine the program line-by-line. Here's the statement in line 1:

```
// This is a simple Java program.
```

Other than the two slash marks that begin this line, it looks pretty much like an ordinary sentence. The `//` marks the beginning of a comment. The compiler ignores everything from the double-slash to the end of the line. That means you can type anything you want on that line and the compiler never complains. Although comments are not required, they are very important to programmers. Most programs are much more complicated than this example, and comments help explain what's going on.

Line 2 is blank. Programmers often insert blank lines in programs to make them easier to read. Line 3 reads:

```
public class Simple
```

This line is known as a *class header*, and it marks the beginning of a *class definition*. One of the uses of a class is to serve as a container for an application. As you progress through this book you will learn more and more about classes. For now, just remember that a Java program must have at least one class definition. This line of code consists of three words: `public`, `class`, and `Simple`. Let's take a closer look at each word.

- `public` is a Java key word, and it must be written in all lowercase letters. It is known as an *access specifier*, and it controls where the class may be accessed from. The `public` specifier means access to the class is unrestricted. (In other words, the class is "open to the public.")
- `class`, which must also be written in lowercase letters, is a Java key word that indicates the beginning of a class definition.

- `Simple` is the class name. This name was made up by the programmer. The class could have been called `Pizza`, or `Dog`, or anything else the programmer wanted. Programmer-defined names may be written in lowercase letters, uppercase letters, or a mixture of both.

In a nutshell, this line of code tells the compiler that a publicly accessible class named `Simple` is being defined. Here are two more points to know about classes:

- You may create more than one class in a file, but you may only have one `public class` per Java file.
- When a Java file has a `public` class, the name of the public class must be the same as the name of the file (without the *.java* extension). For instance, the program in Code Listing 2-1 has a `public class` named `Simple`, so it is stored in a file named *Simple.java*.

NOTE: Java is a case-sensitive language. That means it regards uppercase letters as being entirely different characters than their lowercase counterparts. The word `Public` is not the same as `public`, and `Class` is not the same as `class`. Some words in a Java program must be entirely in lowercase, while other words may use a combination of lower and uppercase characters. Later in this chapter you will see a list of all the Java key words, which must appear in lowercase.

Line 4 contains only a single character:

```
{
```

This is called a left brace, or an opening brace, and is associated with the beginning of the class definition. All of the programming statements that are part of the class are enclosed in a set of braces. If you glance at the last line in the program, line 9, you'll see the closing brace. Everything between the two braces is the *body* of the class named `Simple`. Here is the program code again, this time the body of the class definition is shaded.

```java
// This is a simple Java program.
public class Simple
{
    public static void main(String[] args)
    {
        System.out.println("Programming is great fun!");
    }
}
```

WARNING! Make sure you have a closing brace for every opening brace in your program!

Line 5 reads:

```java
public static void main(String[] args)
```

This line is known as a *method header*. It marks the beginning of a *method*. A method can be thought of as a group of one or more programming statements that collectively has a name. When creating a method, you must tell the compiler several things about it. That is why this line contains so many words. At this point, the only thing you should be concerned about is that the name of the method is main, and the rest of the words are required for the method to be properly defined. This is shown in Figure 2-1.

Recall from Chapter 1 that a stand-alone Java program that runs on your computer is known as an application. Every Java application must have a method named main. The main method is the starting point of an application.

Figure 2-1 The main method header

Name of the Method

public static void **main** (String[] args)

The other parts of this line are necessary
for the method to be properly defined.

> **NOTE:** For the time being, all the programs you will write will consist of a class with a main method whose header looks exactly like the one shown in Code Listing 2-1. As you progress through this book you will learn what public static void and (String[] args) mean. For now, just assume that you are learning a "recipe" for assembling a Java program.

Line 6 has another opening brace:

```
{
```

This opening brace belongs to the main method. Remember that braces enclose statements, and every opening brace must have an accompanying closing brace. If you look at line 8 you will see the closing brace that corresponds with this opening brace. Everything between these braces is the *body* of the main method.

Line 7 appears as follows:

```
System.out.println("Programming is great fun!");
```

To put it simply, this line displays a message on the screen. The message, "Programming is great fun!" is printed without the quotation marks. In programming terms, the group of characters inside the quotation marks is called a *string literal*.

> **NOTE:** This is the only line in the program that causes anything to be printed on the screen. The other lines, like public class Simple and public static void main(String[] args), are necessary for the framework of your program, but they do not cause any screen output. Remember, a program is a set of instructions for the computer. If something is to be displayed on the screen, you must use a programming statement for that purpose.

At the end of the line is a *semicolon*. Just as a period marks the end of a sentence, a semicolon marks the end of a statement in Java. Not every line of code ends with a semicolon, however. Here is a summary of where you do not place a semicolon:

- Comments do not have to end with a semicolon because they are ignored by the compiler.
- Class headers and method headers do not end with a semicolon because they are terminated with a body of code inside braces.
- The brace characters, { and }, are not statements, so you do not place a semicolon after them.

It might seem that the rules for where to put a semicolon are not clear at all. For now, just concentrate on learning the parts of a program. You'll soon get a feel for where you should and should not use semicolons.

As has already been pointed out, lines 8 and 9 contain the closing braces for the `main` method and the class definition:

```
    }
  }
```

Before continuing, let's review the points we just covered, including some of the more elusive rules.

- Java is a case-sensitive language. It does not regard uppercase letters as being the same character as their lowercase equivalents.
- All Java programs must be stored in a file with a name that ends with *.java*.
- Comments are ignored by the compiler.
- A *.java* file may contain many classes, but may only have one `public` class. If a *.java* file has a public class, the class must have the same name as the file. For instance, if the file *Pizza.java* contains a `public class`, the class's name would be `Pizza`.
- Every Java application program must have a method named `main`.
- For every left brace, or opening brace, there must be a corresponding right brace, or closing brace.
- Statements are terminated with semicolons. This does not include comments, class headers, method headers, or braces.

In the sample program you encountered several special characters. Table 2-1 summarizes how they were used.

Table 2-1 Special characters

Characters	Name	Meaning
//	Double slash	Marks the beginning of a comment
( )	Opening and closing parentheses	Used in a method header
{ }	Opening and closing braces	Encloses a group of statements, such as the contents of a class or a method
" "	Quotation marks	Encloses a string of characters, such as a message that is to be printed on the screen
;	Semicolon	Marks the end of a complete programming statement

Checkpoint

2.1   The following program will not compile because the lines have been mixed up.

```
public static void main(String[] args)
}
// A crazy mixed up program
public class Columbus
{
System.out.println("In 1492 Columbus sailed the ocean blue.");
{
}
```

When the lines are properly arranged the program should display the following on the screen:

```
In 1492 Columbus sailed the ocean blue.
```

Rearrange the lines in the correct order. Test the program by entering it on the computer, compiling it, and running it.

2.2   When the program in Question 2.1 is saved to a file, what should the file be named?

2.3   Complete the following program skeleton so it displays the message "Hello World" on the screen.

```
public class Hello
{
    public static void main(String[] args)
    {
        // Insert code here to complete the program
    }
}
```

2.4   On paper, write a program that will display your name on the screen. Place a comment with today's date at the top of the program. Test your program by entering, compiling, and running it.

2.5   All Java source code filenames must end with _____.

a) a semicolon
b) *.class*
c) *.java*
d) none of the above

2.6   Every Java application program must have _____.

a) a method named main
b) more than one class definition
c) one or more comments

2.2 The `print` and `println` **Methods, and the Java API**

CONCEPT: The **print** and **println** methods are used to display text output. They are part of the Java API, which is a collection of prewritten classes and methods for performing specific operations.

In this section you will learn how to write programs that produce output on the screen. The simplest type of output that a program can display on the screen is console output. *Console output* is merely plain text. When you display console output in a system that uses a graphical user interface, such as Windows or Mac OS, the output usually appears in a window similar to the one shown in Figure 2-2.

Figure 2-2   A Console Window

VideoNote
Displaying
Console Output

The word "console" is an old computer term. It comes from the days when the operator of a large computer system interacted with the system by typing on a terminal that consisted of a simple screen and keyboard. This terminal was known as the *console*. The console screen, which displayed only text, was known as the standard output device. Today, the term *standard output device* typically refers to the device that displays console output.

Performing output in Java, as well as many other tasks, is accomplished by using the Java API. The term *API* stands for *Application Programmer Interface*. The API is a standard library of prewritten classes for performing specific operations. These classes and their methods are available to all Java programs. The print and println methods are part of the API and provide ways for output to be displayed on the standard output device.

The program in Code Listing 2-1 (Simple.java) uses the following statement to print a message on the screen:

```
System.out.println("Programming is great fun!");
```

System is a class that is part of the Java API. The System class contains objects and methods that perform system-level operations. One of the objects contained in the System class is named out. The out object has methods, such as print and println, for performing output on the system console, or standard output device. The hierarchical relationship among System, out, print, and println is shown in Figure 2-3.

Figure 2-3   Relationship among the System class, the out object, and the print and println methods

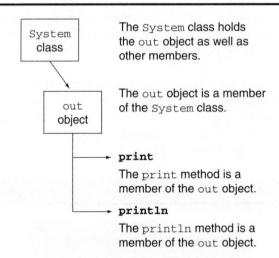

Here is a brief summary of how it all works together:

- The System class is part of the Java API. It has member objects and methods for performing system-level operations, such as sending output to the console.
- The out object is a member of the System class. It provides methods for sending output to the screen.
- The print and println methods are members of the out object. They actually perform the work of writing characters on the screen.

This hierarchy explains why the statement that executes println is so long. The sequence System.out.println specifies that println is a member of out, which is a member of System.

 NOTE: The period that separates the names of the objects is pronounced "dot." System.out.println is pronounced "system dot out dot print line."

The value that is to be displayed on the screen is placed inside the parentheses. This value is known as an *argument*. For example, the following statement executes the println method using the string "King Arthur" as its argument. This will print "King Arthur" on the screen. (The quotation marks are not displayed.)

```
System.out.println("King Arthur");
```

An important thing to know about the println method is that after it displays its message, it advances the cursor to the beginning of the next line. The next item printed on the screen will begin in this position. For example, look at the program in Code Listing 2-2.

Because each string is printed with separate println statements in Code Listing 2-2, they appear on separate lines in the Program Output.

Code Listing 2-2 (TwoLines.java)

```
 1  // This is another simple Java program.
 2
 3  public class TwoLines
 4  {
 5     public static void main(String[] args)
 6     {
 7        System.out.println("Programming is great fun!");
 8        System.out.println("I can't get enough of it!");
 9     }
10  }
```

Program Output

```
Programming is great fun!
I can't get enough of it!
```

The print Method

The print method, which is also part of the System.out object, serves a purpose similar to that of println—to display output on the screen. The print method, however, does not advance the cursor to the next line after its message is displayed. Look at Code Listing 2-3.

Code Listing 2-3 (GreatFun.java)

```
 1  // This is another simple Java program.
 2
 3  public class GreatFun
 4  {
 5     public static void main(String[] args)
 6     {
 7        System.out.print("Programming is ");
 8        System.out.println("great fun!");
 9     }
10  }
```

Program Output

```
Programming is great fun!
```

An important concept to understand about Code Listing 2-3 is that, although the output is broken up into two programming statements, this program will still display the message on one line. The data that you send to the print method is displayed in a continuous stream. Sometimes this can produce less-than-desirable results. The program in Code Listing 2-4 is an example.

Code Listing 2-4   (`Unruly.java`)

```
 1   // An unruly printing program
 2
 3   public class Unruly
 4   {
 5      public static void main(String[] args)
 6      {
 7         System.out.print("These are our top sellers:");
 8         System.out.print("Computer games");
 9         System.out.print("Coffee");
10         System.out.println("Aspirin");
11      }
12   }
```

Program Output

```
These are our top sellers:Computer gamesCoffeeAspirin
```

The layout of the actual output looks nothing like the arrangement of the strings in the source code. First, even though the output is broken up into four lines in the source code (lines 7 through 10), it comes out on the screen as one line. Second, notice that some of the words that are displayed are not separated by spaces. The strings are displayed exactly as they are sent to the print method. If spaces are to be displayed, they must appear in the strings.

There are two ways to fix this program. The most obvious way is to use println methods instead of print methods. Another way is to use escape sequences to separate the output into different lines. An *escape sequence* starts with the backslash character (\), and is followed by one or more *control characters*. It allows you to control the way output is displayed by embedding commands within the string itself. The escape sequence that causes the output cursor to go to the next line is \n. Code Listing 2-5 illustrates its use.

Code Listing 2-5   (`Adjusted.java`)

```
 1   // A well adjusted printing program
 2
 3   public class Adjusted
 4   {
 5      public static void main(String[] args)
 6      {
 7         System.out.print("These are our top sellers:\n");
 8         System.out.print("Computer games\nCoffee\n");
 9         System.out.println("Aspirin");
10      }
11   }
```

Program Output

```
These are our top sellers:
Computer games
Coffee
Aspirin
```

The \n characters are called the newline escape sequence. When the print or println methods encounter \n in a string, they do not print the \n characters on the screen, but interpret them as a special command to advance the output cursor to the next line. There are several other escape sequences as well. For instance, \t is the tab escape sequence. When print or println encounters it in a string, it causes the output cursor to advance to the next tab position. Code Listing 2-6 shows it in use.

Code Listing 2-6   (`Tabs.java`)

```
 1   // Another well-adjusted printing program
 2
 3   public class Tabs
 4   {
 5      public static void main(String[] args)
 6      {
 7         System.out.print("These are our top sellers:\n");
 8         System.out.print("\tComputer games\n\tCoffee\n");
 9         System.out.println("\tAspirin");
10      }
11   }
```

Program Output

```
These are our top sellers:
        Computer games
        Coffee
        Aspirin
```

> **NOTE:** Although you have to type two characters to write an escape sequence, they are stored in memory as a single character.

Table 2-2 lists the common escape sequences and describes them.

Table 2-2   Common escape sequences

Escape Sequence	Name	Description
\n	Newline	Advances the cursor to the next line for subsequent printing
\t	Horizontal tab	Causes the cursor to skip over to the next tab stop
\b	Backspace	Causes the cursor to back up, or move left, one position
\r	Return	Causes the cursor to go to the beginning of the current line, not the next line
\\	Backslash	Causes a backslash to be printed
\'	Single quote	Causes a single quotation mark to be printed
\"	Double quote	Causes a double quotation mark to be printed

> **WARNING!** Do not confuse the backslash (\) with the forward slash (/). An escape sequence will not work if you accidentally start it with a forward slash. Also, do not put a space between the backslash and the control character.

 Checkpoint

2.7 The following program will not compile because the lines have been mixed up.

```java
System.out.print("Success\n");
}
public class Success
{
System.out.print("Success\n");
public static void main(String[] args)
System.out.print("Success ");
}
// It's a mad, mad program.
System.out.println("\nSuccess");
{
```

When the lines are arranged properly the program should display the following output on the screen:

Program Output:

```
Success
Success Success

Success
```

Rearrange the lines in the correct order. Test the program by entering it on the computer, compiling it, and running it.

2.8 Study the following program and show what it will print on the screen.

```java
// The Works of Wolfgang
public class Wolfgang
{
    public static void main(String[] args)
    {
        System.out.print("The works of Wolfgang\ninclude ");
        System.out.print("the following");
        System.out.print("\nThe Turkish March ");
        System.out.print("and Symphony No. 40 ");
        System.out.println("in G minor.");
    }
}
```

2.9 On paper, write a program that will display your name on the first line; your street address on the second line; your city, state, and ZIP code on the third line; and your telephone number on the fourth line. Place a comment with today's date at the top of the program. Test your program by entering, compiling, and running it.

2.3   Variables and Literals

CONCEPT: A variable is a named storage location in the computer's memory. A literal is a value that is written into the code of a program.

As you discovered in Chapter 1, variables allow you to store and work with data in the computer's memory. Part of the job of programming is to determine how many variables a program will need and what types of data they will hold. The program in Code Listing 2-7 is an example of a Java program with a variable.

Code Listing 2-7 (`Variable.java`)

```
1   // This program has a variable.
2
3   public class Variable
4   {
5      public static void main(String[] args)
6      {
7         int value;
8
9         value = 5;
10        System.out.print("The value is ");
11        System.out.println(value);
12     }
13 }
```

Program Output

```
The value is 5
```

Let's look more closely at this program. Here is line 7:

```
int value;
```

VideoNote
Declaring
Variables

This is called a *variable declaration*. Variables must be declared before they can be used. A variable declaration tells the compiler the variable's name and the type of data it will hold. This line indicates the variable's name is value. The word `int` stands for integer, so value will only be used to hold integer numbers. Notice that variable declarations end with a semicolon. The next statement in this program appears in line 9:

```
value = 5;
```

This is called an assignment statement. The equal sign is an operator that stores the value on its right (in this case 5) into the variable named on its left. After this line executes, the value variable will contain the value 5.

NOTE: This line does not print anything on the computer screen. It runs silently behind the scenes.

Now look at lines 10 and 11:

```
System.out.print("The value is ");
System.out.println(value);
```

The statement in line 10 sends the string literal "The value is " to the `print` method. The statement in line 11 sends the name of the `value` variable to the `println` method. When you send a variable name to `print` or `println`, the variable's contents are displayed. Notice there are no quotation marks around `value`. Look at what happens in Code Listing 2-8.

Code Listing 2-8 (`Variable2.java`)

```
1   // This program has a variable.
2
3   public class Variable2
4   {
5      public static void main(String[] args)
6      {
7         int value;
8
9         value = 5;
10        System.out.print("The value is ");
11        System.out.println("value");
12     }
13  }
```

Program Output

```
The value is value
```

When double quotation marks are placed around the word `value` it becomes a string literal, not a variable name. When string literals are sent to `print` or `println`, they are displayed exactly as they appear inside the quotation marks.

Displaying Multiple Items with the + Operator

When the + operator is used with strings, it is known as the *string concatenation operator*. To concatenate means to append, so the string concatenation operator appends one string to another. For example, look at the following statement:

```
System.out.println("This is " + "one string.");
```

This statement will print:

```
This is one string.
```

The + operator produces a string that is the combination of the two strings used as its operands. You can also use the + operator to concatenate the contents of a variable to a string. The following code shows an example:

```
number = 5;
System.out.println("The value is " + number);
```

The second line uses the + operator to concatenate the contents of the `number` variable with the string "The value is ". Although `number` is not a string, the + operator converts its value to a string and then concatenates that value with the first string. The output that will be displayed is:

```
The value is 5
```

Sometimes the argument you use with `print` or `println` is too long to fit on one line in your program code. However, a string literal cannot begin on one line and end on another. For example, the following will cause an error:

```
// This is an error!
System.out.println("Enter a value that is greater than zero
                   and less than 10." );
```

You can remedy this problem by breaking the argument up into smaller string literals, and then using the string concatenation operator to spread them out over more than one line. Here is an example:

```
System.out.println("Enter a value that is " +
                   "greater than zero and less " +
                   "than 10." );
```

In this statement, the argument is broken up into three strings and joined using the + operator. The following example shows the same technique used when the contents of a variable are part of the concatenation:

```
sum = 249;
System.out.println("The sum of the three " +
                   "numbers is " + sum);
```

Be Careful with Quotation Marks

As shown in Code Listing 2-8, placing quotation marks around a variable name changes the program's results. In fact, placing double quotation marks around anything that is not intended to be a string literal will create an error of some type. For example, in Code Listings 2-7 and 2-8, the number 5 was assigned to the variable `value`. It would have been an error to perform the assignment this way:

```
value = "5";     // Error!
```

In this statement, 5 is no longer an integer, but a string literal. Because `value` was declared as an integer variable, you can only store integers in it. In other words, 5 and "5" are not the same thing.

The fact that numbers can be represented as strings frequently confuses students who are new to programming. Just remember that strings are intended for humans to read. They are to be printed on computer screens or paper. Numbers, however, are intended primarily for mathematical operations. You cannot perform math on strings, and before numbers can be displayed on the screen, first they must be converted to strings. (Fortunately, `print` and `println` handle the conversion automatically when you send numbers to them.) Don't fret if this still bothers you. Later in this chapter we will shed more light on the differences among numbers, characters, and strings by discussing their internal storage.

More about Literals

A literal is a value that is written in the code of a program. Literals are commonly assigned to variables or displayed. Code Listing 2-9 contains both literals and a variable.

Code Listing 2-9 (`Literals.java`)

```
1   // This program has literals and a variable.
2
3   public class Literals
4   {
5      public static void main(String[] args)
6      {
7         int apples;
8
9         apples = 20;
10        System.out.println("Today we sold " + apples +
11                           " bushels of apples.");
12     }
13  }
```

Program Output

```
Today we sold 20 bushels of apples.
```

Of course, the variable in this program is `apples`. It is declared as an integer. Table 2-3 shows a list of the literals found in the program.

Table 2-3 Literals

Literal	Type of Literal
20	Integer literal
"Today we sold"	String literal
"bushels of apples."	String literal

Identifiers

An *identifier* is a programmer-defined name that represents some element of a program. Variable names and class names are examples of identifiers. You may choose your own variable names and class names in Java, as long as you do not use any of the Java key words. The *key words* make up the core of the language and each has a specific purpose. Table 1-3 in Chapter 1 and Appendix D on the Student CD shows a complete list of Java key words.

You should always choose names for your variables that give an indication of what they are used for. You may be tempted to declare variables with names like this:

```
int x;
```

The rather nondescript name, x, gives no clue as to what the variable's purpose is. Here is a better example.

```
int itemsOrdered;
```

The name itemsOrdered gives anyone reading the program an idea of what the variable is used for. This method of coding helps produce *self-documenting programs*, which means you get an understanding of what the program is doing just by reading its code. Because real-world programs usually have thousands of lines of code, it is important that they be as self-documenting as possible.

You have probably noticed the mixture of uppercase and lowercase letters in the name itemsOrdered. Although all of Java's key words must be written in lowercase, you may use uppercase letters in variable names. The reason the O in itemsOrdered is capitalized is to improve readability. Normally "items ordered" is used as two words. Variable names cannot contain spaces, however, so the two words must be combined. When "items" and "ordered" are stuck together, you get a variable declaration like this:

```
int itemsordered;
```

Capitalization of the letter O makes itemsOrdered easier to read. Typically, variable names begin with a lowercase letter, and after that, the first letter of each individual word that makes up the variable name is capitalized.

The following are some specific rules that must be followed with all identifiers:

- The first character must be one of the letters a–z, A–Z, an underscore (_), or a dollar sign ($).
- After the first character, you may use the letters a–z or A–Z, the digits 0–9, underscores (_), or dollar signs ($).
- Uppercase and lowercase characters are distinct. This means itemsOrdered is not the same as itemsordered.
- Identifiers cannot include spaces.

NOTE: Although the $ is a legal identifier character, it is normally used for special purposes. So, don't use it in your variable names.

Table 2-4 shows a list of variable names and tells if each is legal or illegal in Java.

Table 2-4   Some variable names

Variable Name	Legal or Illegal?
dayOfWeek	Legal
3dGraph	Illegal because identifiers cannot begin with a digit
june1997	Legal
mixture#3	Illegal because identifiers may only use alphabetic letters, digits, underscores, or dollar signs
week day	Illegal because identifiers cannot contain spaces

Class Names

As mentioned before, it is standard practice to begin variable names with a lowercase letter, and then capitalize the first letter of each subsequent word that makes up the name. It is also a standard practice to capitalize the first letter of a class name, as well as the first letter of each subsequent word it contains. This helps differentiate the names of variables from the names of classes. For example, payRate would be a variable name, and Employee would be a class name.

Checkpoint

2.10 Examine the following program.

```java
// This program uses variables and literals.

public class BigLittle
{
    public static void main(String[] args)
    {
        int little;
        int big;

        little = 2;
        big = 2000;
        System.out.println("The little number is " + little);
        System.out.println("The big number is " + big);
    }
}
```

List the variables and literals found in the program.

2.11 What will the following program display on the screen?

```java
public class CheckPoint
{
    public static void main(String[] args)
    {
        int number;

        number = 712;
        System.out.println("The value is " + "number");
    }
}
```

2.4 Primitive Data Types

CONCEPT: There are many different types of data. Variables are classified according to their data type, which determines the kind of data that may be stored in them.

Computer programs collect pieces of data from the real world and manipulate them in various ways. There are many different types of data. In the realm of numeric data, for example, there are whole and fractional numbers, negative and positive numbers; and numbers so large and others so small that they don't even have a name. Then there is textual information. Names and addresses, for instance, are stored as strings of characters. When you write a program you must determine what types of data it is likely to encounter.

Each variable has a *data type*, which is the type of data that the variable can hold. Selecting the proper data type is important because a variable's data type determines the amount of memory the variable uses, and the way the variable formats and stores data. It is important to select a data type that is appropriate for the type of data that your program will work with. If you are writing a program to calculate the number of miles to a distant star, you need variables that can hold very large numbers. If you are designing software to record microscopic dimensions, you need variables that store very small and precise numbers. If you are writing a program that must perform thousands of intensive calculations, you want variables that can be processed quickly. The data type of a variable determines all of these factors.

Table 2-5 shows all of the Java *primitive data types* for holding numeric data.

The words listed in the left column of Table 2-5 are the key words that you use in variable declarations. A variable declaration takes the following general format:

```
DataType VariableName;
```

Table 2-5   Primitive data types for numeric data

Data Type	Size	Range
byte	1 byte	Integers in the range of −128 to +127
short	2 bytes	Integers in the range of −32,768 to +32,767
int	4 bytes	Integers in the range of −2,147,483,648 to +2,147,483,647
long	8 bytes	Integers in the range of −9,223,372,036,854,775,808 to +9,223,372,036,854,775,807
float	4 bytes	Floating-point numbers in the range of $\pm 3.4 \times 10^{-38}$ to $\pm 3.4 \times 10^{38}$, with 7 digits of accuracy
double	8 bytes	Floating-point numbers in the range of $\pm 1.7 \times 10^{-308}$ to $\pm 1.7 \times 10^{308}$, with 15 digits of accuracy

DataType is the name of the data type and *VariableName* is the name of the variable. Here are some examples of variable declarations:

```
byte inches;
int speed;
short month;
float salesCommission;
double distance;
```

The size column in Table 2-5 shows the number of bytes that a variable of each of the data types uses. For example, an int variable uses 4 bytes, and a double variable uses 8 bytes.

The range column shows the ranges of numbers that may be stored in variables of each data type. For example, an int variable can hold numbers from –2,147,483,648 up to +2,147,483,647. One of the appealing characteristics of the Java language is that the sizes and ranges of all the primitive data types are the same on all computers.

> **NOTE:** These data types are called "primitive" because you cannot use them to create objects. Recall from Chapter 1's discussion on object-oriented programming that an object has attributes and methods. With the primitive data types, you can only create variables, and a variable can only be used to hold a single value. Such variables do not have attributes or methods.

The Integer Data Types

The first four data types listed in Table 2-5, byte, int, short, and long, are all integer data types. An integer variable can hold whole numbers such as 7, 125, –14, and 6928. The program in Code Listing 2-10 shows several variables of different integer data types being used.

Code Listing 2-10   (`IntegerVariables.java`)

```java
 1  // This program has variables of several of the integer types.
 2
 3  public class IntegerVariables
 4  {
 5     public static void main(String[] args)
 6     {
 7        int checking;   // Declare an int variable named checking.
 8        byte miles;     // Declare a byte variable named miles.
 9        short minutes;  // Declare a short variable named minutes.
10        long days;      // Declare a long variable named days.
11
12        checking = -20;
13        miles = 105;
14        minutes = 120;
15        days = 189000;
16        System.out.println("We have made a journey of " + miles +
17                           " miles.");
18        System.out.println("It took us " + minutes + " minutes.");
19        System.out.println("Our account balance is $" + checking);
20        System.out.println("About " + days + " days ago Columbus " +
21                           "stood on this spot.");
22     }
23  }
```

Program Output

```
We have made a journey of 105 miles.
It took us 120 minutes.
Our account balance is $-20
About 189000 days ago Columbus stood on this spot.
```

In most programs you will need more than one variable of any given data type. If a program uses three integers, `length`, `width`, and `area`, they could be declared separately, as follows:

```
int length;
int width;
int area;
```

It is easier, however, to combine the three variable declarations:

```
int length, width, area;
```

You can declare several variables of the same type, simply by separating their names with commas.

Integer Literals

When you write an integer literal in your program code, Java assumes it to be of the `int` data type. For example, in Code Listing 2-10, the literals −20, 105, 120, and 185000 are all treated as `int` values. You can force an integer literal to be treated as a long, however, by suffixing it with the letter L. For example, the value 57L would be treated as a long. You can use either an uppercase or lowercase L. The lowercase l looks too much like the number 1, so you should always use the uppercase L.

> **WARNING!** You cannot embed commas in numeric literals. For example, the following statement will cause an error:
>
> ```
> number = 1,257,649;       // ERROR!
> ```
>
> This statement must be written as:
>
> ```
> number = 1257649;         // Correct.
> ```

Floating-Point Data Types

Whole numbers are not adequate for many jobs. If you are writing a program that works with dollar amounts or precise measurements, you need a data type that allows fractional values. In programming terms, these are called *floating-point* numbers. Values such as 1.7 and −45.316 are floating-point numbers.

In Java there are two data types that can represent floating-point numbers. They are `float` and `double`. The `float` data type is considered a single precision data type. It can store a floating-point number with 7 digits of accuracy. The `double` data type is considered a double precision data type. It can store a floating-point number with 15 digits of accuracy. The `double` data type uses twice as much memory as the `float` data type, however. A `float` variable occupies 4 bytes of memory, whereas a `double` variable uses 8 bytes.

Code listing 2-11 shows a program that uses three `double` variables.

Code Listing 2-11   (Sale.java)

```
1   // This program demonstrates the double data type.
2
3   public class Sale
4   {
```

```
 5      public static void main(String[] args)
 6      {
 7         double price, tax, total;
 8
 9         price = 29.75;
10         tax = 1.76;
11         total = 31.51;
12         System.out.println("The price of the item " +
13                            "is " + price);
14         System.out.println("The tax is " + tax);
15         System.out.println("The total is " + total);
16      }
17   }
```

Program Output

```
The price of the item is 29.75
The tax is 1.76
The total is 31.51
```

Floating-Point Literals

When you write a floating-point literal in your program code, Java assumes it to be of the double data type. For example, in Code Listing 2-11, the literals 29.75, 1.76, and 31.51 are all treated as double values. Because of this, a problem can arise when assigning a floating-point literal to a float variable. Java is a *strongly typed language*, which means that it only allows you to store values of compatible data types in variables. A double value is not compatible with a float variable because a double can be much larger or much smaller than the allowable range for a float. As a result, code such as the following will cause an error:

```
float number;
number = 23.5;              // Error!
```

You can force a double literal to be treated as a float, however, by suffixing it with the letter F or f. The preceding code can be rewritten in the following manner to prevent an error:

```
float number;
number = 23.5F;            // This will work.
```

 WARNING! If you are working with literals that represent dollar amounts, remember that you cannot embed currency symbols (such as $) or commas in the literal. For example, the following statement will cause an error:

```
grossPay = $1,257.00;     // ERROR!
```

This statement must be written as:

```
grossPay = 1257.00;       // Correct.
```

Scientific and E Notation

Floating-point literals can be represented in scientific notation. Take the number 47,281.97. In scientific notation this number is 4.728197×10^4. (10^4 is equal to 10,000, and $4.728197 \times 10,000$ is 47,281.97.)

Java uses E notation to represent values in scientific notation. In E notation, the number 4.728197×10^4 would be 4.728197E4. Table 2-6 shows other numbers represented in scientific and E notation.

Table 2-6   Floating-point representations

Decimal Notation	Scientific Notation	E Notation
247.91	2.4791×10^2	2.4791E2
0.00072	7.2×10^{-4}	7.2E−4
2,900,000	2.9×10^6	2.9E6

NOTE: The E can be uppercase or lowercase.

Code Listing 2-12 demonstrates the use of floating-point literals expressed in E notation.

Code Listing 2-12   (SunFacts.java)

```java
 1  // This program uses E notation.
 2
 3  public class SunFacts
 4  {
 5     public static void main(String[] args)
 6     {
 7        double distance, mass;
 8
 9        distance = 1.495979E11;
10        mass = 1.989E30;
11        System.out.println("The Sun is " + distance +
12                           " meters away.");
13        System.out.println("The Sun's mass is " + mass +
14                           " kilograms.");
15     }
16  }
```

Program Output

```
The Sun is 1.495979E11 meters away.
The Sun's mass is 1.989E30 kilograms.
```

The `boolean` **Data Type**

The `boolean` data type allows you to create variables that may hold one of two possible values: `true` or `false`. Code Listing 2-13 demonstrates the declaration and assignment of a `boolean` variable.

Code Listing 2-13 (`TrueFalse.java`)

```
1   // A program for demonstrating boolean variables
2
3   public class TrueFalse
4   {
5       public static void main(String[] args)
6       {
7           boolean bool;
8
9           bool = true;
10          System.out.println(bool);
11          bool = false;
12          System.out.println(bool);
13      }
14  }
```

Program Output

```
true
false
```

Variables of the `boolean` data type are useful for evaluating conditions that are either true or false. You will not be using them until Chapter 3, however, so for now just remember the following things:

- `boolean` variables may only hold the values `true` or `false`.
- The contents of a `boolean` variable may not be copied to a variable of any type other than `boolean`.

The `char` **Data Type**

The `char` data type is used to store characters. A variable of the `char` data type can hold one character at a time. Character literals are enclosed in *single quotation marks*. The program in Code Listing 2-14 uses a `char` variable. The character literals 'A' and 'B' are assigned to the variable.

Code Listing 2-14 (`Letters.java`)

```
1   // This program demonstrates the char data type.
2
3   public class Letters
4   {
5       public static void main(String[] args)
```

```
 6      {
 7         char letter;
 8
 9         letter = 'A';
10         System.out.println(letter);
11         letter = 'B';
12         System.out.println(letter);
13      }
14   }
```

Program Output

A
B

It is important that you do not confuse character literals with string literals, which are enclosed in double quotation marks. String literals cannot be assigned to char variables.

Unicode

Characters are internally represented by numbers. Each printable character, as well as many non-printable characters, is assigned a unique number. Java uses Unicode, which is a set of numbers that are used as codes for representing characters. Each Unicode number requires two bytes of memory, so char variables occupy two bytes. When a character is stored in memory, it is actually the numeric code that is stored. When the computer is instructed to print the value on the screen, it displays the character that corresponds with the numeric code.

 You may want to refer to Appendix B on the Student CD which shows a portion of the Unicode character set. Notice that the number 65 is the code for A, 66 is the code for B, and so on. Code Listing 2-15 demonstrates that when you work with characters, you are actually working with numbers.

Code Listing 2-15   (`Letters2.java`)

```
 1   // This program demonstrates the close relationship between
 2   // characters and integers.
 3
 4   public class Letters2
 5   {
 6      public static void main(String[] args)
 7      {
 8         char letter;
 9
10         letter = 65;
11         System.out.println(letter);
12         letter = 66;
13         System.out.println(letter);
14      }
15   }
```

Program Output

```
A
B
```

Figure 2-4 illustrates that when you think of the characters A, B, and C being stored in memory, it is really the numbers 65, 66, and 67 that are stored.

Figure 2-4 Characters and how they are stored in memory

Variable Assignment and Initialization

As you have already seen in several examples, a value is put into a variable with an *assignment statement*. For example, the following statement assigns the value 12 to the variable unitsSold:

```
unitsSold = 12;
```

The = symbol is called the assignment operator. Operators perform operations on data. The data that operators work with are called operands. The assignment operator has two operands. In the statement above the operands are unitsSold and 12.

In an assignment statement, the name of the variable receiving the assignment must appear on the left side of the operator, and the value being assigned must appear on the right side. The following statement is incorrect:

```
12 = unitsSold;       // ERROR!
```

The operand on the left side of the = operator must be a variable name. The operand on the right side of the = symbol must be an expression that has a value. The assignment operator takes the value of the right operand and puts it in the variable identified by the left operand. Assuming that length and width are both int variables, the following code illustrates that the assignment operator's right operand may be a literal or a variable:

```
length = 20;
width = length;
```

It is important to note that the assignment operator only changes the contents of its left operand. The second statement assigns the value of the length variable to the width variable. After the statement has executed, length still has the same value, 20.

You may also assign values to variables as part of the declaration statement. This is known as *initialization*. Code Listing 2-16 shows how it is done.

The variable declaration statement in this program is in line 7:

```
int month = 2, days = 28;
```

Code Listing 2-16   (`Initialize.java`)

```
 1   // This program shows variable initialization.
 2
 3   public class Initialize
 4   {
 5      public static void main(String[] args)
 6      {
 7         int month = 2, days = 28;
 8
 9         System.out.println("Month " + month + " has " +
10                            days + " days.");
11      }
12   }
```

Program Output

```
Month 2 has 28 days.
```

This statement declares the `month` variable and initializes it with the value 2, and declares the `days` variable and initializes it with the value 28. As you can see, this simplifies the program and reduces the number of statements that must be typed by the programmer. Here are examples of other declaration statements that perform initialization:

```
double payRate = 25.52;
float interestRate = 12.9F;
char stockCode = 'D';
int customerNum = 459;
```

Of course, there are always variations on a theme. Java allows you to declare several variables and only initialize some of them. Here is an example of such a declaration:

```
int flightNum = 89, travelTime, departure = 10, distance;
```

The variable `flightNum` is initialized to 89 and `departure` is initialized to 10. The `travelTime` and `distance` variables remain uninitialized.

> **WARNING!** When a variable is declared inside a method, it must have a value stored in it before it can be used. If the compiler determines that the program might be using such a variable before a value has been stored in it, an error will occur. You can avoid this type of error by initializing the variable with a value.

Variables Hold Only One Value at a Time

Remember, a variable can hold only one value at a time. When you assign a new value to a variable, the new value takes the place of the variable's previous contents. For example, look at the following code.

```
int x = 5;
System.out.println(x);
x = 99;
System.out.println(x);
```

In this code, the variable x is initialized with the value 5 and its contents are displayed. Then the variable is assigned the value 99. This value overwrites the value 5 that was previously stored there. The code will produce the following output:

```
5
99
```

Checkpoint

2.12   Which of the following are illegal variable names and why?

```
x
99bottles
july97
theSalesFigureForFiscalYear98
r&d
grade_report
```

2.13   Is the variable name Sales the same as sales? Why or why not?

2.14   Refer to the Java primitive data types listed in Table 2-5 for this question.
   a)   If a variable needs to hold whole numbers in the range 32 to 6,000, what primitive data type would be best?
   b)   If a variable needs to hold whole numbers in the range –40,000 to +40,000, what primitive data type would be best?
   c)   Which of the following literals use more memory? 22.1 or 22.1F?

2.15   How would the number 6.31×10^{17} be represented in E notation?

2.16   A program declares a float variable named number, and the following statement causes an error. What can be done to fix the error?

```
number = 7.4;
```

2.17   What values can boolean variables hold?

2.18   Write statements that do the following:
   a)   Declare a char variable named letter.
   b)   Assign the letter A to the letter variable.
   c)   Display the contents of the letter variable.

2.19   What are the Unicode codes for the characters 'C', 'F', and 'W'? (You may need to refer to Appendix B on the Student CD.)

2.20   Which is a character literal, 'B' or "B"?

2.21   What is wrong with the following statement?

```
char letter = "Z";
```

2.5   Arithmetic Operators

CONCEPT: There are many operators for manipulating numeric values and performing arithmetic operations.

Java offers a multitude of operators for manipulating data. Generally, there are three types of operators: *unary*, *binary*, and *ternary*. These terms reflect the number of operands an operator requires.

VideoNote
Simple Math
Expressions

Unary operators require only a single operand. For example, consider the following expression:

```
-5
```

Of course, we understand this represents the value negative five. We can also apply the operator to a variable, as follows:

```
-number
```

This expression gives the negative of the value stored in `number`. The minus sign, when used this way, is called the *negation operator*. Because it only requires one operand, it is a unary operator.

Binary operators work with two operands. The assignment operator is in this category. Ternary operators, as you may have guessed, require three operands. Java has only one ternary operator, which is discussed in Chapter 3.

Arithmetic operations are very common in programming. Table 2-7 shows the arithmetic operators in Java.

Table 2-7   Arithmetic operators

Operator	Meaning	Type	Example
+	Addition	Binary	`total = cost + tax;`
−	Subtraction	Binary	`cost = total - tax;`
*	Multiplication	Binary	`tax = cost * rate;`
/	Division	Binary	`salePrice = original / 2;`
%	Modulus	Binary	`remainder = value % 3;`

Each of these operators works as you probably expect. The addition operator returns the sum of its two operands. Here are some example statements that use the addition operator:

```
amount = 4 + 8;            // Assigns 12 to amount
total = price + tax;       // Assigns price + tax to total
number = number + 1;       // Assigns number + 1 to number
```

The subtraction operator returns the value of its right operand subtracted from its left operand. Here are some examples:

```
temperature = 112 - 14;    // Assigns 98 to temperature
sale = price - discount;   // Assigns price - discount to sale
number = number - 1;       // Assigns number - 1 to number
```

The multiplication operator returns the product of its two operands. Here are some examples:

```
markUp = 12 * 0.25;               // Assigns 3 to markUp
commission = sales * percent;     // Assigns sales * percent to commission
population = population * 2;       // Assigns population * 2 to population
```

The division operator returns the quotient of its left operand divided by its right operand. Here are some examples:

```
points = 100 / 20;                // Assigns 5 to points
teams = players / maxEach;        // Assigns players / maxEach to teams
half = number / 2;                // Assigns number / 2 to half
```

The modulus operator returns the remainder of a division operation involving two integers. The following statement assigns 2 to leftOver:

```
leftOver = 17 % 3;
```

Situations arise where you need to get the remainder of a division. Computations that detect odd numbers or are required to determine how many items are left over after division use the modulus operator.

The program in Code Listing 2-17 demonstrates some of these operators used in a simple payroll calculation.

Code Listing 2-17   (Wages.java)

```
1   // This program calculates hourly wages plus overtime.
2
3   public class Wages
4   {
5      public static void main(String[] args)
6      {
7         double regularWages;        // The calculated regular wages.
8         double basePay = 25;        // The base pay rate.
9         double regularHours = 40;   // The hours worked less overtime.
10        double overtimeWages;       // Overtime wages
11        double overtimePay = 37.5;  // Overtime pay rate
12        double overtimeHours = 10;  // Overtime hours worked
13        double totalWages;          // Total wages
14
15        regularWages = basePay * regularHours;
16        overtimeWages = overtimePay * overtimeHours;
17        totalWages = regularWages + overtimeWages;
18        System.out.println("Wages for this week are $" +
19                           totalWages);
20     }
21  }
```

Program Output

```
Wages for this week are $1375.0
```

Code Listing 2-17 calculates the total wages an hourly paid worker earned in one week. As mentioned in the comments, there are variables for regular wages, base pay rate, regular hours worked, overtime wages, overtime pay rate, overtime hours worked, and total wages.

Line 15 in the program multiplies basePay times regularHours and stores the result, which is 1000, in regularWages:

```
regularWages = basePay * regularHours;
```

Line 16 multiplies `overtimePay` times `overtimeHours` and stores the result, which is 375, in `overtimeWages`:

```
overtimeWages = overtimePay * overtimeHours;
```

Line 17 adds the regular wages and the overtime wages and stores the result, 1375, in `totalWages`:

```
totalWages = regularWages + overtimeWages;
```

The `println` statement in lines 18 and 19 displays the message on the screen reporting the week's wages.

Integer Division

When both operands of a division statement are integers, the statement will result in *integer division*. This means the result of the division will be an integer as well. If there is a remainder, it will be discarded. For example, in the following code, `parts` is assigned the value 5.0:

```
double parts;
parts = 17 / 3;
```

It doesn't matter that `parts` is declared as a `double` because the fractional part of the result is discarded before the assignment takes place. In order for a division operation to return a floating-point value, one of the operands must be of a floating-point data type. For example, the previous code could be written as follows:

```
double parts;
parts = 17.0 / 3;
```

In this code, 17.0 is interpreted as a floating-point number, so the division operation will return a floating-point number. The result of the division is 5.666666666666667.

Operator Precedence

It is possible to build mathematical expressions with several operators. The following statement assigns the sum of 17, x, 21, and y to the variable `answer`:

```
answer = 17 + x + 21 + y;
```

Some expressions are not that straightforward, however. Consider the following statement:

```
outcome = 12 + 6 / 3;
```

What value will be stored in `outcome`? The 6 is used as an operand for both the addition and division operators. The `outcome` variable could be assigned either 6 or 14, depending on when the division takes place. The answer is 14 because the division operator has higher *precedence* than the addition operator.

Mathematical expressions are evaluated from left to right. When two operators share an operand, the operator with the highest precedence works first. Multiplication and division have higher precedence than addition and subtraction, so the statement above works like this:

1. 6 is divided by 3, yielding a result of 2
2. 12 is added to 2, yielding a result of 14

It could be diagrammed as shown in Figure 2-5.

Figure 2-5 Precedence illustrated

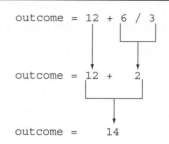

Table 2-8 shows the precedence of the arithmetic operators. The operators at the top of the table have higher precedence than the ones below it.

Table 2-8 Precedence of arithmetic operators (highest to lowest)

Highest Precedence →	- (unary negation)
	* / %
Lowest Precedence →	+ -

The multiplication, division, and modulus operators have the same precedence. The addition and subtraction operators have the same precedence. If two operators sharing an operand have the same precedence, they work according to their *associativity*. Associativity is either *left to right* or *right to left*. Table 2-9 shows the arithmetic operators and their associativity.

Table 2-9 Associativity of arithmetic operators

Operator	Associativity
- (unary negation)	Right to left
* / %	Left to right
+ -	Left to right

Table 2-10 shows some expressions and their values.

Table 2-10 Some expressions and their values

Expression	Value
5 + 2 * 4	13
10 / 2 - 3	2
8 + 12 * 2 - 4	28
4 + 17 % 2 - 1	4
6 - 3 * 2 + 7 - 1	6

Grouping with Parentheses

Parts of a mathematical expression may be grouped with parentheses to force some operations to be performed before others. In the statement below, the sum of a, b, c, and d is divided by 4.0.

```
average = (a + b + c + d) / 4.0;
```

Without the parentheses, however, d would be divided by 4 and the result added to a, b, and c. Table 2-11 shows more expressions and their values.

Table 2-11 More expressions and their values

Expression	Value
(5 + 2) * 4	28
10 / (5 - 3)	5
8 + 12 * (6 - 2)	56
(4 + 17) % 2 - 1	0
(6 - 3) * (2 + 7) / 3	9

In the Spotlight:
Calculating Percentages and Discounts

Determining percentages is a common calculation in computer programming. Although the % symbol is used in general mathematics to indicate a percentage, most programming languages (including Java) do not use the % symbol for this purpose. In a program, you have to convert a percentage to a floating-point number, just as you would if you were using a calculator. For example, 50 percent would be written as 0.5 and 2 percent would be written as 0.02.

Let's look at an example. Suppose you earn $6,000 per month and you are allowed to contribute a portion of your gross monthly pay to a retirement plan. You want to determine the amount of your pay that will go into the plan if you contribute 5 percent, 8 percent, or 10 percent of your gross wages. To make this determination you write a program like the one shown in Code Listing 2-18.

Code Listing 2-18 (`Contribution.java`)

```
 1  // This program calculates the amount of pay that
 2  // will be contributed to a retirement plan if 5%,
 3  // 7%, or 10% of monthly pay is withheld.
 4
 5  public class Contribution
 6  {
 7     public static void main(String[] args)
 8     {
 9        // Variables to hold the monthly pay and
10        // the amount of contribution.
11        double monthlyPay = 6000.0;
12        double contribution;
```

```
13
14        // Calculate and display a 5% contribution.
15        contribution = monthlyPay * 0.05;
16        System.out.println("5 percent is $" +
17                           contribution +
18                           " per month.");
19
20        // Calculate and display an 8% contribution.
21        contribution = monthlyPay * 0.08;
22        System.out.println("8 percent is $" +
23                           contribution +
24                           " per month.");
25
26        // Calculate and display a 10% contribution.
27        contribution = monthlyPay * 0.1;
28        System.out.println("10 percent is $" +
29                           contribution +
30                           " per month.");
31   }
32 }
```

Program Output

```
5 percent is $300.0 per month.
8 percent is $480.0 per month.
10 percent is $600.0 per month.
```

Lines 11 and 12 declare two variables: monthlyPay and contribution. The monthlyPay variable, which is initialized with the value 6000.0, holds the amount of your monthly pay. The contribution variable will hold the amount of a contribution to the retirement plan.

The statements in lines 15 through 18 calculate and display 5 percent of the monthly pay. The calculation is done in line 15, where the monthlyPay variable is multiplied by 0.05. The result is assigned to the contribution variable, which is then displayed by the statement in lines 16 through 18.

Similar steps are taken in lines 21 through 24, which calculate and display 8 percent of the monthly pay, and lines 27 through 30, which calculate and display 10 percent of the monthly pay.

Calculating a Percentage Discount

Another common calculation is determining a percentage discount. For example, suppose a retail business sells an item that is regularly priced at $59, and is planning to have a sale where the item's price will be reduced by 20 percent. You have been asked to write a program to calculate the sale price of the item.

To determine the sale price you perform two calculations:

- First, you get the amount of the discount, which is 20 percent of the item's regular price.

• Second, you subtract the discount amount from the item's regular price. This gives you the sale price.

Code Listing 2-19 shows how this is done in Java.

Code Listing 2-19   (`Discount.java`)

```java
 1 // This program calculates the sale price of an
 2 // item that is regularly priced at $59, with
 3 // a 20 percent discount subtracted.
 4
 5 public class Discount
 6 {
 7    public static void main(String[] args)
 8    {
 9       // Variables to hold the regular price, the
10       // amount of a discount, and the sale price.
11       double regularPrice = 59.0;
12       double discount;
13       double salePrice;
14
15       // Calculate the amount of a 20% discount.
16       discount = regularPrice * 0.2;
17
18       // Calculate the sale price by subtracting
19       // the discount from the regular price.
20       salePrice = regularPrice - discount;
21
22       // Display the results.
23       System.out.println("Regular price: $" + regularPrice);
24       System.out.println("Discount amount $" + discount);
25       System.out.println("Sale price: $" + salePrice);
26    }
27 }
```

Program Output

```
Regular price: $59.0
Discount amount $11.8
Sale price: $47.2
```

Lines 11 through 13 declare three variables. The regularPrice variable holds the item's regular price, and is initialized with the value 59.0. The discount variable will hold the amount of the discount once it is calculated. The salePrice variable will hold the item's sale price.

Line 16 calculates the amount of the 20 percent discount by multiplying regularPrice by 0.2. The result is stored in the discount variable. Line 20 calculates the sale price by subtracting discount from regularPrice. The result is stored in the salePrice variable. The statements in lines 23 through 25 display the item's regular price, the amount of the discount, and the sale price.

The Math Class

The Java API provides a class named Math, which contains numerous methods that are useful for performing complex mathematical operations. In this section we will briefly look at the Math.pow and Math.sqrt methods.

The Math.pow Method

In Java, raising a number to a power requires the Math.pow method. Here is an example of how the Math.pow method is used:

```
result = Math.pow(4.0, 2.0);
```

The method takes two double arguments. It raises the first argument to the power of the second argument, and returns the result as a double. In this example, 4.0 is raised to the power of 2.0. This statement is equivalent to the following algebraic statement:

$$result = 4^2$$

Here is another example of a statement using the Math.pow method. It assigns 3 times 6^3 to x:

```
x = 3 * Math.pow(6.0, 3.0);
```

And the following statement displays the value of 5 raised to the power of 4:

```
System.out.println(Math.pow(5.0, 4.0));
```

The Math.sqrt Method

The Math.sqrt method accepts a double value as its argument and returns the square root of the value. Here is an example of how the method is used:

```
result = Math.sqrt(9.0);
```

In this example the value 9.0 is passed as an argument to the Math.sqrt method. The method will return the square root of 9.0, which is assigned to the result variable. The following statement shows another example. In this statement the square root of 25.0 (which is 5.0) is displayed on the screen:

```
System.out.println(Math.sqrt(25.0));
```

 For more information about the Math class, see Appendix G on the Student CD.

Checkpoint

2.22 Complete the following table by writing the value of each expression in the Value column.

```
Expression                          Value
-------------------------------------------
6 + 3 * 5                           _____
12 / 2 - 4                          _____
9 + 14 * 2 - 6                      _____
5 + 19 % 3 - 1                      _____
(6 + 2) * 3                         _____
14 / (11 - 4)                       _____
9 + 12 * (8 - 3)                    _____
```

2.23   Is the division statement in the following code an example of integer division or floating-point division? What value will be stored in portion?

```
double portion;
portion = 70 / 3;
```

2.6   Combined Assignment Operators

CONCEPT: The combined assignment operators combine the assignment operator with the arithmetic operators.

Quite often, programs have assignment statements of the following form:

```
x = x + 1;
```

On the right side of the assignment operator, 1 is added to x. The result is then assigned to x, replacing the value that was previously there. Effectively, this statement adds 1 to x. Here is another example:

```
balance = balance + deposit;
```

Assuming that balance and deposit are variables, this statement assigns the value of balance + deposit to balance. The effect of this statement is that deposit is added to the value stored in balance. Here is another example:

```
balance = balance - withdrawal;
```

Assuming that balance and withdrawal are variables, this statement assigns the value of balance - withdrawal to balance. The effect of this statement is that withdrawal is subtracted from the value stored in balance.

If you have not seen these types of statements before, they might cause some initial confusion because the same variable name appears on both sides of the assignment operator. Table 2-12 shows other examples of statements written this way.

Table 2-12   Various assignment statements (assume x = 6 in each statement)

Statement	What It Does	Value of x after the Statement
x = x + 4;	Adds 4 to x	10
x = x - 3;	Subtracts 3 from x	3
x = x * 10;	Multiplies x by 10	60
x = x / 2;	Divides x by 2	3
x = x % 4	Assigns the remainder of x / 4 to x.	2

These types of operations are common in programming. For convenience, Java offers a special set of operators designed specifically for these jobs. Table 2-13 shows the *combined assignment operators*, also known as *compound operators*.

Table 2-13 Combined assignment operators

Operator	Example Usage	Equivalent To
+=	x += 5;	x = x + 5;
-=	y -= 2;	y = y - 2;
*=	z *= 10;	z = z * 10;
/=	a /= b;	a = a / b;
%=	c %= 3;	c = c % 3;

As you can see, the combined assignment operators do not require the programmer to type the variable name twice. The following statement:

```
balance = balance + deposit;
```

could be rewritten as

```
balance += deposit;
```

Similarly, the statement

```
balance = balance - withdrawal;
```

could be rewritten as

```
balance -= withdrawal;
```

 Checkpoint

2.24 Write statements using combined assignment operators to perform the following:
   a) Add 6 to x
   b) Subtract 4 from amount
   c) Multiply y by 4
   d) Divide total by 27
   e) Store in x the remainder of x divided by 7

 2.7 Conversion between Primitive Data Types

CONCEPT: Before a value can be stored in a variable, the value's data type must be compatible with the variable's data type. Java performs some conversions between data types automatically, but does not automatically perform any conversion that can result in the loss of data. Java also follows a set of rules when evaluating arithmetic expressions containing mixed data types.

Java is a *strongly typed* language. This means that before a value is assigned to a variable, Java checks the data types of the variable and the value being assigned to it to determine if they are compatible. For example, look at the following statements:

```
int x;
double y = 2.5;
x = y;
```

The assignment statement is attempting to store a double value (2.5) in an int variable. When the Java compiler encounters this line of code, it will respond with an error message. (The Sun JDK displays the message "possible loss of precision.")

Not all assignment statements that mix data types are rejected by the compiler, however. For instance, look at the following program segment:

```
int x;
short y = 2;
x = y;
```

This assignment statement, which stores a short in an int, will work with no problems. So why does Java permit a short to be stored in an int, but does not permit a double to be stored in an int? The obvious reason is that a double can store fractional numbers and can hold values much larger than an int can hold. If Java were to permit a double to be assigned to an int, a loss of data would be likely.

Just like officers in the military, the primitive data types are ranked. One data type outranks another if it can hold a larger number. For example, a float outranks an int, and an int outranks a short. Figure 2-6 shows the numeric data types in order of their rank. The higher a data type appears in the list, the higher is its rank.

Figure 2-6   Primitive data type ranking

In assignment statements where values of lower-ranked data types are stored in variables of higher-ranked data types, Java automatically converts the lower-ranked value to the higher-ranked type. This is called a *widening conversion*. For example, the following code demonstrates a widening conversion, which takes place when an int value is stored in a double variable:

```
double x;
int y = 10;
x = y;              // Performs a widening conversion
```

A *narrowing conversion* is the conversion of a value to a lower-ranked type. For example, converting a double to an int would be a narrowing conversion. Because narrowing conversions can potentially cause a loss of data, Java does not automatically perform them.

Cast Operators

The *cast operator* lets you manually convert a value, even if it means that a narrowing conversion will take place. Cast operators are unary operators that appear as a data type name enclosed in a set of parentheses. The operator precedes the value being converted. Here is an example:

```
x = (int)number;
```

The cast operator in this statement is the word int inside the parentheses. It returns the value in number, converted to an int. This converted value is then stored in x. If number were a floating-point variable, such as a float or a double, the value that is returned would be *truncated*, which means the fractional part of the number is lost. The original value in the number variable is not changed however.

Table 2-14 shows several statements using a cast operator.

Table 2-14   Example uses of cast operators

Statement	Description
littleNum = (short)bigNum;	The cast operator returns the value in bigNum, converted to a short. The converted value is assigned to the variable littleNum.
x = (long)3.7;	The cast operator is applied to the expression 3.7. The operator returns the value 3, which is assigned to the variable x.
number = (int)72.567;	The cast operator is applied to the expression 72.567. The operator returns 72, which is used to initialize the variable number.
value = (float)x;	The cast operator returns the value in x, converted to a float. The converted value is assigned to the variable value.
value = (byte)number;	The cast operator returns the value in number, converted to a byte. The converted value is assigned to the variable value.

Note that when a cast operator is applied to a variable, it does not change the contents of the variable. It only returns the value stored in the variable, converted to the specified data type.

Recall from our earlier discussion that when both operands of a division are integers, the operation will result in integer division. This means that the result of the division will be an integer, with any fractional part of the result thrown away. For example, look at the following code:

```
int pies = 10, people = 4;
double piesPerPerson;
piesPerPerson = pies / people;
```

Although 10 divided by 4 is 2.5, this code will store 2 in the piesPerPerson variable. Because both pies and people are int variables, the result will be an int, and the fractional part will be thrown away. We can modify the code with a cast operator, however, so it gives the correct result as a floating point value:

```
piesPerPerson = (double)pies / people;
```

The variable pies is an int and holds the value 10. The expression (double)pies returns the value in pies converted to a double. This means that one of the division operator's operands is a double, so the result of the division will be a double. The statement could also have been written as follows:

```
piesPerPerson = pies / (double)people;
```

In this statement, the cast operator returns the value of the people variable converted to a double. In either statement, the result of the division is a double.

> ⚠ **WARNING!** The cast operator can be applied to an entire expression enclosed in parentheses. For example, look at the following statement:
>
> ```
> piesPerPerson = (double)(pies / people);
> ```
>
> This statement does not convert the value in `pies` or `people` to a `double`, but converts the result of the expression `pies / people`. If this statement were used, an integer division operation would still have been performed. Here's why: The result of the expression `pies / people` is 2 (because integer division takes place). The value 2 converted to a `double` is 2.0. To prevent the integer division from taking place, one of the operands must be converted to a `double`.

Mixed Integer Operations

One of the nuances of the Java language is the way it internally handles arithmetic operations on `int`, `byte`, and `short` variables. When values of the `byte` or `short` data types are used in arithmetic expressions, they are temporarily converted to `int` values. The result of an arithmetic operation using only a mixture of `byte`, `short`, or `int` values will always be an `int`.

For example, assume that `b` and `c` in the following expression are `short` variables:

```
b + c
```

Although both `b` and `c` are `short` variables, the result of the expression `b + c` is an `int`. This means that when the result of such an expression is stored in a variable, the variable must be an `int` or higher data type. For example, look at the following code:

```
short firstNumber = 10,
      secondNumber = 20,
      thirdNumber;

// The following statement causes an error!
thirdNumber = firstNumber + secondNumber;
```

When this code is compiled, the following statement causes an error:

```
thirdNumber = firstNumber + secondNumber;
```

The error results from the fact that `thirdNumber` is a `short`. Although `firstNumber` and `secondNumber` are also `short` variables, the expression `firstNumber + secondNumber` results in an `int` value. The program can be corrected if `thirdNumber` is declared as an `int`, or if a cast operator is used in the assignment statement, as shown here:

```
thirdNumber = (short)(firstNumber + secondNumber);
```

Other Mixed Mathematical Expressions

In situations where a mathematical expression has one or more values of the `double`, `float`, or `long` data types, Java strives to convert all of the operands in the expression to the same data type. Let's look at the specific rules that govern evaluation of these types of expressions.

1. If one of an operator's operands is a `double`, the value of the other operand will be converted to a `double`. The result of the expression will be a `double`. For example, in the following statement assume that `b` is a `double` and `c` is an `int`:

   ```
   a = b + c;
   ```

   The value in `c` will be converted to a `double` prior to the addition. The result of the addition will be a `double`, so the variable `a` must also be a `double`.

2. If one of an operator's operands is a `float`, the value of the other operand will be converted to a `float`. The result of the expression will be a `float`. For example, in the following statement assume that `x` is a `short` and `y` is a `float`:

   ```
   z = x * y;
   ```

   The value in `x` will be converted to a `float` prior to the multiplication. The result of the multiplication will be a `float`, so the variable `z` must also be either a `double` or a `float`.

3. If one of an operator's operands is a `long`, the value of the other operand will be converted to a `long`. The result of the expression will be a `long`. For example, in the following statement assume that `a` is a `long` and `b` is a `short`:

   ```
   c = a - b;
   ```

   The variable `b` will be converted to a `long` prior to the subtraction. The result of the subtraction will be a `long`, so the variable `c` must also be a `long`, `float`, or `double`.

 Checkpoint

2.25 The following declaration appears in a program:

```
short totalPay, basePay = 500, bonus = 1000;
```

The following statement appears in the same program:

```
totalPay = basePay + bonus;
```

   a) Will the statement compile properly or cause an error?
   b) If the statement causes an error, why? How can you fix it?

2.26 The variable `a` is a `float` and the variable `b` is a `double`. Write a statement that will assign the value of `b` to `a` without causing an error when the program is compiled.

2.8 Creating Named Constants with `final`

CONCEPT: The `final` key word can be used in a variable declaration to make the variable a named constant. Named constants are initialized with a value, and that value cannot change during the execution of the program.

Assume that the following statement appears in a banking program that calculates data pertaining to loans:

```
amount = balance * 0.069;
```

In such a program, two potential problems arise. First, it is not clear to anyone other than the original programmer what 0.069 is. It appears to be an interest rate, but in some situations there are fees associated with loan payments. How can the purpose of this statement be determined without painstakingly checking the rest of the program?

The second problem occurs if this number is used in other calculations throughout the program and must be changed periodically. Assuming the number is an interest rate, what if the rate changes from 6.9 percent to 8.2 percent? The programmer would have to search through the source code for every occurrence of the number.

Both of these problems can be addressed by using named constants. A *named constant* is a variable whose value is read only and cannot be changed during the program's execution. You can create such a variable in Java by using the `final` key word in the variable declaration. The word `final` is written just before the data type. Here is an example:

```
final double INTEREST_RATE = 0.069;
```

This statement looks just like a regular variable declaration except that the word `final` appears before the data type, and the variable name is written in all uppercase letters. It is not required that the variable name appear in all uppercase letters, but many programmers prefer to write them this way so they are easily distinguishable from regular variable names.

An initialization value must be given when declaring a variable with the `final` modifier, or an error will result when the program is compiled. A compiler error will also result if there are any statements in the program that attempt to change the value of a `final` variable.

An advantage of using named constants is that they make programs more self-documenting. The following statement:

```
amount = balance * 0.069;
```

can be changed to read

```
amount = balance * INTEREST_RATE;
```

A new programmer can read the second statement and know what is happening. It is evident that balance is being multiplied by the interest rate. Another advantage to this approach is that widespread changes can easily be made to the program. Let's say the interest rate appears in a dozen different statements throughout the program. When the rate changes, the initialization value in the definition of the named constant is the only value that needs to be modified. If the rate increases to 8.2 percent, the declaration can be changed to the following:

```
final double INTEREST_RATE = 0.082;
```

The program is then ready to be recompiled. Every statement that uses `INTEREST_RATE` will use the new value.

The `Math.PI` Named Constant

The `Math` class, which is part of the Java API, provides a predefined named constant, `Math.PI`. This constant is assigned the value 3.14159265358979323846, which is an approximation of the mathematical value pi. For example, look at the following statement:

```
area = Math.PI * radius * radius;
```

Assuming the radius variable holds the radius of a circle, this statement uses the Math.PI constant to calculate the area of the circle.

> For more information about the Math class, see Appendix G on the Student CD.

2.9 The String Class

CONCEPT: The String class allows you to create objects for holding strings. It also has various methods that allow you to work with strings.

You have already encountered strings and examined programs that display them on the screen, but let's take a moment to make sure you understand what a string is. A string is a sequence of characters. It can be used to represent any type of data that contains text, such as names, addresses, warning messages, and so forth. String literals are enclosed in double-quotation marks, such as the following:

```
"Hello World"
"Joe Mahoney"
```

Although programs commonly encounter strings and must perform a variety of tasks with them, Java does not have a primitive data type for storing them in memory. Instead, the Java API provides a class for handling strings. You use this class to create objects that are capable of storing strings and performing operations on them. Before discussing this class, let's briefly discuss how classes and objects are related.

Objects Are Created from Classes

Chapter 1 introduced you to objects as software entities that can contain attributes and methods. An object's attributes are data values that are stored in the object. An object's methods are procedures that perform operations on the object's attributes. Before an object can be created, however, it must be designed by a programmer. The programmer determines the attributes and methods that are necessary, and then creates a class that describes the object.

You have already seen classes used as containers for applications. A class can also be used to specify the attributes and methods that a particular type of object may have. Think of a class as a "blueprint" that objects may be created from. So a class is not an object, but a description of an object. When the program is running, it can use the class to create, in memory, as many objects as needed. Each object that is created from a class is called an *instance* of the class.

> **TIP:** Don't worry if these concepts seem a little fuzzy to you. As you progress through this book, the concepts of classes and objects will be reinforced again and again.

The String Class

The class that is provided by the Java API for handling strings is named String. The first step in using the String class is to declare a variable of the String class data type. Here is an example of a String variable declaration:

```
String name;
```

> **TIP:** The S in String is written in uppercase letters. By convention, the first character of a class name is always written in uppercase letters.

This statement declares name as a String variable. Remember that String is a class, not a primitive data type. Let's briefly look at the difference between primitive type variables and class type variables.

Primitive Type Variables and Class Type Variables

A variable of any type can be associated with an item of data. *Primitive type variables* hold the actual data items with which they are associated. For example, assume that number is an int variable. The following statement stores the value 25 in the variable:

```
number = 25;
```

This is illustrated in Figure 2-7.

Figure 2-7   A primitive type variable holds the data with which it is associated

The number variable holds the actual data with which it is associated.   25

A *class type variable* does not hold the actual data item that it is associated with, but holds the memory address of the data item it is associated with. If name is a String class variable, then name can hold the memory address of a String object. This is illustrated in Figure 2-8.

Figure 2-8   A String class variable can hold the address of a String object

When a class type variable holds the address of an object, it is said that the variable references the object. For this reason, class type variables are commonly known as *reference variables*.

Creating a `String` Object

Any time you write a string literal in your program, Java will create a `String` object in memory to hold it. You can create a `String` object in memory and store its address in a `String` variable with a simple assignment statement. Here is an example:

```
name = "Joe Mahoney";
```

Here, the string literal causes a `String` object to be created in memory with the value "Joe Mahoney" stored in it. Then the assignment operator stores the address of that object in the `name` variable. After this statement executes, it is said that the `name` variable references a `String` object. This is illustrated in Figure 2-9.

Figure 2-9   The name variable holds the address of a `String` object

You can also use the = operator to initialize a `String` variable, as shown here:

```
String name = "Joe Mahoney";
```

This statement declares name as a `String` variable, creates a `String` object with the value "Joe Mahoney" stored in it, and assigns the object's memory address to the `name` variable. Code Listing 2-20 shows `String` variables being declared, initialized, and then used in a `println` statement.

Code Listing 2-20   (`StringDemo.java`)

```java
 1  // A simple program demonstrating String objects.
 2
 3  public class StringDemo
 4  {
 5     public static void main(String[] args)
 6     {
 7        String greeting = "Good morning ";
 8        String name = "Herman";
 9
10        System.out.println(greeting + name);
11     }
12  }
```

Program Output

```
Good morning Herman
```

Because the String type is a class instead of a primitive data type, it provides numerous methods for working with strings. For example, the String class has a method named length that returns the length of the string stored in an object. Assuming the name variable references a String object, the following statement stores the length of its string in the variable stringSize (assume that stringSize is an int variable):

```
stringSize = name.length();
```

This statement calls the length method of the object that name refers to. To *call* a method means to execute it. The general form of a method call is as follows:

```
referenceVariable.method(arguments...)
```

referenceVariable is the name of a variable that references an object, method is the name of a method, and arguments... is zero or more arguments that are passed to the method. If no arguments are passed to the method, as is the case with the length method, a set of empty parentheses must follow the name of the method.

The String class's length method *returns* an int value. This means that the method sends an int value back to the statement that called it. This value can be stored in a variable, displayed on the screen, or used in calculations. Code Listing 2-21 demonstrates the length method.

Code Listing 2-21   (**StringLength.java**)

```java
 1  // This program demonstrates the String class's length method.
 2
 3  public class StringLength
 4  {
 5     public static void main(String[] args)
 6     {
 7        String name = "Herman";
 8        int stringSize;
 9
10        stringSize = name.length();
11        System.out.println(name + " has " + stringSize +
12                           " characters.");
13     }
14  }
```

Program Output

```
Herman has 6 characters.
```

NOTE: The String class's length method returns the number of characters in the string, including spaces.

You will study the String class methods in detail in Chapter 10, but let's look at a few more examples now. In addition to length, Table 2-15 describes the charAt, toLowerCase, and toUpperCase methods.

Table 2-15 A few `String` class methods

Method	Description and Example

`charAt(index)`	The argument *index* is an int value and specifies a character position in the string. The first character is at position 0, the second character is at position 1, and so forth. The method returns the character at the specified position. The return value is of the type char.
	Example:
	<pre>char letter;
	String name = "Herman";
	letter = name.charAt(3);</pre>After this code executes, the variable `letter` will hold the character 'm'.

`length()`	This method returns the number of characters in the string. The return value is of the type int.
	Example:
	<pre>int stringSize;
	String name = "Herman";
	stringSize = name.length();</pre>After this code executes, the `stringSize` variable will hold the value 6.

`toLowerCase()`	This method returns a new string that is the lowercase equivalent of the string contained in the calling object.
	Example:
	<pre>String bigName = "HERMAN";
	String littleName = bigName.toLowerCase();</pre>After this code executes, the object referenced by `littleName` will hold the string "herman".

`toUpperCase()`	This method returns a new string that is the uppercase equivalent of the string contained in the calling object.
	Example:
	<pre>String littleName = "herman";
	String bigName = littleName.toUpperCase();</pre>After this code executes, the object referenced by `bigName` will hold the string "HERMAN".

The program in Code Listing 2-22 demonstrates these methods.

Code Listing 2-22 (`StringMethods.java`)

```
1   // This program demonstrates a few of the String methods.
2
3   public class StringMethods
4   {
5      public static void main(String[] args)
6      {
7         String message = "Java is Great Fun!";
8         String upper = message.toUpperCase();
```

```
 9          String lower = message.toLowerCase();
10          char letter = message.charAt(2);
11          int stringSize = message.length();
12
13          System.out.println(message);
14          System.out.println(upper);
15          System.out.println(lower);
16          System.out.println(letter);
17          System.out.println(stringSize);
18      }
19  }
```

Program Output

```
Java is Great Fun!
JAVA IS GREAT FUN!
java is great fun!
v
18
```

 Checkpoint

2.27   Write a statement that declares a String variable named city. The variable should be initialized so it references an object with the string "San Francisco".

2.28   Assume that stringLength is an int variable. Write a statement that stores the length of the string referenced by the city variable (declared in Checkpoint 2.27) in stringLength.

2.29   Assume that oneChar is a char variable. Write a statement that stores the first character in the string referenced by the city variable (declared in Checkpoint 2.27) in oneChar.

2.30   Assume that upperCity is a String reference variable. Write a statement that stores the uppercase equivalent of the string referenced by the city variable (declared in Checkpoint 2.27) in upperCity.

2.31   Assume that lowerCity is a String reference variable. Write a statement that stores the lowercase equivalent of the string referenced by the city variable (declared in Checkpoint 2.27) in lowerCity.

2.10 Scope

CONCEPT: A variable's scope is the part of the program that has access to the variable.

Every variable has a *scope*. The scope of a variable is the part of the program where the variable may be accessed by its name. A variable is visible only to statements inside the variable's scope. The rules that define a variable's scope are complex, and you are only introduced to the concept here. In other chapters of the book we revisit this topic and expand on it.

So far, you have only seen variables declared inside the main method. Variables that are declared inside a method are called *local variables*. Later you will learn about variables that are declared outside a method, but for now, let's focus on the use of local variables.

A local variable's scope begins at the variable's declaration and ends at the end of the method in which the variable is declared. The variable cannot be accessed by statements that are outside this region. This means that a local variable cannot be accessed by code that is outside the method, or inside the method but before the variable's declaration. The program in Code Listing 2-23 shows an example.

Code Listing 2-23 (Scope.java)

```
 1  // This program can't find its variable.
 2
 3  public class Scope
 4  {
 5      public static void main(String[] args)
 6      {
 7          System.out.println(value);  // ERROR!
 8          int value = 100;
 9      }
10  }
```

The program does not compile because it attempts to send the contents of the variable value to println before the variable is declared. It is important to remember that the compiler reads your program from top to bottom. If it encounters a statement that uses a variable before the variable is declared, an error will result. To correct the program, the variable declaration must be written before any statement that uses it.

 NOTE: If you compile this program, the compiler will display an error message such as "cannot resolve symbol." This means that the compiler has encountered a name for which it cannot determine a meaning.

Another rule that you must remember about local variables is that you cannot have two local variables with the same name in the same scope. For example, look at the following method.

```
public static void main(String[] args)
{
    // Declare a variable named number and
    // display its value.
    int number = 7;
    System.out.println(number);
```

```
        // Declare another variable named number and
        // display its value.
        int number = 100;                // ERROR!!!
        System.out.println(number);      // ERROR!!!
    }
```

This method declares a variable named number and initializes it with the value 7. The variable's scope begins at the declaration statement and extends to the end of the method. Inside the variable's scope a statement appears that declares another variable named number. This statement will cause an error because you cannot have two local variables with the same name in the same scope.

2.11 Comments

CONCEPT: Comments are notes of explanation that document lines or sections of a program. Comments are part of the program, but the compiler ignores them. They are intended for people who may be reading the source code.

It may surprise you that one of the most important parts of a program has absolutely no impact on the way it runs. In fact, the compiler ignores this part of a program. Of course, it is the comments.

It is crucial that you develop the habit of thoroughly annotating your code with descriptive comments. It might take extra time now, but it will almost certainly save time in the future. Imagine writing a program of medium complexity with about 8,000 to 10,000 lines of code. Once you have written the code and satisfactorily debugged it, you happily put it away and move on to the next project. Ten months later you are asked to make a modification to the program (or worse, track down and fix an elusive bug). You open the file that contains your source code and stare at thousands of statements that now make no sense at all. If only you had left some notes to yourself explaining the program's code. Of course it's too late now. All that's left to do is decide what will take less time: figuring out the old program or completely rewriting it!

This scenario might sound extreme, but it's one you don't want to happen to you. Real-world programs are usually large and complex. Thoroughly documented code will make your life easier, not to mention those of the other programmers who read your code in the future.

Three Ways to Comment in Java

Single-Line Comments

You have already seen the first way to write comments in a Java program. You simply place two forward slashes (//) where you want the comment to begin. The compiler ignores everything from that point to the end of the line. Code Listing 2-24 shows that comments may be placed liberally throughout a program.

Code Listing 2-24 (Comment1.java)

```
1   // PROGRAM: Comment1.java
2   // Written by Herbert Dorfmann
3   // This program calculates company payroll
4
5   public class Comment1
6   {
7      public static void main(String[] args)
8      {
9         double payRate;       // Holds the hourly pay rate
10        double hours;         // Holds the hours worked
11        int employeeNumber;   // Holds the employee number
12
13        // The Remainder of This Program is Omitted.
14     }
15  }
```

In addition to telling who wrote the program and describing the purpose of variables, comments can also be used to explain complex procedures in your code.

Multi-Line Comments

The second type of comment in Java is the multi-line comment. *Multi-line comments* start with /* (a forward slash followed by an asterisk) and end with */ (an asterisk followed by a forward slash). Everything between these markers is ignored. Code Listing 2-25 illustrates how multi-line comments may be used.

Code Listing 2-25 (Comment2.java)

```
1   /*
2      PROGRAM: Comment2.java
3      Written by Herbert Dorfmann
4      This program calculates company payroll
5   */
6
7   public class Comment2
8   {
9      public static void main(String[] args)
10     {
11        double payRate;       // Holds the hourly pay rate
12        double hours;         // Holds the hours worked
13        int employeeNumber;   // Holds the employee number
14
```

```
15          // The Remainder of This Program is Omitted.
16      }
17  }
```

Unlike a comment started with //, a multi-line comment can span several lines. This makes it more convenient to write large blocks of comments because you do not have to mark every line. Consequently, the multi-line comment is inconvenient for writing single-line comments because you must type both a beginning and ending comment symbol.

Remember the following advice when using multi-line comments:

- Be careful not to reverse the beginning symbol with the ending symbol.
- Be sure not to forget the ending symbol.

Many programmers use asterisks or other characters to draw borders or boxes around their comments. This helps to visually separate the comments from surrounding code. These are called block comments. Table 2-16 shows four examples of block comments.

Table 2-16   Block comments

```
/*                                    //*********************************
 *   This program demonstrates the    //    This program demonstrates the *
 *   way to write comments.           //    way to write comments.        *
 */                                   //*********************************


///////////////////////////////////  //---------------------------------
//    This program demonstrates the   //    This program demonstrates the
//    way to write comments.          //    way to write comments.
///////////////////////////////////  //---------------------------------
```

Documentation Comments

The third type of comment is known as a documentation comment. *Documentation comments* can be read and processed by a program named javadoc, which comes with the Sun JDK. The purpose of the javadoc program is to read Java source code files and generate attractively formatted HTML files that document the source code. If the source code files contain any documentation comments, the information in the comments becomes part of the HTML documentation. The HTML documentation files may be viewed in a Web browser such as Internet Explorer or Netscape Navigator.

Any comment that starts with /** and ends with */ is considered a documentation comment. Normally you write a documentation comment just before a class header, giving a brief description of the class. You also write a documentation comment just before each method header, giving a brief description of the method. For example, Code Listing 2-26 shows a program with documentation comments. This program has a documentation comment just before the class header, and just before the main method header.

Code Listing 2-26 (Comment3.java)

```
 1  /**
 2     This class creates a program that calculates company payroll.
 3  */
 4
 5  public class Comment3
 6  {
 7     /**
 8        The main method is the program's starting point.
 9     */
10
11     public static void main(String[] args)
12     {
13        double payRate;        // Holds the hourly pay rate
14        double hours;          // Holds the hours worked
15        int employeeNumber;    // Holds the employee number
16
17        // The Remainder of This Program is Omitted.
18     }
19  }
```

You run the javadoc program from the operating system command prompt. Here is the general format of the javadoc command:

    javadoc *SourceFile*.java

SourceFile.java is the name of a Java source code file, including the .java extension. The file will be read by javadoc and documentation will be produced for it. For example, the following command will produce documentation for the *Comment3.java* source code file, which is shown in Code Listing 2-26:

    javadoc Comment3.java

After this command executes, several documentation files will be created in the same directory as the source code file. One of these files will be named *index.html*. Figure 2-10 shows the *index.html* file being viewed in Internet Explorer. Notice that the text that was written in the documentation comments appears in the file.

TIP: When you write a documentation comment for a method, the HTML documentation file that is produced by javadoc will have two sections for the method: a summary section and a detail section. The first sentence in the method's documentation comment is used as the summary of the method. Note that javadoc considers the end of the sentence as a period followed by a whitespace character. For this reason, when a method description contains more than one sentence, you should always end the first sentence with a period followed by a whitespace character. The method's detail section will contain all of the description that appears in the documentation comment.

Figure 2-10   Documentation generated by `javadoc`

Comment3 - Microsoft Internet Explorer provided by BellSouth

File   Edit   View   Favorites   Tools   Help

Back   Search   Favorites   Media

Links   Address

Google   Search Web   PageRank   68 blocked   AutoFill   Options

All Classes
Comment3

Package **Class** Tree Deprecated Index Help
PREV CLASS   NEXT CLASS   FRAMES   NO FRAMES
SUMMARY: NESTED | FIELD | CONSTR | METHOD   DETAIL: FIELD | CONSTR | METHOD

Class Comment3

java.lang.Object
  └ Comment3

public class **Comment3**   This description is from the documentation comment that appears
extends java.lang.Object   just before the class header.

This class creates a program that calculates company payroll.

Constructor Summary

Comment3()

Method Summary

static void | main(java.lang.String[] args)   This description is from the documentation comment that
              The main method is the program's starting point.   appears just before the main method header.

My Computer

If you look at the JDK documentation, which are HTML files that you view in a Web browser, you will see that they are formatted in the same way as the files generated by `javadoc`. A benefit of using `javadoc` to document your source code is that your documentation will have the same professional look and feel as the standard Java documentation.

 The JDK documentation files shown in Figure 2-10 are on the Student CD that accompanies this book.

From this point forward in the book we will use documentation comments in the example source code. As we progress through various topics, you will see additional uses of documentation comments and the `javadoc` program.

Checkpoint

2.32   How do you write a single line comment? How do you write a multi-line comment? How do you write a documentation comment?

2.33   How are documentation comments different from other types of comments?

2.12 Programming Style

CONCEPT: Programming style refers to the way a programmer uses spaces, indentations, blank lines, and punctuation characters to visually arrange a program's source code.

In Chapter 1, you learned that syntax rules govern the way a language may be used. The syntax rules of Java dictate how and where to place key words, semicolons, commas, braces, and other elements of the language. The compiler checks for syntax errors, and if there are none, generates byte code.

When the compiler reads a program it processes it as one long stream of characters. The compiler doesn't care that each statement is on a separate line, or that spaces separate operators from operands. Humans, on the other hand, find it difficult to read programs that aren't written in a visually pleasing manner. Consider Code Listing 2-27 for example.

Code Listing 2-27 (Compact.java)

```
1  public class Compact {public static void main(String [] args){int
2  shares=220; double averagePrice=14.67; System.out.println(
3  "There were "+shares+" shares sold at $"+averagePrice+
4  " per share.");}}
```

Program Output

```
There were 220 shares sold at $14.67 per share.
```

Although the program is syntactically correct (it doesn't violate any rules of Java), it is very difficult to read. The same program is shown in Code Listing 2-28, written in a more understandable style.

Code Listing 2-28 (Readable.java)

```
1  /**
2      This example is much more readable than Compact.java.
3  */
4
5  public class Readable
6  {
7     public static void main(String[] args)
8     {
9        int shares = 220;
10       double averagePrice = 14.67;
11
12       System.out.println("There were " + shares +
13                          " shares sold at $" +
14                          averagePrice + " per share.");
```

```
15      }
16   }
```

Program Output

There were 220 shares sold at $14.67 per share.

The term *programming style* usually refers to the way source code is visually arranged. It includes techniques for consistently putting spaces and indentations in a program so visual cues are created. These cues quickly tell a programmer important information about a program.

For example, notice in Code Listing 2-28 that inside the class's braces each line is indented, and inside the main method's braces each line is indented again. It is a common programming style to indent all the lines inside a set of braces, as shown in Figure 2-11.

Figure 2-11 Indentation

```
/**
     This example is much more readable than Compact.java.
*/

public class Readable
{
INDENT public static void main(String[] args)
INDENT {
INDENT INDENT int shares = 220;
INDENT INDENT double averagePrice = 14.67;

INDENT INDENT System.out.println("There were " + shares +
INDENT INDENT [Extra spaces inserted here] " shares sold at $" +
INDENT INDENT [Extra spaces inserted here] averagePrice + " per share.");
INDENT }
}
```

Another aspect of programming style is how to handle statements that are too long to fit on one line. Notice that the println statement is spread out over three lines. Extra spaces are inserted at the beginning of the statement's second and third lines, which indicate that they are continuations.

When declaring multiple variables of the same type with a single statement, it is a common practice to write each variable name on a separate line with a comment explaining the variable's purpose. Here is an example:

```
int fahrenheit,    // To hold the Fahrenheit temperature
    celsius,       // To hold the Celsius temperature
    kelvin;        // To hold the Kelvin temperature
```

You may have noticed in the example programs that a blank line is inserted between the variable declarations and the statements that follow them. This is intended to separate the declarations visually from the executable statements.

There are many other issues related to programming style. They will be presented throughout the book.

2.13 Reading Keyboard Input

CONCEPT: Objects of the **Scanner** class can be used to read input from the keyboard.

Previously we discussed the System.out object, and how it refers to the standard output device. The Java API has another object, System.in, which refers to the standard input device. The *standard input device* is normally the keyboard. You can use the System.in object to read keystrokes that have been typed at the keyboard. However, using System.in is not as simple and straightforward as using System.out because the System.in object reads input only as byte values. This isn't very useful because programs normally require values of other data types as input. To work around this, you can use the System.in object in conjunction with an object of the Scanner class. The Scanner class is designed to read input from a source (such as System.in) and it provides methods that you can use to retrieve the input formatted as primitive values or strings.

First, you create a Scanner object and connect it to the System.in object. Here is an example of a statement that does just that:

```
Scanner keyboard = new Scanner(System.in);
```

Let's dissect the statement into two parts. The first part of the statement,

```
Scanner keyboard
```

declares a variable named keyboard. The data type of the variable is Scanner. Because Scanner is a class, the keyboard variable is a class type variable. Recall from our discussion on String objects that a class type variable holds the memory address of an object. Therefore, the keyboard variable will be used to hold the address of a Scanner object. The second part of the statement is as follows:

```
= new Scanner(System.in);
```

The first thing we see in this part of the statement is the assignment operator (=). The assignment operator will assign something to the keyboard variable. After the assignment operator we see the word new, which is a Java key word. The purpose of the new key word is to create an object in memory. The type of object that will be created is listed next. In this case, we see Scanner(System.in) listed after the new key word. This specifies that a Scanner object should be created, and it should be connected to the System.in object. The memory address of the object is assigned (by the = operator) to the variable keyboard. After the statement executes, the keyboard variable will reference the Scanner object that was created in memory.

Figure 2-12 points out the purpose of each part of this statement. Figure 2-13 illustrates how the keyboard variable references an object of the Scanner class.

Figure 2-12   The parts of the statement

Figure 2-13   The keyboard variable references a Scanner object

> **NOTE:** In the preceding code, we chose keyboard as the variable name. There is nothing special about the name keyboard. We simply chose that name because we will use the variable to read input from the keyboard.

The Scanner class has methods for reading strings, bytes, integers, long integers, short integers, floats and doubles. For example, the following code uses an object of the Scanner class to read an int value from the keyboard and assign the value to the number variable.

```
int number;
Scanner keyboard = new Scanner(System.in);
System.out.print("Enter an integer value: ");
number = keyboard.nextInt();
```

The last statement shown here calls the Scanner class's nextInt method. The nextInt method formats an input value as an int, and then returns that value. Therefore, this statement formats the input that was entered at the keyboard as an int, and then returns it. The value is assigned to the number variable.

Table 2-17 lists several of the Scanner class's methods and describes their use.

Table 2-17 Some of the `Scanner` class methods

Method	Example and Description
| nextByte | **Example Usage:**<br><br>```java
byte x;
Scanner keyboard = new Scanner(System.in);
System.out.print("Enter a byte value: ");
x = keyboard.nextByte();
```<br>**Description:** Returns input as a byte. |
| nextDouble | **Example Usage:**<br><br>```java
double number;
Scanner keyboard = new Scanner(System.in);
System.out.print("Enter a double value: ");
number = keyboard.nextDouble();
```<br>**Description:** Returns input as a double. |
| nextFloat | **Example Usage:**<br><br>```java
float number;
Scanner keyboard = new Scanner(System.in);
System.out.print("Enter a float value: ");
number = keyboard.nextFloat();
```<br>**Description:** Returns input as a float. |
| nextInt | **Example Usage:**<br><br>```java
int number;
Scanner keyboard = new Scanner(System.in);
System.out.print("Enter an integer value: ");
number = keyboard.nextInt();
```<br>**Description:** Returns input as an int. |
| nextLine | **Example Usage:**<br><br>```java
String name;
Scanner keyboard = new Scanner(System.in);
System.out.print("Enter your name: ");
name = keyboard.nextLine();
```<br>**Description:** Returns input as a String. |
| nextLong | **Example Usage:**<br><br>```java
long number;
Scanner keyboard = new Scanner(System.in);
System.out.print("Enter a long value: ");
number = keyboard.nextLong();
```<br>**Description:** Returns input as a long. |
| nextShort | **Example Usage:**<br><br>```java
short number;
Scanner keyboard = new Scanner(System.in);
System.out.print("Enter a short value: ");
number = keyboard.nextShort();
```<br>**Description:** Returns input as a short. |
```

Using the `import` Statement

There is one last detail about the `Scanner` class that you must know before you will be ready to use it. The `Scanner` class is not automatically available to your Java programs. Any program that uses the `Scanner` class should have the following statement near the beginning of the file, before any class definition:

```
import java.util.Scanner;
```

This statement tells the Java compiler where in the Java library to find the `Scanner` class, and makes it available to your program.

Code Listing 2-29 shows the `Scanner` class being used to read a `String`, an `int`, and a `double`.

Code Listing 2-29   (`Payroll.java`)

```java
 1   import java.util.Scanner;   // Needed for the Scanner class
 2
 3   /**
 4      This program demonstrates the Scanner class.
 5   */
 6
 7   public class Payroll
 8   {
 9      public static void main(String[] args)
10      {
11         String name;          // To hold a name
12         int hours;            // Hours worked
13         double payRate;       // Hourly pay rate
14         double grossPay;      // Gross pay
15
16         // Create a Scanner object to read input.
17         Scanner keyboard = new Scanner(System.in);
18
19         // Get the user's name.
20         System.out.print("What is your name? ");
21         name = keyboard.nextLine();
22
23         // Get the number of hours worked this week.
24         System.out.print("How many hours did you work this week? ");
25         hours = keyboard.nextInt();
26
27         // Get the user's hourly pay rate.
28         System.out.print("What is your hourly pay rate? ");
29         payRate = keyboard.nextDouble();
30
31         // Calculate the gross pay.
32         grossPay = hours * payRate;
33
```

```
34          // Display the resulting information.
35          System.out.println("Hello " + name);
36          System.out.println("Your gross pay is $" + grossPay);
37      }
38  }
```

Program Output with Example Input Shown in Bold

What is your name? **Joe Mahoney [Enter]**
How many hours did you work this week? **40 [Enter]**
What is your hourly pay rate? **20 [Enter]**
Hello Joe Mahoney
Your gross pay is $800.0

 NOTE: Notice that each `Scanner` class method that we used waits for the user to press the [Enter] key before it returns a value. When the [Enter] key is pressed, the cursor automatically moves to the next line for subsequent output operations.

Reading a Character

Sometimes you will want to read a single character from the keyboard. For example, your program might ask the user a yes/no question, and specify that he or she type Y for yes or N for no. The `Scanner` class does not have a method for reading a single character, however. The approach that we will use in this book for reading a character is to use the `Scanner` class's `nextLine` method to read a string from the keyboard, and then use the `String` class's `charAt` method to extract the first character of the string. This will be the character that the user entered at the keyboard. Here is an example:

```
String input;  // To hold a line of input
char answer;   // To hold a single character

// Create a Scanner object for keyboard input.
Scanner keyboard = new Scanner(System.in);

// Ask the user a question.
System.out.print("Are you having fun? (Y=yes, N=no) ");
input = keyboard.nextLine();  // Get a line of input.
answer = input.charAt(0);     // Get the first character.
```

The `input` variable references a `String` object. The last statement in this code calls the `String` class's `charAt` method to retrieve the character at position 0, which is the first character in the string. After this statement executes, the `answer` variable will hold the character that the user typed at the keyboard.

Mixing Calls to `nextLine` with Calls to Other Scanner Methods

When you call one of the `Scanner` class's methods to read a primitive value, such as `nextInt` or `nextDouble`, and then call the `nextLine` method to read a string, an annoying and hard-to-find problem can occur. For example, look at the program in Code Listing 2-30.

Code Listing 2-30   `(InputProblem.java)`

```
1   import java.util.Scanner;  // Needed for the Scanner class
2
3   /*
4      This program has a problem reading input.
5   */
6
7   public class InputProblem
8   {
9      public static void main(String[] args)
10     {
11        String name;    // To hold the user's name
12        int age;        // To hold the user's age
13        double income;  // To hold the user's income
14
15        // Create a Scanner object to read input.
16        Scanner keyboard = new Scanner(System.in);
17
18        // Get the user's age.
19        System.out.print("What is your age? ");
20        age = keyboard.nextInt();
21
22        // Get the user's income
23        System.out.print("What is your annual income? ");
24        income = keyboard.nextDouble();
25
26        // Get the user's name.
27        System.out.print("What is your name? ");
28        name = keyboard.nextLine();
29
30        // Display the information back to the user.
31        System.out.println("Hello " + name + ". Your age is " +
32                           age + " and your income is $" +
33                           income);
34     }
35  }
```

Program Output with Example Input Shown in Bold

```
What is your age? 24 [Enter]
What is your annual income? 50000.00 [Enter]
What is your name? Hello . Your age is 24 and your income is $50000.0
```

Notice in the example output that the program first allows the user to enter his or her age. The statement in line 20 reads an int from the keyboard and stores the value in the age variable. Next, the user enters his or her income. The statement in line 24 reads a double from the keyboard and stores the value in the income variable. Then the user is asked to enter his or her name, but it appears that the statement in line 28 is skipped. The name is never read from the keyboard. This happens because of a slight difference in behavior between the nextLine method and the other Scanner class methods.

When the user types keystrokes at the keyboard, those keystrokes are stored in an area of memory that is sometimes called the *keyboard buffer*. Pressing the [Enter] key causes a new-line character to be stored in the keyboard buffer. In the example running of the program in Code Listing 2-30, the user was asked to enter his or her age, and the statement in line 20 called the nextInt method to read an integer from the keyboard buffer. Notice that the user typed 24 and then pressed the [Enter] key. The nextInt method read the value 24 from the keyboard buffer, and then stopped when it encountered the newline character. So the value 24 was read from the keyboard buffer, but the newline character was not read. The newline character remained in the keyboard buffer.

Next, the user was asked to enter his or her annual income. The user typed 50000.00 and then pressed the [Enter] key. When the nextDouble method in line 24 executed, it first encountered the newline character that was left behind by the nextInt method. This does not cause a problem because the nextDouble method is designed to skip any leading newline characters it encounters. It skips over the initial newline, reads the value 50000.00 from the keyboard buffer, and stops reading when it encounters the next newline character. This newline character is then left in the keyboard buffer.

Next, the user is asked to enter his or her name. In line 28 the nextLine method is called. The nextLine method, however, is not designed to skip over an initial newline character. If a newline character is the first character that the nextLine method encounters, then nothing will be read. Because the nextDouble method, back in line 24, left a newline character in the keyboard buffer, the nextLine method will not read any input. Instead, it will immediately terminate and the user will not be given a chance to enter his or her name.

Although the details of this problem might seem confusing, the solution is easy. The program in Code Listing 2-31 is a modification of Code Listing 2-30, with the input problem fixed.

Code Listing 2-31 (CorrectedInputProblem.java)

```
 1  import java.util.Scanner;  // Needed for the Scanner class
 2
 3  /*
 4     This program correctly reads numeric and string input.
 5  */
 6
 7  public class CorrectedInputProblem
 8  {
 9     public static void main(String[] args)
10     {
11        String name;   // To hold the user's name
```

```
12        int age;        // To hold the user's age
13        double income; // To hold the user's income
14
15        // Create a Scanner object to read input.
16        Scanner keyboard = new Scanner(System.in);
17
18        // Get the user's age.
19        System.out.print("What is your age? ");
20        age = keyboard.nextInt();
21
22        // Get the user's income
23        System.out.print("What is your annual income? ");
24        income = keyboard.nextDouble();
25
26        // Consume the remaining newline.
27        keyboard.nextLine();
28
29        // Get the user's name.
30        System.out.print("What is your name? ");
31        name = keyboard.nextLine();
32
33        // Display the information back to the user.
34        System.out.println("Hello " + name + ". Your age is " +
35                            age + " and your income is $" +
36                            income);
37    }
38 }
```

Program Output with Example Input Shown in Bold

What is your age? **24 [Enter]**
What is your annual income? **50000.00 [Enter]**
What is your name? **Mary Simpson [Enter]**
Hello Mary Simpson. Your age is 24 and your income is $50000.0

Notice that after the user's income is read by the nextDouble method in line 24, the nextLine method is called in line 27. The purpose of this call is to consume, or remove, the newline character that remains in the keyboard buffer. Then, in line 31, the nextLine method is called again. This time it correctly reads the user's name.

NOTE: Notice that in line 27, where we consume the remaining newline character, we do not assign the method's return value to any variable. This is because we are simply calling the method to remove the newline character, and we do not need to keep the method's return value.

2.14   Dialog Boxes

CONCEPT: The `JOptionPane` class allows you to quickly display a dialog box, which is a small graphical window displaying a message or requesting input.

A *dialog box* is a small graphical window that displays a message to the user or requests input. You can quickly display dialog boxes with the `JOptionPane` class. In this section we will discuss the following types of dialog boxes and how you can display them using `JOptionPane`:

- Message Dialog   A dialog box that displays a message; an OK button is also displayed
- Input Dialog   A dialog box that prompts the user for input and provides a text field where input is typed; an OK button and a Cancel button are also displayed

Figure 2-14 shows an example of each type of dialog box.

Figure 2-14   A message dialog and an input dialog

The `JOptionPane` class is not automatically available to your Java programs. Any program that uses the `JOptionPane` class must have the following statement near the beginning of the file:

```
import javax.swing.JOptionPane;
```

This statement tells the compiler where to find the `JOptionPane` class and makes it available to your program.

Displaying Message Dialogs

The `showMessageDialog` method is used to display a message dialog. Here is a statement that calls the method:

```
JOptionPane.showMessageDialog(null, "Hello World");
```

The first argument is only important in programs that display other graphical windows. You will learn more about this in Chapter 7. Until then, we will always pass the key word null as the first argument. This causes the dialog box to be displayed in the center of the screen. The second argument is the message that we wish to display in the dialog box. This code will cause the dialog box in Figure 2-15 to appear. When the user clicks the OK button, the dialog box will close.

Figure 2-15 Message dialog

Displaying Input Dialogs

An input dialog is a quick and simple way to ask the user to enter data. You use the JOptionPane class's showInputDialog method to display an input dialog. The following code calls the method:

```
String name;
name = JOptionPane.showInputDialog("Enter your name.");
```

The argument passed to the method is a message to display in the dialog box. This statement will cause the dialog box shown in Figure 2-16 to be displayed in the center of the screen. If the user clicks the OK button, name will reference the string value entered by the user into the text field. If the user clicks the Cancel button, name will reference the special value null.

Figure 2-16 Input dialog

An Example Program

The program in Code Listing 2-32 demonstrates how to use both types of dialog boxes. This program uses input dialogs to ask the user to enter his or her first, middle, and last names, and then displays a greeting with a message dialog. When this program executes, the dialog boxes shown in Figure 2-17 will be displayed, one at a time.

Code Listing 2-32 (`NamesDialog.java`)

```java
 1  import javax.swing.JOptionPane;
 2
 3  /**
 4     This program demonstrates using dialogs with
 5     JOptionPane.
 6  */
 7
 8  public class NamesDialog
 9  {
10     public static void main(String[] args)
11     {
12        String firstName;  // The user's first name
13        String middleName; // The user's middle name
14        String lastName;   // The user's last name
15
16        // Get the user's first name.
17        firstName =
18              JOptionPane.showInputDialog("What is " +
19                                    "your first name? ");
20
21        // Get the user's middle name.
22        middleName =
23              JOptionPane.showInputDialog("What is " +
24                                    "your middle name? ");
25
26        // Get the user's last name.
27        lastName =
28              JOptionPane.showInputDialog("What is " +
29                                    "your last name? ");
30
31        // Display a greeting
32        JOptionPane.showMessageDialog(null, "Hello " +
33                          firstName + " " + middleName +
34                          " " + lastName);
35        System.exit(0);
36     }
37  }
```

Notice the last statement in the main method:

```java
System.exit(0);
```

This statement causes the program to end, and is required if you use the JOptionPane class to display dialog boxes. Unlike a console program, a program that uses JOptionPane does not automatically stop executing when the end of the main method is reached, because the JOptionPane class causes an additional task to run in the JVM. If the System.exit method

Figure 2-17   Dialog boxes displayed by the `NamesDialog` program

The first dialog box appears as shown here.
The user types Joe and clicks OK.

The second dialog box appears, as shown here. In
this example the user types Clondike and clicks OK.

The third dialog box appears, as shown here. In
this example the user types Mahoney and clicks OK.

The fourth dialog box appears, as
shown here, displaying a greeting.

is not called, this task, also known as a *thread*, will continue to execute, even after the end of the `main` method has been reached.

The `System.exit` method requires an integer argument. This argument is an exit code that is passed back to the operating system. Although this code is usually ignored, it can be used outside the program to indicate whether the program ended successfully or as the result of a failure. The value 0 traditionally indicates that the program ended successfully.

Converting String Input to Numbers

Unlike the `Scanner` class, the `JOptionPane` class does not have different methods for reading values of different data types as input. The `showInputDialog` method always returns the user's input as a `String`, even if the user enters numeric data. For example, if the user enters the number 72 into an input dialog, the `showInputDialog` method will return the string `"72"`. This can be a problem if you wish to use the user's input in a math operation because, as you know, you cannot perform math on strings. In such a case, you must convert the input to a numeric value. To convert a string value to a numeric value, you use one of the methods listed in Table 2-18.

Table 2-18 Methods for converting strings to numbers

Method	Use this method to . . .	Example Code
`Byte.parseByte`	Convert a string to a byte.	`byte num;` `num = Byte.parseByte(str);`
`Double.parseDouble`	Convert a string to a double.	`double num;` `num = Double.parseDouble(str);`
`Float.parseFloat`	Convert a string to a float.	`float num;` `num = Float.parseFloat(str);`
`Integer.parseInt`	Convert a string to an int.	`int num;` `num = Integer.parseInt(str);`
`Long.parseLong`	Convert a string to a long.	`long num;` `num = Long.parseLong(str);`
`Short.parseShort`	Convert a string to a short.	`short num;` `num = Short.parseShort(str);`

NOTE: The methods in Table 2-18 are part of Java's wrapper classes, which you will learn more about in Chapter 10.

Here is an example of how you would use the `Integer.parseInt` method to convert the value returned from the `JOptionPane.showInputDialog` method to an `int`:

```
int number;
String str;
str = JOptionPane.showInputDialog("Enter a number.");
number = Integer.parseInt(str);
```

After this code executes, the `number` variable will hold the value entered by the user, converted to an `int`. Here is an example of how you would use the `Double.parseDouble` method to convert the user's input to a `double`:

```
double price;
String str;
str = JOptionPane.showInputDialog("Enter the retail price.");
price = Double.parseDouble(str);
```

After this code executes, the `price` variable will hold the value entered by the user, converted to a `double`. Code Listing 2-33 shows a complete program. This is a modification of the `Payroll.java` program in Code Listing 2-29. When this program executes, the dialog boxes shown in Figure 2-18 will be displayed, one at a time.

Code Listing 2-33 (`PayrollDialog.java`)

```java
 1 import javax.swing.JOptionPane;
 2
 3 /**
 4    This program demonstrates using dialogs with
 5    JOptionPane.
 6 */
 7
 8 public class PayrollDialog
 9 {
10    public static void main(String[] args)
11    {
12       String inputString;      // For reading input
13       String name;             // The user's name
14       int hours;               // The number of hours worked
15       double payRate;          // The user's hourly pay rate
16       double grossPay;         // The user's gross pay
17
18       // Get the user's name.
19       name = JOptionPane.showInputDialog("What is " +
20                                          "your name? ");
21
22       // Get the hours worked.
23       inputString =
24         JOptionPane.showInputDialog("How many hours " +
25                                     "did you work this week? ");
26
27       // Convert the input to an int.
28       hours = Integer.parseInt(inputString);
29
30       // Get the hourly pay rate.
31       inputString =
32         JOptionPane.showInputDialog("What is your " +
33                                     "hourly pay rate? ");
34
35       // Convert the input to a double.
36       payRate = Double.parseDouble(inputString);
37
38       // Calculate the gross pay.
39       grossPay = hours * payRate;
40
41       // Display the results.
42       JOptionPane.showMessageDialog(null, "Hello " +
43                     name + ". Your gross pay is $" +
44                     grossPay);
45
46       // End the program.
47       System.exit(0);
48    }
49 }
```

Figure 2-18   Dialog boxes displayed by `PayrollDialog.java`

The first dialog box appears as shown here. The user
enters his or her name and then clicks OK.

> **Input**   ⊠
>
> **?**   **What is your name?**
>
> Joe Mahoney
>
> OK   Cancel

The second dialog box appears, as shown here. The user
enters the number of hours workded and then clicks OK.

> **Input**   ⊠
>
> **?**   **How many hours did you work this week?**
>
> 40
>
> OK   Cancel

The third dialog box appears, as shown here. The user
enters his or her hourly pay rate and then clicks OK.

> **Input**   ⊠
>
> **?**   **What is your hourly pay rate?**
>
> 20
>
> OK   Cancel

The fourth dialog box appears, as shown here.

> **Message**   ⊠
>
> **i**   **Hello Joe Mahoney. Your gross pay is $800.0**
>
> OK

Checkpoint

2.34   What is the purpose of the following types of dialog boxes?
Message dialog
Input dialog

2.35   Write code that will display each of the dialog boxes shown in Figure 2-19.

Figure 2-19   Dialog boxes

a)
> **Message**   ⊠
>
> **i**   **Greetings Earthling.**
>
> OK

b)
> **Input**   ⊠
>
> **?**   **Enter a number.**
>
>
>
> OK   Cancel

2.36 Write code that displays an input dialog asking the user to enter his or her age. Convert the input value to an `int` and store it in an `int` variable named `age`.

2.37 What `import` statement do you write in a program that uses the `JOptionPane` class?

2.15 Common Errors to Avoid

- **Mismatched braces, quotation marks, or parentheses.** In this chapter you saw that the statements making up a class definition are enclosed in a set of braces. Also, you saw that the statements in a method are also enclosed in a set of braces. For every opening brace, there must be a closing brace in the proper location. The same is true of double-quotation marks that enclose string literals and single-quotation marks that enclose character literals. Also, in a statement that uses parentheses, such as a mathematical expression, you must have a closing parenthesis for every opening parenthesis.
- **Misspelling key words.** Java will not recognize a key word that has been misspelled.
- **Using capital letters in key words.** Remember that Java is a case-sensitive language, and all key words are written in lowercase. Using an uppercase letter in a key word is the same as misspelling the key word.
- **Using a key word as a variable name.** The key words are reserved for special uses; they cannot be used for any other purpose.
- **Using inconsistent spelling of variable names.** Each time you use a variable name, it must be spelled exactly as it appears in its declaration statement.
- **Using inconsistent case of letters in variable names.** Because Java is a case-sensitive language, it distinguishes between uppercase and lowercase letters. Java will not recognize a variable name that is not written exactly as it appears in its declaration statement.
- **Inserting a space in a variable name.** Spaces are not allowed in variable names. Instead of using a two-word name such as `gross pay`, use one word, such as `grossPay`.
- **Forgetting the semicolon at the end of a statement.** A semicolon appears at the end of each complete statement in Java.
- **Assigning a `double` literal to a `float` variable.** Java is a strongly typed language, which means that it only allows you to store values of compatible data types in variables. All floating-point literals are treated as `doubles`, and a `double` value is not compatible with a `float` variable. A floating-point literal must end with the letter `f` or `F` in order to be stored in a `float` variable.
- **Using commas or other currency symbols in numeric literals.** Numeric literals cannot contain commas or currency symbols, such as the dollar sign.
- **Unintentionally performing integer division.** When both operands of a division statement are integers, the statement will result in an integer. If there is a remainder, it will be discarded.
- **Forgetting to group parts of a mathematical expression.** If you use more than one operator in a mathematical expression, the expression will be evaluated according to the order of operations. If you wish to change the order in which the operators are used, you must use parentheses to group part of the expression.
- **Inserting a space in a combined assignment operator.** A space cannot appear between the two operators that make a combined assignment operator.
- **Using a variable to receive the result of a calculation when the variable's data type is incompatible with the data type of the result.** A variable that receives the result of a calculation must be of a data type that is compatible with the data type of the result.

- **Incorrectly terminating a multi-line comment or a documentation comment.** Multi-line comments and documentation comments are terminated by the */ characters. Forgetting to place these characters at a comment's desired ending point, or accidentally switching the * and the /, will cause the comment not to have an ending point.
- **Forgetting to use the correct import statement in a program that uses the Scanner class or the JOptionPane class.** In order for the Scanner class to be available to your program, you must have the import java.util.Scanner; statement near the top of your program file. In order for the JOptionPane class to be available to your program, you must have the import javax.swing.JOptionPane; statement near the top of the program file.
- **When using an input dialog to read numeric input, not converting the showInputDialog method's return value to a number.** The showInputDialog method always returns the user's input as a string. If the user enters a numeric value, it must be converted to a number before it can be used in a math statement.

Review Questions and Exercises

Multiple Choice and True/False

1. Every complete statement ends with a _____.
   a. period
   b. parenthesis
   c. semicolon
   d. ending brace

2. The following data

   ```
   72
   'A'
   "Hello World"
   2.8712
   ```

   are all examples of _____.
   a. variables
   b. literals
   c. strings
   d. none of these

3. A group of statements, such as the contents of a class or a method, are enclosed in

   _____.
   a. braces {}
   b. parentheses ()
   c. brackets []
   d. any of these will do

4. Which of the following are *not* valid assignment statements? (Indicate all that apply.)
   a. total = 9;
   b. 72 = amount;
   c. profit = 129
   d. letter = 'W';

Review Questions and Exercises

5. Which of the following are not valid `println` statements? (Indicate all that apply.)
   a. `System.out.println + "Hello World";`
   b. `System.out.println("Have a nice day");`
   c. `out.System.println(value);`
   d. `println.out(Programming is great fun);`

6. The negation operator is _____.
   a. unary
   b. binary
   c. ternary
   d. none of these

7. This key word is used to declare a named constant.
   a. `constant`
   b. `namedConstant`
   c. `final`
   d. `concrete`

8. These characters mark the beginning of a multi-line comment.
   a. `//`
   b. `/*`
   c. `*/`
   d. `/**`

9. These characters mark the beginning of a single-line comment.
   a. `//`
   b. `/*`
   c. `*/`
   d. `/**`

10. These characters mark the beginning of a documentation comment.
    a. `//`
    b. `/*`
    c. `*/`
    d. `/**`

11. Which `Scanner` class method would you use to read a string as input?
    a. `nextString`
    b. `nextLine`
    c. `readString`
    d. `getLine`

12. Which `Scanner` class method would you use to read a double as input?
    a. `nextDouble`
    b. `getDouble`
    c. `readDouble`
    d. None of these; you cannot read a `double` with the `Scanner` class

13. You can use this class to display dialog boxes.
    a. JOptionPane
    b. BufferedReader
    c. InputStreamReader
    d. DialogBox

14. When Java converts a lower-ranked value to a higher-ranked type, it is called a _____
    _____.
    a. 4-bit conversion
    b. escalating conversion
    c. widening conversion
    d. narrowing conversion

15. This type of operator lets you manually convert a value, even if it means that a narrowing conversion will take place.
    a. cast
    b. binary
    c. uploading
    d. dot

16. **True or False:** A left brace in a Java program is always followed by a right brace later in the program.

17. **True or False:** A variable must be declared before it can be used.

18. **True or False:** Variable names may begin with a number.

19. **True or False:** You cannot change the value of a variable whose declaration uses the final key word.

20. **True or False:** Comments that begin with // can be processed by javadoc.

21. **True or False:** If one of an operator's operands is a double, and the other operand is an int, Java will automatically convert the value of the double to an int.

Predict the Output

What will the following code segments print on the screen?

1.
```java
int freeze = 32, boil = 212;
freeze = 0;
boil = 100;
System.out.println(freeze + "\n"+ boil + "\n");
```

2.
```java
int x = 0, y = 2;
x = y * 4;
System.out.println(x + "\n" + y + "\n");
```

3.
```java
System.out.print("I am the incredible");
System.out.print("computing\nmachine");
System.out.print("\nand I will\namaze\n)";
System.out.println("you.");
```

4.
```
System.out.print("Be careful\n)";
System.out.print("This might/n be a trick ");
System.out.println("question.");
```

5.
```
int a, x = 23;
a = x % 2;
System.out.println(x + "\n" + a);
```

Find the Error

There are a number of syntax errors in the following program. Locate as many as you can.

```
*/   What's wrong with this program? /*
public MyProgram
{
    public static void main(String[] args);
    }
        int a, b, c     \\ Three integers
        a = 3
        b = 4
        c = a + b
        System.out.println('The value of c is' + C);
    {
```

Algorithm Workbench

1. Show how the `double` variables `temp`, `weight`, and `age` can be declared in one statement.

2. Show how the `int` variables `months`, `days`, and `years` may be declared in one statement, with `months` initialized to 2 and `years` initialized to 3.

3. Write assignment statements that perform the following operations with the variables `a`, `b`, and `c`.

   a. Adds 2 to `a` and stores the result in `b`
   b. Multiplies `b` times 4 and stores the result in `a`
   c. Divides `a` by 3.14 and stores the result in `b`
   d. Subtracts 8 from `b` and stores the result in `a`
   e. Stores the character 'K' in `c`
   f. Stores the Unicode code for 'B' in `c`

4. Assume the variables `result`, `w`, `x`, `y`, and `z` are all integers, and that $w = 5$, $x = 4$, $y = 8$, and $z = 2$. What value will be stored in `result` in each of the following statements?

   a. `result = x + y;`
   b. `result = z * 2;`
   c. `result = y / x;`
   d. `result = y - z;`
   e. `result = w % 2;`

5. How would each of the following numbers be represented in E notation?
   a. 3.287×10^6
   b. -9.7865×10^{12}
   c. 7.65491×10^{-3}

6. Modify the following program so it prints two blank lines between each line of text.

```java
public class
{
    public static void main(String[] args)
    {
        System.out.print("Hearing in the distance");
        System.out.print("Two mandolins like creatures in the");
        System.out.print("dark");
        System.out.print("Creating the agony of ecstasy.");
        System.out.println("                    - George Barker");
    }
}
```

7. Convert the following pseudocode to Java code. Be sure to declare the appropriate variables.

   Store 20 in the speed variable.
   Store 10 in the time variable.
   Multiply speed by time and store the result in the distance variable.
   Display the contents of the distance variable.

8. Convert the following pseudocode to Java code. Be sure to define the appropriate variables.

   Store 172.5 in the force variable.
   Store 27.5 in the area variable.
   Divide area by force and store the result in the pressure variable.
   Display the contents of the pressure variable.

9. Write the code to set up all the necessary objects for reading keyboard input. Then write code that asks the user to enter his or her desired annual income. Store the input in a `double` variable.

10. Write the code to display a dialog box that asks the user to enter his or her desired annual income. Store the input in a `double` variable.

11. A program has a `float` variable named `total` and a `double` variable named `number`. Write a statement that assigns `number` to `total` without causing an error when compiled.

Short Answer

1. Is the following comment a single-line style comment or a multi-line style comment?

   `/* This program was written by M. A. Codewriter */`

2. Is the following comment a single-line style comment or a multi-line style comment?

   `// This program was written by M. A. Codewriter`

3. Describe what the term "self-documenting program" means.

4. What is meant by "case-sensitive"? Why is it important for a programmer to know that Java is a case-sensitive language?

5. Briefly explain how the print and println methods are related to the System class and the out object.

6. What does a variable declaration tell the Java compiler about a variable?

7. Why are variable names like x not recommended?

8. What things must be considered when deciding on a data type to use for a variable?

9. Briefly describe the difference between variable assignment and variable initialization.

10. What is the difference between comments that start with the // characters and comments that start with the /* characters?

11. Briefly describe what programming style means. Why should your programming style be consistent?

12. Assume that a program uses the named constant PI to represent the value 3.14. The program uses the named constant in several statements. What is the advantage of using the named constant instead of the actual value 3.14 in each statement?

13. Assume the file *SalesAverage.java* is a Java source file that contains documentation comments. Assuming you are in the same folder or directory as the source code file, what command would you enter at the operating system command prompt to generate the HTML documentation files?

14. An expression adds a byte variable and a short variable. Of what data type will the result be?

Programming Challenges

1. Name, Age, and Annual Income

Write a program that declares the following:

- a String variable named name
- an int variable named age
- a double variable named annualPay

Store your age, name, and desired annual income as literals in these variables. The program should display these values on the screen in a manner similar to the following:

```
My name is Joe Mahoney, my age is 26 and
I hope to earn $100000.0 per year.
```

2. Name and Initials

Write a program that has the following String variables: firstName, middleName, and lastName. Initialize these with your first, middle, and last names. The program should also have the following char variables: firstInitial, middleInitial, and lastInitial. Store your first, middle, and last initials in these variables. The program should display the contents of these variables on the screen.

3. Personal Information

Write a program that displays the following information, each on a separate line:

- Your name
- Your address, with city, state, and ZIP
- Your telephone number
- Your college major

Although these items should be displayed on separate output lines, use only a single `println` statement in your program.

4. Star Pattern

Write a program that displays the following pattern:

```
    *
   ***
  *****
 *******
  *****
   ***
    *
```

5. Sum of Two Numbers

Write a program that stores the integers 62 and 99 in variables, and stores their sum in a variable named `total`.

6. Sales Prediction

The East Coast sales division of a company generates 62 percent of total sales. Based on that percentage, write a program that will predict how much the East Coast division will generate if the company has $4.6 million in sales this year. *Hint: Use the value 0.62 to represent 62 percent.*

7. Land Calculation

One acre of land is equivalent to 43,560 square feet. Write a program that calculates the number of acres in a tract of land with 389,767 square feet. *Hint: Divide the size of the tract of land by the size of an acre to get the number of acres.*

8. Sales Tax

Write a program that will ask the user to enter the amount of a purchase. The program should then compute the state and county sales tax. Assume the state sales tax is 4 percent and the county sales tax is 2 percent. The program should display the amount of the purchase, the state sales tax, the county sales tax, the total sales tax, and the total of the sale (which is the sum of the amount of purchase plus the total sales tax). *Hint: Use the value 0.02 to represent 2 percent, and 0.04 to represent 4 percent.*

9. Miles-per-Gallon

VideoNote
The Miles-per-Gallon Problem

A car's miles-per-gallon (MPG) can be calculated with the following formula:

MPG = Miles driven / Gallons of gas used

Write a program that asks the user for the number of miles driven and the gallons of gas used. It should calculate the car's miles-per-gallon and display the result on the screen.

10. Test Average

Write a program that asks the user to enter three test scores. The program should display each test score, as well as the average of the scores.

11. Circuit Board Profit

An electronics company sells circuit boards at a 40 percent profit. If you know the retail price of a circuit board, you can calculate its profit with the following formula:

Profit = Retail price × 0.4

Write a program that asks the user for the retail price of a circuit board, calculates the amount of profit earned for that product, and displays the results on the screen.

12. String Manipulator

Write a program that asks the user to enter the name of his or her favorite city. Use a `String` variable to store the input. The program should display the following:

- The number of characters in the city name
- The name of the city in all uppercase letters
- The name of the city in all lowercase letters
- The first character in the name of the city

13. Restaurant Bill

Write a program that computes the tax and tip on a restaurant bill. The program should ask the user to enter the charge for the meal. The tax should be 6.75 percent of the meal charge. The tip should be 15 percent of the total after adding the tax. Display the meal charge, tax amount, tip amount, and total bill on the screen.

14. Stock Commission

Kathryn bought 600 shares of stock at a price of $21.77 per share. She must pay her stockbroker a 2 percent commission for the transaction. Write a program that calculates and displays the following:

- The amount paid for the stock alone (without the commission)
- The amount of the commission
- The total amount paid (for the stock plus the commission)

15. Energy Drink Consumption

A soft drink company recently surveyed 12,467 of its customers and found that approximately 14 percent of those surveyed purchase one of more energy drinks per week. Of those customers who purchase energy drinks, approximately 64 percent of them prefer citrus-flavored energy drinks. Write a program that displays the following:

- The approximate number of customers in the survey who purchase one or more energy drinks per week
- The approximate number of customers in the survey who prefer citrus-flavored energy drinks

16. Word Game

Write a program that plays a word game with the user. The program should ask the user to enter the following:

- His or her name
- His or her age
- The name of a city
- The name of a college
- A profession
- A type of animal
- A pet's name

After the user has entered these items, the program should display the following story, inserting the user's input into the appropriate locations:

> There once was a person named **NAME** who lived in **CITY**. At the age of **AGE**, **NAME** went to college at **COLLEGE**. **NAME** graduated and went to work as a **PROFESSION**. Then, **NAME** adopted a(n) **ANIMAL** named **PETNAME**. They both lived happily ever after!

17. Stock Transaction Program

Last month Joe purchased some stock in Acme Software, Inc. Here are the details of the purchase:

- The number of shares that Joe purchased was 1,000.
- When Joe purchased the stock, he paid $32.87 per share.
- Joe paid his stockbroker a commission that amounted to 2% of the amount he paid for the stock.

Two weeks later Joe sold the stock. Here are the details of the sale:

- The number of shares that Joe sold was 1,000.
- He sold the stock for $33.92 per share.
- He paid his stockbroker another commission that amounted to 2% of the amount he received for the stock.

Write a program that displays the following information:

- The amount of money Joe paid for the stock.
- The amount of commission Joe paid his broker when he bought the stock.
- The amount that Joe sold the stock for.
- The amount of commission Joe paid his broker when he sold the stock.
- Display the amount of profit that Joe made after selling his stock and paying the two commissions to his broker. (If the amount of profit that your program displays is a negative number, then Joe lost money on the transaction.)

3 Decision Structures

TOPICS

3.1 The if Statement

CONCEPT: The if statement is used to create a decision structure, which allows a program to have more than one path of execution. The if statement causes one or more statements to execute only when a **boolean** expression is **true**.

VideoNote
The if
Statement

In all the programs you have written so far, the statements are executed one after the other, in the order they appear. You might think of sequentially executed statements as the steps you take as you walk down a road. To complete the journey, you must start at the beginning and take each step, one after the other, until you reach your destination. This is illustrated in Figure 3-1.

Figure 3-1   Sequence structure

```
public class SquareArea
{
        public static void main(String[] args)
        {
                double length, width, area;
Step 1 ─────────▶ length = 10;
Step 2 ─────────▶ width = 5;
Step 3 ─────────▶ area = length * width;
Step 4 ─────────▶ System.out.print("The area is " + area);
        }

}
```

The type of code shown in Figure 3-1 is called a *sequence structure*, because the statements are executed in sequence, without branching off in another direction. Programs often need more than one path of execution, however. Many algorithms require a program to execute some statements only under certain circumstances. This can be accomplished with a *decision structure*.

In a decision structure's simplest form, a specific action is taken only when a condition exists. If the condition does not exist, the action is not performed. The flowchart in Figure 3-2 shows the logic of a decision structure. The diamond symbol represents a yes/no question or a true/false condition. If the answer to the question is yes (or if the condition is true), the program flow follows one path which leads to an action being performed. If the answer to the question is no (or the condition is false), the program flow follows another path, which skips the action.

Figure 3-2   Simple decision structure logic

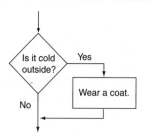

In the flowchart, the action "Wear a coat" is only performed when it is cold outside. If it is not cold outside, the action is skipped. The action is *conditionally executed* because it is only performed when a certain condition (cold outside) exists. Figure 3-3 shows a more elaborate flowchart, where three actions are taken only when it is cold outside.

Figure 3-3   Three-action decision structure logic

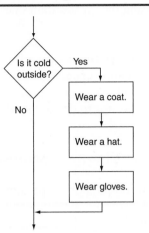

One way to code a decision structure in Java is with the if statement. Here is the general format of the if statement:

```
if (BooleanExpression)
    statement;
```

The if statement is simple in the way it works: The *BooleanExpression* that appears inside the parentheses must be a boolean expression. A *boolean expression* is one that is either true or false. If the boolean expression is true, the very next statement is executed. Otherwise, it is skipped. The statement is conditionally executed because it only executes under the condition that the expression in the parentheses is true.

Using Relational Operators to Form Conditions

Typically, the boolean expression that is tested by an if statement is formed with a relational operator. A *relational operator* determines whether a specific relationship exists between two values. For example, the greater than operator (>) determines whether one value is greater than another. The equal to operator (==) determines whether two values are equal. Table 3-1 lists all of the Java relational operators.

Table 3-1   Relational operators

Relational Operators (in Order of Precedence)	Meaning
>	Greater than
<	Less than
>=	Greater than or equal to
<=	Less than or equal to
==	Equal to
!=	Not equal to

All of the relational operators are binary, which means they use two operands. Here is an example of an expression using the greater than operator:

```
length > width
```

This expression determines whether `length` is greater than `width`. If `length` is greater than `width`, the value of the expression is `true`. Otherwise, the value of the expression is `false`. Because the expression can be only `true` or `false`, it is a `boolean` expression. The following expression uses the less than operator to determine whether `length` is less than `width`:

```
length < width
```

Table 3-2 shows examples of several `boolean` expressions that compare the variables x and y.

Table 3-2   `boolean` expressions using relational operators

Expression	Meaning
x > y	Is x greater than y?
x < y	Is x less than y?
x >= y	Is x greater than or equal to y?
x <= y	Is x less than or equal to y?
x == y	Is x equal to y?
x != y	Is x not equal to y?

Two of the operators, >= and <=, test for more than one relationship. The >= operator determines whether the operand on its left is greater than or equal to the operand on its right. Assuming that a is 4, b is 6, and c is 4, both of the expressions b >= a and a >= c are true and a >= 5 is false. When using this operator, the > symbol must precede the = symbol, and there is no space between them. The <= operator determines whether the operand on its left is less than or equal to the operand on its right. Once again, assuming that a is 4, b is 6, and c is 4, both a <= c and b <= 10 are true, but b <= a is false. When using this operator, the < symbol must precede the = symbol, and there is no space between them.

The == operator determines whether the operand on its left is equal to the operand on its right. If both operands have the same value, the expression is true. Assuming that a is 4, the expression a == 4 is true and the expression a == 2 is false. Notice the equality operator is two = symbols together. Don't confuse this operator with the assignment operator, which is one = symbol.

The != operator is the not equal operator. It determines whether the operand on its left is not equal to the operand on its right, which is the opposite of the == operator. As before, assuming a is 4, b is 6, and c is 4, both a != b and b != c are true because a is not equal to b and b is not equal to c. However, a != c is false because a is equal to c.

Putting It All Together

Let's look at an example of the `if` statement:

```
if (sales > 50000)
    bonus = 500.0;
```

This statement uses the > operator to determine whether sales is greater than 50,000. If the expression sales > 50000 is true, the variable bonus is assigned 500.0. If the expression is false, however, the assignment statement is skipped. The program in Code Listing 3-1 shows another example. The user enters three test scores and the program calculates their average. If the average is greater than 95, the program congratulates the user on obtaining a high score.

Code Listing 3-1 (AverageScore.java)

```java
1   import javax.swing.JOptionPane;  // Needed for JOptionPane
2
3   /**
4      This program demonstrates the if statement.
5   */
6
7   public class AverageScore
8   {
9      public static void main(String[] args)
10     {
11        double score1;    // To hold score #1
12        double score2;    // To hold score #2
13        double score3;    // To hold score #3
14        double average;   // To hold the average score
15        String input;     // To hold the user's input
16
17         // Get the first test score.
18         input = JOptionPane.showInputDialog("Enter score #1:");
19         score1 = Double.parseDouble(input);
20
21         // Get the second score.
22         input = JOptionPane.showInputDialog("Enter score #2:");
23         score2 = Double.parseDouble(input);
24
25         // Get the third test score.
26         input = JOptionPane.showInputDialog("Enter score #3:");
27         score3 = Double.parseDouble(input);
28
29         // Calculate the average score.
30         average = (score1 + score2 + score3) / 3.0;
31
32         // Display the average score.
33         JOptionPane.showMessageDialog(null,
34                              "The average is " + average);
35
36         // If the score was greater than 95, let the user know
37         // that's a great score.
38         if (average > 95)
```

```
39              JOptionPane.showMessageDialog(null,
40                          "That's a great score!");
41
42         System.exit(0);
43     }
44 }
```

Figures 3-4 and 3-5 show examples of interaction with this program. In Figure 3-4 the average of the test scores is not greater than 95. In Figure 3-5 the average is greater than 95.

Figure 3-4   Interaction with the `AverageScore` program

This input dialog box appears first. The user enters 82 and then clicks on the OK button.

This input dialog box appears next. The user enters 76 and then clicks on the OK button.

This input dialog box appears next. The user enters 91 and then clicks on the OK button.

This message dialog box appears next. The average of the three test scores is displayed.

Figure 3-5 Interaction with the AverageScore program

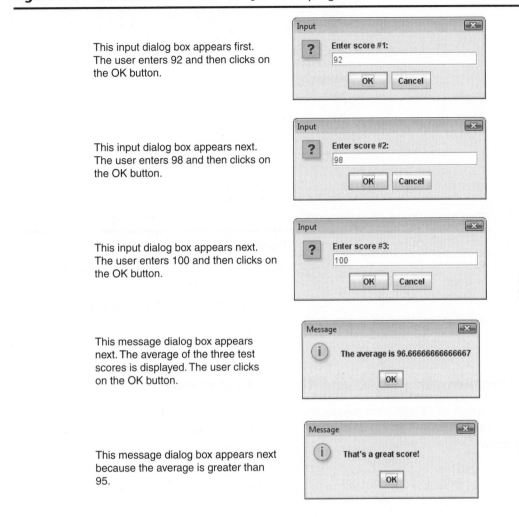

This input dialog box appears first. The user enters 92 and then clicks on the OK button.

This input dialog box appears next. The user enters 98 and then clicks on the OK button.

This input dialog box appears next. The user enters 100 and then clicks on the OK button.

This message dialog box appears next. The average of the three test scores is displayed. The user clicks on the OK button.

This message dialog box appears next because the average is greater than 95.

The code in lines 38 through 40 cause the congratulatory message to be printed:

```
if (average > 95)
    JOptionPane.showMessageDialog(null,
                        "That's a great score!");
```

Figure 3-6 shows the logic of this if statement.

Table 3-3 shows other examples of if statements and their outcomes.

Figure 3-6 Logic of the `if` statement

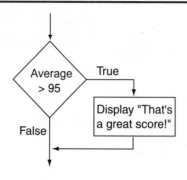

Table 3-3 Other examples of `if` statements

Statement	Outcome
`if (hours > 40)` `overTime = true;`	If `hours` is greater than 40, assigns `true` to the boolean variable `overTime`.
`if (value < 32)` `System.out.println("Invalid number");`	If `value` is less than 32, displays the message "Invalid number"

Programming Style and the `if` Statement

Even though an `if` statement usually spans more than one line, it is really one long statement. For instance, the following `if` statements are identical except for the style in which they are written:

```
if (value > 32)
    System.out.println("Invalid number.");
if (value > 32) System.out.println("Invalid number.");
```

In both of these examples, the compiler considers the `if` statement and the conditionally executed statement as one unit, with a semicolon properly placed at the end. Indentions and spacing are for the human readers of a program, not the compiler. Here are two important style rules you should adopt for writing `if` statements:

- The conditionally executed statement should appear on the line after the `if` statement.
- The conditionally executed statement should be indented one level from the `if` statement.

In most editors, each time you press the tab key, you are indenting one level. By indenting the conditionally executed statement, you are causing it to stand out visually. This is so you can tell at a glance what part of the program the `if` statement executes. This is a standard way of writing `if` statements and is the method you should use.

Be Careful with Semicolons

You do not put a semicolon after the `if (expression)` portion of an `if` statement, as illustrated in Figure 3-7. This is because the `if` statement isn't complete without its conditionally executed statement.

Figure 3-7   Do not prematurely terminate an `if` statement with a semicolon

If you prematurely terminate an `if` statement with a semicolon, the compiler will not display an error message, but will assume that you are placing a *null statement* there. The null statement, which is an empty statement that does nothing, will become the conditionally executed statement. The statement that you intended to be conditionally executed will be disconnected from the `if` statement and will always execute.

For example, look at the following code:

```
int x = 0, y = 10;

// The following if statement is prematurely
// terminated with a semicolon.
if (x > y);
    System.out.println(x + " is greater than " + y);
```

The `if` statement in this code is prematurely terminated with a semicolon. Because the `println` statement is not connected to the `if` statement, it will always execute.

Having Multiple Conditionally Executed Statements

The previous examples of the `if` statement conditionally execute a single statement. The `if` statement can also conditionally execute a group of statements, as long as they are enclosed in a set of braces. Enclosing a group of statements inside braces creates a *block* of statements. Here is an example:

```
if (sales > 50000)
{
    bonus = 500.0;
    commissionRate = 0.12;
    daysOff += 1;
}
```

If `sales` is greater than 50,000, this code will execute all three of the statements inside the braces, in the order they appear. If the braces are accidentally left out, however, the `if` statement conditionally executes only the very next statement. Figure 3-8 illustrates this.

Figure 3-8   An `if` statement missing its braces

```
                        if (sales > 50000)
                           bonus = 500.0;  ◄─────────  Only this statement is
These statements are      ► commissionRate = 0.12;     conditionally executed.
always executed.          ► daysOff += 1;
```

Flags

A flag is a `boolean` variable that signals when some condition exists in the program. When the flag variable is set to `false`, it indicates the condition does not yet exist. When the flag variable is set to `true`, it means the condition does exist.

For example, suppose a program similar to the previous test averaging program has a `boolean` variable named `highScore`. The variable might be used to signal that a high score has been achieved by the following code:

```
if (average > 95)
    highScore = true;
```

Later, the same program might use code similar to the following to test the `highScore` variable, in order to determine if a high score has been achieved:

```
if (highScore)
    System.out.println("That's a high score!");
```

You will find flag variables useful in many circumstances, and we will come back to them in future chapters.

Comparing Characters

You can use the relational operators to test character data as well as numbers. For example, assuming that `ch` is a `char` variable, the following code segment uses the `==` operator to compare it to the character 'A':

```
if (ch == 'A')
    System.out.println("The letter is A.");
```

The `!=` operator can also be used with characters to test for inequality. For example, the following statement determines whether the `char` variable `ch` is not equal to the letter 'A':

```
if (ch != 'A')
    System.out.println("Not the letter A.");
```

You can also use the `>`, `<`, `>=`, and `<=` operators to compare characters. Computers do not actually store characters, such as A, B, C, and so forth, in memory. Instead, they store numeric codes that represent the characters. Recall from Chapter 2 that Java uses Unicode, which is a set of numbers that represents all the letters of the alphabet (both lowercase and uppercase), the printable digits 0 through 9, punctuation symbols, and special characters. When a character is stored in memory, it is actually the Unicode number that is stored. When the computer is instructed to print the value on the screen, it displays the character that corresponds with the numeric code.

> **NOTE:** Unicode is an international encoding system that is extensive enough to represent all the characters of all the world's alphabets.

In Unicode, letters are arranged in alphabetic order. Because 'A' comes before 'B', the numeric code for the character 'A' is less than the code for the character 'B'. (The code for 'A' is 65 and the code for 'B' is 66. Appendix B on the Student CD lists the codes for all of the printable English characters.) In the following if statement, the boolean expression 'A' < 'B' is true:

```java
if ('A' < 'B')
    System.out.println("A is less than B.");
```

In Unicode, the uppercase letters come before the lowercase letters, so the numeric code for 'A' (65) is less than the numeric code for 'a' (97). In addition, the space character (code 32) comes before all the alphabetic characters.

Checkpoint

3.1   Write an if statement that assigns 0 to x when y is equal to 20.

3.2   Write an if statement that multiplies payRate by 1.5 if hours is greater than 40.

3.3   Write an if statement that assigns 0.2 to commission if sales is greater than or equal to 10000.

3.4   Write an if statement that sets the variable fees to 50 if the boolean variable max is true.

3.5   Write an if statement that assigns 20 to the variable y and assigns 40 to the variable z if the variable x is greater than 100.

3.6   Write an if statement that assigns 0 to the variable b and assigns 1 to the variable c if the variable a is less than 10.

3.7   Write an if statement that displays "Goodbye" if the variable myCharacter contains the character 'D'.

3.2 The if-else Statement

> **CONCEPT:** The if-else statement will execute one group of statements if its boolean expression is true, or another group if its boolean expression is false.

VideoNote
The **if-else**
Statement

The if-else statement is an expansion of the if statement. Here is its format:

```java
if (BooleanExpression)
    statement or block
else
    statement or block
```

Like the if statement, a boolean expression is evaluated. If the expression is true, a statement or block of statements is executed. If the expression is false, however, a separate group of statements is executed. The program in Code Listing 3-2 uses the `if-else` statement to handle a classic programming problem: division by zero. In Java, a program crashes when it divides an integer by 0. When a floating-point value is divided by 0, the program doesn't crash. Instead, the special value `Infinity` is produced as the result of the division.

Code Listing 3-2 (`Division.java`)

```
 1   import java.util.Scanner; // Needed for the Scanner class
 2
 3   /**
 4       This program demonstrates the if-else statement.
 5   */
 6
 7   public class Division
 8   {
 9       public static void main(String[] args)
10       {
11           double number1, number2; // Division operands
12           double quotient;         // Result of division
13
14           // Create a Scanner object for keyboard input.
15           Scanner keyboard = new Scanner(System.in);
16
17           // Get the first number.
18           System.out.print("Enter a number: ");
19           number1 = keyboard.nextDouble();
20
21           // Get the second number.
22           System.out.print("Enter another number: ");
23           number2 = keyboard.nextDouble();
24
25           if (number2 == 0)
26           {
27               System.out.println("Division by zero is not possible.");
28               System.out.println("Please run the program again and ");
29               System.out.println("enter a number other than zero.");
30           }
31           else
32           {
33               quotient = number1 / number2;
34               System.out.print("The quotient of " + number1);
35               System.out.print(" divided by " + number2);
36               System.out.println(" is " + quotient);
37           }
38       }
39   }
```

Program Output with Example Input Shown in Bold

```
Enter an integer: 10 [Enter]
Enter another integer: 0 [Enter]
Division by zero is not possible.
Please run the program again and
enter a number other than zero.
```

Program Output with Example Input Shown in Bold

```
Enter an integer: 10 [Enter]
Enter another integer: 5 [Enter]
The quotient of 10 divided by 5 is 2.0
```

The value of number2 is tested before the division is performed. If the user enters 0, the block of statements controlled by the if clause executes, displaying a message that indicates the program cannot perform division by zero. Otherwise, the else clause takes control, which divides number1 by number2 and displays the result. Figure 3-9 shows the logic of the if-else statement.

Figure 3-9   Logic of the if-else statement

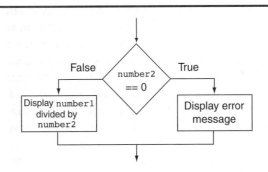

Checkpoint

3.8   Write an if-else statement that assigns 20 to the variable y if the variable x is greater than 100. Otherwise, it should assign 0 to the variable y.

3.9   Write an if-else statement that assigns 1 to x when y is equal to 100. Otherwise it should assign 0 to x.

3.10   Write an if-else statement that assigns 0.10 to commission unless sales is greater than or equal to 50000.0, in which case it assigns 0.2 to commission.

3.11   Write an if-else statement that assigns 0 to the variable b and assigns 1 to the variable c if the variable a is less than 10. Otherwise, it should assign –99 to the variable b and assign 0 to the variable c.

3.3 Nested `if` Statements

CONCEPT: To test more than one condition, an `if` statement can be nested inside another `if` statement.

Sometimes an `if` statement must be nested inside another `if` statement. For example, consider a banking program that determines whether a bank customer qualifies for a special, low interest rate on a loan. To qualify, two conditions must exist: (1) the customer's salary must be at least $30,000, and (2) the customer must have held his or her current job for at least two years. Figure 3-10 shows a flowchart for an algorithm that could be used in such a program.

Figure 3-10   Logic of nested `if` statements

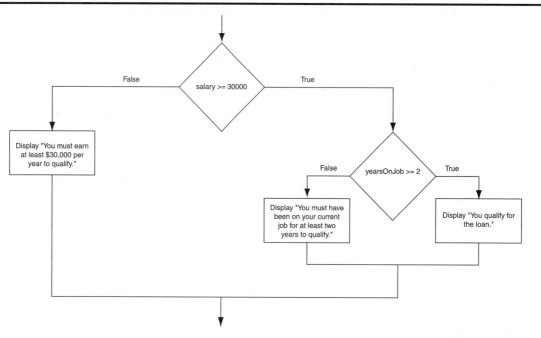

If we follow the flow of execution in the flowchart, we see that the expression `salary >= 30000` is tested. If this expression is false, there is no need to perform further tests; we know that the customer does not qualify for the special interest rate. If the expression is true, however, we need to test the second condition. This is done with a nested decision structure that tests the expression `yearsOnJob >= 2`. If this expression is true, then the customer qualifies for the special interest rate. If this expression is false, then the customer does not qualify. Code Listing 3-3 shows the complete program. Figures 3-11, 3-12, and 3-13 show what happens during three different sessions with the program.

Code Listing 3-3   **(LoanQualifier.java)**

```
1 import javax.swing.JOptionPane; // Needed for JOptionPane class
2
3 /**
```

```
4      This program demonstrates a nested if statement.
5  */
6
7  public class LoanQualifier
8  {
9      public static void main(String[] args)
10     {
11        double salary;          // Annual salary
12        double yearsOnJob;      // Years at current job
13        String input;           // To hold string input
14
15        // Get the user's annual salary.
16        input = JOptionPane.showInputDialog("Enter your " +
17                                            "annual salary.");
18        salary = Double.parseDouble(input);
19
20        // Get the number of years at the current job.
21        input = JOptionPane.showInputDialog("Enter the number of " +
22                                            "years at your current job.");
23        yearsOnJob = Double.parseDouble(input);
24
25        // Determine whether the user qualifies for the loan.
26        if (salary >= 30000)
27        {
28          if (yearsOnJob >= 2)
29          {
30            JOptionPane.showMessageDialog(null, "You qualify " +
31                                                "for the loan.");
32          }
33          else
34          {
35            JOptionPane.showMessageDialog(null, "You must have " +
36                        "been on your current job for at least " +
37                        "two years to qualify.");
38          }
39        }
40        else
41        {
42            JOptionPane.showMessageDialog(null, "You must earn " +
43                        "at least $30,000 per year to qualify.");
44        }
45
46        System.exit(0);
47     }
48 }
```

Figure 3-11 Interaction with the LoanQualifier program

This input dialog box appears first. The user enters 35000 and clicks on the OK button.

This input dialog box appears next. The user enters 1 and clicks on the OK button.

This message dialog box appears next.

Figure 3-12 Interaction with the LoanQualifier program

This input dialog box appears first. The user enters 25000 and clicks on the OK button.

This input dialog box appears next. The user enters 5 and clicks on the OK button.

This message dialog box appears next.

Figure 3-13   Interaction with the LoanQualifier program

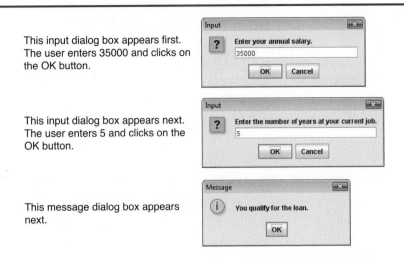

This input dialog box appears first. The user enters 35000 and clicks on the OK button.

This input dialog box appears next. The user enters 5 and clicks on the OK button.

This message dialog box appears next.

The first if statement (which begins in line 26) conditionally executes the second one (which begins in line 28). The only way the program will execute the second if statement is for the salary variable to contain a value that is greater than or equal to 30,000. When this is the case, the second if statement will test the yearsOnJob variable. If it contains a value that is greater than or equal to 2, a dialog box will be displayed informing the user that he or she qualifies for the loan.

It should be noted that the braces used in the if statements in this program are not required. They could have been written as follows:

```
if (salary >= 30000)
  if (yearsOnJob >= 2)
    JOptionPane.showMessageDialog(null, "You qualify " +
                                        "for the loan.");
  else
    JOptionPane.showMessageDialog(null, "You must have " +
              "been on your current job for at least " +
              "two years to qualify.");
else
  JOptionPane.showMessageDialog(null, "You must earn " +
              "at least $30,000 per year to qualify.");
```

Not only do the braces make the statements easier to read, but they also help in debugging code. When debugging a program with nested if-else statements, it's important to know which if clause each else clause belongs to. The rule for matching else clauses with if clauses is this: An else clause goes with the closest previous if clause that doesn't already have its own else clause. This is easy to see when the conditionally executed statements are enclosed in braces and are properly indented, as shown in Figure 3-14. Each else clause lines up with the if clause it belongs to. These visual cues are important because nested if statements can be very long and complex.

Figure 3-14 Alignment of `if` and `else` clauses

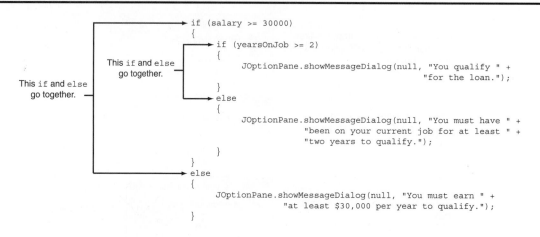

```
                              if (salary >= 30000)
                              {
                                  if (yearsOnJob >= 2)
         This if and else         {
         go together.                 JOptionPane.showMessageDialog(null, "You qualify " +
                                                                            "for the loan.");
This if and else              }
go together.                  else
                              {
                                  JOptionPane.showMessageDialog(null, "You must have " +
                                                                     "been on your current job for at least " +
                                                                     "two years to qualify.");
                              }
                              }
                              else
                              {
                                  JOptionPane.showMessageDialog(null, "You must earn " +
                                                                     "at least $30,000 per year to qualify.");
                              }
```

Testing a Series of Conditions

In the previous example, you saw how a program can use nested decision structures to test more than one condition. It is not uncommon for a program to have a series of conditions to test, and then perform an action depending on which condition is true. One way to accomplish this it to have a decision structure with numerous other decision structures nested inside it. For example, consider the program presented in the following *In the Spotlight* section.

In the Spotlight:
Multiple Nested Decision Structures

Suppose one of your professors uses the following 10-point grading scale for exams:

Test Score	Grade
90 and above	A
80–89	B
70–79	C
60–69	D
Below 60	F

Your professor has asked you to write a program that will allow a student to enter a test score and then display the grade for that score. Here is the algorithm that you will use:

Ask the user to enter a test score.
Determine the grade in the following manner:
If the score is less than 60, then the grade is F.
*   Otherwise, if the score is less than 70, then the grade is D.*
*   Otherwise, if the score is less than 80, then the grade is C.*
*   Otherwise, if the score is less than 90, then the grade is B.*
*   Otherwise, the grade is A.*

You decide that the process of determining the grade will require several nested decisions structures, as shown in Figure 3-15. Code Listing 3-4 shows the complete program. The code for the nested decision structures is in lines 23 through 51. Figures 3-16 and 3-17 shows what happens in two different sessions with the program.

Figure 3-15   Nested decision structure to determine a grade

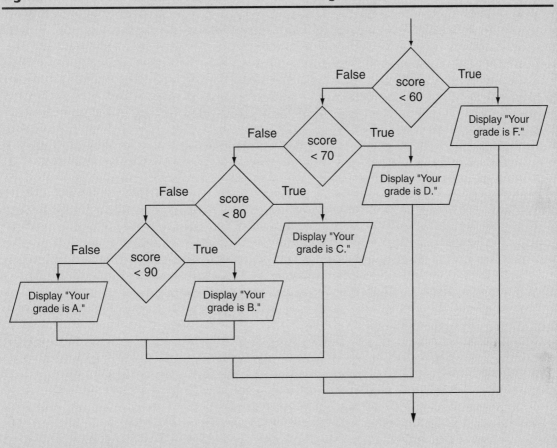

Code Listing 3-4   (NestedDecision.java)

```
1 import javax.swing.JOptionPane;    // Needed for JOptionPane
2
3 /**
4    This program asks the user to enter a numeric test
5    score and displays a letter grade for the score. The
6    program uses nested decision structures
7    to determine the grade.
8 */
9
10 public class NestedDecision
11 {
```

```
12    public static void main(String[] args)
13    {
14        int testScore;   // Numeric test score
15        String input;    // To hold the user's input
16
17        // Get the numeric test score.
18        input = JOptionPane.showInputDialog("Enter your numeric " +
19                    "test score and I will tell you the grade: ");
20        testScore = Integer.parseInt(input);
21
22        // Display the grade.
23        if (testScore < 60)
24        {
25            JOptionPane.showMessageDialog(null, "Your grade is F.");
26        }
27        else
28        {
29            if (testScore < 70)
30            {
31                JOptionPane.showMessageDialog(null, "Your grade is D.");
32            }
33            else
34            {
35                if (testScore < 80)
36                {
37                    JOptionPane.showMessageDialog(null, "Your grade is C.");
38                }
39                else
40                {
41                    if (testScore < 90)
42                    {
43                        JOptionPane.showMessageDialog(null, "Your grade is B.");
44                    }
45                    else
46                    {
47                        JOptionPane.showMessageDialog(null, "Your grade is A.");
48                    }
49                }
50            }
51        }
52
53    System.exit(0);
54    }
55 }
```

Figure 3-16   Interaction with the NestedDecision program

This input dialog box appears first. The user enters 80 and then clicks the OK button.

> **Input**
>
> **?**   Enter your numeric test score and I will tell you the grade:
>
> 80
>
> OK   Cancel

This message dialog box appears next.

> **Message**
>
> (i)   Your grade is B.
>
> OK

Figure 3-17   Interaction with the NestedDecision program

This input dialog box appears first. The user enters 72 and then clicks the OK button.

> **Input**
>
> **?**   Enter your numeric test score and I will tell you the grade:
>
> 72
>
> OK   Cancel

This message dialog box appears next.

> **Message**
>
> (i)   Your grade is C.
>
> OK

Checkpoint

3.12   Write nested if statements that perform the following test: If amount1 is greater than 10 and amount2 is less than 100, display the greater of the two.

3.13   Write code that tests the variable x to determine whether it is greater than 0. If x is greater than 0, the code should test the variable y to determine whether it is less than 20. If y is less than 20, the code should assign 1 to the variable z. If y is not less than 20, the code should assign 0 to the variable z.

3.4   The if-else-if Statement

CONCEPT: The if-else-if statement tests a series of conditions. It is often simpler to test a series of conditions with the if-else-if statement than with a set of nested if-else statements.

Even though Code Listing 3-4 is a simple example, the logic of the nested decision structure is fairly complex. You can alternatively test a series of conditions using the if-else-if

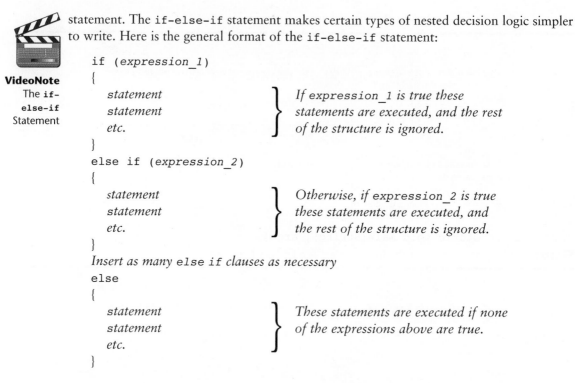

statement. The `if-else-if` statement makes certain types of nested decision logic simpler to write. Here is the general format of the `if-else-if` statement:

```
if (expression_1)
{
    statement
    statement
    etc.
}
else if (expression_2)
{
    statement
    statement
    etc.
}
Insert as many else if clauses as necessary
else
{
    statement
    statement
    etc.
}
```

If expression_1 is true these statements are executed, and the rest of the structure is ignored.

Otherwise, if expression_2 is true these statements are executed, and the rest of the structure is ignored.

These statements are executed if none of the expressions above are true.

When the statement executes, *expression_1* is tested. If *expression_1* is true, the block of statements that immediately follows is executed, and the rest of the structure is ignored. If *expression_1* is false, however, the program jumps to the next `else if` clause and tests *expression_2*. If it is true, the block of statements that immediately follows is executed, and then the rest of the structure is ignored. This process continues, from the top of the structure to the bottom, until one of the expressions is found to be true. If none of the expressions are true, the last `else` clause takes over and the block of statements immediately following it is executed.

The last `else` clause, which does not have an `if` statement following it, is referred to as the *trailing else*. The trailing `else` is optional, but in most cases you will use it.

> **NOTE:** The general format shows braces surrounding each block of conditionally executed statements. As with other forms of the `if` statement, the braces are required only when more than one statement is conditionally executed.

Code Listing 3-5 shows an example of the `if-else-if` statement. This program is a modification of Code Listing 3-4, which appears in the previous *In the Spotlight* section. The output of this program is the same as Code Listing 3-4.

Code Listing 3-5 (TestResults.Java)

```java
1 import javax.swing.JOptionPane;        // Needed for JOptionPane
2
3 /**
4    This program asks the user to enter a numeric test
5    score and displays a letter grade for the score. The
6    program uses an if-else-if statement to determine
7    the letter grade.
8 */
9
10 public class TestResults
11 {
12   public static void main(String[] args)
13   {
14     int testScore;      // Numeric test score
15     String input;       // To hold the user's input
16
17     // Get the numeric test score.
18     input = JOptionPane.showInputDialog("Enter your numeric " +
19                     "test score and I will tell you the grade: ");
20     testScore = Integer.parseInt(input);
21
22     // Display the grade.
23     if (testScore < 60)
24        JOptionPane.showMessageDialog(null, "Your grade is F.");
25     else if (testScore < 70)
26        JOptionPane.showMessageDialog(null, "Your grade is D.");
27     else if (testScore < 80)
28        JOptionPane.showMessageDialog(null, "Your grade is C.");
29     else if (testScore < 90)
30        JOptionPane.showMessageDialog(null, "Your grade is B.");
31     else
32        JOptionPane.showMessageDialog(null, "Your grade is A.");
33
34     System.exit(0);
35   }
36 }
```

Let's analyze how the if-else-if statement in lines 23 through 32 works. First, the expression testScore < 60 is tested in line 23:

```java
→   if (testScore < 60)
       JOptionPane.showMessageDialog(null, "Your grade is F.");
    else if (testScore < 70)
       JOptionPane.showMessageDialog(null, "Your grade is D.");
    else if (testScore < 80)
```

```
        JOptionPane.showMessageDialog(null, "Your grade is c.");
    else if (testScore < 90)
        JOptionPane.showMessageDialog(null, "Your grade is B.");
    else
        JOptionPane.showMessageDialog(null, "Your grade is A.");
```

If `testScore` is less than 60, the message `"Your grade is F."` is displayed and the rest of the `if-else if` statement is skipped. If `testScore` is not less than 60, the `else` clause in line 25 takes over and causes the next `if` statement to be executed:

```
    if (testScore < 60)
        JOptionPane.showMessageDialog(null, "Your grade is F.");

→   else if (testScore < 70)

        JOptionPane.showMessageDialog(null, "Your grade is D.");
    else if (testScore < 80)
        JOptionPane.showMessageDialog(null, "Your grade is c.");
    else if (testScore < 90)
        JOptionPane.showMessageDialog(null, "Your grade is B.");
    else
        JOptionPane.showMessageDialog(null, "Your grade is A.");
```

The first `if` statement handled all of the grades less than 60, so when this `if` statement executes, `testScore` will have a value of 60 or greater. If `testScore` is less than 70, the message `"Your grade is D."` is displayed and the rest of the `if-else-if` statement is skipped. This chain of events continues until one of the expressions is found to be true, or the last `else` clause at the end of the statement is encountered.

Notice the alignment and indentation that is used with the `if-else-if` statement: The starting `if` clause, the `else if` clauses, and the trailing `else` clause are all aligned, and the conditionally executed statements are indented.

Using the Trailing `else` to Catch Errors

The trailing `else` clause, which appears at the end of the `if-else-if` statement, is optional, but in many situations you will use it to catch errors. For example, Code Listing 3-5 will assign the grade `'A'` to any test score that is 90 or greater. What if the highest possible test score is 100? We can modify the code as shown in Code Listing 3-6 so the trailing `else` clause catches any value greater than 100 and displays an error message. Figure 3-18 shows what happens when the user enters a test score that is greater than 100.

Code Listing 3-6   (`TrailingElse.java`)

```
1 import javax.swing.JOptionPane; // Needed for JOptionPane
2
3 /**
4    This program asks the user to enter a numeric test
5    score and displays a letter grade for the score. The
6    program displays an error message if an invalid
7    numeric score is entered.
8 */
9
```

```
10  public class TrailingElse
11  {
12     public static void main(String[] args)
13     {
14        int testScore;     // Numeric test score
15        String input;      // To hold the user's input
16
17        // Get the numeric test score.
18        input = JOptionPane.showInputDialog("Enter your numeric " +
19                       "test score and I will tell you the grade: ");
20        testScore = Integer.parseInt(input);
21
22        // Display the grade.
23        if (testScore < 60)
24           JOptionPane.showMessageDialog(null, "Your grade is F.");
25        else if (testScore < 70)
26           JOptionPane.showMessageDialog(null, "Your grade is D.");
27        else if (testScore < 80)
28           JOptionPane.showMessageDialog(null, "Your grade is C.");
29        else if (testScore < 90)
30           JOptionPane.showMessageDialog(null, "Your grade is B.");
31        else if (testScore <= 100)
32           JOptionPane.showMessageDialog(null, "Your grade is A.");
33        else
34           JOptionPane.showMessageDialog(null, "Invalid score.");
35
36        System.exit(0);
37     }
38  }
```

Figure 3-18   Interaction with the `NestedDecision` program

This input dialog box appears first. The user enters 105 and then clicks the OK button.

This message dialog box appears next.

The `if-else-if` Statement Compared to a Nested Decision Structure

You never have to use the `if-else-if` statement because its logic can be coded with nested `if-else` statements. However, a long series of nested `if-else` statements has two particular disadvantages when you are debugging code:

- The code can grow complex and become difficult to understand.

- Because indenting is important in nested statements, a long series of nested `if-else` statements can become too long to be displayed on the computer screen without horizontal scrolling. Also, long statements tend to "wrap around" when printed on paper, making the code even more difficult to read.

The logic of an `if-else-if` statement is usually easier to follow than that of a long series of nested `if-else` statements. And, because all of the clauses are aligned in an `if-else-if` statement, the lengths of the lines in the statement tend to be shorter.

Checkpoint

3.14 What will the following program display?

```java
public class CheckPoint
{
    public static void main(String[] args)
    {
        int funny = 7, serious = 15;
        funny = serious % 2;
        if (funny != 1)
        {
            funny = 0;
            serious = 0;
        }
        else if (funny == 2)
        {
            funny = 10;
            serious = 10;
        }
        else
        {
            funny = 1;
            serious = 1;
        }
        System.out.println(funny + " " + serious);
    }
}
```

3.15 The following program is used in a bookstore to determine how many discount coupons a customer gets. Complete the table that appears after the program.

```java
import javax.swing.JOptionPane;
public class CheckPoint
{
    public static void main(String[] args)
    {
        int books, coupons;
        String input;
        input = JOptionPane.showInputDialog("How many books " +
                                    "are being purchased? ");
        books = Integer.parseInt(input);
```

```
        if (books < 1)
            coupons = 0;
        else if (books < 3)
            coupons = 1;
        else if (books < 5)
            coupons = 2;
        else
            coupons = 3;
        JOptionPane.showMessageDialog(null,
                "The number of coupons to give is " +
                coupons);
        System.exit(0);
    }
}
```

If the customer purchases this many books . . .	this many coupons are given.
1	_____
2	_____
3	_____
4	_____
5	_____
10	_____

3.5 Logical Operators

CONCEPT: Logical operators connect two or more relational expressions into one or reverse the logic of an expression.

Java provides two binary logical operators, && and ||, which are used to combine two boolean expressions into a single expression. It also provides the unary ! operator, which reverses the truth of a boolean expression. Table 3-4 describes these logical operators.

Table 3-4 Logical operators

Operator	Meaning	Effect
&&	AND	Connects two boolean expressions into one. Both expressions must be true for the overall expression to be true.
||	OR	Connects two boolean expressions into one. One or both expressions must be true for the overall expression to be true. It is only necessary for one to be true, and it does not matter which one.
!	NOT	The ! operator reverses the truth of a boolean expression. If it is applied to an expression that is true, the operator returns false. If it is applied to an expression that is false, the operator returns true.

Table 3-5 shows examples of several `boolean` expressions that use logical operators.

Table 3-5   `boolean` expressions using logical operators

Expression	Meaning
`x > y && a < b`	Is x greater than y AND is a less than b?
`x == y || x == z`	Is x equal to y OR is x equal to z?
`!(x > y)`	Is the expression x > y NOT true?

Let's take a close look at each of these operators.

The && Operator

The `&&` operator is known as the logical AND operator. It takes two `boolean` expressions as operands and creates a `boolean` expression that is `true` only when both subexpressions are `true`. Here is an example of an `if` statement that uses the `&&` operator:

```
if (temperature < 20 && minutes > 12)
{
      System.out.println("The temperature is in the " +
                         "danger zone.");
}
```

In this statement the two `boolean` expressions `temperature < 20` and `minutes > 12` are combined into a single expression. The message will only be displayed if `temperature` is less than 20 AND `minutes` is greater than 12. If either `boolean` expression is `false`, the entire expression is `false` and the message is not displayed.

Table 3-6 shows a truth table for the `&&` operator. The truth table lists expressions showing all the possible combinations of `true` and `false` connected with the `&&` operator. The resulting values of the expressions are also shown.

Table 3-6 Truth table for the `&&` operator

Expression	Value of the Expression
`true && false`	`false`
`false && true`	`false`
`false && false`	`false`
`true && true`	`true`

As the table shows, both sides of the `&&` operator must be `true` for the operator to return a `true` value.

The `&&` operator performs *short-circuit evaluation*. Here's how it works: If the expression on the left side of the `&&` operator is `false`, the expression on the right side will not be checked. Because the entire expression is `false` if only one of the subexpressions is `false`, it would waste CPU time to check the remaining expression. So, when the `&&` operator finds that the expression on its left is `false`, it short-circuits and does not evaluate the expression on its right.

The `&&` operator can be used to simplify programs that otherwise would use nested `if` statements. The program in Code Listing 3-7 is a different version of the `LoanQualifier` program in Code Listing 3-3, written to use the `&&` operator. Figures 3-19 and 3-20 show the interaction during two different sessions with the program.

Code Listing 3-7 (`LogicalAnd.java`)

```java
1   import javax.swing.JOptionPane;  // Needed for JOptionPane class
2
3   /**
4      This program demonstrates the logical && operator.
5   */
6
7   public class LogicalAnd
8   {
9      public static void main(String[] args)
10     {
11        double salary;          // Annual salary
12        double yearsOnJob;      // Years at current job
13        String input;           // To hold string input
14
15        // Get the user's annual salary.
16         input = JOptionPane.showInputDialog("Enter your " +
17                                             "annual salary.");
18         salary = Double.parseDouble(input);
19
20        // Get the number of years at the current job.
21        input = JOptionPane.showInputDialog("Enter the number of " +
22                                            "years at your current job.");
23        yearsOnJob = Double.parseDouble(input);
24
25        // Determine whether the user qualifies for the loan.
26        if (salary >= 30000 && yearsOnJob >= 2)
27        {
28                JOptionPane.showMessageDialog(null, "You qualify " +
29                                                "for the loan.");
30        }
31        else
32        {
33                JOptionPane.showMessageDialog(null, "You do not " +
34                                                "qualify for the loan.");
35        }
36
37        System.exit(0);
38     }
39  }
```

Figure 3-19 Interaction with the `LogicalAnd` program

This input dialog box appears first. The user enters 50000 and clicks on the OK button.

This input dialog box appears next. The user enters 1 and clicks on the OK button.

This message dialog box appears next.

Figure 3-20 Interaction with the `LogicalAnd` program

This input dialog box appears first. The user enters 50000 and clicks on the OK button.

This input dialog box appears next. The user enters 4 and clicks on the OK button.

This message dialog box appears next.

The message `"You qualify for the loan."` is displayed only when both the expressions `salary >= 30000` and `yearsOnJob >= 2` are `true`. If either of these expressions is `false`, the message `"You do not qualify for the loan."` is displayed.

You can also use logical operators with `boolean` variables. For example, assuming that `isValid` is a `boolean` variable, the following `if` statement determines whether `isValid` is true and `x` is greater than 90.

```
if (isValid && x > 90)
```

The || Operator

The || operator is known as the logical OR operator. It takes two boolean expressions as operands and creates a boolean expression that is true when either of the subexpressions is true. Here is an example of an if statement that uses the || operator:

```
if (temperature < 20 || temperature > 100)
{
        System.out.println("The temperature is in the " +
                            "danger zone.");
}
```

The message will be displayed if temperature is less than 20 OR temperature is greater than 100. If either relational test is true, the entire expression is true.

Table 3-7 shows a truth table for the || operator.

All it takes for an OR expression to be true is for one side of the || operator to be true. It doesn't matter if the other side is false or true. Like the && operator, the || operator performs short-circuit evaluation. If the expression on the left side of the || operator is true, the expression on the right side will not be checked. Because it is only necessary for one of the expressions to be true, it would waste CPU time to check the remaining expression.

Table 3-7 Truth table for the || operator

Expression	Value
true || false	true
false || true	true
false || false	false
true || true	true

The program in Code Listing 3-8 is a different version of the previous program, shown in Code Listing 3-5. This version uses the || operator to determine whether salary >= 30000 is true OR yearsOnJob >= 2 is true. If either expression is true, then the person qualifies for the loan. Figure 3-21 shows example interaction with the program.

Code Listing 3-8   (LogicalOr.java)

```
 1   import javax.swing.JOptionPane;   // Needed for JOptionPane class
 2
 3   /**
 4      This program demonstrates the logical || operator.
 5   */
 6
 7   public class LogicalOr
 8   {
 9      public static void main(String[] args)
10      {
```

```
11          double salary;          // Annual salary
12          double yearsOnJob;      // Years at current job
13          String input;           // To hold string input
14
15      // Get the user's annual salary.
16      input = JOptionPane.showInputDialog("Enter your " +
17                                          "annual salary.");
18      salary = Double.parseDouble(input);
19
20      // Get the number of years at the current job.
21      input = JOptionPane.showInputDialog("Enter the number of " +
22                                          "years at your current job.");
23      yearsOnJob = Double.parseDouble(input);
24
25      // Determine whether the user qualifies for loan.
26      if (salary >= 30000 || yearsOnJob >= 2)
27      {
28              JOptionPane.showMessageDialog(null, "You qualify " +
29                                          "for the loan.");
30      }
31      else
32      {
33              JOptionPane.showMessageDialog(null, "You do not " +
34                                          "qualify for the loan.");
35      }
36
37      System.exit(0);
38     }
39 }
```

Figure 3-21 Interaction with the LogicalOr program

This input dialog box appears first. The user enters 20000 and clicks on the OK button.

This input dialog box appears next. The user enters 7 and clicks on the OK button.

This message dialog box appears next.

The ! Operator

The ! operator performs a logical NOT operation. It is a unary operator that takes a boolean expression as its operand and reverses its logical value. In other words, if the expression is true, the ! operator returns false, and if the expression is false, it returns true. Here is an if statement using the ! operator:

```
if (!(temperature > 100))
    System.out.println("This is below the maximum temperature.");
```

First, the expression (temperature > 100) is tested and a value of either true or false is the result. Then the ! operator is applied to that value. If the expression (temperature > 100) is true, the ! operator returns false. If the expression (temperature > 100) is false, the ! operator returns true. The previous code is equivalent to asking: "Is the temperature not greater than 100?"

Table 3-8 shows a truth table for the ! operator.

Table 3-8   Truth table for the ! operator

Expression	Value
!true	false
!false	true

The Precedence and Associativity of Logical Operators

Like other operators, the logical operators have orders of precedence and associativity. Table 3-9 shows the precedence of the logical operators, from highest to lowest.

Table 3-9   Logical operators in order of precedence

!
&&
||

The ! operator has a higher precedence than many of Java's other operators. You should always enclose its operand in parentheses unless you intend to apply it to a variable or a simple expression with no other operators. For example, consider the following expressions (assume x is an int variable with a value stored in it):

```
!(x > 2)
!x > 2
```

The first expression applies the ! operator to the expression x > 2. It is asking "is x not greater than 2?" The second expression, however, attempts to apply the ! operator to x only. It is asking "is the logical complement of x greater than 2?" Because the ! operator can only be applied to boolean expressions, this statement would cause a compiler error.

The `&&` and `||` operators rank lower in precedence than the relational operators, so precedence problems are less likely to occur. If you are unsure, however, it doesn't hurt to use parentheses anyway.

`(a > b) && (x < y)`	*is the same as*	`a > b && x < y`
`(x == y) || (b > a)`	*is the same as*	`x == y || b > a`

The logical operators evaluate their expressions from left to right. In the following expression, `a < b` is evaluated before `y == z`.

```
a < b || y == z
```

In the following expression, `y == z` is evaluated first, however, because the `&&` operator has higher precedence than `||`.

```
a < b || y == z && m > j
```

This expression is equivalent to the following:

```
(a < b) || ((y == z) && (m > j))
```

Table 3-10 shows the precedence of all the operators we have discussed so far. This table includes the assignment, arithmetic, relational, and logical operators.

Table 3-10   Precedence of all operators discussed so far

Order of Precedence	Operators	Description
1	`– (unary negation)  !`	Unary negation, logical NOT
2	`*   /   %`	Multiplication, division, modulus
3	`+   –`	Addition, subtraction
4	`<   >   <=   >=`	Less than, greater than, less than or equal to, greater than or equal to
5	`==   !=`	Equal to, not equal to
6	`&&`	Logical AND
7	`||`	Logical OR
8	`=   +=   –=   *=   /=   %=`	Assignment and combined assignment

Checking Numeric Ranges with Logical Operators

Sometimes you will need to write code that determines whether a numeric value is within a specific range of values or outside a specific range of values. When determining whether a number is inside a range, it's best to use the `&&` operator. For example, the following `if` statement checks the value in `x` to determine if it is in the range of 20 through 40:

```
if (x >= 20 && x <= 40)
    System.out.println(x + " is in the acceptable range.");
```

The `boolean` expression in the `if` statement will be `true` only when `x` is greater than or equal to 20 AND less than or equal to 40. The value in `x` must be within the range of 20 through 40 for this expression to be `true`.

When determining whether a number is outside a range, it's best to use the || operator. The following statement determines whether x is outside the range of 20 through 40:

```
if (x < 20 || x > 40)
    System.out.println(x + " is outside the acceptable range.");
```

It's important not to get the logic of these logical operators confused. For example, the boolean expression in the following if statement would never test true:

```
if (x < 20 && x > 40)
    System.out.println(x + " is outside the acceptable range.");
```

Obviously, x cannot be less than 20 and at the same time be greater than 40.

 Checkpoint

3.16   The following truth table shows various combinations of the values true and false connected by a logical operator. Complete the table by circling T or F to indicate if the result of such a combination is true or false.

Logical Expression	Result (true or false)	
true && false	T	F
true && true	T	F
false && true	T	F
false && false	T	F
true || false	T	F
true || true	T	F
false || true	T	F
false || false	T	F
!true	T	F
!false	T	F

3.17   Assume the variables a = 2, b = 4, and c = 6. Circle the T or F for each of the following conditions to indicate if it is true or false.

a == 4 || b > 2	T	F
6 <= c && a > 3	T	F
1 != b && c != 3	T	F
a >= -1 || a <= b	T	F
!(a > 2)	T	F

3.18   Write an if statement that displays the message "The number is valid" if the variable speed is within the range 0 through 200.

3.19   Write an if statement that displays the message "The number is not valid" if the variable speed is outside the range 0 through 200.

 ## 3.6 Comparing `String` **Objects**

CONCEPT: You cannot use relational operators to compare **String** objects. Instead you must use a **String** method.

You saw in the preceding sections how numeric values can be compared using the relational operators. You should not use the relational operators to compare String objects, however.

Remember that a `String` object is referenced by a variable that contains the object's memory address. When you use a relational operator with the reference variable, the operator works on the memory address that the variable contains, not the contents of the `String` object. For example, suppose a program has the following declarations:

```
String name1 = "Mark";
String name2 = "Mary";
```

And later, the same program has the following `if` statement:

```
        if (name1 == name2)
```

The expression `name1 == name2` will be `false`, but not because the strings "Mark" and "Mary" are different. The expression will be `false` because the variables `name1` and `name2` reference different objects. Figure 3-22 illustrates how the variables reference the `String` objects.

Figure 3-22 The `name1` and `name2` variables reference different `String` objects

To compare the contents of two `String` objects correctly, you should use the `String` class's `equals` method. The general form of the method is as follows:

```
    StringReference1.equals(StringReference2)
```

StringReference1 is a variable that references a `String` object, and *StringReference2* is another variable that references a `String` object. The method returns `true` if the two strings are equal, or `false` if they are not equal. Here is an example:

```
    if (name1.equals(name2))
```

Assuming that `name1` and `name2` reference `String` objects, the expression in the `if` statement will return `true` if they are the same, or `false` if they are not the same. The program in Code Listing 3-9 demonstrates.

Code Listing 3-9 (`StringCompare.java`)

```
1   /**
2       This program correctly compares two String objects using
3       the equals method.
```

```
 4  */
 5
 6  public class StringCompare
 7  {
 8      public static void main(String[] args)
 9      {
10          String name1 = "Mark",
11                 name2 = "Mark",
12                 name3 = "Mary";
13
14          // Compare "Mark" and "Mark"
15
16          if (name1.equals(name2))
17          {
18              System.out.println(name1 + " and " + name2 +
19                                  " are the same.");
20          }
21          else
22          {
23              System.out.println(name1 + " and " + name2 +
24                                  " are NOT the same.");
25          }
26
27          // Compare "Mark" and "Mary"
28
29          if (name1.equals(name3))
30          {
31              System.out.println(name1 + " and " + name3 +
32                                  " are the same.");
33          }
34          else
35          {
36              System.out.println(name1 + " and " + name3 +
37                                  " are NOT the same.");
38          }
39      }
40  }
```

Program Output

```
Mark and Mark are the same.
Mark and Mary are NOT the same.
```

You can also compare String objects to string literals. Simply pass the string literal as the argument to the equals method, as follows:

```
if (name1.equals("Mark"))
```

To determine if two strings are not equal, simply apply the ! operator to the `equals` method's return value. Here is an example:

```
if (!name1.equals("Mark"))
```

The `boolean` expression in this `if` statement performs a not-equal-to operation. It determines whether the object referenced by `name1` is not equal to "Mark".

The `String` class also provides the `compareTo` method, which can be used to determine whether one string is greater than, equal to, or less than another string. The general form of the method is as follows:

```
StringReference.compareTo(OtherString)
```

StringReference is a variable that references a `String` object, and *OtherString* is either another variable that references a `String` object or a string literal. The method returns an integer value that can be used in the following manner:

- If the method's return value is negative, the string referenced by *StringReference* (the calling object) is less than the *OtherString* argument.
- If the method's return value is 0, the two strings are equal.
- If the method's return value is positive, the string referenced by *StringReference* (the calling object) is greater than the *OtherString* argument.

For example, assume that `name1` and `name2` are variables that reference `String` objects. The following `if` statement uses the `compareTo` method to compare the strings:

```
if (name1.compareTo(name2) == 0)
   System.out.println("The names are the same.");
```

Also, the following expression compares the string referenced by `name1` to the string literal "Joe":

```
if (name1.compareTo("Joe") == 0)
   System.out.println("The names are the same.");
```

The program in Code Listing 3-10 more fully demonstrates the `compareTo` method.

Code Listing 3-10   (`StringCompareTo.java`)

```
 1  /**
 2      This program compares two String objects using
 3      the compareTo method.
 4  */
 5
 6  public class StringCompareTo
 7  {
 8     public static void main(String[] args)
 9     {
10        String name1 = "Mary",
11               name2 = "Mark";
12
13        // Compare "Mary" and "Mark"
```

```
14
15          if (name1.compareTo(name2) < 0)
16          {
17              System.out.println(name1 + " is less than " + name2);
18          }
19          else if (name1.compareTo(name2) == 0)
20          {
21              System.out.println(name1 + " is equal to " + name2);
22          }
23          else if (name1.compareTo(name2) > 0)
24          {
25              System.out.println(name1 + " is greater than " + name2);
26          }
27      }
28  }
```

Program Output

Mary is greater than Mark

Let's take a closer look at this program. When you use the compareTo method to compare two strings, the strings are compared character by character. This is often called a *lexicographical comparison*. The program uses the compareTo method to compare the strings "Mary" and "Mark", beginning with the first, or leftmost, characters. This is illustrated in Figure 3-23.

Figure 3-23 String comparison of "Mary" and "Mark"

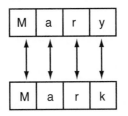

Here is how the comparison takes place:

1. The "M" in "Mary" is compared with the "M" in "Mark." Because these are the same, the next characters are compared.
2. The "a" in "Mary" is compared with the "a" in "Mark." Because these are the same, the next characters are compared.
3. The "r" in "Mary" is compared with the "r" in "Mark." Because these are the same, the next characters are compared.
4. The "y" in "Mary" is compared with the "k" in "Mark." Because these are not the same, the two strings are not equal. The character "y" is greater than "k", so it is determined that "Mary" is greater than "Mark."

If one of the strings in a comparison is shorter than the other, Java can only compare the corresponding characters. If the corresponding characters are identical, then the shorter string is considered less than the longer string. For example, suppose the strings "High" and "Hi" were being compared. The string "Hi" would be considered less than "High" because it is shorter.

Ignoring Case in String Comparisons

The `equals` and `compareTo` methods perform case sensitive comparisons, which means that uppercase letters are not considered the same as their lowercase counterparts. In other words, "A" is not the same as "a". This can obviously lead to problems when you want to perform case insensitive comparisons.

The `String` class provides the `equalsIgnoreCase` and `compareToIgnoreCase` methods. These methods work like the `equals` and `compareTo` methods, except the case of the characters in the strings is ignored. For example, the program in Code Listing 3-11 asks the user to enter the "secret word," which is similar to a password. The secret word is "PROSPERO", and the program performs a case-insensitive string comparison to determine whether the user has entered it.

Code Listing 3-11 (`SecretWord.java`)

```
 1   import java.util.Scanner; // Needed for the Scanner class
 2
 3   /**
 4      This program demonstrates a case insensitive string comparison.
 5   */
 6
 7   public class SecretWord
 8   {
 9      public static void main(String[] args)
10      {
11         String input;     // To hold the user's input
12
13         // Create a Scanner object for keyboard input.
14         Scanner keyboard = new Scanner(System.in);
15
16         // Prompt the user to enter the secret word.
17         System.out.print("Enter the secret word: ");
18         input = keyboard.nextLine();
19
20         // Determine whether the user entered the secret word.
21         if (input.equalsIgnoreCase("PROSPERO"))
22         {
23            System.out.println("Congratulations! You know the " +
24                               "secret word!");
25         }
26         else
27         {
```

```
28              System.out.println("Sorry, that is NOT the " +
29                                 "secret word!");
30         }
31     }
32 }
```

Program Output with Example Input Shown in Bold

Enter the secret word: **Ferdinand [Enter]**
Sorry, that is NOT the secret word!

Program Output with Example Input Shown in Bold

Enter the secret word: **Prospero [Enter]**
Congratulations! You know the secret word!

The `compareToIgnoreCase` method works exactly like the `compareTo` method, except the case of the characters in the strings being compared is ignored.

Checkpoint

3.20   Assume the variable `name` references a `String` object. Write an `if` statement that displays "Do I know you?" if the `String` object contains "Timothy".

3.21   Assume the variables `name1` and `name2` reference two different `String` objects, containing different strings. Write code that displays the strings referenced by these variables in alphabetical order.

3.22   Modify the statement you wrote in response to Checkpoint 3.20 so it performs a case insensitive comparison.

3.7 More about Variable Declaration and Scope

CONCEPT: The scope of a variable is limited to the block in which it is declared.

Recall from Chapter 2 that a local variable is a variable that is declared inside a method. Java allows you to create local variables just about anywhere in a method. For example, look at the program in Code Listing 3-12. The `main` method declares two `String` reference variables: `firstName` and `lastName`. Notice that the declarations of these variables appear near the code that first uses the variables.

Code Listing 3-12   (`VariableScope.java`)

```java
1  import javax.swing.JOptionPane;   // Needed for JOptionPane
2
3  /**
4     This program demonstrates how variables may be declared
5     in various locations throughout a program.
```

```
 6   */
 7
 8   public class VariableScope
 9   {
10      public static void main(String[] args)
11      {
12         // Get the user's first name.
13         String firstName;
14         firstName = JOptionPane.showInputDialog("Enter your " +
15                                                 "first name.");
16
17         // Get the user's last name.
18         String lastName;
19         lastName = JOptionPane.showInputDialog("Enter your " +
20                                                "last name.");
21
22         JOptionPane.showMessageDialog(null, "Hello " + firstName +
23                                             " " + lastName);
24         System.exit(0);
25      }
26   }
```

Although it is a common practice to declare all of a method's local variables at the beginning of the method, it is possible to declare them at later points. Sometimes programmers declare certain variables near the part of the program where they are used in order to make their purpose more evident.

Recall from Chapter 2 that a variable's scope is the part of the program where the variable's name may be used. A local variable's scope always starts at the variable's declaration, and ends at the closing brace of the block of code in which it is declared. In Code Listing 3-12, the firstName variable is visible only to the code in lines 13 through 24. The lastName variable is visible only to the code in lines 18 through 24.

> **NOTE:** When a program is running and it enters the section of code that constitutes a variable's scope, it is said that the variable "comes into scope." This simply means the variable is now visible and the program may reference it. Likewise, when a variable "leaves scope" it may not be used.

3.8 The Conditional Operator (Optional)

CONCEPT: You can use the conditional operator to create short expressions that work like if-else statements.

The *conditional operator* is powerful and unique. Because it takes three operands, it is considered a ternary operator. The conditional operator provides a shorthand method of expressing a simple `if-else` statement. The operator consists of the question mark (?) and the colon (:). You use the operator to write a conditional expression, in the following format:

```
BooleanExpression ? Value1: Value2;
```

The `BooleanExpression` is like the `boolean` expression in the parentheses of an `if` statement. If the `BooleanExpression` is true, then the value of the conditional expression is `Value1`. Otherwise, the value of the conditional expression is `Value2`. Here is an example of a statement using the conditional operator:

```
y = x < 0 ? 10: 20;
```

This preceding statement performs the same operation as the following `if-else` statement:

```
if (x < 0)
    y = 10;
else
    y = 20;
```

The conditional operator gives you the ability to pack decision-making power into a concise line of code. With a little imagination it can be applied to many other programming problems. For instance, consider the following statement:

```
System.out.println("Your grade is: " +
            (score < 60 ? "Fail." : "Pass."));
```

Converted to an `if-else` statement, it would be written as follows:

```
if (score < 60)
    System.out.println("Your grade is: Fail.");
else
    System.out.println("Your grade is: Pass.");
```

NOTE: The parentheses are placed around the conditional expression because the + operator has higher precedence than the ?: operator. Without the parentheses, the + operator would concatenate the value in score with the string "Your grade is: ".

To see an example program that uses the conditional operator, see the program called *ConsultantCharges.java* in this chapter's source code folder on the Student CD.

Checkpoint

3.23 Rewrite the following `if-else` statements as statements that use the conditional operator.

```
a)  if (x > y)
        z = 1;
    else
        z = 20;
```

```
    b)  if (temp > 45)
            population = base * 10;
        else
            population = base * 2;
    c)  if (hours > 40)
            wages *= 1.5;
        else
            wages *= 1;
    d)  if (result >= 0)
            System.out.println("The result is positive.)";
        else
            System.out.println("The result is negative.");
```

3.9   The switch **Statement**

CONCEPT: The switch statement lets the value of a variable or expression
determine where the program will branch to.

A branch occurs when one part of a program causes another part to execute. The if-else-
if statement allows your program to branch into one of several possible paths. It tests
a series of boolean expressions, and branches if one of those expressions is true. The
switch statement is a similar mechanism. It, however, tests the value of an integer or character expression and then uses that value to determine which set of statements to branch
to. Here is the format of the switch statement:

```
switch (SwitchExpression)
{
        case CaseExpression:
            // place one or more
            // statements here
            break;
        case CaseExpression:
            // place one or more
            // statements here
            break;
        // case statements may be repeated as many
        // times as necessary
        default:
            // place one or more
            // statements here
}
```

The first line of the statement starts with the word switch, followed by a SwitchExpression
inside parentheses. The SwitchExpression is an expression that must result in a value of
one of these types: char, byte, short, or int.

On the next line is the beginning of a block containing several case statements. Each
case statement is formatted in the following manner:

```
case CaseExpression:
        // place one or more
        // statements here
        break;
```

The case statement starts with the key word case, followed by a *CaseExpression*. The *CaseExpression* is a literal or a final variable which must be of the char, byte, short, or int types. The *CaseExpression* is followed by a colon.

After the case statement, one or more valid programming statements may appear. These statements are branched to if the value of the *SwitchExpression* matches the case statement's *CaseExpression*. The last statement in the group of statements should be the key word break. The break statement causes the program to jump out of the switch statement and resume processing at the statement following it.

NOTE: The *CaseExpressions* of each case statement must be unique.

A default section normally comes after all the case statements. This section is branched to if none of the case expressions match the switch expression.

NOTE: The default section is optional. If you leave it out, however, your program will have nowhere to branch to if the *SwitchExpression* doesn't match any of the *CaseExpressions*.

The program in Code Listing 3-13 shows how a simple switch statement works.

Code Listing 3-13   (SwitchDemo.java)

```java
 1  import java.util.Scanner;      // Needed for Scanner class
 2
 3  /**
 4      This program demonstrates the switch statement.
 5  */
 6
 7  public class SwitchDemo
 8  {
 9     public static void main(String[] args)
10     {
11        int number;         // A number entered by the user
12
13        // Create a Scanner object for keyboard input.
14        Scanner keyboard = new Scanner(System.in);
15
16        // Get one of the numbers 1, 2, or 3 from the user.
17        System.out.print("Enter 1, 2, or 3: ");
18        number = keyboard.nextInt();
19
```

```
20          // Determine the number entered.
21          switch (number)
22          {
23             case 1:
24                 System.out.println("You entered 1.");
25                 break;
26             case 2:
27                 System.out.println("You entered 2.");
28                 break;
29             case 3:
30                 System.out.println("You entered 3.");
31                 break;
32             default:
33                 System.out.println("That's not 1, 2, or 3!");
34          }
35       }
36   }
```

Program Output with Example Input Shown in Bold

```
Enter 1, 2, or 3: 2 [Enter]
You entered 2.
```

Program Output with Example Input Shown in Bold

```
Enter 1, 2, or 3: 5 [Enter]
That's not 1, 2, or 3!
```

The first case statement is case 1, the second is case 2, and the third is case 3. These statements mark where the program is to branch to if the variable number contains the values 1, 2, or 3. The default section is branched to if the user enters anything other than 1, 2, or 3.

Notice the break statements that are in the case 1, case 2, and case 3 sections.

```
switch (number)
{
    case 1:
            System.out.println("You entered 1.");
            break;←
    case 2:
            System.out.println("You entered 2.");
            break;←
    case 3:
             System.out.println("You entered 3.");
             break;←
    default:
            System.out.println("That's not 1, 2, or 3!");
}
```

The case statements show the program where to start executing in the block and the break statements show the program where to stop. Without the break statements, the program would execute all of the lines from the matching case statement to the end of the block.

> **NOTE:** The default section (or the last case section if there is no default) does not need a break statement. Some programmers prefer to put one there anyway for consistency.

The program in Code Listing 3-14 is a modification of Code Listing 3-13, without the break statements.

Code Listing 3-14   (NoBreaks.java)

```java
 1  import java.util.Scanner;     // Needed for Scanner class
 2
 3  /**
 4     This program demonstrates the switch statement.
 5  */
 6
 7  public class NoBreaks
 8  {
 9     public static void main(String[] args)
10     {
11        int number;        // A number entered by the user
12
13        // Create a Scanner object for keyboard input.
14        Scanner keyboard = new Scanner(System.in);
15
16        // Get one of the numbers 1, 2, or 3 from the user.
17        System.out.print("Enter 1, 2, or 3: ");
18        number = keyboard.nextInt();
19
20        // Determine the number entered.
21        switch (number)
22        {
23           case 1:
24              System.out.println("You entered 1.");
25           case 2:
26              System.out.println("You entered 2.");
27           case 3:
28              System.out.println("You entered 3.");
29           default:
30              System.out.println("That's not 1, 2, or 3!");
31        }
32     }
33  }
```

Program Output with Example Input Shown in Bold

```
Enter 1, 2, or 3: 1 [Enter]
You entered 1.
```

```
You entered 2.
You entered 3.
That's not 1, 2, or 3!
```

Program Output with Example Input Shown in Bold

Enter 1, 2, or 3: **3 [Enter]**
You entered 3.
That's not 1, 2, or 3!

Without the break statement, the program "falls through" all of the statements below the one with the matching case expression. Sometimes this is what you want. For instance, the program in Code Listing 3-15 asks the user to select a grade of pet food. The available choices are A, B, and C. The switch statement will recognize either uppercase or lowercase letters.

Code Listing 3-15   (PetFood.java)

```java
 1   import java.util.Scanner; // Needed for the Scanner class
 2
 3   /**
 4      This program demonstrates a switch statement.
 5   */
 6
 7   public class PetFood
 8   {
 9      public static void main(String[] args)
10      {
11         String input;     // To hold the user's input
12         char foodGrade;   // Grade of pet food
13
14         // Create a Scanner object for keyboard input.
15         Scanner keyboard = new Scanner(System.in);
16
17         // Prompt the user for a grade of pet food.
18         System.out.println("Our pet food is available in " +
19                            "three grades:");
20         System.out.print("A, B, and C. Which do you want " +
21                          "pricing for? ");
22         input = keyboard.nextLine();
23         foodGrade = input.charAt(0);
24
25         // Display pricing for the selected grade.
26         switch(foodGrade)
27         {
```

```
28          case 'a':
29          case 'A':
30              System.out.println("30 cents per lb.");
31              break;
32          case 'b':
33          case 'B':
34              System.out.println("20 cents per lb.");
35              break;
36          case 'c':
37          case 'C':
38              System.out.println("15 cents per lb.");
39              break;
40          default:
41              System.out.println("Invalid choice.");
42      }
43  }
44 }
```

Program Output with Example Input Shown in Bold

```
Our pet food is available in three grades:
A, B, and C. Which do you want pricing for? b [Enter]
20 cents per lb.
```

Program Output with Example Input Shown in Bold

```
Our pet food is available in three grades:
A, B, and C. Which do you want pricing for? B [Enter]
20 cents per lb.
```

When the user enters 'a' the corresponding case has no statements associated with it, so the program falls through to the next case, which corresponds with 'A'.

```
case 'a':
case 'A':
        System.out.println("30 cents per lb.");
        break;
```

The same technique is used for 'b' and 'c'.

 Checkpoint

3.24 Complete the following program skeleton by writing a switch statement that displays "one" if the user has entered 1, "two" if the user has entered 2, and "three" if the user has entered 3. If a number other than 1, 2, or 3 is entered, the program should display an error message.

```
import java.util.Scanner;
public class CheckPoint
{
```

```
        public static void main(String[] args)
        {
            int userNum;
            Scanner keyboard = new Scanner(System.in);
            System.out.print("Enter one of the numbers " +
                                "1, 2, or 3: ");
            userNum = keyboard.nextInt();

            //
            // Write the switch statement here.
            //
        }
    }
```

3.25 Rewrite the following `if-else-if` statement as a `switch` statement.

```
if (selection == 'A')
    System.out.println("You selected A.");
else if (selection == 'B')
    System.out.println("You selected B.");
else if (selection == 'C')
    System.out.println("You selected C.");
else if (selection == 'D')
    System.out.println("You selected D.");
else
    System.out.println("Not good with letters, eh?");
```

3.26 Explain why you cannot convert the following `if-else-if` statement into a `switch` statement.

```
if (temp == 100)
    x = 0;
else if (population > 1000)
    x = 1;
else if (rate < .1)
    x = -1;
```

3.27 What is wrong with the following `switch` statement?

```
// This code has errors!!!
switch (temp)
{
    case temp < 0 :
        System.out.println("Temp is negative.");
        break;
    case temp = 0:
        System.out.println("Temp is zero.");
        break;
    case temp > 0 :
        System.out.println("Temp is positive.");
        break;
}
```

3.28   What will the following code display?

```
int funny = 7, serious = 15;
funny = serious * 2;
switch (funny)
{   case 0 :
        System.out.println("That is funny.");
        break;
    case 30:
        System.out.println("That is serious.");
        break;
    case 32:
        System.out.println("That is seriously funny.");
        break;
    default:
        System.out.println(funny);
}
```

3.10 Creating Objects with the `DecimalFormat` Class

CONCEPT: The `DecimalFormat` class can be used to format the appearance of floating-point numbers rounded to a specified number of decimal places.

In Java, a value of the `double` data type can be displayed with as many as 15 decimal places, and a value of the `float` data type can be displayed with up to 6 decimal places. For example, look at the following code:

```
double number = 10.0 / 6.0;
System.out.println(number);
```

This code will display:

```
1.666666666666667
```

Quite often, you want to control the number of decimal places that are displayed. For example, when displaying dollar amounts, you normally display two decimal places. You can use the `DecimalFormat` class, which is part of the API, to control the way floating-point numbers are formatted. First, to use the `DecimalFormat` class you must have the following import statement at the top of your program:

```
import java.text.DecimalFormat;
```

The `DecimalFormat` class is not automatically available to your Java programs. This statement makes the class available.

Recall from Chapter 2's discussion of the `String` class that a class is a description of an object. It specifies the attributes and methods that an object has. In this book, a class is frequently referred to as a "blueprint" that objects may be created from. When a program is running, it can use a class to create, in memory, as many objects as needed. Each object that is created from a class is called an *instance* of the class.

To use the `DecimalFormat` class, you create an object, or an instance, of the class. The following statement shows an example:

```
DecimalFormat formatter = new DecimalFormat("#0.00");
```

Let's dissect the statement into two parts. The first part of the statement is as follows:

```
DecimalFormat formatter =
```

This declares a variable named `formatter`. The data type of the variable is `DecimalFormat`. Because the word `DecimalFormat` is not the name of a primitive data type, Java assumes it to be the name of a class. Recall from Chapter 2 that a variable of a class type is known as a reference variable, and it is used to hold the memory address of an object. When a reference variable holds an object's memory address, it is said that the variable references the object. So, the `formatter` variable will be used to reference a `DecimalFormat` object. The = operator that appears next assigns the address of an object that is created by the second part of the statement as follows:

```
new DecimalFormat("#0.00");
```

This part of the statement uses the key word new, which creates an object in memory. After the word new, the name `DecimalFormat` appears, followed by some data enclosed in a set of parentheses. The name `DecimalFormat` specifies that an object of the `DecimalFormat` class should be created.

Now let's look at the data appearing inside the parentheses. When an object is created, a special method known as a *constructor* is automatically executed. The purpose of the constructor is to initialize the object's attributes with appropriate data and perform any necessary setup operations. In other words, it constructs the object. The data that appears inside the parentheses is an argument that is passed to the constructor. When you create a `DecimalFormat` object, you pass a string that contains a *formatting pattern* to the constructor. A formatting pattern consists of special characters specifying how floating-point numbers should be formatted. In this example the string `"#0.00"` is being passed to the constructor. This string will be assigned to one of the object's internal attributes. After the statement executes, the `formatter` variable will reference the object that was created in memory. This is illustrated in Figure 3-24.

Figure 3-24 The `formatter` variable references a `DecimalFormat` object

Each character in the formatting pattern corresponds with a position in a number. The first two characters, #0, correspond to the two digits before the decimal point, the period indicates the decimal point, and the characters 00 correspond to two digits after the decimal point. The # character specifies that a digit should be displayed in this position if it is present. If there is no digit in this position, no digit should be displayed. The 0 character also specifies that a digit should be displayed in this position if it is present. However, if there is no digit present in this position, a 0 should be displayed. The two zeros that appear after the decimal point indicate that numbers should be rounded to two decimal places.

Once you have properly created a `DecimalFormat` object, you call its `format` method and pass the number you wish to format as an argument. The method returns a string containing the formatted number. For example, look at the program in Code Listing 3-16.

Code Listing 3-16   **(Format1.java)**

```
1   import java.text.DecimalFormat;
2
3   /**
4       This program demonstrates the DecimalFormat class.
5   */
6
7   public class Format1
8   {
9      public static void main(String[] args)
10     {
11         double number1 = 0.166666666666667;
12         double number2 = 1.666666666666667;
13         double number3 = 16.666666666666667;
14         double number4 = 166.666666666666667;
15
16         // Create a DecimalFormat object.
17         DecimalFormat formatter = new DecimalFormat("#0.00");
18
19         // Display the formatted variable contents.
20         System.out.println(formatter.format(number1));
21         System.out.println(formatter.format(number2));
22         System.out.println(formatter.format(number3));
23         System.out.println(formatter.format(number4));
24     }
25  }
```

Program Output

```
0.17
1.67
16.67
166.67
```

Notice the difference between the # character and the 0 character in the formatting pattern. The # symbol causes no digits to be displayed, while the 0 character causes leading zeros to be displayed. For example, look at the program in Code Listing 3-17. This is the same program as shown in Code Listing 3-16, but using a different format pattern.

Code Listing 3-17 (Format2.java)

```java
1   import java.text.DecimalFormat;
2
3   /**
4      This program demonstrates the DecimalFormat class.
5   */
6
7   public class Format2
8   {
9      public static void main(String[] args)
10     {
11        double number1 = 0.166666666666667;
12        double number2 = 1.666666666666667;
13        double number3 = 16.666666666666667;
14        double number4 = 166.666666666666667;
15
16         // Create a DecimalFormat object.
17         DecimalFormat formatter = new DecimalFormat("000.00");
18
19         // Display the formatted variable contents.
20         System.out.println(formatter.format(number1));
21         System.out.println(formatter.format(number2));
22         System.out.println(formatter.format(number3));
23         System.out.println(formatter.format(number4));
24     }
25  }
```

Program Output

```
000.17
001.67
016.67
166.67
```

You can also insert a comma into the format pattern to create grouping separators in formatted numbers. The program in Code Listing 3-18 demonstrates.

Code Listing 3-18 (Format3.java)

```java
1   import java.text.DecimalFormat;
2
3   /**
4      This program demonstrates the DecimalFormat class.
5   */
6
```

```
 7  public class Format3
 8  {
 9     public static void main(String[] args)
10     {
11        double number1 = 123.899;
12        double number2 = 1233.899;
13        double number3 = 12345.899;
14        double number4 = 123456.899;
15        double number5 = 1234567.899;
16
17         // Create a DecimalFormat object.
18         DecimalFormat formatter = new DecimalFormat("#,##0.00");
19
20         // Display the formatted variable contents.
21         System.out.println(formatter.format(number1));
22         System.out.println(formatter.format(number2));
23         System.out.println(formatter.format(number3));
24         System.out.println(formatter.format(number4));
25         System.out.println(formatter.format(number5));
26      }
27  }
```

Program Output

```
123.90
1,233.90
12,345.90
123,456.90
1,234,567.90
```

You can also format numbers as percentages by writing the % character at the last position in the format pattern. This causes a number to be multiplied by 100, and the % character is appended to its end. The program in Code Listing 3-19 demonstrates.

Code Listing 3-19   (Format4.java)

```
 1  import java.text.DecimalFormat;
 2
 3  /**
 4     This program demonstrates the DecimalFormat class.
 5  */
 6
 7  public class Format4
 8  {
 9     public static void main(String[] args)
10     {
11        double number1 = 0.12;
12        double number2 = 0.05;
```

```
13
14          // Create a DecimalFormat object.
15          DecimalFormat formatter = new DecimalFormat("#0%");
16
17          // Display the formatted variable contents.
18          System.out.println(formatter.format(number1));
19          System.out.println(formatter.format(number2));
20      }
21  }
```

Program Output

```
12%
5%
```

Checkpoint

3.29   What is the purpose of the new key word?

3.30   What is a constructor?

3.31   Assume that the double variable number holds the value 459.6329. What format
        pattern would you use to display the number as 00459.633?

3.32   Assume that the double variable number holds the value 0.179. What format pat-
        tern would you use to display the number as .18?

3.33   Assume that the double variable number holds the value 7634869.1. What format
        pattern would you use to display the number as 7,634,869.10?

CASE STUDY ON CD-ROM: The Student CD contains a valuable case study,
Calculating Sales Commission, that demonstrates how sales commissions may be calculated using various commission rates. The commission rate is determined by the amount
of sales.

3.11 The printf Method

CONCEPT: The **System.out.printf** method allows you to format output in a
variety of ways.

You can perform formatted console output with the System.out.printf method. The
method's general format is as follows:

```
System.out.printf(FormatString, ArgumentList)
```

In the general format, *FormatString* is a string that contains text and/or special formatting specifiers. *ArgumentList* is a list of zero or more additional arguments, which will be
formatted according to the format specifiers listed in the format string.

The simplest way you can use the printf method is with only a format string, and no additional arguments. Here is an example:

```java
System.out.printf("I love Java programming.\n");
```

The format string in this example is "I love Java programming.\n". It does not contain any format specifiers, so this method call simply prints the string "I love Java programming.\n". Using the method in this fashion is like using the System.out.print method. Now let's look at an example that uses a format specifier and an additional argument:

```java
int hours = 40;
System.out.printf("I worked %d hours this week.\n", hours);
```

In this example, the %d is a format specifier for a decimal integer. When this string is printed, the %d will not be displayed. Instead, the value of the hours argument will be printed in place of the format specifier. Here is the output of the code:

```
I worked 40 hours this week.
```

In this example, the %d format specifier was used because the hours variable is an int. An error will occur if you use %d with a non-integer value. Here's another example:

```java
int dogs = 2;
int cats = 4;
System.out.printf("We have %d dogs and %d cats.\n",
                  dogs, cats);
```

First, notice that this example uses two %d format specifiers in the format string. Also notice that two arguments appear after the format string. The value of the first integer argument, dogs, will be printed in place of the first %d, and the value of the second integer argument, cats, will be printed in place of the second %d. The code will produce the following output:

```
We have 2 dogs and 4 cats.
```

These examples show the one-to-one correspondence between the format specifiers and the arguments that appear after the format string. The following code shows another example:

```java
int value1 = 3;
int value2 = 6;
int value3 = 9;
System.out.printf("%d %d %d\n", value1, value2, value3);
```

In the printf method call, there are three format specifiers and three additional arguments after the format string. This code will produce the following output:

```
3 6 9
```

Now let's actually apply some formatting to the values we are displaying. A format specifier may also include a field width. Here is an example:

```java
int number = 9;
System.out.printf("The value is %6d\n", number);
```

The format specifier %6d indicates that the argument number should be printed in a field that is 6 places wide. If the value in number is shorter than 6 places, it will be right justified. Here is the output of the code:

```
The value is      9
```

If the value of the argument is wider than the specified field width, the field width will be expanded to accommodate the value. For example, look at the following code:

```
int number = 97654;
System.out.printf("The value is %2d\n", number);
```

In this code the field width is two spaces, but the value being displayed, 97654, requires five spaces. Because the field width will be automatically expanded to accommodate the number, this code will produce the following output:

```
The value is 97654
```

Field widths can help when you need to print values aligned in columns. For example, look at the following code:

```
int num1 = 97654, num2 = 598;
int num3 = 86,    num4 = 56012;
int num5 = 246,   num6 = 2;
System.out.printf("%7d %7d\n", num1, num2);
System.out.printf("%7d %7d\n", num3, num4);
System.out.printf("%7d %7d\n", num5, num6);
```

The %7d format specifier prints an integer in a field that is seven spaces wide. So, this code displays the values of the variables in a table with three rows and two columns. Each column has a width of seven spaces. Here is the output of the code:

```
 97654     598
    86   56012
   246       2
```

If you wish to print a floating-point value, use the %f format specifier. Here is an example:

```
double number = 1278.92;
System.out.printf("The number is %f\n", number);
```

This code produces the following output:

```
The number is 1278.920000
```

You can also use a field width when printing floating-point values. For example the following code prints the value of number in a field that is 18 spaces wide:

```
System.out.printf("The number is %18f\n", number);
```

In addition to the field width, you can also specify the number of digits that appear after the decimal point. Here is an example:

```
double grossPay = 874.12;
System.out.printf("Your pay is %.2f\n", grossPay);
```

In this code, the `%.2f` specifier indicates that the value should appear with two digits after the decimal point. The output of the code is as follows:

```
Your pay is 874.12
```

When you specify the number of digits to appear after the decimal point, the number will be rounded. For example, look at the following code:

```
double number = 1278.92714;
System.out.printf("The number is %.2f\n", number);
```

This code will produce the following output:

```
The number is 1278.93
```

You can specify both the field width and the number of decimal places together, as shown here:

```
double grossPay = 874.12;
System.out.printf("Your pay is %8.2f\n", grossPay);
```

The output of the code is as follows:

```
Your pay is   874.12
```

You can also use commas to group digits in a number. To do this, place a comma after the `%` symbol in the format specifier. Here is an example:

```
double grossPay = 1253874.12;
System.out.printf("Your pay is %,.2f\n", grossPay);
```

This code will produce the following output:

```
Your pay is 1,253,874.12
```

If you wish to print a string argument, use the `%s` format specifier. Here is an example:

```
String name = "Ringo";
System.out.printf("Your name is %s\n", name);
```

This code produces the following output:

```
Your name is Ringo
```

You can also use a field width when printing strings. For example, look at the following code:

```
String name1 = "George",  name2 = "Franklin";
String name3 = "Jay",     name4 = "Ozzy";
String name5 = "Carmine", name6 = "Dee";
System.out.printf("%10s %10s\n", name1, name2);
System.out.printf("%10s %10s\n", name3, name4);
System.out.printf("%10s %10s\n", name5, name6);
```

The `%10s` format specifier prints a string in a field that is ten spaces wide. This code displays the values of the variables in a table with three rows and two columns. Each column has a width of ten spaces. Here is the output of the code:

```
    George    Franklin
       Jay        Ozzy
   Carmine         Dee
```

The format specifiers we have shown in this section are the very basic ones. Java provides much more powerful format specifiers for more complex formatting needs. The API documentation gives an overview of them all.

3.12 Common Errors to Avoid

The following list describes several errors that are commonly committed when learning this chapter's topics.

- **Using = instead of == to compare primitive values.** Remember, = is the assignment operator and == tests for equality.
- **Using == instead of the `equals` method to compare `String` objects.** You cannot use the == operator to compare the contents of a `String` object with another string. Instead you must use the `equals` or `compareTo` methods.
- **Forgetting to enclose an `if` statement's `boolean` expression in parentheses.** Java requires that the `boolean` expression being tested by an `if` statement is enclosed in a set of parentheses. An error will result if you omit the parentheses or use any other grouping characters.
- **Writing a semicolon at the end of an `if` clause.** When you write a semicolon at the end of an `if` clause, Java assumes that the conditionally executed statement is a null or empty statement.
- **Forgetting to enclose multiple conditionally executed statements in braces.** Normally the `if` statement conditionally executes only one statement. To conditionally execute more than one statement, you must enclose them in braces.
- **Omitting the trailing `else` in an `if-else-if` statement.** This is not a syntax error, but can lead to logical errors. If you omit the trailing else from an `if-else-if` statement, no code will be executed if none of the statement's `boolean` expressions are `true`.
- **Not writing complete `boolean` expressions on both sides of a logical `&&` or `||` operator.** You must write a complete `boolean` expression on both sides of a logical `&&` or `||` operator. For example, the expression x > 0 && < 10 is not valid because < 10 is not a complete expression. The expression should be written as x > 0 && x < 10.
- **Trying to perform case insensitive string comparisons with the `String` class's `equals` and `compareTo` methods.** To perform case insensitive string comparisons, use the `String` class's `equalsIgnoreCase` and `compareToIgnoreCase` methods.
- **Using a `SwitchExpression` that is not an `int`, `short`, `byte`, or `char`.** The switch statement can only evaluate expressions that are of the `int`, `short`, `byte`, or `char` data types.
- **Using a `CaseExpression` that is not a literal or a `final` variable.** Because the compiler must determine the value of a `CaseExpression` at compile time, `CaseExpressions` must be either literal values or `final` variables.
- **Forgetting to write a colon at the end of a `case` statement.** A colon must appear after the `CaseExpression` in each `case` statement.
- **Forgetting to write a `break` statement in a `case` section.** This is not a syntax error, but it can lead to logical errors. The program does not branch out of a `switch` statement until it reaches a `break` statement or the end of the `switch` statement.
- **Forgetting to write a `default` section in a `switch` statement.** This is not a syntax error, but can lead to a logical error. If you omit the `default` section, no code will be executed if none of the `CaseExpressions` match the `SwitchExpression`.

- **Reversing the ? and the : when using the conditional operator.** When using the conditional operator, the ? character appears first in the conditional expression, then the : character.
- **Forgetting to pass a formatting string to a `DecimalFormat` object's constructor.** The formatting string specifies how the object should format any numbers that are passed to the `format` method.

Review Questions and Exercises

Multiple Choice and True/False

1. The `if` statement is an example of a _____.

   a. sequence structure
   b. decision structure
   c. pathway structure
   d. class structure

2. This type of expression has a value of either `true` or `false`.

   a. `binary` expression
   b. `decision` expression
   c. `unconditional` expression
   d. `boolean` expression

3. >, <, and == are _____.

   a. relational operators
   b. logical operators
   c. conditional operators
   d. ternary operators

4. &&, ||, and ! are _____.

   a. relational operators
   b. logical operators
   c. conditional operators
   d. ternary operators

5. This is an empty statement that does nothing.

   a. missing statement
   b. virtual statement
   c. null statement
   d. conditional statement

6. To create a block of statements, you enclose the statements in these.

   a. parentheses `( )`
   b. square brackets `[ ]`
   c. angled brackets `<>`
   d. braces `{ }`

7. This is a `boolean` variable that signals when some condition exists in the program.

   a. flag
   b. signal
   c. sentinel
   d. siren

8. How does the character 'A' compare to the character 'B'?

   a. 'A' is greater than 'B'
   b. 'A' is less than 'B'
   c. 'A' is equal to 'B'
   d. You cannot compare characters

9. This is an `if` statement that appears inside another `if` statement.

   a. nested `if` statement
   b. tiered `if` statement
   c. dislodged `if` statement
   d. structured `if` statement

10. An `else` clause always goes with _____.

    a. the closest previous `if` clause that doesn't already have its own `else` clause
    b. the closest `if` clause
    c. the `if` clause that is randomly selected by the compiler
    d. none of these

11. When determining whether a number is inside a range, it's best to use this operator.

    a. `&&`
    b. `!`
    c. `||`
    d. `? :`

12. This determines whether two different `String` objects contain the same string.

    a. the `==` operator
    b. the `=` operator
    c. the `equals` method
    d. the `stringCompare` method

13. The conditional operator takes this many operands.

    a. one
    b. two
    c. three
    d. four

14. This section of a `switch` statement is branched to if none of the `case` expressions match the `switch` expression.

    a. `else`
    b. `default`
    c. `case`
    d. `otherwise`

15. This key word creates an object.

    a. `create`
    b. `object`
    c. `new`
    d. `construct`

16. **True or False:** The = operator and the == operator perform the same operation.

17. **True or False:** A conditionally executed statement should be indented one level from the `if` clause.

18. **True or False:** All lines in a conditionally executed block should be indented one level.

19. **True or False:** When an `if` statement is nested in the `if` clause of another statement, the only time the inner `if` statement is executed is when the `boolean` expression of the outer `if` statement is `true`.

20. **True or False:** When an `if` statement is nested in the `else` clause of another statement, the only time the inner `if` statement is executed is when the `boolean` expression of the outer `if` statement is `true`.

21. **True or False:** The scope of a variable is limited to the block in which it is defined.

Find the Error

Find the errors in the following code:

1.
```
// Warning! This code contains ERRORS!
if (x == 1);
    y = 2;
else if (x == 2);
    y = 3;
else if (x == 3);
    y = 4;
```

2.
```
// Warning! This code contains an ERROR!
if (average = 100)
    System.out.println("Perfect Average!");
```

3.
```
// Warning! This code contains ERRORS!
if (num2 == 0)
    System.out.println("Division by zero is not possible.");
    System.out.println("Please run the program again ");
    System.out.println("and enter a number besides zero.");
else
    Quotient = num1 / num2;
    System.out.print("The quotient of " + Num1);
    System.out.print(" divided by " + Num2 + " is ");
    System.out.println(Quotient);
```

4. ```
// Warning! This code contains ERRORS!
switch (score)
{
    case (score > 90):
        grade = 'A';
        break;
    case(score > 80):
        grade = 'b';
        break;
    case(score > 70):
        grade = 'C';
        break;
    case (score > 60):
        grade = 'D';
        break;
    default:
        grade = 'F';
}
```

5. The following statement should determine whether x is not greater than 20. What is wrong with it?

   ```
   if (!x > 20)
   ```

6. The following statement should determine whether count is within the range of 0 through 100. What is wrong with it?

   ```
   if (count >= 0 || count <= 100)
   ```

7. The following statement should determine whether count is outside the range of 0 through 100. What is wrong with it?

   ```
   if (count < 0 && count > 100)
   ```

8. The following statement should assign 0 to z if a is less than 10, otherwise it should assign 7 to z. What is wrong with it?

   ```
   z = (a < 10) : 0 ? 7;
   ```

9. Assume that partNumber references a String object. The following if statement should perform a case-insensitive comparison. What is wrong with it?

   ```
   if (partNumber.equals("BQ789W4"))
       available = true;
   ```

10. The following statement should create a DecimalFormat object. What is wrong with it?

    ```
    DecimalFormat fmt = DecimalFormat("00.00");
    ```

Algorithm Workbench

1. Write an if statement that assigns 100 to x when y is equal to 0.

2. Write an if-else statement that assigns 0 to x when y is equal to 10. Otherwise it should assign 1 to x.
    ```

3. Using the following chart, write an `if-else-if` statement that assigns .10, .15, or .20 to `commission`, depending on the value in `sales`.

Sales	Commission Rate
Up to $10,000	10%
$10,000 to $15,000	15%
Over $15,000	20%

4. Write an `if` statement that sets the variable `hours` to 10 when the `boolean` flag variable `minimum` is equal to `true`.

5. Write nested `if` statements that perform the following tests: If `amount1` is greater than 10 and `amount2` is less than 100, display the greater of the two.

6. Write an `if` statement that prints the message "The number is valid" if the variable `grade` is within the range 0 through 100.

7. Write an `if` statement that prints the message "The number is valid" if the variable `temperature` is within the range –50 through 150.

8. Write an `if` statement that prints the message "The number is not valid" if the variable `hours` is outside the range 0 through 80.

9. Write an `if-else` statement that displays the `String` objects `title1` and `title2` in alphabetical order.

10. Convert the following `if-else-if` statement into a `switch` statement:

```
if (choice == 1)
{
    System.out.println("You selected 1.");
}
else if (choice == 2 || choice == 3)
{
    System.out.println("You selected 2 or 3.");
}
else if (choice == 4)
{
    System.out.println("You selected 4.");
}
else
{
    System.out.println("Select again please.");
}
```

11. Match the conditional expression with the `if-else` statement that performs the same operation.

```
a. q = x < y ? a + b : x * 2;
b. q = x < y ? x * 2 : a + b;
c. q = x < y ? 0 : 1;
```

```
_____        if (x < y)
                 q = 0;
             else
                 q = 1;
```

```
_____      if (x < y)
               q = a + b;
           else
               q = x * 2;
_____      if (x < y)
               q = x * 2;
           else
               q = a + b;
```

12. Assume that the `double` variable `number` holds the value 0.0329. What format pattern would you use with the `DecimalFormat` class to display the number as 00000.033?

13. Assume that the `double` variable `number` holds the value 0.0329. What format pattern would you use with the `DecimalFormat` class to display the number as 0.03?

14. Assume that the `double` variable `number` holds the value 456198736.3382. What format pattern would you use with the `DecimalFormat` class to display the number as 456,198,736.34?

Short Answer

1. Explain what is meant by the term "conditionally executed."

2. Explain why a misplaced semicolon can cause an `if` statement to operate incorrectly.

3. Why is it good advice to indent all the statements inside a set of braces?

4. What happens when you compare two `String` objects with the `==` operator?

5. Explain the purpose of a flag variable. Of what data type should a flag variable be?

6. What risk does a programmer take when not placing a trailing `else` at the end of an `if-else-if` statement?

7. Briefly describe how the `&&` operator works.

8. Briefly describe how the `||` operator works.

9. Why are the relational operators called "relational"?

10. When does a constructor execute? What is its purpose?

Programming Challenges

myCodeMate **1. Roman Numerals**

Write a program that prompts the user to enter a number within the range of 1 through 10. The program should display the Roman numeral version of that number. If the number is outside the range of 1–10, the program should display an error message.

2. Magic Dates

The date June 10, 1960, is special because when we write it in the following format, the month times the day equals the year:

6/10/60

Write a program that asks the user to enter a month (in numeric form), a day, and a two-digit year. The program should then determine whether the month times the day is equal to the year. If so, it should display a message saying the date is magic. Otherwise it should display a message saying the date is not magic.

3. Body Mass Index

Write a program that calculates and displays a person's body mass index (BMI). The BMI is often used to determine whether a person with a sedentary lifestyle is overweight or underweight for his or her height. A person's BMI is calculated with the following formula:

$$BMI = weight \times 703 / height^2$$

where *weight* is measured in pounds and *height* is measured in inches. The program should display a message indicating whether the person has optimal weight, is underweight, or is overweight. A sedentary person's weight is considered optimal if his or her BMI is between 18.5 and 25. If the BMI is less than 18.5, the person is considered underweight. If the BMI value is greater than 25, the person is considered overweight.

4. Test Scores and Grade

Write a program that has variables to hold three test scores. The program should ask the user to enter three test scores and then assign the values entered to the variables. The program should display the average of the test scores and the letter grade that is assigned for the test score average. Use the grading scheme in the following table:

Test Score Average	Letter Grade
90–100	A
80–89	B
70–79	C
60–69	D
Below 60	F

5. Mass and Weight

Scientists measure an object's mass in kilograms and its weight in Newtons. If you know the amount of mass that an object has, you can calculate its weight, in Newtons, with the following formula:

$$Weight = mass \times 9.8$$

Write a program that asks the user to enter an object's mass, and then calculate its weight. If the object weighs more than 1000 Newtons, display a message indicating that it is too heavy. If the object weighs less than 10 Newtons, display a message indicating that the object is too light.

6. Time Calculator

Write a program that asks the user to enter a number of seconds.

- There are 60 seconds in a minute. If the number of seconds entered by the user is greater than or equal to 60, the program should display the number of minutes in that many seconds.
- There are 3600 seconds in an hour. If the number of seconds entered by the user is greater than or equal to 3600, the program should display the number of hours in that many seconds.

VideoNote
The Time
Calculator
Problem

- There are 86400 seconds in a day. If the number of seconds entered by the user is greater than or equal to 86400, the program should display the number of days in that many seconds.

7. Sorted Names

Write a program that asks the user to enter three names, and then displays the names sorted in ascending order. For example, if the user entered "Charlie", "Leslie", and "Andy", the program would display:

    Andy
    Charlie
    Leslie

 ### 8. Software Sales

A software company sells a package that retails for $99. Quantity discounts are given according to the following table:

Quantity	Discount
10–19	20%
20–49	30%
50–99	40%
100 or more	50%

Write a program that asks the user to enter the number of packages purchased. The program should then display the amount of the discount (if any) and the total amount of the purchase after the discount.

9. Shipping Charges

The Fast Freight Shipping Company charges the following rates:

Weight of Package	Rate per 500 Miles Shipped
2 pounds or less	$1.10
Over 2 pounds but not more than 6 pounds	$2.20
Over 6 pounds but not more than 10 pounds	$3.70
Over 10 pounds	$3.80

The shipping charges per 500 miles are not prorated. For example, if a 2-pound package is shipped 550 miles, the charges would be $2.20. Write a program that asks the user to enter the weight of a package and then displays the shipping charges.

 ### 10. Fat Gram Calculator

Write a program that asks the user to enter the number of calories and fat grams in a food item. The program should display the percentage of the calories that come from fat. One gram of fat has 9 calories, therefore:

    Calories from fat = fat grams * 9

The percentage of calories from fat can be calculated as follows:

    Calories from fat ÷ total calories

If the calories from fat are less than 30 percent of the total calories of the food, it should also display a message indicating the food is low in fat.

> **NOTE:** The number of calories from fat cannot be greater than the total number of calories in the food item. If the program determines that the number of calories from fat is greater than the number of calories in the food item, it should display an error message indicating that the input is invalid.

11. Running the Race

Write a program that asks for the names of three runners and the time, in minutes, it took each of them to finish a race. The program should display the names of the runners in the order that they finished.

12. The Speed of Sound

The following table shows the approximate speed of sound in air, water, and steel:

Medium	Speed
Air	1100 feet per second
Water	4900 feet per second
Steel	16,400 feet per second

Write a program that asks the user to enter "air", "water", or "steel", and the distance that a sound wave will travel in the medium. The program should then display the amount of time it will take. You can calculate the amount of time it takes sound to travel in air with the following formula:

$$Time = distance / 1100$$

You can calculate the amount of time it takes sound to travel in water with the following formula:

$$Time = distance / 4900$$

You can calculate the amount of time it takes sound to travel in steel with the following formula:

$$Time = distance / 16400$$

13. Internet Service Provider

An Internet service provider has three different subscription packages for its customers:

Package A: For $9.95 per month 10 hours of access are provided. Additional hours are $2.00 per hour.

Package B: For $13.95 per month 20 hours of access are provided. Additional hours are $1.00 per hour.

Package C: For $19.95 per month unlimited access is provided.

Write a program that calculates a customer's monthly bill. It should ask the user to enter the letter of the package the customer has purchased (A, B, or C) and the number of hours that were used. It should then display the total charges.

14. Internet Service Provider, Part 2

Modify the program you wrote for Programming Challenge 13 so it also calculates and displays the amount of money Package A customers would save if they purchased Packages B or C, and the amount of money Package B customers would save if they purchased Package C. If there would be no savings, no message should be printed.

15. Bank Charges

A bank charges a base fee of $10 per month, plus the following check fees for a commercial checking account:

$.10 each for less than 20 checks
$.08 each for 20–39 checks
$.06 each for 40–59 checks
$.04 each for 60 or more checks

Write a program that asks for the number of checks written for the month. The program should then calculate and display the bank's service fees for the month.

16. Book Club Points

Serendipity Booksellers has a book club that awards points to its customers based on the number of books purchased each month. The points are awarded as follows:

- If a customer purchases 0 books, he or she earns 0 points.
- If a customer purchases 1 book, he or she earns 5 points.
- If a customer purchases 2 books, he or she earns 15 points.
- If a customer purchases 3 books, he or she earns 30 points.
- If a customer purchases 4 or more books, he or she earns 60 points.

Write a program that asks the user to enter the number of books that he or she has purchased this month and then displays the number of points awarded.

CHAPTER

4 Loops and Files

TOPICS

4.1 The Increment and Decrement Operators

CONCEPT: ++ and -- are operators that add and subtract one from their operands.

To *increment* a value means to increase it by one, and to *decrement* a value means to decrease it by one. Both of the following statements increment the variable number:

```
number = number + 1;
number += 1;
```

And number is decremented in both of the following statements:

```
number = number - 1;
number -= 1;
```

Java provides a set of simple unary operators designed just for incrementing and decrementing variables. The increment operator is ++ and the decrement operator is --. The following statement uses the ++ operator to increment number:

```
number++;
```

And the following statement decrements number:

```
number--;
```

NOTE: The expression number++ is pronounced "number plus plus," and number-- is pronounced "number minus minus."

The program in Code Listing 4-1 demonstrates the ++ and -- operators.

Code Listing 4-1 (`IncrementDecrement.java`)

```
 1  /**
 2      This program demonstrates the ++ and -- operators.
 3  */
 4
 5  public class IncrementDecrement
 6  {
 7      public static void main(String[] args)
 8      {
 9          int number = 4;   // number starts out with 4
10
11          // Display the value in number.
12          System.out.println("number is " + number);
13          System.out.println("I will increment number.");
14
15          // Increment number.
16          number++;
17
18          // Display the value in number again.
19          System.out.println("Now, number is " + number);
20          System.out.println("I will decrement number.");
21
22          // Decrement number.
23          number--;
24
25          // Display the value in number once more.
26          System.out.println("Now, number is " + number);
27      }
28  }
```

Program Output

```
number is 4
I will increment number.
Now, number is 5
I will decrement number.
Now, number is 4
```

The statements in Code Listing 4-1 show the increment and decrement operators used in *postfix mode*, which means the operator is placed after the variable. The operators also work in *prefix mode*, where the operator is placed before the variable name as follows:

```
++number;

--number;
```

In both postfix and prefix mode, these operators add one to or subtract one from their operand. Code Listing 4-2 demonstrates this.

Code Listing 4-2   (`Prefix.java`)

```java
1   /**
2       This program demonstrates the ++ and -- operators
3       in prefix mode.
4   */
5
6   public class Prefix
7   {
8       public static void main(String[] args)
9       {
10          int number = 4;   // number starts out with 4
11
12          // Display the value in number.
13          System.out.println("number is " + number);
14          System.out.println("I will increment number.");
15
16          // Increment number.
17          ++number;
18
19          // Display the value in number again.
20          System.out.println("Now, number is " + number);
21          System.out.println("I will decrement number.");
22
23          // Decrement number.
24          --number;
25
26          // Display the value in number once again.
27          System.out.println("Now, number is " + number);
28      }
29  }
```

Program Output

```
number is 4
I will increment number.
Now, number is 5
I will decrement number.
Now, number is 4
```

The Difference between Postfix and Prefix Modes

In Code Listings 4-1 and 4-2, the statements number++ and ++number increment the variable number, while the statements number-- and --number decrement the variable number. In these simple statements it doesn't matter whether the operator is used in postfix or prefix mode. The difference is important, however, when these operators are used in statements that do more than just increment or decrement. For example, look at the following code:

```
number = 4;
System.out.println(number++);
```

The statement that calls the println method does two things: (1) calls println to display the value of number, and (2) increments number. But which happens first? The println method will display a different value if number is incremented first than if number is incremented last. The answer depends upon the mode of the increment operator.

Postfix mode causes the increment to happen after the value of the variable is used in the expression. In the previously shown statement, the println method will display 4 and then number will be incremented to 5. Prefix mode, however, causes the increment to happen first. Here is an example:

```
number = 4;
System.out.println(++number);
```

In these statements, number is incremented to 5, then println will display the value in number (which is 5). For another example, look at the following code:

```
int x = 1, y;
y = x++;                  // Postfix increment
```

The first statement declares the variable x (initialized with the value 1) and the variable y. The second statement does the following:

- It assigns the value of x to the variable y.
- The variable x is incremented.

The value that will be stored in y depends on when the increment takes place. Because the ++ operator is used in postfix mode, it acts after the assignment takes place. So, this code will store 1 in y. After the code has executed, x will contain 2. Let's look at the same code, but with the ++ operator used in prefix mode as follows:

```
int x = 1, y;
y = ++x;                  // Prefix increment
```

The first statement declares the variable x (initialized with the value 1) and the variable y. In the second statement, the ++ operator is used in prefix mode, so it acts on the variable before the assignment takes place. So, this code will store 2 in y. After the code has executed, x will also contain 2.

Checkpoint

4.1 What will the following program segments display?

a) ```
x = 2;
y = x++;
System.out.println(y);
```

b) ```
x = 2;
System.out.println(x++);
```

c) ```
x = 2;
System.out.println(--x);
```

d) ```
x = 8;
y = x--;
System.out.println(y);
```

4.2 The while Loop

— **CONCEPT:** A loop is part of a program that repeats.

In Chapter 3, you were introduced to the concept of control structures, which direct the flow of a program. A *loop* is a control structure that causes a statement or group of statements to repeat. Java has three looping control structures: the while loop, the do-while loop, and the for loop. The difference among each of these is how they control the repetition. In this section we will focus on the while loop.

VideoNote
The **while**
Loop

The while loop has two important parts: (1) a boolean expression that is tested for a true or false value, and (2) a statement or block of statements that is repeated as long as the expression is true. Figure 4-1 shows the logic of a while loop.

Figure 4-1 Logic of a while Loop

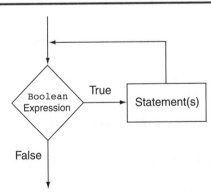

Here is the general format of the while loop:

```
while (BooleanExpression)
    Statement;
```

In the general format, *BooleanExpression* is any valid boolean expression, and *Statement* is any valid Java statement. The first line shown in the format is sometimes called the *loop header*. It consists of the key word while followed by the *BooleanExpression* enclosed in parentheses.

Here's how the loop works: the *BooleanExpression* is tested, and if it is true, the *Statement* is executed. Then, the *BooleanExpression* is tested again. If it is true, the *Statement* is executed. This cycle repeats until the *BooleanExpression* is false.

The statement that is repeated is known as the *body* of the loop. It is also considered a conditionally executed statement, because it is only executed under the condition that the *BooleanExpression* is true.

Notice there is no semicolon at the end of the loop header. Like the if statement, the while loop is not complete without the conditionally executed statement that follows it.

If you wish the while loop to repeat a block of statements, the format is as follows:

```
while (BooleanExpression)
{
    Statement;
    Statement;
    // Place as many statements here
    // as necessary.
}
```

The while loop works like an if statement that executes over and over. As long as the expression in the parentheses is true, the conditionally executed statement or block will repeat. The program in Code Listing 4-3 uses the while loop to print "Hello" five times.

Code Listing 4-3   (WhileLoop.java)

```
 1   /**
 2       This program demonstrates the while loop.
 3   */
 4
 5   public class WhileLoop
 6   {
 7       public static void main(String[] args)
 8       {
 9           int number = 1;
10
11           while (number <= 5)
12           {
13               System.out.println("Hello");
14               number++;
15           }
```

```
16
17          System.out.println("That's all!");
18      }
19  }
```

Program Output

```
Hello
Hello
Hello
Hello
Hello
That's all!
```

Let's take a closer look at this program. An integer variable, number, is declared and initialized with the value 1. The while loop begins with the following statement:

```
while (number <= 5)
```

This statement tests the variable number to determine whether it is less than or equal to 5. If it is, then the statements in the body of the loop are executed as follows:

```
System.out.println("Hello");
number++;
```

The first statement in the body of the loop prints the word "Hello". The second statement uses the increment operator to add one to number. This is the last statement in the body of the loop, so after it executes, the loop starts over. It tests the boolean expression again, and if it is true, the statements in the body of the loop are executed. This cycle repeats until the boolean expression number <= 5 is false, as illustrated in Figure 4-2.

Figure 4-2 The while Loop

Each repetition of a loop is known as an *iteration*. This loop will perform five iterations because the variable number is initialized with the value 1, and it is incremented each time the body of the loop is executed. When the expression number <= 5 is tested and found to be `false`, the loop will terminate and the program will resume execution at the statement that immediately follows the loop. Figure 4-3 shows the logic of this loop.

In this example, the `number` variable is referred to as the *loop control variable* because it controls the number of times that the loop iterates.

Figure 4-3 Logic of the example `while` loop

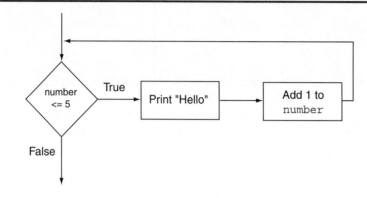

The `while` Loop Is a Pretest Loop

The `while` loop is known as a *pretest* loop, which means it tests its expression before each iteration. Notice the variable declaration of `number` in Code Listing 4-3:

```
int number = 1;
```

The `number` variable is initialized with the value 1. If `number` had been initialized with a value that is greater than 5, as shown in the following program segment, the loop would never execute:

```
int number = 6;
while (number <= 5)
{
    System.out.println("Hello");
    number++;
}
```

An important characteristic of the `while` loop is that the loop will never iterate if the `boolean` expression is `false` to start with. If you want to be sure that a `while` loop executes the first time, you must initialize the relevant data in such a way that the `boolean` expression starts out as `true`.

Infinite Loops

In all but rare cases, loops must contain a way to terminate within themselves. This means that something inside the loop must eventually make the `boolean` expression `false`. The loop in Code Listing 4-3 stops when the expression `number <= 5` is `false`.

If a loop does not have a way of stopping, it is called an infinite loop. An *infinite loop* continues to repeat until the program is interrupted. Here is an example of an infinite loop:

```java
int number = 1;
while (number <= 5)
{
    System.out.println("Hello");
}
```

This is an infinite loop because it does not contain a statement that changes the value of the number variable. Each time the boolean expression is tested, number will contain the value 1.

It's also possible to create an infinite loop by accidentally placing a semicolon after the first line of the while loop. Here is an example:

```java
int number = 1;
while (number <= 5);   // This semicolon is an ERROR!
{
    System.out.println("Hello");
    number++;
}
```

The semicolon at the end of the first line is assumed to be a null statement and disconnects the while statement from the block that comes after it. To the compiler, this loop looks like the following:

```java
while (number <= 5);
```

This while loop will forever execute the null statement, which does nothing. The program will appear to have "gone into space" because there is nothing to display screen output or show activity.

Don't Forget the Braces with a Block of Statements

If you are using a block of statements, don't forget to enclose all of the statements in a set of braces. If the braces are accidentally left out, the while statement conditionally executes only the very next statement. For example, look at the following code:

```java
int number = 1;
// This loop is missing its braces!
while (number <= 5)
    System.out.println("Hello");
    number++;
```

In this code the number++ statement is not in the body of the loop. Because the braces are missing, the while statement only executes the statement that immediately follows it. This loop will execute infinitely because there is no code in its body that changes the number variable.

Programming Style and the `while` Loop

It's possible to create loops that look like the following:

```
while (number <= 5) { System.out.println("Hello"); number++; }
```

Avoid this style of programming. The programming style you should use with the `while` loop is similar to that of the `if` statement as follows:

- If there is only one statement repeated by the loop, it should appear on the line after the `while` statement and be indented one additional level. The statement can optionally appear inside a set of braces.
- If the loop repeats a block, each line inside the braces should be indented.

This programming style should visually set the body of the loop apart from the surrounding code. In general, you'll find a similar style being used with the other types of loops presented in this chapter.

In the Spotlight:
Designing a Program with a while Loop

A project currently underway at Chemical Labs, Inc., requires that a substance be continually heated in a vat. A technician must check the substance's temperature every 15 minutes. If the substance's temperature does not exceed 102.5 degrees Celsius, then the technician does nothing. However, if the temperature is greater than 102.5 degrees Celsius, the technician must turn down the vat's thermostat, wait 5 minutes, and check the temperature again. The technician repeats these steps until the temperature does not exceed 102.5 degrees Celsius. The director of engineering has asked you to write a program that guides the technician through this process.

Here is the algorithm:

1. *Prompt the user to enter the substance's temperature.*
2. *Repeat the following steps as long as the temperature is greater than 102.5 degrees Celsius:*
   (a) *Tell the technician to turn down the thermostat, wait 5 minutes, and check the temperature again.*
   (b) *Prompt the user to enter the substance's temperature.*
3. *After the loop finishes, tell the technician that the temperature is acceptable and to check it again in 15 minutes.*

After reviewing this algorithm, you realize that Steps 2(a) and 2(b) should not be performed if the test condition (temperature is greater than 102.5) is false to begin with. The `while` loop will work well in this situation, because it will not execute even once if its condition is false. Code Listing 4-4 shows the program.

Code Listing 4-4

```
1  /**
2     This program assists a technician in the process
```

```
 3     of checking a substance's temperature.
 4  */
 5  import java.util.Scanner;
 6
 7  public class CheckTemperature
 8  {
 9    public static void main(String[] args)
10    {
11       final double MAX_TEMP = 102.5;    // Maximim temperature
12       double temperature;               // To hold the temperature
13
14       // Create a Scanner object for keyboard input.
15       Scanner keyboard = new Scanner(System.in);
16
17       // Get the current temperature.
18       System.out.print("Enter the substance's Celsius temperature: ");
19       temperature = keyboard.nextDouble();
20
21       // As long as necessary, instruct the technician
22       // to adjust the temperature.
23       while (temperature > MAX_TEMP)
24       {
25          System.out.println("The temperature is too high. Turn the");
26          System.out.println("thermostat down and wait 5 minutes.");
27          System.out.println("Then, take the Celsius temperature again");
28          System.out.print("and enter it here: ");
29          temperature = keyboard.nextDouble();
30       }
31
32       // Remind the technician to check the temperature
33       // again in 15 minutes.
34       System.out.println("The temperature is acceptable.");
35       System.out.println("Check it again in 15 minutes.");
36    }
37  }
```

Program Output with Example Input Shown in Bold

```
Enter the substance's Celsius temperature: 104.7 [Enter]
The temperature is too high. Turn the
thermostat down and wait 5 minutes.
Then take the Celsius temperature again
and enter it here: 103.2 [Enter]
The temperature is too high. Turn the
thermostat down and wait 5 minutes.
Then take the Celsius temperature again
and enter it here: 102.1 [Enter]
The temperature is acceptable.
Check it again in 15 minutes.
```

Checkpoint

4.2   How many times will `"Hello World"` be printed in the following program segment?

```
int count = 10;
while (count < 1)
{
    System.out.println("Hello World");
    count++;
}
```

4.3   How many times will `"I love Java programming!"` be printed in the following program segment?

```
int count = 0;
while (count < 10)
    System.out.println("I love Java programming!);
```

4.3   Using the `while` Loop for Input Validation

CONCEPT: The `while` loop can be used to create input routines that repeat until acceptable data is entered.

Perhaps the most famous saying of the computer industry is "garbage in, garbage out." The integrity of a program's output is only as good as its input, so you should try to make sure garbage does not go into your programs. *Input validation* is the process of inspecting data given to a program by the user and determining if it is valid. A good program should give clear instructions about the kind of input that is acceptable, and not assume the user has followed those instructions.

The `while` loop is especially useful for validating input. If an invalid value is entered, a loop can require that the user re-enter it as many times as necessary. For example, the following loop asks for a number in the range of 1 through 100:

```
input = JOptionPane.showInputDialog("Enter a number " +
                    "in the range of 1 through 100.");
number = Integer.parseInt(input);
// Validate the input.
while (number < 1 || number > 100)
{
    input = JOptionPane.showInputDialog("Invalid input. " +
                    "Enter a number in the range of " +
                    "1 through 100.");
    number = Integer.parseInt(input);
}
```

This code first allows the user to enter a number. This takes place just before the loop. If the input is valid, the loop will not execute. If the input is invalid, however, the loop will display an error message and require the user to enter another number. The loop will continue to

execute until the user enters a valid number. The general logic of performing input validation is shown in Figure 4-4.

Figure 4-4   Input validation logic

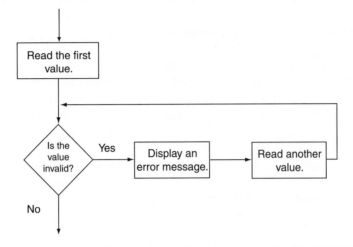

The read operation that takes place just before the loop is called a *priming read*. It provides
the first value for the loop to test. Subsequent values are obtained by the loop.

The program in Code Listing 4-5 calculates the number of soccer teams a youth league may
create, based on a given number of players and a maximum number of players per team.
The program uses `while` loops (in lines 28 through 36 and lines 44 through 49) to validate
the user's input. Figure 4-5 shows an example of interaction with the program.

Code Listing 4-5   (`SoccerTeams.java`)

```
 1   import javax.swing.JOptionPane;
 2
 3   /**
 4      This program calculates the number of soccer teams
 5      that a youth league may create from the number of
 6      available players. Input validation is demonstrated
 7      with while loops.
 8   */
 9
10   public class SoccerTeams
11   {
12      public static void main(String[] args)
13      {
14         final int MIN_PLAYERS = 9;    // Minimum players per team
15         final int MAX_PLAYERS = 15;   // Maximum players per team
16         int players;                  // Number of available players
17         int teamSize;                 // Number of players per team
18         int teams;                    // Number of teams
```

```
19          int leftOver;              // Number of left over players
20          String input;              // To hold the user input
21
22          // Get the number of players per team.
23          input = JOptionPane.showInputDialog("Enter the number of " +
24                                               "players per team.");
25          teamSize = Integer.parseInt(input);
26
27          // Validate the number entered.
28          while (teamSize < MIN_PLAYERS || teamSize > MAX_PLAYERS)
29          {
30              input = JOptionPane.showInputDialog("The number must " +
31                                       "be at least " + MIN_PLAYERS +
32                                       " and no more than " +
33                                       MAX_PLAYERS + ".\n Enter " +
34                                       "the number of players.");
35              teamSize = Integer.parseInt(input);
36          }
37
38          // Get the number of available players.
39          input = JOptionPane.showInputDialog("Enter the available " +
40                                               "number of players.");
41          players = Integer.parseInt(input);
42
43          // Validate the number entered.
44          while (players < 0)
45          {
46              input = JOptionPane.showInputDialog("Enter 0 or " +
47                                               "greater.");
48              players = Integer.parseInt(input);
49          }
50
51          // Calculate the number of teams.
52          teams = players / teamSize;
53
54          // Calculate the number of left over players.
55          leftOver = players % teamSize;
56
57          // Display the results.
58          JOptionPane.showMessageDialog(null, "There will be " +
59                                           teams + " teams with " +
60                                           leftOver +
61                                           " players left over.");
62          System.exit(0);
63      }
64  }
```

Figure 4-5   Interaction with the `SoccerTeams` program

This input dialog box appears first. The user enters 4 (an invalid value) and clicks the OK button.

> **Input**
>
> **?** Enter the number of players per team.
>
> 4
>
> OK   Cancel

This input dialog box appears next. The user enters 12 and clicks the OK button.

> **Input**
>
> **?** The number must be at least 9 and no more than 15.
> Enter the number of players.
>
> 12
>
> OK   Cancel

This input dialog box appears next. The user enters −142 (an invalid value) and clicks the OK button.

> **Input**
>
> **?** Enter the available number of players.
>
> -142
>
> OK   Cancel

This input dialog box appears next. The user enters 142 and clicks the OK button.

> **Input**
>
> **?** Enter 0 or greater.
>
> 142
>
> OK   Cancel

This message dialog box appears next.

> **Message**
>
> **i** There will be 11 teams with 10 players left over.
>
> OK

Checkpoint

4.4   Write an input validation loop that asks the user to enter a number in the range of 10 through 24.

4.5   Write an input validation loop that asks the user to enter 'Y', 'y', 'N', or 'n'.

4.6   Write an input validation loop that asks the user to enter "Yes" or "No".

4.4 The do-while Loop

CONCEPT: The `do-while` loop is a posttest loop, which means its **boolean** expression is tested after each iteration.

The `do-while` loop looks something like an inverted `while` loop. Here is the `do-while` loop's format when the body of the loop contains only a single statement:

```
do
    Statement;
while (BooleanExpression);
```

Here is the format of the `do-while` loop when the body of the loop contains multiple statements:

```
do
{
    Statement;
    Statement;
    // Place as many statements here as necessary.
} while (BooleanExpression);
```

NOTE: The do-while loop must be terminated with a semicolon.

The `do-while` loop is a *posttest* loop. This means it does not test its **boolean** expression until it has completed an iteration. As a result, the `do-while` loop always performs at least one iteration, even if the **boolean** expression is **false** to begin with. This differs from the behavior of a `while` loop, which you will recall is a pretest loop. For example, in the following `while` loop the `println` statement will not execute at all:

```
int x = 1;
while (x < 0)
    System.out.println(x);
```

But the `println` statement in the following `do-while` loop will execute once because the `do-while` loop does not evaluate the expression `x < 0` until the end of the iteration:

```
int x = 1;
do
    System.out.println(x);
while (x < 0);
```

Figure 4-6 illustrates the logic of the `do-while` loop.

You should use the `do-while` loop when you want to make sure the loop executes at least once. For example, the program in Code Listing 4-6 averages a series of three test scores for a student. After the average is displayed, it asks the user if he or she wants to average another set of test scores. The program repeats as long as the user enters **Y** for yes.

Figure 4-6   Logic of the do-while loop

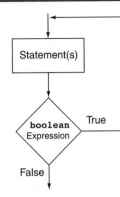

| Code Listing 4-6 | (TestAverage1.java) |

```java
1   import java.util.Scanner;    // Needed for the Scanner class
2
3   /**
4      This program demonstrates a user controlled loop.
5   */
6
7   public class TestAverage1
8   {
9      public static void main(String[] args)
10     {
11        int score1, score2, score3;    // Three test scores
12        double average;                // Average test score
13        char repeat;                   // To hold 'y' or 'n'
14        String input;                  // To hold input
15
16        System.out.println("This program calculates the " +
17                           "average of three test scores.");
18
19        // Create a Scanner object for keyboard input.
20        Scanner keyboard = new Scanner(System.in);
21
22        // Get as many sets of test scores as the user wants.
23        do
24        {
25           // Get the first test score in this set.
26           System.out.print("Enter score #1: ");
27           score1 = keyboard.nextInt();
28
29           // Get the second test score in this set.
30           System.out.print("Enter score #2: ");
31           score2 = keyboard.nextInt();
32
```

```
33              // Get the third test score in this set.
34              System.out.print("Enter score #3: ");
35              score3 = keyboard.nextInt();
36
37              // Consume the remaining newline.
38              keyboard.nextLine();
39
40              // Calculate and print the average test score.
41              average = (score1 + score2 + score3) / 3.0;
42              System.out.println("The average is " + average);
43              System.out.println();    // Prints a blank line
44
45              // Does the user want to average another set?
46              System.out.println("Would you like to average " +
47                              "another set of test scores?");
48              System.out.print("Enter Y for yes or N for no: ");
49              input = keyboard.nextLine();  // Read a line.
50              repeat = input.charAt(0);     // Get the first char.
51
52          } while (repeat == 'Y' || repeat == 'y');
53      }
54  }
```

Program Output with Example Input Shown in Bold

```
This program calculates the average of three test scores.
Enter score #1: 89 [Enter]
Enter score #2: 90 [Enter]
Enter score #3: 97 [Enter]
The average is 92.0

Would you like to average another set of test scores?
Enter Y for yes or N for no: y [Enter]
Enter score #1: 78 [Enter]
Enter score #2: 65 [Enter]
Enter score #3: 88 [Enter]
The average is 77.0

Would you like to average another set of test scores?
Enter Y for yes or N for no: n [Enter]
```

When this program was written, the programmer had no way of knowing the number of times the loop would iterate. This is because the loop asks the user if he or she wants to repeat the process. This type of loop is known as a *user controlled loop,* because it allows the user to decide the number of iterations.

4.5 The for Loop

CONCEPT: The **for** loop is ideal for performing a known number of iterations.

In general, there are two categories of loops: conditional loops and count-controlled loops. A *conditional loop* executes as long as a particular condition exists. For example, an input validation loop executes as long as the input value is invalid. When you write a conditional loop, you have no way of knowing the number of times it will iterate.

Sometimes you do know the exact number of iterations that a loop must perform. A loop that repeats a specific number of times is known as a *count-controlled loop*. For example, if a loop asks the user to enter the sales amounts for each month in the year, it will iterate 12 times. In essence, the loop counts to 12 and asks the user to enter a sales amount each time it makes a count.

A count-controlled loop must possess three elements:

1. It must initialize a control variable to a starting value.
2. It must test the control variable by comparing it to a maximum value. When the control variable reaches its maximum value, the loop terminates.
3. It must update the control variable during each iteration. This is usually done by incrementing the variable.

In Java, the **for** loop is ideal for writing count-controlled loops. It is specifically designed to initialize, test, and update a loop control variable. Here is the format of the **for** loop when used to repeat a single statement:

```
for (Initialization; Test; Update)
    Statement;
```

The format of the **for** loop when used to repeat a block is as follows:

```
for (Initialization; Test; Update)
{
    Statement;
    Statement;
    // Place as many statements here as necessary.
}
```

The first line of the **for** loop is known as the *loop header*. After the key word **for**, there are three expressions inside the parentheses, separated by semicolons. (Notice there is not a semicolon after the third expression.) The first expression is the *initialization expression*. It is normally used to initialize a control variable to its starting value. This is the first action performed by the loop, and it is only done once. The second expression is the *test expression*. This is a **boolean** expression that controls the execution of the loop. As long as this expression is **true**, the body of the **for** loop will repeat. The **for** loop is a pretest loop, so it evaluates the test expression before each iteration. The third expression is the *update expression*. It executes at the end of each iteration. Typically, this is a statement that increments the loop's control variable.

Here is an example of a simple `for` loop that prints "Hello" five times:

```
for (count = 1; count <= 5; count++)
    System.out.println("Hello");
```

In this loop, the initialization expression is `count = 1`, the test expression is `count <= 5`, and the update expression is `count++`. The body of the loop has one statement, which is the `println` statement. Figure 4-7 illustrates the sequence of events that takes place during the loop's execution. Notice that Steps 2 through 4 are repeated as long as the test expression is `true`.

Figure 4-7   Sequence of events in the `for` loop

Figure 4-8 shows the loop's logic in the form of a flowchart.

Figure 4-8   Logic of the `for` loop

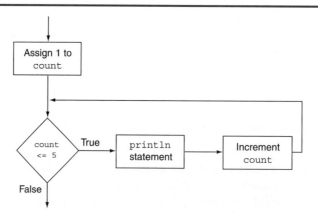

Notice how the control variable, `count`, is used to control the number of times that the loop iterates. During the execution of the loop, this variable takes on the values 1 through 5, and when the test expression `count <= 5` is `false`, the loop terminates. Because this variable keeps a count of the number of iterations, it is often called a *counter variable*.

Also notice that in this example the `count` variable is used only in the loop header, to control the number of loop iterations. It is not used for any other purpose. It is also possible to use the control variable within the body of the loop. For example, look at the following code:

```
for (number = 1; number <= 10; number++)
    System.out.print(number + " ");
```

The control variable in this loop is `number`. In addition to controlling the number of iterations, it is also used in the body of the loop. This loop will produce the following output:

```
1 2 3 4 5 6 7 8 9 10
```

As you can see, the loop displays the contents of the `number` variable during each iteration. The program in Code Listing 4-7 shows another example of a `for` loop that uses its control variable within the body of the loop. This program displays a table showing the numbers 1 through 10 and their squares.

Code Listing 4-7   (`Squares.java`)

```
 1   /**
 2       This program demonstrates the for loop.
 3   */
 4
 5   public class Squares
 6   {
 7       public static void main(String[] args)
 8       {
 9           int number; // Loop control variable
10
11           System.out.println("Number    Number Squared");
12           System.out.println("-----------------------");
13
14           for (number = 1; number <= 10; number++)
15           {
16               System.out.println(number + "\t\t" +
17                                   number * number);
18           }
19       }
20   }
```

Program Output

```
Number    Number Squared
-----------------------
1               1
2               4
3               9
4               16
5               25
6               36
7               49
8               64
9               81
10              100
```

Figure 4-9 illustrates the sequence of events performed by this `for` loop.

Figure 4-9 Sequence of events with the `for` loop in Code Listing 4-7

Figure 4-10 shows the logic of the loop.

Figure 4-10 Logic of the `for` loop in Code Listing 4-7

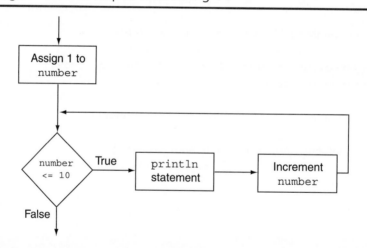

The `for` Loop Is a Pretest Loop

Because the `for` loop tests its `boolean` expression before it performs an iteration, it is a pretest loop. It is possible to write a `for` loop in such a way that it will never iterate. Here is an example:

```
for (count = 11; count <= 10; count++)
    System.out.println("Hello");
```

Because the variable `count` is initialized to a value that makes the `boolean` expression `false` from the beginning, this loop terminates as soon as it begins.

Avoid Modifying the Control Variable in the Body of the `for` Loop

Be careful not to place a statement that modifies the control variable in the body of the `for` loop. All modifications of the control variable should take place in the update expression, which is automatically executed at the end of each iteration. If a statement in the body of the loop also modifies the control variable, the loop probably will not terminate when you expect it to. The following loop, for example, increments x twice for each iteration:

```
for (x = 1; x <= 10; x++)
{
   System.out.println(x);
   x++;   // Wrong!
}
```

Other Forms of the Update Expression

You are not limited to using increment statements in the update expression. Here is a loop that displays all the even numbers from 2 through 100 by adding 2 to its counter:

```
for (number = 2; number <= 100; number += 2)
   System.out.println(number);
```

And here is a loop that counts backward from 10 to 0:

```
for (number = 10; number >= 0; number--)
   System.out.println(number);
```

Declaring a Variable in the `for` Loop's Initialization Expression

Not only may the control variable be initialized in the initialization expression, but also it may be declared there. The following code shows an example. The following is a modified version of the loop in Code Listing 4-7:

```
for (int number = 1; number <= 10; number++)
{
   System.out.println(number + "\t\t" +
                      number * number);
}
```

In this loop, the number variable is both declared and initialized in the initialization expression. If the control variable is used only in the loop, it makes sense to declare it in the loop header. This makes the variable's purpose clearer.

When a variable is declared in the initialization expression of a `for` loop, the scope of the variable is limited to the loop. This means you cannot access the variable in statements outside the loop. For example, the following program segment will not compile because the last println statement cannot access the variable count:

```
    for (int count = 1; count <= 10; count++)
        System.out.println(count);
    System.out.println("count is now " + count);    // ERROR!
```

Creating a User Controlled for Loop

Sometimes you want the user to determine the maximum value of the control variable in a for loop, and therefore determine the number of times the loop iterates. For example, look at the program in Code Listing 4-8. It is a modification of Code Listing 4-7. Instead of displaying the numbers 1 through 10 and their squares, this program allows the user to enter the maximum value to display.

Code Listing 4-8   (UserSquares.java)

```
 1  import java.util.Scanner;      // Needed for the Scanner class
 2
 3  /**
 4     This program demonstrates a user controlled for loop.
 5  */
 6
 7  public class UserSquares
 8  {
 9     public static void main(String[] args)
10     {
11        int number;     // Loop control variable
12        int maxValue;   // Maximum value to display
13
14        System.out.println("I will display a table of " +
15                           "numbers and their squares.");
16
17        // Create a Scanner object for keyboard input.
18        Scanner keyboard = new Scanner(System.in);
19
20        // Get the maximum value to display.
21        System.out.print("How high should I go? ");
22        maxValue = keyboard.nextInt();
23
24        // Display the table.
25        System.out.println("Number    Number Squared");
26        System.out.println("-----------------------");
27        for (number = 1; number <= maxValue; number++)
28        {
29            System.out.println(number + "\t\t" +
30                               number * number);
31        }
32     }
33  }
```

Program Output with Example Input Shown in Bold

```
I will display a table of numbers and their squares.
How high should I go? 7 [Enter]
Number    Number Squared
----------------------
1                1
2                4
3                9
4                16
5                25
6                36
7                49
```

In lines 21 and 22, which are before the loop, this program asks the user to enter the highest value to display. This value is stored in the maxValue variable as follows:

```
System.out.print("How high should I go? ");
maxValue = keyboard.nextInt();
```

In line 27, the for loop's test expression uses the value in the maxValue variable as the upper limit for the control variable as follows:

```
for (number = 1; number <= maxValue; number++)
```

In this loop, the number variable takes on the values 1 through maxValue, and then the loop terminates.

Using Multiple Statements in the Initialization and Update Expressions

It is possible to execute more than one statement in the initialization expression and the update expression. When using multiple statements in either of these expressions, simply separate the statements with commas. For example, look at the loop in the following code, which has two statements in the initialization expression:

```
int x, y;
for (x = 1, y = 1; x <= 5; x++)
{
    System.out.println(x + " plus " + y +
                       " equals " + (x + y));
}
```

This loop's initialization expression is as follows:

```
x = 1, y = 1
```

This initializes two variables, x and y. The output produced by this loop is as follows:

```
1 plus 1 equals 2
2 plus 1 equals 3
3 plus 1 equals 4
```

```
4 plus 1 equals 5
5 plus 1 equals 6
```

We can further modify the loop to execute two statements in the update expression. Here is an example:

```
int x, y;
for (x = 1, y = 1; x <= 5; x++, y++)
{
    System.out.println(x + " plus " + y +
                          " equals " + (x + y));
}
```

The loop's update expression is as follows:

```
x++, y++
```

This update expression increments both the x and y variables. The output produced by this loop is as follows:

```
1 plus 1 equals 2
2 plus 2 equals 4
3 plus 3 equals 6
4 plus 4 equals 8
5 plus 5 equals 10
```

Connecting multiple statements with commas works well in the initialization and update expressions, but don't try to connect multiple boolean expressions this way in the test expression. If you wish to combine multiple boolean expressions in the test expression, you must use the && or || operators.

In the Spotlight:

Designing a Count-Controlled for Loop

Your friend Amanda just inherited a European sports car from her uncle. Amanda lives in the United States, and she is afraid she will get a speeding ticket because the car's speedometer indicates kilometers per hour (KPH). She has asked you to write a program that displays a table of speeds in kilometers per hour with their values converted to miles per hour (MPH). The formula for converting KPH to MPH is

$$MPH = KPH * 0.6214$$

In the formula, *MPH* is the speed in miles per hour and *KPH* is the speed in kilometers per hour.

The table that your program displays should show speeds from 60 kilometers per hour through 130 kilometers per hour, in increments of 10, along with their values converted to miles per hour. The table should look something like this:

KPH	MPH
60	37.3
70	43.5
80	49.7
etc.	
130	80.8

After thinking about this table of values, you decide that you will write a `for` loop that uses a counter variable to hold the KPH speeds. The counter's starting value will be 60, its ending value will be 130, and you will add 10 to the counter variable after each iteration. Inside the loop you will use the counter variable to calculate a speed in MPH. Code Listing 4-9 shows the code.

Code Listing 4-9   (SpeedConverter.java)

```java
 1  /**
 2     This program displays a table of speeds in
 3     kph converted to mph.
 4  */
 5
 6  public class SpeedConverter
 7  {
 8     public static void main(String[] args)
 9     {
10        // Constants
11        final int STARTING_KPH = 60;      // Starting speed
12        final int MAX_KPH = 130;          // Maximum speed
13        final int INCREMENT = 10;         // Speed increment
14
15        // Variables
16        int kph;         // To hold the speed in kph
17        double mph;      // To hold the speed in mph
18
19        // Display the table headings.
20        System.out.println("KPH\t\tMPH");
21        System.out.println("----------------");
22
23        // Display the speeds.
24        for (kph = STARTING_KPH; kph <= MAX_KPH; kph += INCREMENT)
25        {
26           // Calculate the mph.
27           mph = kph * 0.6214;
28
29           // Display the speeds in kph and mph.
30           System.out.printf("%d\t\t%.1f\n", kph, mph);
31        }
32     }
33  }
```

Program Output

```
KPH      MPH
-----------
60       37.3
70       43.5
80       49.7
90       55.9
100      62.1
110      68.4
120      74.6
130      80.8
```

 Checkpoint

4.7   Name the three expressions that appear inside the parentheses in the `for` loop's header.

4.8.   You want to write a `for` loop that displays "I love to program" 50 times. Assume that you will use a control variable named `count`.
   a)   What initialization expression will you use?
   b)   What test expression will you use?
   c)   What update expression will you use?
   d)   Write the loop.

4.9   What will the following program segments display?
   a)   ```
        for (int count = 0; count < 6; count++)
            System.out.println(count + count);
        ```
   b)   ```
        for (int value = -5; value < 5; value++)
            System.out.println(value);
        ```
   c)   ```
        int x;
        for (x = 5; x <= 14; x += 3)
            System.out.println(x);
        System.out.println(x);
        ```

4.10   Write a `for` loop that displays your name 10 times.

4.11   Write a `for` loop that displays all of the odd numbers, 1 through 49.

4.12   Write a `for` loop that displays every fifth number, zero through 100.

## 4.6  Running Totals and Sentinel Values

**CONCEPT:** A running total is a sum of numbers that accumulates with each iteration of a loop. The variable used to keep the running total is called an accumulator. A sentinel is a value that signals when the end of a list of values has been reached.

Many programming tasks require you to calculate the total of a series of numbers. For example, suppose you are writing a program that calculates a business's total sales for a week. The program would read the sales for each day as input and calculate the total of those numbers.

Programs that calculate the total of a series of numbers typically use two elements:

- A loop that reads each number in the series.
- A variable that accumulates the total of the numbers as they are read.
        ```

The variable used to accumulate the total of the numbers is called an *accumulator*. It is often said that the loop keeps a *running total* because it accumulates the total as it reads each number in the series. Figure 4-11 shows the general logic of a loop that calculates a running total.

Figure 4-11 Logic for calculating a running total

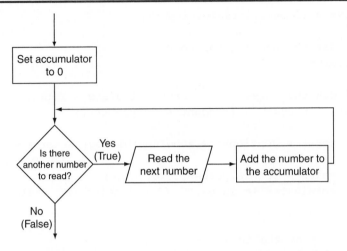

When the loop finishes, the accumulator will contain the total of the numbers that were read by the loop. Notice that the first step in the flowchart is to set the accumulator variable to 0. This is a critical step. Each time the loop reads a number, it adds it to the accumulator. If the accumulator starts with any value other than 0, it will not contain the correct total when the loop finishes.

Let's look at a program that calculates a running total. Code Listing 4-10 calculates a company's total sales over a period of time by taking daily sales figures as input and calculating a running total of them as they are gathered. Figure 4-12 shows an example of interaction with the program.

Code Listing 4-10 (`TotalSales.java`)

```java
 1   import java.text.DecimalFormat;
 2   import javax.swing.JOptionPane;
 3
 4   /**
 5      This program calculates a running total.
 6   */
 7
 8   public class TotalSales
 9   {
10      public static void main(String[] args)
11      {
12         int days;              // The number of days
13         double sales;          // A day's sales figure
14         double totalSales;     // Accumulator
15         String input;          // To hold the user's input
16
```

```
17              // Create a DecimalFormat object to format output.
18              DecimalFormat dollar = new DecimalFormat("#,##0.00");
19
20              // Get the number of days.
21              input = JOptionPane.showInputDialog("For how many days " +
22                                          "do you have sales figures?");
23              days = Integer.parseInt(input);
24
25              // Set the accumulator to 0.
26              totalSales = 0.0;
27
28              // Get the sales figures and calculate a running total.
29              for (int count = 1; count <= days; count++)
30              {
31                  input = JOptionPane.showInputDialog("Enter the sales " +
32                                          "for day " + count + ":");
33                  sales = Double.parseDouble(input);
34                  totalSales += sales;    // Add sales to totalSales.
35              }
36
37              // Display the total sales.
38              JOptionPane.showMessageDialog(null, "The total sales are $" +
39                                          dollar.format(totalSales));
40
41              System.exit(0);
42      }
43  }
```

Figure 4-12 Interaction with the `TotalSales` program

Let's take a closer look at this program. In lines 20 through 23 the user is asked to enter the number of days for which he or she has sales figures. The number is read from an input dialog box and assigned to the days variable. Then, in line 26 the totalSales variable is assigned 0.0. In general programming terms, the `totalSales` variable is referred to as an *accumulator*. An *accumulator* is a variable that is initialized with a starting value, which is usually zero, and then accumulates a sum of numbers by having the numbers added to it. As you will see, it is critical that the accumulator is set to zero before values are added to it.

Next, the `for` loop in lines 29 through 35 executes. During each iteration of the loop, the user enters the amount of sales for a specific day, which are assigned to the `sales` variable. This is done in lines 31 through 33. Then, in line 34 the contents of `sales` is added to the existing value in the `totalSales` variable. (Note that line 34 does not assign `sales` to `totalSales`, but adds `sales` to `totalSales`. Put another way, this line increases `totalSales` by the amount in `sales`.)

Because `totalSales` was initially assigned 0.0, after the first iteration of the loop, `totalSales` will be set to the same value as `sales`. After each subsequent iteration, `totalSales` will be increased by the amount in `sales`. After the loop has finished, `totalSales` will contain the total of all the daily sales figures entered. Now it should be clear why we assigned 0.0 to `totalSales` before the loop executed. If `totalSales` started at any other value, the total would be incorrect.

Using a Sentinel Value

The program in Code Listing 4-10 requires the user to know in advance the number of days for which he or she has sales figures. Sometimes the user has a very long list of input values, and doesn't know the exact number of items. In other cases, the user might be entering values from several lists and it is impractical to require that every item in every list is counted.

A technique that can be used in these situations is to ask the user to enter a sentinel value at the end of the list. A *sentinel value* is a special value that cannot be mistaken as a member of the list, and signals that there are no more values to be entered. When the user enters the sentinel value, the loop terminates.

The program in Code Listing 4-11 shows an example. It calculates the total points earned by a soccer team over a series of games. It allows the user to enter the series of game points, and then –1 to signal the end of the list.

Code Listing 4-11 (`SoccerPoints.java`)

```java
1   import java.util.Scanner;      // Needed for the Scanner class
2
3   /**
4      This program calculates the total number of points a
5      soccer team has earned over a series of games. The user
6      enters a series of point values, then -1 when finished.
7   */
8
9   public class SoccerPoints
10  {
11     public static void main(String[] args)
12     {
13        int points;                // Game points
14        int totalPoints = 0;       // Accumulator initialized to 0
```

```
15
16          // Create a Scanner object for keyboard input.
17          Scanner keyboard = new Scanner(System.in);
18
19          // Display general instructions.
20          System.out.println("Enter the number of points your team");
21          System.out.println("has earned for each game this season.");
22          System.out.println("Enter -1 when finished.");
23          System.out.println();
24
25          // Get the first number of points.
26          System.out.print("Enter game points or -1 to end: ");
27          points = keyboard.nextInt();
28
29          // Accumulate the points until -1 is entered.
30          while (points != -1)
31          {
32             // Add points to totalPoints.
33             totalPoints += points;
34
35             // Get the next number of points.
36             System.out.print("Enter game points or -1 to end: ");
37             points = keyboard.nextInt();
38          }
39
40          // Display the total number of points.
41          System.out.println("The total points are " +
42                             totalPoints);
43       }
44    }
```

Program Output with Example Input Shown in Bold

```
Enter the number of points your team
has earned for each game this season.
Enter -1 when finished.

Enter game points or -1 to end: 7 [Enter]
Enter game points or -1 to end: 9 [Enter]
Enter game points or -1 to end: 4 [Enter]
Enter game points or -1 to end: 6 [Enter]
Enter game points or -1 to end: 8 [Enter]
Enter game points or -1 to end: -1 [Enter]
The total points are 34
```

The value –1 was chosen for the sentinel because it is not possible for a team to score negative points. Notice that this program performs a priming read to get the first value. This makes it possible for the loop to terminate immediately if the user enters –1 as the first value. Also note that the sentinel value is not included in the running total.

Checkpoint

4.13 Write a `for` loop that repeats seven times, asking the user to enter a number. The loop should also calculate the sum of the numbers entered.

4.14 In the following program segment, which variable is the loop control variable (also known as the counter variable) and which is the accumulator?

```java
int a, x = 0, y = 0;
while (x < 10)
{
    a = x * 2;
    y += a;
    x++;
}
System.out.println("The sum is " + y);
```

4.15 Why should you be careful when choosing a sentinel value?

4.7 Nested Loops

CONCEPT: A loop that is inside another loop is called a nested loop.

Nested loops are necessary when a task performs a repetitive operation and that task itself must be repeated. A clock is a good example of something that works like a nested loop. The program in Code Listing 4-12 uses nested loops to simulate a clock.

Code Listing 4-12   (`Clock.java`)

```java
 1  import java.text.DecimalFormat;
 2
 3  /**
 4     This program uses nested loops to simulate a clock.
 5  */
 6
 7  public class Clock
 8  {
 9     public static void main(String[] args)
10     {
11        // Create a DecimalFormat object to format output.
12        DecimalFormat fmt = new DecimalFormat("00");
13
14        // Simulate the clock.
15        for (int hours = 1; hours <= 12; hours++)
16        {
17            for (int minutes = 0; minutes <= 59; minutes++)
18            {
19                for (int seconds = 0; seconds <= 59; seconds++)
```

```
20                         {
21                             System.out.print(fmt.format(hours) + ":");
22                             System.out.print(fmt.format(minutes) + ":");
23                             System.out.println(fmt.format(seconds));
24                         }
25                     }
26                 }
27         }
28 }
```

Program Output

```
01:00:00
01:00:01
01:00:02
01:00:03
```

(The loop continues to count . . .)

```
12:59:57
12:59:58
12:59:59
```

The innermost loop (which begins at line 19) will iterate 60 times for each single iteration of the middle loop. The middle loop (which begins at line 17) will iterate 60 times for each single iteration of the outermost loop. When the outermost loop (which begins at line 15) has iterated 12 times, the middle loop will have iterated 720 times and the innermost loop will have iterated 43,200 times.

The simulated clock example brings up a few points about nested loops:

- An inner loop goes through all of its iterations for each iteration of an outer loop.
- Inner loops complete their iterations before outer loops do.
- To get the total number of iterations of a nested loop, multiply the number of iterations of all the loops.

> For an additional example, see the `TestAverage2.java` file in this chapter's source code folder on the Student CD. It asks the user for the number of students and the number of test scores per student. A nested inner loop asks for all the test scores for one student, iterating once for each test score. The outer loop iterates once for each student.

4.8 The break and continue Statements (Optional)

CONCEPT: The break statement causes a loop to terminate early. The continue statement causes a loop to stop its current iteration and begin the next one.

The break statement, which was used with the switch statement in Chapter 3, can also be placed inside a loop. When it is encountered, the loop stops and the program jumps to the statement immediately following the loop. Although it is perfectly acceptable to use the `break` statement in a `switch` statement, it is considered taboo to use it in a loop. This is because it bypasses the normal condition that is required to terminate the loop, and it makes code difficult to understand and debug. For this reason, you should avoid using the `break` statement in a loop when possible.

The `continue` statement causes the current iteration of a loop to end immediately. When `continue` is encountered, all the statements in the body of the loop that appear after it are ignored, and the loop prepares for the next iteration. In a `while` loop, this means the program jumps to the `boolean` expression at the top of the loop. As usual, if the expression is still `true`, the next iteration begins. In a `do-while` loop, the program jumps to the `boolean` expression at the bottom of the loop, which determines whether the next iteration will begin. In a `for` loop, `continue` causes the update expression to be executed, and then the test expression is evaluated.

The `continue` statement should also be avoided. Like the `break` statement, it bypasses the loop's logic and makes the code difficult to understand and debug.

4.9 Deciding Which Loop to Use

CONCEPT: Although most repetitive algorithms can be written with any of the three types of loops, each works best in different situations.

Each of Java's three loops is ideal to use in different situations. The following is a short summary of when each loop should be used:

- **The `while` loop.** The `while` loop is a pretest loop. It is ideal in situations where you do not want the loop to iterate if the condition is `false` from the beginning. It is also ideal if you want to use a sentinel value to terminate the loop.
- **The `do-while` loop.** The `do-while` loop is a posttest loop. It is ideal in situations where you always want the loop to iterate at least once.
- **The `for` loop.** The `for` loop is a pretest loop that has built-in expressions for initializing, testing, and updating. These expressions make it very convenient to use a loop control variable as a counter. The `for` loop is ideal in situations where the exact number of iterations is known.

4.10 Introduction to File Input and Output

CONCEPT: The Java API provides several classes that you can use for writing data to a file and reading data from a file. To write data to a file, you can use the **PrintWriter** class, and optionally, the **FileWriter** class. To read data from a file, you can use the **Scanner** class and the **File** class.

The programs you have written so far require you to re-enter data each time the program runs. This is because the data stored in variables and objects in RAM disappears once the program stops running. To retain data between the times it runs, a program must have a way of saving the data.

Data may be saved in a *file*, which is usually stored on a computer's disk. Once the data is saved in a file, it will remain there after the program stops running. The data can then be retrieved and used at a later time. In general, there are three steps that are taken when a file is used by a program:

1. The file must be *opened*. When the file is opened, a connection is created between the file and the program.
2. Data is then written to the file or read from the file.
3. When the program is finished using the file, the file must be *closed*.

In this section we will discuss how to write Java programs that write data to files and read data from files. The terms input file and output file are commonly used. An *input file* is a file that a program reads data from. It is called an input file because the data stored in it serves as input to the program. An *output file* is a file that a program writes data to. It is called an output file because the program stores output in the file.

In general, there are two types of files: text and binary. A *text file* contains data that has been encoded as text, using a scheme such as Unicode. Even if the file contains numbers, those numbers are stored in the file as a series of characters. As a result, the file may be opened and viewed in a text editor such as Notepad. A *binary file* contains data that has not been converted to text. As a consequence, you cannot view the contents of a binary file with a text editor. In this chapter, we will discuss how to work with text files. Binary files are discussed in Chapter 12.

The Java API provides a number of classes that you will use to work with files. To use these classes, you will place the following import statement near the top of your program:

```
import java.io.*;
```

Using the PrintWriter Class to Write Data to a File

To write data to a file you will create an instance of the PrintWriter class. The PrintWriter class allows you to open a file for writing. It also allows you to write data to the file using the same print and println methods that you have been using to display data on the screen. You pass the name of the file that you wish to open, as a string, to the PrintWriter class's constructor. For example, the following statement creates a PrintWriter object and passes the file name *StudentData.txt* to the constructor.

```
PrintWriter outputFile = new PrintWriter("StudentData.txt");
```

This statement will create an empty file named *StudentData.txt* and establish a connection between it and the PrintWriter object that is referenced by outputFile. The file will be created in the current directory or folder.

You may also pass a reference to a String object as an argument to the PrintWriter constructor. For example, in the following code the user specifies the name of the file.

```
String filename;
filename = JOptionPane.showInputDialog("Enter the filename.");
PrintWriter outputFile = new PrintWriter(filename);
```

> **WARNING!** If the file that you are opening with the `PrintWriter` object already exists, it will be erased and an empty file by the same name will be created.

Once you have created an instance of the `PrintWriter` class and opened a file, you can write data to the file using the `print` and `println` methods. You already know how to use `print` and `println` with `System.out` to display data on the screen. They are used the same way with a `PrintWriter` object to write data to a file. For example, assuming that `outputFile` references a `PrintWriter` object, the following statement writes the string `"Jim"` to the file:

```
outputFile.println("Jim");
```

When the program is finished writing data to the file, it must close the file. To close the file use the `PrintWriter` class's `close` method. Here is an example of the method's use:

```
outputFile.close();
```

Your application should always close files when finished with them. This is because the system creates one or more buffers when a file is opened. A *buffer* is a small "holding section" of memory. When a program writes data to a file, that data is first written to the buffer. When the buffer is filled, all the information stored there is written to the file. This technique increases the system's performance because writing data to memory is faster than writing it to a disk. The `close` method writes any unsaved data remaining in the file buffer.

Once a file is closed, the connection between it and the `PrintWriter` object is removed. In order to perform further operations on the file, it must be opened again.

More About the `PrintWriter` Class's `println` Method

The `PrintWriter` class's `println` method writes a line of data to a file. For example, assume an application creates a file and writes three students' first names and their test scores to the file with the following code:

```
PrintWriter outputFile = new PrintWriter("StudentData.txt");
outputFile.println("Jim");
outputFile.println(95);
outputFile.println("Karen");
outputFile.println(98);
outputFile.println("Bob");
outputFile.println(82);
outputFile.close();
```

The `println` method writes data to the file and then writes a newline character immediately after the data. You can visualize the data written to the file in the following manner:

Jim*<newline>*95*<newline>*Karen*<newline>*98*<newline>*Bob*<newline>*82*<newline>*

The newline characters are represented here as *<newline>*. You do not actually see the newline characters, but when the file is opened in a text editor such as Notepad, its contents will appear as shown in Figure 4-13. As you can see from the figure, each newline character causes the data that follows it to be displayed on a new line.

Figure 4-13   File contents displayed in Notepad

```
StudentData.txt - Notepad
File  Edit  Format  View  Help
Jim
95
Karen
98
Bob
82
```

In addition to separating the contents of a file into lines, the newline character also serves as a delimiter. A *delimiter* is an item that separates other items. When you write data to a file using the println method, newline characters will separate the individual items of data. Later you will see that the individual items of data in a file must be separated in order for them to be read from the file.

The PrintWriter Class's print Method

The print method is used to write an item of data to a file without writing the newline character. For example, look at the following code:

```
String name = "Jeffrey Smith";
String phone = "554-7864";
int idNumber = 47895;
PrintWriter outputFile = new PrintWriter("PersonalData.txt");
outputFile.print(name + " ");
outputFile.print(phone + " ");
outputFile.println(idNumber);
outputFile.close();
```

This code uses the print method to write the contents of the name object to the file, followed by a space (" "). Then it uses the print method to write the contents of the phone object to the file, followed by a space. Then it uses the println method to write the contents of the idNumber variable, followed by a newline character. Figure 4-14 shows the contents of the file displayed in Notepad.

Figure 4-14   Contents of file displayed in Notepad

```
PersonalData.txt - Notepad
File  Edit  Format  View  Help
Jeffrey Smith 555-7864 47895
```

Adding a `throws` Clause to the Method Header

When an unexpected event occurs in a Java program, it is said that the program throws an exception. For now, you can think of an *exception* as a signal indicating that the program cannot continue until the unexpected event has been dealt with. For example, suppose you create a `PrintWriter` object and pass the name of a file to its constructor. The `PrintWriter` object attempts to create the file, but unexpectedly, the disk is full and the file cannot be created. Obviously the program cannot continue until this situation has been dealt with, so an exception is thrown, which causes the program to suspend normal execution.

When an exception is thrown, the method that is executing must either deal with the exception or throw it again. If the `main` method throws an exception, the program halts and an error message is displayed. Because `PrintWriter` objects are capable of throwing exceptions, we must either write code that deals with the possible exceptions, or allow our methods to rethrow the exceptions when they occur. In Chapter 12 you will learn all about exceptions and how to respond to them, but for now, we will simply allow our methods to rethrow any exceptions that might occur.

To allow a method to rethrow an exception that has not been dealt with, you simply write a `throws` clause in the method header. The `throws` clause must indicate the type of exception that might be thrown. The following is an example:

```
public static void main(String[] args) throws IOException
```

This header indicates that the `main` method is capable of throwing an exception of the `IOException` type. This is the type of exception that `PrintWriter` objects are capable of throwing. So, any method that uses `PrintWriter` objects and does not respond to their exceptions must have this `throws` clause listed in its header.

In addition, any method that calls a method that uses a `PrintWriter` object should have a `throws IOException` clause in its header. For example, suppose the `main` method does not perform any file operations, but calls a method named `buildFile` that opens a file and writes data to it. Both the `buildFile` and `main` methods should have a `throws IOException` clause in their headers. Otherwise a compiler error will occur.

An Example Program

Let's look at an example program that writes data to a file. The program in Code Listing 4-13 writes the names of your friends to a file.

Code Listing 4-13   (`FileWriteDemo.java`)

```java
1   import java.util.Scanner;        // Needed for Scanner class
2   import java.io.*;                // Needed for File I/O classes
3
4   /**
5      This program writes data to a file.
6   */
7
8   public class FileWriteDemo
9   {
```

```
10      public static void main(String[] args) throws IOException
11      {
12          String filename;        // File name
13          String friendName;      // Friend's name
14          int numFriends;         // Number of friends
15
16          // Create a Scanner object for keyboard input.
17          Scanner keyboard = new Scanner(System.in);
18
19          // Get the number of friends.
20          System.out.print("How many friends do you have? ");
21          numFriends = keyboard.nextInt();
22
23          // Consume the remaining newline character.
24          keyboard.nextLine();
25
26          // Get the filename.
27          System.out.print("Enter the filename: ");
28          filename = keyboard.nextLine();
29
30          // Open the file.
31          PrintWriter outputFile = new PrintWriter(filename);
32
33          // Get data and write it to the file.
34          for (int i = 1; i <= numFriends; i++)
35          {
36              // Get the name of a friend.
37              System.out.print("Enter the name of friend " +
38                               "number " + i + ": ");
39              friendName = keyboard.nextLine();
40
41              // Write the name to the file.
42              outputFile.println(friendName);
43          }
44
45          // Close the file.
46          outputFile.close();
47          System.out.println("Data written to the file.");
48      }
49  }
```

Program Output with Example Input Shown in Bold

How many friends do you have? **5 [Enter]**
Enter the filename: **MyFriends.txt [Enter]**
Enter the name of friend number 1: **Joe [Enter]**
Enter the name of friend number 2: **Rose [Enter]**
Enter the name of friend number 3: **Greg [Enter]**

```
Enter the name of friend number 4: Kirk [Enter]
Enter the name of friend number 5: Renee [Enter]
Data written to the file.
```

The import statement in line 2 is necessary because this program uses the PrintWriter class. In addition, the main method header, in line 10, has a throws IOException clause because objects of the PrintWriter class can potentially throw an IOException.

This program asks the user to enter the number of friends he or she has (in lines 20 through 21), then a name for the file that will be created (in lines 27 and 28). The filename variable references the name of the file, and is used in the following statement, in line 31:

```
PrintWriter outputFile = new PrintWriter(filename);
```

This statement opens the file and creates a PrintWriter object that can be used to write data to the file. The for loop in lines 34 through 43 performs an iteration for each friend that the user has, each time asking for the name of a friend. The user's input is referenced by the friendName variable. Once the name is entered, it is written to the file with the following statement, which appears in line 42:

```
outputFile.println(friendName);
```

After the loop finishes, the file is closed in line 46. After the program is executed with the input shown in the example run, the file *MyFriends.txt* will be created. If we open the file in Notepad, we will see its contents as shown in Figure 4-15.

Figure 4-15   Contents of the file displayed in Notepad

Review

Before moving on, let's review the basic steps necessary when writing a program that writes data to a file:

1. You need the import java.io.*; statement in the top section of your program.
2. Because we have not yet learned how to respond to exceptions, any method that uses a PrintWriter object must have a throws IOException clause in its header.
3. You create a PrintWriter object and pass the name of the file as a string to the constructor.

4. You use the `PrintWriter` class's `print` and `println` methods to write data to the file.
5. When finished writing to the file, you use the `PrintWriter` class's `close` method to close the file.

Appending Data to a File

When you pass the name of a file to the `PrintWriter` constructor, and the file already exists, it will be erased and a new empty file with the same name will be created. Sometimes, however, you want to preserve an existing file and append new data to its current contents. Appending to a file means writing new data to the end of the data that already exists in the file.

To append data to an existing file, you first create an instance of the `FileWriter` class. You pass two arguments to the `FileWriter` constructor: a string containing the name of the file, and the `boolean` value `true`. Here is an example:

```
FileWriter fwriter = new FileWriter("MyFriends.txt", true);
```

This statement creates a `FileWriter` object and opens the file *MyFriends.txt* for writing. Any data written to the file will be appended to the file's existing contents. (If the file does not exist, it will be created.)

You still need to create a `PrintWriter` object so you can use the `print` and `println` methods to write data to the file. When you create the `PrintWriter` object, you pass a reference to the `FileWriter` object as an argument to the `PrintWriter` constructor. For example, look at the following code:

```
FileWriter fwriter = new FileWriter("MyFriends.txt", true);
PrintWriter outputFile = new PrintWriter(fwriter);
```

This creates a `PrintWriter` object that can be used to write data to the file *MyFriends.txt*. Any data that is written to the file will be appended to the file's existing contents. For example, assume the file *MyFriends.txt* exists and contains the following data:

```
Joe
Rose
Greg
Kirk
Renee
```

The following code opens the file and appends additional data to its existing contents:

```
FileWriter fwriter = new FileWriter("MyFriends.txt", true);
PrintWriter outputFile = new PrintWriter(fwriter);
outputFile.println("Bill");
outputFile.println("Steven");
outputFile.println("Sharon");
outputFile.close();
```

After this code executes, the *MyFriends.txt* file will contain the following data:

```
Joe
Rose
Greg
Kirk
Renee
Bill
Steven
Sharon
```

 NOTE: The `FileWriter` class also throws an `IOException` if the file cannot be opened for any reason.

Specifying the File Location

When you open a file you may specify its path along with its filename. On a Windows computer, paths contain backslash characters. Remember that when a single backslash character appears in a string literal, it marks the beginning of an escape sequence such as `"\n"`. Two backslash characters in a string literal represent a single backslash. So, when you provide a path in a string literal, and the path contains backslash characters, you must use two backslash characters in the place of each single backslash character.

For example, the path `"E:\\Names.txt"` specifies that *Names.txt* is in the root folder of drive E:, and the path `"C:\\MyData\\Data.txt"` specifies that *Data.txt* is in the *\MyData* folder on drive C:. In the following statement, the file *Pricelist.txt* is created in the root folder of drive A:.

```
PrintWriter outputFile = new PrintWriter("A:\\PriceList.txt");
```

You only need to use double backslashes if the file's path is in a string literal. If your program asks the user to enter a path into a `String` object, which is then passed to the `PrintWriter` or `FileWriter` constructor, the user does not have to enter double backslashes.

 TIP: Java allows you to substitute forward slashes for backslashes in a Windows path. For example, the path `"C:\\MyData\\Data.txt"` could be written as `"C:/MyData/Data.txt"`. This eliminates the need to use double backslashes.

On a UNIX or Linux computer, you can provide a path without any modifications. Here is an example:

```
PrintWriter outputFile = new PrintWriter("/home/rharrison/names.txt");
```

Reading Data from a File

In Chapter 2 you learned how to use the `Scanner` class to read input from the keyboard. To read keyboard input, recall that we create a `Scanner` object, passing `System.in` to the `Scanner` class constructor. Here is an example:

```
Scanner keyboard = new Scanner(System.in);
```

Recall that the `System.in` object represents the keyboard. Passing `System.in` as an argument to the `Scanner` constructor specifies that the keyboard is the `Scanner` object's source of input.

You can also use the `Scanner` class to read input from a file. Instead of passing `System.in` to the `Scanner` class constructor, you pass a reference to a `File` object. Here is an example:

```
File myFile = new File("Customers.txt");
Scanner inputFile = new Scanner(myFile);
```

The first statement creates an instance of the `File` class. The `File` class is in the Java API, and is used to represent a file. Notice that we have passed the string `"Customers.txt"` to the constructor. This creates a `File` object that represents the file *Customers.txt*.

In the second statement we pass a reference to this `File` object as an argument to the `Scanner` class constructor. This creates a `Scanner` object that uses the file *Customers.txt* as its source of input. You can then use the same `Scanner` class methods that you learned about in Chapter 2 to read items from the file. (See Table 2-17 for a list of commonly used methods.)

When you are finished reading from the file, you use the `Scanner` class's `close` method to close the file. For example, assuming the variable `inputFile` references a `Scanner` object, the following statement closes the file that is the object's source of input:

```
inputFile.close();
```

Reading Lines From a File with the `nextLine` Method

The `Scanner` class's `nextLine` method reads a line of input, and returns the line as a `String`. The program in Code Listing 4-14 demonstrates how the `nextLine` method can be used to read a line from a file. This program asks the user to enter a filename. It then displays the first line in the file on the screen.

Code Listing 4-14   (ReadFirstLine.java)

```
 1   import java.util.Scanner;  // Needed for Scanner class
 2   import java.io.*;          // Needed for File and IOException
 3
 4   /**
 5      This program reads the first line from a file.
 6   */
 7
 8   public class ReadFirstLine
 9   {
10      public static void main(String[] args) throws IOException
11      {
12         // Create a Scanner object for keyboard input.
13         Scanner keyboard = new Scanner(System.in);
14
```

```
15          // Get the file name.
16          System.out.print("Enter the name of a file: ");
17          String filename = keyboard.nextLine();
18
19          // Open the file.
20          File file = new File(filename);
21          Scanner inputFile = new Scanner(file);
22
23          // Read the first line from the file.
24          String line = inputFile.nextLine();
25
26          // Display the line.
27          System.out.println("The first line in the file is:");
28          System.out.println(line);
29
30          // Close the file.
31          inputFile.close();
32      }
33 }
```

Program Output with Example Input Shown in Bold

Enter the name of a file: **MyFriends.txt [Enter]**
The first line in the file is:
Joe

This program gets the name of a file from the user in line 17. A `File` object is created in line 20 to represent the file, and a `Scanner` object is created in line 21 to read data from the file. Line 24 reads a line from the file. After this statement executes, the `line` variable references a `String` object holding the line that was read from the file. The line is displayed on the screen in line 28, and the file is closed in line 31.

It's worth pointing out that this program creates two separate `Scanner` objects. The `Scanner` object that is created in line 13 reads data from the keyboard, and the `Scanner` object that is created in line 21 reads data from a file.

When a file is opened for reading, a special value known as a *read position* is internally maintained for that file. A file's read position marks the location of the next item that will be read from the file. When a file is opened, its read position is set to the first item in the file. When the item is read, the read position is advanced to the next item in the file. As subsequent items are read, the internal read position advances through the file. For example, consider the file *Quotation.txt*, shown in Figure 4-16. As you can see from the figure, the file has three lines.

You can visualize that the data is stored in the file in the following manner:

```
Imagination is more<newline>important than knowledge<newline>
Albert Einstein<newline>
```

Suppose a program opens the file with the following code:

```
File file = new File("Quotation.txt");
Scanner inputFile = new Scanner(file);
```

Figure 4-16 File with three lines

When this code opens the file, its read position is at the beginning of the first line, as illustrated in Figure 4-17.

Figure 4-17 Initial read position

Read position ⟶ Imagination is more
important than knowledge.
Albert Einstein

Now, suppose the program uses the following statement to read a line from the file

```
String str = inputFile.nextLine();
```

This statement will read a line from the file, beginning at the current read position. After the statement executes, the object referenced by `str` will contain the string "Imagination is more". The file's read position will be advanced to the next line, as illustrated in Figure 4-18.

Figure 4-18 Read position after first line is read

Imagination is more
Read position ⟶ important than knowledge.
Albert Einstein

If the `nextLine` method is called again, the second line will be read from the file and the file's read position will be advanced to the third line. After all the lines have been read, the read position will be at the end of the file.

NOTE: The string that is returned from the `nextLine` method will not contain the newline character.

Adding a `throws` Clause to the Method Header

When you pass a `File` object reference to the `Scanner` class constructor, the constructor will throw an exception of the `IOException` type if the specified file is not found. So, you will need to write a throws `IOException` clause in the header of any method that passes a `File` object reference to the `Scanner` class constructor.

Detecting the End of a File

Quite often a program must read the contents of a file without knowing the number of items that are stored in the file. For example, the *MyFriends.txt* file that was created by the program in Code Listing 4-13 can have any number of names stored in it. This is because the program asks the user for the number of friends that he or she has. If the user enters 5 for the number of friends, the program creates a file with five names in it. If the user enters 100, the program creates a file with 100 names in it.

The `Scanner` class has a method named `hasNext` that can be used to determine whether the file has more data that can be read. You call the `hasNext` method before you call any other methods to read from the file. If there is more data that can be read from the file, the `hasNext` method returns `true`. If the end of the file has been reached and there is no more data to read, the `hasNext` method returns `false`.

Code Listing 4-15 shows an example. The program reads the file containing the names of your friends, which was created by the program in Code Listing 4-13.

Code Listing 4-15   (FileReadDemo.java)

```
 1   import java.util.Scanner;  // Needed for the Scanner class
 2   import java.io.*;          // Needed for the File and IOException
 3
 4   /**
 5      This program reads data from a file.
 6   */
 7
 8   public class FileReadDemo
 9   {
10      public static void main(String[] args) throws IOException
11      {
12         // Create a Scanner object for keyboard input.
13         Scanner keyboard = new Scanner(System.in);
14
15         // Get the filename.
16         System.out.print("Enter the filename: ");
17         String filename = keyboard.nextLine();
```

```
18
19          // Open the file.
20          File file = new File(filename);
21          Scanner inputFile = new Scanner(file);
22
23          // Read lines from the file until no more are left.
24          while (inputFile.hasNext())
25          {
26              // Read the next name.
27              String friendName = inputFile.nextLine();
28
29              // Display the last name read.
30              System.out.println(friendName);
31          }
32
33          // Close the file.
34          inputFile.close();
35      }
36  }
```

Program Output with Example Input Shown in Bold

Enter the filename: **MyFriends.txt [Enter]**
Joe
Rose
Greg
Kirk
Renee

The file is opened and a Scanner object to read it is created in line 21. The loop in lines 24 through 31 reads all of the lines from the file and displays them. In line 24 the loop calls the Scanner object's hasNext method. If the method returns true, then the file has more data to read. In that case, the next line is read from the file in line 27, and is displayed in line 30. The loop repeats until the hasNext method returns false in line 24. Figure 4-19 shows the logic of reading a file until the end is reached.

Reading Primitive Values from a File

Recall from Chapter 2 that the Scanner class provides methods for reading primitive values. These methods are named nextByte, nextDouble, nextFloat, nextInt, nextLong, and nextShort. Table 2-17 gives more information on each of these methods, which can be used to read primitive values from a file.

The program in Code Listing 4-16 demonstrates how the nextDouble method can be used to read floating-point values from a file. The program reads the contents of a file named *Numbers.txt*, which is on the Student CD. The contents of the *Numbers.txt* file are shown in Figure 4-20. As you can see, the file contains a series of floating-point numbers. The program reads all of the numbers from the file and calculates their total.

Figure 4-19   Logic of reading a file until the end is reached

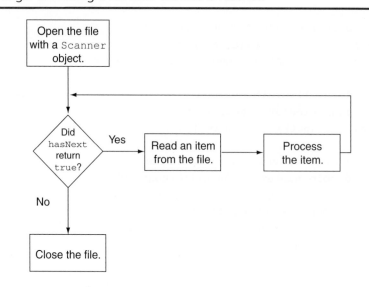

Figure 4-20   Contents of *Numbers.txt*

Code Listing 4-16   (`FileSum.java`)

```
1    import java.util.Scanner;
2    import java.io.*;
3
4    /**
5        This program reads a series of numbers from a file and
6        accumulates their sum.
7    */
8
9    public class FileSum
10   {
11       public static void main(String[] args) throws IOException
12       {
```

```
13              double sum = 0.0;    // Accumulator, initialized to 0
14
15              // Open the file for reading.
16              File file = new File("Numbers.txt");
17              Scanner inputFile = new Scanner(file);
18
19              // Read all of the values from the file
20              // and calculate their total.
21              while (inputFile.hasNext())
22              {
23                  // Read a value from the file.
24                  double number = inputFile.nextDouble();
25
26                  // Add the number to sum.
27                  sum = sum + number;
28              }
29
30              // Close the file.
31              inputFile.close();
32
33              // Display the sum of the numbers.
34              System.out.println("The sum of the numbers in " +
35                                 "Numbers.txt is " + sum);
36          }
37  }
```

Program Output

The sum of the numbers in Numbers.txt is 41.4

Review

Let's quickly review the steps necessary when writing a program that reads data from a file:

1. You will need the import java.util.Scanner; statement in the top section of your program, so you can use the Scanner class. You will also need the import java.io.*; statement in the top section of your program. This is required by the File class.
2. Because we have not yet learned how to respond to exceptions, any method that uses a Scanner object to open a file must have a throws IOException clause in its header.
3. You create a File object and pass the name of the file as a string to the constructor.
4. You create a Scanner object and pass a reference to the File object as an argument to the constructor.
5. You use the Scanner class's nextLine method to read a line from the file. The method returns the line of data as a string. To read primitive values, use methods such as nextInt, nextDouble, and so forth.

6. Call the `Scanner` class's `hasNext` method to determine whether there is more data to read from the file. If the method returns `true`, then there is more data to read. If the method returns `false`, you have reached the end of the file.
7. When finished writing to the file, you use the `Scanner` class's `close` method to close the file.

Checking for a File's Existence

It's usually a good idea to make sure that a file exists before you try to open it for input. If you attempt to open a file for input, and the file does not exist, the program will throw an exception and halt. For example, the program you saw in Code Listing 4-16 will throw an exception at line 17 if the file *Numbers.txt* does not exist. Here is an example of the error message that will be displayed when this happens:

```
Exception in thread "main" java.io.FileNotFoundException: Numbers.txt (The
system cannot find the file specified)
    at java.io.FileInputStream.open(Native Method)
    at java.io.FileInputStream.<init>(FileInputStream.java:106)
    at java.util.Scanner.<init>(Scanner.java:636)
    at FileSum.main(FileSum.java:17)
```

Rather than allowing the exception to be thrown and permitting this cryptic error message to be displayed, your program can check for the file's existence before it attempts to open the file. If the file does not exist, the program can display a more user-friendly error message and gracefully shut down.

After you create a `File` object representing the file that you want to open, you can use the `File` class's `exists` method to determine whether the file exists. The method returns `true` if the file exists, or `false` if the file does not exist. Code Listing 4-17 shows how to use the method. This is a modification of the *FileSum* program in Code Listing 4-16. This version of the program checks for the existence of the file *Numbers.txt* before it attempts to open it.

Code Listing 4-17   (FileSum2.java)

```java
 1   import java.util.Scanner;
 2   import java.io.*;
 3
 4   /**
 5       This version of the program confirms that the
 6       Numbers.txt file exists before opening it.
 7   */
 8
 9   public class FileSum2
10   {
11       public static void main(String[] args) throws IOException
12       {
13           double sum = 0.0;    // Accumulator, initialized to 0
```

```
14
15          // Make sure the file exists.
16          File file = new File("Numbers.txt");
17          if (!file.exists())
18          {
19              System.out.println("The file Numbers.txt is not found.");
20              System.exit(0);
21          }
22
23          // Open the file for reading.
24          Scanner inputFile = new Scanner(file);
25
26          // Read all of the values from the file
27          // and calculate their total.
28          while (inputFile.hasNext())
29          {
30              // Read a value from the file.
31              double number = inputFile.nextDouble();
32
33              // Add the number to sum.
34              sum = sum + number;
35          }
36
37          // Close the file.
38          inputFile.close();
39
40          // Display the sum of the numbers.
41          System.out.println("The sum of the numbers in " +
42                          "Numbers.txt is " + sum);
43      }
44  }
```

Program Output (Assuming Numbers.txt Does Not Exist)

```
The file Numbers.txt is not found.
```

In line 16 the program creates a File object to represent the *Numbers.txt* file. In line 17, the if statement calls the file.exists() method. Notice the use of the ! operator. If the method returns false, indicating that the file does not exist, the code in lines 19 and 20 executes. Line 19 displays an error message, and line 20 calls the System.exit(0) method to shut the program down.

The previous example shows you how to make sure that a file exists before trying to open it for input. But, when you are opening a file for output, sometimes you want to make sure the file does *not* exist. When you use a PrintWriter object to open a file, the file will be erased if it already exists. If you do not want to erase the existing file, you have to check for its existence before creating the PrintWriter object. Code Listing 4-18 shows you how to use the File class's exists method in this type of situation. This is a modification of the program you saw in Code Listing 4-13.

Code Listing 4-18   (`FileWriteDemo2.java`)

```java
 1   import java.util.Scanner;          // Needed for Scanner class
 2   import java.io.*;                   // Needed for File and IOException
 3
 4   /**
 5      This program writes data to a file. It makes sure the
 6      specified file does not exist before opening it.
 7   */
 8
 9   public class FileWriteDemo2
10   {
11      public static void main(String[] args) throws IOException
12      {
13         String filename;          // Filename
14         String friendName;        // Friend's name
15         int numFriends;           // Number of friends
16
17         // Create a Scanner object for keyboard input.
18         Scanner keyboard = new Scanner(System.in);
19
20         // Get the number of friends.
21         System.out.print("How many friends do you have? ");
22         numFriends = keyboard.nextInt();
23
24         // Consume the remaining newline character.
25         keyboard.nextLine();
26
27         // Get the filename.
28         System.out.print("Enter the filename: ");
29         filename = keyboard.nextLine();
30
31         // Make sure the file does not exist.
32         File file = new File(filename);
33         if (file.exists())
34         {
35            System.out.println("The file " + filename +
36                               " already exists.");
37            System.exit(0);
38         }
39
40         // Open the file.
41         PrintWriter outputFile = new PrintWriter(file);
42
43         // Get data and write it to the file.
44         for (int i = 1; i <= numFriends; i++)
45         {
46            // Get the name of a friend.
```

```
47                    System.out.print("Enter the name of friend " +
48                                 "number " + i + ": ");
49              friendName = keyboard.nextLine();
50
51              // Write the name to the file.
52              outputFile.println(friendName);
53          }
54
55          // Close the file.
56          outputFile.close();
57          System.out.println("Data written to the file.");
58      }
59  }
```

Program Output with Example Input Shown in Bold

How many friends do you have? **2 [Enter]**
Enter the filename: **MyFriends.txt [Enter]**
The file MyFriends.txt already exists.

Line 32 creates a `File` object representing the file. The `if` statement in line 33 calls the `file.exists()` method. If the method returns `true`, then the file exists. In this case the code in lines 35 through 37 executes. This code displays an error message and shuts the program down. If the file does not exist, the rest of the program executes.

Notice that in line 41 we pass a reference to the `File` object to the `PrintWriter` constructor. In previous programs that created an instance `PrintWriter`, we passed a filename to the constructor. If you have a reference to a `File` object that represents the file you wish to open, as we do in this program, you have the option of passing it to the `PrintWriter` constructor.

 Checkpoint

4.16   What is the difference between an input file and an output file?

4.17   What `import` statement will you need in a program that performs file operations?

4.18   What class do you use to write data to a file?

4.19   Write code that does the following: Opens a file named *MyName.txt*, writes your first name to the file, and then closes the file.

4.20   What classes do you use to read data from a file?

4.21   Write code that does the following: Opens a file named *MyName.txt*, reads the first line from the file and displays it, and then closes the file.

4.22   You are opening an existing file for output. How do you open the file without erasing it, and at the same time make sure that new data that is written to the file is appended to the end of the file's existing data?

4.23   What clause must you write in the header of a method that performs a file operation?

4.11 The Random Class

Some applications, such as games and simulations, require the use of randomly generated numbers. The Java API has a class, Random, for this purpose. The Random class uses an algorithm to generate a sequence of random numbers. First, you should have the following import statement in your code:

```
import java.util.Random;
```

To use the Random class, you create an object, or an instance, of the class. The following statement shows an example:

```
Random randomNumbers = new Random();
```

This statement creates an instance of the Random class in memory and assigns its address to the randomNumbers variable. You can then use the instance to generate random numbers. Table 4-1 shows some of the Random class's methods.

Table 4-1   Some of the Random class's methods

Method	Description
nextDouble()	Returns the next random number as a double. The number will be within the range of 0.0 and 1.0.
nextFloat()	Returns the next random number as a float. The number will be within the range of 0.0 and 1.0.
nextInt()	Returns the next random number as an int. The number will be within the range of an int, which is –2,147,483,648 to +2,147,483,648.
nextInt(int *n*)	This method accepts an integer argument, *n*. It returns a random number as an int. The number will be within the range of 0 and *n*.
nextLong()	Returns the next random number as a long. The number will be within the range of a long, which is –9,223,372,036,854,775,808 to +9,223,372,036,854,775,808.

The program in Code Listing 4-19 demonstrates using the Random class.

Code Listing 4-19   (MathTutor.java)

```java
1   import java.util.Scanner;  // Needed for the Scanner class
2   import java.util.Random;   // Needed for the Random class
3
4   /**
5      This program demonstrates the Random class.
6   */
7
8   public class MathTutor
```

```
 9   {
10       public static void main(String[] args)
11       {
12           int number1;        // A number
13           int number2;        // Another number
14           int sum;            // The sum of the numbers
15           int userAnswer;     // The user's answer
16
17           // Create a Scanner object for keyboard input.
18           Scanner keyboard = new Scanner(System.in);
19
20           // Create a Random class object.
21           Random randomNumbers = new Random();
22
23           // Get two random numbers.
24           number1 = randomNumbers.nextInt(100);
25           number2 = randomNumbers.nextInt(100);
26
27           // Display an addition problem.
28           System.out.println("What is the answer to the " +
29                               "following problem?");
30           System.out.print(number1 + " + " +
31                               number2 + " = ? ");
32
33           // Calculate the answer.
34           sum = number1 + number2;
35
36           // Get the user's answer.
37           userAnswer = keyboard.nextInt();
38
39           // Display the user's results.
40           if (userAnswer == sum)
41               System.out.println("Correct!");
42           else
43           {
44               System.out.println("Sorry, wrong answer. " +
45                                   "The correct answer is " +
46                                   sum);
47           }
48       }
49   }
```

Program Output with Example Input Shown in Bold

```
What is the answer to the following problem?
52 + 19 = ? 71 [Enter]
Correct!
```

Program Output with Example Input Shown in Bold

```
What is the answer to the following problem?
27 + 73 = ? 101 [Enter]
Sorry, wrong answer. The correct answer is 100
```

4.12 Common Errors to Avoid

The following list describes several errors that are commonly committed when learning this chapter's topics.

- **Using the increment or decrement operator in the wrong mode.** When the increment or decrement operator is placed in front of (to the left of) its operand, it is used in prefix mode. When either of these operators is placed behind (to the right of) its operand, it is used in postfix mode.
- **Forgetting to enclose the `boolean` expression in a `while` loop or a `do-while` loop inside parentheses.**
- **Placing a semicolon at the end of a `while` or `for` loop's header.** When you write a semicolon at the end of a `while` or `for` loop's header, Java assumes that the conditionally executed statement is a `null` or empty statement. This usually results in an infinite loop.
- **Forgetting to write the semicolon at the end of the `do-while` loop.** The do-while loop must be terminated with a semicolon.
- **Forgetting to enclose multiple statements in the body of a loop in braces.** Normally a loop conditionally executes only one statement. To conditionally execute more than one statement, you must place the statements in braces.
- **Using commas instead of semicolons to separate the initialization, test, and update expressions in a `for` loop.**
- **Forgetting to write code in the body of a `while` or `do-while` loop that modifies the loop control variable.** If a `while` or do-while loop's `boolean` expression never becomes `false`, the loop will repeat indefinitely. You must have code in the body of the loop that modifies the loop control variable so that the `boolean` expression will at some point become `false`.
- **Using a sentinel value that can also be a valid data value.** Remember, a sentinel is a special value that cannot be mistaken as a member of a list of data items and signals that there are no more data items from the list to be processed. If you choose as a sentinel a value that might also appear in the list, the loop will prematurely terminate if it encounters the value in the list.
- **Forgetting to initialize an accumulator to zero.** In order for an accumulator to keep a correct running total, it must be initialized to zero before any values are added to it.

Review Questions and Exercises

Multiple Choice and True/False

1. What will the `println` statement in the following program segment display?

   ```
   int x = 5;
   System.out.println(x++);
   ```

   a. 5
   b. 6
   c. 0
   d. None of these

2. What will the `println` statement in the following program segment display?

   ```
   int x = 5;
   System.out.println(++x);
   ```

   a. 5
   b. 6
   c. 0
   d. None of these

3. In the expression `number++`, the ++ operator is in what mode?

   a. prefix
   b. pretest
   c. postfix
   d. posttest

4. What is each repetition of a loop known as?

   a. cycle
   b. revolution
   c. orbit
   d. iteration

5. This is a variable that controls the number of iterations performed by a loop.

   a. loop control variable
   b. accumulator
   c. iteration register variable
   d. repetition meter

6. The `while` loop is this type of loop.

   a. pretest
   b. posttest
   c. prefix
   d. postfix

7. The `do-while` loop is this type of loop.

   a. pretest
   b. posttest
   c. prefix
   d. postfix

8. The `for` loop is this type of loop.
   a. pretest
   b. posttest
   c. prefix
   d. postfix

9. This type of loop has no way of ending and repeats until the program is interrupted.
   a. indeterminate
   b. interminable
   c. infinite
   d. timeless

10. This type of loop always executes at least once.
    a. `while`
    b. `do-while`
    c. `for`
    d. any of these

11. This expression is executed by the `for` loop only once, regardless of the number of iterations.
    a. initialization expression
    b. test expression
    c. update expression
    d. pre-increment expression

12. This is a variable that keeps a running total.
    a. sentinel
    b. sum
    c. total
    d. accumulator

13. This is a special value that signals when there are no more items from a list of items to be processed. This value cannot be mistaken as an item from the list.
    a. sentinel
    b. flag
    c. signal
    d. accumulator

14. To open a file for writing, you use the following class.
    a. `PrintWriter`
    b. `FileOpen`
    c. `OutputFile`
    d. `FileReader`

15. To open a file for reading, you use the following classes.
    a. `File` and `Writer`
    b. `File` and `Output`
    c. `File` and `Input`
    d. `File` and `Scanner`

16. When a program is finished using a file, it should do this.
    a. erase the file
    b. close the file
    c. throw an exception
    d. reset the read position

17. This class allows you to use the `print` and `println` methods to write data to a file.
    a. `File`
    b. `FileReader`
    c. `OutputFile`
    d. `PrintWriter`

18. This class allows you to read a line from a file.
    a. `FileWriter`
    b. `Scanner`
    c. `InputFile`
    d. `FileReader`

19. **True or False:** The `while` loop is a pretest loop.

20. **True or False:** The `do-while` loop is a pretest loop.

21. **True or False:** The `for` loop is a posttest loop.

22. **True or False:** It is not necessary to initialize accumulator variables.

23. **True or False:** One limitation of the `for` loop is that only one variable may be initialized in the initialization expression.

24. **True or False:** A variable may be defined in the initialization expression of the `for` loop.

25. **True or False:** In a nested loop, the inner loop goes through all of its iterations for every iteration of the outer loop.

26. **True or False:** To calculate the total number of iterations of a nested loop, add the number of iterations of all the loops.

Find the Error

Find the errors in the following code:

1.
```
// This code contains ERRORS!
// It adds two numbers entered by the user.
int num1, num2;
String input;
char again;

Scanner keyboard = new Scanner(System.in);
while (again == 'y' || again == 'Y')
   System.out.print("Enter a number: ");
   num1 = keyboard.nextInt();
   System.out.print("Enter another number: ";
```

```
        num2 = keyboard.nextInt();
        System.out.println("Their sum is "+ (num1 + num2));
        System.out.println("Do you want to do this again? ");
        keyboard.nextLine();  // Consume remaining newline
        input = keyboard.nextLine();
        again = input.charAt(0);
```

2.  ```
    // This code contains ERRORS!
    int count = 1, total;
    while (count <= 100)
        total += count;
    System.out.print("The sum of the numbers 1 - 100 is ");
    System.out.println(total);
    ```

3.  ```
    // This code contains ERRORS!
    int choice, num1, num2;
    Scanner keyboard = new Scanner(System.in);
    do
    {
        System.out.print("Enter a number: ");
        num1 = keyboard.nextInt();
        System.out.print("Enter another number: ");
        num2 = keyboard.nextInt();
        System.out.println("Their sum is " + (num1 + num2));
        System.out.println("Do you want to do this again? ");
        System.out.print("1 = yes, 0 = no ");
        choice = keyboard.nextInt();
    } while (choice = 1)
    ```

4.  ```
    // This code contains ERRORS!
    // Print the numbers 1 through 10.
    for (int count = 1, count <= 10, count++;)
    {
            System.out.println(count);
            count++;
    }
    ```

Algorithm Workbench

1. Write a `while` loop that lets the user enter a number. The number should be multiplied by 10, and the result stored in the variable `product`. The loop should iterate as long as `product` contains a value less than 100.

2. Write a `do-while` loop that asks the user to enter two numbers. The numbers should be added and the sum displayed. The loop should ask the user if he or she wishes to perform the operation again. If so, the loop should repeat, otherwise it should terminate.

3. Write a `for` loop that displays the following set of numbers:

    `0, 10, 20, 30, 40, 50 . . . 1000`
    ```

4. Write a loop that asks the user to enter a number. The loop should iterate 10 times and keep a running total of the numbers entered.

5. Write a for loop that calculates the total of the following series of numbers:

$$\frac{1}{30} + \frac{2}{29} + \frac{3}{28} + \cdots \frac{30}{1}$$

6. Write a nested loop that displays 10 rows of '#' characters. There should be 15 '#' characters in each row.

7. Convert the while loop in the following code to a do-while loop:

```
Scanner keyboard = new Scanner(System.in);
int x = 1;
while (x > 0)
{
    System.out.print("Enter a number: ");
    x = keyboard.nextInt();
}
```

8. Convert the do-while loop in the following code to a while loop:

```
Scanner keyboard = new Scanner(System.in);
String input;
char sure;
do
{
    System.out.print("Are you sure you want to quit? ";
    input = keyboard.next();
    sure = input.charAt(0);
} while (sure != 'Y' && sure != 'N');
```

9. Convert the following while loop to a for loop:

```
int count = 0;
while (count < 50)
{
    System.out.println("count is " + count);
    count++;
}
```

10. Convert the following for loop to a while loop:

```
for (int x = 50; x > 0; x--)
{
    System.out.println(x + " seconds to go.");
}
```

11. Write an input validation loop that asks the user to enter a number in the range of 1 through 4.

12. Write an input validation loop that asks the user to enter the words "yes" or "no".

13. Write code that does the following: Opens a file named *NumberList.txt*, uses a loop to write the numbers 1 through 100 to the file, and then closes the file.

14. Write code that does the following: Opens the *NumberList.txt* file that was created by the code in Question 13, reads all of the numbers from the file and displays them, and then closes the file.

15. Modify the code you wrote in Question 14 so it adds all of the numbers read from the file and displays their total.

16. Write code that opens a file named *NumberList.txt* for writing, but does not erase the file's contents if it already exists.

Short Answer

1. Briefly describe the difference between the prefix and postfix modes used by the increment and decrement operators.

2. Why should you indent the statements in the body of a loop?

3. Describe the difference between pretest loops and posttest loops.

4. Why are the statements in the body of a loop called conditionally executed statements?

5. Describe the difference between the `while` loop and the `do-while` loop.

6. Which loop should you use in situations where you want the loop to repeat until the `boolean` expression is `false`, and the loop should not execute if the test expression is `false` to begin with?

7. Which loop should you use in situations where you want the loop to repeat until the `boolean` expression is `false`, but the loop should execute at least once?

8. Which loop should you use when you know the number of required iterations?

9. Why is it critical that accumulator variables are properly initialized?

10. What is an infinite loop? Write the code for an infinite loop.

11. Describe a programming problem that would require the use of an accumulator.

12. What does it mean to let the user control a loop?

13. What is the advantage of using a sentinel?

14. Why must the value chosen for use as a sentinel be carefully selected?

15. Describe a programming problem requiring the use of nested loops.

16. How does a file buffer increase a program's performance?

17. Why should a program close a file when it's finished using it?

18. What is a file's read position? Where is the read position when a file is first opened for reading?

19. When writing data to a file, what is the difference between the `print` and the `println` methods?

20. What does the `Scanner` class's `hasNext` method return when the end of the file has been reached?

21. What is a potential error that can occur when a file is opened for reading?

22. What does it mean to append data to a file?

23. How do you open a file so that new data will be written to the end of the file's existing data?

Programming Challenges

1. Sum of Numbers

Write a program that asks the user for a positive nonzero integer value. The program should use a loop to get the sum of all the integers from 1 up to the number entered. For example, if the user enters 50, the loop will find the sum of 1, 2, 3, 4, . . . 50.

2. Distance Traveled

The distance a vehicle travels can be calculated as follows:

*Distance = Speed * Time*

For example, if a train travels 40 miles-per-hour for three hours, the distance traveled is 120 miles. Write a program that asks for the speed of a vehicle (in miles-per-hour) and the number of hours it has traveled. It should use a loop to display the distance a vehicle has traveled for each hour of a time period specified by the user. For example, if a vehicle is traveling at 40 mph for a three-hour time period, it should display a report similar to the one that follows:

```
Hour      Distance Traveled
------------------------------
1                 40
2                 80
3                 120
```

Input Validation: Do not accept a negative number for speed and do not accept any value less than 1 for time traveled.

3. Distance File

Modify the program you wrote for Programming Challenge 2 (Distance Traveled) so it writes the report to a file instead of the screen. Open the file in Notepad or another text editor to confirm the output.

4. Pennies for Pay

VideoNote
The Pennies for
Pay Problem

Write a program that calculates the amount a person would earn over a period of time if his or her salary is one penny the first day, two pennies the second day, and continues to double each day. The program should display a table showing the salary for each day, and then show the total pay at the end of the period. The output should be displayed in a dollar amount, not the number of pennies.

Input Validation: Do not accept a number less than 1 for the number of days worked.

5. Letter Counter

Write a program that asks the user to enter a string, and then asks the user to enter a character. The program should count and display the number of times that the specified character appears in the string.

6. File Letter Counter

Write a program that asks the user to enter the name of a file, and then asks the user to enter a character. The program should count and display the number of times that the specified character appears in the file. Use Notepad or another text editor to create a simple file that can be used to test the program.

7. Hotel Occupancy

A hotel's occupancy rate is calculated as follows:

   Occupancy rate = number of rooms occupied ÷ total number of rooms

Write a program that calculates the occupancy rate for each floor of a hotel. The program should start by asking for the number of floors in the hotel. A loop should then iterate once for each floor. During each iteration, the loop should ask the user for the number of rooms on the floor and the number of them that are occupied. After all the iterations, the program should display the number of rooms the hotel has, the number of them that are occupied, the number that are vacant, and the occupancy rate for the hotel.

Input Validation: Do not accept a value less than 1 for the number of floors. Do not accept a number less than 10 for the number of rooms on a floor.

8. Average Rainfall

Write a program that uses nested loops to collect data and calculate the average rainfall over a period of years. First the program should ask for the number of years. The outer loop will iterate once for each year. The inner loop will iterate 12 times, once for each month. Each iteration of the inner loop will ask the user for the inches of rainfall for that month. After all iterations, the program should display the number of months, the total inches of rainfall, and the average rainfall per month for the entire period.

Input Validation: Do not accept a number less than 1 for the number of years. Do not accept negative numbers for the monthly rainfall.

9. Population

Write a program that will predict the size of a population of organisms. The program should ask for the starting number of organisms, their average daily population increase (as a percentage), and the number of days they will multiply. For example, a population might begin with two organisms, have an average daily increase of 50 percent, and will be allowed to multiply for seven days. The program should use a loop to display the size of the population for each day.

Input Validation: Do not accept a number less than 2 for the starting size of the population. Do not accept a negative number for average daily population increase. Do not accept a number less than 1 for the number of days they will multiply.

10. Largest and Smallest

Write a program with a loop that lets the user enter a series of integers. The user should enter −99 to signal the end of the series. After all the numbers have been entered, the program should display the largest and smallest numbers entered.

11. Celsius to Fahrenheit Table

Write a program that displays a table of the Celsius temperatures 0 through 20 and their Fahrenheit equivalents. The formula for converting a temperature from Celsius to Fahrenheit is

$$F = \frac{9}{5} C + 32$$

where F is the Fahrenheit temperature and C is the Celsius temperature. Your program must use a loop to display the table.

12. Bar Chart

Write a program that asks the user to enter today's sales for five stores. The program should display a bar chart comparing each store's sales. Create each bar in the bar chart by displaying a row of asterisks. Each asterisk should represent $100 of sales. Here is an example of the program's output:

```
Enter today's sales for store 1: 1000 [Enter]
Enter today's sales for store 2: 1200 [Enter]
Enter today's sales for store 3: 1800 [Enter]
Enter today's sales for store 4: 800 [Enter]
Enter today's sales for store 5: 1900 [Enter]

SALES BAR CHART
Store 1: **********
Store 2: ************
Store 3: ******************
Store 4: ********
Store 5: *******************
```

13. File Head Display

Write a program that asks the user for the name of a file. The program should display only the first five lines of the file's contents. If the file contains less than five lines, it should display the file's entire contents.

14. Line Numbers

Write a program that asks the user for the name of a file. The program should display the contents of the file with each line preceded with a line number followed by a colon. The line numbering should start at 1.

15. Uppercase File Converter

Write a program that asks the user for the names of two files. The first file should be opened for reading and the second file should be opened for writing. The program should read the contents of the first file, change all characters to uppercase, and store the results in the second file. The second file will be a copy of the first file, except that all the characters will be uppercase. Use Notepad or another text editor to create a simple file that can be used to test the program.

16. Budget Analysis

Write a program that asks the user to enter the amount that he or she has budgeted for a month. A loop should then prompt the user to enter each of his or her expenses for the month, and keep a running total. When the loop finishes, the program should display the amount that the user is over or under budget.

17. Random Number Guessing Game

Write a program that generates a random number and asks the user to guess what the number is. If the user's guess is higher than the random number, the program should display "Too high, try again." If the user's guess is lower than the random number, the program should display "Too low, try again." The program should use a loop that repeats until the user correctly guesses the random number.

18. Random Number Guessing Game Enhancement

Enhance the program that you wrote for Programming Challenge 17 so it keeps a count of the number of guesses that the user makes. When the user correctly guesses the random number, the program should display the number of guesses.

19. Square Display

Write a program that asks the user for a positive integer no greater than 15. The program should then display a square on the screen using the character 'X'. The number entered by the user will be the length of each side of the square. For example, if the user enters 5, the program should display the following:

```
XXXXX
XXXXX
XXXXX
XXXXX
XXXXX
```

If the user enters 8, the program should display the following:

```
XXXXXXXX
XXXXXXXX
XXXXXXXX
XXXXXXXX
XXXXXXXX
XXXXXXXX
XXXXXXXX
XXXXXXXX
```

5 Methods

TOPICS

5.1 Introduction to Methods

CONCEPT: Methods can be used to break a complex program into small, manageable pieces. A **void** method simply executes a group of statements and then terminates. A value-returning method returns a value to the statement that called it.

In a general sense, a method is a collection of statements that performs a specific task. So far you have experienced methods in two ways: (1) you have created a method named main in every program you've written, and (2) you have executed predefined methods from the Java API, such as System.out.println, Integer.parseInt, and Math.pow. In this chapter you will learn how to create your own methods, other than main, that can be executed just as you execute the API methods.

Methods are commonly used to break a problem into small manageable pieces. Instead of writing one long method that contains all of the statements necessary to solve a problem, several small methods that each solve a specific part of the problem can be written. These small methods can then be executed in the desired order to solve the problem. This approach is sometimes called *divide and conquer* because a large problem is divided into several smaller problems that are easily solved. Figure 5-1 illustrates this idea by comparing two programs: one that uses a long, complex method containing all of the statements necessary to solve a problem, and another that divides a problem into smaller problems, each of which are handled by a separate method.

Figure 5-1 Using methods to divide and conquer a problem

Another reason to write methods is that they simplify programs. If a specific task is performed in several places in a program, a method can be written once to perform that task, and then be executed any time it is needed. This benefit of using methods is known as *code reuse* because you are writing the code to perform a task once and then reusing it each time you need to perform the task.

First, we will look at the general ways in which methods operate. At the end of the chapter we will discuss in greater detail how methods can be used in problem solving.

`void` **Methods and Value-Returning Methods**

In this chapter you will learn about two general categories of methods: `void` methods and value-returning methods. A *void method* is one that simply performs a task and then terminates. `System.out.println` is an example of a `void` method. For example, look at the following code:

```
1       int number = 7;
2       System.out.println(number);
3       number = 0;
```

The statement in line 1 declares the `number` variable and initializes it with the value 7. The statement in line 2 calls the `System.out.println` method, passing `number` as an argument. The method does its job, which is to display a value on the screen, and then terminates. The code then resumes at line 3.

A *value-returning method* not only performs a task, but also sends a value back to the code that called it. The `Integer.parseInt` method is an example of a value-returning method. For example, look at the following code:

```
1       int number;
2       String str = "700";
3       number = Integer.parseInt(str);
```

The statement in line 1 declares the `number` variable. Line 2 creates a `String` object with the value `"700"` and assigns its address to the `str` variable. Line 3 is an assignment statement, which assigns a value to the `number` variable. Notice that on the right side of the = operator is a call to the `Integer.parseInt` method, passing `str` as an argument. The method executes, and then returns a value to this line of code. The value that is returned from the method is assigned to the `number` variable.

As demonstrated in this code, value-returning methods return a value to the calling statement. The calling statement normally does something with this value, such as assign it to a variable. The following code shows another example that uses the `Integer.parseInt` method's return value in a math operation:

```
1       int number;
2       String str = "700";
3       number = Integer.parseInt(str) * 2;
```

Line 3 in this code multiplies the `Inter.parseInt` method's return value by 2 and assigns the result to the `number` variable. After the code executes, `number` will be assigned the value 1400.

Defining a `void` Method

To create a method you must write its *definition*, which consists of two general parts: a header and a body. You learned about both of these in Chapter 2, but let's briefly review. The *method header*, which appears at the beginning of a method definition, lists several important things about the method, including the method's name. The *method body* is a collection of statements that are performed when the method is executed. These statements are enclosed inside a set of curly braces. Figure 5-2 points out the header and body of a `main` method.

Figure 5-2 The header and body of a `main` method

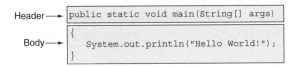

As you already know, every complete Java program must have a `main` method. Java programs can have other methods as well. Here is an example of a simple method that displays a message on the screen:

```
public static void displayMessage()
{
    System.out.println("Hello from the displayMessage method.");
}
```

This method has a header and a body. Figure 5-3 shows the different parts of the method header.

Figure 5-3 Parts of the method header

Let's take a closer look at the parts identified in the figure as follows:

- **Method modifiers**—The key words `public` and `static` are modifiers. You don't need to be too concerned with these modifiers now, but if your curiosity is getting the best of you, here's a brief explanation: The word `public` means that the method is publicly available to code outside the class. The word `static` means that the method belongs to the class, not a specific object. You will learn more about these modifiers in later chapters. For this chapter, every method that we write will begin with `public static`.

- **Return type**—Recall our previous discussion of `void` and value-returning methods. When the key word `void` appears here, it means that the method is a `void` method, and does not return a value. As you will see later, a value-returning method lists a data type here.

- **Method name**—You should give each method a descriptive name. In general, the same rules that apply to variable names also apply to method names. This method is named `displayMessage`, so we can easily guess what the method does: it displays a message.

- **Parentheses**—In the header, the method name is always followed by a set of parentheses. As you will learn later in this chapter, methods can be capable of receiving arguments. When this is the case, a list of one or more variable declarations will appear inside the parentheses. The method in this example does not receive any arguments, so the parentheses are empty.

NOTE: The method header is never terminated with a semicolon.

Calling a Method

A method executes when it is called. The main method is automatically called when a program starts, but other methods are executed by method call statements. When a method is called, the JVM branches to that method and executes the statements in its body. Here is an example of a method call statement that calls the `displayMessage` method we previously examined:

```
displayMessage();
```

The statement is simply the name of the method followed by a set of parentheses. Because it is a complete statement, it is terminated with a semicolon.

> **TIP:** Notice that the method modifiers and the `void` return type are not written in the method call statement. They are only written in the method header.

The program in Code Listing 5-1 demonstrates.

Code Listing 5-1 (`SimpleMethod.java`)

```java
1   /**
2       This program defines and calls a simple method.
3   */
4
5   public class SimpleMethod
6   {
7       public static void main(String[] args)
8       {
9           System.out.println("Hello from the main method.");
10          displayMessage();
11          System.out.println("Back in the main method.");
12      }
13
14      /**
15          The displayMessage method displays a greeting.
16      */
17
18      public static void displayMessage()
19      {
20          System.out.println("Hello from the displayMessage method.");
21      }
22  }
```

Program Output

```
Hello from the main method.
Hello from the displayMessage method.
Back in the main method.
```

Notice how the program flows. It starts, of course, in the `main` method. When the call to the `displayMessage` method in line 10 is encountered, the JVM branches to that method and performs the statement in its body (at line 20). Once the `displayMessage` method has finished executing, the JVM branches back to the `main` method and resumes at line 11 with the statement that follows the method call. This is illustrated in Figure 5-4.

Figure 5-4 Branching in the `SimpleMethod.java` program

Method call statements may be used in control structures like loops, `if` statements, and `switch` statements. The program in Code Listing 5-2 places the `displayMessage` method call inside a loop.

Code Listing 5-2 (`LoopCall.java`)

```
1   /**
2       This program defines and calls a simple method.
3   */
4
5   public class LoopCall
6   {
7      public static void main(String[] args)
8      {
9         System.out.println("Hello from the main method.");
10        for (int i = 0; i < 5; i++)
11           displayMessage();
12        System.out.println("Back in the main method.");
13     }
14
15     /**
16         The displayMessage method displays a greeting.
17     */
18
19     public static void displayMessage()
20     {
21        System.out.println("Hello from the displayMessage method.");
22     }
23  }
```

Program Output

```
Hello from the main method.
Hello from the displayMessage method.
Hello from the displayMessage method.
Hello from the displayMessage method.
Hello from the displayMessage method.
Hello from the displayMessage method.
Back in the main method.
```

The program in Code Listing 5-3 shows another example. It asks the user to enter his or her annual salary and credit rating. The program then determines whether the user qualifies for a credit card. One of two void methods, qualify or noQualify, is called to display a message. Figures 5-5 and 5-6 show example interactions with the program.

Code Listing 5-3   (`CreditCard.java`)

```java
 1   import javax.swing.JOptionPane;
 2
 3   /**
 4       This program uses two void methods.
 5   */
 6
 7   public class CreditCard
 8   {
 9       public static void main(String[] args)
10       {
11           double salary;      // Annual salary
12           int creditRating;   // Credit rating
13           String input;       // To hold the user's input
14
15           // Get the user's annual salary.
16           input = JOptionPane.showInputDialog("What is " +
17                                   "your annual salary?");
18           salary = Double.parseDouble(input);
19
20           // Get the user's credit rating (1 through 10).
21           input = JOptionPane.showInputDialog("On a scale of " +
22                   "1 through 10, what is your credit rating?\n" +
23                   "(10 = excellent, 1 = very bad)");
24           creditRating = Integer.parseInt(input);
25
26           // Determine whether the user qualifies.
27           if (salary >= 20000 && creditRating >= 7)
28               qualify();
29           else
30               noQualify();
```

```
31
32          System.exit(0);
33      }
34
35      /**
36          The qualify method informs the user that he
37          or she qualifies for the credit card.
38      */
39
40      public static void qualify()
41      {
42          JOptionPane.showMessageDialog(null, "Congratulations! " +
43                              "You qualify for the credit card!");
44      }
45
46      /**
47          The noQualify method informs the user that he
48          or she does not qualify for the credit card.
49      */
50
51      public static void noQualify()
52      {
53          JOptionPane.showMessageDialog(null, "I'm sorry.  You " +
54                              "do not qualify for the credit card.");
55      }
56  }
```

Figure 5-5   Interaction with the `CreditCard.java` program

Figure 5-6   Interaction with the `CreditCard.java` program

Hierarchical Method Calls

Methods can also be called in a hierarchical, or layered fashion. In other words, method A can call method B, which can then call method C. When method C finishes, the JVM returns to method B. When method B finishes, the JVM returns to method A. The program in Code Listing 5-4 demonstrates this with three methods: `main`, `deep`, and `deeper`. The `main` method calls the `deep` method, which then calls the `deeper` method.

Code Listing 5-4   (`DeepAndDeeper.java`)

```
 1  /**
 2      This program demonstrates hierarchical method calls.
 3  */
 4
 5  public class DeepAndDeeper
 6  {
 7     public static void main(String[] args)
 8     {
 9        System.out.println("I am starting in main.");
10        deep();
11        System.out.println("Now I am back in main.");
12     }
13
14     /**
15         The deep method displays a message and then calls
16         the deeper method.
17     */
18
19     public static void deep()
20     {
21        System.out.println("I am now in deep.");
```

```
22              deeper();
23              System.out.println("Now I am back in deep.");
24         }
25
26         /**
27             The deeper method simply displays a message.
28         */
29
30         public static void deeper()
31         {
32              System.out.println("I am now in deeper.");
33         }
34  }
```

Program Output

```
I am starting in main.
I am now in deep.
I am now in deeper.
Now I am back in deep.
Now I am back in main
```

Using Documentation Comments with Methods

You should always document a method by writing comments that appear just before the method's definition. The comments should provide a brief explanation of the method's purpose. Notice that the programs we've looked at in this chapter use documentation comments. Recall from Chapter 2 that documentation comments begin with /** and end with */. These types of comments can be read and processed by a program named javadoc, which produces attractive HTML documentation. As we progress through this chapter you will learn more about documentation comments and how they can be used with methods.

 Checkpoint

5.1   What is the difference between a void method and a value-returning method?

5.2   Is the following line of code a method header or a method call?

```
calcTotal();
```

5.3   Is the following line of code a method header or a method call?

```
public static void calcTotal()
```

5.4   What message will the following program display if the user enters 5? What if the user enters 10? What if the user enters 100?

```
import javax.swing.JOptionPane;
public class Checkpoint
{
    public static void main(String[] args)
    {
```

```java
        String input;
        int number;

        input = JOptionPane.showInputDialog("Enter a number.");
        number = Integer.parseInt(input);

        if (number < 10)
            method1();
        else
            method2();

        System.exit(0);
    }

    public static void method1()
    {
        JOptionPane.showMessageDialog(null, "Able was I.");
    }

    public static void method2()
    {
        JOptionPane.showMessageDialog(null, "I saw Elba.");
    }
}
```

5.5   Write a void method that displays your full name. The method should be named
      `myName`.

5.2   Passing Arguments to a Method

CONCEPT: A method may be written so it accepts arguments. Data can then be
passed into the method when it is called.

Values that are sent into a method are called *arguments*. You're already familiar with how to
use arguments in a method call. For example, look at the following statement:

```java
System.out.println("Hello");
```

VideoNote
Passing Arguments
to a Method

This statement calls the `System.out.println` method and passes `"Hello"` as an argument.
Here is another example:

```java
number = Integer.parseInt(str);
```

This statement calls the `Integer.parseInt` method and passes the contents of the `str` variable as an argument. By using parameter variables, you can design your own methods that
accept data this way. A *parameter variable*, sometimes simply referred to as a *parameter*, is
a special variable that holds a value being passed into a method. Here is the definition of a
method that uses a parameter:

```
public static void displayValue(int num)
{
    System.out.println("The value is " + num);
}
```

Notice the integer variable declaration that appears inside the parentheses (int num). This is the declaration of a parameter variable, which enables the displayValue method to accept an integer value as an argument. Here is an example of a call to the displayValue method, passing 5 as an argument:

```
displayValue(5);
```

This statement executes the displayValue method. The argument that is listed inside the parentheses is copied into the method's parameter variable, num. This is illustrated in Figure 5-7.

Figure 5-7   Passing 5 to the displayValue method

```
displayValue(5);              The argument 5 is copied into
                              the parameter variable num.


public static void displayValue(int num)
{
    System.out.println("The value is " + num);
}
```

Inside the displayValue method, the variable num will contain the value of whatever argument was passed into it. If we pass 5 as the argument, the method will display as follows:

```
The value is 5
```

You may also pass the contents of variables and the values of expressions as arguments. For example, the following statements call the displayValue method with various arguments passed:

```
displayValue(x);
displayValue(x * 4);
displayValue(Integer.parseInt("700"));
```

The first statement is simple. It passes the value in the variable x as the argument to the displayValue method. The second statement is also simple, but it does a little more work: it passes the result of the expression x * 4 as the argument to the displayValue method. The third statement does even more work. It passes the value returned from the Integer.parseInt method as the argument to the displayValue method. (The Integer.parseInt method is called first, and its return value is passed to the displayValue method.) The program in Code Listing 5-5 demonstrates these method calls.

Code Listing 5-5 (`PassArg.java`)

```
 1   /**
 2       This program demonstrates a method with a parameter.
 3   */
 4
 5   public class PassArg
 6   {
 7       public static void main(String[] args)
 8       {
 9          int x = 10;
10
11          System.out.println("I am passing values to displayValue.");
12          displayValue(5);                        // Pass 5
13          displayValue(x);                        // Pass 10
14          displayValue(x * 4);                    // Pass 40
15          displayValue(Integer.parseInt("700"));  // Pass 700
16          System.out.println("Now I am back in main.");
17       }
18
19       /**
20          The displayValue method displays the value
21          of its integer parameter.
22       */
23
24       public static void displayValue(int num)
25       {
26          System.out.println("The value is " + num);
27       }
28   }
```

Program Output

```
I am passing values to displayValue.
The value is 5
The value is 10
The value is 40
The value is 700
Now I am back in main.
```

WARNING! When passing a variable as an argument, simply write the variable name inside the parentheses of the method call. Do not write the data type of the argument variable in the method call. For example, the following statement will cause an error:

```
    displayValue(int x);    // Error!
```

The method call should appear as follows:

```
    displayValue(x);        // Correct
```

NOTE: In this text, the values that are passed into a method are called arguments, and the variables that receive those values are called parameters. There are several variations of these terms in use. In some circles these terms are switched in meaning. Also, some call the arguments *actual parameters* and call the parameters *formal parameters*. Others use the terms actual argument and formal argument. Regardless of which set of terms you use, it is important to be consistent.

Argument and Parameter Data Type Compatibility

When you pass an argument to a method, be sure that the argument's data type is compatible with the parameter variable's data type. Java will automatically perform a widening conversion if the argument's data type is ranked lower than the parameter variable's data type. For example, the displayValue method has an int parameter variable. Both of the following code segments will work because the short and byte arguments are automatically converted to an int:

```
short s = 1;
displayValue(s);     // Converts short to int

byte b = 2;
displayValue(b);     // Converts byte to int
```

However, Java will not automatically convert an argument to a lower-ranking data type. This means that a long, float, or double value cannot be passed to a method that has an int parameter variable. For example, the following code will cause a compiler error:

```
double d = 1.0;
displayValue(d);  // Error! Can't convert double to int.
```

TIP: You can use a cast operator to convert a value manually to a lower-ranking data type. For example, the following code will compile:

```
double d = 1.0;
displayValue((int)d);  // This will work.
```

Parameter Variable Scope

Recall from Chapter 2 that a variable's scope is the part of the program where the variable may be accessed by its name. A variable is visible only to statements inside the variable's scope. A parameter variable's scope is the method in which the parameter is declared. No statement outside the method can access the parameter variable by its name.

Passing Multiple Arguments

Often it is useful to pass more than one argument to a method. Here is a method that accepts two arguments:

```
public static void showSum(double num1, double num2)
{
   double sum;     // To hold the sum

   sum = num1 + num2;
   System.out.println("The sum is " + sum);
}
```

Notice that two parameter variables, num1 and num2, are declared inside the parentheses in the method header. This is often referred to as a *parameter list*. Also notice that a comma separates the declarations. Here is an example of a statement that calls the method:

```
showSum(5, 10);
```

This statement passes the arguments 5 and 10 into the method. The arguments are passed into the parameter variables in the order that they appear in the method call. In other words, the first argument is passed into the first parameter variable, the second argument is passed into the second parameter variable, and so forth. So, this statement causes 5 to be passed into the num1 parameter and 10 to be passed into the num2 parameter. This is illustrated in Figure 5-8.

Figure 5-8   Multiple arguments passed into multiple parameters

Suppose we were to reverse the order in which the arguments are listed in the method call, as shown here:

```
showSum(10, 5);
```

This would cause 10 to be passed into the num1 parameter and 5 to be passed into the num2 parameter. The following code segment shows one more example. This time we are passing variables as arguments.

```
double value1 = 2.5;
double value2 = 3.5;
showSum(value1, value2);
```

When the showSum methods executes as a result of this code, the num1 parameter will contain 2.5 and the num2 parameter will contain 3.5.

> **WARNING!** Each parameter variable in a parameter list must have a data type listed before its name. For example, a compiler error would occur if the parameter list for the showSum method were defined as shown in the following header:
>
> ```
> public static void showSum(double num1, num2) // Error!
> ```
>
> A data type for both the num1 and num2 parameter variables must be listed, as shown here:
>
> ```
> public static void showSum(double num1, double num2)
> ```

> See the program TwoArgs.java in this chapter's source code folder on the Student CD for a complete program that demonstrates the showSum method.

Arguments Are Passed by Value

In Java, all arguments of the primitive data types are *passed by value*, which means that only a copy of an argument's value is passed into a parameter variable. A method's parameter variables are separate and distinct from the arguments that are listed inside the parentheses of a method call. If a parameter variable is changed inside a method, it has no effect on the original argument. For example, look at the program in Code Listing 5-6.

Code Listing 5-6   (PassByValue.java)

```
 1  /**
 2      This program demonstrates that only a copy of an argument
 3      is passed into a method.
 4  */
 5
 6  public class PassByValue
 7  {
 8     public static void main(String[] args)
 9     {
10        int number = 99; // number starts with 99
11
12        // Display the value in number.
13        System.out.println("number is " + number);
14
15        // Call changeMe, passing the value in number
16        // as an argument.
17        changeMe(number);
18
19        // Display the value in number again.
20        System.out.println("number is " + number);
```

```
21      }
22
23      /**
24          The changeMe method accepts an argument and then
25          changes the value of the parameter.
26      */
27
28      public static void changeMe(int myValue)
29      {
30          System.out.println("I am changing the value.");
31
32          // Change the myValue parameter variable to 0.
33          myValue = 0;
34
35          // Display the value in myValue.
36          System.out.println("Now the value is " + myValue);
37      }
38  }
```

Program Output

```
number is 99
I am changing the value.
Now the value is 0
number is 99
```

Even though the parameter variable myValue is changed in the changeMe method, the argument number is not modified. The myValue variable contains only a copy of the number variable.

Passing Object References to a Method

So far you've seen examples of methods that accept primitive values as arguments. You can also write methods that accept references to objects as arguments. For example, look at the following method, which is from the program ShowStringLength.java on the Student CD:

```java
public static void showLength(String str)
{
    System.out.println(str + " is " + str.length() +
                        " characters long.");
}
```

This method accepts a String object reference as its argument, and displays a message showing the number of characters in the object. The following code shows an example of how to call the method:

```java
String name = "Warren";
showLength(name);
```

When this code executes, the showLength method will display the following:

```
Warren is 6 characters long.
```

When an object, such as a String, is passed as an argument, it is actually a reference to the object that is passed. In this example code, the name variable is a String reference variable. It is passed as an argument to the showLength method. The showLength method has a parameter variable, str, which is also a String reference variable, that receives the argument.

Recall that a reference variable holds the memory address of an object. When the showLength method is called, the address that is stored in name is passed into the str parameter variable. This is illustrated in Figure 5-9. This means that when the showLength method is executing, both name and str reference the same object. This is illustrated in Figure 5-10.

Figure 5-9 Passing a reference as an argument

Figure 5-10 Both name and str reference the same object

This might lead you to the conclusion that a method can change the contents of any String object that has been passed to it as an argument. After all, the parameter variable references the same object as the argument. However, String objects in Java are *immutable*, which means that they cannot be changed. For example, look at the program in Code Listing 5-7. It passes a String object to a method, which appears to change the object. In reality, the object is not changed.

Code Listing 5-7   (`PassString.java`)

```
 1   /**
 2       This program demonstrates that String arguments
 3       cannot be changed.
 4   */
 5
 6   public class PassString
 7   {
 8       public static void main(String[] args)
 9       {
10          // Create a String object containing "Shakespeare".
11          // The name variable references the object.
12          String name = "Shakespeare";
13
14          // Display the String referenced by the name variable.
15          System.out.println("In main, the name is " +
16                             name);
17
18          // Call the changeName method, passing the
19          // contents of the name variable as an argument.
20          changeName(name);
21
22          // Display the String referenced by the name variable.
23          System.out.println("Back in main, the name is " +
24                             name);
25      }
26
27      /**
28          The changeName method accepts a String as its argument
29          and assigns the str parameter to a new String.
30      */
31
32      public static void changeName(String str)
33      {
34          // Create a String object containing "Dickens".
35          // Assign its address to the str parameter variable.
36          str = "Dickens";
37
38          // Display the String referenced by str.
39          System.out.println("In changeName, the name " +
40                             "is now " + str);
41      }
42   }
```

Program Output

```
In main, the name is Shakespeare
In changeName, the name is now Dickens
Back in main, the name is Shakespeare
```

Let's take a closer look at this program. After line 12 executes, the name variable references a String object containing "Shakespeare". In line 20 the changeName method is called and the name variable is passed as an argument. This passes the address of the String object into the str parameter variable. At this point, both name and str reference the same object, as shown in Figure 5-11.

Figure 5-11   Before line 36 executes both name and str reference the same object

In the changeName method, line 36 executes as follows:

```
str = "Dickens";
```

At first, you might think that this statement changes the String object's contents to "Dickens". What actually happens is that a new String object containing "Dickens" is created and its address is stored in the str variable. After this statement executes, the name variable and the str parameter variable reference different objects. This is shown in Figure 5-12.

Figure 5-12   After line 36 executes, name and str reference different objects

In Chapter 10 we will discuss the immutability of String objects in greater detail. Until then, just remember the following point: String objects cannot be changed. Any time you use the = operator to assign a string literal to a String reference variable, a new String object is created in memory.

Using the `@param` Tag in Documentation Comments

When writing the documentation comments for a method, you can provide a description of each parameter by using a `@param` tag. When the `javadoc` utility sees a `@param` tag inside a method's documentation comments, it knows that the documentation for a parameter variable appears next. The file *TwoArgs2.java* on the Student CD has the following method, which uses `@param` tags in its documentation comments:

```
/**
   The showSum method displays the sum of two numbers.
   @param num1 The first number.
   @param num2 The second number.
*/

   public static void showSum(double num1, double num2)
   {
      double sum;    // To hold the sum

      sum = num1 + num2;
      System.out.println("The sum is " + sum);
   }
```

The general format of a `@param` tag comment is as follows:

```
@param parameterName Description
```

In the general format, `parameterName` is the name of the parameter and `Description` is a description of the parameter. Remember the following points about `@param` tag comments:

- All `@param` tags in a method's documentation comment must appear after the general description of the method.
- The description can span several lines. It ends at the end of the documentation comment (the `*/` symbol), or at the beginning of another tag.

When a method's documentation comments contain one or more `@param` tags, the `javadoc` utility will create a Parameters section in the method's documentation. This is where the descriptions of the method's parameters will be listed. Figure 5-13 shows the documentation generated by `javadoc` for the `showSum` method in the *TwoArgs2.java* file.

Figure 5-13 Documentation for the `showSum` method in *TwoArgs2.java*

showSum

```
public static void showSum(double num1,
                           double num2)
```

The showSum method displays the sum of two numbers.

Parameters:
        num1 - The first number.
        num2 - The second number.

Checkpoint

5.6 What is the difference between an argument and a parameter?

5.7 Look at the following method header:

```
public static void myMethod(int num)
```

Which of the following calls to the method will cause a compiler error?

a) `myMethod(7);`
b) `myMethod(6.2);`
c) `long x = 99;`
   `myMethod(x);`
d) `short s = 2;`
   `myMethod(s);`

5.8 Suppose a method named showValues accepts two int arguments. Which of the following method headers is written correctly?

a) `public static void showValues()`
b) `public static void showValues(int num1, num2)`
c) `public static void showValues(num1, num2)`
d) `public static void showValues(int num1, int num2)`

5.9 In Java, method arguments are passed by value. What does this mean?

5.10 What will the following program display?

```java
public class Checkpoint
{
    public static void main(String[] args)
    {
        int num1 = 99;
        double num2 = 1.5;

        System.out.println(num1 + " " + num2);
        myMethod(num1, num2);
        System.out.println(num1 + " " + num2);
    }

    public static void myMethod(int i, double d)
    {
        System.out.println(i + " " + d);
        i = 0;
        d = 0.0;
        System.out.println(i + " " + d);
    }
}
```

5.3 **More about Local Variables**

CONCEPT: A local variable is declared inside a method and is not accessible to statements outside the method. Different methods can have local variables with the same names because the methods cannot see each other's local variables.

In Chapter 2 we introduced the concept of local variables, which are variables that are declared inside a method. They are called *local* because they are local to the method in which they are declared. Statements outside a method cannot access that method's local variables.

Because a method's local variables are hidden from other methods, the other methods may have their own local variables with the same name. For example, look at the program in Code Listing 5-8. In addition to the main method, this program has two other methods: texas and california. These two methods each have a local variable named birds.

Code Listing 5-8   (LocalVars.java)

```
 1   /**
 2       This program demonstrates that two methods may have
 3       local variables with the same name.
 4   */
 5
 6   public class LocalVars
 7   {
 8       public static void main(String[] args)
 9       {
10          texas();
11          california();
12       }
13
14       /**
15          The texas method has a local variable named birds.
16       */
17
18       public static void texas()
19       {
20          int birds = 5000;
21
22          System.out.println("In texas there are " +
23                             birds + " birds.");
24       }
25
26       /**
27          The california method also has a local variable named birds.
28       */
```

```
29      public static void california()
30      {
31          int birds = 3500;
32
33          System.out.println("In california there are " +
34                          birds + " birds.");
35      }
36  }
```

Program Output

```
In texas there are 5000 birds.
In california there are 3500 birds.
```

Although there are two variables named birds, the program can only see one of them at a time because they are in different methods. When the texas method is executing, the birds variable declared inside texas is visible. When the california method is executing, the birds variable declared inside california is visible.

Local Variable Lifetime

A method's local variables exist only while the method is executing. This is known as the *lifetime* of a local variable. When the method begins, its local variables and its parameter variables are created in memory, and when the method ends, the local variables and parameter variables are destroyed. This means that any value stored in a local variable is lost between calls to the method in which the variable is declared.

Initializing Local Variables with Parameter Values

It is possible to use a parameter variable to initialize a local variable. Sometimes this simplifies the code in a method. For example, recall the following showSum method we discussed earlier:

```java
public static void showSum(double num1, double num2)
{
    double sum;     // To hold the sum

    sum = num1 + num2;
    System.out.println("The sum is " + sum);
}
```

In the body of the method, the sum variable is declared and then a separate assignment statement assigns num1 + num2 to sum. We can combine these statements into one, as shown in the following modified version of the method.

```java
public static void showSum(double num1, double num2)
{
    double sum = num1 + num2;
    System.out.println("The sum is " + sum);
}
```

Because the scope of a parameter variable is the entire method in which it is declared, we can use parameter variables to initialize local variables.

> **WARNING!** Local variables are not automatically initialized with a default value. They must be given a value before they can be used. If you attempt to use a local variable before it has been given a value, a compiler error will result. For example, look at the following method:
>
> ```
> public static void myMethod()
> {
>    int x;
>    System.out.println(x);   //Error! x has no value.
> }
> ```
>
> This code will cause a compiler error because the variable x has not been given a value, and it is being used as an argument to the System.out.println method.

5.4 Returning a Value from a Method

CONCEPT: A method may send a value back to the statement that called the method.

You've seen that data may be passed into a method by way of parameter variables. Data may also be returned from a method, back to the statement that called it. Methods that return a value are appropriately known as *value-returning methods*.

You are already experienced at using value-returning methods. For instance, you have used the wrapper class parse methods, such as Integer.parseInt. Here is an example:

```
int num;
num = Integer.parseInt("700");
```

VideoNote
Returning a Value
from a Method

The second line in this code calls the Integer.parseInt method, passing "700" as the argument. The method returns the integer value 700, which is assigned to the num variable by the = operator. You have also seen the Math.pow method, which returns a value. Here is an example:

```
double x;
x = Math.pow(4.0, 2.0);
```

The second line in this code calls the Math.pow method, passing 4.0 and 2.0 as arguments. The method calculates the value of 4.0 raised to the power of 2.0 and returns that value. The value, which is 16.0, is assigned to the x variable by the = operator.

In this section we will discuss how you can write your own value-returning methods.

Defining a Value-Returning Method

When you are writing a value-returning method, you must decide what type of value the method will return. This is because you must specify the data type of the return value in the method header. Recall that a void method, which does not return a value, uses the key word void as its return type in the method header. A value-returning method will use int, double, boolean, or any other valid data type in its header. Here is an example of a method that returns an int value:

```
public static int sum(int num1, int num2)
{
    int result;

    result = num1 + num2;
    return result;
}
```

The name of this method is sum. Notice in the method header that the return type is int, as shown in Figure 5-14.

Figure 5-14 Return type in the method header

Return Type

```
public static int sum(int num1, int num2)
```

This code defines a method named sum that accepts two int arguments. The arguments are passed into the parameter variables num1 and num2. Inside the method, a local variable, result, is declared. The parameter variables num1 and num2 are added, and their sum is assigned to the result variable. The last statement in the method is as follows:

```
return result;
```

This is a return statement. You must have a return statement in a value-returning method. It causes the method to end execution and it returns a value to the statement that called the method. In a value-returning method, the general format of the return statement is as follows:

```
return Expression;
```

Expression is the value to be returned. It can be any expression that has a value, such as a variable, literal, or mathematical expression. In this case, the sum method returns the value in the result variable. However, we could have eliminated the result variable and returned the expression num1 + num2, as shown in the following code:

```
public static int sum(int num1, int num2)
{
    return num1 + num2;
}
```

NOTE: The return statement's expression must be of the same data type as the return type specified in the method header, or compatible with it. Otherwise, a compiler error will occur. Java will automatically widen the value of the return expression, if necessary, but it will not automatically narrow it.

Calling a Value-Returning Method

The program in Code Listing 5-9 shows an example of how to call the sum method. Notice that the documentation comments for the sum method have a new tag, @return. This tag will be explained later.

Code Listing 5-9   (`ValueReturn.java`)

```
1   /**
2       This program demonstrates a value-returning method.
3   */
4
5   public class ValueReturn
6   {
7      public static void main(String[] args)
8      {
9         int total, value1 = 20, value2 = 40;
10
11        // Call the sum method, passing the contents of
12        // value1 and value2 as arguments. Assign the
13        // return value to the total variable.
14        total = sum(value1, value2);
15
16        // Display the contents of all these variables.
17        System.out.println("The sum of " + value1 +
18                           " and " + value2 + " is " +
19                           total);
20     }
21
22     /**
23         The sum method returns the sum of its two parameters.
24         @param num1 The first number to be added.
25         @param num2 The second number to be added.
26         @return The sum of num1 and num2.
27     */
28
29     public static int sum(int num1, int num2)
30     {
31        int result;  // result is a local variable
32
33        // Assign the value of num1 + num2 to result.
34        result = num1 + num2;
35
36        // Return the value in the result variable.
37        return result;
38     }
39  }
```

Program Output

```
The sum of 20 and 40 is 60
```

The statement in line 14 calls the `sum` method, passing `value1` and `value2` as arguments. It assigns the value returned by the `sum` method to the `total` variable. In this case, the method will return 60. Figure 5-15 shows how the arguments are passed into the method and how a value is passed back from the method.

Figure 5-15   Arguments passed to `sum` and a value returned

When you call a value-returning method, you usually want to do something meaningful with the value it returns. The `ValueReturn.java` program shows a method's return value being assigned to a variable. This is commonly how return values are used, but you can do many other things with them. For example, the following code shows a math expression that uses a call to the `sum` method:

```
int x = 10, y = 15;
double average;
average = sum(x, y) / 2.0;
```

In the last statement, the `sum` method is called with x and y as its arguments. The method's return value, which is 25, is divided by 2.0. The result, 12.5, is assigned to `average`. Here is another example:

```
int x = 10, y = 15;
System.out.println("The sum is " + sum(x, y));
```

This code sends the `sum` method's return value to `System.out.println`, so it can be displayed on the screen. The message "The sum is 25" will be displayed.

Remember, a value-returning method returns a value of a specific data type. You can use the method's return value anywhere that you can use a regular value of the same data type. This means that anywhere an `int` value can be used, a call to an `int` value-returning method can be used. Likewise, anywhere a `double` value can be used, a call to a `double` value-returning method can be used. The same is true for all other data types.

Using the `@return` Tag in Documentation Comments

When writing the documentation comments for a value-returning method, you can provide a description of the return value by using a `@return` tag. When the `javadoc` utility sees a `@return` tag inside a method's documentation comments, it knows that a description of the method's return value appears next.

The general format of a @return tag comment is as follows:

@return *Description*

Description is a description of the return value. Remember the following points about @return tag comments:

- The @return tag in a method's documentation comment must appear after the general description of the method.
- The description can span several lines. It ends at the end of the documentation comment (the */ symbol), or at the beginning of another tag.

When a method's documentation comments contain a @return tag, the javadoc utility will create a Returns section in the method's documentation. This is where the description of the method's return value will be listed. Figure 5-16 shows the documentation generated by javadoc for the sum method in the *ValueReturn.java* file.

Figure 5-16   Documentation for the sum method in ValueReturn.java

sum

```
public static int sum(int num1,
                      int num2)
```

The sum method returns the sum of its two parameters.

Parameters:
    num1 - The first number to be added.
    num2 - The second number to be added.
Returns:
    The sum of num1 and num2.

In the Spotlight:
Using Methods

Your friend Michael runs a catering company. Some of the ingredients that his recipes require are measured in cups. When he goes to the grocery store to buy those ingredients, however, they are sold only by the fluid ounce. He has asked you to write a simple program that converts cups to fluid ounces.

You design the following algorithm:

1. *Get the number of cups from the user.*
2. *Convert the number of cups to fluid ounces.*
3. *Display the result.*

This algorithm lists the top level of tasks that the program needs to perform, and becomes the basis of the class's main method. The class will also have the following methods:

- getCups—This method will prompt the user to enter the number of cups, and then return that value as a double.

- cupsToOunces—This method will accept the number of cups as an argument and then return the equivalent number of fluid ounces as a double.
- displayResults—This method displays a message indicating the results of the conversion.

Code Listing 5-10 shows the program. Figure 5-17 shows interaction with the program during execution.

Code Listing 5-10   (CupConverter.java)

```java
 1  import javax.swing.JOptionPane;
 2
 3  /**
 4     This program converts cups to fluid ounces.
 5  */
 6
 7  public class CupConverter
 8  {
 9     public static void main(String[] args)
10     {
11        double cups;    // To hold the number of cups
12        double ounces;  // To hold the number of ounces
13
14        // Get the number of cups.
15        cups = getCups();
16
17        // Convert the cups to fluid ounces.
18        ounces = cupsToOunces(cups);
19
20        // Display the results.
21        displayResults(cups, ounces);
22        System.exit(0);
23     }
24
25     /**
26        The getCups method prompts the user to enter a number
27        of cups.
28        @return The number of cups entered by the user.
29     */
30
31     public static double getCups()
32     {
33        String input;      // To hold input.
34        double numCups;    // To hold cups.
35
```

```
36            // Get the number of cups from the user.
37            input = JOptionPane.showInputDialog(
38                    "This program converts measurements\n" +
39                    "in cups to fluid ounces. For your\n" +
40                    "reference the formula is:\n" +
41                    "    1 cup = 8 fluid ounces\n\n" +
42                    "Enter the number of cups.");
43
44            // Convert the input to a double.
45            numCups = Double.parseDouble(input);
46
47            // Return the number of cups.
48            return numCups;
49        }
50
51        /**
52            The cupsToOunces method converts a number of
53            cups to fluid ounces, using the formula
54            1 cup = 8 fluid ounces.
55            @param numCups The number of cups to convert.
56            @return The number of ounces.
57        */
58
59        public static double cupsToOunces(double numCups)
60        {
61            return numCups * 8.0;
62        }
63
64        /**
65            The displayResults method displays a message showing
66            the results of the conversion.
67            @param cups A number of cups.
68            @param ounces A number of ounces.
69        */
70
71        public static void displayResults(double cups, double ounces)
72        {
73            // Display the number of ounces.
74            JOptionPane.showMessageDialog(null,
75                    cups + " cups equals " +
76                    ounces + " fluid ounces.");
77        }
78    }
```

Figure 5-17   Interaction with the `CupConverter` program

This input dialog appears first.
The user enters 2 and clicks OK.

This message dialog shows
the results.

Input   ❌

❓   This program converts measurements
in cups to fluid ounces. For your
reference the formula is:
    1 cup = 8 fluid ounces

Enter the number of cups.

2

    OK   Cancel

Message   ❌

ⓘ   2.0 cups equals 16.0 fluid ounces.

    OK

Returning a `boolean` Value

Frequently there is a need for a method that tests an argument and returns a `true` or `false` value indicating whether or not a condition exists. Such a method would return a `boolean` value. For example, the following method accepts an argument and returns `true` if the argument is within the range of 1 through 100, or `false` otherwise:

```java
public static boolean isValid(int number)
{
   boolean status;

   if (number >= 1 && number <= 100)
      status = true;
   else
      status = false;
   return status;
}
```

The following code shows an `if-else` statement that uses a call to the method:

```java
int value = 20;
if (isValid(value))
   System.out.println("The value is within range.");
else
   System.out.println("The value is out of range.");
```

When this code executes, the message "The value is within range." will be displayed.

Returning a Reference to an Object

A value-returning method can also return a reference to a non-primitive type, such as a `String` object. The program in Code Listing 5-11 shows such an example.

Code Listing 5-11   (`ReturnString.java`)

```java
 1   /**
 2       This program demonstrates a method that
 3       returns a reference to a String object.
 4   */
 5
 6   public class ReturnString
 7   {
 8      public static void main(String[] args)
 9      {
10         String customerName;
11
12         customerName = fullName("John", "Martin");
13         System.out.println(customerName);
14      }
15
16      /**
17          The fullName method accepts two String arguments
18          containing a first and last name. It concatenates
19          them into a single String object.
20          @param first The first name.
21          @param last The last name.
22          @return A reference to a String object containing
23                  the first and last names.
24      */
25
26      public static String fullName(String first, String last)
27      {
28         String name;
29
30         name = first + " " + last;
31         return name;
32      }
33   }
```

Program Output

```
John Martin
```

Line 12 calls the `fullName` method, passing "John" and "Martin" as arguments. The method returns a reference to a `String` object containing "John Martin". The reference is assigned to the `customerName` variable. This is illustrated in Figure 5-18.

Figure 5-18   The `fullName` method returning a reference to a `String` object

 Checkpoint

5.11   Look at the following method header. What type of value does the method return?

```
public static double getValue(int a, float b, String c)
```

5.12   Write the header for a method named `days`. The method should return an `int` and have three `int` parameter variables: `years`, `months`, and `weeks`.

5.13   Write the header for a method named `distance`. The method should return a `double` and have two `double` parameter variables: `rate` and `time`.

5.14   Write the header for a method named `lightYears`. The method should return a `long` and have one `long` parameter variable: `miles`.

5.5   Problem Solving with Methods

CONCEPT: A large, complex problem can be solved a piece at a time by methods.

At the beginning of this chapter we introduced the idea of using methods to "divide and conquer" a problem. Often the best way to solve a complex problem is to break it down into smaller problems, and then solve the smaller problems. The process of breaking down a problem into smaller pieces is called *functional decomposition*.

In functional decomposition, instead of writing one long method that contains all of the statements necessary to solve a problem, small methods are written, which each solve a specific part of the problem. These small methods can then be executed in the desired order to solve the problem.

Let's look at an example. The program in Code Listing 5-12 reads 30 days of sales amounts from a file, and then displays the total sales and average daily sales. Here's a brief pseudo-code model of the algorithm:

Ask the user to enter the name of the file.
Get the total of the sales amounts in the file.
Calculate the average daily sales.
Display the total and average daily sales.

 The file `MonthlySales.txt`, on the Student CD is used to test the program. Figure 5-19 shows interaction with the program during execution.

Code Listing 5-12   (`SalesReport.java`)

```java
 1 import java.util.Scanner;              // For the Scanner class
 2 import java.io.*;                      // For file I/O classes
 3 import java.text.DecimalFormat;        // For the DecimalFormat class
 4 import javax.swing.JOptionPane;        // For the JOptionPane class
 5
 6 /**
 7    This program opens a file containing the sales
 8    amounts for 30 days. It calculates and displays
 9    the total sales and average daily sales.
10 */
11
12 public class SalesReport
13 {
14    public static void main(String[] args) throws IOException
15    {
16       final int NUM_DAYS = 30;          // Number of days of sales
17       String filename;                  // The name of the file to open
18       double totalSales;                // Total sales for period
19       double averageSales;              // Average daily sales
20
21       // Get the name of the file.
22       filename = getFileName();
23
24       // Get the total sales from the file.
25       totalSales = getTotalSales(filename);
26
27       // Calculate the average.
28       averageSales = totalSales / NUM_DAYS;
29
30       // Display the total and average.
31       displayResults(totalSales, averageSales);
32
33       System.exit(0);
34    }
35
36    /**
37       The getFileName method prompts the user to enter
38       the name of the file to open.
39       @return A reference to a String object containing
40               the name of the file.
41    */
42
43    public static String getFileName()
44    {
45       String file;                          // To hold the file name
46
```

```
47          // Prompt the user to enter a file name.
48          file = JOptionPane.showInputDialog("Enter " +
49                          "the name of the file\n" +
50                          "containing 30 days of " +
51                          "sales amounts.");
52
53          // Return the name.
54          return file;
55       }
56
57       /**
58          The getTotalSales method opens a file and
59          reads the daily sales amounts, accumulating
60          the total. The total is returned.
61          @param filename The name of the file to open.
62          @return The total of the sales amounts.
63       */
64
65       public static double getTotalSales(String filename)
66                                       throws IOException
67       {
68          double total = 0.0;                // Accumulator
69          double sales;                      // A daily sales amount
70
71          // Open the file.
72          File file = new File(filename);
73          Scanner inputFile = new Scanner(file);
74
75          // This loop processes the lines read from the file,
76          // until the end of the file is encountered.
77          while (inputFile.hasNext())
78          {
79             // Read a double from the file.
80             sales = inputFile.nextDouble();
81
82             // Add sales to the value already in total.
83             total += sales;
84          }
85
86          // Close the file.
87          inputFile.close();
88
89          // Return the total sales.
90          return total;
91       }
92
93       /**
```

```
 94          The displayResults method displays the total and
 95          average daily sales.
 96          @param total The total sales.
 97          @param avg The average daily sales.
 98       */
 99
100      public static void displayResults(double total, double avg)
101      {
102         // Create a DecimalFormat object capable of formatting
103         // a dollar amount.
104         DecimalFormat dollar = new DecimalFormat("#,###.00");
105
106         // Display the total and average sales.
107         JOptionPane.showMessageDialog(null, "The total sales for " +
108                         "the period is $" + dollar.format(total) +
109                         "\nThe average daily sales were $" +
110                         dollar.format(avg));
111      }
112 }
```

Instead of writing the entire program in the main method, the algorithm was broken down into the following methods:

- getFileName—This method displays an input dialog box asking the user to enter the name of the file containing 30 days of sales amounts. The method returns a reference to a String object containing the name entered by the user.
- getTotalSales—This method accepts the name of a file as an argument. The file is opened, the sales amounts are read from it, and the total of the sales amounts is accumulated. The method returns the total as a double.
- displayResults—This method accepts as arguments the total sales and the average daily sales. It displays a message dialog box indicating these values.

Figure 5-19   Interaction with the SalesReport.java program

Calling Methods That Throw Exceptions

One last thing about the *SalesReport.java* program should be discussed. Notice that the main method header (in line 14) and the getTotalSales method header (in lines 65 through 66) both have a throws IOException clause. The getTotalSales method has the clause because it uses a Scanner object to open a file. As you know from Chapter 4, any method that uses a Scanner object to open a file should have a throws IOException clause in its header. Let's quickly review why this is so.

When a Scanner object has a problem opening a file, it throws an exception known as IOException. Java requires that either (a) the exception is handled in the method that caused it to occur, or (b) the method terminates and throws the exception again. For now you must write your methods to throw the exception again because you will not learn how to handle exceptions until Chapter 12. By writing a throws IOException clause in a method's header, you are telling the compiler that the method does not handle the exception. Instead, it throws the exception again.

That explains why the getTotalSales method has the throws IOException clause, but it doesn't explain why the main method has one. After all, main doesn't use a Scanner object to perform any file operations. The reason main has to have the clause is because main calls the getTotalSales method. If the Scanner object in getTotalSales throws an IOException, the getTotalSales method terminates and throws the IOException again. That means that main must either handle the exception, or terminate and throw it once again. When the main method throws the exception, the JVM displays an error message on the screen.

> **TIP:** Until you learn how to handle exceptions in Chapter 12, just remember this when writing programs that throw exceptions: If a method calls another method that has a throws clause in its header, then the calling method should have the same throws clause.

5.6   Common Errors to Avoid

- **Putting a semicolon at the end of a method header.** Method headers are never terminated with a semicolon.
- **Writing modifiers or return types in a method call statement.** Method modifiers and return types are written in method headers, but never in method calls.
- **Forgetting to write the empty parentheses in a call to a method that accepts no arguments.** You must always write the parentheses in a method call statement, even if the method doesn't accept arguments.
- **Forgetting to pass arguments to methods that require them.** If a method has parameter variables, you must provide arguments when calling the method.
- **Passing an argument of a data type that cannot be automatically converted to the data type of the parameter variable.** Java will automatically perform a widening conversion if the argument's data type is ranked lower than the parameter variable's data type. But Java will not automatically convert an argument to a lower-ranking data type.
- **Attempting to access a parameter variable with code outside the method where the variable is declared.** A parameter variable is only visible within the method it is declared in.

- **Not writing the data type of each parameter variable in a method header.** Each parameter variable declaration inside the parentheses of a method header must include the variable's data type.
- **Changing the contents of a method's parameter variable and expecting the argument that was passed into the parameter to change as well.** Method arguments are passed by value, which means that a copy of the argument is passed into a parameter variable. Changes to the parameter variable have no effect on the argument.
- **Using a variable to receive a method's return value when the variable's data type is incompatible with the data type of the return value.** A variable that receives a method's return value must be of a data type that is compatible with the data type of the return value.
- **Not writing a `return` statement in a value-returning method.** If a method's return type is anything other than `void`, it should return a value.
- **Not writing a required `throws` clause in a method that calls another method.** Any method that calls a method with a `throws` clause in its header must either handle the potential exception or have the same `throws` clause. You will learn how to handle exceptions in Chapter 12.

Review Questions and Exercises

Multiple Choice and True/False

1. This type of method does not return a value.

   a. null
   b. void
   c. empty
   d. anonymous

2. This appears at the beginning of a method definition.

   a. semicolon
   b. parentheses
   c. body
   d. header

3. The body of a method is enclosed in _____.

   a. curly braces { }
   b. square brackets [ ]
   c. parentheses ( )
   d. quotation marks " "

4. A method header can contain _____.

   a. method modifiers
   b. the method return type
   c. the method name
   d. a list of parameter declarations
   e. all of these
   f. none of these

5. A value that is passed into a method when it is called is known as a(n) _____.

   a. parameter
   b. argument
   c. signal
   d. return value

6. A variable that receives a value that is passed into a method is known as a(n) _____.

   a. parameter
   b. argument
   c. signal
   d. return value

7. This `javadoc` tag is used to document a parameter variable.

   a. `@parameter`
   b. `@param`
   c. `@paramvar`
   d. `@arg`

8. This statement causes a method to end and sends a value back to the statement that called the method.

   a. `end`
   b. `send`
   c. `exit`
   d. `return`

9. This `javadoc` tag is used to document a method's return value.

   a. `@methodreturn`
   b. `@ret`
   c. `@return`
   d. `@returnval`

10. **True or False:** You terminate a method header with a semicolon.

11. **True or False:** When passing an argument to a method, Java will automatically perform a widening conversion (convert the argument to a higher-ranking data type) if necessary.

12. **True or False:** When passing an argument to a method, Java will automatically perform a narrowing conversion (convert the argument to a lower-ranking data type) if necessary.

13. **True or False:** A parameter variable's scope is the entire program that contains the method in which the parameter is declared.

14. **True or False:** When code in a method changes the value of a parameter, it also changes the value of the argument that was passed into the parameter.

15. **True or False:** When an object, such as a `String`, is passed as an argument, it is actually a reference to the object that is passed.

16. **True or False:** The contents of a `string` object cannot be changed.

17. **True or False:** When passing multiple arguments to a method, the order in which the arguments are passed is not important.

18. **True or False:** No two methods in the same program can have a local variable with the same name.

19. **True or False:** It is possible for one method to access a local variable that is declared in another method.

20. **True or False:** You must have a `return` statement in a value-returning method.

Find the Error

1. Find the error in the following method definition:

```
// This method has an error!
public static void sayHello();
{
    System.out.println("Hello");
}
```

2. Look at the following method header:

```
public static void showValue(int x)
```

The following code has a call to the `showValue` method. Find the error.

```
int x = 8;
showValue(int x);    // Error!
```

3. Find the error in the following method definition:

```
// This method has an error!
public static double timesTwo(double num)
{
    double result = num * 2;
}
```

4. Find the error in the following method definition:

```
// This method has an error!
public static int half(double num)
{
    double result = num / 2.0;
    return result;
}
```

Algorithm Workbench

1. Examine the following method header, and then write an example call to the method:

```
public static void doSomething(int x)
```

2. Here is the code for the `displayValue` method, shown earlier in this chapter:

```java
public static void displayValue(int num)
{
    System.out.println("The value is " + num);
}
```

For each of the following code segments, indicate whether it will successfully compile or cause an error:

a. `displayValue(100);`
b. `displayValue(6.0);`
c. `short s = 5;`
   `displayValue(s);`
d. `long num = 1;`
   `displayValue(num);`
e. `displayValue(6.2f);`
f. `displayValue((int) 7.5);`

3. Look at the following method header:

```java
public static void myMethod(int a, int b, int c)
```

Now look at the following call to `myMethod`:

```java
myMethod(3, 2, 1);
```

When this call executes, what value will be stored in a? What value will be stored in b? What value will be stored in c?

4. What will the following program display?

```java
public class ChangeParam
{
    public static void main(String[] args)
    {
        int x = 1;
        double y = 3.4;
        System.out.println(x + " " + y);
        changeUs(x, y);
        System.out.println(x + " " + y);
    }

    public static void changeUs(int a, double b)
    {
        a = 0;
        b = 0.0;
        System.out.println(a + " " + b);
    }
}
```

5. A program contains the following method definition:

```
public static int cube(int num)
{
        return num * num * num;
}
```

Write a statement that passes the value 4 to this method and assigns its return value to a variable named `result`.

6. A program contains the following method:

```
public static void display(int arg1, double arg2, char arg3)
{
        System.out.println("The values are " + arg1 + ", " +
                            arg2 + ", and " + arg3);
}
```

Write a statement that calls this method and passes the following variables as arguments:

```
char initial = 'T';
int age = 25;
double income = 50000.00;
```

7. Write a method named `timesTen`. The method should accept a `double` argument, and return a `double` value that is ten times the value of the argument.

Short Answer

1. What is the "divide and conquer" approach to problem solving?

2. What is the difference between a void method and a value-returning method?

3. What is the difference between an argument and a parameter variable?

4. Where do you declare a parameter variable?

5. Explain what is meant by the phrase "pass by value."

6. Why do local variables lose their values between calls to the method in which they are declared?

Programming Challenges

1. showChar Method

Write a method named `showChar`. The method should accept two arguments: a reference to a `String` object and an integer. The integer argument is a character position within the `String`, with the first character being at position 0. When the method executes, it should display the character at that character position. Here is an example of a call to the method:

```
showChar("New York", 2);
```

In this call, the method will display the character w because it is in position 2. Demonstrate the method in a complete program.

2. Retail Price Calculator

VideoNote
The Retail
Price Calculator
Problem

Write a program that asks the user to enter an item's wholesale cost and its markup percentage. It should then display the item's retail price. For example:

- If an item's wholesale cost is 5.00 and its markup percentage is 100 percent, then the item's retail price is 10.00.
- If an item's wholesale cost is 5.00 and its markup percentage is 50 percent, then the item's retail price is 7.50.

The program should have a method named `calculateRetail` that receives the wholesale cost and the markup percentage as arguments, and returns the retail price of the item.

3. Rectangle Area—Complete the Program

The Student CD contains a partially written program named `AreaRectangle.java`. Your job is to complete the program. When it is complete, the program will ask the user to enter the width and length of a rectangle, and then display the rectangle's area. The program calls the following methods, which have not been written:

- `getLength`—This method should ask the user to enter the rectangle's length, and then return that value as a `double`.
- `getWidth`—This method should ask the user to enter the rectangle's width, and then return that value as a `double`.
- `getArea`—This method should accept the rectangle's length and width as arguments, and return the rectangle's area. The area is calculated by multiplying the length by the width.
- `displayData`—This method should accept the rectangle's length, width, and area as arguments, and display them in an appropriate message on the screen.

myCodeMate   4. Paint Job Estimator

A painting company has determined that for every 115 square feet of wall space, one gallon of paint and eight hours of labor will be required. The company charges $18.00 per hour for labor. Write a program that allows the user to enter the number of rooms to be painted and the price of the paint per gallon. It should also ask for the square feet of wall space in each room. The program should have methods that return the following data:

- The number of gallons of paint required
- The hours of labor required
- The cost of the paint
- The labor charges
- The total cost of the paint job

Then it should display the data on the screen.

5. Falling Distance

When an object is falling because of gravity, the following formula can be used to determine the distance the object falls in a specific time period:

$$d = \frac{1}{2} gt^2$$

The variables in the formula are as follows: d is the distance in meters, g is 9.8, and t is the amount of time, in seconds, that the object has been falling.

Write a method named `fallingDistance` that accepts an object's falling time (in seconds) as an argument. The method should return the distance, in meters, that the object has fallen during that time interval. Demonstrate the method by calling it in a loop that passes the values 1 through 10 as arguments, and displays the return value.

6. Celsius Temperature Table

The formula for converting a temperature from Fahrenheit to Celsius is

$$C = \frac{5}{9}(F - 32)$$

where F is the Fahrenheit temperature and C is the Celsius temperature. Write a method named `celsius` that accepts a Fahrenheit temperature as an argument. The method should return the temperature, converted to Celsius. Demonstrate the method by calling it in a loop that displays a table of the Fahrenheit temperatures 0 through 20 and their Celsius equivalents.

7. Test Average and Grade

Write a program that asks the user to enter five test scores. The program should display a letter grade for each score and the average test score. Write the following methods in the program:

- `calcAverage`—This method should accept five test scores as arguments and return the average of the scores.
- `determineGrade`—This method should accept a test score as an argument and return a letter grade for the score, based on the following grading scale:

Score	Letter Grade
90–100	A
80–89	B
70–79	C
60–69	D
Below 60	F

8. Conversion Program

Write a program that asks the user to enter a distance in meters. The program will then present the following menu of selections:

1. Convert to kilometers
2. Convert to inches
3. Convert to feet
4. Quit the program

The program will convert the distance to kilometers, inches, or feet, depending on the user's selection. Here are the specific requirements:

- Write a `void` method named `showKilometers`, which accepts the number of meters as an argument. The method should display the argument converted to kilometers. Convert the meters to kilometers using the following formula:

```
kilometers = meters * 0.001
```

- Write a void method named showInches, which accepts the number of meters as an argument. The method should display the argument converted to inches. Convert the meters to inches using the following formula:

  inches = meters * 39.37

- Write a void method named showFeet, which accepts the number of meters as an argument. The method should display the argument converted to feet. Convert the meters to feet using the following formula:

  feet = meters * 3.281

- Write a void method named menu that displays the menu of selections. This method should not accept any arguments.
- The program should continue to display the menu until the user enters 4 to quit the program.
- The program should not accept negative numbers for the distance in meters.
- If the user selects an invalid choice from the menu, the program should display an error message.

  Here is an example session with the program, using console input. The user's input is shown in bold.

```
Enter a distance in meters: 500 [Enter]
1. Convert to kilometers
2. Convert to inches
3. Convert to feet
4. Quit the program

Enter your choice: 1 [Enter]
500 meters is 0.5 kilometers.

1. Convert to kilometers
2. Convert to inches
3. Convert to feet
4. Quit the program

Enter your choice: 3 [Enter]
500 meters is 1640.5 feet.

1. Convert to kilometers
2. Convert to inches
3. Convert to feet
4. Quit the program

Enter your choice: 4 [Enter]
Bye!
```

9. Distance Traveled Modification

The distance a vehicle travels can be calculated as follows:

$Distance = Speed * Time$

Write a method named `distance` that accepts a vehicle's speed and time as arguments, and returns the distance the vehicle has traveled. Modify the "Distance Traveled" program you wrote in Chapter 4 (Programming Challenge 2) to use the method.

10. Stock Profit

The profit from the sale of a stock can be calculated as follows:

$$\text{Profit} = ((NS \times SP) - SC) - ((NS \times PP) + PC)$$

where NS is the number of shares, PP is the purchase price per share, PC is the purchase commission paid, SP is the sale price per share, and SC is the sale commission paid. If the calculation yields a positive value, then the sale of the stock resulted in a profit. If the calculation yields a negative number, then the sale resulted in a loss.

Write a method that accepts as arguments the number of shares, the purchase price per share, the purchase commission paid, the sale price per share, and the sale commission paid. The method should return the profit (or loss) from the sale of stock. Demonstrate the method in a program that asks the user to enter the necessary data and displays the amount of the profit or loss.

11. Multiple Stock Sales

Use the method that you wrote for Programming Challenge 10 (Stock Profit) in a program that calculates the total profit or loss from the sale of multiple stocks. The program should ask the user for the number of stock sales, and the necessary data for each stock sale. It should accumulate the profit or loss for each stock sale and then display the total.

12. Kinetic Energy

In physics, an object that is in motion is said to have kinetic energy. The following formula can be used to determine a moving object's kinetic energy:

$$KE = \tfrac{1}{2}\ mv^2$$

The variables in the formula are as follows: KE is the kinetic energy, m is the object's mass in kilograms, and v is the object's velocity, in meters per second.

Write a method named `kineticEnergy` that accepts an object's mass (in kilograms) and velocity (in meters per second) as arguments. The method should return the amount of kinetic energy that the object has. Demonstrate the method by calling it in a program that asks the user to enter values for mass and velocity.

myCodeMate ### 13. `isPrime` Method

A prime number is a number that is only evenly divisible by itself and 1. For example, the number 5 is prime because it can only be evenly divided by 1 and 5. The number 6, however, is not prime because it can be divided evenly by 1, 2, 3, and 6.

Write a method named `isPrime`, which takes an integer as an argument and returns `true` if the argument is a prime number, or `false` otherwise. Demonstrate the method in a complete program.

> **TIP:** Recall that the % operator divides one number by another, and returns the remainder of the division. In an expression such as num1 % num2, the % operator will return 0 if num1 is evenly divisible by num2.

14. Prime Number List

Use the isPrime method that you wrote in Programming Challenge 13 in a program that stores a list of all the prime numbers from 1 through 100 in a file.

15. Coin Toss

Write a method named coinToss that simulates the tossing of a coin. When you call the method, it should generate a random number in the range of 0 through 1. If the random number is 0, the method should display "heads." If the random number is 1, the method should display "tails." Demonstrate the method in a program that asks the user for the number of times that the coin should be tossed, and then simulates the tossing of the coin that number of times.

16. Present Value

Suppose you want to deposit a certain amount of money into a savings account, and then leave it alone to draw interest for the next 10 years. At the end of 10 years, you would like to have $10,000 in the account. How much do you need to deposit today to make that happen? You can use the following formula, which is known as the present value formula, to find out:

$$P = \frac{F}{(1 + r)^n}$$

The terms in the formula are as follows:

- P is the **present value**, or the amount that you need to deposit today.
- F is the **future value** that you want in the account. (In this case, F is $10,000.)
- r is the **annual interest rate**.
- n is the **number of years** that you plan to let the money sit in the account.

Write a method named presentValue that performs this calculation. The method should accept the future value, annual interest rate, and number of years as arguments. It should return the present value, which is the amount that you need to deposit today. Demonstrate the method in a program that lets the user experiment with different values for the formula's terms.

17. Rock, Paper, Scissors Game

Write a program that lets the user play the game of Rock, Paper, Scissors against the computer. The program should work as follows.

1. When the program begins, a random number in the range of 1 through 3 is generated. If the number is 1, then the computer has chosen rock. If the number is 2, then the computer has chosen paper. If the number is 3, then the computer has chosen scissors. (Don't display the computer's choice yet.)

2. The user enters his or her choice of "rock", "paper", or "scissors" at the keyboard. (You can use a menu if you prefer.)

3. The computer's choice is displayed.

4. A winner is selected according to the following rules:

    • If one player chooses rock and the other player chooses scissors, then rock wins. (The rock smashes the scissors.)

    • If one player chooses scissors and the other player chooses paper, then scissors wins. (Scissors cuts paper.)

    • If one player chooses paper and the other player chooses rock, then paper wins. (Paper wraps rock.)

    • If both players make the same choice, the game must be played again to determine the winner.

Be sure to divide the program into methods that perform each major task.

CHAPTER 6

A First Look at Classes

6.1 Classes and Objects

CONCEPT: A class is the blueprint for an object. It specifies the fields and methods a particular type of object has. From the class, one or more objects may be created.

There are primarily two methods of programming in use today: procedural and object oriented. The earliest programming languages were procedural, meaning a program was made of one or more procedures. A *procedure* is a set of programming language statements that, together, perform a specific task. The statements might gather input from the user, manipulate data stored in the computer's memory, and perform calculations or any other operation necessary to complete its task. The programs that you have written so far have been procedural in nature.

Procedures typically operate on data items that are separate from the procedures. In a procedural program, the data items are commonly passed from one procedure to another. As you might imagine, the focus of procedural programming is on the creation of procedures that operate on the program's data. The separation of data and the code that operates on the data can lead to problems, however, as the program becomes larger and more complex. For example, the data is stored in a particular format that consists of variables and more complex structures that are created from variables. The procedures that operate on the data must be designed with that format in mind. But, what happens if the format of the data is altered? Quite often, a program's specifications change, resulting in a redesigned data format. When the structure of the data changes, the code that operates on the data must also be changed to accept the new format. This results in added work for programmers and a greater opportunity for bugs to appear in the code.

This has helped influence the shift from procedural programming to object-oriented programming (OOP). Whereas procedural programming is centered on creating procedures, object-oriented programming is centered on creating objects. An *object* is a software entity that contains data and procedures. The data contained in an object is known as the object's *fields*. The procedures that an object performs are nothing more than methods. The object is, conceptually, a self-contained unit consisting of data (fields) and procedures (methods). This is illustrated in Figure 6-1.

Figure 6-1   An object contains data and procedures

NOTE: An object's fields are sometimes called attributes. The term "field" is most often used by Java programmers, however.

OOP addresses the problem of code/data separation through encapsulation and data hiding. *Encapsulation* refers to the combining of data and code into a single object. *Data hiding* refers to an object's ability to hide its data from code that is outside the object. Only the object's methods may then directly access and make changes to the object's data. An object typically hides its data, but allows outside code to access its methods. As shown in Figure 6-2, the object's methods provide programming statements outside the object with indirect access to the object's data.

When an object's internal data is hidden from outside code and access to that data is restricted to the object's methods, the data is protected from accidental corruption. In addition, the programming code outside the object does not need to know about the format or internal structure of the object's data. The code only needs to interact with the object's methods. When a programmer changes the structure of an object's internal data, he or she also modifies the object's methods so they may properly operate on the data. The way in which outside code interacts with the methods, however, does not change.

Figure 6-2   Code outside the object interacts with the object's methods

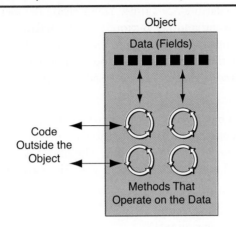

Object Reusability

In addition to solving the problems of code/data separation, the use of OOP has also been encouraged by the trend of *object reusability*. An object is not a stand-alone program, but is used by programs that need its service. For example, Sharon is a programmer who has developed an object for rendering 3D images. She is a math whiz and knows a lot about computer graphics, so her object is coded to perform all the necessary 3D mathematical operations and handle the computer's video hardware. Tom, who is writing a program for an architectural firm, needs his application to display 3D images of buildings. Because he is working under a tight deadline and does not possess a great deal of knowledge about computer graphics, he can use Sharon's object to perform the 3D rendering (for a small fee, of course!).

An Everyday Example of an Object

Think of your alarm clock as an object. It has the following fields:

- The current second (a value in the range of 0–59)
- The current minute (a value in the range of 0–59)
- The current hour (a value in the range of 1–12)
- The time the alarm is set for (a valid hour and minute)
- Whether the alarm is on or off ("on" or "off ")

As you can see, the fields are merely data values that define the *state* that the alarm clock is currently in. You, the user of the alarm clock object, cannot directly manipulate these fields because they are *private*. To change a field's value, you must use one of the object's methods. Here are some of the alarm clock object's methods:

- Set time
- Set alarm time
- Turn alarm on
- Turn alarm off

Each method manipulates one or more of the fields. For example, the "Set time" method allows you to set the alarm clock's time. You activate the method by pressing a button on top of the clock. By using another button, you can activate the "Set alarm time" method. In addition, another button allows you to execute the "Turn alarm on" and "Turn alarm off" methods. Notice that all of these methods can be activated by you, who are outside of the alarm clock. Methods that can be accessed by entities outside the object are known as *public methods*.

The alarm clock also has *private methods*, which are part of the object's private, internal workings. External entities (such as you, the user of the alarm clock) do not have direct access to the alarm clock's private methods. The object is designed to execute these methods automatically and hide the details from you. Here are the alarm clock object's private methods:

- Increment the current second
- Increment the current minute
- Increment the current hour
- Sound alarm

Every second the "Increment the current second" method executes. This changes the value of the current second field. If the current second field is set to 59 when this method executes, the method is programmed to reset the current second to 0, and then cause the "Increment current minute" method to execute. This method adds 1 to the current minute, unless it is set to 59. In that case, it resets the current minute to 0 and causes the "Increment current hour" method to execute. (It might also be noted that the "Increment current minute" method compares the new time to the alarm time. If the two times match and the alarm is turned on, the "Sound alarm" method is executed.)

Classes and Objects

Now let's discuss how objects are created in software. Before an object can be created, it must be designed by a programmer. The programmer determines the fields and methods that are necessary, and then creates a class. You already know that a class can be used as a container for a program. Classes also have another use in Java: A class can specify the fields and methods that a particular type of object may have. Think of a class as a "blueprint" that objects may be created from. So, a class is not an object, but it can be a description of an object. When the program is running, it can use the class to create, in memory, as many objects of a specific type as needed. Each object that is created from a class is called an *instance* of the class.

For example, Jessica is an entomologist (someone who studies insects) and she also enjoys writing computer programs. She designs a program to catalog different types of insects. As part of the program, she creates a class named `Insect`, which specifies fields and methods for holding and manipulating data common to all types of insects. The `Insect` class is not an object, but a specification that objects may be created from. Next, she writes programming statements that create a `housefly` object, which is an instance of the `Insect` class. The `housefly` object is an entity that occupies computer memory and stores data about a `housefly`. It has the fields and methods specified by the `Insect` class. Then she writes programming statements that create a `mosquito` object. The `mosquito` object is also an instance of the `Insect` class. It has its own area in memory, and stores data about a mosquito. Although the `housefly` and `mosquito` objects are two separate entities in the computer's memory, they were both created from the `Insect` class. This means that each of the objects have the fields and methods described by the `Insect` class. This is illustrated in Figure 6-3.

Figure 6-3 The `housefly` and `mosquito` objects are instances of the `Insect` class

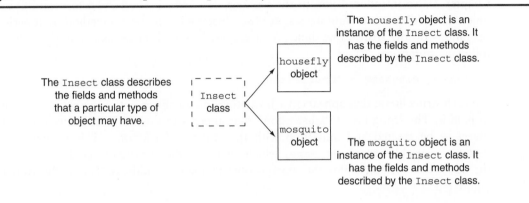

The cookie cutter metaphor is often used to describe the difference between classes and objects. While a cookie cutter itself is not a cookie, it describes a cookie. The cookie cutter can be used to make several cookies, as shown in Figure 6-4. Think of a class as a cookie cutter and the objects created from the class as cookies.

Figure 6-4 The cookie cutter metaphor

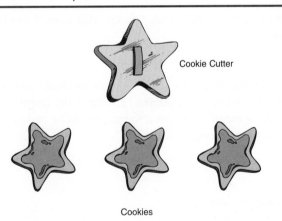

So, a class is not an object, but a description of an object. Once a class has been written, you can use the class to create as many objects as needed. Each object is considered an instance of the class. All of the objects that are created from the same class will have the fields and methods described by the class.

Objects versus Primitive Variables

Chapter 2 introduced you to the Java primitive data types: `byte`, `short`, `int`, `long`, `char`, `float`, `double`, and `boolean`. You use these data types to create variables, which are storage locations in the computer's memory. A primitive data type is called "primitive" because a variable created with a primitive data type has no built-in capabilities other than storing a value.

Chapter 2 also introduced you to the `String` class, which allows you to create `String` objects. In addition to storing strings, `String` objects have numerous methods that perform operations on the strings they hold. As a review, let's look at an example. Consider the following statement:

```
String cityName = "Charleston";
```

For each string literal that appears in a Java program, a `String` object is created in memory to hold it. The string literal "Charleston" that appears in this statement causes a `String` object to be created and initialized with the string "Charleston". This statement also declares a variable named `cityName`, which references the `String` object. This means that the `cityName` variable holds the `String` object's memory address. This is illustrated in Figure 6-5.

Figure 6-5   The `cityName` variable references a `String` object

Assume that the same program has an `int` variable named `stringSize`. Look at the following statement:

```
stringSize = cityName.length();
```

This statement calls the `String` class's `length` method, which returns the length of a string. The expression `cityName.length()` returns the length of the string referenced by `cityName`. After this statement executes, the `stringSize` variable will contain the value 10, which is the length of the string "Charleston".

Suppose we create several objects from the `String` class, as demonstrated with the following code:

```
String person = "Jenny";
String pet = "Fido";
String favoriteColor = "Blue";
```

As illustrated in Figure 6-6, this code creates three `String` objects in memory, which are referenced by the `person`, `pet`, and `favoriteColor` variables.

Figure 6-6   Three variables referencing three `String` objects

Although each of the three `String` objects holds different data, they are all identical in design. For example, we can call the `length` method for each of the objects as follows:

```
personSize = person.length();
petSize = pet.length();
colorSize = favoriteColor.length();
```

After these statements execute, `personSize` will hold the length of the string referenced by `person`, `petSize` will hold the length of the string referenced by `pet`, and `colorSize` will hold the length of the string referenced by `favoriteColor`.

As you saw in Chapter 2, the `String` class has other methods in addition to `length`. These examples illustrate one of the differences between an object created from a class and a variable created from a primitive data type. Class objects normally have methods that perform useful operations on their data. Primitive variables, however, only store data and have no methods. Any operations performed on a primitive variable must be written in code that is external to the variable.

Building a Simple Class Step by Step

In this section we will write a class named `Rectangle`. Each object that is created from the `Rectangle` class will be able to hold data about a rectangle. Specifically, a `Rectangle` object will have the following fields:

- `length`. The `length` field will hold the rectangle's length.
- `width`. The `width` field will hold the rectangle's width.

The `Rectangle` class will also have the following methods:

- `setLength`. The `setLength` method will store a value in an object's `length` field.
- `setWidth`. The `setWidth` method will store a value in an object's `width` field.
- `getLength`. The `getLength` method will return the value in an object's `length` field.
- `getWidth`. The `getWidth` method will return the value in an object's `width` field.

- • getArea. The getArea method will return the area of the rectangle, which is the result of an object's length multiplied by its width.

When designing a class it is often helpful to draw a UML diagram. UML stands for Unified Modeling Language. It provides a set of standard diagrams for graphically depicting object-oriented systems. Figure 6-7 shows the general layout of a UML diagram for a class. Notice that the diagram is a box that is divided into three sections. The top section is where you write the name of the class. The middle section holds a list of the class's fields. The bottom section holds a list of the class's methods.

Figure 6-7 General layout of a UML diagram for a class

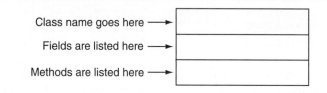

Class name goes here ⟶

Fields are listed here ⟶

Methods are listed here ⟶

Following this layout, Figure 6-8 shows a UML diagram for our Rectangle class. Throughout this book we frequently use UML diagrams to illustrate classes.

Figure 6-8 UML diagram for the Rectangle class

Rectangle

length
width

setLength()
setWidth()
getLength()
getWidth()
getArea()

Writing the Code for a Class

Now that we have identified the fields and methods that we want the Rectangle class to have, let's write the Java code. First, we use an editor to create a new file named *Rectangle.java*. In the *Rectangle.java* file we will start by writing a general class "skeleton" as follows:

VideoNote
Writing Classes and
Creating Objects

```
public class Rectangle
{
}
```

The key word public, which appears in the first line, is an access specifier. An access specifier indicates how the class may be accessed. The public access specifier indicates that the class will be publicly available to code that is written outside the *Rectangle.java* file. Almost all of the classes that we write in this book are public.

Following the access specifier is the key word `class`, followed by `Rectangle`, which is the name of the class. On the next line an opening brace appears, which is followed by a closing brace. The contents of the class, which are the fields and methods, will be written inside these braces. The general format of a class definition is as follows:

```
AccessSpecifier class Name
{
    Members
}
```

In general terms, the fields and methods that belong to a class are referred to as the class's *members*.

Writing the Code for the Class Fields

Let's continue writing our `Rectangle` class by filling in the code for some of its members. First we will write the code for the class's two fields, `length` and `width`. We will use variables of the `double` data type for the fields. The new lines of code are shown in bold, as follows:

```
public class Rectangle
{
    private double length;
    private double width;
}
```

These two lines of code that we have added declare the variables `length` and `width`. Notice that both declarations begin with the key word `private`, preceding the data type. The key word `private` is an access specifier. It indicates that these variables may not be accessed by statements outside the class.

Recall from our earlier discussion that an object can perform data hiding, which means that critical data stored inside the object is protected from code outside the object. In Java, a class's private members are hidden and can be accessed only by methods that are members of the same class. When an object's internal data is hidden from outside code, and access to that data is restricted to the object's methods, the data is protected from accidental corruption. It is a common practice in object-oriented programming to make all of a class's fields private and to provide access to those fields through methods.

When writing classes, you will primarily use the `private` and `public` access specifiers for class members. Table 6-1 summarizes these access specifiers.

Table 6-1 Summary of the `private` and `public` access specifiers for class members

Access Specifier	Description
private	When the `private` access specifier is applied to a class member, the member cannot be accessed by code outside the class. The member can be accessed only by methods that are members of the same class.
public	When the `public` access specifier is applied to a class member, the member can be accessed by code inside the class or outside.

Writing the `setLength` Method

Now we will begin writing the class methods. We will start with the `setLength` method. This method will allow code outside the class to store a value in the `length` field. Code Listing 6-1 shows the `Rectangle` class at this stage of its development. The `setLength` method is in lines 17 through 20. (This file is stored in the Student CD source code folder *Chapter 06\Rectangle Class Phase 1*.)

Code Listing 6-1 (`Rectangle.java`)

```
 1  /**
 2      Rectangle class, phase 1
 3      Under construction!
 4  */
 5
 6  public class Rectangle
 7  {
 8      private double length;
 9      private double width;
10
11      /**
12          The setLength method stores a value in the
13          length field.
14          @param len The value to store in length.
15      */
16
17      public void setLength(double len)
18      {
19          length = len;
20      }
21  }
```

In lines 11 through 15, we write a block comment that gives a brief description of the method. It's important always to write comments that describe a class's methods so that in the future, anyone reading the code will understand it. The definition of the method appears in lines 17 through 20. Here is the method header:

```
public void setLength(double len)
```

The method header looks very much like any other method header that you learned to write in Chapter 5. Let's look at the parts as follows:

- `public`. The key word `public` is an access specifier. It indicates that the method may be called by statements outside the class.
- `void`. This is the method's return type. The key word `void` indicates that the method returns no data to the statement that called it.
- `setLength`. This is the name of the method.
- `(double len)`. This is the declaration of a parameter variable of the `double` data type, named `len`.

Figure 6-9 labels each part of the header for the `setLength` method.

Figure 6-9 Header for the `setLength` method

Notice that the word `static` does not appear in the method header. When a method is designed to work on an instance of a class, it is referred to as an *instance method*, and you do not write the word `static` in the header. Because this method will store a value in the `length` field of an instance of the `Rectangle` class, it is an instance method. We will discuss this in greater detail later.

After the header, the body of the method appears inside a set of braces:

```
{
    length = len;
}
```

The body of this method has only one statement, which assigns the value of `len` to the `length` field. When the method executes, the `len` parameter variable will hold the value of an argument that is passed to the method. That value is assigned to the `length` field.

Before adding the other methods to the class, it might help if we demonstrate how the `setLength` method works. First, notice that the `Rectangle` class does not have a `main` method. This class is not a complete program, but is a blueprint that `Rectangle` objects may be created from. Other programs will use the `Rectangle` class to create objects. The programs that create and use these objects will have their own `main` methods. We can demonstrate the class's `setLength` method by saving the current contents of the *Rectangle.java* file and then creating the program shown in Code Listing 6-2.

Code Listing 6-2   (`LengthDemo.java`)

```
1   /**
2       This program demonstrates the Rectangle class's
3       setLength method.
4   */
5
6   public class LengthDemo
7   {
8       public static void main(String[] args)
9       {
10          // Create a Rectangle object and assign its
11          // address to the box variable.
```

```
12          Rectangle box = new Rectangle();
13
14          // Indicate what we are doing.
15          System.out.println("Sending the value 10.0 " +
16                             "to the setLength method.");
17
18          // Call the box object's setLength method.
19          box.setLength(10.0);
20
21          // Indicate we are done.
22          System.out.println("Done.");
23     }
24  }
```

Program Output

```
Sending the value 10.0 to the setLength method.
Done.
```

The program in Code Listing 6-2 must be saved as *LengthDemo.java* in the same folder or directory as the file *Rectangle.java*. The following command can then be used with the Sun JDK to compile the program:

```
javac LengthDemo.java
```

When the compiler reads the source code for LengthDemo.java and sees that a class named Rectangle is being used, it looks in the current folder or directory for the file *Rectangle.class*. That file does not exist, however, because we have not yet compiled *Rectangle.java*. So, the compiler searches for the file Rectangle.java and compiles it. This creates the file *Rectangle.class*, which makes the Rectangle class available. The compiler then finishes compiling LengthDemo.java. The resulting *LengthDemo.class* file may be executed with the following command:

```
java LengthDemo
```

The output of the program is shown at the bottom of Code Listing 6-2.

Let's look at each statement in this program's main method. First, the program uses the following statement, in line 12, to create a Rectangle object and associate it with a variable:

```
Rectangle box = new Rectangle();
```

Let's dissect the statement into two parts. The first part of the statement,

```
Rectangle box
```

declares a variable named box. The data type of the variable is Rectangle. (Because the word Rectangle is not the name of a primitive data type, Java assumes it to be the name of a class.) Recall that a variable of a class type is a reference variable, and it holds the memory address of an object. When a reference variable holds an object's memory address, it is said that the variable references the object. So, the variable `box` will be used to reference a `Rectangle` object. The second part of the statement is as follows:

```
= new Rectangle();
```

This part of the statement uses the key word `new`, which creates an object in memory. After the word `new`, the name of a class followed by a set of parentheses appears. This specifies the class that the object should be created from. In this case, an object of the `Rectangle` class is created. The memory address of the object is then assigned (by the = operator) to the variable `box`. After the statement executes, the variable `box` will reference the object that was created in memory. This is illustrated in Figure 6-10.

Figure 6-10   The box variable references a `Rectangle` class object

Notice that Figure 6-10 shows the `Rectangle` object's `length` and `width` fields set to 0. All of a class's numeric fields are initialized to 0 by default.

> **TIP:** The parentheses in this statement are required. It would be an error to write the statement as follows:
>
> ```
> Rectangle box = new Rectangle;   // ERROR!!
> ```

The statement in lines 15 and 16 uses the `System.out.println` method to display a message on the screen. The next statement, in line 19, calls the `box` object's `setLength` method as follows:

```
box.setLength(10.0);
```

This statement passes the argument 10.0 to the `setLength` method. When the method executes, the value 10.0 is copied into the `len` parameter variable. The method assigns the value of `len` to the `length` field and then terminates. Figure 6-11 shows the state of the `box` object after the method executes.

Figure 6-11   The state of the box object after the `setLength` method executes

Writing the setWidth Method

Now that we've seen how the setLength method works, let's add the setWidth method to the Rectangle class. The setWidth method is similar to setLength. It accepts an argument, which is assigned to the width field. Code Listing 6-3 shows the updated Rectangle class. The setWidth method is in lines 28 through 31. (This file is stored in the Student CD source code folder *Chapter 06\Rectangle Class Phase 2*.)

Code Listing 6-3 (Rectangle.java)

```java
1   /**
2       Rectangle class, phase 2
3       Under construction!
4   */
5
6   public class Rectangle
7   {
8       private double length;
9       private double width;
10
11      /**
12          The setLength method stores a value in the
13          length field.
14          @param len The value to store in length.
15      */
16
17      public void setLength(double len)
18      {
19          length = len;
20      }
21
22      /**
23          The setWidth method stores a value in the
24          width field.
25          @param w The value to store in width.
26      */
27
28      public void setWidth(double w)
29      {
30          width = w;
31      }
32  }
```

The `setWidth` method has a parameter variable named `w`, which is assigned to the `width` field. For example, assume that `box` references a `Rectangle` object and the following statement is executed:

```
box.setWidth(20.0);
```

After this statement executes, the `box` object's `width` field will be set to 20.0.

Writing the `getLength` and `getWidth` Methods

Because the `length` and `width` fields are private, we wrote the `setLength` and `setWidth` methods to allow code outside the `Rectangle` class to store values in the fields. We must also write methods that allow code outside the class to get the values that are stored in these fields. That's what the `getLength` and `getWidth` methods will do. The `getLength` method will return the value stored in the `length` field, and the `getWidth` method will return the value stored in the `width` field.

Here is the code for the `getLength` method:

```
public double getLength()
{
     return length;
}
```

Assume that `size` is a `double` variable and that `box` references a `Rectangle` object, and the following statement is executed:

```
size = box.getLength();
```

This statement assigns the value that is returned from the `getLength` method to the `size` variable. After this statement executes, the `size` variable will contain the same value as the `box` object's `length` field.

The `getWidth` method is similar to `getLength`. The code for the method follows:

```
public double getWidth()
{
     return width;
}
```

This method returns the value that is stored in the `width` field. For example, assume that `size` is a `double` variable and that `box` references a `Rectangle` object, and the following statement is executed:

```
size = box.getWidth();
```

This statement assigns the value that is returned from the `getWidth` method to the `size` variable. After this statement executes, the `size` variable will contain the same value as the `box` object's `width` field.

Code Listing 6-4 shows the `Rectangle` class with all of the members we have discussed so far. The code for the `getLength` and `getWidth` methods is shown in lines 33 through 53. (This file is stored in the Student CD source code folder *Chapter 06\Rectangle Class Phase 3.*)

Code Listing 6-4 (`Rectangle.java`)

```
 1 /**
 2    Rectangle class, phase 3
 3    Under construction!
 4 */
 5
 6 public class Rectangle
 7 {
 8    private double length;
 9    private double width;
10
11    /**
12       The setLength method stores a value in the
13       length field.
14       @param len The value to store in length.
15    */
16
17    public void setLength(double len)
18    {
19       length = len;
20    }
21
22    /**
23       The setWidth method stores a value in the
24       width field.
25       @param w The value to store in width.
26    */
27
28    public void setWidth(double w)
29    {
30       width = w;
31    }
32
33    /**
34       The getLength method returns a Rectangle
35       object's length.
36       @return The value in the length field.
37    */
38
39    public double getLength()
40    {
41       return length;
42    }
43
44    /**
45       The getWidth method returns a Rectangle
46       object's width.
```

```
47            @return The value in the width field.
48      */
49
50      public double getWidth()
51      {
52         return width;
53      }
54 }
```

Before continuing we should demonstrate how these methods work. Look at the program in Code Listing 6-5. (This file is also stored in the Student CD source code folder *Chapter 06\Rectangle Class Phase 3.*)

Code Listing 6-5 (`LengthWidthDemo.java`)

```
1  /**
2      This program demonstrates the Rectangle class's
3      setLength, setWidth, getLength, and getWidth methods.
4  */
5
6  public class LengthWidthDemo
7  {
8      public static void main(String[] args)
9      {
10         // Create a Rectangle object.
11         Rectangle box = new Rectangle();
12
13         // Call the object's setLength method, passing 10.0
14         // as an argument.
15         box.setLength(10.0);
16
17         // Call the object's setWidth method, passing 20.0
18         // as an argument.
19         box.setWidth(20.0);
20
21         // Display the object's length and width.
22         System.out.println("The box's length is " +
23                            box.getLength());
24         System.out.println("The box's width is " +
25                            box.getWidth());
26      }
27 }
```

Program Output

```
The box's length is 10.0
The box's width is 20.0
```

Let's take a closer look at the program. In line 11 this program creates a `Rectangle` object, which is referenced by the `box` variable. Then the following statements execute in lines 15 and 19:

```
box.setLength(10.0);
box.setWidth(20.0);
```

After these statements execute, the `box` object's `length` field is set to 10.0 and its `width` field is set to 20.0. The state of the object is shown in Figure 6-12.

Figure 6-12 State of the `box` object

Next, the following statement in lines 22 and 23 executes as follows:

```
System.out.println("The box's length is " +
                   box.getLength());
```

This statement calls the `box.getLength()` method, which returns the value 10.0. The following message is displayed on the screen:

```
The box's length is 10.0
```

Then the following statement executes in lines 24 and 25:

```
System.out.println("The box's width is " +
                   box.getWidth());
```

This statement calls the `box.getWidth()` method, which returns the value 20.0. The following message is displayed on the screen:

```
The box's width is 20.0
```

Writing the `getArea` Method

The last method we will write for the `Rectangle` class is `getArea`. This method returns the area of a rectangle, which is its length multiplied by its width. Here is the code for the `getArea` method:

```
public double getArea()
{
    return length * width;
}
```

This method returns the result of the mathematical expression `length * width`. For example, assume that `area` is a `double` variable and that `box` references a `Rectangle` object, and the following code is executed:

```
box.setLength(10.0);
box.setWidth(20.0);
area = box.getArea();
```

The last statement assigns the value that is returned from the getArea method to the area variable. After this statement executes, the area variable will contain the value 200.0.

Code Listing 6-6 shows the Rectangle class with all of the members we have discussed so far. The getArea method appears in lines 61 through 64. (This file is stored in the Student CD source code folder *Chapter 06\Rectangle Class Phase 4.*)

Code Listing 6-6   (`Rectangle.java`)

```java
 1  /**
 2      Rectangle class, phase 4
 3      Under construction!
 4  */
 5
 6  public class Rectangle
 7  {
 8      private double length;
 9      private double width;
10
11      /**
12         The setLength method stores a value in the
13         length field.
14         @param len The value to store in length.
15      */
16
17      public void setLength(double len)
18      {
19          length = len;
20      }
21
22      /**
23         The setWidth method stores a value in the
24         width field.
25         @param w The value to store in width.
26      */
27
28      public void setWidth(double w)
29      {
30          width = w;
31      }
32
33      /**
34         The getLength method returns a Rectangle
35         object's length.
```

```
36          @return The value in the length field.
37      */
38
39      public double getLength()
40      {
41          return length;
42      }
43
44      /**
45          The getWidth method returns a Rectangle
46          object's width.
47          @return The value in the width field.
48      */
49
50      public double getWidth()
51      {
52          return width;
53      }
54
55      /**
56          The getArea method returns a Rectangle
57          object's area.
58          @return The product of length times width.
59      */
60
61      public double getArea()
62      {
63          return length * width;
64      }
65  }
```

The program in Code Listing 6-7 demonstrates all the methods of the Rectangle class, including getArea. (This file is also stored in the Student CD source code folder *Chapter 06\Rectangle Class Phase 4.*)

Code Listing 6-7   (RectangleDemo.java)

```
1   /**
2       This program demonstrates the Rectangle class's
3       setLength, setWidth, getLength, getWidth, and
4       getArea methods.
5   */
6
7   public class RectangleDemo
8   {
9       public static void main(String[] args)
```

```
10     {
11         // Create a Rectangle object.
12         Rectangle box = new Rectangle();
13
14         // Set length to 10.0 and width to 20.0.
15         box.setLength(10.0);
16         box.setWidth(20.0);
17
18         // Display the length.
19         System.out.println("The box's length is " +
20                             box.getLength());
21
22         // Display the width.
23         System.out.println("The box's width is " +
24                             box.getWidth());
25
26         // Display the area.
27         System.out.println("The box's area is " +
28                             box.getArea());
29     }
30 }
```

Program Output

```
The box's length is 10.0
The box's width is 20.0
The box's area is 200.0
```

Accessor and Mutator Methods

As mentioned earlier, it is a common practice to make all of a class's fields private and to provide public methods for accessing and changing those fields. This ensures that the object owning those fields is in control of all changes being made to them. A method that gets a value from a class's field but does not change it is known as an *accessor method*. A method that stores a value in a field or changes the value of a field in some other way is known as a *mutator method*. In the Rectangle class, the methods getLength and getWidth are accessors, and the methods setLength and setWidth are mutators.

 NOTE: Mutator methods are sometimes called "setters" and accessor methods are sometimes called "getters."

Avoiding Stale Data

In the Rectangle class, the getLength and getWidth methods return the values stored in fields, but the getArea method returns the result of a calculation. You might be wondering why the area of the rectangle is not stored in a field, like the length and the width. The area is not stored in a field because it could potentially become stale. When the value of an item is dependent on other data and that item is not updated when the other data is changed, it is said that the item has become *stale*. If the area of the rectangle were stored in a field, the value of the field would become incorrect as soon as either the `length` or `width` fields changed.

When designing a class, you should take care not to store in a field calculated data that can potentially become stale. Instead, provide a method that returns the result of the calculation.

Showing Access Specification in UML Diagrams

In Figure 6-8 we presented a UML diagram for the `Rectangle` class. The diagram listed all of the members of the class but did not indicate which members were private and which were public. In a UML diagram, you have the option to place a – character before a member name to indicate that it is private, or a + character to indicate that it is public. Figure 6-13 shows the UML diagram modified to include this notation.

Figure 6-13   UML diagram for the `Rectangle` class

Data Type and Parameter Notation in UML Diagrams

The Unified Modeling Language also provides notation that you may use to indicate the data types of fields, methods, and parameter variables. To indicate the data type of a field, place a colon followed by the name of the data type after the name of the field. For example, the `length` field in the `Rectangle` class is a `double`. It could be listed in the UML diagram as follows:

```
- length : double
```

The return type of a method can be listed in the same manner: After the method's name, place a colon followed by the return type. The `Rectangle` class's `getLength` method returns a `double`, so it could be listed in the UML diagram as follows:

```
+ getLength() : double
```

Parameter variables and their data types may be listed inside a method's parentheses. For example, the `Rectangle` class's `setLength` method has a `double` parameter named `len`, so it could be listed in the UML diagram as follows:

```
+ setLength(len : double) : void
```

Figure 6-14 shows a UML diagram for the `Rectangle` class with parameter and data type notation.

Figure 6-14   UML diagram for the `Rectangle` class with parameter and data type notation

Rectangle
– length : double – width : double
+ setLength(len : double) : void + setWidth(w : double) : void + getLength() : double + getWidth() : double + getArea() : double

Layout of Class Members

Notice that in the `Rectangle` class, the field variables are declared first and then the methods are defined. You are not required to write field declarations before the method definitions. In fact, some programmers prefer to write the definitions for the public methods first and write the declarations for the private fields last. Regardless of which style you use, you should be consistent. In this book we always write the field declarations first, followed by the method definitions. Figure 6-15 shows this layout.

Figure 6-15   Typical layout of class members

```
public class ClassName
{

        Field declarations

        Method definitions

}
```

 Checkpoint

6.1   You hear someone make the following comment: "A blueprint is a design for a house. A carpenter can use the blueprint to build the house. If the carpenter wishes, he or she can build several identical houses from the same blueprint." Think of this as a metaphor for classes and objects. Does the blueprint represent a class, or does it represent an object?

6.2 In this chapter we use the metaphor of a cookie cutter and cookies that are made from the cookie cutter to describe classes and objects. In this metaphor, are objects the cookie cutter, or the cookies?

6.3 When a variable is said to reference an object, what is actually stored in the variable?

6.4 A string literal, such as `"Joe"`, causes what type of object to be created?

6.5 Look at the UML diagram in Figure 6-16 and answer the following questions:
   a) What is the name of the class?
   b) What are the fields?
   c) What are the methods?
   d) What are the private members?
   e) What are the public members?

6.6 Assume that limo is a variable that references an instance of the class shown in Figure 6-16. Write a statement that calls `setMake` and passes the argument `"Cadillac"`.

Figure 6-16 UML diagram

```
┌─────────────────────┐
│        Car          │
├─────────────────────┤
│ – make              │
│ – yearModel         │
├─────────────────────┤
│ + setMake()         │
│ + setYearModel()    │
│ + getMake()         │
│ + getYearModel()    │
└─────────────────────┘
```

6.7 What does the key word new do?

6.8 What is an accessor? What is a mutator?

6.9 What is a stale data item?

6.2 Instance Fields and Methods

CONCEPT: Each instance of a class has its own set of fields, which are known as instance fields. You can create several instances of a class and store different values in each instance's fields. The methods that operate on an instance of a class are known as instance methods.

The program in Code Listing 6-7 creates one instance of the `Rectangle` class. It is possible to create many instances of the same class, each with its own data. For example, the `RoomAreas.java` program in Code Listing 6-8 creates three instances of the `Rectangle` class, referenced by the variables `kitchen`, `bedroom`, and `den`. Figure 6-17 shows example interaction with the program. (The file in Code Listing 6-8 is stored in the Student CD source code folder *Chapter 06\Rectangle Class Phase 4*.)

Code Listing 6-8   (`RoomAreas.java`)

```java
1    import javax.swing.JOptionPane;
2
3    /**
4        This program creates three instances of the
5        Rectangle class.
6    */
7
8    public class RoomAreas
9    {
10       public static void main(String[] args)
11       {
12          double number;          // To hold a number
13          double totalArea;       // The total area
14          String input;           // To hold user input
15
16          // Create three Rectangle objects.
17          Rectangle kitchen = new Rectangle();
18          Rectangle bedroom = new Rectangle();
19          Rectangle den = new Rectangle();
20
21          // Get and store the dimensions of the kitchen.
22          input = JOptionPane.showInputDialog("What is the " +
23                                     "kitchen's length?");
24          number = Double.parseDouble(input);
25          kitchen.setLength(number);
26          input = JOptionPane.showInputDialog("What is the " +
27                                     "kitchen's width?");
28          number = Double.parseDouble(input);
29          kitchen.setWidth(number);
30
31          // Get and store the dimensions of the bedroom.
32          input = JOptionPane.showInputDialog("What is the " +
33                                     "bedroom's length?");
34          number = Double.parseDouble(input);
35          bedroom.setLength(number);
36          input = JOptionPane.showInputDialog("What is the " +
37                                     "bedroom's width?");
38          number = Double.parseDouble(input);
39          bedroom.setWidth(number);
40
41          // Get and store the dimensions of the den.
42          input = JOptionPane.showInputDialog("What is the " +
43                                     "den's length?");
44          number = Double.parseDouble(input);
45          den.setLength(number);
```

```
46          input = JOptionPane.showInputDialog("What is the " +
47                                              "den's width?");
48          number = Double.parseDouble(input);
49          den.setWidth(number);
50
51          // Calculate the total area of the rooms.
52          totalArea = kitchen.getArea() + bedroom.getArea()
53                      + den.getArea();
54
55          // Display the total area of the rooms.
56          JOptionPane.showMessageDialog(null, "The total area " +
57                                        "of the rooms is " + totalArea);
58
59          System.exit(0);
60     }
61 }
```

Figure 6-17 Interaction with the `RoomAreas.java` program

In lines 17, 18, and 19, the following code creates three objects, each an instance of the Rectangle class:

```
Rectangle kitchen = new Rectangle();
Rectangle bedroom = new Rectangle();
Rectangle den = new Rectangle();
```

Figure 6-18 illustrates how the kitchen, bedroom, and den variables reference the objects.

Figure 6-18   The kitchen, bedroom, and den variables reference Rectangle objects

In the example session with the program, the user enters 10 and 14 as the length and width of the kitchen, 15 and 12 as the length and width of the bedroom, and 20 and 30 as the length and width of the den. Figure 6-19 shows the states of the objects after these values are stored in them.

Figure 6-19   States of the objects after data has been stored in them

Notice from Figure 6-19 that each instance of the `Rectangle` class has its own `length` and `width` variables. For this reason, the variables are known as *instance variables*, or *instance fields*. Every instance of a class has its own set of instance fields and can store its own values in those fields.

The methods that operate on an instance of a class are known as *instance methods*. All of the methods in the `Rectangle` class are instance methods because they perform operations on specific instances of the class. For example, look at the following statement in line 25 of the `RoomAreas.java` program:

```
kitchen.setLength(number);
```

This statement calls the `setLength` method, which stores a value in the `kitchen` object's `length` field. Now look at the following statement in line 35:

```
bedroom.setLength(number);
```

This statement also calls the `setLength` method, but this time it stores a value in the `bedroom` object's `length` field. Likewise, the following statement in line 45 calls the `setLength` method to store a value in the `den` object's `length` field:

```
den.setLength(number);
```

The `setLength` method stores a value in a specific instance of the `Rectangle` class. This is true of all of the methods that are members of the `Rectangle` class.

NOTE: As previously mentioned, instance methods do not have the key word `static` in their headers.

Checkpoint

6.10 Assume that r1 and r2 are variables that reference `Rectangle` objects, and the following statements are executed:

```
r1.setLength(5.0);
r2.setLength(10.0);
r1.setWidth(20.0);
r2.setWidth(15.0);
```

Fill in the boxes in Figure 6-20 that represent each object's length and width fields.

Figure 6-20 Fill in the boxes for each field

6.3 Constructors

CONCEPT: A constructor is a method that is automatically called when an object is created.

VideoNote
Initializing an Object with a Constructor

A constructor is a method that is automatically called when an instance of a class is created. Constructors normally perform initialization or setup operations, such as storing initial values in instance fields. They are called "constructors" because they help construct an object.

A constructor method has the same name as the class. For example, Code Listing 6-9 shows the first few lines of a new version of the `Rectangle` class. In this version of the class, a constructor has been added. (This file is stored in the Student CD source code folder *Chapter 06\Rectangle Class Phase 5*.)

Code Listing 6-9 `(Rectangle.java)`

```
1  /**
2      Rectangle class, phase 5
3  */
4
5  public class Rectangle
6  {
7      private double length;
8      private double width;
9
10     /**
11         Constructor
12         @param len The length of the rectangle.
13         @param w The width of the rectangle.
14     */
15
16     public Rectangle(double len, double w)
17     {
18         length = len;
19         width = w;
20     }
```

. . . The remainder of the class has not changed, and is not shown.

This constructor accepts two arguments, which are passed into the `len` and `w` parameter variables. The parameter variables are then assigned to the `length` and `width` fields.

Notice that the constructor's header doesn't specify a return type—not even `void`. This is because constructors are not executed by explicit method calls and cannot return a value.

The method header for a constructor takes the following general format:

```
AccessSpecifier ClassName(Parameters...)
```

Here is an example statement that declares the variable box, creates a Rectangle object, and passes the values 7.0 and 14.0 to the constructor.

```
Rectangle box = new Rectangle(7.0, 14.0);
```

After this statement executes, box will reference a Rectangle object whose length field is set to 7 and whose width field is set to 14. The program in Code Listing 6-10 demonstrates the Rectangle class constructor. (This file is also stored in the Student CD source code folder *Chapter 06\Rectangle Class Phase 5.*)

Code Listing 6-10 (ConstructorDemo.java)

```java
 1  /**
 2      This program demonstrates the Rectangle class's
 3      constructor.
 4  */
 5
 6  public class ConstructorDemo
 7  {
 8      public static void main(String[] args)
 9      {
10          // Create a Rectangle object, passing 5.0 and
11          // 15.0 as arguments to the constructor.
12          Rectangle box = new Rectangle(5.0, 15.0);
13
14          // Display the length.
15          System.out.println("The box's length is " +
16                              box.getLength());
17
18          // Display the width.
19          System.out.println("The box's width is " +
20                              box.getWidth());
21
22          // Display the area.
23          System.out.println("The box's area is " +
24                              box.getArea());
25      }
26  }
```

Program Output

```
The box's length is 5.0
The box's width is 15.0
The box's area is 75.0
```

Showing Constructors in a UML Diagram

There is more than one accepted way of showing a class's constructor in a UML diagram. In this book, we simply show a constructor just as any other method, except we list no return type. Figure 6-21 shows a UML diagram for the `Rectangle` class with the constructor listed.

Figure 6-21   UML diagram for the `Rectangle` class showing the constructor

```
                  ┌─────────────────────────────────────────┐
                  │                Rectangle                │
                  ├─────────────────────────────────────────┤
                  │ − length : double                       │
                  │ − width : double                        │
                  ├─────────────────────────────────────────┤
                  │ + Rectangle(len : double, w : double)   │
                  │ + setLength(len : double) : void        │
                  │ + setWidth(w : double) : void           │
                  │ + getLength() : double                  │
                  │ + getWidth() : double                   │
                  │ + getArea() : double                    │
                  └─────────────────────────────────────────┘
```

Uninitialized Local Reference Variables

The program in Code Listing 6-10 initializes the `box` variable with the address of a `Rectangle` object. Reference variables can also be declared without being initialized, as in the following statement:

```
Rectangle box;
```

Note that this statement does not create a `Rectangle` object. It only declares a variable named `box` that can be used to reference a `Rectangle` object. Because the `box` variable does not yet hold an object's address, it is an *uninitialized reference variable*.

After declaring the reference variable, the following statement can be used to assign it the address of an object. This statement creates a `Rectangle` object, passes the values 7.0 and 14.0 to its constructor, and assigns the object's address to the `box` variable:

```
box = new Rectangle(7.0, 14.0);
```

Once this statement executes, the `box` variable will reference a `Rectangle` object.

You need to be careful when using uninitialized reference variables. Recall from Chapter 5 that local variables *must* be initialized or assigned a value before they can be used. This is also true for local reference variables. A local reference variable must reference an object before it can be used. Otherwise a compiler error will occur.

The Default Constructor

When an object is created, its constructor is *always* called. But what if we do not write a constructor in the object's class? If you do not write a constructor in a class, Java automatically provides one when the class is compiled. The constructor that Java provides is known as the *default constructor*. The default constructor doesn't accept arguments. It sets all of the object's numeric fields to 0 and `boolean` fields to `false`. If the object has any fields that are reference variables, the default constructor sets them to the special value `null`, which means that they do not reference anything.

The *only* time that Java provides a default constructor is when you do not write your own constructor for a class. For example, at the beginning of this chapter we developed the `Rectangle` class without writing a constructor for it. When we compiled the class, the compiler generated a default constructor that set both the `length` and `width` fields to 0.0. Assume that the following code uses that version of the class to create a `Rectangle` object:

```
// We wrote no constructor for the Rectangle class.
Rectangle r = new Rectangle();  // Calls the default constructor
```

When we created `Rectangle` objects using that version of the class, we did not pass any arguments to the default constructor because the default constructor doesn't accept arguments.

Later we added our own constructor to the class. The constructor that we added accepts arguments for the `length` and `width` fields. When we compiled the class at that point, Java did not provide a default constructor. The constructor that we added became the only constructor that the class has. When we create `Rectangle` objects with that version of the class, we *must* pass the length and width arguments to the constructor. Using that version of the class, the following statement would cause an error because we have not provided arguments for the constructor:

```
// Now we wrote our own constructor for the Rectangle class.
Rectangle box = new Rectangle(); // Error! Must now pass arguments.
```

Because we have added our own constructor, which requires two arguments, the class no longer has a default constructor.

Writing Your Own No-Arg Constructor

A constructor that does not accept arguments is known as a *no-arg constructor*. The default constructor doesn't accept arguments, so it is considered a no-arg constructor. In addition, you can write your own no-arg constructor. For example, suppose we wrote the following constructor for the `Rectangle` class:

```
public Rectangle()
{
   length = 1.0;
   width = 1.0;
}
```

If we were using this constructor in our `Rectangle` class, we would not pass any arguments when creating a `Rectangle` object. The following code shows an example. After this code executes, the `Rectangle` object's `length` and `width` fields would both be set to 1.0.

```
// Now we have written our own no-arg constructor.
Rectangle r = new Rectangle();  // Calls the no-arg constructor
```

The `String` Class Constructor

The `String` class has a constructor that accepts a string literal as its argument, which is used to initialize the `String` object. The following statement creates a `String` object, passes the string literal "Joe Mahoney" to the constructor, and then stores the `String` object's address in the `name` variable. After the statement executes, the `String` object referenced by `name` will contain "Joe Mahoney".

```
String name = new String("Joe Mahoney");
```

Because string operations are so common in programming, Java provides the shortcut notation for creating and initializing `String` objects that we discussed earlier. For example, the following statement creates a `String` object initialized with "Joe Mahoney" and assigns its address to the `name` variable.

```
String name = "Joe Mahoney";
```

In the Spotlight:
Creating the `CellPhone` Class

Wireless Solutions, Inc., is a business that sells cell phones and wireless service. You are a programmer in the company's information technology (IT) department, and your team is designing a program to manage all of the cell phones that are in inventory. You have been asked to design a class that represents a cell phone. The data that should be kept as fields in the class are as follows:

- The name of the phone's manufacturer will be assigned to the `manufact` field.
- The phone's model number will be assigned to the `model` field.
- The phone's retail price will be assigned to the `retailPrice` field.

The class will also have the following methods:

- A constructor that accepts arguments for the manufacturer, model number, and retail price.
- A `setManufact` method that accepts an argument for the manufacturer. This method will allow us to change the value of the `manufact` field after the object has been created, if necessary.
- A `setModel` method that accepts an argument for the model. This method will allow us to change the value of the `model` field after the object has been created, if necessary.
- A `setRetailPrice` method that accepts an argument for the retail price. This method will allow us to change the value of the `retailPrice` field after the object has been created, if necessary.
- A `getManufact` method that returns the phone's manufacturer.
- A `getModel` method that returns the phone's model number.
- A `getRetailPrice` method that returns the phone's retail price.

Figure 6-22 shows a UML diagram for the class. Code Listing 6-11 shows the class definition.

Figure 6-22 UML diagram for the CellPhone class

CellPhone
– manufact : String – model : String – retailPrice : double
+ CellPhone(man : String, mod : String,   price : double); + setManufact(man : String) : void + setModel(mod : String) : void + setRetailPrice(price : double) : void + getManufact() : String + getModel() : String + getRetailPrice() : double

Code Listing 6-11 (CellPhone.java)

```java
 1  /**
 2      The CellPhone class holds data about a cell phone.
 3  */
 4
 5  public class CellPhone
 6  {
 7     // Fields
 8     private String manufact;      // Manufacturer
 9     private String model;         // Model
10     private double retailPrice;   // Retail price
11
12     /**
13         Constructor
14         @param man The phone's manufacturer.
15         @param mod The phone's model number.
16         @param price The phone's retail price.
17     */
18
19     public CellPhone(String man, String mod, double price)
20     {
21        manufact = man;
22        model = mod;
23        retailPrice = price;
24     }
25
26     /**
27         The setManufact method sets the phone's
28         manufacturer name.
29         @param man The phone's manufacturer.
30     */
31
```

```
32      public void setManufact(String man)
33      {
34         manufact = man;
35      }
36
37      /**
38         The setModel method sets the phone's
39         model number.
40         @param mod The phone's model number.
41      */
42
43      public void setMod(String mod)
44      {
45         model = mod;
46      }
47
48      /**
49         The setRetailPrice method sets the phone's
50         retail price.
51         @param price The phone's retail price.
52      */
53
54      public void setRetailPrice(double price)
55      {
56         retailPrice = price;
57      }
58
59      /**
60         getManufact method
61         @return The name of the phone's manufacturer.
62      */
63
64      public String getManufact()
65      {
66         return manufact;
67      }
68
69      /**
70         getModel method
71         @return The phone's model number.
72      */
73
74      public String getModel()
75      {
76         return model;
77      }
78
```

```
79      /**
80         getretailPrice method
81         @return The phone's retail price.
82      */
83
84      public double getRetailPrice()
85      {
86         return retailPrice;
87      }
88   }
```

The `CellPhone` class will be used by several programs that your team is developing. To perform a simple test of the class, you write the program shown in Code Listing 6-12. This is a simple program that prompts the user for the phone's manufacturer, model number, and retail price. An instance of the `CellPhone` class is created and the data is assigned to its attributes.

Code Listing 6-12   (`CellPhoneTest.java`)

```
1    import java.util.Scanner;
2
3    /**
4       This program runs a simple test
5       of the CellPhone class.
6    */
7
8    public class CellPhoneTest
9    {
10      public static void main(String[] args)
11      {
12         String testMan;   // To hold a manufacturer
13         String testMod;   // To hold a model number
14         double testPrice; // To hold a price
15
16         // Create a Scanner object for keyboard input.
17         Scanner keyboard = new Scanner(System.in);
18
19         // Get the manufacturer name.
20         System.out.print("Enter the manufacturer: ");
21         testMan = keyboard.nextLine();
22
23         // Get the model number.
24         System.out.print("Enter the model number: ");
25         testMod = keyboard.nextLine();
26
27         // Get the retail price.
```

```
28        System.out.print("Enter the retail price: ");
29        testPrice = keyboard.nextDouble();
30
31        // Create an instance of the CellPhone class,
32        // passing the data that was entered as arguments
33        // to the constructor.
34        CellPhone phone = new CellPhone(testMan, testMod, testPrice);
35
36        // Get the data from the phone and display it.
37        System.out.println();
38        System.out.println("Here is the data that you provided:");
39        System.out.println("Manufacturer: " + phone.getManufact());
40        System.out.println("Model number: " + phone.getModel());
41        System.out.println("Retail price: " + phone.getRetailPrice());
42    }
43 }
```

Program Output (with Input Shown in Bold)

```
Enter the manufacturer: Acme Electronics [Enter]
Enter the model number: M1000 [Enter]
Enter the retail price: 199.99 [Enter]

Here is the data that you provided:
Manufacturer: Acme Electronics
Model Number: M1000
Retail Price: $199.99
```

 Checkpoint

6.11 How is a constructor named?

6.12 What is a constructor's return type?

6.13 Assume that the following is a constructor, which appears in a class:

```
ClassAct(int number)
{
     item = number;
}
```

a) What is the name of the class that this constructor appears in?

b) Write a statement that creates an object from the class and passes the value 25 as an argument to the constructor.

6.4 Overloading Methods and Constructors

CONCEPT: Two or more methods in a class may have the same name as long as their parameter lists are different. This also applies to constructors.

Method overloading is an important part of object-oriented programming. When a method is *overloaded*, it means that multiple methods in the same class have the same name, but use different types of parameters. Method overloading is important because sometimes you need several different ways to perform the same operation. For example, suppose a class has the following two methods:

```
public int add(int num1, int num2)
{
    int sum = num1 + num2;
    return sum;
}
public String add(String str1, String str2)
{
    String combined = str1 + str2;
    return combined;
}
```

Both of these methods are named add. They both take two arguments, which are added together. The first one accepts two int arguments and returns their sum. The second accepts two String references and returns a reference to a String that is a concatenation of the two arguments. When we write a call to the add method, the compiler must determine which one of the overloaded methods we intended to call.

The process of matching a method call with the correct method is known as *binding*. When an overloaded method is being called, Java uses the method's name and parameter list to determine which method to bind the call to. If two int arguments are passed to the add method, the version of the method with two int parameters is called. Likewise, when two String arguments are passed to add, the version with two String parameters is called.

Java uses a method's signature to distinguish it from other methods of the same name. A method's *signature* consists of the method's name and the data types of the method's parameters, in the order that they appear. For example, here are the signatures of the add methods that were previously shown:

```
add(int, int)
add(String, String)
```

Note that the method's return type is *not* part of the signature. For this reason, the following add method cannot be added to the same class with the previous ones:

```
public int add(String str1, String str2)
{
    int sum = Integer.parstInt(str1) + Integer.parseInt(str2);
    return sum;
}
```

Because the return type is not part of the signature, this method's signature is the same as that of the other add method that takes two String arguments. For this reason, an error message will be issued when a class containing all of these methods is compiled.

Constructors can also be overloaded, which means that a class can have more than one constructor. The rules for overloading constructors are the same for overloading other methods: Each version of the constructor must have a different parameter list. As long as each constructor has a unique signature, the compiler can tell them apart. For example, the Rectangle class that we discussed earlier could have the following two constructors:

```
public Rectangle()
{
   length = 0.0;
   width = 0.0;
}
public Rectangle(double len, double w)
{
   length = len;
   width = w;
}
```

The first constructor shown here accepts no arguments, and assigns 0.0 to the length and width fields. The second constructor accepts two arguments, which are assigned to the length and width fields. The following code shows an example of how each constructor is called:

```
Rectangle box1 = new Rectangle();
Rectangle box2 = new Rectangle(5.0, 10.0);
```

The first statement creates a Rectangle object, referenced by the box1 variable, and executes the no-arg constructor. Its length and width fields will be set to 0.0. The second statement creates another Rectangle object, referenced by the box2 variable, and executes the second constructor. Its length and width fields will be set to 5.0 and 10.0 respectively.

Recall that Java provides a default constructor only when you do not write any constructors for a class. If a class has a constructor that accepts arguments, but it does not have a no-arg constructor, you cannot create an instance of the class without passing arguments to the constructor. Therefore, any time you write a constructor for a class, and that constructor accepts arguments, you should also write a no-arg constructor if you want to be able to create instances of the class without passing arguments to the constructor.

The BankAccount Class

Now we will look at the BankAccount class. Objects that are created from this class will simulate bank accounts, allowing us to have a starting balance, make deposits, make withdrawals, and get the current balance. A UML diagram for the BankAccount class is shown in Figure 6-23. In the figure, the overloaded constructors and overloaded methods are pointed out. Note that the extra annotation is not part of the UML diagram. It is there to draw attention to the items that are overloaded.

Figure 6-23   UML diagram for the `BankAccount` class

As you can see from the diagram, the class has three overloaded constructors. Also, the class has two overloaded methods named `deposit`, two overloaded methods named `withdraw`, and two overloaded methods named `setBalance`. The last method, `getBalance`, is not overloaded. Code listing 6-13 shows the code for the class.

Code Listing 6-13   (`BankAccount.java`)

```
 1   /**
 2       The BankAccount class simulates a bank account.
 3   */
 4
 5   public class BankAccount
 6   {
 7      private double balance;        // Account balance
 8
 9      /**
10         This constructor sets the starting balance
11         at 0.0.
12      */
13
14      public BankAccount()
15      {
16         balance = 0.0;
17      }
18
19      /**
20         This constructor sets the starting balance
21         to the value passed as an argument.
22         @param startBalance The starting balance.
23      */
24
```

```
25      public BankAccount(double startBalance)
26      {
27         balance = startBalance;
28      }
29
30      /**
31         This constructor sets the starting balance
32         to the value in the String argument.
33         @param str The starting balance, as a String.
34      */
35
36      public BankAccount(String str)
37      {
38         balance = Double.parseDouble(str);
39      }
40
41      /**
42         The deposit method makes a deposit into
43         the account.
44         @param amount The amount to add to the
45                       balance field.
46      */
47
48      public void deposit(double amount)
49      {
50         balance += amount;
51      }
52
53      /**
54         The deposit method makes a deposit into
55         the account.
56         @param str The amount to add to the
57                    balance field, as a String.
58      */
59
60      public void deposit(String str)
61      {
62         balance += Double.parseDouble(str);
63      }
64
65      /**
66         The withdraw method withdraws an amount
67         from the account.
68         @param amount The amount to subtract from
69                       the balance field.
70      */
71
72      public void withdraw(double amount)
```

```
73    {
74        balance -= amount;
75    }
76
77    /**
78        The withdraw method withdraws an amount
79        from the account.
80        @param str The amount to subtract from
81                    the balance field, as a String.
82    */
83
84    public void withdraw(String str)
85    {
86        balance -= Double.parseDouble(str);
87    }
88
89    /**
90        The setBalance method sets the account balance.
91        @param b The value to store in the balance field.
92    */
93
94    public void setBalance(double b)
95    {
96        balance = b;
97    }
98
99    /**
100        The setBalance method sets the account balance.
101        @param str The value, as a String, to store in
102                    the balance field.
103    */
104
105    public void setBalance(String str)
106    {
107        balance = Double.parseDouble(str);
108    }
109
110    /**
111        The getBalance method returns the
112        account balance.
113        @return The value in the balance field.
114    */
115
116    public double getBalance()
117    {
118        return balance;
119    }
120 }
```

The class has one field, `balance`, which is a `double`. This field holds an account's current balance. Here is a summary of the class's overloaded constructors:

- The first constructor is a no-arg constructor. It sets the `balance` field to 0.0. If we wish to execute this constructor when we create an instance of the class, we simply pass no constructor arguments. Here is an example:

```
BankAccount account = new BankAccount();
```

- The second constructor has a `double` parameter variable, `startBalance`, which is assigned to the `balance` field. If we wish to execute this constructor when we create an instance of the class, we pass a `double` value as a constructor argument. Here is an example:

```
BankAccount account = new BankAccount(1000.0);
```

- The third constructor has a `String` parameter variable, `str`. It is assumed that the `String` contains a string representation of the account's balance. The method uses the `Double.parseDouble` method to convert the string to a `double`, and then assigns it to the `balance` field. If we wish to execute this constructor when we create an instance of the class, we pass a reference to a `String` as a constructor argument. Here is an example:

```
BankAccount account = new BankAccount("1000.0");
```

This constructor is provided as a convenience. If the class is used in a program that reads the account balance from a dialog box, or from a text file, the amount does not have to be converted from a string before it is passed to the constructor.

Here is a summary of the overloaded `deposit` methods:

- The first `deposit` method has a parameter, `amount`, which is a `double`. When the method is called, an amount that is to be deposited into the account is passed into this parameter. The value of the parameter is then added to value in the `balance` field.
- The second `deposit` method has a parameter, `str`, which is a reference to a `String`. It is assumed that the `String` contains a string representation of the amount to be deposited. The method uses the `Double.parseDouble` method to convert the string to a `double`, and then adds it to the `balance` field. For example, if we call the method and pass "500.0" as the argument, it will add 500.0 to the balance field. As with the overloaded constructors, this method is provided as a convenience for programs that read the amount to be deposited from a dialog box or a text file.

Here is a summary of the overloaded `withdraw` methods:

- The first `withdraw` method has a parameter, `amount`, which is a `double`. When the method is called, an amount that is to be withdrawn from the account is passed into this parameter. The value of the parameter is then subtracted from the value in the `balance` field.
- The second `withdraw` method has a parameter, `str`, which is a reference to a `String`. It is assumed that the `String` contains a string representation of the amount to be withdrawn. This amount is converted to a `double`, and then subtracted from the `balance` field. As with the overloaded constructors and `deposit` methods, this method is provided as a convenience.

Here is a summary of the overloaded setBalance methods:

- The first setBalance method accepts a double argument, which is assigned to the balance field.
- The second setBalance method accepts a String reference as an argument. It is assumed that the String contains a string representation of the account's balance. The String is converted to a double and then assigned to the balance field. As with many of the other overloaded methods, this method is provided as a convenience.

The remaining method is getBalance. It returns the value in the balance field, which is the current account balance. The AccountTest.java program, shown in Code Listing 6-14, demonstrates the BankAccount class. Its output is shown in Figure 6-24.

Code Listing 6-14   **(AccountTest.java)**

```java
 1  import javax.swing.JOptionPane; // For the JOptionPane class
 2  import java.text.DecimalFormat; // For the DecimalFormat class
 3
 4  /**
 5     This program demonstrates the BankAccount class.
 6  */
 7
 8  public class AccountTest
 9  {
10     public static void main(String[] args)
11     {
12        String input;    // To hold user input
13
14        // Create a DecimalFormat object for displaying dollars.
15        DecimalFormat dollar = new DecimalFormat("#,###.00");
16
17        // Get the starting balance.
18        input = JOptionPane.showInputDialog("What is your " +
19                          "account's starting balance?");
20
21        // Create a BankAccount object.
22        BankAccount account = new BankAccount(input);
23
24        // Get the amount of pay.
25        input = JOptionPane.showInputDialog("How much were " +
26                            "you paid this month? ");
27
28        // Deposit the user's pay into the account.
29        account.deposit(input);
30
31        // Display the new balance.
32        JOptionPane.showMessageDialog(null,
33                          "Your pay has been deposited.\n" +
34                          "Your current balance is $ " +
```

```
35                        dollar.format(account.getBalance()));
36
37      // Withdraw some cash from the account.
38      input = JOptionPane.showInputDialog("How much would " +
39                              "you like to withdraw? ");
40      account.withdraw(input);
41
42      // Display the new balance
43      JOptionPane.showMessageDialog(null,
44                  "Now your balance is $" +
45                  dollar.format(account.getBalance()));
46
47      System.exit(0);
48   }
49 }
```

Figure 6-24 Interaction with the `AccountTest` program

Overloaded Methods Make Classes More Useful

You might be wondering why all those overloaded methods appear in the BankAccount class, especially since many of them weren't used by the demonstration program in Code Listing 6-14. After all, wouldn't it be simpler if the class had only the methods we were going to use?

An object's purpose is to provide a specific service. The service provided by the BankAccount class is that it simulates a bank account. Any program that needs a simulated bank account can simply create a BankAccount object and then use its methods to put the simulation into action. Because the BankAccount class has numerous overloaded methods, it is much more flexible than it would be if it provided only one way to perform every operation. By providing overloaded constructors, deposit methods, withdraw methods, and setBalance methods, we made the BankAccount class useful to programs other than our simple demonstration program. This is an important consideration to keep in mind when you design classes of your own.

6.5 Scope of Instance Fields

CONCEPT: Instance fields are visible to all of the class's instance methods.

Recall from Chapter 2 that a variable's scope is the part of a program where the variable may be accessed by its name. A variable's name is visible only to statements inside the variable's scope. The location of a variable's declaration determines the variable's scope.

In this chapter you have seen variables declared as instance fields in a class. An instance field can be accessed by any instance method in the same class as the field. If an instance field is declared with the `public` access specifier, it can also be accessed by code outside the class.

Shadowing

In Chapter 2 you saw that you cannot have two local variables with the same name in the same scope. This applies to parameter variables as well. A parameter variable is, in essence, a local variable. So, you cannot give a parameter variable and a local variable in the same method the same name.

However, you can have a local variable or a parameter variable with the same name as a field. When you do, the name of the local or parameter variable *shadows* the name of the field. This means that the field name is hidden by the name of the local or parameter variable.

For example, assume that the `Rectangle` class's `setLength` method had been written in the following manner:

```
public void setLength(double len)
{
    int length;          // Local variable
    length = len;
}
```

In this code a local variable is given the same name as a field. Therefore, the local variable's name shadows the field's name. When the statement `length = len;` is executed, the value of `len` is assigned to the local variable `length`, not to the field. The unintentional shadowing of field names can cause elusive bugs, so you need to be careful not to give local variables the same names as fields.

Checkpoint

6.14 Is it required that overloaded methods have different return values, different parameter lists, or both?

6.15 What is a method's signature?

6.16 Look at the following class:

```
public class CheckPoint
{
```

```java
public void message(int x)
{
    System.out.print("This is the first version ");
    System.out.println("of the method.");
}
public void message(String x)
{
    System.out.print("This is the second version ");
    System.out.println("of the method.");
}
}
```

What will the following code display?

```java
CheckPoint cp = new CheckPoint();
cp.message("1");
cp.message(1);
```

6.17   How many default constructors may a class have?

6.6   Packages and `import` Statements

CONCEPT: The classes in the Java API are organized into packages. An `import` statement tells the compiler which package a class is located in.

In Chapter 2 you were introduced to the Java API, which is a standard library of prewritten classes. Each class in the Java API is designed for a specific purpose, and you can use the classes in your own programs. You've already used a few classes from the API, such as the `String` class, the `Scanner` class, the `JOptionPane` class, the `DecimalFormat` class, and the `Random` class.

All of the classes in the Java API are organized into packages. A *package* is simply a group of related classes. Each package also has a name. For example, the `Scanner` class is in the `java.util` package.

Many of the classes in the Java API are not automatically available to your program. Quite often, you have to *import* an API class in order to use it. You use the `import` key word to import a class. For example, the following statement is required to import the `Scanner` class:

```java
import java.util.Scanner;
```

This statement tells the compiler that the `Scanner` class is located in the `java.util` package. Without this statement, the compiler will not be able to locate the `Scanner` class, and the program will not compile.

Explicit and Wildcard `import` Statements

There are two types of `import` statements: explicit and wildcard. An *explicit `import`* statement identifies the package location of a single class. For example, the following statement explicitly identifies the location of the `Scanner` class:

```
import java.util.Scanner;
```

The `java.util` package contains several other classes as well as the `Scanner` class. For example, the `Random` class is also part of the `java.util` package. If a program needs to use the `Scanner` class and the `Random` class, it will have to import both of these classes. One way to do this is to write explicit `import` statements for each class, as follows:

```
import java.util.Scanner;
import java.util.Random;
```

Another way to import both of these classes is to use a wildcard `import` statement. A *wildcard import* statement tells the compiler to import all of the classes in a package. Here is an example:

```
import java.util.*;
```

The `.*` that follows the package name tells the compiler to import all the classes that are part of the `java.util` package. Using a wildcard `import` statement does not affect the performance or the size of your program. It merely tells the compiler that you want to make every class in a particular package available to your program.

The `java.lang` Package

The Java API does have one package, `java.lang`, which is automatically imported into every Java program. This package contains general classes, such as `String` and `System`, that are fundamental to the Java programming language. You do not have to write an `import` statement for any class that is part of the `java.lang` package.

Other API Packages

There are numerous packages in the Java API. Table 6-2 lists a few of them.

Table 6-2 A few of the standard Java packages

Package	Description
`java.applet`	Provides the classes necessary to create an applet.
`java.awt`	Provides classes for the Abstract Windowing Toolkit. These classes are used in drawing images and creating graphical user interfaces.
`java.io`	Provides classes that perform various types of input and output.
`java.lang`	Provides general classes for the Java language. This package is automatically imported.
`java.net`	Provides classes for network communications.
`java.security`	Provides classes that implement security features.
`java.sql`	Provides classes for accessing databases using structured query language.
`java.text`	Provides various classes for formatting text.
`java.util`	Provides various utility classes.
`javax.swing`	Provides classes for creating graphical user interfaces.

See Appendix H on the Student CD for a more detailed look at packages.

6.7 Focus on Object-Oriented Design: Finding the Classes and Their Responsibilities

So far you have learned the basics of writing a class, creating an object from the class, and using the object to perform operations. Although this knowledge is necessary to create an object-oriented application, it is not the first step. The first step is to analyze the problem that you are trying to solve and determine the classes that you will need. In this section we will discuss a simple technique for finding the classes in a problem and determining their responsibilities.

Finding the Classes

When developing an object-oriented application, one of your first tasks is to identify the classes that you will need to create. Typically, your goal is to identify the different types of real-world objects that are present in the problem, and then create classes for those types of objects within your application.

Over the years, software professionals have developed numerous techniques for finding the classes in a given problem. One simple and popular technique involves the following steps:

1. Get a written description of the problem domain.
2. Identify all the nouns (including pronouns and noun phrases) in the description. Each of these is a potential class.
3. Refine the list to include only the classes that are relevant to the problem.

Let's take a closer look at each of these steps.

Writing a Description of the Problem Domain

The *problem domain* is the set of real-world objects, parties, and major events related to the problem. If you adequately understand the nature of the problem you are trying to solve, you can write a description of the problem domain yourself. If you do not thoroughly understand the nature of the problem, you should have an expert write the description for you.

For example, suppose we are programming an application that the manager of Joe's Automotive Shop will use to print service quotes for customers. Here is a description that an expert, perhaps Joe himself, might have written:

> Joe's Automotive Shop services foreign cars, and specializes in servicing cars made by Mercedes, Porsche, and BMW. When a customer brings a car to the shop, the manager gets the customer's name, address, and telephone number. Then the manager determines the make, model, and year of the car, and gives the customer a service quote. The service quote shows the estimated parts charges, estimated labor charges, sales tax, and total estimated charges.

The problem domain description should include any of the following:

- Physical objects such vehicles, machines, or products
- Any role played by a person, such as manager, employee, customer, teacher, student, and so forth.
- The results of a business event, such as a customer order, or in this case a service quote
- Recordkeeping items, such as customer histories and payroll records

Identify All of the Nouns

The next step is to identify all of the nouns and noun phrases. (If the description contains pronouns, include them too.) Here's another look at the previous problem domain description. This time the nouns and noun phrases appear in bold.

> **Joe's Automotive Shop** services **foreign cars**, and specializes in servicing **cars** made by **Mercedes**, **Porsche**, and **BMW**. When a **customer** brings a **car** to the **shop**, the **manager** gets the **customer's name**, **address**, and **telephone number**. Then the **manager** determines the **make**, **model**, and **year** of the **car**, and gives the **customer** a **service quote**. The **service quote** shows the **estimated parts charges**, **estimated labor charges**, **sales tax**, and **total estimated charges**.

Notice that some of the nouns are repeated. The following list shows all of the nouns without duplication.

address	foreign cars	Porsche
BMW	Joe's Automotive Shop	sales tax
car	make	service quote
cars	manager	shop
customer	Mercedes	telephone number
estimated labor charges	model	total estimated charges
estimated parts charges	name	year

Refining the List of Nouns

The nouns that appear in the problem description are merely candidates to become classes. It might not be necessary to make classes for them all. The next step is to refine the list to include only the classes that are necessary to solve the particular problem at hand. We will look at the common reasons that a noun can be eliminated from the list of potential classes.

1. Some of the nouns really mean the same thing.

In this example, the following sets of nouns refer to the same thing:

- cars and foreign cars
  These all refer to the general concept of a car.

- Joe's Automotive Shop and shop
  Both of these refer to the company "Joe's Automotive Shop."

We can settle on a single class for each of these. In this example we will arbitrarily eliminate **foreign cars** from the list, and use the word **cars**. Likewise, we will eliminate **Joe's**

Automotive Shop from the list and use the word **shop**. The updated list of potential classes is as follows:

address	~~foreign cars~~	Porsche
BMW	~~Joe's Automotive Shop~~	sales tax
car	make	service quote
cars	manager	shop
customer	Mercedes	telephone number
estimated labor charges	model	total estimated charges
estimated parts charges	name	year

Because **cars** and **foreign cars** mean the same thing in this problem, we have eliminated **foreign cars**. Also, because **Joe's Automotive Shop** and **shop** mean the same thing, we have eliminated **Joe's Automotive Shop**.

2. Some nouns might represent items that we do not need to be concerned with in order to solve the problem.

A quick review of the problem description reminds us of what our application should do: print a service quote. In this example we can eliminate two unnecessary classes from the list:

- We can cross **shop** off the list because our application only needs to be concerned with individual service quotes. It doesn't need to work with or determine any company-wide information. If the problem description asked us to keep a total of all the service quotes, then it would make sense to have a class for the shop.
- We will not need a class for the **manager** because the problem statement does not direct us to process any information about the manager. If there were multiple shop managers, and the problem description had asked us to record which manager generated each service quote, then it would make sense to have a class for the manager.

At this point the updated list of potential classes is as follows:

address	~~foreign cars~~	Porsche
BMW	~~Joe's Automotive Shop~~	sales tax
car	make	service quote
cars	~~manager~~	~~shop~~
customer	Mercedes	telephone number
estimated labor charges	model	total estimated charges
estimated parts charges	name	year

Our problem description does not direct us to process any information about the **shop**, or any information about the **manager**, so we have eliminated those from the list.

3. Some of the nouns might represent objects, not classes.

We can eliminate **Mercedes, Porsche,** and **BMW** as classes because, in this example, they all represent specific cars, and can be considered instances of a **cars** class. Also, we can eliminate the word **car** from the list. In the description it refers to a specific car brought to the shop by a customer. Therefore, it would also represent an instance of a **cars** class. At this point the updated list of potential classes is as follows:

address	~~foreign cars~~	~~Porsche~~
~~BMW~~	~~Joe's Automotive Shop~~	sales tax
~~car~~	make	service quote
cars	~~manager~~	~~shop~~
customer	~~Mercedes~~	telephone number
estimated labor charges	model	total estimated charges
estimated parts charges	name	year

We have eliminated **Mercedes, Porsche, BMW,** and **car** because they are all instances of a cars class. That means that these nouns identify objects, not classes.

> **TIP:** Some object-oriented designers take note of whether a noun is plural or singular. Sometimes a plural noun will indicate a class and a singular noun will indicate an object.

4. Some of the nouns might represent simple values that can be stored in a primitive variable and do not require a class.

Remember, a class contains fields and methods. Fields are related items that are stored within an object of the class, and define the object's state. Methods are actions or behaviors that may be performed by an object of the class. If a noun represents a type of item that would not have any identifiable fields or methods, then it can probably be eliminated from the list. To help determine whether a noun represents an item that would have fields and methods, ask the following questions about it:

- Would you use a group of related values to represent the item's state?
- Are there any obvious actions to be performed by the item?

If the answers to both of these questions are no, then the noun probably represents a value that can be stored in a primitive variable. If we apply this test to each of the nouns that remain in our list, we can conclude that the following are probably not classes: **address, estimated labor charges, estimated parts charges, make, model, name, sales tax, telephone number, total estimated charges** and **year.** These are all simple string or numeric values that can be stored in primitive variables. Here is the updated list of potential classes:

~~address~~	~~foreign cars~~	~~Porsche~~
~~BMW~~	~~Joe's Automotive Shop~~	~~sales tax~~
~~car~~	~~make~~	service quote
cars	~~manager~~	~~shop~~
customer	~~Mercedes~~	~~telephone number~~
~~estimated labor charges~~	~~model~~	~~total estimated charges~~
~~estimated parts charges~~	~~name~~	~~year~~

We have eliminated **address, estimated labor charges, estimated parts charges, make, model, name, sales tax, telephone number, total estimated charges,** and **year** as classes because they represent simple values that can be stored in primitive variables.

As you can see from the list, we have eliminated everything except **cars, customer,** and **service quote.** This means that in our application, we will need classes to represent cars, customers, and service quotes. Ultimately, we will write a Car class, a Customer class, and a ServiceQuote class.

Identifying a Class's Responsibilities

Once the classes have been identified, the next task is to identify each class's responsibilities. A class's *responsibilities* are as follows:

- The things that the class is responsible for knowing
- The actions that the class is responsible for doing

When you have identified the things that a class is responsible for knowing, you have identified the class's attributes. These values will be stored in fields. Likewise, when you have identified the actions that a class is responsible for doing, you have identified its methods.

It is often helpful to ask the questions "In the context of this problem, what must the class know? What must the class do?" The first place to look for the answers is in the description of the problem domain. Many of the things that a class must know and do will be mentioned. Some class responsibilities, however, might not be directly mentioned in the problem domain, so brainstorming is often required. Let's apply this methodology to the classes we previously identified from our problem domain.

The Customer class

In the context of our problem domain, what must the Customer class know? The description directly mentions the following items, which are all attributes of a customer:

- The customer's name
- The customer's address
- The customer's telephone number

These are all values that can be represented as strings and stored in the class's fields. The Customer class can potentially know many other things. One mistake that can be made at this point is to identify too many things that an object is responsible for knowing. In some applications, a Customer class might know the customer's email address. This particular problem domain does not mention that the customer's email address is used for any purpose, so we should not include it as a responsibility.

Now let's identify the class's methods. In the context of our problem domain, what must the Customer class do? The only obvious actions are as follows:

- Create an object of the Customer class
- Set and get the customer's name
- Set and get the customer's address
- Set and get the customer's telephone number

From this list we can see that the Customer class will have a constructor, as well as accessor and mutator methods for each of its fields. Figure 6-25 shows a UML diagram for the Customer class.

Figure 6-25   UML diagram for the `Customer` class

Customer
– name : String – address : String – phone : String
+ Customer() + setName(n : String) : void + setAddress(a : String) : void + setPhone(p : String) : void + getName() : String + getAddress() : String + getPhone() : String

The `Car` Class

In the context of our problem domain, what must an object of the `Car` class know? The following items are all attributes of a car, and are mentioned in the problem domain:

- The car's make
- The car's model
- The car's year

Now let's identify the class's methods. In the context of our problem domain, what must the `Car` class do? Once again, the only obvious actions are the standard set of methods that we will find in most classes (constructors, accessors, and mutators). Specifically, the actions are:

- Create an object of the `Car` class
- Set and get the car's make
- Set and get the car's model
- Set and get the car's year

Figure 6-26 shows a UML diagram for the `Car` class at this point.

Figure 6-26   UML diagram for the `Car` class

Car
– make : String – model : String – year : int
+ Car() + setMake(m : String) : void + setModel(m : String) : void + setYear(y : int) : void + getMake() : String + getModel() : String + getYear() : int

The `ServiceQuote` Class

In the context of our problem domain, what must an object of the `ServiceQuote` class know? The problem domain mentions the following items:

- The estimated parts charges
- The estimated labor charges
- The sales tax
- The total estimated charges

Careful thought and a little brainstorming will reveal that two of these items are the results of calculations: sales tax and total estimated charges. These items are dependent on the values of the estimated parts and labor charges. In order to avoid the risk of holding stale data, we will not store these values in fields. Rather, we will provide methods that calculate these values and return them. The other methods that we will need for this class are a constructor and the accessors and mutators for the estimated parts charges and estimated labor charges fields. Figure 6-27 shows a UML diagram for the `ServiceQuote` class.

Figure 6-27   UML diagram for the `ServiceQuote` class

```
                    ServiceQuote
        ─────────────────────────────────────
        – partsCharges : double
        – laborCharges : double
        ─────────────────────────────────────
        + ServiceQuote()
        + setPartsCharges(c : double):
             void
        + setLaborCharges(c : double):
             void
        + getPartsCharges() : double
        + getLaborCharges() : double
        + getSalesTax() : double
        + getTotalCharges() : double
```

This Is Only the Beginning

You should consider the process that we have discussed in this section merely as a starting point. It's important to realize that designing an object-oriented application is an iterative process. It may take you several attempts to identify all of the classes that you will need, and determine all of their responsibilities. As the design process unfolds, you will gain a deeper understanding of the problem, and consequently you will see ways to improve the design.

 Checkpoint

6.18   What is a problem domain?

6.19   When designing an object-oriented application, who should write a description of the problem domain?

6.20   How do you identify the potential classes in a problem domain description?

6.21   What are a class's responsibilities?

6.22   What two questions should you ask to determine a class's responsibilities?

6.23   Will all of a class's actions always be directly mentioned in the problem domain description?

 See the `Amortization` Class Case Study on the student CD for an in-depth example using this chapter's topics.

6.8   Common Errors to Avoid

- **Putting a semicolon at the end of a method header.** A semicolon never appears at the end of a method header.
- **Declaring a variable to reference an object, but forgetting to use the new key word to create the object.** Declaring a variable to reference an object does not create an object. You must use the new key word to create the object.
- **Forgetting the parentheses that must appear after the class name, which appears after the new key word.** The name of a class appears after the new key word, and a set of parentheses appears after the class name. You must write the parentheses even if no arguments are passed to the constructor.
- **Forgetting to provide arguments when a constructor requires them.** When using a constructor that has parameter variables, you must provide arguments for them.
- **Inserting a space before or after the period in a method call.** In a method call, a space cannot appear before or after the period (dot operator).
- **Trying to overload methods by giving them different return types.** Overloaded methods must have unique parameter lists.
- **Forgetting to write a no-arg constructor for a class that you want to be able to create instances of without passing arguments to the constructor.** If you write a constructor that accepts arguments, you must also write a no-arg constructor for the same class if you want to be able to create instances of the class without passing arguments to the constructor.
- **Unintentionally declaring a local variable with the same name as a field of the same class in a method.** When a method's local variable has the same name as a field in the same class, the local variable's name shadows the field's name.

Review Questions and Exercises

Multiple Choice and True/False

1. This is a collection of programming statements that specify the fields and methods that a particular type of object may have.
   a. class
   b. method
   c. parameter
   d. instance

2. A class is analogous to a _____.

   a. cookie
   b. cookie cutter
   c. bakery
   d. soft drink

3. An object is a(n) _____.

   a. blueprint
   b. cookie cutter
   c. variable
   d. instance

4. This is a member of a class that holds data.

   a. method
   b. instance
   c. field
   d. constructor

5. This key word causes an object to be created in memory.

   a. `create`
   b. `new`
   c. `object`
   d. `construct`

6. This is a method that gets a value from a class's field, but does not change it.

   a. accessor
   b. constructor
   c. void
   d. mutator

7. This is a method that stores a value in a field or in some other way changes the value of a field.

   a. accessor
   b. constructor
   c. void
   d. mutator

8. When the value of an item is dependent on other data, and that item is not updated when the other data is changed, what has the value become?

   a. bitter
   b. stale
   c. asynchronous
   d. moldy

9. This is a method that is automatically called when an instance of a class is created.

   a. accessor
   b. constructor
   c. void
   d. mutator

10. When a local variable has the same name as a field, the local variable's name does this to the field's name.

    a. shadows
    b. complements
    c. deletes
    d. merges with

11. This is automatically provided for a class if you do not write one yourself.

    a. accessor method
    b. default instance
    c. default constructor
    d. variable declaration

12. Two or more methods in a class may have the same name, as long as this is different.

    a. their return values
    b. their access specifier
    c. their parameter lists
    d. their memory address

13. The process of matching a method call with the correct method is known as _____.

    a. matching
    b. binding
    c. linking
    d. connecting

14. A class's responsibilities are _____.

    a. the objects created from the class
    b. things the class knows
    c. actions the class performs
    d. both b and c

15. **True or False:** The occurrence of a string literal in a Java program causes a `String` object to be created in memory, initialized with the string literal.

16. **True or False:** Each instance of a class has its own set of instance fields.

17. **True or False:** When you write a constructor for a class, it still has the default constructor that Java automatically provides.

18. **True or False:** A class may not have more than one constructor.

19. **True or False:** To find the classes needed for an object-oriented application, you identify all of the verbs in a description of the problem domain.

Find the Error

1. Find the error in the following class:

```
public class MyClass
{
```

```
    private int x;
    private double y;
    public void MyClass(int a, double b)
    {
        x = a;
        y = b;
    }
}
```

2. Assume that the following method is a member of a class. Find the error.

```
public void total(int value1, value2, value3)
{
    return value1 + value2 + value3;
}
```

3. The following statement attempts to create a `Rectangle` object. Find the error.

```
Rectangle box = new Rectangle;
```

4. Find the error in the following class:

```
public class TwoValues
{
    private int x, y;
    public TwoValues()
    {
        x = 0;
    }
    public TwoValues()
    {
        x = 0;
        y = 0;
    }
}
```

5. Find the error in the following class:

```
public class FindTheError
{
    public int square(int number)
    {
        return number * number;
    }
    public double square(int number)
    {
        return number * number;
    }
}
```

Algorithm Workbench

1. Design a class named `Pet`, which should have the following fields:

   - `name`. The `name` field holds the name of a pet.
   - `animal`. The `animal` field holds the type of animal that a pet is. Example values are "Dog", "Cat", and "Bird".
   - `age`. The `age` field holds the pet's age.

   The `Pet` class should also have the following methods:

   - `setName`. The `setName` method stores a value in the `name` field.
   - `setAnimal`. The `setAnimal` method stores a value in the `animal` field.
   - `setAge`. The `setAge` method stores a value in the `age` field.
   - `getName`. The `getName` method returns the value of the `name` field.
   - `getAnimal`. The `getAnimal` method returns the value of the `animal` field.
   - `getAge`. The `getAge` method returns the value of the `age` field.

   a. Draw a UML diagram of the class. Be sure to include notation showing each field and method's access specification and data type. Also include notation showing any method parameters and their data types.
   b. Write the Java code for the `Pet` class.

2. Look at the following partial class definition, and then respond to the questions that follow it:

   ```
   public class Book
   {
       private String title;
       private String author;
       private String publisher;
       private int copiesSold;
   }
   ```

   a. Write a constructor for this class. The constructor should accept an argument for each of the fields.
   b. Write accessor and mutator methods for each field.
   c. Draw a UML diagram for the class, including the methods you have written.

3. Consider the following class declaration:

   ```
   public class Square
   {
       private double sideLength;
       public double getArea()
       {
           return sideLength * sideLength;
       }
       public double getSideLength()
       {
           return sideLength;
       }
   }
   ```

a. Write a no-arg constructor for this class. It should assign the `sideLength` field the value 0.0.

b. Write an overloaded constructor for this class. It should accept an argument that is copied into the `sideLength` field.

4. Look at the following description of a problem domain:

The bank offers the following types of accounts to its customers: savings accounts, checking accounts, and money market accounts. Customers are allowed to deposit money into an account (thereby increasing its balance), withdraw money from an account (thereby decreasing its balance), and earn interest on the account. Each account has an interest rate.

Assume that you are writing an application that will calculate the amount of interest earned for a bank account.

a. Identify the potential classes in this problem domain.

b. Refine the list to include only the necessary class or classes for this problem.

c. Identify the responsibilities of the class or classes.

Short Answer

1. What is the difference between a class and an instance of a class?

2. A contractor uses a blueprint to build a set of identical houses. Are classes analogous to the blueprint or the houses?

3. What is an accessor method? What is a mutator method?

4. Is it a good idea to make fields private? Why or why not?

5. If a class has a private field, what has access to the field?

6. What is the purpose of the new key word?

7. Assume a program named `MailList.java` is stored in the `DataBase` folder on your hard drive. The program creates objects of the `Customer` and `Account` classes. Describe the steps that the compiler goes through in locating and compiling the `Customer` and `Account` classes.

8. Why are constructors useful for performing "start-up" operations?

9. Under what circumstances does Java automatically provide a default constructor for a class?

10. What do you call a constructor that accepts no arguments?

11. When the same name is used for two or more methods in the same class, how does Java tell them apart?

12. How does method overloading improve the usefulness of a class?

Programming Challenges

myCodeMate

1. Employee Class

Write a class named `Employee` that has the following fields:

- `name`. The `name` field references a `String` object that holds the employee's name.

- idNumber. The idNumber is an int variable that holds the employee's ID number.
- department. The department field references a String object that holds the name of the department where the employee works.
- position. The position field references a String object that holds the employee's job title.

The class should have the following constructors:

- A constructor that accepts the following values as arguments and assigns them to the appropriate fields: employee's name, employee's ID number, department, and position.
- A constructor that accepts the following values as arguments and assigns them to the appropriate fields: employee's name and ID number. The department and position fields should be assigned an empty string ("").
- A no-arg constructor that assigns empty strings ("") to the name, department, and position fields, and 0 to the idNumber field.

Write appropriate mutator methods that store values in these fields and accessor methods that return the values in these fields. Once you have written the class, write a separate program that creates three Employee objects to hold the following data:

Name	ID Number	Department	Position
Susan Meyers	47899	Accounting	Vice President
Mark Jones	39119	IT	Programmer
Joy Rogers	81774	Manufacturing	Engineer

The program should store this data in the three objects and then display the data for each employee on the screen.

2. Car Class

Write a class named Car that has the following fields:

- **yearModel.** The yearModel field is an int that holds the car's year model.
- **make.** The make field references a String object that holds the make of the car.
- **speed.** The speed field is an int that holds the car's current speed.

In addition, the class should have the following constructor and other methods.

- Constructor. The constructor should accept the car's year model and make as arguments. These values should be assigned to the object's yearModel and make fields. The constructor should also assign 0 to the speed field.
- Accessors. Appropriate accessor methods should get the values stored in an object's yearModel, make, and speed fields.
- accelerate. The accelerate method should add 5 to the speed field each time it is called.
- brake. The brake method should subtract 5 from the speed field each time it is called.

Demonstrate the class in a program that creates a Car object, and then calls the accelerate method five times. After each call to the accelerate method, get the current speed of the car and display it. Then call the brake method five times. After each call to the brake method, get the current speed of the car and display it.

3. Personal Information Class

Design a class that holds the following personal data: name, address, age, and phone number. Write appropriate accessor and mutator methods. Demonstrate the class by writing a program that creates three instances of it. One instance should hold your information, and the other two should hold your friends' or family members' information.

4. RetailItem Class

Write a class named `RetailItem` that holds data about an item in a retail store. The class should have the following fields:

- `description`. The `description` field references a `String` object that holds a brief description of the item.
- `unitsOnHand`. The `unitsOnHand` field is an `int` variable that holds the number of units currently in inventory.
- `price`. The `price` field is a `double` that holds the item's retail price.

Write a constructor that accepts arguments for each field, appropriate mutator methods that store values in these fields, and accessor methods that return the values in these fields. Once you have written the class, write a separate program that creates three `RetailItem` objects and stores the following data in them:

	Description	Units on Hand	Price
Item #1	Jacket	12	59.95
Item #2	Designer Jeans	40	34.95
Item #3	Shirt	20	24.95

5. Payroll Class

Design a `Payroll` class that has fields for an employee's name, ID number, hourly pay rate, and number of hours worked. Write the appropriate accessor and mutator methods and a constructor that accepts the employee's name and ID number as arguments. The class should also have a method that returns the employee's gross pay, which is calculated as the number of hours worked multiplied by the hourly pay rate. Write a program that demonstrates the class by creating a `Payroll` object, then asking the user to enter the data for an employee. The program should display the amount of gross pay earned.

6. TestScores Class

Design a `TestScores` class that has fields to hold three test scores. The class should have a constructor, accessor and mutator methods for the test score fields, and a method that returns the average of the test scores. Demonstrate the class by writing a separate program that creates an instance of the class. The program should ask the user to enter three test scores, which are stored in the `TestScores` object. Then the program should display the average of the scores, as reported by the `TestScores` object.

7. Circle Class

Write a `Circle` class that has the following fields:

- `radius`: a double
- `PI`: a final double initialized with the value 3.14159

The class should have the following methods:

- **Constructor.** Accepts the radius of the circle as an argument.
- **Constructor.** A no-arg constructor that sets the `radius` field to 0.0.
- **setRadius.** A mutator method for the radius field.
- **getRadius.** An accessor method for the radius field.
- **getArea.** Returns the area of the circle, which is calculated as

  `area = PI * radius * radius`
- **getDiameter.** Returns the diameter of the circle, which is calculated as

  `diameter = radius * 2`
- **getCircumference.** Returns the circumference of the circle, which is calculated as

  `circumference = 2 * PI * radius`

Write a program that demonstrates the `Circle` class by asking the user for the circle's radius, creating a `Circle` object, and then reporting the circle's area, diameter, and circumference.

8. BankCharges Class

A bank charges $10 per month plus the following check fees for a commercial checking account:

$.10 each for less than 20 checks
$.08 each for 20–39 checks
$.06 each for 40–59 checks
$.04 each for 60 or more checks

The bank also charges an extra $15 if the balance of the account falls below $400 (before any check fees are applied). Design a class that stores the beginning balance of an account and the number of checks written. It should also have a method that returns the bank's service fees for the month.

9. Freezing and Boiling Points

The following table lists the freezing and boiling points of several substances.

Substance	Freezing Point	Boiling Point
Ethyl Alcohol	−173	172
Oxygen	−362	−306
Water	32	212

Design a class that stores a temperature in a `temperature` field and has the appropriate accessor and mutator methods for the field. In addition to appropriate constructors, the class should have the following methods:

- **isEthylFreezing.** This method should return the `boolean` value `true` if the temperature stored in the `temperature` field is at or below the freezing point of ethyl alcohol. Otherwise, the method should return `false`.
- **isEthylBoiling.** This method should return the `boolean` value `true` if the temperature stored in the `temperature` field is at or above the boiling point of ethyl alcohol. Otherwise, the method should return `false`.
- **isOxygenFreezing.** This method should return the `boolean` value `true` if the temperature stored in the `temperature` field is at or below the freezing point of oxygen. Otherwise, the method should return `false`.

- **isOxygenBoiling.** This method should return the `boolean` value `true` if the temperature stored in the `temperature` field is at or above the boiling point of oxygen. Otherwise, the method should return `false`.
- **isWaterFreezing.** This method should return the `boolean` value `true` if the temperature stored in the `temperature` field is at or below the freezing point of water. Otherwise, the method should return `false`.
- **isWaterBoiling.** This method should return the `boolean` value `true` if the temperature stored in the `temperature` field is at or above the boiling point of water. Otherwise, the method should return `false`.

Write a program that demonstrates the class. The program should ask the user to enter a temperature, and then display a list of the substances that will freeze at that temperature and those that will boil at that temperature. For example, if the temperature is –20 the class should report that water will freeze and oxygen will boil at that temperature.

10. SavingsAccount Class

Design a `SavingsAccount` class that stores a savings account's annual interest rate and balance. The class constructor should accept the amount of the savings account's starting balance. The class should also have methods for subtracting the amount of a withdrawal, adding the amount of a deposit, and adding the amount of monthly interest to the balance. The monthly interest rate is the annual interest rate divided by twelve. To add the monthly interest to the balance, multiply the monthly interest rate by the balance, and add the result to the balance.

Test the class in a program that calculates the balance of a savings account at the end of a period of time. It should ask the user for the annual interest rate, the starting balance, and the number of months that have passed since the account was established. A loop should then iterate once for every month, performing the following:

- a. Ask the user for the amount deposited into the account during the month. Use the class method to add this amount to the account balance.
- b. Ask the user for the amount withdrawn from the account during the month. Use the class method to subtract this amount from the account balance.
- c. Use the class method to calculate the monthly interest.

After the last iteration, the program should display the ending balance, the total amount of deposits, and the total amount of withdrawals, and the total interest earned.

11. Deposit and Withdrawal Files

Use Notepad or another text editor to create a text file named `Deposits.txt`. The file should contain the following numbers, one per line:

```
100.00
124.00
78.92
37.55
```

Next, create a text file named `Withdrawals.txt`. The file should contain the following numbers, one per line:

```
29.88
110.00
27.52
50.00
12.90
```

The numbers in the `Deposits.txt` file are the amounts of deposits that were made to a savings account during the month, and the numbers in the `Withdrawals.txt` file are the amounts of withdrawals that were made during the month. Write a program that creates an instance of the `SavingsAccount` class that you wrote in Programming Challenge 10. The starting balance for the object is 500.00. The program should read the values from the `Deposits.txt` file and use the object's method to add them to the account balance. The program should read the values from the `Withdrawals.txt` file and use the object's method to subtract them from the account balance. The program should call the class method to calculate the monthly interest, and then display the ending balance and the total interest earned.

12. Coin Toss Simulator

Write a class named `Coin`. The `Coin` class should have the following field:

- A `String` named `sideUp`. The `sideUp` field will hold either "heads" or "tails" indicating the side of the coin that is facing up.

The `Coin` class should have the following methods:

- A no-arg constructor that randomly determines the side of the coin that is facing up ("heads" or "tails") and initializes the `sideUp` field accordingly.
- A `void` method named `toss` that simulates the tossing of the coin. When the toss method is called, it randomly determines the side of the coin that is facing up ("heads" or "tails") and sets the `sideUp` field accordingly.
- A method named `getSideUp` that returns the value of the `sideUp` field.

Write a program that demonstrates the `Coin` class. The program should create an instance of the class and display the side that is initially facing up. Then, use a loop to toss the coin 20 times. Each time the coin is tossed, display the side that is facing up. The program should keep count of the number of times heads is facing up and the number of times tails is facing up, and display those values after the loop finishes.

7 A First Look at GUI Applications

7.1 Introduction

CONCEPT: In Java, you use the Java Foundation Classes (JFC) to create a graphical user interface for your application. Within the JFC you use the Abstract Windowing Toolkit (AWT) or Swing classes to create a graphical user interface.

In this chapter we discuss the basics of creating a Java application with a *graphical user interface* or *GUI* (pronounced "gooey"). A GUI is a graphical window or a system of graphical windows that is presented by an application for interaction with the user. In addition to accepting input from the keyboard, GUIs typically accept input from a mouse as well.

A window in a GUI commonly consists of several *components* that present data to the user and/or allow interaction with the application. Some of the common GUI components are buttons, labels, text fields, check boxes, and radio buttons. Figure 7-1 shows an example of a window with a variety of components. Table 7-1 describes the components that appear in the window.

Figure 7-1 Various GUI components

Table 7-1 Some GUI components

Component	Description
Label	An area that can display text.
Text field	An area in which the user may type a single line of input from the keyboard.
Combo box	A component that displays a drop-down list of items from which the user may select. A combo box also provides a text field in which the user may type input. It is called a combo box because it is the combination of a list and a text field.
Check box	A component that has a box that may be checked or unchecked.
List	A list from which the user may select an item.
Radio button	A component that can be either selected or deselected. Radio buttons usually appear in groups and allow the user to select one of several options.
Slider	A component that allows the user to select a value by moving a slider along a track.
Button	A button that can cause an action to occur when it is clicked.

The JFC, AWT, and Swing

Java programmers use the *Java Foundation Classes (JFC)* to create GUI applications. The JFC consists of several sets of classes, many of which are beyond the scope of this book. The two sets of JFC classes that we focus on are the AWT and Swing classes. First, we discuss the differences between them.

Java has been equipped, since its earliest version, with a set of classes for drawing graphics and creating GUIs. These classes are part of the *Abstract Windowing Toolkit (AWT)*. The AWT allows programmers to create applications and applets that interact with the user via windows and other GUI components.

Programmers are limited in what they can do with the AWT classes, however. This is because the AWT classes do not actually draw user interface components on the screen. Instead, the AWT classes communicate with another layer of software, known as the *peer classes*, which directs the underlying operating system to draw its own built-in components. Each version of Java that is developed for a particular operating system has its own set of peer classes. Although this means that Java programs have a look that is consistent with other applications on the same system, it also leads to some problems.

One problem is that not all operating systems offer the same set of GUI components. For example, one operating system might provide a sophisticated slider bar component that is not found on any other platform. Other operating systems might have their own unique components as well. In order for the AWT to retain its portability, it has to offer only those components that are common to all the operating systems that support Java.

Another problem is in the behavior of components across various operating systems. A component on one operating system might have slightly different behavior than the same component on a different operating system. In addition, the peer classes for some operating systems reportedly have bugs. As a result, programmers cannot be completely sure how their AWT programs will behave on different operating systems until they test each one.

A third problem is that programmers cannot easily customize the AWT components. Because these components rely on the appearance and behavior of the underlying operating system components, there is little that can be done by the programmer to change their properties.

To remedy these problems, Swing was introduced with the release of Java 2. *Swing* is a library of classes that do not replace the AWT, but provide an improved alternative for creating GUI applications and applets. Very few of the Swing classes rely on an underlying system of peer classes. Instead, Swing draws most of its own components on the screen. This means that Swing components can have a consistent look and predictable behavior on any operating system.

NOTE: Swing applications can have the look of a specific operating system. The programmer may choose from a variety of "look and feel" themes.

Swing components can also be easily customized. The Swing library provides many sophisticated components that are not found in the AWT. In this chapter and in Chapter 13 we primarily use Swing to develop GUI applications. In Chapter 14 we use AWT to develop applets.

NOTE: AWT components are commonly called heavyweight components because they are coupled with their underlying peer classes. Very few of the Swing components are coupled with peer classes, so they are referred to as lightweight components.

Event-Driven Programming

Programs that operate in a GUI environment must be *event-driven*. An *event* is an action that takes place within a program, such as the clicking of a button. Part of writing a GUI application is creating event listeners. An *event listener* is an object that automatically executes one of its methods when a specific event occurs. If you wish for an application to perform an operation when a particular event occurs, you must create an event listener object that responds when that event takes place.

The `javax.swing` and `java.awt` Packages

In this chapter we use the Swing classes for all of the graphical components that we create in our GUIs. The Swing classes are part of the `javax.swing` package. (Take note of the letter x that appears after the word `java`.) The following `import` statement will be used in every applicaton:

```
import javax.swing.*;
```

We also use some of the AWT classes to determine when events, such as the clicking of a mouse, take place in our applications. The AWT classes are part of the `java.awt` package. (Note that there is no x after `java` in this package name.) Programs that use the AWT classes will have the following `import` statement:

```
import java.awt.*;
```

7.2 Creating Windows

CONCEPT: You can use Swing classes to create windows containing various GUI components.

VideoNote
Creating a
Simple GUI
Application

The `JOptionPane` dialog boxes that you learned about in Chapter 2 allow you to easily display messages and gather input. If an application is to provide a full graphical user interface, however, much more is needed. Often, applications need one or more windows with various components that allow the user to enter and/or select data and interact with the application. For example, the window that is displayed in Figure 7-1 has several different components within it.

A window is a component, but because a window contains other components, it is more appropriately considered a container. A *container* is simply a component that holds other components. In GUI terminology, a container that can be displayed as a window is known as a *frame*. A frame appears as a basic window that has a border around it, a title bar, and a set of buttons for minimizing, maximizing, and closing the window. In a Swing application, you create a frame object from the `JFrame` class.

There are a number of steps involved in creating a window, so let's look at an example. The program in Code Listing 7-1 displays the window shown in Figure 7-2.

Code Listing 7-1   (`ShowWindow.java`)

```
1   import javax.swing.*;    // Needed for Swing classes
2
3   /**
4      This program displays a simple window with a title. The
5      application exits when the user clicks the close button.
6   */
7
8   public class ShowWindow
9   {
10     public static void main(String[] args)
11     {
12        final int WINDOW_WIDTH = 350;    // Window width in pixels
13        final int WINDOW_HEIGHT = 250;   // Window height in pixels
14
15        // Create a window.
16        JFrame window = new JFrame();
17
18        // Set the title.
19        window.setTitle("A Simple Window");
20
21        // Set the size of the window.
22        window.setSize(WINDOW_WIDTH, WINDOW_HEIGHT);
23
24        // Specify what happens when the close button is clicked.
25        window.setDefaultCloseOperation(JFrame.EXIT_ON_CLOSE);
26
27        // Display the window.
28        window.setVisible(true);
29     }
30  }
```

Figure 7-2   Window displayed by `ShowWindow.java`

The window shown in Figure 7-2 was produced on a system running Windows XP. Notice that the window has a border and a title bar with "A Simple Window" displayed in it. In addition, it has the standard Windows XP buttons in the upper-right corner: a minimize button, a maximize button, and a close button. These standard features are sometimes referred to as *decorations*. If you run this program, you will see the window displayed on your screen. When you click on the close button, the window disappears and the program terminates.

Let's take a closer look at the code. First, notice that the following import statement is used in line 1:

```
import javax.swing.*;   // Needed for Swing classes
```

Any program that uses a Swing class, such as JFrame, must have this import statement. In lines 12 and 13 the two constants WINDOW_WIDTH and WINDOW_HEIGHT are declared as follows:

```
final int WINDOW_WIDTH = 350;   // Window width in pixels
final int WINDOW_HEIGHT = 250;  // Window height in pixels
```

We use these constants later in the program to set the size of the window. The window's size is measured in pixels. A *pixel* is one of the small dots that make up a screen display; the resolution of your monitor is measured in pixels. For example, if your monitor's resolution is 1024 by 768, that means the width of your screen is 1024 pixels, and the height of your screen is 768 pixels.

Next, we create an instance of the JFrame class with the following statement in line 16:

```
JFrame window = new JFrame();
```

This statement creates a JFrame object in memory and assigns its address to the window variable. This statement does not display the window on the screen, however. A JFrame is initially invisible.

In line 19 we call the JFrame object's setTitle method as follows:

```
window.setTitle("A Simple Window");
```

The string that is passed as an argument to setTitle will appear in the window's title bar when it is displayed. In line 22 we call the JFrame object's setSize method to set the window's size as follows:

```
window.setSize(WINDOW_WIDTH, WINDOW_HEIGHT);
```

The two arguments passed to setSize specify the window's width and height in pixels. In this program we pass the constants WINDOW_WIDTH and WINDOW_HEIGHT, which we declared earlier, to set the size of the window to 350 pixels by 250 pixels.

In line 25 we specify the action that we wish to take place when the user clicks on the close button, which appears in the upper-right corner of the window as follows:

```
window.setDefaultCloseOperation(JFrame.EXIT_ON_CLOSE);
```

There are a number of actions that can take place when the user clicks on the close button. The setDefaultCloseOperation method takes an int argument, which specifies the action. In this statement, we pass the constant JFrame.EXIT_ON_CLOSE, which causes the application to end with a `System.exit` method call. If we had passed `JFrame.HIDE_ON_CLOSE`, the window would be hidden from view, but the application would not end. The default action is `JFrame.HIDE_ON_CLOSE`.

Last, in line 28, we use the following code to display the window:

```
window.setVisible(true);
```

The `setVisible` method takes a `boolean` argument. If the argument is `true`, the window is made visible. If the argument is `false`, the window is hidden.

Using Inheritance to Extend the `JFrame` Class

The program in Code Listing 7-1 performs a very simple operation: It creates an instance of the `JFrame` class and displays it. Most of the time, your GUI applications will be much more involved than this. As you progress through this chapter, you will add numerous components and capabilities to the windows that you create.

Instead of simply creating an instance of the `JFrame` class, as shown in Code Listing 7-1, a more common technique is to use *inheritance* to create a new class that *extends* the `JFrame` class. Although we will thoroughly explore the topic of inheritance in Chapter 11, we will introduce it here, and discuss how it is used in a GUI application.

When a new class extends an existing class, it inherits many of the existing class's members just as if they were part of the new class. For example, you saw how the program in Code Listing 7-1 created a `JFrame` object and then called four of its methods: `setTitle`, `setSize`, `setDefaultCloseOperation`, and `setVisible`. These methods are all members of the `JFrame` class. If you create a new class that extends the `JFrame` class, the new class will automatically inherit these methods. Then these methods can be called from an instance of the new class just as if they were written into its declaration. You can add your own custom code to the new class, making it a specialized, or extended, version of the `JFrame` class. Programs can then create instances of your new specialized class instead of the more generic `JFrame` class.

Let's look at the `SimpleWindow` class in Code Listing 7-2. This is an example of a class that extends the `JFrame` class.

Code Listing 7-2   (`SimpleWindow.java`)

```
 1  import javax.swing.*;   // Needed for Swing classes
 2
 3  /**
 4     This class extends the JFrame class. Its constructor displays
 5     a simple window with a title. The application exits when the
 6     user clicks the close button.
 7  */
 8
 9  public class SimpleWindow extends JFrame
10  {
11     /**
```

```
12          Constructor
13    */
14
15    public SimpleWindow()
16    {
17        final int WINDOW_WIDTH = 350;    // Window width in pixels
18        final int WINDOW_HEIGHT = 250;   // Window height in pixels
19
20        // Set this window's title.
21        setTitle("A Simple Window");
22
23        // Set the size of this window.
24        setSize(WINDOW_WIDTH, WINDOW_HEIGHT);
25
26        // Specify what happens when the close button is clicked.
27        setDefaultCloseOperation(JFrame.EXIT_ON_CLOSE);
28
29        // Display the window.
30        setVisible(true);
31    }
32 }
```

Notice the class header in line 9 as follows:

```
public class SimpleWindow extends JFrame
```

The words extends JFrame indicate that the SimpleWindow class extends the JFrame class. This means that the SimpleWindow class inherits members of the JFrame class, such as the setTitle, setSize, setDefaultCloseOperation, and setVisible methods, just as if they were written into the SimpleWindow class declaration. Now look at the constructor. In lines 17 and 18 we declare the WINDOW_WIDTH and WINDOW_HEIGHT constants, which will be used to establish the size of the window as follows:

```
final int WINDOW_WIDTH = 350;    // Window width in pixels
final int WINDOW_HEIGHT = 250;   // Window height in pixels
```

In line 21 we call the setTitle method to set the text for the window's title bar as follows:

```
setTitle("A Simple Window");
```

Notice that we are calling the method without an object reference and a dot preceding it. This is because the method was inherited from the JFrame class, and we can call it just as if it were written into the SimpleWindow class declaration.

The rest of the constructor calls the setSize, setDefaultCloseOperation, and setVisible methods. All that is necessary to display the window is to create an instance of the SimpleWindow class, as shown in the program in Code Listing 7-3. When this program runs, the window that was previously shown in Figure 7-2 is displayed. Remember, the `SimpleWindow` class is an extended version of the `JFrame` class. When we create an instance of the `SimpleWindow` class, we are really creating an instance of the `JFrame` class, with some customized code added to its constructor.

Code Listing 7-3   (`SimpleWindowDemo.java`)

```
 1   /**
 2       This program creates an instance of the
 3       SimpleWindow class.
 4   */
 5
 6   public class SimpleWindowDemo
 7   {
 8      public static void main(String[] args)
 9      {
10         SimpleWindow myWindow = new SimpleWindow();
11      }
12   }
```

Adding Components to a Window

Swing provides numerous GUI components that can be added to a window. Three fundamental components are the label, the text field, and the button. These are summarized in Table 7-2.

Table 7-2   Label, text field, and button controls

Component	Swing Class	Description
Label	`JLabel`	An area that can display text
Text field	`JTextField`	An area in which the user may type a single line of input from the keyboard
Button	`JButton`	A button that can cause an action to occur when it is clicked

In Swing, labels are created with the `JLabel` class, text fields are created with the `JTextField` class, and buttons are created with the `JButton` class. To demonstrate these components, we will build a simple GUI application: The Kilometer Converter. This application will present a window in which the user will be able to enter a distance in kilometers, and then click a button to see that distance converted to miles. The conversion formula is as follows:

Miles = Kilometers × `0.6214`

When designing a GUI application, it is usually helpful to draw a sketch showing the window you are creating. Figure 7-3 shows a sketch of what the Kilometer Converter application's window will look like. As you can see from the sketch, the window will have a label, a text field, and a button. When the user clicks the button, the distance in miles will be displayed in a separate JOptionPane dialog box.

Figure 7-3   Sketch of the Kilometer Converter window

Content Panes and Panels

Before we start writing code, you should be familiar with content panes and panels. A *content pane* is a container that is part of every JFrame object. You cannot see the content pane and it does not have a border, but any component that is to be displayed in a JFrame must be added to its content pane.

A *panel* is also a container that can hold GUI components. Unlike JFrame objects, panels cannot be displayed by themselves. However, they are commonly used to hold and organize collections of related components. With Swing, you create panels with the JPanel class. In our Kilometer Converter application, we will create a panel to hold the label, text field, and button. Then we will add the panel to the JFrame object's content pane. This is illustrated in Figure 7-4.

Figure 7-4   A panel is added to the content pane

Code Listing 7-4 shows the initial code for the KiloConverterWindow class. We will be adding to this code as we develop the application. This version of the class is stored in the Student CD source code folder *Chapter 07\KiloConverter Phase 1*.

Code Listing 7-4   (`KiloConverterWindow.java`)

```java
 1 import javax.swing.*;
 2
 3 /**
 4    The KiloConverterWindow class displays a JFrame that
 5    lets the user enter a distance in kilometers. When
 6    the Calculate button is clicked, a dialog box is
 7    displayed with the distance converted to miles.
 8 */
 9
10 public class KiloConverterWindow extends JFrame
11 {
12    private JPanel panel;                   // To reference a panel
13    private JLabel messageLabel;            // To reference a label
14    private JTextField kiloTextField;       // To reference a text field
15    private JButton calcButton;             // To reference a button
16    private final int WINDOW_WIDTH = 310;   // Window width
17    private final int WINDOW_HEIGHT = 100;  // Window height
18
19    /**
20       Constructor
21    */
22
23    public KiloConverterWindow()
24    {
25       // Set the window title.
26       setTitle("Kilometer Converter");
27
28       // Set the size of the window.
29       setSize(WINDOW_WIDTH, WINDOW_HEIGHT);
30
31       // Specify what happens when the close button is clicked.
32       setDefaultCloseOperation(JFrame.EXIT_ON_CLOSE);
33
34       // Build the panel and add it to the frame.
35       buildPanel();
36
37       // Add the panel to the frame's content pane.
38       add(panel);
39
40       // Display the window.
41       setVisible(true);
42    }
43
```

```
44    /**
45       The buildPanel method adds a label, text field, and
46       a button to a panel.
47    */
48
49    private void buildPanel()
50    {
51       // Create a label to display instructions.
52       messageLabel = new JLabel("Enter a distance " +
53                                 "in kilometers");
54
55       // Create a text field 10 characters wide.
56       kiloTextField = new JTextField(10);
57
58       // Create a button with the caption "Calculate".
59       calcButton = new JButton("Calculate");
60
61       // Create a JPanel object and let the panel
62       // field reference it.
63       panel = new JPanel();
64
65       // Add the label, text field, and button
66       // components to the panel.
67       panel.add(messageLabel);
68       panel.add(kiloTextField);
69       panel.add(calcButton);
70    }
71 }
```

Let's take a closer look at this class. First, notice in line 10 that the `KiloConverterWindow` class extends the `JFrame` class as follows:

```
public class KiloConverterWindow extends JFrame
```

Next, in lines 12 through 17, notice in the following that the class declares a number of fields, and according to good class design principles, the fields are private:

```
private JPanel panel;                // To reference a panel
private JLabel messageLabel;         // To reference a label
private JTextField kiloTextField;    // To reference a text field
private JButton calcButton;          // To reference a button
private final int WINDOW_WIDTH = 310;    // Window width
private final int WINDOW_HEIGHT = 100;   // Window height
```

The statement in line 12 declares a `JPanel` reference variable named `panel`, which we will use to reference the panel that will hold the other components. The `messageLabel` variable, declared in line 13, will reference a `JLabel` object that displays a message instructing the user to enter a distance in kilometers. The `kiloTextField` variable, declared in line 14, will reference a `JTextField` object that will hold a value typed by the user. The `calcButton` variable, declared in line 15, will reference a JButton object that will calculate and display the kilometers converted to miles when clicked. The WINDOW_WIDTH and WINDOW_HEIGHT fields, declared in lines 16 and 17, are constants that hold the width and height of the window.

Now let's look at the constructor. In line 26 the setTitle method, which was inherited from the JFrame class, is called to set the text for the window's title bar. Next, in line 29, the inherited setSize method is called to establish the size of the window. In line 32, the inherited setDefaultCloseOperation method is called to establish the action that should occur when the window's close button is clicked.

Line 35 calls the buildPanel method. The buildPanel method is defined in this class, in lines 49 through 70. The purpose of the buildPanel method is to create a label, a text field, and a button, and then add those components to a panel. Let's look at the method.

First, look at the method header in line 49 and notice that it is declared private. When a method is private, only other methods in the same class can call it. This method is not meant to be called by code outside the class, so it is declared private. In lines 52 and 53, the method uses the following statement to create a JLabel object and assign its address to the message field:

```
messageLabel = new JLabel("Enter a distance " +
                          "in kilometers");
```

The string that is passed to the JLabel constructor is the text that will be displayed in the label. The following statement appears in line 56. It creates a JTextField object, and assigns its address to the kiloTextField field:

```
kiloTextField = new JTextField(10);
```

The argument that is passed to the JTextField constructor is the width of the text field in columns. One column is enough space to hold the letter "m," which is the widest letter in the alphabet.

The following statement appears in line 59; it creates a JButton object, and assigns its address to the calcButton field:

```
calcButton = new JButton("Calculate");
```

The string that is passed as an argument to the JButton constructor is the text that will be displayed on the button.

Next, in line 63, the method uses the following statement to create a JPanel object and assign its address to the panel field, which is a private field in the class:

```
panel = new JPanel();
```

A JPanel object is used to hold other components. You add a component to a JPanel object with the add method. The following code, in lines 67 through 69, adds the objects referenced by the messageLabel, kiloTextField, and calcButton variables to the JPanel object:

```
panel.add(messageLabel);
panel.add(kiloTextField);
panel.add(calcButton);
```

At this point, the panel is fully constructed in memory. The `buildPanel` method ends, and control returns to the class constructor. Here's the next statement in the constructor, which appears in line 38:

```
add(panel);
```

This statement calls the `add` method, which was inherited from the `JFrame` class. The purpose of the `add` method is to add an object to the content pane. This statement adds the object referenced by `panel` to the content pane.

The constructor's last statement, in line 41, calls the inherited `setVisible` method to display the window on the screen as follows:

```
setVisible(true);
```

All we must do to demonstrate the `KiloConverterWindow` class is to create an instance of it, as shown in Code Listing 7-5. (This program is stored in the Student CD source code folder *Chapter 07\KiloConverter Phase 1*.) When this program is executed, the window shown in Figure 7-5 is displayed on the screen.

Code Listing 7-5   (`KilometerConverterDemo.java`)

```java
 1  /**
 2      This program creates an instance of the
 3      KiloConverterWindow class, which displays
 4      a window on the screen.
 5  */
 6
 7  public class KilometerConverterDemo
 8  {
 9      public static void main(String[] args)
10      {
11          KiloConverterWindow kc = new KiloConverterWindow();
12      }
13  }
```

Figure 7-5   Kilometer Converter window

Figure 7-6 shows the window again, this time pointing out each of the components.

Although you can type input into the text field, the application does nothing when you click the Calculate button because we have not written an event handler that will execute when the button is clicked. That's the next step.

Figure 7-6   Components in the Kilometer Converter window

NOTE: Recall that the size of the window in the `KiloConverterWindow` class is set to 310 pixels wide by 100 pixels high. This is set with the `WINDOW_WIDTH` and `WINDOW_HEIGHT` constants. Figures 7-5 and 7-6 show the window as it appears on a system set at a video resolution of 1024 by 768 pixels. If your video resolution is lower, the window might not appear exactly as shown in the figures. If this is the case, you can increase the values of the `WINDOW_WIDTH` and `WINDOW_HEIGHT` constants and recompile the program. This is true for other applications in this chapter as well.

Handling Events with Action Listeners

VideoNote
Handling Events

An *event* is an action that takes place within a program, such as the clicking of a button. When an event takes place, the component that is responsible for the event creates an event object in memory. The *event object* contains information about the event. The component that generated the event object is known as the *event source*. For example, when the user clicks a button, the `JButton` component generates an event object. The `JButton` component that generated the event object is the event source.

But what happens to the event object once it is generated by a source component? It is possible that the source component is connected to one or more event listeners. An *event listener* is an object that responds to events. If the source component is connected to an event listener, then the event object is automatically passed, as an argument, to a specific method in the event listener. The method then performs any actions that it was programmed to perform in response to the event. This process is sometimes referred to as *event firing*.

When you are writing a GUI application, it is your responsibility to write the classes for the event listeners that your application needs. For example, if you write an application with a `JButton` component, an event will be generated each time the user clicks the button. Therefore, you should write an event listener class that can handle the event. In your application you would create an instance of the event listener class and connect it to the `JButton` component. Before looking at a specific example, we must discuss two important topics that arise when writing event listeners: private inner classes and interfaces.

Writing Event Listener Classes as Private Inner Classes

Java allows you to write a class definition inside of another class definition. A class that is defined inside of another class is known as an *inner class*. Figure 7-7 illustrates a class definition inside of another class definition.

Figure 7-7 A class with an inner class

```
public class Outer
{
```
Fields and methods of the Outer class appear here.

```
    private class Inner
    {
```
Fields and methods of the Inner class appear here.

```
    }
}
```

When an inner class is private, as shown in the figure, it is accessible only to code in the class that contains it. For example, the Inner class shown in the figure would only be accessible to methods that belong to the Outer class. Code outside the Outer class would not be able to access the Inner class. A common technique for writing an event listener class is to write it as a private inner class, inside the class that creates the GUI. Although this is not the only way to write event listener classes, it is the approach we take in this book.

Event Listeners Must Implement an Interface

There is a special requirement that all event listener classes must meet: they must *implement an interface*. Although we will discuss interfaces in detail in Chapter 11, we will introduce the concept here for the purposes of writing an event listener class.

For now, you can think of an interface as something like a class, containing one or more method headers. Interfaces do not have actual methods, however, only their headers. When you write a class that implements an interface, you are agreeing that the class will have all of the methods that are specified in the interface.

Java provides numerous interfaces that you can use with event listener classes. There are several different types of events that can occur within a GUI application, and the specific interface that you use depends on the type of event you want to handle. JButton components generate *action events*, and an event listener class that can handle action events is also known as an *action listener* class. When you write an action listener class for a JButton component, it must implement an interface known as ActionListener. We won't discuss how to write an interface until Chapter 11, but in case you are curious, this is what the code for the ActionListener interface looks like:

```
public interface ActionListener
{
    public void actionPerformed(ActionEvent e);
}
```

As you can see, the ActionListener interface contains the header for only one method: actionPerformed. Notice that the method has public access, is void, and has a parameter of the ActionEvent type. When you write a class that implements this interface, it *must* have a method named actionPerformed, with a header exactly like the one in the interface.

NOTE: The `ActionListener` interface, as well as other event listener interfaces, is in the `java.awt.event` package. We will use the following `import` statement in order to use those interfaces:

```
import java.awt.event.*;
```

You use the `implements` key word in a class header to indicate that it implements an interface. Here is an example of a class named `MyButtonListener` that implements the `ActionListener` interface:

```
private class MyButtonListener implements ActionListener
{
    public void actionPerformed(ActionEvent e)
    {
        Write code here to handle the event.
    }
}
```

Remember, when you write a class that implements an interface, you are "promising" that the class will have the methods specified in the interface. Notice that this class lives up to its promise. It has a method named `actionPerformed`, with a header that matches the `actionPerformed` header in the `ActionListener` interface exactly.

 NOTE: In your action listener class, the only part of the `actionPerformed` method header that does not have to match that which is shown in the `ActionListener` interface exactly is the name of the parameter variable. Instead of using the name e, you can use any legal variable name that you wish.

Registering an Event Listener Object

Once you have written an event listener class, you can create an object of that class, and then connect the object with a GUI component. The process of connecting an event listener object to a GUI component is known as *registering* the event listener.

When a `JButton` component generates an event, it automatically executes the `actionPerformed` method of the event listener object that is registered with it, passing the event object as an argument. This is illustrated in Figure 7-8.

Figure 7-8   A `JButton` component firing an action event

Writing an Event Listener for the `KiloConverterWindow` Class

Now that we've gone over the basics of event listeners, let's continue to develop the `KiloConverterWindow` class. Code Listing 7-6 shows the class with an action listener added to it. This version of the class is stored in the Student CD source code folder *Chapter 07\KiloConverter Phase 2*. The action listener is a private inner class named `CalcButtonListener`. The new code is shown in bold.

Code Listing 7-6   (`KiloConverterWindow.java`)

```
 1 import javax.swing.*;    // Needed for Swing classes
 2 import java.awt.event.*; // Needed for ActionListener Interface
 3
 4 /**
 5    The KiloConverterWindow class displays a JFrame that
 6    lets the user enter a distance in kilometers. When
 7    the Calculate button is clicked, a dialog box is
 8    displayed with the distance converted to miles.
 9 */
10
11 public class KiloConverterWindow extends JFrame
12 {
13    private JPanel panel;            // To reference a panel
14    private JLabel messageLabel;     // To reference a label
15    private JTextField kiloTextField; // To reference a text field
16    private JButton calcButton;      // To reference a button
17    private final int WINDOW_WIDTH = 310;  // Window width
18    private final int WINDOW_HEIGHT = 100; // Window height
19
20    /**
21       Constructor
22    */
23
24    public KiloConverterWindow()
25    {
26       // Set the window title.
27       setTitle("Kilometer Converter");
28
29       // Set the size of the window.
30       setSize(WINDOW_WIDTH, WINDOW_HEIGHT);
31
32       // Specify what happens when the close button is clicked.
33       setDefaultCloseOperation(JFrame.EXIT_ON_CLOSE);
34
35       // Build the panel and add it to the frame.
36       buildPanel();
37
```

```
38        // Add the panel to the frame's content pane.
39        add(panel);
40
41        // Display the window.
42        setVisible(true);
43     }
44
45     /**
46        The buildPanel method adds a label, text field, and
47        and a button to a panel.
48     */
49
50     private void buildPanel()
51     {
52        // Create a label to display instructions.
53        messageLabel = new JLabel("Enter a distance " +
54                                  "in kilometers");
55
56        // Create a text field 10 characters wide.
57        kiloTextField = new JTextField(10);
58
59        // Create a button with the caption "Calculate".
60        calcButton = new JButton("Calculate");
61
62        // Add an action listener to the button.
63        calcButton.addActionListener(new CalcButtonListener());
64
65        // Create a JPanel object and let the panel
66        // field reference it.
67        panel = new JPanel();
68
69        // Add the label, text field, and button
70        // components to the panel.
71        panel.add(messageLabel);
72        panel.add(kiloTextField);
73        panel.add(calcButton);
74     }
75
76     /**
77        CalcButtonListener is an action listener class for
78        the Calculate button.
79     */
80
81     private class CalcButtonListener implements ActionListener
82     {
83        /**
84           The actionPerformed method executes when the user
85           clicks on the Calculate button.
86           @param e The event object.
```

```
87        */
88
89        public void actionPerformed(ActionEvent e)
90        {
91            String input;  // To hold the user's input
92            double miles;  // The number of miles
93
94            // Get the text entered by the user into the
95            // text field.
96            input = kiloTextField.getText();
97
98            // Convert the input to miles.
99            miles = Double.parseDouble(input) * 0.6214;
100
101            // Display the result.
102            JOptionPane.showMessageDialog(null, input +
103                    " kilometers is " + miles + " miles.");
104        }
105    }
106 }
```

First, notice that we've added the import java.awt.event.*; statement in line 2. This is necessary for our program to use the ActionListener interface. Next, look at the following code in line 81:

```
private class CalcButtonListener implements ActionListener
```

This is the header for an inner class that we will use to create event listener objects. The name of this class is CalcButtonListener and it implements the ActionListener interface. We could have named the class anything we wanted to, but because it will handle the JButton component's action events, it must implement the ActionListener interface. The class has one method, actionPerformed, which is required by the ActionListener interface. The header for the actionPerformed method appears in line 89 as follows:

```
public void actionPerformed(ActionEvent e)
```

This method will be executed when the user clicks the JButton component. It has one parameter, e, which is an ActionEvent object. This parameter receives the event object that is passed to the method when it is called. Although we do not actually use the e parameter in this method, we still have to list it inside the method header's parentheses because it is required by the ActionListener interface.

The actionPerformed method declares two local variables in lines 91 and 92: input, a reference to a String object; and miles, a double. The following statement appears in line 96:

```
input = kiloTextField.getText();
```

All JTextField objects have a getText method that returns the text contained in the text field. This will be any value entered into the text field by the user. The value is returned as a string. So, this statement retrieves any value entered by the user into the text field and assigns it to input.

The following statement appears in line 99:

```
miles = Double.parseDouble(input) * 0.6214;
```

This statement converts the value in `input` to a `double`, and then multiplies it by 0.6214. This will convert the number of kilometers entered by the user to miles. The result is stored in the `miles` variable. The method's last statement, in lines 102 and 103, uses `JOptionPane` to display a dialog box showing the distance converted to miles as follows:

```
JOptionPane.showMessageDialog(null, input +
          " kilometers is " + miles + " miles.");
```

Writing an action listener class is only part of the process of handling a `JButton` component's action events. We must also create an object from the class and then register the object with the `JButton` component. When we register the action listener object with the `JButton` component, we are creating a connection between the two objects.

`JButton` components have a method named `addActionListener`, which is used for registering action event listeners. In line 63, which is in the `buildPanel` method, the following statement creates a `CalcButtonListener` object and registers that object with the `calcButton` object:

```
calcButton.addActionListener(new CalcButtonListener());
```

You pass the address of an action listener object as the argument to the `addActionListener` method. This statement uses the expression `new  CalcButtonListener()` to create an instance of the `CalcButtonListener` class. The address of that instance is then passed to the `addActionListener` method. Now, when the user clicks the Calculate button, the `CalcButtonListener` object's `actionPerformed` method will be executed.

TIP: Instead of the one statement in line 63, we could have written the following two statements:

```
CalcButtonListener listener = new CalcButtonListener();
calcButton.addActionListener(listener);
```

The first statement shown here declares a `CalcButtonListener` variable named `listener`, creates a new `CalcButtonListener` object, and assigns the object's address to the `listener` variable. The second statement passes the address in listener to the `addActionListener` method. These two statements accomplish the same thing as the one statement in line 63, but it declares a variable, `listener`, that we will not use again in the program. A better way is to use the one statement that appears in line 63 as follows:

```
calcButton.addActionListener(new CalcButtonListener());
```

Recall that the new key word creates an object and returns the object's address. This statement uses the new key word to create a `CalcButtonListener` object, and passes the object's address directly to the `addActionListener` method. Because we do not need to refer to the object again in the program, we do not assign the object's address to a variable. It is known as an *anonymous object*.

NOTE: To demonstrate this class we can again run the `KilometerConverterDemo` program that was previously shown in Code Listing 7-5. For convenience, a copy of the program is stored on the Student CD in the same folder as the updated `KilometerConverterDemo` class.

When this program is executed, the first window shown in Figure 7-9 is displayed on the screen. If the user enters 2 in the text field and clicks the Calculate button, the second window shown in the figure (a dialog box) appears. To exit the application, the user clicks the OK button on the dialog box, and then clicks the close button in the upper-right corner of the main window.

Figure 7-9   Windows displayed by the `KiloConverterWindow` class

This window appears first. The user enters 2 in the text field and then clicks the Calculate button.

This dialog box appears next.

Background and Foreground Colors

Many of the Swing component classes have methods named `setBackground` and `setForeground`. You call these methods to change a component's color. The background color is the color of the component itself, and the foreground color is the color of text that might be displayed on the component.

The argument that you pass to the `setBackground` and `setForeground` methods is a color code. Table 7-3 lists several predefined constants that you can use for colors. To use these constants, you must have the `import java.awt.*;` statement in your code.

Table 7-3   Color constants

Color.BLACK	Color.BLUE
Color.CYAN	Color.DARK_GRAY
Color.GRAY	Color.GREEN
Color.LIGHT_GRAY	Color.MAGENTA
Color.ORANGE	Color.PINK
Color.RED	Color.WHITE
Color.YELLOW	

For example, the following code creates a button with the text "OK" displayed on it. The `setBackground` and `setForeground` methods are called to make the button blue and the text yellow.

```
JButton okButton = new JButton("OK");
okButton.setBackground(Color.BLUE);
okButton.setForeground(Color.YELLOW);
```

The ColorWindow class in Code Listing 7-7 displays a window with a label and three buttons. When the user clicks a button, it changes the background color of the panel that contains the components and the foreground color of the label.

Code Listing 7-7   (ColorWindow.java)

```
 1 import javax.swing.*;    // Needed for Swing classes
 2 import java.awt.*;       // Needed for Color class
 3 import java.awt.event.*; // Needed for event listener interface
 4
 5 /**
 6    This class demonstrates how to set the background color of
 7    a panel and the foreground color of a label.
 8 */
 9
10 public class ColorWindow extends JFrame
11 {
12    private JLabel messageLabel;    // To display a message
13    private JButton redButton;      // Changes color to red
14    private JButton blueButton;     // Changes color to blue
15    private JButton yellowButton;   // Changes color to yellow
16    private JPanel panel;           // A panel to hold components
17    private final int WINDOW_WIDTH = 200; // Window width
18    private final int WINDOW_HEIGHT = 125; // Window height
19
20    /**
21       Constructor
22    */
23
24    public ColorWindow()
25    {
26       // Set the title bar text.
27       setTitle("Colors");
28
29       // Set the size of the window.
30       setSize(WINDOW_WIDTH, WINDOW_HEIGHT);
31
32       // Specify an action for the close button.
33       setDefaultCloseOperation(JFrame.EXIT_ON_CLOSE);
34
35       // Create a label.
36       messageLabel = new JLabel("Click a button to " +
37                                 "select a color.");
```

```
38
39          // Create the three buttons.
40          redButton = new JButton("Red");
41          blueButton = new JButton("Blue");
42          yellowButton = new JButton("Yellow");
43
44          // Register an event listener with all 3 buttons.
45          redButton.addActionListener(new RedButtonListener());
46          blueButton.addActionListener(new BlueButtonListener());
47          yellowButton.addActionListener(new YellowButtonListener());
48
49          // Create a panel and add the components to it.
50          panel = new JPanel();
51          panel.add(messageLabel);
52          panel.add(redButton);
53          panel.add(blueButton);
54          panel.add(yellowButton);
55
56          // Add the panel to the content pane.
57          add(panel);
58
59          // Display the window.
60          setVisible(true);
61       }
62
63       /**
64          Private inner class that handles the event when
65          the user clicks the Red button.
66       */
67
68       private class RedButtonListener implements ActionListener
69       {
70          public void actionPerformed(ActionEvent e)
71          {
72             // Set the panel's background to red.
73             panel.setBackground(Color.RED);
74
75             // Set the label's text to blue.
76             messageLabel.setForeground(Color.BLUE);
77          }
78       }
79
80       /**
81          Private inner class that handles the event when
82          the user clicks the Blue button.
83       */
84
85       private class BlueButtonListener implements ActionListener
```

```
 86     {
 87        public void actionPerformed(ActionEvent e)
 88        {
 89           // Set the panel's background to blue.
 90           panel.setBackground(Color.BLUE);
 91
 92           // Set the label's text to yellow.
 93           messageLabel.setForeground(Color.YELLOW);
 94        }
 95     }
 96
 97     /**
 98        Private inner class that handles the event when
 99        the user clicks the Yellow button.
100     */
101
102     private class YellowButtonListener implements ActionListener
103     {
104        public void actionPerformed(ActionEvent e)
105        {
106           // Set the panel's background to yellow.
107           panel.setBackground(Color.YELLOW);
108
109           // Set the label's text to black.
110           messageLabel.setForeground(Color.BLACK);
111        }
112     }
113 }
```

Notice that this class has three action listener classes, one for each button. The action-listener classes are `RedButtonListener`, `BlueButtonListener`, and `YellowButtonListener`. The following statements, in lines 45 through 47, register instances of these classes with the appropriate button components:

```
redButton.addActionListener(new RedButtonListener());
blueButton.addActionListener(new BlueButtonListener());
yellowButton.addActionListener(new YellowButtonListener());
```

The program in Code Listing 7-8 creates an instance of the class. Figure 7-10 shows the window that is displayed.

Code Listing 7-8   (`ColorDemo.java`)

```
1  /**
2     This program creates an instance of the ColorWindow class,
3     which causes it to display its window.
4  */
```

```
 5
 6   public class ColorDemo
 7   {
 8       public static void main(String[] args)
 9       {
10           ColorWindow cw = new ColorWindow();
11       }
12   }
```

Figure 7-10 The window produced by the `ColorWindow` class

The window components first appear in their default colors.

When the user clicks on the Red button, the panel turns red and the label turns blue.

When the user clicks on the Blue button, the panel turns blue and the label turns yellow.

When the user clicks on the Yellow button, the panel turns yellow and the label turns black.

Changing the Background Color of a `JFrame` Object's Content Pane

Recall that a `JFrame` object has a content pane, which is a container for all the components that are added to the `JFrame`. When you add a component to a `JFrame` object, you are actually adding it to the object's content pane. In the example shown in this section, we added a label and some buttons to a panel, and then added the panel to the `JFrame` object's content pane. When we changed the background color, we changed the background color of the panel. In this example, the color of the content pane does not matter because it is completely filled up by the panel. The color of the panel covers up the color of the content pane.

In some cases, where you have not filled up the `JFrame` object's content pane with a panel, you might want to change the background color of the content pane. If you wish to change the background color of a `JFrame` object's content pane, you must call the content pane's `setBackground` method, not the `JFrame` object's `setBackground` method. For example, in a class that extends the `JFrame` class, the following statement can be used to change the content pane's background to blue:

```
getContentPane().setBackground(Color.BLUE);
```

In this statement, the getConentPane method is called to get a reference to the JFrame object's content pane. This reference is then used to call the content pane's setBackground method. As a result, the content pane's background color will change to blue.

The ActionEvent Object

The action listener's actionPerformed method has a parameter variable named e that is declared as follows:

```
ActionEvent e
```

ActionEvent is a class that is defined in the Java API. When an action event occurs, an object of the ActionEvent class is created, the action listener's actionPerformed method is called, and a reference to the ActionEvent object is passed into the e parameter variable. So, when the actionPerformed method executes, the e parameter references the event object that was generated in response to the event.

Earlier it was mentioned that the event object contains information about the event. If you wish, you can retrieve certain information about the event by calling one of the event object's methods. Two of the ActionEvent methods are listed in Table 7-4.

Table 7-4 ActionEvent methods

Method Name	Description
getActionCommand()	Returns the action command for this event as a String
getSource()	Returns a reference to the object that generated this event

The getActionCommand Method

The first method listed in Table 7-4, getActionCommand, returns the *action command* that is associated with the event. When a JButton component generates an event, the action command is the text that appears on the button. The getActionCommand returns this text as a String. You can use the getActionCommand method to determine which button was clicked when several buttons share the same action listener class.

To demonstrate, look at the EventObjectWindow class in Code Listing 7-9. It produces a window with three buttons. The buttons have the text "Button 1", "Button 2", and "Button 3". The action listener class displays the contents of the event object's action command when any of these buttons are clicked.

Code Listing 7-9   (EventObjectWindow.java)

```
 1 import javax.swing.*;    // Needed for Swing classes
 2 import java.awt.event.*; // Needed for event listener interface
 3
 4 /**
```

```
 5       This class demonstrates how to retrieve the action command
 6       from an event object.
 7  */
 8
 9  public class EventObjectWindow extends JFrame
10  {
11       private JButton button1;      // Button 1
12       private JButton button2;      // Button 2
13       private JButton button3;      // Button 3
14       private JPanel panel;         // A panel to hold components
15       private final int WINDOW_WIDTH = 300; // Window width
16       private final int WINDOW_HEIGHT = 70; // Window height
17
18       /**
19          Constructor
20       */
21
22       public EventObjectWindow()
23       {
24          // Set the title bar text.
25          setTitle("Event Object Demonstration");
26
27          // Set the size of the window.
28          setSize(WINDOW_WIDTH, WINDOW_HEIGHT);
29
30          // Specify what happens when the close button is clicked.
31          setDefaultCloseOperation(JFrame.EXIT_ON_CLOSE);
32
33          // Create the three buttons.
34          button1 = new JButton("Button 1");
35          button2 = new JButton("Button 2");
36          button3 = new JButton("Button 3");
37
38          // Register an event listener with all three buttons.
39          button1.addActionListener(new ButtonListener());
40          button2.addActionListener(new ButtonListener());
41          button3.addActionListener(new ButtonListener());
42
43          // Create a panel and add the buttons to it.
44          panel = new JPanel();
45          panel.add(button1);
46          panel.add(button2);
47          panel.add(button3);
48
49          // Add the panel to the content pane.
50          add(panel);
51
52          // Display the window.
```

```
53          setVisible(true);
54     }
55
56     /**
57        Private inner class that handles the event when
58        the user clicks a button.
59     */
60
61     private class ButtonListener implements ActionListener
62     {
63        public void actionPerformed(ActionEvent e)
64        {
65           // Get the action command.
66           String actionCommand = e.getActionCommand();
67
68           // Determine which button was clicked and display
69           // a message.
70           if (actionCommand.equals("Button 1"))
71           {
72              JOptionPane.showMessageDialog(null, "You clicked " +
73                                               "the first button.");
74           }
75           else if (actionCommand.equals("Button 2"))
76           {
77              JOptionPane.showMessageDialog(null, "You clicked " +
78                                               "the second button.");
79           }
80           else if (actionCommand.equals("Button 3"))
81           {
82              JOptionPane.showMessageDialog(null, "You clicked " +
83                                               "the third button.");
84           }
85        }
86     }
87 }
```

Previously you saw the `ColorWindow` class, in Code Listing 7-7, which had three buttons and three different action listener classes. The `EventObjectWindow` class also has three buttons, but only one action listener class. In lines 39 through 41, we create and register three separate instances of the class with the three buttons as follows:

```
button1.addActionListener(new ButtonListener());
button2.addActionListener(new ButtonListener());
button3.addActionListener(new ButtonListener());
```

The program in Code Listing 7-10 creates an instance of the `EventObjectWindow` class, which displays its window. Figure 7-11 shows the output of the application when the user clicks Button 1, Button 2, and Button 3.

Code Listing 7-10   `(EventObjectDemo.java)`

```
 1   /**
 2       This program creates an instance of the EventObjectWindow
 3       class, which causes it to display its window.
 4   */
 5
 6   public class EventObjectDemo
 7   {
 8       public static void main(String[] args)
 9       {
10           EventObjectWindow eow = new EventObjectWindow();
11       }
12   }
```

Figure 7-11   Output of `EventObjectWindow` class

This window appears first.

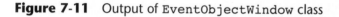

The user clicks Button 1 and this dialog box appears next. The user clicks the OK button to dismiss the dialog box.

The user clicks Button 2 and this dialog box appears next. The user clicks the OK button to dismiss the dialog box.

The user clicks Button 3 and this dialog box appears next. The user clicks the OK button to dismiss the dialog box.

TIP: The text that is displayed on a button is the default action command. You can change the action command by calling the `JButton` class's `setActionCommand` method. For example, assuming that `myButton` references a `JButton` component, the following statement would change the component's action command to "The button was clicked":

```
myButton.setActionCommand("The button was clicked");
```

NOTE: Changing a `JButton` component's action command does not change the text that is displayed on the button. For a demonstration of how to change the action command, see the files *ActionCommandWindow.java* and *ActionCommandDemo.java* on the Student CD.

The `getSource` Method

The second `ActionEvent` method listed in Table 7-4, `getSource`, returns a reference to the component that is the source of the event. As with the `getActionCommand` method, if you have several buttons and use objects of the same action listener class to respond to their events, you can use the `getSource` method to determine which button was clicked. For example, the `ButtonListener` class's `actionPerformed` method in Code Listing 7-9 could have been written as follows, to achieve the same result:

```java
public void actionPerformed(ActionEvent e)
{
    // Determine which button was clicked and display
    // a message.
    if (e.getSource() == button1)
    {
        JOptionPane.showMessageDialog(null, "You clicked " +
                                      "the first button.");
    }
    else if (e.getSource() == button2)
    {
        JOptionPane.showMessageDialog(null, "You clicked " +
                                      "the second button.");
    }
    else if (e.getSource() == button3)
    {
        JOptionPane.showMessageDialog(null, "You clicked " +
                                      "the third button.");
    }
}
```

On the Student CD, the *EventObjectWindow2.java* file uses this code. You can run *EventObjectWindowDemo2.java* to see it in action.

Checkpoint

7.1   What is a frame? How do you create a frame with Swing?

7.2   How do you set a frame's size?

7.3   How do you display a frame on the screen?

7.4   What is a content pane?

7.5   What is the difference between a frame and a panel?

7.6   What is an event listener?

7.7 If you are writing an event listener class for a JButton component, what interface must the class implement? What method must the class have? When is this method executed?

7.8 How do you register an event listener with a JButton component?

7.9 How do you change the background color of a component? How do you change the color of text displayed by a label or a button?

7.3 Equipping GUI Classes with a main Method

CONCEPT: The main method that Java uses as the starting point of an application can be written directly into a GUI class.

You know that a Java application always starts execution with a method named main. The applications that we have looked at so far in this chapter consist of two separate files: one file containing a class that defines a GUI window, and another file with a main method that creates an object of the GUI window class, thus displaying it. The purpose of the second file is simply to demonstrate the GUI window.

It is possible to eliminate the second file by writing the main method directly into the GUI class. The EmbeddedMain class in Code Listing 7-11 shows an example.

Code Listing 7-11 (EmbeddedMain.java)

```
 1 import javax.swing.*; // Needed for Swing classes
 2
 3 /**
 4    This class defines a GUI window and has its own
 5    main method.
 6 */
 7
 8 public class EmbeddedMain extends JFrame
 9 {
10    final int WINDOW_WIDTH = 220;  // Window width in pixels
11    final int WINDOW_HEIGHT = 70;  // Window height in pixels
12
13    /**
14       Constructor
15    */
16
17    public EmbeddedMain()
18    {
19       // Set this window's title.
20       setTitle("A Simple Window");
21
22       // Set the size of this window.
23       setSize(WINDOW_WIDTH, WINDOW_HEIGHT);
```

```
24
25        // Specify an action for the close button.
26        setDefaultCloseOperation(JFrame.EXIT_ON_CLOSE);
27
28        // Create a label to display a message.
29        JLabel messageLabel =
30              new JLabel("This class has its own main method.");
31
32        // Add the label to the content pane.
33        add(messageLabel);
34
35        // Display the window.
36        setVisible(true);
37    }
38
39    /**
40       The main method creates an instance of the EmbeddedMain
41       class, which causes it to display its window.
42    */
43
44    public static void main(String[] args)
45    {
46        EmbeddedMain em = new EmbeddedMain();
47    }
48 }
```

The `EmbeddedMain` class contains its own `main` method which creates an instance of the class. Notice that the `main` method has exactly the same header as any other `main` method that we have written. We can compile the *EmbeddedMain.java* file and then run the resulting *.class* file. When we do, we see the window shown in Figure 7-12.

Figure 7-12   Window displayed by the `EmbeddedMain` class

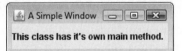

Notice that in line 46 the `main` method declares a variable named `em` to reference the instance of the class. Once the instance is created, however, the variable is not used again. Because we do not need the variable, we can instantiate the class anonymously as shown here:

```
public static void main(String[] args)
{
    new EmbeddedMain();
}
```

7.4   Layout Managers

CONCEPT: A layout manager is an object that governs the positions and sizes of components in a container. The layout manager automatically repositions and, in some cases, resizes the components when the container is resized.

An important part of designing a GUI application is determining the layout of the components that are displayed in the application's windows. The term *layout* refers to the positioning and sizing of components. In Java, you do not normally specify the exact location of a component within a window. Instead, you let a layout manager control the positions of components for you. A *layout manager* is an object that has its own rules about how components are to be positioned and sized, and it makes adjustments when necessary. For example, when the user resizes a window, the layout manager determines where the components should be moved to.

In order to use a layout manager with a group of components, you must place the components in a container, and then create a layout manager object. The layout manager object and the container work together. In this chapter we discuss the three layout managers described in Table 7-5. To use any of these classes, your code should have the following import statement: import java.awt.*;

Table 7-5   Layout managers

Layout Manager	Description
FlowLayout	Arranges components in rows; this is the default layout manager for JPanel objects
BorderLayout	Arranges components in five regions: north, south, east, west, and center; this is the default layout manager for a JFrame object's content pane
GridLayout	Arranges components in a grid with rows and columns

Adding a Layout Manager to a Container

You add a layout manager to a container, such as a content pane or a panel, by calling the setLayout method and passing a reference to a layout manager object as the argument. For example, the following code creates a JPanel object, then sets a BorderLayout object as its layout manager:

```
JPanel panel = new JPanel();
panel.setLayout(new BorderLayout());
```

Likewise, the following code might appear in the constructor of a class that extends the JFrame class. It sets a FlowLayout object as the layout manager for the content pane:

```
setLayout(new FlowLayout());
```

Once you establish a layout manager for a container, the layout manager governs the positions and sizes of the components that are added to the container.

The `FlowLayout` Manager

The `FlowLayout` manager arranges components in rows. This is the default layout manager for `JPanel` objects. Here are some rules that the `FlowLayout` manager follows:

- You can add multiple components to a container that uses a `FlowLayout` manager.
- When you add components to a container that uses a `FlowLayout` manager, the components appear horizontally, from left to right, in the order that they were added to the component.
- When there is no more room in a row but more components are added, the new components "flow" to the next row.

For example, the `FlowWindow` class shown in Code Listing 7-12 extends `JFrame`. This class creates a 200 pixel wide by 105 pixel high window. In the constructor, the `setLayout` method is called to give the content pane a `FlowLayout` manager. Then, three buttons are created and added to the content pane. The `main` method creates an instance of the `FlowWindow` class, which displays the window.

Code Listing 7-12   **(FlowWindow.java)**

```java
 1 import javax.swing.*; // Needed for Swing classes
 2 import java.awt.*;    // Needed for FlowLayout class
 3
 4 /**
 5    This class demonstrates how to use a FlowLayout manager
 6    with the content pane.
 7 */
 8
 9 public class FlowWindow extends JFrame
10 {
11    private final int WINDOW_WIDTH = 200;  // Window width
12    private final int WINDOW_HEIGHT = 105; // Window height
13
14    /**
15       Constructor
16    */
17
18    public FlowWindow()
19    {
20       // Set the title bar text.
21       setTitle("Flow Layout");
22
23       // Set the size of the window.
24       setSize(WINDOW_WIDTH, WINDOW_HEIGHT);
25
26       // Specify an action for the close button.
27       setDefaultCloseOperation(JFrame.EXIT_ON_CLOSE);
28
29       // Add a FlowLayout manager to the content pane.
30       setLayout(new FlowLayout());
```

```
31
32          // Create three buttons.
33          JButton button1 = new JButton("Button 1");
34          JButton button2 = new JButton("Button 2");
35          JButton button3 = new JButton("Button 3");
36
37          // Add the three buttons to the content pane.
38          add(button1);
39          add(button2);
40          add(button3);
41
42          // Display the window.
43          setVisible(true);
44      }
45
46      /**
47          The main method creates an instance of the FlowWindow
48          class, causing it to display its window.
49      */
50
51      public static void main(String[] args)
52      {
53          new FlowWindow();
54      }
55 }
```

Figure 7-13 shows the window that is displayed by this class. Notice that the buttons appear from left to right in the order they were added to the content pane. Because there is only enough room for the first two buttons in the first row, the third button is positioned in the second row. By default, the content of each row is centered and there is a five pixel gap between the components.

Figure 7-13   The window displayed by the `FlowWindow` class

If the user resizes the window, the layout manager repositions the components according to its rules. Figure 7-14 shows the appearance of the window in three different sizes.

Figure 7-14   The arrangement of the buttons after resizing

Adjusting the `FlowLayout` Alignment

The `FlowLayout` manager allows you to align components in the center of each row or along the left or right edges of each row. An overloaded constructor allows you to pass one of the following constants as an argument to set an alignment: `FlowLayout.CENTER`, `FlowLayout.LEFT`, or `FlowLayout.RIGHT`. Here is an example that sets left alignment:

```
setLayout(new FlowLayout(FlowLayout.LEFT));
```

Figure 7-15 shows examples of windows that use a `FlowLayout` manager with left, center, and right alignment.

Adjusting the `FlowLayout` Component Gaps

By default, the `FlowLayout` manager inserts a gap of five pixels between components, both horizontally and vertically. You can adjust this gap by passing values for the horizontal and vertical gaps as arguments to an overloaded `FlowLayout` constructor. The constructor has the following format:

```
FlowLayout(int alignment, int horizontalGap, int verticalGap)
```

You pass one of the alignment constants discussed in the previous section to the `alignment` parameter. The `horizontalGap` parameter is the number of pixels to separate components horizontally, and the `verticalGap` parameter is the number of pixels to separate components vertically. Here is an example of the constructor call:

```
setLayout(new FlowLayout(FlowLayout.LEFT, 10, 7));
```

This statement causes components to be left aligned with a horizontal gap of 10 pixels and a vertical gap of seven pixels.

Figure 7-15   Left, center, and right alignment

The `BorderLayout` Manager

The `BorderLayout` manager divides a container into five regions. The regions are known as north, south, east, west, and center. The arrangement of these regions is shown in Figure 7-16.

Figure 7-16   The regions of a `BorderLayout` manager

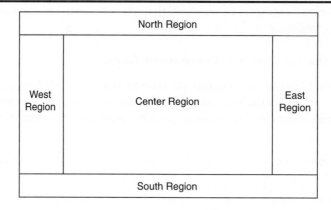

When a component is placed into a container that is managed by a `BorderLayout` manager, the component must be placed into one of these five regions. Only one component at a time may be placed into a region. When adding a component to the container, you specify the region by passing one of the following constants as a second argument to the container's add method: `BorderLayout.NORTH`, `BorderLayout.SOUTH`, `BorderLayout.EAST`, `BorderLayout.WEST`, or `BorderLayout.CENTER`.

For example, look at the following code:

```
JPanel panel = new JPanel();
JButton button = new JButton("Click Me");
panel.setLayout(new BorderLayout());
panel.add(button, BorderLayout.NORTH);
```

The first statement creates a `JPanel` object, referenced by the `panel` variable. The second statement creates a `JButton` object, referenced by the `button` variable. The third statement sets the `JPanel` object's layout manager to a `BorderLayout` object. The fourth statement adds the `JButton` object to the `JPanel` object's north region.

If you do not pass a second argument to the `add` method, the component will be added to the center region. Here are some rules that the `BorderLayout` manager follows:

- Each region can hold only one component at a time.
- When a component is added to a region, the component is stretched so it fills up the entire region.

Look at the `BorderWindow` class shown in Code Listing 7-13, which extends `JFrame`. This class creates a 400 pixel wide by 300 pixel high window. In the constructor, the `setLayout` method is called to give the content pane a `BorderLayout` manager. Then, five buttons are created and each is added to a different region.

Code Listing 7-13   (`BorderWindow.java`)

```
 1 import javax.swing.*; // Needed for Swing classes
 2 import java.awt.*;    // Needed for BorderLayout class
 3
 4 /**
 5    This class demonstrates the BorderLayout manager.
 6 */
 7
 8 public class BorderWindow extends JFrame
 9 {
10    private final int WINDOW_WIDTH = 400;   // Window width
11    private final int WINDOW_HEIGHT = 300;  // Window height
12
13    /**
14       Constructor
15    */
16
17    public BorderWindow()
18    {
19       // Set the title bar text.
20       setTitle("Border Layout");
21
22       // Set the size of the window.
23       setSize(WINDOW_WIDTH, WINDOW_HEIGHT);
24
25       // Specify an action for the close button.
26       setDefaultCloseOperation(JFrame.EXIT_ON_CLOSE);
27
28       // Add a BorderLayout manager to the content pane.
29       setLayout(new BorderLayout());
30
31       // Create five buttons.
32       JButton button1 = new JButton("North Button");
33       JButton button2 = new JButton("South Button");
34       JButton button3 = new JButton("East Button");
35       JButton button4 = new JButton("West Button");
36       JButton button5 = new JButton("Center Button");
37
38       // Add the five buttons to the content pane.
39       add(button1, BorderLayout.NORTH);
40       add(button2, BorderLayout.SOUTH);
41       add(button3, BorderLayout.EAST);
42       add(button4, BorderLayout.WEST);
43       add(button5, BorderLayout.CENTER);
44
45       // Display the window.
46       setVisible(true);
```

```
47      }
48
49      /**
50         The main method creates an instance of the BorderWindow
51         class, causing it to display its window.
52      */
53
54      public static void main(String[] args)
55      {
56         new BorderWindow();
57      }
58 }
```

> **NOTE:** A JFrame object's content pane is automatically given a BorderLayout manager. We have explicitly added it in Code Listing 7-13 so it is clear that we are using a BorderLayout manager.

Figure 7-17 shows the window that is displayed. Normally the size of a button is just large enough to accommodate the text that is displayed on the button. Notice that the buttons displayed in this window did not retain their normal size. Instead, they were stretched to fill all of the space in their regions. If the user resizes the window, the sizes of the components will be changed as well. This is shown in Figure 7-18.

Figure 7-17 The window displayed by the BorderWindow class

Here are the rules that govern how a BorderLayout manager resizes components:

- A component that is placed in the north or south regions may be resized horizontally so it fills up the entire region.
- A component that is placed in the east or west regions may be resized vertically so it fills up the entire region.

Figure 7-18   The window resized

- A component that is placed in the center region may be resized both horizontally and vertically so it fills up the entire region.

> **TIP:** You do not have to place a component in every region of a border layout. To achieve the desired positioning, you might want to place components in only a few of the layout regions. In Chapter 13 you will see examples of applications that do this.

By default there is no gap between the regions. You can use an overloaded version of the BorderLayout constructor to specify horizontal and vertical gaps, however. Here is the constructor's format:

```
BorderLayout(int horizontalGap, int verticalGap)
```

The horizontalGap parameter is the number of pixels to separate the regions horizontally, and the verticalGap parameter is the number of pixels to separate the regions vertically. Here is an example of the constructor call:

```
setLayout(new BorderLayout(5, 10));
```

This statement causes the regions to appear with a horizontal gap of five pixels and a vertical gap of 10 pixels.

Nesting Panels Inside a Container's Regions

You might think that the BorderLayout manager is limiting because it allows only one component per region, and the components that are placed in its regions are automatically resized to fill up any extra space. These limitations are easy to overcome, however, by adding components to panels and then nesting the panels inside the regions.

For example, suppose we wish to modify the BorderWindow class in Code Listing 7-13 so the buttons retain their original size. We can accomplish this by placing each button in a separate JPanel object and then adding the JPanel objects to the content pane's five regions. This is illustrated in Figure 7-19. As a result, the BorderLayout manager resizes the JPanel objects to fill up the space in the regions, not the buttons contained within the JPanel objects.

Figure 7-19   Nesting `JPanel` objects inside each region

1. Five `JPanel` objects are created and a `JButton` object is added to each one.

2. The `JPanel` objects are then added to the content pane, one to each region.

The `BorderPanelWindow` class in Code Listing 7-14 demonstrates this technique. This class also introduces a new way of sizing windows. Notice that the constructor does not explicitly set the size of the window with the `setSize` method. Instead, it calls the `pack` method just before calling the `setVisible` method. The `pack` method, which is inherited from `JFrame`, automatically sizes the window to accommodate the components contained within it. Figure 7-20 shows the window that the class displays.

Code Listing 7-14   (`BorderPanelWindow.java`)

```
 1 import java.awt.*;     // Needed for BorderLayout class
 2 import javax.swing.*;  // Needed for Swing classes
 3
 4 /**
 5    This class demonstrates how JPanels can be nested
 6    inside each region of a content pane governed by
 7    a BorderLayout manager.
 8 */
 9
10 public class BorderPanelWindow extends JFrame
11 {
12    /**
13       Constructor
14    */
15
16    public BorderPanelWindow()
17    {
18       // Set the title bar text.
19       setTitle("Border Layout");
20
21       // Specify an action for the close button.
22       setDefaultCloseOperation(JFrame.EXIT_ON_CLOSE);
23
24       // Add a BorderLayout manager to the content pane.
```

```
25          setLayout(new BorderLayout());
26
27          // Create five panels.
28          JPanel panel1 = new JPanel();
29          JPanel panel2 = new JPanel();
30          JPanel panel3 = new JPanel();
31          JPanel panel4 = new JPanel();
32          JPanel panel5 = new JPanel();
33
34          // Create five buttons.
35          JButton button1 = new JButton("North Button");
36          JButton button2 = new JButton("South Button");
37          JButton button3 = new JButton("East Button");
38          JButton button4 = new JButton("West Button");
39          JButton button5 = new JButton("Center Button");
40
41          // Add the buttons to the panels.
42          panel1.add(button1);
43          panel2.add(button2);
44          panel3.add(button3);
45          panel4.add(button4);
46          panel5.add(button5);
47
48          // Add the five panels to the content pane.
49          add(panel1, BorderLayout.NORTH);
50          add(panel2, BorderLayout.SOUTH);
51          add(panel3, BorderLayout.EAST);
52          add(panel4, BorderLayout.WEST);
53          add(panel5, BorderLayout.CENTER);
54
55          // Pack and display the window.
56          pack();
57          setVisible(true);
58       }
59
60       /**
61          The main method creates an instance of the
62          BorderPanelWindow class, causing it to display
63          its window.
64       */
65
66       public static void main(String[] args)
67       {
68          new BorderPanelWindow();
69       }
70 }
```

Figure 7-20 Window displayed by the `BorderPanelWindow` class

> **NOTE:** There are multiple layout managers at work in the `BorderPanelWindow` class. The content pane uses a `BorderLayout` manager, and each of the `JPanel` objects use a `FlowLayout` manager.

The `GridLayout` Manager

The `GridLayout` manager creates a grid with rows and columns, much like a spreadsheet. As a result, the container that is managed by a `GridLayout` object is divided into equally sized cells. Figure 7-21 illustrates a container with three rows and five columns. This means that the container is divided into 15 cells.

Figure 7-21 The `GridLayout` manager divides a container into cells

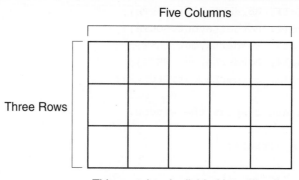

Here are some rules that the `GridLayout` manager follows:

- Each cell can hold only one component.
- All of the cells are the same size. This is the size of the largest component placed within the layout.
- A component that is placed in a cell is automatically resized to fill up any extra space.

You pass the number of rows and columns that a container should have as arguments to the GridLayout constructor. Here is the general format of the constructor:

```
GridLayout(int rows, int columns)
```

Here is an example of the constructor call:

```
setLayout(new GridLayout(2, 3));
```

This statement gives the container two rows and three columns, for a total of six cells. You can pass 0 as an argument for the rows or the columns, but not both. Passing 0 for both arguments will cause an error.

When adding components to a container that is governed by the GridLayout manager, you cannot specify a cell. Instead, the components are assigned to cells in the order they are added. The first component added to the container is assigned to the first cell, which is in the upper-left corner. As other components are added, they are assigned to the remaining cells in the first row, from left to right. When the first row is filled up, components are assigned to the cells in the second row, and so forth.

The GridWindow class shown in Code Listing 7-15 demonstrates. It creates a 400 pixel wide by 200 pixel high window, governed by a GridLayout manager. The content pane is divided into two rows and three columns, and a button is added to each cell. Figure 7-22 shows the window displayed by the class.

Code Listing 7-15   (`GridWindow.java`)

```
 1 import javax.swing.*; // Needed for Swing classes
 2 import java.awt.*;    // Needed for GridLayout class
 3
 4 /**
 5    This class demonstrates the GridLayout manager.
 6 */
 7
 8 public class GridWindow extends JFrame
 9 {
10    private final int WINDOW_WIDTH = 400;   // Window width
11    private final int WINDOW_HEIGHT = 200;  // Window height
12
13    /**
14       Constructor
15    */
16
17    public GridWindow()
18    {
19       // Set the title bar text.
20       setTitle("Grid Layout");
21
```

```
22        // Set the size of the window.
23        setSize(WINDOW_WIDTH, WINDOW_HEIGHT);
24
25        // Specify an action for the close button.
26        setDefaultCloseOperation(JFrame.EXIT_ON_CLOSE);
27
28        // Add a GridLayout manager to the content pane.
29        setLayout(new GridLayout(2, 3));
30
31        // Create six buttons.
32        JButton button1 = new JButton("Button 1");
33        JButton button2 = new JButton("Button 2");
34        JButton button3 = new JButton("Button 3");
35        JButton button4 = new JButton("Button 4");
36        JButton button5 = new JButton("Button 5");
37        JButton button6 = new JButton("Button 6");
38
39        // Add the six buttons to the content pane.
40        add(button1);   // Goes into row 1, column 1
41        add(button2);   // Goes into row 1, column 2
42        add(button3);   // Goes into row 1, column 3
43        add(button4);   // Goes into row 2, column 1
44        add(button5);   // Goes into row 2, column 2
45        add(button6);   // Goes into row 2, column 3
46
47        // Display the window.
48        setVisible(true);
49    }
50
51    /**
52       The main method creates an instance of the GridWindow
53       class, causing it to display its window.
54    */
55
56    public static void main(String[] args)
57    {
58        new GridWindow();
59    }
60 }
```

As previously mentioned, the GridLayout manager limits each cell to only one component and resizes components to fill up all of the space in a cell. To get around these limitations you can nest panels inside the cells and add other components to the panels. For example, the GridPanelWindow class shown in Code Listing 7-16 is a modification of the GridWindow class. It creates six panels and adds a button and a label to each panel. These panels are then added to the content pane's cells. Figure 7-23 shows the window displayed by this class.

Figure 7-22   Window displayed by the `GridWindow` class

Code Listing 7-16   (`GridPanelWindow.java`)

```java
 1 import javax.swing.*; // Needed for Swing classes
 2 import java.awt.*;    // Needed for GridLayout class
 3
 4 /**
 5    This class demonstrates how panels may be added to
 6    the cells created by a GridLayout manager.
 7 */
 8
 9 public class GridPanelWindow extends JFrame
10 {
11    private final int WINDOW_WIDTH = 400;   // Window width
12    private final int WINDOW_HEIGHT = 200;  // Window height
13
14    /**
15       Constructor
16    */
17
18    public GridPanelWindow()
19    {
20       // Set the title bar text.
21       setTitle("Grid Layout");
22
23       // Set the size of the window.
24       setSize(WINDOW_WIDTH, WINDOW_HEIGHT);
25
26       // Specify an action for the close button.
27       setDefaultCloseOperation(JFrame.EXIT_ON_CLOSE);
28
29       // Add a GridLayout manager to the content pane.
30       setLayout(new GridLayout(2, 3));
31
32       // Create six buttons.
33       JButton button1 = new JButton("Button 1");
```

```
34          JButton button2 = new JButton("Button 2");
35          JButton button3 = new JButton("Button 3");
36          JButton button4 = new JButton("Button 4");
37          JButton button5 = new JButton("Button 5");
38          JButton button6 = new JButton("Button 6");
39
40          // Create six labels.
41          JLabel label1 = new JLabel("This is cell 1.");
42          JLabel label2 = new JLabel("This is cell 2.");
43          JLabel label3 = new JLabel("This is cell 3.");
44          JLabel label4 = new JLabel("This is cell 4.");
45          JLabel label5 = new JLabel("This is cell 5.");
46          JLabel label6 = new JLabel("This is cell 6.");
47
48          // Create six panels.
49          JPanel panel1 = new JPanel();
50          JPanel panel2 = new JPanel();
51          JPanel panel3 = new JPanel();
52          JPanel panel4 = new JPanel();
53          JPanel panel5 = new JPanel();
54          JPanel panel6 = new JPanel();
55
56          // Add the labels to the panels.
57          panel1.add(label1);
58          panel2.add(label2);
59          panel3.add(label3);
60          panel4.add(label4);
61          panel5.add(label5);
62          panel6.add(label6);
63
64          // Add the buttons to the panels.
65          panel1.add(button1);
66          panel2.add(button2);
67          panel3.add(button3);
68          panel4.add(button4);
69          panel5.add(button5);
70          panel6.add(button6);
71
72          // Add the panels to the content pane.
73          add(panel1);  // Goes into row 1, column 1
74          add(panel2);  // Goes into row 1, column 2
75          add(panel3);  // Goes into row 1, column 3
76          add(panel4);  // Goes into row 2, column 1
77          add(panel5);  // Goes into row 2, column 2
78          add(panel6);  // Goes into row 2, column 3
79
80          // Display the window.
81          setVisible(true);
```

```
82      }
83
84      /**
85          The main method creates an instance of the
86          GridPanelWindow class, displaying its window.
87      */
88
89      public static void main(String[] args)
90      {
91          new GridPanelWindow();
92      }
93  }
```

Figure 7-23   Window displayed by the GridPanelWindow class

Because we have containers nested inside the content pane, there are multiple layout managers at work in the GridPanelWindow class. The content pane uses a GridLayout manager, and each of the JPanel objects uses a FlowLayout manager.

Checkpoint

7.10   How do you add a layout manager to a container?

7.11   Which layout manager divides a container into regions known as north, south, east, west, and center?

7.12   Which layout manager arranges components in a row, from left to right, in the order they were added to the container?

7.13   Which layout manager arranges components in rows and columns?

7.14   How many components can you have at one time in a BorderLayout region? In a GridLayout cell?

7.15   How do you prevent the BorderLayout manager from resizing a component that has been placed in its region?

7.16   How can you cause a content pane to be automatically sized to accommodate the components contained within it?

7.17   What is the default layout manager for a JFrame object's content pane? For a JPanel object?

7.5 Radio Buttons and Check Boxes

CONCEPT: Radio buttons normally appear in groups of two or more and allow the user to select one of several possible options. Check boxes, which may appear alone or in groups, allow the user to make yes/no or on/off selections.

Radio Buttons

Radio buttons are useful when you want the user to select one choice from several possible options. Figure 7-24 shows a group of radio buttons.

Figure 7-24   Radio buttons

A radio button may be selected or deselected. Each radio button has a small circle that appears filled in when the radio button is selected and appears empty when the radio button is deselected. You use the JRadioButton class to create radio buttons. Here are the general formats of two JRadioButton constructors:

```
JRadioButton(String text)
JRadioButton(String text, boolean selected)
```

The first constructor shown creates a deselected radio button. The argument passed to the text parameter is the string that is displayed next to the radio button. For example, the following statement creates a radio button with the text "Choice 1" displayed next to it. The radio button initially appears deselected.

```
JRadioButton radio1 = new JRadioButton("Choice 1");
```

The second constructor takes an additional boolean argument, which is passed to the selected parameter. If true is passed as the selected argument, the radio button initially appears selected. If false is passed, the radio button initially appears deselected. For example, the following statement creates a radio button with the text "Choice 1" displayed next to it. The radio button initially appears selected.

```
JRadioButton radio1 = new JRadioButton("Choice 1", true);
```

Radio buttons are normally grouped together. When a set of radio buttons are grouped together, only one of the radio buttons in the group may be selected at any time. Clicking a radio button selects it and automatically deselects any other radio button in the same group. Because only one radio button in a group can be selected at any given time, the buttons are said to be *mutually exclusive*.

> **NOTE:** The name "radio button" refers to the old car radios that had push buttons for selecting stations. Only one of the buttons could be pushed in at a time. When you pushed a button in, it automatically popped out any other button that was pushed in.

Grouping with the `ButtonGroup` class

Once you have created the `JRadioButton` objects that you wish to appear in a group, you must create an instance of the `ButtonGroup` class, and then add the `JRadioButton` objects to it. The `ButtonGroup` object creates the mutually exclusive relationship among the radio buttons that it contains. The following code shows an example:

```
// Create three radio buttons.
JRadioButton radio1 = new JRadioButton("Choice 1", true);
JRadioButton radio2 = new JRadioButton("Choice 2");
JRadioButton radio3 = new JRadioButton("Choice 3");

// Create a ButtonGroup object.
ButtonGroup group = new ButtonGroup();

// Add the radio buttons to the ButtonGroup object.
group.add(radio1);
group.add(radio2);
group.add(radio3);
```

Although you add radio buttons to a `ButtonGroup` object, `ButtonGroup` objects are not containers like `JPanel` objects, or content frames. The function of a `ButtonGroup` object is to deselect all the other radio buttons when one of them is selected. If you wish to add the radio buttons to a panel or a content frame, you must add them individually, as shown here:

```
// Add the radio buttons to the JPanel referenced by panel.
panel.add(radio1);
panel.add(radio2);
panel.add(radio3);
```

Responding to Radio Button Events

Just like `JButton` objects, `JRadioButton` objects generate an action event when they are clicked. To respond to a radio button action event, you must write an action listener class and then register an instance of that class with the `JRadioButton` object. To demonstrate, we will look at the `MetricConverterWindow` class, which is similar to the `KiloConverterWindow` class shown earlier. The `MetricConverterWindow` class presents a window in which the user can enter a distance in kilometers, and then click radio buttons to see that distance converted to miles, feet, or inches. The conversion formulas are as follows:

$Miles = Kilometers \times 0.6214$
$Feet = Kilometers \times 3281.0$
$Inches = Kilometers \times 39370.0$

Figure 7-25 shows a sketch of what the window will look like. As you can see from the sketch, the window will have a label, a text field, and three radio buttons. When the user clicks on one of the radio buttons, the distance will be converted to the selected units and displayed in a separate JOptionPane dialog box.

Figure 7-25 Metric Converter window

The MetricConverterWindow class is shown in Code Listing 7-17. The class initially displays the window shown at the top of Figure 7-26. The figure also shows the dialog boxes that are displayed when the user clicks any of the radio buttons.

Code Listing 7-17 (MetricConverterWindow.java)

```java
 1 import javax.swing.*;
 2 import java.awt.event.*;
 3 import java.awt.*;
 4
 5 /**
 6    The MetricConverterWindow class lets the user enter a
 7    distance in kilometers. Radio buttons can be selected to
 8    convert the kilometers to miles, feet, or inches.
 9 */
10
11 public class MetricConverterWindow extends JFrame
12 {
13    private JPanel panel;                    // A holding panel
14    private JLabel messageLabel;             // A message to the user
15    private JTextField kiloTextField;        // To hold user input
16    private JRadioButton milesButton;        // To convert to miles
17    private JRadioButton feetButton;         // To convert to feet
18    private JRadioButton inchesButton;       // To convert to inches
19    private ButtonGroup radioButtonGroup;    // To group radio buttons
20    private final int WINDOW_WIDTH = 400;    // Window width
21    private final int WINDOW_HEIGHT = 100;   // Window height
22
23    /**
24       Constructor
25    */
26
27    public MetricConverterWindow()
28    {
```

```
29          // Set the title.
30          setTitle("Metric Converter");
31
32          // Set the size of the window.
33          setSize(WINDOW_WIDTH, WINDOW_HEIGHT);
34
35          // Specify an action for the close button.
36          setDefaultCloseOperation(JFrame.EXIT_ON_CLOSE);
37
38          // Build the panel and add it to the frame.
39          buildPanel();
40
41          // Add the panel to the frame's content pane.
42          add(panel);
43
44          // Display the window.
45          setVisible(true);
46      }
47
48      /**
49          The buildPanel method adds a label, text field, and
50          and three buttons to a panel.
51      */
52
53      private void buildPanel()
54      {
55          // Create the label, text field, and radio buttons.
56          messageLabel = new JLabel("Enter a distance in kilometers");
57          kiloTextField = new JTextField(10);
58          milesButton = new JRadioButton("Convert to miles");
59          feetButton = new JRadioButton("Convert to feet");
60          inchesButton = new JRadioButton("Convert to inches");
61
62          // Group the radio buttons.
63          radioButtonGroup = new ButtonGroup();
64          radioButtonGroup.add(milesButton);
65          radioButtonGroup.add(feetButton);
66          radioButtonGroup.add(inchesButton);
67
68          // Add action listeners to the radio buttons.
69          milesButton.addActionListener(new RadioButtonListener());
70          feetButton.addActionListener(new RadioButtonListener());
71          inchesButton.addActionListener(new RadioButtonListener());
72
73          // Create a panel and add the components to it.
74          panel = new JPanel();
75          panel.add(messageLabel);
76          panel.add(kiloTextField);
```

```
77              panel.add(milesButton);
78              panel.add(feetButton);
79              panel.add(inchesButton);
80       }
81
82       /**
83          Private inner class that handles the event when
84          the user clicks one of the radio buttons.
85       */
86
87       private class RadioButtonListener implements ActionListener
88       {
89          public void actionPerformed(ActionEvent e)
90          {
91             String input;          // To hold the user's input
92             String convertTo = ""; // The units we're converting to
93             double result = 0.0;   // To hold the conversion
94
95             // Get the kilometers entered.
96             input = kiloTextField.getText();
97
98             // Determine which radio button was clicked.
99             if (e.getSource() == milesButton)
100            {
101               // Convert to miles.
102               convertTo = " miles.";
103               result = Double.parseDouble(input) * 0.6214;
104            }
105            else if (e.getSource() == feetButton)
106            {
107               // Convert to feet.
108               convertTo = " feet.";
109               result = Double.parseDouble(input) * 3281.0;
110            }
111            else if (e.getSource() == inchesButton)
112            {
113               // Convert to inches.
114               convertTo = " inches.";
115               result = Double.parseDouble(input) * 39370.0;
116            }
117
118            // Display the conversion.
119            JOptionPane.showMessageDialog(null, input +
120                    " kilometers is " + result + convertTo);
121         }
122      }
```

```
123
124     /**
125         The main method creates an instance of the
126         MetricConverterWindow class, displaying its window.
127     */
128
129     public static void main(String[] args)
130     {
131         new MetricConverterWindow();
132     }
133 }
```

Figure 7-26 Window and dialog boxes displayed by the `MetricConverterWindow` class

This window appears first. The user enters 2 into the text field.

This dialog box appears when the user clicks the "Convert to miles" radio button.

This dialog box appears when the user clicks the "Convert to feet" radio button.

This dialog box appears when the user clicks the "Convert to inches" radio button.

Determining in Code Whether a Radio Button Is Selected

In many applications you will merely want to know if a radio button is selected. The `JRadioButton` class's `isSelected` method returns a `boolean` value indicating whether the radio button is selected. If the radio button is selected, the method returns `true`. Otherwise, it returns `false`. In the following code, the `radio` variable references a radio button. The `if` statement calls the `isSelected` method to determine whether the radio button is selected.

```
if (radio.isSelected())
{
    // Code here executes if the radio
    // button is selected.
}
```

Selecting a Radio Button in Code

It is also possible to select a radio button in code with the `JRadioButton` class's `doClick` method. When the method is called, the radio button is selected just as if the user had clicked on it. As a result, an action event is generated. In the following statement, the `radio` variable references a radio button. When this statement executes, the radio button will be selected.

```
radio.doClick();
```

Check Boxes

A *check box* appears as a small box with a label appearing next to it. The window shown in Figure 7-27 has three check boxes.

Figure 7-27 Check boxes

Like radio buttons, check boxes may be selected or deselected at run time. When a check box is selected, a small check mark appears inside the box. Although check boxes are often displayed in groups, they are not usually grouped in a `ButtonGroup` like radio buttons. This is because check boxes are not normally used to make mutually exclusive selections. Instead, the user is allowed to select any or all of the check boxes that are displayed in a group.

You create a check box with the `JCheckBox` class. Here are the general formats of two `JCheckBox` constructors:

```
JCheckBox(String text)
JCheckBox(String text, boolean selected)
```

The first constructor shown creates a deselected check box. The argument passed to the `text` parameter is the string that is displayed next to the check box. For example, the following statement creates a check box with the text "Macaroni" displayed next to it. The check box initially appears deselected.

```
JCheckBox check1 = new JCheckBox("Macaroni");
```

The second constructor takes an additional `boolean` argument, which is passed to the `selected` parameter. If `true` is passed as the `selected` argument, the radio check box initially appears selected. If `false` is passed, the check box initially appears deselected. For example, the following statement creates a check box with the text "Macaroni" displayed next to it. The radio check box initially appears selected.

```
JCheckBox check1 = new JCheckBox("Macaroni", true);
```

Responding to Check Box Events

When a `JCheckBox` object is selected or deselected, it generates an *item event*. You handle item events in a manner similar to the way you handle the action events that are generated by `JButton` and `JRadioButton` objects. First, you write an *item listener* class, which must meet the following requirements:

- It must implement the `ItemListener` interface.
- It must have a method named `itemStateChanged` with the following header:

```
public void itemStateChanged(ItemEvent e)
```

NOTE: When implementing the `ItemListener` interface, your code must have the following import statement: `import java.awt.event.*;`

Once you have written an item listener class, you create an object of that class, and then register the item listener object with the `JCheckBox` component. When a `JCheckBox` component generates an event, it automatically executes the `itemStateChanged` method of the item listener object that is registered to it, passing the event object as an argument.

Determining in Code Whether a Check Box Is Selected

As with `JRadioButton`, you use the `isSelected` method to determine whether a `JCheckBox` component is selected. The method returns a `boolean` value. If the check box is selected, the method returns `true`. Otherwise, it returns `false`. In the following code, the `checkBox` variable references a `JCheckBox` component. The `if` statement calls the `isSelected` method to determine whether the check box is selected.

```
if (checkBox.isSelected())
{
    // Code here executes if the check
    // box is selected.
}
```

The `ColorCheckBoxWindow` class, shown in Code Listing 7-18 demonstrates how check boxes are used. It displays the window shown in Figure 7-28. When the "Yellow background" check box is selected, the background color of the content pane, the label, and the check boxes turns yellow. When this check box is deselected, the background colors go back to light gray. When the "Red foreground" check box is selected, the color of the text displayed in the label and the check boxes turns red. When this check box is deselected, the foreground colors go back to black.

Code Listing 7-18 (`ColorCheckBoxWindow.java`)

```
 1 import javax.swing.*;
 2 import java.awt.*;
 3 import java.awt.event.*;
 4
 5 /**
 6    The ColorCheckBoxWindow class demonstrates how check boxes
 7    can be used.
 8 */
 9
10 public class ColorCheckBoxWindow extends JFrame
11 {
12    private JLabel messageLabel;           // A message to the user
13    private JCheckBox yellowCheckBox;      // To select yellow background
14    private JCheckBox redCheckBox;         // To select red foreground
15    private final int WINDOW_WIDTH = 300;      // Window width
16    private final int WINDOW_HEIGHT = 100;     // Window height
17
18    /**
19       Constructor
20    */
21
22    public ColorCheckBoxWindow()
23    {
24       // Set the text for the title bar.
25       setTitle("Color Check Boxes");
26
27       // Set the size of the window.
28       setSize(WINDOW_WIDTH, WINDOW_HEIGHT);
29
30       // Specify an action for the close button.
31       setDefaultCloseOperation(JFrame.EXIT_ON_CLOSE);
32
33       // Create a label.
34       messageLabel = new JLabel("Select the check " +
35                                 "boxes to change colors.");
36
37       // Create the check boxes.
38       yellowCheckBox = new JCheckBox("Yellow background");
39       redCheckBox = new JCheckBox("Red foreground");
40
41       // Add an item listener to the check boxes.
42       yellowCheckBox.addItemListener(new CheckBoxListener());
43       redCheckBox.addItemListener(new CheckBoxListener());
44
45       // Add a FlowLayout manager to the content pane.
46       setLayout(new FlowLayout());
```

```
47
48          // Add the label and check boxes to the content pane.
49          add(messageLabel);
50          add(yellowCheckBox);
51          add(redCheckBox);
52
53          // Display the window.
54          setVisible(true);
55       }
56
57       /**
58          Private inner class that handles the event when
59          the user clicks one of the check boxes.
60       */
61
62       private class CheckBoxListener implements ItemListener
63       {
64          public void itemStateChanged(ItemEvent e)
65          {
66             // Determine which check box was clicked.
67             if (e.getSource() == yellowCheckBox)
68             {
69                // Is the yellow check box selected? If so, we
70                // want to set the background color to yellow.
71                if (yellowCheckBox.isSelected())
72                {
73                   // The yellow check box was selected. Set
74                   // the background color for the content
75                   // pane and the two check boxes to yellow.
76                   getContentPane().setBackground(Color.YELLOW);
77                   yellowCheckBox.setBackground(Color.YELLOW);
78                   redCheckBox.setBackground(Color.YELLOW);
79                }
80                else
81                {
82                   // The yellow check box was deselected. Set
83                   // the background color for the content
84                   // pane and the two check boxes to light gray.
85                   getContentPane().setBackground(Color.LIGHT_GRAY);
86                   yellowCheckBox.setBackground(Color.LIGHT_GRAY);
87                   redCheckBox.setBackground(Color.LIGHT_GRAY);
88                }
89             }
90             else if (e.getSource() == redCheckBox)
91             {
92                // Is the red check box selected? If so, we want
93                // to set the foreground color to red.
94                if (redCheckBox.isSelected())
```

```
 95                   {
 96                       // The red check box was selected. Set the
 97                       // foreground color for the label and the
 98                       // two check boxes to red.
 99                       messageLabel.setForeground(Color.RED);
100                       yellowCheckBox.setForeground(Color.RED);
101                       redCheckBox.setForeground(Color.RED);
102                   }
103                   else
104                   {
105                       // The red check box was deselected. Set the
106                       // foreground color for the label and the
107                       // two check boxes to black.
108                       messageLabel.setForeground(Color.BLACK);
109                       yellowCheckBox.setForeground(Color.BLACK);
110                       redCheckBox.setForeground(Color.BLACK);
111                   }
112               }
113           }
114       }
115
116       /**
117           The main method creates an instance of the
118           ColorCheckBoxWindow class, displaying its window.
119       */
120
121       public static void main(String[] args)
122       {
123           new ColorCheckBoxWindow();
124       }
125 }
```

Figure 7-28 Window displayed by the ColorCheckBoxWindow class

Selecting a Check Box in Code

As with radio buttons, it is possible to select check boxes in code with the JCheckBox class's doClick method. When the method is called, the radio check box is selected just as if the user had clicked on it. As a result, an item event is generated. In the following statement, the checkBox variable references a JCheckBox object. When this statement executes, the check box will be selected.

```
checkBox.doClick();
```

✓ Checkpoint

7.18   You want the user to be able to select only one item from a group of items. Which type of component would you use for the items, radio buttons or check boxes?

7.19   You want the user to be able to select any number of items from a group of items. Which type of component would you use for the items, radio buttons or check boxes?

7.20   What is the purpose of a ButtonGroup object?

7.21   Do you normally add radio buttons, check boxes, or both to a ButtonGroup object?

7.22   What type of event does a radio button generate when the user clicks on it?

7.23   What type of event does a check box generate when the user clicks on it?

7.24   How do you determine in code whether a radio button is selected?

7.25   How do you determine in code whether a check box is selected?

7.6 Borders

CONCEPT: A component can appear with several different styles of borders around it. A Border object specifies the details of a border. You use the BorderFactory class to create Border objects.

Sometimes it is helpful to place a border around a component or a group of components on a panel. You can give windows a more organized look by grouping related components inside borders. For example, Figure 7-29 shows a group of check boxes that are enclosed in a border. In addition, notice that the border has a title.

Figure 7-29   A group of check boxes with a titled border

JPanel components have a method named setBorder, which is used to add a border to the panel. The setBorder method accepts a Border object as its argument. A Border object contains detailed information describing the appearance of a border.

Rather than creating Border objects yourself, you should use the BorderFactory class to create them for you. The BorderFactory class has methods that return various types of borders. Table 7-6 describes borders that can be created with the `BorderFactory` class. The table also lists the `BorderFactory` methods that can be called to create the borders. Note that there are several overloaded versions of each method.

NOTE: If you use the `BorderFactory` class in your code, you should have the following import statement: `import javax.swing.*;`

Table 7-6 Borders produced by the `BorderFactory` class

Border	`BorderFactory` Method	Description
Compound border	createCompoundBorder	A border that has two parts: an inside edge and an outside edge. The inside and outside edges can be any of the other borders.
Empty border	createEmptyBorder	A border that contains only empty space.
Etched border	createEtchedBorder	A border with a 3-D appearance that looks "etched" into the background.
Line border	createLineBorder	A border that appears as a line.
Lowered bevel border	createLoweredBevelBorder	A border that looks like beveled edges. It has a 3-D appearance that gives the illusion of being sunken into the surrounding background.
Matte border	createMatteBorder	A line border that can have edges of different thicknesses.
Raised bevel border	createRaisedBevelBorder	A border that looks like beveled edges. It has a 3-D appearance that gives the illusion of being raised above the surrounding background.
Titled border	createTitledBorder	An etched border with a title.

In this chapter we will concentrate on empty borders, line borders, and titled borders.

Empty Borders

An empty border is simply empty space around the edges of a component. To create an empty border, call the `BorderFactory` class's `createEmtpyBorder` method. Here is the method's general format:

```
BorderFactory.createEmptyBorder(int top, int left,
                                int bottom, int right);
```

The arguments passed into `top`, `left`, `bottom`, and `right` specify in pixels the size of the border's top, left, bottom, and right edges. The method returns a reference to a `Border` object. The following is an example of a statement that uses the method. Assume that the `panel` variable references a `JPanel` object.

```
panel.setBorder(BorderFactory.createEmptyBorder(5, 5, 5, 5));
```

After this statement executes, the JPanel referenced by panel will have an empty border of five pixels around each edge.

> **NOTE:** You do not create an instance of the BorderFactory class. Instead, you simply call its methods with BorderFactory. preceding the name of the method. Instead of calling the methods from an object, you call them directly from the class. This is similar to the way the Math class and wrapper class methods we have discussed are called. Methods that are called from the class instead of an object are called *static methods*. You will learn more about static methods in Chapter 9.

Line Borders

A line border is a line of a specified color and thickness that appears around the edges of a component. To create a line border, call the BorderFactory class's createLineBorder method. Here is the method's general format:

```
BorderFactory.createLineBorder(Color color, int thickness);
```

The arguments passed into color and thickness specify the color of the line and the size of the line in pixels. The method returns a reference to a Border object. The following is an example of a statement that uses the method. Assume that the panel variable references a JPanel object.

```
panel.setBorder(BorderFactory.createLineBorder(Color.RED, 1));
```

After this statement executes, the JPanel referenced by panel will have a red line border that is one pixel thick around its edges.

Titled Borders

A titled border is an etched border with a title displayed on it. To create a titled border, call the BorderFactory class's createTitledBorder method. Here is the method's general format:

```
BorderFactory.createTitledBorder(String title);
```

The argument passed into title is the text that is to be displayed as the border's title. The method returns a reference to a Border object. The following is an example of a statement that uses the method. Assume that the panel variable references a JPanel object.

```
panel.setBorder(BorderFactory.createTitledBorder("Choices"));
```

After this statement executes, the JPanel referenced by panel will have an etched border with the title "Choices" displayed on it.

Checkpoint

7.26   What method do you use to set a border around a component?

7.27   What is the preferred way of creating a Border object?

7.7 Focus on Problem Solving: Extending Classes from `JPanel`

CONCEPT: By writing a class that is extended from the **JPanel** class, you can create a custom panel component that can hold other components and their related code.

In the applications that you have studied so far in this chapter, we have used the `extends JFrame` clause in the class header to extend the class from the `JFrame` class. Recall that the extended class is then a specialized version of the `JFrame` class, and we use its constructor to create the panels, buttons, and all of the other components needed. This approach works well for simple applications. But for applications that use many components, this approach can be cumbersome. Bundling all of the code and event listeners for a large number of components into a single class can lead to a large and complex class. A better approach is to encapsulate smaller groups of related components and their event listeners into their own classes.

A commonly used technique is to extend a class from the `JPanel` class. This allows you to create your own specialized panel component, which can contain other components and related code such as event listeners. A complex application that uses numerous components can be constructed from several specialized panel components. In this section we will examine such an application.

The Brandi's Bagel House Application

Brandi's Bagel House has a bagel and coffee delivery service for the businesses in her neighborhood. Customers may call in and order white and whole wheat bagels with a variety of toppings. In addition, customers may order three different types of coffee. (Delivery for coffee alone is not available, however.) Here is a complete price list:

Bagels: *White bagel $1.25, whole wheat bagel $1.50*
Toppings: *Cream cheese $0.50, butter $0.25, peach jelly $0.75, blueberry jam $0.75*
Coffee: *Regular coffee $1.25, decaf coffee $1.25, cappuccino $2.00*

Brandi, the owner, needs an "order calculator" application that her staff can use to calculate the price of an order as it is called in. The application should display the subtotal, the amount of a 6 percent sales tax, and the total of the order. Figure 7-30 shows a sketch of the application's window. The user selects the type of bagel, toppings, and coffee, then clicks the Calculate button. A dialog box appears displaying the subtotal, amount of sales tax, and total. The user can exit the application by either clicking the Exit button or the standard close button in the upper-right corner.

The layout shown in the sketch can be achieved using a `BorderLayout` manager with the window's content pane. The label that displays "Welcome to Brandi's Bagel House" is in the north region, the radio buttons for the bagel types are in the west region, the check boxes for the toppings are in the center region, the radio buttons for the coffee selection are in the east region, and the Calculate and Exit buttons are in the south region. To construct this window we create the following specialized panel classes that are extended from `JPanel`:

Figure 7-30   Sketch of the Order Calculator window

- **GreetingsPanel.** This panel contains the label that appears in the window's north region.
- **BagelPanel.** This panel contains the radio buttons for the types of bagels.
- **ToppingsPanel.** This panel contains the check boxes for the types of bagels.
- **CoffeePanel.** This panel contains the radio buttons for the coffee selections.

(We will not create a specialized panel for the Calculate and Exit buttons. The reason is explained later.) After these classes have been created, we can create objects from them and add the objects to the correct regions of the window's content pane. Let's take a closer look at each of these classes.

The GreetingPanel Class

The GreetingPanel class holds the label displaying the text "Welcome to Brandi's Bagel House". Code Listing 7-19 shows the class, which extends JPanel.

Code Listing 7-19   (GreetingPanel.java)

```
1   import javax.swing.*;
2
3   /**
4      The GreetingPanel class displays a greeting in a panel.
5   */
6
7   public class GreetingPanel extends JPanel
8   {
9      private JLabel greeting; // To display a greeting
10
11     /**
12        Constructor
13     */
14
15     public GreetingPanel()
16     {
17        // Create the label.
```

```
18                greeting = new JLabel("Welcome to Brandi's Bagel House");
19
20                // Add the label to this panel.
21                add(greeting);
22            }
23    }
```

In line 21 the add method is called to add the JLabel component referenced by greeting. Notice that we are calling the method without an object reference and a dot preceding it. This is because the method was inherited from the JPanel class, and we can call it just as if it were written into the GreetingPanel class declaration.

When we create an instance of this class, we are creating a JPanel component that displays a label with the text "Welcome to Brandi's Bagel House". Figure 7-31 shows how the component will appear when it is placed in the window's north region.

Figure 7-31   Appearance of the GreetingPanel component

Welcome to Brandi's Bagel House

The BagelPanel Class

The BagelPanel class holds the radio buttons for the types of bagels. Notice that this panel uses a GridLayout manager with two rows and one column. Code Listing 7-20 shows the class, which is extended from JPanel.

Code Listing 7-20   (BagelPanel.java)

```java
1    import javax.swing.*;
2    import java.awt.*;
3
4    /**
5       The BagelPanel class allows the user to select either
6       a white or whole wheat bagel.
7    */
8
9    public class BagelPanel extends JPanel
10   {
11       // The following constants are used to indicate
12       // the cost of each type of bagel.
13       public final double WHITE_BAGEL = 1.25;
14       public final double WHEAT_BAGEL = 1.50;
15
16       private JRadioButton whiteBagel;  // To select white
17       private JRadioButton wheatBagel;  // To select wheat
```

```
18      private ButtonGroup bg;                  // Radio button group
19
20      /**
21         Constructor
22      */
23
24      public BagelPanel()
25      {
26         // Create a GridLayout manager with
27         // two rows and one column.
28         setLayout(new GridLayout(2, 1));
29
30         // Create the radio buttons.
31         whiteBagel = new JRadioButton("White", true);
32         wheatBagel = new JRadioButton("Wheat");
33
34         // Group the radio buttons.
35         bg = new ButtonGroup();
36         bg.add(whiteBagel);
37         bg.add(wheatBagel);
38
39         // Add a border around the panel.
40         setBorder(BorderFactory.createTitledBorder("Bagel"));
41
42         // Add the radio buttons to the panel.
43         add(whiteBagel);
44         add(wheatBagel);
45      }
46
47      /**
48         getBagelCost method
49         @return The cost of the selected bagel.
50      */
51
52      public double getBagelCost()
53      {
54         double bagelCost = 0.0;
55
56         if (whiteBagel.isSelected())
57            bagelCost = WHITE_BAGEL;
58         else
59            bagelCost = WHEAT_BAGEL;
60
61         return bagelCost;
62      }
63   }
```

Notice that the `whiteBagel` radio button is automatically selected when it is created. This is the default choice. This class does not have an inner event listener class because we do not want to execute any code when the user selects a bagel. Instead, we want this class to be able to report the cost of the selected bagel. That is the purpose of the `getBagelCost` method, which returns the cost of the selected bagel as a `double`. (This method will be called by the Calculate button's event listener.) Figure 7-32 shows how the component appears when it is placed in the window's west region.

Figure 7-32   Appearance of the `BagelPanel` component

The `ToppingPanel` Class

The `ToppingPanel` class holds the check boxes for the available toppings. Code Listing 7-21 shows the class, which is also extended from `JPanel`.

Code Listing 7-21   (`ToppingPanel.java`)

```
 1   import javax.swing.*;
 2   import java.awt.*;
 3
 4   /**
 5      The ToppingPanel class allows the user to select
 6      the toppings for the bagel.
 7   */
 8
 9   public class ToppingPanel extends JPanel
10   {
11      // The following constants are used to indicate
12      // the cost of toppings.
13      public final double CREAM_CHEESE = 0.50;
14      public final double BUTTER = 0.25;
15      public final double PEACH_JELLY = 0.75;
16      public final double BLUEBERRY_JAM = 0.75;
17
18      private JCheckBox creamCheese;      // To select cream cheese
19      private JCheckBox butter;           // To select butter
20      private JCheckBox peachJelly;       // To select peach jelly
21      private JCheckBox blueberryJam;     // To select blueberry jam
22
```

```
23      /**
24         Constructor
25      */
26
27      public ToppingPanel()
28      {
29         // Create a GridLayout manager with
30         // four rows and one column.
31         setLayout(new GridLayout(4, 1));
32
33         // Create the check boxes.
34         creamCheese = new JCheckBox("Cream cheese");
35         butter = new JCheckBox("Butter");
36         peachJelly = new JCheckBox("Peach jelly");
37         blueberryJam = new JCheckBox("Blueberry jam");
38
39         // Add a border around the panel.
40         setBorder(BorderFactory.createTitledBorder("Toppings"));
41
42         // Add the check boxes to the panel.
43         add(creamCheese);
44         add(butter);
45         add(peachJelly);
46         add(blueberryJam);
47      }
48
49      /**
50         getToppingCost method
51         @return The cost of the selected toppings.
52      */
53
54      public double getToppingCost()
55      {
56         double toppingCost = 0.0;
57
58         if (creamCheese.isSelected())
59            toppingCost += CREAM_CHEESE;
60         if (butter.isSelected())
61            toppingCost += BUTTER;
62         if (peachJelly.isSelected())
63            toppingCost += PEACH_JELLY;
64         if (blueberryJam.isSelected())
65            toppingCost += BLUEBERRY_JAM;
66
67         return toppingCost;
68      }
69   }
```

As with the `BagelPanel` class, this class does not have an inner event listener class because we do not want to execute any code when the user selects a topping. Instead, we want this class to be able to report the total cost of all the selected toppings. That is the purpose of the `getToppingCost` method, which returns the cost of all the selected toppings as a `double`. (This method will be called by the Calculate button's event listener.) Figure 7-33 shows how the component appears when it is placed in the window's center region.

Figure 7-33   Appearance of the `ToppingPanel` component

The `CoffeePanel` Class

The `CoffeePanel` class holds the radio buttons for the available coffee selections. Code Listing 7-22 shows the class, which extends `JPanel`.

Code Listing 7-22   (`CoffeePanel.java`)

```
 1   import javax.swing.*;
 2   import java.awt.*;
 3
 4   /**
 5      The CoffeePanel class allows the user to select coffee.
 6   */
 7
 8   public class CoffeePanel extends JPanel
 9   {
10      // The following constants are used to indicate
11      // the cost of coffee.
12      public final double NO_COFFEE = 0.0;
13      public final double REGULAR_COFFEE = 1.25;
14      public final double DECAF_COFFEE = 1.25;
15      public final double CAPPUCCINO = 2.00;
16
17      private JRadioButton noCoffee;       // To select no coffee
18      private JRadioButton regularCoffee;  // To select regular coffee
19      private JRadioButton decafCoffee;    // To select decaf
20      private JRadioButton cappuccino;     // To select cappuccino
21      private ButtonGroup bg;              // Radio button group
22
23      /**
24         Constructor
```

```java
25      */
26
27      public CoffeePanel()
28      {
29         // Create a GridLayout manager with
30         // four rows and one column.
31         setLayout(new GridLayout(4, 1));
32
33         // Create the radio buttons.
34         noCoffee = new JRadioButton("None");
35         regularCoffee = new JRadioButton("Regular coffee", true);
36         decafCoffee = new JRadioButton("Decaf coffee");
37         cappuccino = new JRadioButton("Cappuccino");
38
39         // Group the radio buttons.
40         bg = new ButtonGroup();
41         bg.add(noCoffee);
42         bg.add(regularCoffee);
43         bg.add(decafCoffee);
44         bg.add(cappuccino);
45
46         // Add a border around the panel.
47         setBorder(BorderFactory.createTitledBorder("Coffee"));
48
49         // Add the radio buttons to the panel.
50         add(noCoffee);
51         add(regularCoffee);
52         add(decafCoffee);
53         add(cappuccino);
54      }
55
56      /**
57         getCoffeeCost method
58         @return The cost of the selected coffee.
59      */
60
61      public double getCoffeeCost()
62      {
63         double coffeeCost = 0.0;
64
65         if (noCoffee.isSelected())
66            coffeeCost = NO_COFFEE;
67         else if (regularCoffee.isSelected())
68            coffeeCost = REGULAR_COFFEE;
69         else if (decafCoffee.isSelected())
70            coffeeCost = DECAF_COFFEE;
71         else if (cappuccino.isSelected())
72            coffeeCost = CAPPUCCINO;
```

```
73
74          return coffeeCost;
75     }
76 }
```

As with the `BagelPanel` and `ToppingPanel` classes, this class does not have an inner event listener class because we do not want to execute any code when the user selects coffee. Instead, we want this class to be able to report the cost of the selected coffee. The `getCoffeeCost` method returns the cost of the selected coffee as a `double`. (This method will be called by the Calculate button's event listener.) Figure 7-34 shows how the component appears when it is placed in the window's east region.

Figure 7-34   Appearance of the `CoffeePanel` component

Putting It All Together

The last step in creating this application is to write a class that builds the application's window and adds the Calculate and Exit buttons. This class, which we name `OrderCalculatorGUI`, is extended from `JFrame` and uses a `BorderLayout` manager with its content pane. Figure 7-35 shows how instances of the `GreetingPanel`, `BagelPanel`, `ToppingPanel`, and `CoffeePanel` classes are placed in the content pane.

Figure 7-35   Placement of the custom panels

We have not created a custom panel class to hold the Calculate and Exit buttons. The reason is that the Calculate button's event listener must call the `getBagelCost`, `getToppingCost`, and `getCoffeeCost` methods. In order to call those methods, the event listener must have access to the `BagelPanel`, `ToppingPanel`, and `CoffeePanel` objects that are created in the `OrderCalculatorGUI` class. The approach taken in this example is to have the `OrderCalculatorGUI` class itself create the buttons. The code for the `OrderCalculatorGUI` class is shown in Code Listing 7-23.

Code Listing 7-23 (`OrderCalculatorGUI.java`)

```
 1 import javax.swing.*;
 2 import java.awt.*;
 3 import java.awt.event.*;
 4 import java.text.DecimalFormat;
 5
 6 /**
 7    The OrderCalculatorGUI class creates the GUI for the
 8    Brandi's Bagel House application.
 9 */
10
11 public class OrderCalculatorGUI extends JFrame
12 {
13    private BagelPanel bagels;           // Bagel panel
14    private ToppingPanel toppings;       // Topping panel
15    private CoffeePanel coffee;          // Coffee panel
16    private GreetingPanel banner;        // To display a greeting
17    private JPanel buttonPanel;          // To hold the buttons
18    private JButton calcButton;          // To calculate the cost
19    private JButton exitButton;          // To exit the application
20    private final double TAX_RATE = 0.06;// Sales tax rate
21
22
23    /**
24       Constructor
25    */
26
27    public OrderCalculatorGUI()
28    {
29       // Display a title.
30       setTitle("Order Calculator");
31
32       // Specify an action for the close button.
33       setDefaultCloseOperation(JFrame.EXIT_ON_CLOSE);
34
```

```
35          // Create a BorderLayout manager.
36          setLayout(new BorderLayout());
37
38          // Create the custom panels.
39          banner = new GreetingPanel();
40          bagels = new BagelPanel();
41          toppings = new ToppingPanel();
42          coffee = new CoffeePanel();
43
44          // Create the button panel.
45          buildButtonPanel();
46
47          // Add the components to the content pane.
48          add(banner, BorderLayout.NORTH);
49          add(bagels, BorderLayout.WEST);
50          add(toppings, BorderLayout.CENTER);
51          add(coffee, BorderLayout.EAST);
52          add(buttonPanel, BorderLayout.SOUTH);
53
54          // Pack the contents of the window and display it.
55          pack();
56          setVisible(true);
57       }
58
59       /**
60          The buildButtonPanel method builds the button panel.
61       */
62
63       private void buildButtonPanel()
64       {
65          // Create a panel for the buttons.
66          buttonPanel = new JPanel();
67
68          // Create the buttons.
69          calcButton = new JButton("Calculate");
70          exitButton = new JButton("Exit");
71
72          // Register the action listeners.
73          calcButton.addActionListener(new CalcButtonListener());
74          exitButton.addActionListener(new ExitButtonListener());
75
76          // Add the buttons to the button panel.
77          buttonPanel.add(calcButton);
78          buttonPanel.add(exitButton);
79       }
80
81       /**
82          Private inner class that handles the event when
83          the user clicks the Calculate button.
```

```
 84     */
 85
 86     private class CalcButtonListener implements ActionListener
 87     {
 88        public void actionPerformed(ActionEvent e)
 89        {
 90           // Variables to hold the subtotal, tax, and total
 91           double subtotal, tax, total;
 92
 93           // Calculate the subtotal.
 94           subtotal = bagels.getBagelCost() +
 95                      toppings.getToppingCost() +
 96                      coffee.getCoffeeCost();
 97
 98           // Calculate the sales tax.
 99           tax = subtotal * TAX_RATE;
100
101           // Calculate the total.
102           total = subtotal + tax;
103
104           // Create a DecimalFormat object to format output.
105           DecimalFormat dollar = new DecimalFormat("0.00");
106
107           // Display the charges.
108           JOptionPane.showMessageDialog(null, "Subtotal: $" +
109                      dollar.format(subtotal) + "\n" +
110                      "Tax: $" + dollar.format(tax) + "\n" +
111                      "Total: $" + dollar.format(total));
112        }
113     }
114
115     /**
116        Private inner class that handles the event when
117        the user clicks the Exit button.
118     */
119
120     private class ExitButtonListener implements ActionListener
121     {
122        public void actionPerformed(ActionEvent e)
123        {
124           System.exit(0);
125        }
126     }
127 }
```

The program shown in Code Listing 7-24 creates an instance of the `OrderCalculatorGUI` class, which displays the window shown in Figure 7-36. Figure 7-37 shows the `JOptionPane` dialog box that is displayed when the user selects a wheat bagel with butter, cream cheese, and decaf coffee.

Code Listing 7-24 (Bagel.java)

```
1   /**
2      This program creates an instance of the OrderCalculatorGUI class
3     which displays the GUI for the Brandi's Bagel House application.
4   */
5
6   public class Bagel
7   {
8      public static void main(String[] args)
9      {
10         new OrderCalculatorGUI();
11     }
12  }
```

Figure 7-36 The Order Calculator window

Figure 7-37 The subtotal, tax, and total displayed

7.8 Splash Screens

CONCEPT: A splash screen is a graphic image that is displayed while an application loads into memory and starts up.

Most major applications display a splash screen, which is a graphic image that is displayed while the application is loading into memory. Splash screens usually show company logos and keep the user's attention while the application starts up. Splash screens are particularly important for large applications that take a long time to load, because they assure the user that the program is not malfunctioning.

Beginning with Java 6, you can display splash screens with your Java applications. First, you have to use a graphics program to create the image that you want to display. Java supports splash screens in the GIF, PNG, or JPEG formats. (If you are using Windows, you can create images with Microsoft Paint, which supports all of these formats.)

To display the splash screen you use the `java` command in the following way when you run the application:

```
java -splash:GraphicFileName ClassFileName
```

`GraphicFileName` is the name of the file that contains the graphic image, and `ClassFileName` is the name of the *.class* file that you are running. For example, on the Student CD, in the same folder as the *Brandi's Bagel House* application, you will find a file named *BrandiLogo.jpg*. This image, which is shown in Figure 7-38, is a logo for the *Brandi's Bagel House* application. To display the splash screen when the application starts, you would use the following command:

```
java -splash:BrandiLogo.jpg Bagel
```

When you run this command, the graphic file will immediately be displayed in the center of the screen. It will remain displayed until the application's window appears.

Figure 7-38   Splash screen for the *Brandi's Bagel House* application

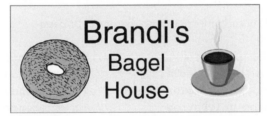

7.9 Using Console Output to Debug a GUI Application

CONCEPT: When debugging a GUI application, you can use `System.out.println` to send diagnostic messages to the console.

When an application is not performing correctly, programmers sometimes write statements that display *diagnostic messages* into the application. For example, if an application is not giving the correct result for a calculation, diagnostic messages can be displayed at various points in the program's execution showing the values of all the variables used in the calculation. If the trouble is caused by a variable that has not been properly initialized, or that has not been assigned the correct value, the diagnostic messages reveal this problem. This helps the programmer to see what is going on "under the hood" while an application is running.

The System.out.println method can be a valuable tool for displaying diagnostic messages in a GUI application. Because the System.out.println method sends its output to the console, diagnostic messages can be displayed without interfering with the application's GUI windows.

Code Listing 7-25 shows an example. This is a modified version of the KiloConverterWindow class, discussed earlier in this chapter. Inside the actionPerformed method, which is in the CalcButtonListener inner class, calls to the System.out.println method have been written. The new code, which appears in lines 98 through 103 and 112 through 114, is shown in bold. These new statements display the value that the application has retrieved from the text field, and is working within its calculation. (This file is stored in the Student CD source code folder *Chapter 07\KiloConverter Phase 3*.)

Code Listing 7-25 (KiloConverterWindow.java)

```java
1  import javax.swing.*;    // Needed for Swing classes
2  import java.awt.event.*; // Needed for ActionListener Interface
3
4  /**
5     The KiloConverterWindow class displays a JFrame that
6     lets the user enter a distance in kilometers. When
7     the Calculate button is clicked, a dialog box is
8     displayed with the distance converted to miles.
9  */
10
11 public class KiloConverterWindow extends JFrame
12 {
13    private JPanel panel;               // To reference a panel
14    private JLabel messageLabel;        // To reference a label
15    private JTextField kiloTextField;   // To reference a text field
16    private JButton calcButton;         // To reference a button
17    private final int WINDOW_WIDTH = 310;   // Window width
18    private final int WINDOW_HEIGHT = 100;  // Window height
19
20    /**
21       Constructor
22    */
23
24    public KiloConverterWindow()
25    {
26       // Set the window title.
27       setTitle("Kilometer Converter");
28
29       // Set the size of the window.
30       setSize(WINDOW_WIDTH, WINDOW_HEIGHT);
31
32       // Specify what happens when the close button is clicked.
```

```
33          setDefaultCloseOperation(JFrame.EXIT_ON_CLOSE);
34
35          // Build the panel and add it to the frame.
36          buildPanel();
37
38          // Add the panel to the frame's content pane.
39          add(panel);
40
41          // Display the window.
42          setVisible(true);
43      }
44
45      /**
46         The buildPanel method adds a label, text field,
47         and a button to a panel.
48      */
49
50      private void buildPanel()
51      {
52          // Create a label to display instructions.
53          messageLabel = new JLabel("Enter a distance " +
54                                    "in kilometers");
55
56          // Create a text field 10 characters wide.
57          kiloTextField = new JTextField(10);
58
59          // Create a button with the caption "Calculate".
60          calcButton = new JButton("Calculate");
61
62          // Add an action listener to the button.
63          calcButton.addActionListener(new CalcButtonListener());
64
65          // Create a JPanel object and let the panel
66          // field reference it.
67          panel = new JPanel();
68
69          // Add the label, text field, and button
70          // components to the panel.
71          panel.add(messageLabel);
72          panel.add(kiloTextField);
73          panel.add(calcButton);
74      }
75
76      /**
77         CalcButtonListener is an action listener class for
78         the Calculate button.
79      */
80
```

```java
81    private class CalcButtonListener implements ActionListener
82    {
83       /**
84          The actionPerformed method executes when the user
85          clicks on the Calculate button.
86          @param e The event object.
87       */
88
89       public void actionPerformed(ActionEvent e)
90       {
91          String input;  // To hold the user's input
92          double miles;  // The number of miles
93
94          // Get the text entered by the user into the
95          // text field.
96          input = kiloTextField.getText();
97
98          // For debugging, display the text entered, and
99          // its value converted to a double.
100         System.out.println("Reading " + input +
101                          " from the text field.");
102         System.out.println("Converted value: " +
103                          Double.parseDouble(input));
104
105         // Convert the input to miles.
106         miles = Double.parseDouble(input) * 0.6214;
107
108         // Display the result.
109         JOptionPane.showMessageDialog(null, input +
110                 " kilometers is " + miles + " miles.");
111
112         // For debugging, display a message indicating
113         // the application is ready for more input.
114         System.out.println("Ready for the next input.");
115      }
116   } // End of CalcButtonListener class
117
118   /**
119      The main method creates an instance of the
120      KiloConverterWindow class, which displays
121      its window on the screen.
122   */
123
124   public static void main(String[] args)
125   {
126      new KiloConverterWindow();
127   }
128 }
```

Let's take a closer look. In lines 100 through 101 a message is displayed to the console showing the value that was read from the text field. In lines 102 through 103 another message is displayed showing the value after it is converted to a `double`. Then, in line 114, a message is displayed indicating that the application is ready for its next input. Figure 7-39 shows an example session with the application on a computer running Windows XP. Both the console window and the application windows are shown.

Figure 7-39 Messages displayed to the console during the application's execution

1. A command is typed in the console window to execute the application. The application's window appears.

2. The user types a value into the text field and clicks the Calculate button. Debugging messages appear in the console window, and a message dialog appears showing the value converted to miles.

3. The user dismisses the dialog box and a message is displayed in the console window indicating that the application is ready for the next input.

The messages that are displayed to the console are meant only for the programmer to see, while he or she is debugging the application. Once the programmer is satisfied that the application is running correctly, the calls to `System.out.println` can be taken out.

7.10   Common Errors to Avoid

- Misspelling `javax.swing` in an `import` statement. Don't forget the letter x that appears after `java` in this import statement.
- Forgetting to specify the action taken when the user clicks on a `JFrame`'s close button. By default, a window is hidden from view when the close button is clicked, but the application is not terminated. If you wish to exit the application when a `JFrame`'s close button is clicked, you must call the `setDefaultCloseOperation` method and pass `JFrame.EXIT_ON_CLOSE` as the argument.
- Forgetting to write an event listener for each event you wish an application to respond to. In order to respond to an event, you must write an event listener that implements the proper type of interface, registered to the component that generates the event.
- Forgetting to register an event listener. Even if you write an event listener, it will not execute unless it has been registered with the correct component.
- When writing an event listener method that is required by an interface, not using the method header specified by the interface. The header of an `actionPerformed` method must match that specified by the `ActionListener` interface. Also, the header of an `itemStateChanged` method must match that specified by the `ItemListener` method.
- Placing components directly into the regions of a container governed by a `BorderLayout` manager when you do not want the components resized or you want to add more than one component per region. If you do not want the components that you place in a `BorderLayout` region to be resized, place them in a `JPanel` component and then add the `JPanel` component to the region.
- Placing components directly into the cells of a container governed by a `GridLayout` manager when you do not want the components resized or you want to add more than one component per cell. If you do not want the components that you place in a `GridLayout` cell to be resized, place them in a `JPanel` component, and then add the `JPanel` component to the cell.
- Forgetting to add `JRadioButton` components to a `ButtonGroup` object. A mutually exclusive relationship is created between radio buttons only when they are added to a `ButtonGroup` object.

Review Questions and Exercises

Multiple Choice and True/False

1. With Swing, you use this class to create a frame.
   a. `Frame`
   b. `SwingFrame`
   c. `JFrame`
   d. `JavaFrame`

2. This is the part of a `JFrame` object that holds the components that have been added to the `JFrame` object.

    a. content pane
    b. viewing area
    c. component array
    d. object collection

3. This is a `JPanel` object's default layout manager.

    a. `BorderLayout`
    b. `GridLayout`
    c. `FlowLayout`
    d. None

4. This is the default layout manager for a `JFrame` object's content pane.

    a. `BorderLayout`
    b. `GridLayout`
    c. `FlowLayout`
    d. None

5. If a container is governed by a `BorderLayout` manager and you add a component to it, but you do not pass the second argument specifying the region, this is the region in which the component will be added.

    a. north
    b. south
    c. east
    d. center

6. Components in this/these regions of a `BorderLayout` manager are resized horizontally so they fill up the entire region.

    a. north and south
    b. east and west
    c. center only
    d. north, south, east, and west

7. Components in this/these regions of a `BorderLayout` manager are resized vertically so they fill up the entire region.

    a. north and south
    b. east and west
    c. center only
    d. north, south, east, and west

8. Components in this/these regions of a `BorderLayout` manager are resized both horizontally and vertically so they fill up the entire region.

    a. north and south
    b. east and west
    c. center only
    d. north, south, east, and west

9. This is the default alignment of a `FlowLayout` manager.
   - a. left
   - b. center
   - c. right
   - d. no alignment

10. Adding radio button components to this type of object creates a mutually exclusive relationship between them.
    - a. `MutualExclude`
    - b. `RadioGroup`
    - c. `LogicalGroup`
    - d. `ButtonGroup`

11. You use this class to create `Border` objects.
    - a. `BorderFactory`
    - b. `BorderMaker`
    - c. `BorderCreator`
    - d. `BorderSource`

12. **True or False:** A panel cannot be displayed by itself.

13. **True or False:** You can place multiple components inside a `GridLayout` cell.

14. **True or False:** You can place multiple components inside a `BorderLayout` region.

15. **True or False:** You can place multiple components inside a container governed by a `FlowLayout` manager.

16. **True or False:** You can place a panel inside a region governed by a `BorderLayout` manager.

17. **True or False:** A component placed in a `GridLayout` manager's cell will not be resized to fill up any extra space in the cell.

18. **True or False:** You normally add `JCheckBox` components to a `ButtonGroup` object.

19. **True or False:** A mutually exclusive relationship is automatically created among all `JRadioButton` components in the same container.

20. **True or False:** You can write a class that extends the `JPanel` class.

Find the Error

1. The following statement is in a class that uses Swing components:

```
import java.swing.*;
```

2. The following is an inner class that will be registered as an action listener for a `JButton` component:

```
private class ButtonListener implements ActionListener
{
    public void actionPerformed()
    {
        // Code appears here.
    }
}
```

3. The intention of the following statement is to give the `panel` object a `GridLayout` manager with 10 columns and 5 rows:

```
panel.setLayout(new GridLayout(10, 5));
```

4. The `panel` variable references a `JPanel` governed by a `BorderLayout` manager. The following statement attempts to add the button component to the north region of panel:

```
panel.add(button, NORTH);
```

5. The `panel` variable references a `JPanel` object. The intention of the following statement is to create a titled border around `panel`:

```
panel.setBorder(new BorderFactory("Choices"));
```

Algorithm Workbench

1. The variable `myWindow` references a `JFrame` object. Write a statement that sets the size of the object to 500 pixels wide and 250 pixels high.

2. The variable `myWindow` references a `JFrame` object. Write a statement that causes the application to end when the user clicks on the `JFrame` object's close button.

3. The variable `myWindow` references a `JFrame` object. Write a statement that displays the object's window on the screen.

4. The variable `myButton` references a `JButton` object. Write the code to set the object's background color to white and foreground color to red.

5. Assume that a class inherits from the `JFrame` class. Write code that can appear in the class constructor, which gives the content pane a `FlowLayout` manager. Components added to the content pane should be aligned with the left edge of each row.

6. Assume that a class inherits from the `JFrame` class. Write code that can appear in the class constructor, which gives the content pane a `GridLayout` manager with five rows and 10 columns.

7. Assume that the variable `panel` references a `JPanel` object that uses a `BorderLayout` manager. In addition, the variable `button` references a `JButton` object. Write code that adds the `button` object to the `panel` object's west region.

8. Write code that creates three radio buttons with the text "Option 1", "Option 2", and "Option 3". The radio button that displays the text "Option 1" should be initially selected. Make sure these components are grouped so that a mutually exclusive relationship exists among them.

9. Assume that panel references a `JPanel` object. Write code that creates a two pixel thick blue line border around it.

Short Answer

1. If you do not change the default close operation, what happens when the user clicks on the close button on a `JFrame` object?

2. Why is it sometimes necessary to place a component inside a panel and then place the panel inside a container governed by a `BorderLayout` manager?

3. In what type of situation would you present a group of items to the user with radio buttons? With check boxes?

4. How can you create a specialized panel component that can be used to hold other components and their related code?

Programming Challenges

1. Retail Price Calculator

Create a GUI application where the user enters the wholesale cost of an item and its markup percentage into text fields. (For example, if an item's wholesale cost is $5 and its markup percentage is 100 percent, then its retail price is $10.) The application should have a button that displays the item's retail price when clicked.

2. Monthly Sales Tax

VideoNote
The Monthly
Sales Tax
Problem

A retail company must file a monthly sales tax report listing the total sales for the month, and the amount of state and county sales tax collected. The state sales tax rate is 4 percent and the county sales tax rate is 2 percent. Create a GUI application that allows the user to enter the total sales for the month into a text field. From this figure, the application should calculate and display the following:

- The amount of county sales tax
- The amount of state sales tax
- The total sales tax (county plus state)

In the application's code, represent the county tax rate (0.02) and the state tax rate (0.04) as named constants.

3. Property Tax

A county collects property taxes on the assessment value of property, which is 60 percent of the property's actual value. If an acre of land is valued at $10,000, its assessment value is $6,000. The property tax is then $0.64 for each $100 of the assessment value. The tax for the acre assessed at $6,000 will be $38.40. Create a GUI application that displays the assessment value and property tax when a user enters the actual value of a property.

4. Travel Expenses

Create a GUI application that calculates and displays the total travel expenses of a business person on a trip. Here is the information that the user must provide:

- Number of days on the trip
- Amount of airfare, if any
- Amount of car rental fees, if any
- Number of miles driven, if a private vehicle was used
- Amount of parking fees, if any
- Amount of taxi charges, if any
- Conference or seminar registration fees, if any
- Lodging charges, per night

The company reimburses travel expenses according to the following policy:

- $37 per day for meals
- Parking fees, up to $10.00 per day
- Taxi charges up to $20.00 per day
- Lodging charges up to $95.00 per day
- If a private vehicle is used, $0.27 per mile driven

The application should calculate and display the following:

- Total expenses incurred by the business person
- The total allowable expenses for the trip
- The excess that must be paid by the business person, if any
- The amount saved by the business person if the expenses are under the total allowed

5. Theater Revenue

A movie theater only keeps a percentage of the revenue earned from ticket sales. The remainder goes to the movie company. Create a GUI application that allows the user to enter the following data into text fields:

- Price per adult ticket
- Number of adult tickets sold
- Price per child ticket
- Number of child tickets sold

The application should calculate and display the following data for one night's box office business at a theater:

- **Gross revenue for adult tickets sold.** This is the amount of money taken in for all adult tickets sold.
- **Net revenue for adult tickets sold.** This is the amount of money from adult ticket sales left over after the payment to the movie company has been deducted.
- **Gross revenue for child tickets sold.** This is the amount of money taken in for all child tickets sold.
- **Net revenue for child tickets sold.** This is the amount of money from child ticket sales left over after the payment to the movie company has been deducted.
- **Total gross revenue.** This is the sum of gross revenue for adult and child tickets sold.
- **Total net revenue.** This is the sum of net revenue for adult and child tickets sold.

Assume the theater keeps 20 percent of its box office receipts. Use a constant in your code to represent this percentage.

6. Joe's Automotive

Joe's Automotive performs the following routine maintenance services:

- Oil change—$26.00
- Lube job—$18.00
- Radiator flush—$30.00
- Transmission flush—$80.00
- Inspection—$15.00

- Muffler replacement—$100.00
- Tire rotation—$20.00

Joe also performs other nonroutine services and charges for parts and for labor ($20 per hour). Create a GUI application that displays the total for a customer's visit to Joe's.

7. Long Distance Calls

A long-distance provider charges the following rates for telephone calls:

Rate Category	Rate per Minute
Daytime (6:00 A.M. through 5:59 P.M.)	$0.07
Evening (6:00 P.M. through 11:59 P.M.)	$0.12
Off-Peak (12:00 A.M. through 5:59 A.M.)	$0.05

Create a GUI application that allows the user to select a rate category (from a set of radio buttons), and enter the number of minutes of the call into a text field. A dialog box should display the charge for the call.

8. Latin Translator

Look at the following list of Latin words and their meanings.

Latin	English
sinister	left
dexter	right
medium	center

Write a GUI application that translates the Latin words to English. The window should have three buttons, one for each Latin word. When the user clicks a button, the program displays the English translation in a label.

9. MPG Calculator

Write a GUI application that calculates a car's gas mileage. The application should let the user enter the number of gallons of gas the car holds, and the number of miles it can be driven on a full tank. When a *Calculate MPG* button is clicked, the application should display the number of miles that the car may be driven per gallon of gas. Use the following formula to calculate MPG:

$$MPG = \frac{miles}{gallons}$$

10. Celsius to Fahrenheit

Write a GUI application that converts Celsius temperatures to Fahrenheit temperatures. The user should be able to enter a Celsius temperature, click a button, and then see the equivalent Fahrenheit temperature. Use the following formula to make the conversion:

$$F = \frac{9}{5}C + 32$$

F is the Fahrenheit temperature and C is the Celsius temperature.

8

Arrays and the **ArrayList** Class

TOPICS

8.1 Introduction to Arrays

CONCEPT: An array can hold multiple values of the same data type simultaneously.

The primitive variables you have worked with so far are designed to hold one value at a time. Each of the variable declarations in Figure 8-1 causes only enough memory to be reserved to hold one value of the specified data type.

An array, however, is an object that can store a group of values, all of the same type. Creating and using an array in Java is similar to creating and using any other type of object: You declare a reference variable and use the new key word to create an instance of the array in memory. Here is an example of a statement that declares an array reference variable:

```
int[] numbers;
```

This statement declares numbers as an array reference variable. The numbers variable can reference an array of int values. Notice that this statement looks like a regular int variable declaration except for the set of brackets that appear after the key word int. The brackets indicate that this variable is a reference to an int array. Declaring an array reference variable does not create an array. The next step in the process is to use the new key word to create an array and assign its address to the numbers variable. The following statement shows an example:

```
numbers = new int[6];
```

Figure 8-1 Variable declarations and their memory allocations

```
int count;
```
Enough memory to hold one `int`.

1234

```
double number;
```
Enough memory to hold one `double`.

1234.55

```
char letter;
```
Enough memory to hold one `char`.

A

The number inside the brackets is the array's *size declarator*. It indicates the number of elements, or values, the array can hold. When this statement is executed, `numbers` will reference an array that can hold six elements, each one an `int`. This is shown in Figure 8-2.

Figure 8-2 The numbers array

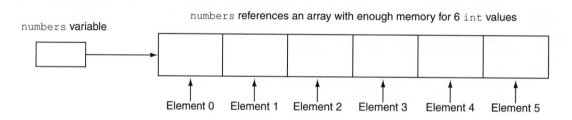

`numbers` **variable**

`numbers` **references an array with enough memory for 6 `int` values**

Element 0   Element 1   Element 2   Element 3   Element 4   Element 5

As with any other type of object, it is possible to declare a reference variable and create an instance of an array with one statement. Here is an example:

```
int[] numbers = new int[6];
```

Arrays of any data type can be declared. The following are all valid array declarations:

```
float[] temperatures = new float[100];
char[] letters = new char[41];
long[] units = new long[50];
double[] sizes = new double[1200];
```

An array's size declarator must be a non-negative integer expression. It can be a literal value, as shown in the previous examples, or a variable. It is a common practice to use a `final` variable as a size declarator. Here is an example:

```
final int NUM_ELEMENTS = 6;
int[] numbers = new int[NUM_ELEMENTS];
```

This practice can make programs easier to maintain. When we store the size of an array in a variable, we can use the variable instead of a literal number when we refer to the size of the array. If we ever need to change the array's size, we need only to change the value of the variable. The variable should be final so its contents cannot be changed during the program's execution.

NOTE: Once an array is created, its size cannot be changed.

Accessing Array Elements

Although an array has only one name, the elements in the array may be accessed and used as individual variables. This is possible because each element is assigned a number known as a *subscript*. A subscript is used as an index to pinpoint a specific element within an array. The first element is assigned the subscript 0, the second element is assigned 1, and so forth. The six elements in the numbers array (described earlier) would have the subscripts 0 through 5. This is shown in Figure 8-3.

Figure 8-3   Subscripts for the numbers array

The numbers array has six elements, numbered 0 through 5.

Subscript numbering always starts at zero. The subscript of the last element in an array is one less than the total number of elements in the array. This means that for the numbers array, which has six elements, 5 is the subscript for the last element.

Each element in the numbers array, when accessed by its subscript, can be used as an int variable. For example, look at the following code. The first statement stores 20 in the first element of the array (element 0), and the second statement stores 30 in the fourth element (element 3).

```
numbers[0] = 20;
numbers[3] = 30;
```

NOTE: The expression numbers[0] is pronounced "numbers sub zero." You read these assignment statements as "numbers sub zero is assigned twenty" and "numbers sub three is assigned thirty."

Figure 8-4 illustrates the contents of the array after these statements execute.

Figure 8-4 Contents of the array after 20 is assigned to numbers[0] and 30 is assigned to numbers[3]

numbers[0] numbers[1] numbers[2] numbers[3] numbers[4] numbers[5]

| 20 | 0 | 0 | 30 | 0 | 0 |

NOTE: By default, Java initializes array elements with 0. In Figure 8-4, values have not been stored in elements 1, 2, 4, and 5, so they are shown as 0s.

By this point you should understand the difference between the array size declarator and a subscript. When you use the new key word to create an array object, the number inside the brackets is the size declarator. It indicates the number of elements in the array. The number inside the brackets in an assignment statement or any statement that works with the contents of an array is a subscript. It is used to access a specific element in the array.

Inputting and Outputting Array Contents

You can read values from the keyboard and store them in an array element just as you can a regular variable. You can also output the contents of an array element with print and println. Code Listing 8-1 shows an array being used to store and display values entered by the user. Figure 8-5 shows the contents of the hours array with the values entered by the user in the example output.

Code Listing 8-1 (`ArrayDemo1.java`)

```java
 1  import java.util.Scanner;    // Needed for Scanner class
 2
 3  /**
 4     This program shows values being stored in an array's
 5     elements and displayed.
 6  */
 7
 8  public class ArrayDemo1
 9  {
10     public static void main(String[] args)
11     {
12        final int EMPLOYEES = 3;          // Number of employees
13        int[] hours = new int[EMPLOYEES];// Array of hours
14
15        // Create a Scanner object for keyboard input.
16        Scanner keyboard = new Scanner(System.in);
17
18        System.out.println("Enter the hours worked by " +
```

```
19                              EMPLOYEES + " employees.");
20
21          // Get the hours worked by employee 1.
22          System.out.print("Employee 1: ");
23          hours[0] = keyboard.nextInt();
24
25          // Get the hours worked by employee 2.
26          System.out.print("Employee 2: ");
27          hours[1] = keyboard.nextInt();
28
29          // Get the hours worked by employee 3.
30          System.out.print("Employee 3: ");
31          hours[2] = keyboard.nextInt();
32
33          // Display the values entered.
34          System.out.println("The hours you entered are:");
35          System.out.println(hours[0]);
36          System.out.println(hours[1]);
37          System.out.println(hours[2]);
38      }
39   }
```

Program Output with Example Input Shown in Bold
```
Enter the hours worked by 3 employees.
Employee 1: 40 [Enter]
Employee 2: 20 [Enter]
Employee 3: 15 [Enter]
The hours you entered are:
40
20
15
```

Figure 8-5   Contents of the hours array

VideoNote
Accessing Array
Elements in
a Loop
Subscript numbers can be stored in variables. This makes it possible to use a loop to "cycle through" an entire array, performing the same operation on each element. For example, Code Listing 8-1 could be simplified by using two for loops: one for inputting the values into the array and the other for displaying the contents of the array. This is shown in Code Listing 8-2.

Code Listing 8-2 (`ArrayDemo2.java`)

```java
 1  import java.util.Scanner;    // Needed for Scanner class
 2
 3  /**
 4     This program shows an array being processed with loops.
 5  */
 6
 7  public class ArrayDemo2
 8  {
 9     public static void main(String[] args)
10     {
11        final int EMPLOYEES = 3;                  // Number of employees
12        int[] hours = new int[EMPLOYEES];         // Array of hours
13
14        // Create a Scanner object for keyboard input.
15        Scanner keyboard = new Scanner(System.in);
16
17        System.out.println("Enter the hours worked by " +
18                        EMPLOYEES + " employees.");
19
20        // Get the hours for each employee.
21        for (int index = 0; index < EMPLOYEES; index++)
22        {
23           System.out.print("Employee " + (index + 1) + ": ");
24           hours[index] = keyboard.nextInt();
25        }
26
27        System.out.println("The hours you entered are:");
28
29        // Display the values entered.
30        for (int index = 0; index < EMPLOYEES; index++)
31           System.out.println(hours[index]);
32     }
33  }
```

Program Output with Example Input Shown in Bold

```
Enter the hours worked by 3 employees.
Employee 1: 40 [Enter]
Employee 2: 20 [Enter]
Employee 3: 15 [Enter]
The hours you entered are:
40
20
15
```

Let's take a closer look at the first loop in this program, which appears in lines 21 through 25. Notice that the loop's control variable, index, is used as a subscript in line 24:

```java
hours[index] = keyboard.nextInt();
```

The variable index starts at 0. During the loop's first iteration, the user's input is stored in hours[0]. Then, index is incremented, so its value becomes 1. During the next iteration, the user's input is stored in hours[1]. This continues until values have been stored in all of the elements of the array. Notice that the loop correctly starts and ends the control variable with valid subscript values (0 through 2), as illustrated in Figure 8-6. This ensures that only valid subscripts are used.

Figure 8-6 Annotated loop

The variable index starts at 0, which is the first valid subscript value.

The loop ends before the variable index reaches 3, which is the first invalid subscript value.

```java
for (int index = 0; index < EMPLOYEES; index++)
{
    System.out.print("Employee " + (index + 1) + ": ");
    hours[index] = keyboard.nextInt();
}
```

Java Performs Bounds Checking

Java performs array bounds checking, which means that it does not allow a statement to use a subscript that is outside the range of valid subscripts for an array. For example, the following statement creates an array with 10 elements. The valid subscripts for the array are 0 through 9.

```java
int[] values = new int[10];
```

Java will not allow a statement to use a subscript that is less than 0 or greater than 9 with this array. Bounds checking occurs at runtime. The Java compiler does not display an error message when it processes a statement that uses an invalid subscript. Instead, when the statement executes, the program throws an exception and immediately terminates. For instance, the program in Code Listing 8-3 declares a three-element array, but attempts to store four values in the array. In line 17, when the program attempts to store a value in values[3], it halts and an error message is displayed.

Code Listing 8-3 (InvalidSubscript.java)

```java
1  /**
2     This program uses an invalid subscript with an array.
3  */
4
```

```
 5   public class InvalidSubscript
 6   {
 7      public static void main(String[] args)
 8      {
 9         int[] values = new int[3];
10
11         System.out.println("I will attempt to store four " +
12                            "numbers in a three-element array.");
13
14         for (int index = 0; index < 4; index++)
15         {
16            System.out.println("Now processing element " + index);
17            values[index] = 10;
18         }
19      }
20   }
```

Program Output

```
I will attempt to store four numbers in a three-element array.
Now processing element 0
Now processing element 1
Now processing element 2
Now processing element 3
Exception in thread "main"
java.lang.ArrayIndexOutOfBoundsException: 3
        at InvalidSubscript.main(InvalidSubscript.java:17)
```

 NOTE: The error message you see may be different, depending on your system.

Watch Out for Off-by-One Errors

Because array subscripts start at 0 rather than 1, you have to be careful not to perform an off-by-one error. For example, look at the following code:

```
// This code has an off-by-one error.
final int SIZE = 100;
int[] numbers = new int[SIZE];
for (int index = 1; index <= SIZE; index++)
   numbers[index] = 0;
```

The intent of this code is to create an array of integers with 100 elements, and store the value 0 in each element. However, this code has an off-by-one error. The loop uses its control variable, index, as a subscript with the numbers array. During the loop's execution, the variable index takes on the values 1 through 100, when it should take on the values 0 through 99. As a result, the first element, which is at subscript 0, is skipped. In addition, the loop attempts to use 100 as a subscript during the last iteration. Because 100 is an invalid subscript, the program will throw an exception and halt.

Array Initialization

Like regular variables, Java allows you to initialize an array's elements when you create the array. Here is an example:

```
int[] days = {31, 28, 31, 30, 31, 30, 31, 31, 30, 31, 30, 31};
```

This statement declares the reference variable days, creates an array in memory, and stores initial values in the array. The series of values inside the braces and separated with commas is called an initialization list. These values are stored in the array elements in the order they appear in the list. (The first value, 31, is stored in days[0], the second value, 28, is stored in days[1], and so forth.) Note that you do not use the new key word when you use an initialization list. Java automatically creates the array and stores the values in the initialization list in it.

The Java compiler determines the size of the array by the number of items in the initialization list. Because there are 12 items in the example statement's initialization list, the array will have 12 elements. The program in Code Listing 8-4 demonstrates an array being initialized.

Code Listing 8-4   (`ArrayInitialization.java`)

```java
 1  /**
 2      This program shows an array being initialized.
 3  */
 4
 5  public class ArrayInitialization
 6  {
 7     public static void main(String[] args)
 8     {
 9        int[] days = { 31, 28, 31, 30, 31, 30,
10                       31, 31, 30, 31, 30, 31 };
11
12        for (int index = 0; index < 12; index++)
13        {
14           System.out.println("Month " + (index + 1) +
15                              " has " + days[index] +
16                              " days.");
17        }
18     }
19  }
```

Program Output

```
Month 1 has 31 days.
Month 2 has 28 days.
Month 3 has 31 days.
Month 4 has 30 days.
Month 5 has 31 days.
```

```
Month 6 has 30 days.
Month 7 has 31 days.
Month 8 has 31 days.
Month 9 has 30 days.
Month 10 has 31 days.
Month 11 has 30 days.
Month 12 has 31 days.
```

Java allows you to spread the initialization list across multiple lines. Both of the following array declarations are equivalent:

```
double[] coins = { 0.05, 0.1, 0.25 };

double[] coins = { 0.05,
                   0.1,
                   0.25 };
```

Alternate Array Declaration Notation

Java allows you to use two different styles when declaring array reference variables. The first style is the one used in this book, with the brackets immediately following the data type, as shown here:

```
int[] numbers;
```

In the second style the brackets are placed after the variable name, as shown here:

```
int numbers[];
```

Both of these statements accomplish the same thing: They declare that `numbers` is a reference to an `int` array. The difference between the two styles is noticed when more than one variable is declared in the same statement. For example, look at the following statement:

```
int[] numbers, codes, scores;
```

This statement declares three variables: `numbers`, `codes`, and `scores`. All three are references to `int` arrays. This makes perfect sense because `int[]` is the data type for all the variables declared in the statement. Now look at the following statement, which uses the alternate notation:

```
int numbers[], codes, scores;
```

This statement declares the same three variables, but only `numbers` is a reference to an `int` array. The `codes` and `scores` variables are regular `int` variables. This is because `int` is the data type for all the variables declared in the statement, and only `numbers` is followed by the brackets. To declare all three of these variables as references to `int` arrays using the alternate notation, you need to write a set of brackets after each variable name. Here is an example:

```
int numbers[], codes[], scores[];
```

The first style is the standard notation for most Java programmers, so that is the style used in this book.

Checkpoint

8.1 Write statements that create the following arrays:
  a) A 100-element `int` array referenced by the variable `employeeNumbers`.
  b) A 25-element `double` array referenced by the variable `payRates`.
  c) A 14-element `float` array referenced by the variable `miles`.
  d) A 1000-element `char` array referenced by the variable `letters`.

8.2 What's wrong with the following array declarations?
```
int[] readings = new int[-1];
double[] measurements = new double[4.5];
```

8.3 What would the valid subscript values be in a four-element array of `doubles`?

8.4 What is the difference between an array's size declarator and a subscript?

8.5 What does it mean for a subscript to be out-of-bounds?

8.6 What happens in Java when a program tries to use a subscript that is out-of-bounds?

8.7 What is the output of the following code?
```
int[] values = new int[5];
for (int count = 0; count < 5; count++)
    values[count] = count + 1;
for (int count = 0; count < 5; count++)
    System.out.println(values[count]);
```

8.8 Write a statement that creates and initializes a `double` array with the following values: 1.7, 6.4, 8.9, 3.1, and 9.2. How many elements are in the array?

8.2 Processing Array Elements

CONCEPT: Individual array elements are processed like any other type of variable.

Processing array elements is no different from processing other variables. For example, the following statement multiplies `hours[3]` by the variable `payRate`:

```
grossPay = hours[3] * payRate;
```

The following are examples of pre-increment and post-increment operations on array elements:

```
int[] score = {7, 8, 9, 10, 11};
++score[2];    // Pre-increment operation
score[4]++;    // Post-increment operation
```

When using increment and decrement operators, be careful not to use the operator on the subscript when you intend to use it on the array element. For example, the following statement decrements the variable `count`, but does nothing to the value stored in the array element `amount[count]`:

```
amount[count--];
```

Code Listing 8-5 demonstrates the use of array elements in a simple mathematical statement. A loop steps through each element of the array, using the elements to calculate the gross pay of five employees.

Code Listing 8-5 (`PayArray.java`)

```
 1   import java.util.Scanner; // Needed for Scanner class
 2
 3   /**
 4       This program stores in an array the hours worked by
 5       five employees who all make the same hourly wage.
 6   */
 7
 8   public class PayArray
 9   {
10       public static void main(String[] args)
11       {
12           final int EMPLOYEES = 5;    // Number of employees
13           double payRate;             // Hourly pay rate
14           double grossPay;            // Gross pay
15
16           // Create an array to hold employee hours.
17           int[] hours = new int[EMPLOYEES];
18
19           // Create a Scanner object for keyboard input.
20           Scanner keyboard = new Scanner(System.in);
21
22           // Get the hours worked by each employee.
23           System.out.println("Enter the hours worked by " +
24                               EMPLOYEES + " employees who all earn " +
25                               "the same hourly rate.");
26
27           for (int index = 0; index < EMPLOYEES; index++)
28           {
29               System.out.print( "Employee #" + (index + 1) + ": ");
30               hours[index] = keyboard.nextInt();
31           }
32
33           // Get the hourly pay rate.
34           System.out.print("Enter the hourly rate for each employee: ");
35           payRate = keyboard.nextDouble();
36
37           // Display each employee's gross pay.
38           System.out.println( "Here is each employee's gross pay:");
39           for (int index = 0; index < EMPLOYEES; index++)
40           {
41               grossPay = hours[index] * payRate;
```

```
42                System.out.println("Employee #" + (index + 1) +
43                             ": $" + grossPay);
44         }
45     }
46 }
```

Program Output with Example Input Shown in Bold

Enter the hours worked by 5 employees who all earn the same hourly rate.
Employee #1: **10 [Enter]**
Employee #2: **20 [Enter]**
Employee #3: **30 [Enter]**
Employee #4: **40 [Enter]**
Employee #5: **50 [Enter]**
Enter the hourly rate for each employee: **10 [Enter]**
Here is each employee's gross pay:
Employee #1: $100.0
Employee #2: $200.0
Employee #3: $300.0
Employee #4: $400.0
Employee #5: $500.0

In line 41, the following statement assigns the value of hours[index] times payRate to the grossPay variable:

```
grossPay = hours[index] * payRate;
```

Array elements may also be used in relational expressions. For example, the following if statement determines whether cost[20] is less than cost[0]:

```
if (cost[20] < cost[0])
```

And the following while loop iterates as long as value[count] does not equal 0:

```
while (value[count] != 0)
{
     Statements
}
```

> On the Student CD you will find the file *Overtime.java*, which is a modification of the *PayArray.java* program in Code Listing 8-5. The *Overtime.java* program includes over-time wages in the gross pay. If an employee works more than 40 hours, an overtime pay rate of 1.5 times the regular pay rate is used for the excess hours.

Array Length

Each array in Java has a public field named length. This field contains the number of elements in the array. For example, consider an array created by the following statement:

```
double[] temperatures = new double[25];
```

Because the `temperatures` array has 25 elements, the following statement would assign 25 to the variable `size`:

```
size = temperatures.length;
```

The `length` field can be useful when processing the entire contents of an array. For example, the following loop steps through an array and displays the contents of each element. The array's `length` field is used in the test expression as the upper limit for the loop control variable:

```
for (int i = 0; i < temperatures.length; i++)
    System.out.println(temperatures[i]);
```

 WARNING! Be careful not to cause an off-by-one error when using the `length` field as the upper limit of a subscript. The `length` field contains the number of elements in an array. The largest subscript in an array is `length − 1`.

 NOTE: You cannot change the value of an array's `length` field.

The Enhanced `for` Loop

Java provides a specialized version of the `for` loop that, in many circumstances, simplifies array processing. It is known as the *enhanced `for` loop*. Here is the general format of the enhanced `for` loop:

```
for (dataType elementVariable : array)
    statement;
```

The enhanced `for` loop is designed to iterate once for every element in an array. Each time the loop iterates, it copies an array element to a variable. Let's look at the syntax more closely as follows:

- *dataType elementVariable* is a variable declaration. This variable will receive the value of a different array element during each loop iteration. During the first loop iteration, it receives the value of the first element; during the second iteration, it receives the value of the second element, and so on. This variable must be of the same data type as the array elements, or a type that the elements can automatically be converted to.
- *array* is the name of an array on which you wish the loop to operate. The loop will iterate once for every element in the array.
- *statement* is a statement that executes during a loop iteration.

For example, assume that we have the following array declaration:

```
int[] numbers = { 3, 6, 9 };
```

We can use the following enhanced `for` loop to display the contents of the `numbers` array:

```
for (int val : numbers)
    System.out.println(val);
```

Because the `numbers` array has three elements, this loop will iterate three times. The first time it iterates, the `val` variable will receive the value in `numbers[0]`. During the second iteration, `val` will receive the value in `numbers[1]`. During the third iteration, `val` will receive the value in `numbers[2]`. The code's output will be as follows:

```
3
6
9
```

If you need to execute more than one statement in the enhanced `for` loop, simply enclose the block of statements in a set of braces. Here is an example:

```
int[] numbers = { 3, 6, 9 };
for (int val : numbers)
{
    System.out.print("The next value is ");
    System.out.println(val);
}
```

This code will produce the following output:

```
The next value is 3
The next value is 6
The next value is 9
```

The Enhanced `for` Loop versus the Traditional `for` Loop

When you need to access the values that are stored in an array, from the first element to the last element, the enhanced `for` loop is simpler to use than the traditional `for` loop. With the enhanced `for` loop you do not have to be concerned about the size of the array, and you do not have to create an "index" variable to hold subscripts. However, there are circumstances in which the enhanced `for` loop is not adequate. You cannot use the enhanced `for` loop as follows:

- if you need to change the contents of an array element
- if you need to work through the array elements in reverse order
- if you need to access some of the array elements, but not all of them
- if you need to simultaneously work with two or more arrays within the loop
- if you need to refer to the subscript number of a particular element

In any of these circumstances, you should use the traditional `for` loop to process the array.

Letting the User Specify an Array's Size

Java allows you to use an integer variable to specify an array's size declarator. This makes it possible to allow the user to specify an array's size. Code Listing 8-6 demonstrates this, as well as the use of the `length` field. It stores a number of test scores in an array and then displays them.

Code Listing 8-6   (`DisplayTestScores.java`)

```java
 1 import java.util.Scanner; // Needed for Scanner class
 2
 3 /**
 4    This program demonstrates how the user may specify an
 5    array's size.
 6 */
 7
 8 public class DisplayTestScores
 9 {
10    public static void main(String[] args)
11    {
12       int numTests;      // The number of tests
13       int[] tests;       // Array of test scores
14
15       // Create a Scanner object for keyboard input.
16       Scanner keyboard = new Scanner(System.in);
17
18       // Get the number of test scores.
19       System.out.print("How many tests do you have? ");
20       numTests = keyboard.nextInt();
21
22       // Create an array to hold that number of scores.
23       tests = new int[numTests];
24
25       // Get the individual test scores.
26       for (int index = 0; index < tests.length; index++)
27       {
28          System.out.print("Enter test score " +
29                           (index + 1) + ": ");
30          tests[index] = keyboard.nextInt();
31       }
32
33       // Display the test scores.
34       System.out.println();
35       System.out.println("Here are the scores you entered:");
36       for (int index = 0; index < tests.length; index++)
37          System.out.print(tests[index] + " ");
38    }
39 }
```

Program Output with Example Input Shown in Bold

```
How many tests do you have? 5 [Enter]
Enter test score 1: 72 [Enter]
```

```
Enter test score 2: 85 [Enter]
Enter test score 3: 81 [Enter]
Enter test score 4: 94 [Enter]
Enter test score 5: 99 [Enter]


Here are the scores you entered:
72 85 81 94 99
```

This program allows the user to determine the size of the array. In line 23 the following statement creates the array, using the `numTests` variable to determine its size:

```
tests = new int[numTests];
```

The program then uses two `for` loops. The first, in lines 26 through 31, allows the user to input each test score. The second, in lines 36 and 37, displays all of the test scores. Both loops use the `length` member to control their number of iterations as follows:

```
for (int index = 0; index < tests.length; index++)
```

Reassigning Array Reference Variables

It is possible to reassign an array reference variable to a different array, as demonstrated by the following code:

```
// Create an array referenced by the numbers variable.
int[] numbers = new int[10];
// Reassign numbers to a new array.
numbers = new int[5];
```

The first statement creates a ten-element integer array and assigns its address to the `numbers` variable. This is illustrated in Figure 8-7.

Figure 8-7   The `numbers` variable references a ten-element array

The second statement allocates a five-element integer array and assigns its address to the `numbers` variable. The address of the five-element array takes the place of the address of the ten-element array. After this statement executes, the `numbers` variable references the five-element array instead of the ten-element array. This is illustrated in Figure 8-8. Because the ten-element array is no longer referenced, it cannot be accessed.

Figure 8-8 The `numbers` variable references a five-element array

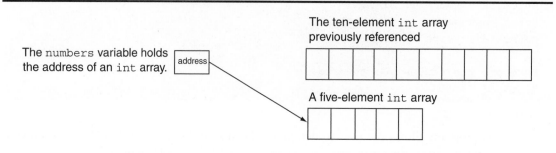

Copying Arrays

Because an array is an object, there is a distinction between an array and the variable that references it. The array and the reference variable are two separate entities. This is important to remember when you wish to copy the contents of one array to another. You might be tempted to write something like the following code, thinking that you are copying an array:

```
int[] array1 = { 2, 4, 6, 8, 10 };
int[] array2 = array1;   // This does not copy array1.
```

The first statement creates an array and assigns its address to the `array1` variable. The second statement assigns `array1` to `array2`. This does not make a copy of the array referenced by `array1`. Rather, it makes a copy of the address that is stored in `array1` and stores it in `array2`. After this statement executes, both the `array1` and `array2` variables will reference the same array. This type of assignment operation is called a *reference copy*. Only the address of the array object is copied, not the contents of the array object. This is illustrated in Figure 8-9.

Figure 8-9 Both `array1` and `array2` reference the same array

Code Listing 8-7 demonstrates the assigning of an array's address to two reference variables. Regardless of which variable the program uses, it is working with the same array.

Code Listing 8-7   (`SameArray.java`)

```java
 1   /**
 2       This program demonstrates that two variables can
 3       reference the same array.
 4   */
 5
 6   public class SameArray
 7   {
 8       public static void main(String[] args)
 9       {
10           int[] array1 = { 2, 4, 6, 8, 10 };
11           int[] array2 = array1;
12
13           // Change one of the elements using array1.
14           array1[0] = 200;
15
16           // Change one of the elements using array2.
17           array2[4] = 1000;
18
19           // Display all the elements using array1
20           System.out.println("The contents of array1:");
21           for (int value : array1)
22               System.out.print(value + " ");
23           System.out.println();
24
25           // Display all the elements using array2
26           System.out.println("The contents of array2:");
27           for (int value : array2)
28               System.out.print(value + " ");
29           System.out.println();
30       }
31   }
```

Program Output

```
The contents of array1:
200 4 6 8 1000
The contents of array2:
200 4 6 8 1000
```

The program in Code Listing 8-7 illustrates that you cannot copy an array by merely assigning one array reference variable to another. Instead, to copy an array you need to copy the individual elements of one array to another. Usually, this is best done with a loop, such as the following:

```
int[] firstArray = { 5, 10, 15, 20, 25 };
int[] secondArray = new int[5];

for (int index = 0; index < firstArray.length; index++)
   secondArray[index] = firstArray[index];
```

The loop in this code copies each element of `firstArray` to the corresponding element of `secondArray`.

 Checkpoint

8.9   Look at the following statements:
```
int[] numbers1 = { 1, 3, 6, 9 };
int[] numbers2 = { 2, 4, 6, 8 };
int result;
```
Write a statement that multiplies element 0 of the `numbers1` array by element 3 of the `numbers2` array and assigns the result to the `result` variable.

8.10 A program uses a variable named `array` that references an array of integers. You do not know the number of elements in the array. Write a `for` loop that stores −1 in each element of the array.

8.11 A program has the following declaration:
```
double[] values;
```
Write code that asks the user for the size of the array and then creates an array of the specified size, referenced by the `values` variable.

8.12 Look at the following statements:
```
int[] a = { 1, 2, 3, 4, 5, 6, 7 };
int[] b = new int[7];
```
Write code that copies the a array to the b array.

8.3 Passing Arrays As Arguments to Methods

CONCEPT: An array can be passed as an argument to a method. To pass an array, you pass the value in the variable that references the array.

VideoNote
Passing an
Array to
a Method

Quite often you'll want to write methods that process the data in arrays. As you will see, methods can be written to store values in an array, display an array's contents, total all of an array's elements, calculate their average, and so forth. Usually, such methods accept an array as an argument.

When a single element of an array is passed to a method, it is handled like any other variable. For example, Code Listing 8-8 shows a loop that passes each element of the array `numbers` to the method `showValue`.

Code Listing 8-8 (`PassElements.java`)

```
 1   /**
 2       This program demonstrates passing individual array
 3       elements as arguments to a method.
 4   */
 5
 6   public class PassElements
 7   {
 8       public static void main(String[] args)
 9       {
10           int[] numbers = {5, 10, 15, 20, 25, 30, 35, 40};
11
12           for (int index = 0; index < numbers.length; index++)
13               showValue(numbers[index]);
14       }
15
16       /**
17           The showValue method displays its argument.
18           @param n The value to display.
19       */
20
21       public static void showValue(int n)
22       {
23           System.out.print(n + " ");
24       }
25   }
```

Program Output

5 10 15 20 25 30 35 40

Each time showValue is called in this program, an array element is passed to the method. The showValue method has an int parameter variable named n, which receives the argument. The method simply displays the contents of n. If the method were written to accept the entire array as an argument, however, the parameter would have to be set up differently. For example, consider the following method definition. The parameter array is declared as an array reference variable. This indicates that the argument will be an array, not a single value.

```
public static void showArray(int[] array)
{
   for (int i = 0; i < array.length; i++)
      System.out.print(array[i] + " ");
}
```

When you pass an array as an argument, you simply pass the value in the variable that references the array, as shown here:

```
showArray(numbers);
```

When an entire array is passed into a method, it is passed just as an object is passed: The actual array itself is not passed, but a reference to the array is passed into the parameter. Consequently, this means the method has direct access to the original array. This is illustrated in Figure 8-10.

Figure 8-10   An array passed as an argument

Code Listing 8-9 shows the `showArray` method in use, as well as another method, `getValues`. The `getValues` method accepts an array as an argument. It asks the user to enter a value for each element.

Code Listing 8-9   (`PassArray.java`)

```
 1 import java.util.Scanner;  // Needed for Scanner class
 2
 3 /**
 4    This program demonstrates passing an array
 5    as an argument to a method.
 6 */
 7
 8 public class PassArray
 9 {
10    public static void main(String[] args)
11    {
12       final int ARRAY_SIZE = 4;  // Size of the array
13
```

```
14          // Create an array.
15          int[] numbers = new int[ARRAY_SIZE];
16
17          // Pass the array to the getValues method.
18          getValues(numbers);
19
20          System.out.println("Here are the " +
21                      "numbers that you entered:");
22
23          // Pass the array to the showArray method.
24          showArray(numbers);
25      }
26
27      /**
28          The getValues method accepts a reference
29          to an array as its argument. The user is
30          asked to enter a value for each element.
31          @param array A reference to the array.
32      */
33
34      private static void getValues(int[] array)
35      {
36          // Create a Scanner objects for keyboard input.
37          Scanner keyboard = new Scanner(System.in);
38
39          System.out.println("Enter a series of " +
40                      array.length + " numbers.");
41
42          // Read values into the array
43          for (int index = 0; index < array.length; index++)
44          {
45              System.out.print("Enter number " +
46                          (index + 1) + ": ");
47              array[index] = keyboard.nextInt();
48          }
49      }
50
51      /**
52          The showArray method accepts an array as
53          an argument and displays its contents.
54          @param array A reference to the array.
55      */
56
57      public static void showArray(int[] array)
58      {
59          // Display the array elements.
60          for (int index = 0; index < array.length; index++)
61              System.out.print(array[index] + " ");
```

```
62    }
63 }
```

Program Output with Example Input Shown in Bold
```
Enter a series of 4 numbers.
Enter number 1: 2 [Enter]
Enter number 2: 4 [Enter]
Enter number 3: 6 [Enter]
Enter number 4: 8 [Enter]
Here are the numbers that you entered:
2 4 6 8
```

 Checkpoint

8.13 Look at the following method header:
```
public static void myMethod(double[] array)
```
Here is an array declaration:
```
double[] numbers = new double[100];
```
Write a statement that passes the `numbers` array to the `myMethod` method.

8.14 Write a method named `zero`, which accepts an `int` array as an argument and stores the value 0 in each element.

8.4 Some Useful Array Algorithms and Operations

Comparing Arrays

In the previous section you saw that you cannot copy an array by simply assigning its reference variable to another array's reference variable. In addition, you cannot use the == operator to compare two array reference variables and determine whether the arrays are equal. For example, the following code appears to compare two arrays, but in reality does not:

```
int[] firstArray = { 5, 10, 15, 20, 25 };
int[] secondArray = { 5, 10, 15, 20, 25 };
if (firstArray == secondArray)        // This is a mistake.
    System.out.println("The arrays are the same.");
else
    System.out.println("The arrays are not the same.");
```

When you use the == operator with reference variables, including those that reference arrays, the operator compares the memory addresses that the variables contain, not the contents of the objects referenced by the variables. Because the two array variables in this code reference different objects in memory, they will contain different addresses. Therefore, the result of the boolean expression `firstArray == secondArray` is `false` and the code reports that the arrays are not the same.

To compare the contents of two arrays, you must compare the elements of the two arrays.

For example, look at the following code:

```
int[] firstArray = { 2, 4, 6, 8, 10 };
int[] secondArray = { 2, 4, 6, 8, 10 };
boolean arraysEqual = true;  // Flag variable
int index = 0;               // Loop control variable

// First determine whether the arrays are the same size.
if (firstArray.length != secondArray.length)
   arraysEqual = false;

// Next determine whether the elements contain the same data.
while (arraysEqual && index < firstArray.length)
{
   if (firstArray[index] != secondArray[index])
      arraysEqual = false;
   index++;
}

if (arraysEqual)
   System.out.println("The arrays are equal.");
else
   System.out.println("The arrays are not equal.");
```

This code determines whether `firstArray` and `secondArray` contain the same values. A `boolean` flag variable, `arraysEqual`, which is initialized to `true`, is used to signal whether the arrays are equal. Another variable, `index`, which is initialized to 0, is used as a loop control variable.

First, this code determines whether the two arrays are the same length. If they are not the same length, then the arrays cannot be equal, so the flag variable `arraysEqual` is set to `false`. Then a `while` loop begins. The loop executes as long as `arraysEqual` is `true` and the control variable `index` is less than `firstArray.length`. During each iteration, it compares a different set of corresponding elements in the arrays. When it finds two corresponding elements that have different values, the flag variable `arraysEqual` is set to `false`. After the loop finishes, an `if` statement examines the `arraysEqual` variable. If the variable is `true`, then the arrays are equal and a message indicating so is displayed. Otherwise, they are not equal, so a different message is displayed.

Summing the Values in a Numeric Array

To sum the values in an array you must use a loop with an accumulator variable. The loop adds the value in each array element to the accumulator. For example, assume that the following statement appears in a program and that values have been stored in the `units` array:

```
int[] units = new int[25];
```

The following loop adds the values of each element of the `units` array to the `total` variable. When the code is finished, `total` will contain the sum of all of the `units` array's elements.

```
int total = 0;        // Initialize accumulator
for (int index = 0; index < units.length; index++)
   total += units[index];
```

Getting the Average of the Values in a Numeric Array

The first step in calculating the average of all the values in an array is to sum the values. The second step is to divide the sum by the number of elements in the array. Assume that the following statement appears in a program and that values have been stored in the `scores` array:

```
double[] scores = new double[10];
```

The following code calculates the average of the values in the `scores` array. When the code completes, the average will be stored in the `average` variable.

```
double total = 0;     // Initialize accumulator
double average;       // Will hold the average
for (int index = 0; index < scores.length; index++)
   total += scores[index];
average = total / scores.length;
```

Notice that the last statement, which divides `total` by `scores.length`, is not inside the loop. This statement should only execute once, after the loop has finished its iterations.

Finding the Highest and Lowest Values in a Numeric Array

The algorithms for finding the highest and lowest values in an array are very similar. First, let's look at code for finding the highest value in an array. Assume that the following statement exists in a program and that values have been stored in the `numbers` array:

```
int[] numbers = new int[50];
```

The code to find the highest value in the array is as follows:

```
int highest = numbers[0];
for (int index = 1; index < numbers.length; index++)
{
   if (numbers[index] > highest)
      highest = numbers[index];
}
```

First we copy the value in the first array element to the variable `highest`. Then the loop compares all of the remaining array elements, beginning at subscript 1, to the value in `highest`. Each time it finds a value in the array that is greater than `highest`, it copies that value to `highest`. When the loop has finished, `highest` will contain the highest value in the array.

The following code finds the lowest value in the array. As you can see, it is nearly identical to the code for finding the highest value.

```
    int lowest = numbers[0];
    for (int index = 1; index < numbers.length; index++)
    {
       if (numbers[index] < lowest)
          lowest = numbers[index];
    }
```

When the loop has finished, `lowest` will contain the lowest value in the array.

The SalesData Class

To demonstrate these algorithms, look at the `SalesData` class shown in Code Listing 8-10. An instance of the class keeps sales amounts for any number of days in an array, which is a private field. Public methods are provided that return the total, average, highest, and lowest amounts of sales. The program in Code Listing 8-11 demonstrates the class, and Figure 8-11 shows an example of interaction with the program.

Code Listing 8-10 (SalesData.java)

```
1   /**
2       This class keeps the sales figures for a number of
3       days in an array and provides methods for getting
4       the total and average sales, and the highest and
5       lowest amounts of sales.
6   */
7
8   public class SalesData
9   {
10      private double[] sales; // The sales data
11
12      /**
13          The constructor copies the elements in
14          an array to the sales array.
15          @param s The array to copy.
16      */
17
18      public SalesData(double[] s)
19      {
20          // Create an array as large as s.
21          sales = new double[s.length];
22
23          // Copy the elements from s to sales.
24          for (int index = 0; index < s.length; index++)
25              sales[index] = s[index];
26      }
```

```
27
28        /**
29            getTotal method
30            @return The total of the elements in
31            the sales array.
32        */
33
34        public double getTotal()
35        {
36            double total = 0.0;        // Accumulator
37
38            // Accumulate the sum of the elements
39            // in the sales array.
40            for (int index = 0; index < sales.length; index++)
41                total += sales[index];
42
43            // Return the total.
44            return total;
45        }
46
47        /**
48            getAverage method
49            @return The average of the elements
50            in the sales array.
51        */
52
53        public double getAverage()
54        {
55            return getTotal() / sales.length;
56        }
57
58        /**
59            getHighest method
60            @return The highest value stored
61            in the sales array.
62        */
63
64        public double getHighest()
65        {
66            double highest = sales[0];
67
68            for (int index = 1; index < sales.length; index++)
69            {
70                if (sales[index] > highest)
71                    highest = sales[index];
72            }
```

```
73
74          return highest;
75      }
76
77      /**
78          getLowest method
79          @return The lowest value stored
80          in the sales array.
81      */
82
83      public double getLowest()
84      {
85          double lowest = sales[0];
86
87          for (int index = 1; index < sales.length; index++)
88          {
89              if (sales[index] < lowest)
90                  lowest = sales[index];
91          }
92
93          return lowest;
94      }
95  }
```

Code Listing 8-11   (Sales.java)

```
 1 import javax.swing.JOptionPane;
 2 import java.text.DecimalFormat;
 3
 4 /**
 5    This program gathers sales amounts for the week.
 6    It uses the SalesData class to display the total,
 7    average, highest, and lowest sales amounts.
 8 */
 9
10 public class Sales
11 {
12    public static void main(String[] args)
13    {
14       final int ONE_WEEK = 7; // Number of elements
15
16       // Create an array to hold sales amounts for a week.
17       double[] sales = new double[ONE_WEEK];
18
```

```java
19          // Get the week's sales figures.
20          getValues(sales);
21
22          // Create a SalesData object, initialized
23          // with the week's sales figures.
24          SalesData week = new SalesData(sales);
25
26          // Create a DecimalFormat object.
27          DecimalFormat dollar = new DecimalFormat("#,##0.00");
28
29          // Display the total, average, highest, and lowest
30          // sales amounts for the week.
31          JOptionPane.showMessageDialog(null,
32                  "The total sales were $" +
33                  dollar.format(week.getTotal()) +
34                  "\nThe average sales were $" +
35                  dollar.format(week.getAverage()) +
36                  "\nThe highest sales were $" +
37                  dollar.format(week.getHighest()) +
38                  "\nThe lowest sales were $" +
39                  dollar.format(week.getLowest()));
40
41      System.exit(0);
42   }
43
44   /**
45      The getValues method asks the user to enter sales
46      amounts for each element of an array.
47      @param array The array to store the values in.
48   */
49
50   private static void getValues(double[] array)
51   {
52      String input;  // To hold user input.
53
54      // Get sales for each day of the week.
55      for (int i = 0; i < array.length; i++)
56      {
57         input = JOptionPane.showInputDialog("Enter " +
58             "the sales for day " + (i + 1) + ".");
59         array[i] = Double.parseDouble(input);
60      }
61   }
62 }
```

Figure 8-11   Interaction with the `Sales.java` program

In the Spotlight:

Creating an Object that Processes an Array

Dr. LaClaire gives a set of exams during the semester in her chemistry class. At the end of the semester, she drops each student's lowest test score before averaging the scores. She has asked you to write a program that will read a student's test scores as input, and calculate the average with the lowest score dropped.

The following pseudocode shows the steps for calculating the average of a set of test scores, with the lowest score dropped:

> *Calculate the total of the scores.*
> *Find the lowest score.*
> *Subtract the lowest score from the total. This gives the adjusted total.*
> *Divide the adjusted total by (number of scores − 1). This is the average.*

You decide to create a class named `Grader`, with a constructor that accepts a double array of test scores. The `Grader` class will have a method named `getLowestScore` that returns the lowest score in the array, and a method named `getAverage` that returns the average of the test scores with the lowest score dropped. Figure 8-12 shows a UML diagram for the class.

Figure 8-12   UML diagram for the `Grader` class

Grader
- testScores: double[ ]
+ Grader(scoreArray : double[ ]); + getLowestScore() : double + getAverage() : double

Code Listing 8-12 shows the code for the class.

Code Listing 8-12   (`Grader.java`)

```
 1 /**
 2     The Grader class calculates the average
 3     of an array of test scores, with the
 4     lowest score dropped.
 5 */
 6
 7 public class Grader
 8 {
 9     // The testScores field is a variable
10     // that will reference an array
11     // of test scores.
12     private double[] testScores;
13
14     /**
15        Constructor
16        @param scoreArray An array of test scores.
17     */
18
19     public Grader(double[] scoreArray)
20     {
21        // Assign the array argument to
22        // the testScores field.
23        testScores = scoreArray;
24     }
25
26     /**
27        getLowestScore method
28        @return The lowest test score.
29     */
30
31     public double getLowestScore()
32     {
33        double lowest;     // To hold the lowest score
```

```
34
35        // Get the first test score in the array.
36        lowest = testScores[0];
37
38        // Step through the rest of the array. When
39        // a value less than lowest is found, assign
40        // it to lowest.
41        for (int index = 1; index < testScores.length; index++)
42        {
43           if (testScores[index] < lowest)
44               lowest = testScores[index];
45        }
46
47        // Return the lowest test score.
48        return lowest;
49     }
50
51     /**
52        getAverage method
53        @return The average of the test scores
54                with the lowest score dropped.
55     */
56
57     public double getAverage()
58     {
59        double total = 0;    // To hold the score total
60        double lowest;       // To hold the lowest score
61        double average;      // To hold the average
62
63        // If the array contains less than two test
64        // scores, display an error message and set
65        // average to 0.
66        if (testScores.length < 2)
67        {
68           System.out.println("ERROR: You must have at " +
69                              "least two test scores!");
70           average = 0;
71        }
72        else
73        {
74           // First, calculate the total of the scores.
75           for (double score : testScores)
76               total += score;
77
78           // Next, get the lowest score.
79           lowest = getLowestScore();
80
81           // Subtract the lowest score from the total.
82           total -= lowest;
```

```
83
84          // Get the adjusted average.
85          average = total / (testScores.length - 1);
86      }
87
88      // Return the adjusted average.
89      return average;
90   }
91 }
```

- Line 12 declares a field named `testScores`, which will be used to reference a `double` array of test scores.
- The constructor appears in lines 19 through 24. It accepts a `double` array as an argument, which is assigned to the `testScores` field.
- The `getLowestScore` method appears in lines 31 through 49. It finds the lowest value in the `testScores` array and returns that value.
- The `getAverage` method appears in lines 57 through 90. This method first determines if there are less than 2 elements in the `testScores` array (in line 66). If that is the case, we cannot drop the lowest score so an error message is displayed and the `average` variable is set to 0. Otherwise, the code in lines 74 through 85 calculates the average of the test scores with the lowest score dropped, and assigns that value to the `average` variable. Line 89 returns the value of the `average` variable.

Code Listing 8-13 shows the program that Dr. LaClaire will use to calculate a student's adjusted average. The program gets a series of test scores, stores those scores in an array, and uses an instance of the `Grader` class to calculate the average.

Code Listing 8-13 (`CalcAverage.java`)

```
1 import java.util.Scanner;
2
3 /**
4    This program gets a set of test scores and
5    uses the Grader class to calculate the average
6    with the lowest score dropped.
7 */
8
9 public class CalcAverage
10 {
11    public static void main(String[] args)
12    {
13       int numScores;    // To hold the number of scores
14
15       // Create a Scanner object for keyboard input.
16       Scanner keyboard = new Scanner(System.in);
17
18       // Get the number of test scores.
19       System.out.print("How many test scores do you have? ");
```

```
20          numScores = keyboard.nextInt();
21
22          // Create an array to hold the test scores.
23          double[] scores = new double[numScores];
24
25          // Get the test scores and store them
26          // in the scores array.
27          for (int index = 0; index < numScores; index++)
28          {
29              System.out.print("Enter score #" +
30                                  (index + 1) + ": ");
31              scores[index] = keyboard.nextDouble();
32          }
33
34          // Create a Grader object, passing the
35          // scores array as an argument to the
36          // constructor.
37          Grader myGrader = new Grader(scores);
38
39          // Display the adjusted average.
40          System.out.println("Your adjusted average is " +
41                                  myGrader.getAverage());
42
43          // Display the lowest score.
44          System.out.println("Your lowest test score was " +
45                                  myGrader.getLowestScore());
46
47      }
48 }
```

Program Output with Example Input Shown in Bold

```
How many test scores do you have? 4 [Enter]
Enter scores #1: 100 [Enter]
Enter scores #2: 100 [Enter]
Enter scores #3: 40 [Enter]
Enter scores #4: 100 [Enter]
Your adjusted average is 100.0
Your lowest test score was 40.0
```

Partially Filled Arrays

Sometimes you need to store a series of items in an array, but you do not know the number of items that there are. As a result, you do not know the exact number of elements needed for the array. One solution is to make the array large enough to hold the largest possible number of items. This can lead to another problem, however. If the actual number of items stored in the array is less than the number of elements, the array will be only partially filled. When you process a partially filled array, you must only process the elements that contain valid data items.

A partially filled array is normally used with an accompanying integer variable that holds the number of items stored in the array. For example, suppose a program uses the following code to create an array with 100 elements, and an `int` variable named `count`, which will hold the number of items stored in the array:

```
final int ARRAY_SIZE = 100;
int[] array = new int[ARRAY_SIZE];
int count = 0;
```

Each time we add an item to the array, we must increment `count`. The following code demonstrates:

```
Scanner keyboard = new Scanner(System.in);
System.out.print("Enter a number or -1 to quit: ");
number = keyboard.nextInt();
while (number != -1 && count < array.length)
{
    array[count] = number;
    count++;
    System.out.print("Enter a number or -1 to quit: ");
    number = keyboard.nextInt();
}
```

Each iteration of this sentinel-controlled loop allows the user to enter a number to be stored in the array, or –1 to quit. The `count` variable is used as the subscript of the next available element in the array, and then incremented. When the user enters –1, or `count` reaches the size of the array, the loop stops. The following code displays all of the valid items in the array:

```
for (int index = 0; index < count; index++)
{
    System.out.println(array[index]);
}
```

Notice that this code uses `count` to determine the maximum array subscript to use.

> **NOTE:** If a partially filled array is passed as an argument to a method, the variable that holds the count of items in the array must also be passed as an argument. Otherwise, the method will not be able to determine the number of items that are stored in the array.

Working with Arrays and Files

Saving the contents of an array to a file is a straightforward procedure: Use a loop to step through each element of the array, writing its contents to the file. For example, assume a program declares an array as follows:

```
int[] numbers = { 10, 20, 30, 40, 50 };
```

The following code opens a file named *Values.txt* and writes the contents of each element of the numbers array to the file:

```
int[] numbers = { 10, 20, 30, 40, 50 };
```

```
// Open the file.
PrintWriter outputFile = new PrintWriter("Values.txt");

// Write the array elements to the file.
for (int index = 0; index < numbers.length; index++)
   outputFile.println(numbers[index]);
// Close the file.
outputFile.close();
```

The following code demonstrates how to open the *Values.txt* file and read its contents back into the numbers array.

```
final int SIZE = 5;
int[] numbers = new int[SIZE];
int index = 0;     // Loop control variable

// Open the file.
File file = new File("Values.txt");
Scanner inputFile = new Scanner(file);

// Read the file contents into the array.
while (inputFile.hasNext() && index < numbers.length)
{
   numbers[index] = inputFile.nextInt();
   index++;
}

// Close the file.
inputFile.close();
```

The file is opened, then a while loop reads all of the values from the file into the numbers array. The loop repeats as long as inputFile.hasNext() returns true, and index is less than numbers.length. The inputFile.hasNext() method is called to make sure there is a value remaining in the file. This prevents an error in case the file does not contain enough values to fill the array. The second condition (index < numbers.length) prevents the loop from writing outside the array boundaries.

8.5 Returning Arrays from Methods

CONCEPT: In addition to accepting arrays as arguments, methods may also return arrays.

A method can return a reference to an array. To do so, the return type of the method must be declared properly. For example, look at the following method definition:

```
public static double[] getArray()
{
   double[] array = { 1.2, 2.3, 4.5, 6.7, 8.9 };
   return array;
}
```

The `getArray` method returns an array of `doubles`. Notice that the return type listed in the method header is `double[]`. The method header is illustrated in Figure 8-13. It indicates that the method returns a reference to a `double` array.

Figure 8-13 Array reference return type

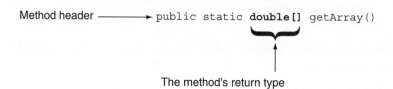

Inside the method an array of `doubles` is created, initialized with some values, and referenced by the `array` variable. Then the `return` statement returns the `array` variable. By returning the `array` variable, the method is returning a reference to the array. The method's return value can be stored in any compatible reference variable, as demonstrated in Code Listing 8-14.

Code Listing 8-14 (ReturnArray.java)

```
 1  /**
 2      This program demonstrates how a reference to an
 3      array can be returned from a method.
 4  */
 5
 6  public class ReturnArray
 7  {
 8     public static void main(String[] args)
 9     {
10        double[] values;
11
12        values = getArray();
13        for (double num : values)
14           System.out.print(num + "   ");
15     }
16
17     /**
18         getArray method
19         @return A reference to an array of doubles.
20     */
21
22     public static double[] getArray()
23     {
24        double[] array = { 1.2, 2.3, 4.5, 6.7, 8.9 };
25
26        return array;
```

```
27    }
28  }
```

Program Output

```
1.2   2.3   4.5   6.7   8.9
```

The following statement, which appears in line 12, assigns the array returned by the getArray method to the array variable values:

```
values = getArray();
```

Then the for loop in lines 13 and 14 displays the value of each element of the values array.

8.6 String Arrays

CONCEPT: An array of **String** objects may be created, but if the array is uninitialized, each **String** in the array must be created individually.

Java also allows you to create arrays of String objects. Here is a statement that creates an array of String objects initialized with values:

```
String[] names = { "Bill", "Susan", "Steven", "Jean" };
```

In memory, an array of String objects is arranged differently than an array of a primitive data type. In order to use a String object, you must have a reference to the String object. So, an array of String objects is really an array of references to String objects. Figure 8-14 illustrates how the names variable will reference an array of references to String objects.

Figure 8-14   The names variable references a String array

Each element in the names array is a reference to a String object. The names[0] element references a String object containing "Bill", the names[1] element references a String object containing "Susan", and so forth. The program in Code Listing 8-15 demonstrates an array of String objects.

Code Listing 8-15 (`MonthDays.java`)

```java
 1  /**
 2      This program demonstrates an array of String objects.
 3  */
 4
 5  public class MonthDays
 6  {
 7      public static void main(String[] args)
 8      {
 9          String[] months = { "January", "February", "March",
10                              "April", "May", "June", "July",
11                              "August", "September", "October",
12                              "November", "December" };
13
14          int[] days = { 31, 28, 31, 30, 31, 30, 31,
15                         31, 30, 31, 30, 31 };
16
17          for (int index = 0; index < months.length; index++)
18          {
19              System.out.println(months[index] + " has " +
20                                 days[index] + " days.");
21          }
22      }
23  }
```

Program Output

```
January has 31 days.
February has 28 days.
March has 31 days.
April has 30 days.
May has 31 days.
June has 30 days.
July has 31 days.
August has 31 days.
September has 30 days.
October has 31 days.
November has 30 days.
December has 31 days.
```

As with the primitive data types, an initialization list automatically causes an array of String objects to be created in memory. If you do not provide an initialization list, you must use the new key word to create the array. Here is an example:

```java
final int SIZE = 4;
String[] names = new String[SIZE];
```

This statement creates an array of four references to `String` objects, as shown in Figure 8-15. Notice that the array is an array of four uninitialized `String` references. Because they do not reference any objects, they are set to `null`.

Figure 8-15   An uninitialized String array

When you create an uninitialized array of `String` objects, you must assign a value to each element in the array that you intend to use. Here is an example:

```
final int SIZE = 4;
String[] names = new String[SIZE];
names[0] = "Bill";
names[1] = "Susan";
names[2] = "Steven";
names[3] = "Jean";
```

After these statements execute, each element of the `names` array will reference a `String` object.

Calling `String` Methods from an Array Element

Recall from Chapter 2 that `String` objects have several methods. For example, the `toUpperCase` method returns the uppercase equivalent of a `String` object. Because each element of a `String` array is a `String` object, you can use an element to call a `String` method. For example, the following statement uses element 0 of the `names` array to call the `toUpperCase` method:

```
System.out.println(names[0].toUpperCase());
```

The following code shows another example. It uses element 3 of the `names` array to call the `charAt` method. When this code executes, the first character of the string stored in `names[3]` will be assigned to the `letter` variable.

```
// Declare a char variable named letter.
char letter;
// Assign the first character in names[3] to letter.
letter = names[3].charAt(0);
```

> **TIP:** Arrays have a field named `length` and `String` objects have a method named `length`. When working with `String` arrays, do not confuse the two. The following loop displays the length of each string held in names, which is assumed to be a `String` array. Note that the loop uses both the array's `length` field and each element's `length` method.
>
> ```
> for (int i = 0; i < names.length; i++)
>     System.out.println(names[i].length());
> ```
>
> Because the array's `length` member is a field, you do not write a set of parentheses after its name. You do write the parentheses after the name of the `String` class's `length` method.

Checkpoint

8.15   a)   Write a statement that declares a `String` array initialized with the following strings: "Mercury", "Venus", "Earth", and "Mars".

b)   Write a loop that displays the contents of each element in the array you declared in A.

c)   Write a loop that displays the first character of the strings stored in each element of the array you declared in A. (*Hint:* Use the `String` class's `charAt` method discussed in Chapter 2.)

8.7   Arrays of Objects

CONCEPT: You may create arrays of objects that are instances of classes that you have written.

Like any other data type, you can create arrays of class objects. For example, recall the `BankAccount` class that we developed in Chapter 6. An array of `BankAccount` objects could be created to represent all of the bank accounts owned by a single person. The following code declares an array of five `BankAccount` objects:

```
final int NUM_ACCOUNTS = 5;
BankAccount[] accounts = new BankAccount[NUM_ACCOUNTS];
```

The variable that references the array is named `accounts`. As with `String` arrays, each element in this array is a reference variable, as illustrated in Figure 8-16.

Notice from the figure that each element of the array is initialized with the value `null`. This is a special value in Java that indicates the array elements do not yet reference objects. You must individually create the objects that each element will reference. The following code uses a loop to create objects for each element:

```
for (int index = 0; index < accounts.length; index++)
    accounts[index] = new BankAccount();
```

Figure 8-16 The accounts variable references an array of references

In this code, the no-arg constructor is called for each object. Recall that the `BankAccount` class has a no-arg constructor that assigns 0.0 to the `balance` field. After the loop executes, each element of the `accounts` array will reference a `BankAccount` object, as shown in Figure 8-17.

Figure 8-17 Each element of the array references an object

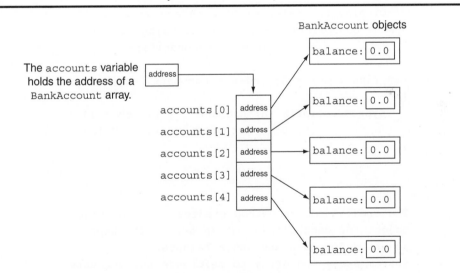

Objects in an array are accessed with subscripts, just like any other data type in an array. For example, the following code uses the `accounts[2]` element to call the `setBalance` and `withdraw` methods:

```
accounts[2].setBalance(2500.0);
accounts[2].withdraw(500.0);
```

Code Listing 8-16 shows a complete program that uses an array of objects.

Code Listing 8-16 (ObjectArray.java)

```java
 1 import java.util.Scanner; // Needed for the Scanner class
 2
 3 /**
 4    This program works with an array of three
 5    BankAccount objects.
 6 */
 7
 8 public class ObjectArray
 9 {
10    public static void main(String[] args)
11    {
12       final int NUM_ACCOUNTS = 3;   // Number of accounts
13
14       // Create an array that can reference
15       // BankAccount objects.
16       BankAccount[] accounts = new BankAccount[NUM_ACCOUNTS];
17
18       // Create objects for the array.
19       createAccounts(accounts);
20
21       // Display the balances of each account.
22       System.out.println("Here are the balances " +
23                          "of each account:");
24
25       for (int index = 0; index < accounts.length; index++)
26       {
27          System.out.println("Account " + (index + 1) +
28                    ": $" + accounts[index].getBalance());
29       }
30    }
31
32    /**
33       The createAccounts method creates a BankAccount
34       object for each element of an array. The user
35       is asked for each account's balance.
36       @param array The array to reference the accounts
37    */
38
39    private static void createAccounts(BankAccount[] array)
40    {
41       double balance;   // To hold an account balance
42
43       // Create a Scanner object.
44       Scanner keyboard = new Scanner(System.in);
45
```

```
46              // Create the accounts.
47              for (int index = 0; index < array.length; index++)
48              {
49                 // Get the account's balance.
50                 System.out.print("Enter the balance for " +
51                                 "account " + (index + 1) + ": ");
52                 balance = keyboard.nextDouble();
53
54                 // Create the account.
55                 array[index] = new BankAccount(balance);
56              }
57           }
58  }
```

Program Output with Example Input Shown in Bold

Enter the balance for account 1: **2500.0 [Enter]**
Enter the balance for account 2: **5000.0 [Enter]**
Enter the balance for account 3: **1500.0 [Enter]**
Here are the balances for each account:
Account 1: $2500.0
Account 2: $5000.0
Account 3: $1500.0

 Checkpoint

8.16   Recall that we discussed a `Rectangle` class in Chapter 6. Write code that declares
a `Rectangle` array with five elements. Instantiate each element with a `Rectangle`
object. Use the `Rectangle` constructor to initialize each object with values for the
`length` and `width` fields.

8.8 # The Sequential Search Algorithm

CONCEPT: A search algorithm is a method of locating a specific item in a larger
collection of data. This section discusses the sequential search algorithm,
which is a simple technique for searching the contents of an array.

It is very common for programs not only to store and process information stored in arrays,
but also to search arrays for specific items. This section shows you how to use the simplest
of all search algorithms—the sequential search.

The sequential search algorithm uses a loop to sequentially step through an array, starting
with the first element. It compares each element with the value being searched for and stops
when the value is found or the end of the array is encountered. If the value being searched
for is not in the array, the algorithm unsuccessfully searches to the end of the array.

The SearchArray program shown in Code Listing 8-17 searches the five-element array tests to find a score of 100. It uses a method, sequentialSearch, to find the value in the array. The array that is passed as an argument into the array parameter is searched for an occurrence of the number passed into value. If the number is found, its array subscript is returned. Otherwise, –1 is returned indicating the value did not appear in the array.

Code Listing 8-17 (SearchArray.java)

```java
 1  /**
 2      This program sequentially searches an
 3      int array for a specified value.
 4  */
 5
 6  public class SearchArray
 7  {
 8      public static void main(String[] args)
 9      {
10          int[] tests = { 87, 75, 98, 100, 82 };
11          int results;
12
13          // Search the array for the value 100.
14          results = sequentialSearch(tests, 100);
15
16          // Determine whether 100 was found and
17          // display an appropriate message.
18          if (results == -1)
19          {
20              System.out.println("You did not " +
21                          "earn 100 on any test.");
22          }
23          else
24          {
25              System.out.println("You earned 100 " +
26                          "on test " + (results + 1));
27          }
28      }
29
30      /**
31          The sequentialSearch method searches an array for
32          a value.
33          @param array The array to search.
34          @param value The value to search for.
35          @return The subscript of the value if found in the
36                      array, otherwise -1.
37      */
```

```
38
39      public static int sequentialSearch(int[] array,
40                                      int value)
41      {
42          int index;         // Loop control variable
43          int element;       // Element the value is found at
44          boolean found;     // Flag indicating search results
45
46          // Element 0 is the starting point of the search.
47          index = 0;
48
49          // Store the default values element and found.
50          element = -1;
51          found = false;
52
53          // Search the array.
54          while (!found && index < array.length)
55          {
56              if (array[index] == value)
57              {
58                  found = true;
59                  element = index;
60              }
61              index++;
62          }
63
64          return element;
65      }
66  }
```

Program Output

```
You earned 100 on test 4
```

NOTE: The reason –1 is returned when the search value is not found in the array is because –1 is not a valid subscript.

See the `PinTester` Class Case Study on the Student CD for another example using arrays. Also, see the Student CD for the Bonus Section on Parallel Arrays to learn about another programming technique using arrays.

8.9 Two-Dimensional Arrays

CONCEPT: A two-dimensional array is an array of arrays. It can be thought of as having rows and columns.

An array is useful for storing and working with a set of data. Sometimes, though, it's necessary to work with multiple sets of data. For example, in a grade-averaging program a teacher might record all of one student's test scores in an array of `doubles`. If the teacher has 30 students, that means she'll need 30 arrays to record the scores for the entire class. Instead of defining 30 individual arrays, however, it would be better to define a two-dimensional array.

The arrays that you have studied so far are one-dimensional arrays. They are called *one-dimensional* because they can only hold one set of data. Two-dimensional arrays, which are sometimes called *2D arrays*, can hold multiple sets of data. Although a two-dimensional array is actually an array of arrays, it's best to think of it as having rows and columns of elements, as shown in Figure 8-18. This figure shows an array of test scores, having three rows and four columns.

Figure 8-18 Rows and columns

The array shown in the figure has three rows (numbered 0 through 2) and four columns (numbered 0 through 3). There are a total of 12 elements in the array.

To declare a two-dimensional array, two sets of brackets and two size declarators are required: The first one is for the number of rows and the second one is for the number of columns. Here is an example declaration of a two-dimensional array with three rows and four columns:

```
double[][] scores = new double[3][4];
```

The two sets of brackets in the data type indicate that the `scores` variable will reference a two-dimensional array. The numbers 3 and 4 are size declarators. The first size declarator specifies the number of rows, and the second size declarator specifies the number of columns. Notice that each size declarator is enclosed in its own set of brackets. This is illustrated in Figure 8-19.

Figure 8-19   Declaration of a two-dimensional array

When processing the data in a two-dimensional array, each element has two subscripts: one for its row and another for its column. In the scores array, the elements in row 0 are referenced as follows:

```
scores[0][0]
scores[0][1]
scores[0][2]
scores[0][3]
```

The elements in row 1 are as follows:

```
scores[1][0]
scores[1][1]
scores[1][2]
scores[1][3]
```

And the elements in row 2 are as follows:

```
scores[2][0]
scores[2][1]
scores[2][2]
scores[2][3]
```

Figure 8-20 illustrates the array with the subscripts shown for each element.

Figure 8-20   Subscripts for each element of the scores array

The scores variable holds the address of a 2D array of doubles.	address		column 0	column 1	column 2	column 3
		row 0	scores[0][0]	scores[0][1]	scores[0][2]	scores[0][3]
		row 1	scores[1][0]	scores[1][1]	scores[1][2]	scores[1][3]
		row 2	scores[2][0]	scores[2][1]	scores[2][2]	scores[2][3]

To access one of the elements in a two-dimensional array, you must use both subscripts. For example, the following statement stores the number 95 in scores[2][1]:

```
scores[2][1] = 95;
```

Programs that process two-dimensional arrays can do so with nested loops. For example, the following code prompts the user to enter a score, once for each element in the array:

```
final int ROWS = 3;
final int COLS = 4;
double[][] scores = new double[ROWS][COLS];
for (int row = 0; row < ROWS; row++)
{
   for (int col = 0; col < COLS; col++)
   {
      System.out.print("Enter a score: ");
      scores[row][col] = keyboard.nextDouble();
   }
}
```

And the following code displays all the elements in the `scores` array:

```
for (int row = 0; row < ROWS; row++)
{
   for (int col = 0; col < COLS; col++)
   {
      System.out.println(scores[row][col]);
   }
}
```

The program in Code Listing 8-18 uses a two-dimensional array to store corporate sales data. The array has three rows (one for each division of the company) and four columns (one for each quarter).

Code Listing 8-18 (CorpSales.java)

```
 1 import java.util.Scanner;
 2 import java.text.DecimalFormat;
 3
 4 /**
 5    This program demonstrates a two-dimensional array.
 6 */
 7
 8 public class CorpSales
 9 {
10    public static void main(String[] args)
11    {
12       final int DIVS = 3; // Three divisions in the company
13       final int QTRS = 4; // Four quarters
14       double totalSales = 0.0;   // Accumulator
15
16       // Create an array to hold the sales for each
17       // division, for each quarter.
18       double[][] sales = new double[DIVS][QTRS];
```

```
19
20          // Create a Scanner object for keyboard input.
21          Scanner keyboard = new Scanner(System.in);
22
23          // Display an introduction.
24          System.out.println("This program will calculate the " +
25                              "total sales of");
26          System.out.println("all the company's divisions. " +
27                              "Enter the following sales data:");
28
29          // Nested loops to fill the array with quarterly
30          // sales figures for each division.
31          for (int div = 0; div < DIVS; div++)
32          {
33             for (int qtr = 0; qtr < QTRS; qtr++)
34             {
35                System.out.print("Division " + (div + 1) +
36                                  ", Quarter " + (qtr + 1) +
37                                  ": $");
38                sales[div][qtr] = keyboard.nextDouble();
39             }
40             System.out.println();   // Print blank line.
41          }
42
43          // Nested loops to add all the elements of the array.
44          for (int div = 0; div < DIVS; div++)
45          {
46             for (int qtr = 0; qtr < QTRS; qtr++)
47             {
48                totalSales += sales[div][qtr];
49             }
50          }
51
52          // Create a DecimalFormat object to format output.
53          DecimalFormat dollar = new DecimalFormat("#,##0.00");
54
55          // Display the total sales.
56          System.out.println("The total sales for the company " +
57                              "are $" + dollar.format(totalSales));
58       }
59 }
```

Program Output with Example Input Shown in Bold

```
This program will calculate the total sales of
all the company's divisions. Enter the following sales data:
Division 1, Quarter 1: $35698.77 [Enter]
Division 1, Quarter 2: $36148.63 [Enter]
```

```
Division 1, Quarter 3: $31258.95 [Enter]
Division 1, Quarter 4: $30864.12 [Enter]

Division 2, Quarter 1: $41289.64 [Enter]
Division 2, Quarter 2: $43278.52 [Enter]
Division 2, Quarter 3: $40928.18 [Enter]
Division 2, Quarter 4: $42818.98 [Enter]

Division 3, Quarter 1: $28914.56 [Enter]
Division 3, Quarter 2: $27631.52 [Enter]
Division 3, Quarter 3: $30596.64 [Enter]
Division 3, Quarter 4: $29834.21 [Enter]

The total sales for the company are $419,262.72
```

Look at the following array declaration in line 18:

```
double[][] sales = new double[DIVS][QTRS];
```

As mentioned earlier, the array has three rows (one for each division) and four columns (one for each quarter) to store the company's sales data. The row subscripts are 0, 1, and 2, and the column subscripts are 0, 1, 2, and 3. Figure 8-21 illustrates how the quarterly sales data is stored in the array.

Figure 8-21   Division and quarter data stored in the `sales` array

Initializing a Two-Dimensional Array

When initializing a two-dimensional array, you enclose each row's initialization list in its own set of braces. Here is an example:

```
int[][] numbers = { {1, 2, 3}, {4, 5, 6}, {7, 8, 9} };
```

As with one-dimensional arrays, you do not use the new key word when you provide an initialization list. Java automatically creates the array and fills its elements with the initialization values. In this example, the initialization values for row 0 are {1, 2, 3}, the initialization values for row 1 are {4, 5, 6}, and the initialization values for row 2 are {7, 8, 9}. So, this statement declares an array with three rows and three columns. For more clarity, the same statement could also be written as follows:

```
int[][] numbers = { {1, 2, 3},
                    {4, 5, 6},
                    {7, 8, 9} };
```

In either case, the values are assigned to the numbers array as illustrated in Figure 8-22.

Figure 8-22 The numbers array

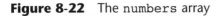

The length Field in a Two-Dimensional Array

A one-dimensional array has a length field that holds the number of elements in the array. A two-dimensional array, however, has multiple length fields. It has a length field that holds the number of rows, and then each row has a length field that holds the number of columns. This makes sense when you think of a two-dimensional array as an array of one-dimensional arrays. Figure 8-22 shows the numbers array depicted in rows and columns. Figure 8-23 shows another way of thinking of the numbers array: as an array of arrays.

Figure 8-23 The numbers array is an array of arrays

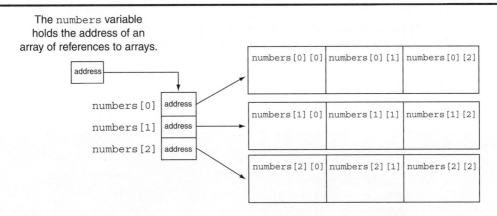

As you can see from the figure, the numbers variable references a one-dimensional array with three elements. Each of the three elements is a reference to another one-dimensional array. The elements in the array referenced by numbers[0] are numbers[0][0], numbers[0][1], and numbers[0][2]. This pattern continues with numbers[1] and numbers[2]. The figure shows a total of four arrays. Each of the arrays in the figure has its own length field. The program in Code Listing 8-19 uses these length fields to display the number of rows and columns in a two-dimensional array.

Code Listing 8-19   (`Lengths.java`)

```java
 1 /**
 2     This program uses the length fields of a 2D array
 3     to display the number of rows, and the number of
 4     columns in each row.
 5 */
 6
 7 public class Lengths
 8 {
 9     public static void main(String[] args)
10     {
11         // Declare a 2D array with 3 rows
12         // and 4 columns.
13
14         int[][] numbers = { { 1,   2,   3,   4 },
15                             { 5,   6,   7,   8 },
16                             { 9,  10,  11,  12 } };
17
18         // Display the number of rows.
19         System.out.println("The number of " +
20                 "rows is " + numbers.length);
21
22         // Display the number of columns in each row.
23         for (int index = 0; index < numbers.length; index++)
24         {
25             System.out.println("The number of " +
26                 "columns in row " + index + " is " +
27                 numbers[index].length);
28         }
29     }
30 }
```

Program Output

```
The number of rows is 3
The number of columns in row 0 is 4
The number of columns in row 1 is 4
The number of columns in row 2 is 4
```

Displaying All the Elements of a Two-Dimensional Array

As you have seen in previous example programs, a pair of nested loops can be used to display all the elements of a two-dimensional array. For example, the following code creates the numbers array with three rows and four columns, and then displays all the elements in the array:

```
int[][] numbers = { { 1,  2,  3,  4 },
                    { 5,  6,  7,  8 },
                    { 9, 10, 11, 12 } };

for (int row = 0; row < 3; row++)
{
   for (int col = 0; col < 4; col++)
      System.out.println(numbers[row][col]);
}
```

Although this code will display all of the elements, it is limited in the following way: The loops are specifically written to display an array with three rows and four columns. A better approach is to use the array's length fields for the upper limit of the subscripts in the loop test expressions. Here are the modified loops:

```
for (int row = 0; row < numbers.length; row++)
{
   for (int col = 0; col < numbers[row].length; col++)
      System.out.println(numbers[row][col]);
}
```

Let's take a closer look at the header for the outer loop:

```
for (int row = 0; row < numbers.length; row++)
```

This loop controls the subscript for the number array's rows. Because numbers.length holds the number of rows in the array, we have used it as the upper limit for the row subscripts. Here is the header for the inner loop:

```
for (int col = 0; col < numbers[row].length; col++)
```

This loop controls the subscript for the number array's columns. Because each row's length field holds the number of columns in the row, we have used it as the upper limit for the column subscripts. By using the length fields in algorithms that process two-dimensional arrays, you can write code that works with arrays of any number of rows and columns.

Summing All the Elements of a Two-Dimensional Array

To sum all the elements of a two-dimensional array, you can use a pair of nested loops to add the contents of each element to an accumulator. The following code shows an example:

```
int[][] numbers = { { 1,  2,  3,  4 },
                    { 5,  6,  7,  8 },
                    { 9, 10, 11, 12 } };
```

```
int total = 0;      // Accumulator, set to 0
// Sum the array elements.
for (int row = 0; row < numbers.length; row++)
{
   for (int col = 0; col < numbers[row].length; col++)
      total += numbers[row][col];
}

// Display the sum.
System.out.println("The total is " + total);
```

Summing the Rows of a Two-Dimensional Array

Sometimes you may need to calculate the sum of each row in a two-dimensional array. For example, suppose a two-dimensional array is used to hold a set of test scores for a set of students. Each row in the array is a set of test scores for one student. To get the sum of a student's test scores (perhaps so an average may be calculated), you use a loop to add all the elements in one row. The following code shows an example:

```
int[][] numbers = { { 1,  2,  3,  4 },
                    { 5,  6,  7,  8 },
                    { 9, 10, 11, 12 } };
int total;         // Accumulator

for (int row = 0; row < numbers.length; row++)
{
   // Set the accumulator to 0.
   total = 0;

   // Sum a row.
   for (int col = 0; col < numbers[row].length; col++)
      total += numbers[row][col];

   // Display the row's total.
   System.out.println("Total of row " + row +
                      " is " + total);
}
```

Notice that the `total` variable, which is used as an accumulator, is set to zero just before the inner loop executes, because the inner loop sums the elements of a row and stores the sum in `total`. Therefore, the `total` variable must be set to zero before each iteration of the inner loop.

Summing the Columns of a Two-Dimensional Array

Sometimes you may need to calculate the sum of each column in a two-dimensional array. For example, suppose a two-dimensional array is used to hold a set of test scores for a set of students, and you wish to calculate the class average for each of the test scores. To do this, you calculate the average of each column in the array. This is accomplished with a set of nested loops. The outer loop controls the column subscript and the inner loop controls the row subscript. The inner loop calculates the sum of a column, which is stored in an accumulator. The following code demonstrates:

```java
int[][] numbers = { { 1,  2,  3,  4 },
                    { 5,  6,  7,  8 },
                    { 9, 10, 11, 12 } };
int total;        // Accumulator

for (int col = 0; col < numbers[0].length; col++)
{
   // Set the accumulator to 0.
   total = 0;

   // Sum a column.
   for (int row = 0; row < numbers.length; row++)
      total += numbers[row][col];

   // Display the columns's total.
   System.out.println("Total of column " + col +
                      " is " + total);
}
```

Passing Two-Dimensional Arrays to Methods

When a two-dimensional array is passed to a method, the parameter must be declared as a reference to a two-dimensional array. The following method header shows an example:

```java
private static void showArray(int[][] array)
```

This method's parameter, array, is declared as a reference to a two-dimensional int array. Any two-dimensional int array can be passed as an argument to the method. Code Listing 8-20 demonstrates two such methods.

Code Listing 8-20   (`Pass2Darray.java`)

```java
 1 /**
 2    This program demonstrates methods that accept
 3    a two-dimensional array as an argument.
 4 */
 5
 6 public class Pass2Darray
 7 {
 8    public static void main(String[] args)
 9    {
10       int[][] numbers = { { 1,  2,  3,  4 },
11                           { 5,  6,  7,  8 },
12                           { 9, 10, 11, 12 } };
```

```
13
14          // Display the contents of the array.
15          System.out.println("Here are the values " +
16                             " in the array.");
17          showArray(numbers);
18
19          // Display the sum of the array's values.
20          System.out.println("The sum of the values " +
21                             "is " + arraySum(numbers));
22      }
23
24      /**
25         The showArray method displays the contents
26         of a two-dimensional int array.
27         @param array The array to display.
28      */
29
30      private static void showArray(int[][] array)
31      {
32         for (int row = 0; row < array.length; row++)
33         {
34            for (int col = 0; col < array[row].length; col++)
35               System.out.print(array[row][col] + " ");
36            System.out.println();
37         }
38      }
39
40      /**
41         The arraySum method returns the sum of the
42         values in a two-dimensional int array.
43         @param array The array to sum.
44         @return The sum of the array elements.
45      */
46
47      private static int arraySum(int[][] array)
48      {
49         int total = 0;    // Accumulator
50
51         for (int row = 0; row < array.length; row++)
52         {
53            for (int col = 0; col < array[row].length; col++)
54               total += array[row][col];
55         }
56
```

```
57          return total;
58      }
59 }
```

Program Output

```
Here are the values in the array.
1  2  3  4
5  6  7  8
9  10  11  12
The sum of the values is 78
```

Ragged Arrays

Because the rows in a two-dimensional array are also arrays, each row can have its own length. When the rows of a two-dimensional array are of different lengths, the array is known as a ragged array. You create a ragged array by first creating a two-dimensional array with a specific number of rows, but no columns. Here is an example:

```
int[][] ragged = new int[4][];
```

This statement partially creates a two-dimensional array. The array can have four rows, but the rows have not yet been created. Next, you create the individual rows as shown in the following code:

```
ragged[0] = new int[3];    // Row 0 has 3 columns.
ragged[1] = new int[4];    // Row 1 has 4 columns.
ragged[2] = new int[5];    // Row 2 has 5 columns.
ragged[3] = new int[6];    // Row 3 has 6 columns.
```

This code creates the four rows. Row 0 has three columns, row 1 has four columns, row 2 has five columns, and row 3 has six columns. The following code displays the number of columns in each row:

```
for (int index = 0; index < ragged.length; index++)
{
    System.out.println("The number of columns " +
                       "in row " + index + " is " +
                       ragged[index].length);
}
```

This code will display the following output:

```
The number of columns in row 0 is 3
The number of columns in row 1 is 4
The number of columns in row 2 is 5
The number of columns in row 3 is 6
```

8.10 Arrays with Three or More Dimensions

CONCEPT: Java does not limit the number of dimensions that an array may have. It is possible to create arrays with multiple dimensions, to model data that occurs in multiple sets.

Java allows you to create arrays with virtually any number of dimensions. Here is an example of a three-dimensional array declaration:

```
double[][][] seats = new double[3][5][8];
```

This array can be thought of as three sets of five rows, with each row containing eight elements. The array might be used to store the prices of seats in an auditorium, where there are eight seats in a row, five rows in a section, and a total of three sections.

Figure 8-24 illustrates the concept of a three-dimensional array as "pages" of two-dimensional arrays.

Figure 8-24   A three-dimensional array

Arrays with more than three dimensions are difficult to visualize, but can be useful in some programming problems. For example, in a factory warehouse where cases of widgets are stacked on pallets, an array with four dimensions could be used to store a part number for each widget. The four subscripts of each element could represent the pallet number, case number, row number, and column number of each widget. Similarly, an array with five dimensions could be used if there were multiple warehouses.

Checkpoint

8.17   A video rental store keeps videos on 50 racks with 10 shelves each. Each shelf holds 25 videos. Declare a three-dimensional array large enough to represent the store's storage system.

8.11 The Selection Sort and the Binary Search Algorithms

CONCEPT: A sorting algorithm is used to arrange data into some order. A search algorithm is a method of locating a specific item in a larger collection of data. The selection sort and the binary search are popular sorting and searching algorithms.

The Selection Sort Algorithm

Often the data in an array must be sorted in some order. Customer lists, for instance, are commonly sorted in alphabetical order. Student grades might be sorted from highest to lowest. Product codes could be sorted so all the products of the same color are stored together. In this section we explore how to write your own sorting algorithm. A sorting algorithm is a technique for scanning through an array and rearranging its contents in some specific order. The algorithm that we will explore is called the selection sort.

The *selection sort* works like this: The smallest value in the array is located and moved to element 0. Then the next smallest value is located and moved to element 1. This process continues until all of the elements have been placed in their proper order. Let's see how the selection sort works when arranging the elements of the following array in Figure 8-25.

Figure 8-25   Values in an array

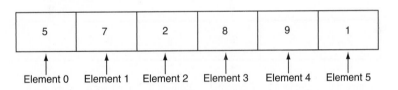

The selection sort scans the array, starting at element 0, and locates the element with the smallest value. The contents of this element are then swapped with the contents of element 0. In this example, the 1 stored in element 5 is swapped with the 5 stored in element 0. After the exchange, the array would appear as shown in Figure 8-26.

Figure 8-26   Values in array after first swap

The algorithm then repeats the process, but because element 0 already contains the smallest value in the array, it can be left out of the procedure. This time, the algorithm begins the scan at element 1. In this example, the contents of element 2 are exchanged with that of element 1. The array would then appear as shown in Figure 8-27.

Figure 8-27   Values in array after second swap

Once again the process is repeated, but this time the scan begins at element 2. The algorithm will find that element 5 contains the next smallest value. This element's value is swapped with that of element 2, causing the array to appear as shown in Figure 8-28.

Figure 8-28   Values in array after third swap

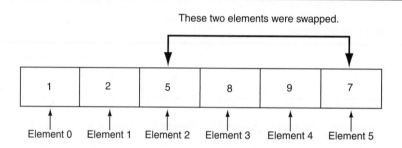

Next, the scanning begins at element 3. Its value is swapped with that of element 5, causing the array to appear as shown in Figure 8-29.

Figure 8-29   Values in array after fourth swap

At this point there are only two elements left to sort. The algorithm finds that the value in element 5 is smaller than that of element 4, so the two are swapped. This puts the array in its final arrangement as shown in Figure 8-30.

Figure 8-30 Values in array after fifth swap

Here is the selection sort algorithm in pseudocode:

For `startScan` *is each subscript in array from 0 through the next-to-last subscript*
  Set `minIndex` *variable to* `startScan`.
  Set `minValue` *variable to* `array[startScan]`.
  For `index` *is each subscript in array from (`startScan` + 1) through the last subscript*
    If `array[index]` *is less than* `minValue`
      Set `minValue` *to* `array[index]`.
      Set `minIndex` *to* `index`.
    End If.
    Increment `index`.
  End For.
  Set `array[minIndex]` *to* `array[startScan]`.
  Set `array[startScan]` *to* `minValue`.
End For.

The following method performs a selection sort on an integer array. The array that is passed as an argument is sorted in ascending order.

```
public static void selectionSort(int[] array)
{
    int startScan, index, minIndex, minValue;

    for (startScan = 0; startScan < (array.length-1); startScan++)
    {
        minIndex = startScan;
        minValue = array[startScan];
        for(index = startScan + 1; index < array.length; index++)
        {
            if (array[index] < minValue)
            {
                minValue = array[index];
```

```
                minIndex = index;
          }
      }
      array[minIndex] = array[startScan];
      array[startScan] = minValue;
    }
  }
```

 The `SelectionSortDemo.java` program on the Student CD demonstrates the `selectionSort` method.

The Binary Search Algorithm

This chapter previously presented the sequential search algorithm for searching an array. The advantage of the sequential search is its simplicity. It is easy to understand and implement. Furthermore, it doesn't require the data in the array to be stored in any particular order. Its disadvantage, however, is its inefficiency. If the array being searched contains 20,000 elements, the algorithm will have to look at all 20,000 elements in order to find a value stored in the last element. In an average case, an item is just as likely to be found near the end of the array as near the beginning. Typically, for an array of N items, the sequential search will locate an item in N/2 attempts. If an array has 50,000 elements, the sequential search will make a comparison with 25,000 of them in a typical case.

This is assuming, of course, that the search item is consistently found in the array. (N/2 is the average number of comparisons. The maximum number of comparisons is always N.) When the sequential search fails to locate an item, it must make a comparison with every element in the array. As the number of failed search attempts increases, so does the average number of comparisons. Obviously, the sequential search should not be used on large arrays if speed is important.

The binary search is a clever algorithm that is much more efficient than the sequential search. Its only requirement is that the values in the array must be sorted in ascending order. Instead of testing the array's first element, this algorithm starts with the element in the middle. If that element happens to contain the desired value, then the search is over. Otherwise, the value in the middle element is either greater than or less than the value being searched for. If it is greater, then the desired value (if it is in the list) will be found somewhere in the first half of the array. If it is less, then the desired value (again, if it is in the list) will be found somewhere in the last half of the array. In either case, half of the array's elements have been eliminated from further searching.

If the desired value wasn't found in the middle element, the procedure is repeated for the half of the array that potentially contains the value. For instance, if the last half of the array is to be searched, the algorithm tests its middle element. If the desired value isn't found there, the search is narrowed to the quarter of the array that resides before or after that element. This process continues until the value being searched for is either found, or there are no more elements to test. Here is the pseudocode for a method that performs a binary search on an array:

Set first *to 0.*
Set last *to the last subscript in the array.*
Set position to –1.
Set found *to false.*
While found *is not true and* first *is less than or equal to* last
   Set middle *to the subscript half-way between*
                     array[first]*and* array[last].
 If array[middle] *equals the desired value*
   Set found *to true.*
   Set position to middle.
 Else If array[middle] *is greater than the desired value*
   Set last *to* middle – 1.
 Else
   Set first *to* middle + 1.
 End If.
End While.
Return position.

This algorithm uses three variables to mark positions within the array: first, last, and middle. The first and last variables mark the boundaries of the portion of the array currently being searched. They are initialized with the subscripts of the array's first and last elements. The subscript of the element halfway between first and last is calculated and stored in the middle variable. If the element in the middle of the array does not contain the search value, the first or last variables are adjusted so that only the top or bottom half of the array is searched during the next iteration. This cuts the portion of the array being searched in half each time the loop fails to locate the search value.

The following method performs a binary search on an integer array. The first parameter, array, is searched for an occurrence of the number stored in value. If the number is found, its array subscript is returned. Otherwise, –1 is returned indicating the value did not appear in the array.

```java
public static int binarySearch(int[] array, int value)
{
    int first;        // First array element
    int last;         // Last array element
    int middle;       // Mid point of search
    int position;     // Position of search value
    boolean found;    // Flag
    // Set the inital values.
    first = 0;
    last = array.length - 1;
    position = -1;
    found = false;
    // Search for the value.
    while (!found && first <= last)
    {
```

```
         // Calculate mid point
         middle = (first + last) / 2;
         // If value is found at midpoint...
         if (array[middle] == value)
         {
            found = true;
            position = middle;
         }
         // else if value is in lower half...
         else if (array[middle] > value)
            last = middle - 1;
         // else if value is in upper half....
         else
            first = middle + 1;
      }
      // Return the position of the item, or -1
      // if it was not found.
      return position;
   }
```

 The `BinarySearchDemo` program on the Student CD demonstrates this method.

Checkpoint

8.18 What value in an array does the selection sort algorithm look for first? When the selection sort finds this value, what does it do with it?

8.19 How many times will the selection sort swap the smallest value in an array with another value?

8.20 Describe the difference between the sequential search and the binary search.

8.21 On average, with an array of 20,000 elements, how many comparisons will the sequential search perform? (Assume the items being searched for are consistently found in the array.)

8.22 If a sequential search is performed on an array, and it is known that some items are searched for more frequently than others, how can the contents of the array be reordered to improve the average performance of the search?

8.12 Command-Line Arguments and Variable-Length Argument Lists

CONCEPT: When you invoke a Java program from the operating system command line, you can specify arguments that are passed into the **main** method of the program. In addition, you can write a method that takes a variable number of arguments. When the method runs, it can determine the number of arguments that were passed to it and act accordingly.

Command-Line Arguments

Every program you have seen in this book and every program you have written uses a static `main` method with a header that looks like this:

```
public static void main(String[] args)
```

Inside the parentheses of the method header is the declaration of a parameter named `args`. This parameter is an array name. As its declaration indicates, it is used to reference an array of `String`s. The array that is passed into the `args` parameter comes from the operating system command-line. For example, look at Code Listing 8-21.

Code Listing 8-21 (`CommandLine.java`)

```java
 1  /**
 2      This program displays the arguments passed to
 3      it from the operating system command line.
 4  */
 5
 6  public class CommandLine
 7  {
 8      public static void main(String[] args)
 9      {
10          for (int index = 0; index < args.length; index++)
11              System.out.println(args[index]);
12      }
13  }
```

If this program is compiled and then executed with the following command:

```
java CommandLine How does this work?
```

its output will be as follows:

```
How
does
this
work?
```

Any items typed on the command-line, separated by spaces, and after the name of the class are considered to be one or more arguments that are to be passed into the `main` method. In the previous example, four arguments are passed into `args`. The word "How" is passed into `args[0]`, "does" is passed into `args[1]`, "this" is passed into `args[2]`, and "work?" is passed into `args[3]`. The `for` loop in `main` simply displays each argument.

NOTE: It is not required that the name of `main`'s parameter array be `args`. You can name it anything you wish. It is a standard convention, however, for the name `args` to be used.

Variable-Length Argument Lists

Java provides a mechanism known as *variable-length argument lists,* which makes it possible to write a method that takes a variable number of arguments. In other words, you can write a method that accepts any number of arguments when it is called. When the method runs, it can determine the number of arguments that were passed to it and act accordingly.

For example, suppose we need to write a method named `sum` that can accept any number of `int` values and then return the sum of those values. We might call the method as shown here:

```
result = sum(10, 20);
```

Here we pass two arguments to the method: 10 and 20. After this code executes, the value 30 would be stored in the `result` variable. But, the method does not have to accept two arguments each time it is called. We could call the method again with a different number of arguments, as shown here:

```
int firstVal = 1, secondVal = 2, thirdVal = 3, fourthVal = 4;
result = sum(firstVal, secondVal, thirdVal, fourthVal);
```

Here we pass four arguments to the method: `firstVal` (which is set to 1), `secondVal` (which is set to 2), `thirdVal` (which is set to 3), and `fourthVal` (which is set to 4). After this code executes, the value 10 would be stored in the `result` variable. Here's the code for the `sum` method:

```
public static int sum(int... numbers)
{
   int total = 0;  // Accumulator

   // Add all the values in the numbers array.
   for (int val : numbers)
      total += val;

   // Return the total.
   return total;
}
```

Notice the declaration of the `numbers` parameter in the method header. The ellipsis (three periods) that follows the data type indicates that `numbers` is a special type of parameter known as a *vararg parameter.* A vararg parameter can take a variable number of arguments.

In fact, vararg parameters are actually arrays. In the `sum` method, the `numbers` parameter is an array of `int`s. All of the arguments that are passed to the `sum` method are stored in the elements of the `numbers` array. As you can see from the code, the method uses the enhanced `for` loop to step through the elements of the `numbers` array, adding up the values stored in its elements. (The *VarargsDemo1.java* program on the Student CD demonstrates the `sum` method.)

You can also write a method to accept a variable number of object references as arguments. For example, the program in Code Listing 8-22 shows a method that accepts a variable number of references to `BankAccount` objects. The method returns the total of the objects' `balance` fields.

Code Listing 8-22   (`VarargsDemo2.java`)

```java
 1 /**
 2     This program demonstrates a method that accepts
 3     a variable number of arguments (varargs).
 4 */
 5
 6 public class VarargsDemo2
 7 {
 8     public static void main(String[] args)
 9     {
10         double total;  // To hold the total balances
11
12         // Create BankAccount object with $100.
13         BankAccount account1 = new BankAccount(100.0);
14
15         // Create BankAccount object with $500.
16         BankAccount account2 = new BankAccount(500.0);
17
18         // Create BankAccount object with $1500.
19         BankAccount account3 = new BankAccount(1500.0);
20
21         // Call the method with one argument.
22         total = totalBalance(account1);
23         System.out.println("Total: $" + total);
24
25         // Call the method with two arguments.
26         total = totalBalance(account1, account2);
27         System.out.println("Total: $" + total);
28
29         // Call the method with three arguments.
30         total = totalBalance(account1, account2, account3);
31         System.out.println("Total: $" + total);
32     }
33
34     /**
35         The totalBalance method takes a variable number
36         of BankAccount objects and returns the total
37         of their balances.
38         @param accounts The target account or accounts.
39         @return The sum of the account balances
40     */
41
42     public static double totalBalance(BankAccount... accounts)
43     {
44         double total = 0.0;  // Accumulator
45
46         // Add all the values in the accounts array.
```

```
47          for (BankAccount acctObject : accounts)
48              total += acctObject.getBalance();
49
50          // Return the total.
51          return total;
52      }
53  }
```

Program Output

```
Total: $100.0
Total: $600.0
Total: $2100.0
```

You can write a method to accept a mixture of fixed arguments and a variable-length argument list. For example, suppose we want to write a method named `courseAverage`, which accepts the name of a course as a `String`, and a variable-length list of test scores as `doubles`. We could write the method header as follows:

```
public static void courseAverage(String course, double... scores)
```

This method has a regular `String` parameter named `course`, and a vararg parameter named `scores`. When we call this method, we always pass a `String` argument, then a list of `double` values. (This method is demonstrated in the program *VarargsDemo3.java*, which is on the Student CD.) Note that when a method accepts a mixture of fixed arguments and a variable-length argument list, the vararg parameter must be the last one declared.

> You can also pass an array to a vararg parameter. This is demonstrated in the program *VarargsDemo4.java*, which is on the Student CD.

8.13 The `ArrayList` Class

CONCEPT: `ArrayList` is a class in the Java API that is similar to an array and allows you to store objects. Unlike an array, an **`ArrayList`** object's size is automatically adjusted to accommodate the number of items being stored in it.

The Java API provides a class named `ArrayList`, which can be used for storing and retrieving objects. Once you create an `ArrayList` object, you can think of it as a container for holding other objects. An `ArrayList` object is similar to an array of objects, but offers many advantages over an array. Here are a few:

- An `ArrayList` object automatically expands as items are added to it.
- In addition to adding items to an `ArrayList`, you can remove items as well.
- An `ArrayList` object automatically shrinks as items are removed from it.

The `ArrayList` class is in the `java.util` package, so the following `import` statement is required:

```
import java.util.ArrayList;
```

Creating and Using an `ArrayList` Object

Here is an example of how you create an `ArrayList` object:

```
ArrayList<String> nameList = new ArrayList<String>();
```

This statement creates a new `ArrayList` object and stores its address in the `nameList` variable. Notice that in this example the word `String` is written inside angled brackets `<>` immediately after the word `ArrayList`. This specifies that the `ArrayList` can hold `String` objects. If we try to store any other type of object in this `ArrayList`, an error will occur. (Later in this section, you will see an example that creates an `ArrayList` for holding other types of objects.)

To add items to the `ArrayList` object, you use the add method. For example, the following statements add a series of `String` objects to `nameList`:

```
nameList.add("James");
nameList.add("Catherine");
nameList.add("Bill");
```

After these statements execute, `nameList` will hold three references to `String` objects. The first will reference "James", the second will reference "Catherine", and the third will reference "Bill".

The items that are stored in an `ArrayList` have a corresponding index. The index specifies the item's location in the `ArrayList`, so it is much like an array subscript. The first item that is added to an `ArrayList` is stored at index 0. The next item that is added to the `ArrayList` is stored at index 1, and so forth. After the previously shown statements execute, "James" will be stored at index 0, "Catherine" will be stored at index 1, and "Bill" will be stored at index 2.

The `ArrayList` class has a `size` method that reports the number of items stored in an `ArrayList`. It returns the number of items as an `int`. For example, the following statement uses the method to display the number of items stored in `nameList`:

```
System.out.println("The ArrayList has " +
                    nameList.size() +
                    " objects stored in it.");
```

Assuming that `nameList` holds the `Strings` "James", "Catherine", and "Bill", the following statement will display:

```
The ArrayList has 3 objects stored in it.
```

The `ArrayList` class's `get` method returns the item stored at a specific index. You pass the index as an argument to the method. For example, the following statement will display the item stored at index 1 of `nameList`:

```
System.out.println(nameList.get(1));
```

The program in Code Listing 8-23 demonstrates the topics discussed so far.

Code Listing 8-23   (`ArrayListDemo1.java`)

```
 1   import java.util.ArrayList; // Needed for ArrayList class
 2
 3   /**
 4      This program demonstrates an ArrayList.
 5   */
 6
 7   public class ArrayListDemo1
 8   {
 9      public static void main(String[] args)
10      {
11         // Create an ArrayList to hold some names.
12         ArrayList<String> nameList = new ArrayList<String>();
13
14         // Add some names to the ArrayList.
15         nameList.add("James");
16         nameList.add("Catherine");
17         nameList.add("Bill");
18
19         // Display the size of the ArrayList.
20         System.out.println("The ArrayList has " +
21                            nameList.size() +
22                            " objects stored in it.");
23
24         // Now display the items in nameList.
25         for (int index = 0; index < nameList.size(); index++)
26            System.out.println(nameList.get(index));
27      }
28   }
```

Program Output

```
The ArrayList has 3 objects stored in it.
James
Catherine
Bill
```

Notice in line 25 that the `for` loop uses the value returned from `nameList`'s `size` method to control the number of times the loop iterates. This is to prevent a bounds checking error from occurring. The last item stored in an `ArrayList` will have an index that is 1 less than the `size` of the `ArrayList`. If you pass a value larger than this to the `get` method, an error will occur.

Using the Enhanced `for` Loop with an `ArrayList`

Earlier in this chapter, you saw how the enhanced `for` loop can be used to iterate over each `element` in an array. You can also use the enhanced `for` loop to iterate over each item in an

ArrayList. Code Listing 8-24 demonstrates. The enhanced for loop is used in lines 26 and 27 to display all of the items stored in the ArrayList.

Code Listing 8-24 (`ArrayListDemo2.java`)

```java
 1 import java.util.ArrayList; // Needed for ArrayList class
 2
 3 /**
 4    This program demonstrates how the enhanced for loop
 5    can be used with an ArrayList.
 6 */
 7
 8 public class ArrayListDemo2
 9 {
10    public static void main(String[] args)
11    {
12       // Create an ArrayList to hold some names.
13       ArrayList<String> nameList = new ArrayList<String>();
14
15       // Add some names to the ArrayList.
16       nameList.add("James");
17       nameList.add("Catherine");
18       nameList.add("Bill");
19
20       // Display the size of the ArrayList.
21       System.out.println("The ArrayList has " +
22                          nameList.size() +
23                          " objects stored in it.");
24
25       // Now display the items in nameList.
26       for (String name : nameList)
27          System.out.println(name);
28    }
29 }
```

Program Output
```
The ArrayList has 3 objects stored in it.
James
Catherine
Bill
```

The ArrayList Class's toString method

The ArrayList class has a toString method that returns a string representing all of the items stored in an ArrayList object. For example, suppose we have set up the nameList object as previously shown, with the `String`s "James", "Catherine", and "Bill". We could use the following statement to display all of the names:

```
System.out.println(nameList);
```

The contents of the `ArrayList` will be displayed in the following manner:

```
[James, Catherine, Bill]
```

This is demonstrated in the program *ArrayListToString.java*, which is on the Student CD.

Removing an Item from an `ArrayList`

The `ArrayList` class has a remove method that removes an item at a specific index. You pass the index as an argument to the method. The program in Code Listing 8-25 demonstrates.

Code Listing 8-25   (`ArrayListDemo3.java`)

```java
 1  import java.util.ArrayList; // Needed for ArrayList class
 2
 3  /**
 4      This program demonstrates an ArrayList.
 5  */
 6
 7  public class ArrayListDemo3
 8  {
 9     public static void main(String[] args)
10     {
11        // Create an ArrayList to hold some names.
12        ArrayList<String> nameList = new ArrayList<String>();
13
14        // Add some names to the ArrayList.
15        nameList.add("James");
16        nameList.add("Catherine");
17        nameList.add("Bill");
18
19        // Display the items in nameList and their indices.
20        for (int index = 0; index < nameList.size(); index++)
21        {
22           System.out.println("Index: " + index + " Name: " +
23                              nameList.get(index));
24        }
25
26        // Now remove the item at index 1.
27        nameList.remove(1);
28
29        System.out.println("The item at index 1 is removed. " +
30                           "Here are the items now.");
31
32        // Display the items in nameList and their indices.
```

```
33            for (int index = 0; index < nameList.size(); index++)
34            {
35                System.out.println("Index: " + index + " Name: " +
36                                    nameList.get(index));
37            }
38        }
39 }
```

Program Output

```
Index: 0 Name: James
Index: 1 Name: Catherine
Index: 2 Name: Bill
The item at index 1 is removed. Here are the items now.
Index: 0 Name: James
Index: 1 Name: Bill
```

Note that when the item at index 1 was removed (in line 27), the item that was previously stored at index 2 was shifted in position to index 1. When an item is removed from an `ArrayList`, the items that come after it are shifted downward in position to fill the empty space. This means that the index of each item after the removed item will be decreased by one.

Note that an error will occur if you call the `remove` method with an invalid index.

Inserting an Item

The `add` method, as previously shown, adds an item at the last position in an `ArrayList` object. The `ArrayList` class has an overloaded version of the `add` method that allows you to add an item at a specific index. This causes the item to be inserted into the `ArrayList` object at a specific position. The program in Code Listing 8-26 demonstrates.

Code Listing 8-26   (`ArrayListDemo4.java`)

```
 1 import java.util.ArrayList; // Needed for ArrayList class
 2
 3 /**
 4     This program demonstrates inserting an item.
 5 */
 6
 7 public class ArrayListDemo4
 8 {
 9     public static void main(String[] args)
10     {
11         // Create an ArrayList to hold some names.
12         ArrayList<String> nameList = new ArrayList<String>();
13
14         // Add some names to the ArrayList.
15         nameList.add("James");
16         nameList.add("Catherine");
```

```
17              nameList.add("Bill");
18
19          // Display the items in nameList and their indices.
20          for (int index = 0; index < nameList.size(); index++)
21          {
22              System.out.println("Index: " + index + " Name: " +
23                                  nameList.get(index));
24          }
25
26          // Now insert an  item at index 1.
27          nameList.add(1, "Mary");
28
29          System.out.println("Mary was added at index 1. " +
30                              "Here are the items now.");
31
32          // Display the items in nameList and their indices.
33          for (int index = 0; index < nameList.size(); index++)
34          {
35              System.out.println("Index: " + index + " Name: " +
36                                  nameList.get(index));
37          }
38      }
39  }
```

Program Output

```
Index: 0 Name: James
Index: 1 Name: Catherine
Index: 2 Name: Bill
Mary was added at index 1. Here are the items now.
Index: 0 Name: James
Index: 1 Name: Mary
Index: 2 Name: Catherine
Index: 3 Name: Bill
```

Note that when a new item was added at index 1 (in line 27), the item that was previously stored at index 1 was shifted in position to index 2. When an item is added at a specific index, the items that come after it are shifted upward in position to accommodate the new item. This means that the index of each item after the new item will be increased by one.

Note that an error will occur if you call the add method with an invalid index.

Replacing an Item

The ArrayList class's set method can be used to replace an item at a specific index with another item. For example, the following statement will replace the item currently at index 1 with the String "Becky":

```
nameList.set(1, "Becky");
```

This is demonstrated in the program *ArrayListDemo5.java*, which is on the Student CD. Note that an error will occur if you specify an invalid index.

Capacity

Previously you learned that an `ArrayList` object's size is the number of items stored in the `ArrayList` object. When you add an item to the `ArrayList` object, its size increases by one, and when you remove an item from the `ArrayList` object, its size decreases by one.

An `ArrayList` object also has a *capacity*, which is the number of items it can store without having to increase its size. When an `ArrayList` object is first created, using the no-arg constructor, it has an initial capacity of 10 items. This means that it can hold up to 10 items without having to increase its size. When the eleventh item is added, the `ArrayList` object must increase its size to accommodate the new item. You can specify a different starting capacity, if you desire, by passing an `int` argument to the `ArrayList` constructor. For example, the following statement creates an `ArrayList` object with an initial capacity of 100 items:

```
ArrayList<String> list = new ArrayList<String>(100);
```

All of the examples we have looked at so far use `ArrayList` objects to hold `String`s. You can create an `ArrayList` to hold any type of object. For example, the following statement creates an `ArrayList` that can hold `BankAccount` objects:

```
ArrayList<BankAccount> accountList = new ArrayList<BankAccount>();
```

By specifying `BankAccount` inside the angled brackets, we are declaring that the `ArrayList` can hold only `BankAccount` objects. Code Listing 8-27 demonstrates such an `ArrayList`.

Code Listing 8-27   (`ArrayListDemo6.java`)

```java
 1 import java.util.ArrayList; // Needed for ArrayList class
 2
 3 /**
 4    This program demonstrates how to store BankAccount
 5    objects in an ArrayList.
 6 */
 7
 8 public class ArrayListDemo6
 9 {
10    public static void main(String[] args)
11    {
12       // Create an ArrayList to hold BankAccount objects.
13       ArrayList<BankAccount> list = new ArrayList<BankAccount>();
14
15       // Add three BankAccount objects to the ArrayList.
16       list.add(new BankAccount(100.0));
17       list.add(new BankAccount(500.0));
18       list.add(new BankAccount(1500.0));
19
```

```
20          // Display each item.
21          for (int index = 0; index < list.size(); index++)
22          {
23              BankAccount account = list.get(index);
24              System.out.println("Account at index " + index +
25                          "\nBalance: " + account.getBalance());
26          }
27     }
28 }
```

Program Output

```
Account at index 0
Balance: 100.0
Account at index 1
Balance: 500.0
Account at index 2
Balance: 1500.0
```

 Checkpoint

8.23 What import statement must you include in your code in order to use the ArrayList class?

8.24 Write a statement that creates an ArrayList object and assigns its address to a variable named frogs.

8.25 Write a statement that creates an ArrayList object and assigns its address to a variable named lizards. The ArrayList should be able to store String objects only.

8.26 How do you add items to an ArrayList object?

8.27 How do you remove an item from an ArrayList object?

8.28 How do you retrieve a specific item from an ArrayList object?

8.29 How do you insert an item at a specific location in an ArrayList object?

8.30 How do you determine an ArrayList object's size?

8.31 What is the difference between an ArrayList object's size and its capacity?

8.14 Common Errors to Avoid

The following list describes several errors that are commonly committed when learning this chapter's topics:

- **Using an invalid subscript.** Java does not allow you to use a subscript value that is outside the range of valid subscripts for an array.
- **Confusing the contents of an integer array element with the element's subscript.** An element's subscript and the value stored in the element are not the same thing. The subscript identifies an element, which holds a value.

- **Causing an off-by-one error.** When processing arrays, the subscripts start at zero and end at one less than the number of elements in the array. Off-by-one errors are commonly caused when a loop uses an initial subscript of one and/or uses a maximum subscript that is equal to the number of elements in the array.
- **Using the = operator to copy an array.** Assigning one array reference variable to another with the = operator merely copies the address in one variable to the other. To copy an array, you should copy the individual elements of one array to another.
- **Using the == operator to compare two arrays.** You cannot use the == operator to compare two array reference variables and determine whether the arrays are equal. When you use the == operator with reference variables, the operator compares the memory addresses that the variables contain, not the contents of the objects referenced by the variables.
- **Reversing the row and column subscripts when processing a two-dimensional array.** When thinking of a two-dimensional array as having rows and columns, the first subscript accesses a row and the second subscript accesses a column. If you reverse these subscripts, you will access the wrong element.

Review Questions and Exercises

Multiple Choice and True/False

1. In an array declaration, this indicates the number of elements that the array will have.
   a. subscript
   b. size declarator
   c. element sum
   d. reference variable

2. Each element of an array is accessed by a number known as a(n) _____.
   a. subscript
   b. size declarator
   c. address
   d. specifier

3. The first subscript in an array is always _____.
   a. 1
   b. 0
   c. −1
   d. 1 less than the number of elements

4. The last subscript in an array is always _____.
   a. 100
   b. 0
   c. −1
   d. 1 less than the number of elements

5. Array bounds checking happens _____.
   a. when the program is compiled
   b. when the program is saved
   c. when the program runs
   d. when the program is loaded into memory

6. This array field holds the number of elements that the array has.
   a. `size`
   b. `elements`
   c. `length`
   d. `width`

7. This search algorithm steps through an array, comparing each item with the search value.
   a. binary search
   b. sequential search
   c. selection search
   d. iterative search

8. This search algorithm repeatedly divides the portion of an array being searched in half.
   a. binary search
   b. sequential search
   c. selection search
   d. iterative search

9. This is the typical number of comparisons performed by the sequential search on an array of N elements (assuming the search values are consistently found).
   a. 2N
   b. N
   c. N^2
   d. N/2

10. When initializing a two-dimensional array, you enclose each row's initialization list in _____.
    a. braces
    b. parentheses
    c. brackets
    d. quotation marks

11. To insert an item at a specific location in an `ArrayList` object, you use this method.
    a. `store`
    b. `insert`
    c. `add`
    d. `get`

12. To delete an item from an `ArrayList` object, you use this method.
    a. `remove`
    b. `delete`
    c. `erase`
    d. `get`

13. To determine the number of items stored in an `ArrayList` object, you use this method.
    a. `size`
    b. `capacity`
    c. `items`
    d. `length`

14. **True or False:** Java does not allow a statement to use a subscript that is outside the range of valid subscripts for an array.

15. **True or False:** An array's size declarator can be a negative integer expression.

16. **True or False:** Both of the following declarations are legal and equivalent:

    ```
    int[] numbers;
    int numbers[];
    ```

17. **True or False:** The subscript of the last element in a single-dimensional array is one less than the total number of elements in the array.

18. **True or False:** The values in an initialization list are stored in the array in the order that they appear in the list.

19. **True or False:** The Java compiler does not display an error message when it processes a statement that uses an invalid subscript.

20. **True or False:** When an array is passed to a method, the method has access to the original array.

21. **True or False:** The first size declarator in the declaration of a two-dimensional array represents the number of columns. The second size declarator represents the number of rows.

22. **True or False:** A two-dimensional array has multiple `length` fields.

23. **True or False:** An `ArrayList` automatically expands in size to accommodate the items stored in it.

Find the Error

1. ```
int[] collection = new int[-20];
```

2. ```
int[] hours = 8, 12, 16;
```

3. ```
int[] table = new int[10];
for (int x = 1; x <= 10; x++)
{
    table[x] = 99;
}
```

4. ```
String[] names = { "George", "Susan" };
int totalLength = 0;
for (int i = 0; i < names.length(); i++)
    totalLength += names[i].length;
```

5. ```
String[] words = { "Hello", "Goodbye" };
System.out.println(words.toUpperCase());
```
```

Algorithm Workbench

1. The variable `names` references an integer array with 20 elements. Write a `for` loop that prints each element of the array.

2. The variables `numberArray1` and `numberArray2` reference arrays that each have 100 elements. Write code that copies the values in `numberArray1` to `numberArray2`.

3. a. Write a statement that declares a `String` array initialized with the following strings:
   "Einstein", "Newton", "Copernicus", and "Kepler".
   b. Write a loop that displays the contents of each element in the array that you declared in Question 3(a).
   c. Write code that displays the total length of all the strings in the array that you declared in Question 3(a).

4. In a program you need to store the populations of 12 countries.

   a. Define two arrays that may be used in parallel to store the names of the countries and their populations.
   b. Write a loop that uses these arrays to print each country's name and its population.

5. In a program you need to store the identification numbers of ten employees (as `int` values) and their weekly gross pay (as `double` values).

   a. Define two arrays that may be used in parallel to store the 10 employee identification numbers and gross pay amounts.
   b. Write a loop that uses these arrays to print each of the employees' identification number and weekly gross pay.

6. Declare a two-dimensional `int` array named `grades`. It should have 30 rows and 10 columns.

7. Write code that calculates the average of all the elements in the `grades` array that you declared in Question 6.

8. Look at the following array declaration:

   ```
   int[][] numberArray = new int[9][11];
   ```

   a. Write a statement that assigns 145 to the first column of the first row of this array.
   b. Write a statement that assigns 18 to the last column of the last row of this array.

9. The `values` variable references a two-dimensional double array with 10 rows and 20 columns. Write code that sums all the elements in the array and stores the sum in the variable `total`.

10. An application uses a two-dimensional array declared as follows:

    ```
    int[][] days = new int[29][5];
    ```

    a. Write code that sums each row in the array and displays the results.
    b. Write code that sums each column in the array and displays the results.

11. Write code that creates an `ArrayList` that can hold `String` objects. Add the names of three cars to the `ArrayList`, and then display the contents of the `ArrayList`.

Short Answer

1. What is the difference between a size declarator and a subscript?

2. Look at the following array definition:

```
int[] values = new int[10];
```

a. How many elements does the array have?
b. What is the subscript of the first element in the array?
c. What is the subscript of the last element in the array?

3. Look at the following array definition:

```
int[] values = { 4, 7, 6, 8, 2 };
```

What does each of the following code segments display?

```
System.out.println(values[4]);        a. _____
```

```
x = values[2] + values[3];
System.out.println(x);                b. _____
```

```
x = ++values[1];
System.out.println(x);                c. _____
```

4. How do you define an array without providing a size declarator?

5. Assuming that `array1` and `array2` are both array reference variables, why is it not possible to assign the contents of the array referenced by `array2` to the array referenced by `array1` with the following statement?

```
array1 = array2;
```

6. How do you establish an array without providing a size declarator?

7. The following statement creates a `BankAccount` array:

```
BankAccount[] acc = new BankAccount[10];
```

Is it okay or not okay to execute the following statements?

```
acc[0].setBalance(5000.0);
acc[0].withdraw(100.0);
```

8. If a sequential search method is searching for a value that is stored in the last element of a 10,000-element array, how many elements will the search code have to read to locate the value?

9. Look at the following array definition:

```
double[][] sales = new double[8][10];
```

a. How many rows does the array have?
b. How many columns does the array have?
c. How many elements does the array have?
d. Write a statement that stores a number in the last column of the last row in the array.

Programming Challenges

myCodeMate | ### 1. Rainfall Class

Write a `RainFall` class that stores the total rainfall for each of 12 months into an array of `doubles`. The program should have methods that return the following:

- the total rainfall for the year
- the average monthly rainfall
- the month with the most rain
- the month with the least rain

Demonstrate the class in a complete program.

Input Validation: Do not accept negative numbers for monthly rainfall figures.

2. Payroll Class

Write a `Payroll` class that uses the following arrays as fields:

- **employeeId.** An array of seven integers to hold employee identification numbers. The array should be initialized with the following numbers:

  ```
  5658845 4520125 7895122 8777541
  8451277 1302850 7580489
  ```

- **hours.** An array of seven integers to hold the number of hours worked by each employee
- **payRate.** An array of seven `doubles` to hold each employee's hourly pay rate
- **wages.** An array of seven `doubles` to hold each employee's gross wages

The class should relate the data in each array through the subscripts. For example, the number in element 0 of the `hours` array should be the number of hours worked by the employee whose identification number is stored in element 0 of the `employeeId` array. That same employee's pay rate should be stored in element 0 of the `payRate` array.

In addition to the appropriate accessor and mutator methods, the class should have a method that accepts an employee's identification number as an argument and returns the gross pay for that employee.

Demonstrate the class in a complete program that displays each employee number and asks the user to enter that employee's hours and pay rate. It should then display each employee's identification number and gross wages.

Input Validation: Do not accept negative values for hours or numbers less than 6.00 for pay rate.

3. Charge Account Validation

Create a class with a method that accepts a charge account number as its argument. The method should determine whether the number is valid by comparing it to the following list of valid charge account numbers:

```
5658845    4520125    7895122    8777541    8451277    1302850
8080152    4562555    5552012    5050552    7825877    1250255
1005231    6545231    3852085    7576651    7881200    4581002
```

VideoNote
The Charge
Account
Validation
Problem

These numbers should be stored in an array or an `ArrayList` object. Use a sequential search to locate the number passed as an argument. If the number is in the array, the method should return `true`, indicating the number is valid. If the number is not in the array, the method should return `false`, indicating the number is invalid.

Write a program that tests the class by asking the user to enter a charge account number. The program should display a message indicating whether the number is valid or invalid.

4. Charge Account Modification

Modify the charge account validation class that you wrote for Programming Challenge 3 so it reads the list of valid charge account numbers from a file. Use Notepad or another text editor to create the file.

5. Driver's License Exam

The local Driver's License Office has asked you to write a program that grades the written portion of the driver's license exam. The exam has 20 multiple choice questions. Here are the correct answers:

1. B	6. A	11. B	16. C
2. D	7. B	12. C	17. C
3. A	8. A	13. D	18. B
4. A	9. C	14. A	19. D
5. C	10. D	15. D	20. A

A student must correctly answer 15 of the 20 questions to pass the exam.

Write a class named `DriverExam` that holds the correct answers to the exam in an array field. The class should also have an array field that holds the student's answers. The class should have the following methods:

- `passed`. Returns true if the student passed the exam, or false if the student failed
- `totalCorrect`. Returns the total number of correctly answered questions
- `totalIncorrect`. Returns the total number of incorrectly answered questions
- `questionsMissed`. An int array containing the question numbers of the questions that the student missed

Demonstrate the class in a complete program that asks the user to enter a student's answers, and then displays the results returned from the `DriverExam` class's methods.

Input Validation: Only accept the letters A, B, C, or D as answers.

6. Quarterly Sales Statistics

Write a program that lets the user enter four quarterly sales figures for six divisions of a company. The figures should be stored in a two-dimensional array. Once the figures are entered, the program should display the following data for each quarter:

- A list of the sales figures by division
- Each division's increase or decrease from the previous quarter (this will not be displayed for the first quarter)
- The total sales for the quarter
- The company's increase or decrease from the previous quarter (this will not be displayed for the first quarter)

- The average sales for all divisions that quarter
- The division with the highest sales for that quarter

Input Validation: Do not accept negative numbers for sales figures.

7. Grade Book

A teacher has five students who have taken four tests. The teacher uses the following grading scale to assign a letter grade to a student, based on the average of his or her four test scores:

Test Score	Letter Grade
90–100	A
80–89	B
70–79	C
60–69	D
0–59	F

Write a class that uses a `String` array or an `ArrayList` object to hold the five students' names, an array of five characters to hold the five students' letter grades, and five arrays of four `doubles` each to hold each student's set of test scores. The class should have methods that return a specific student's name, average test score, and a letter grade based on the average.

Demonstrate the class in a program that allows the user to enter each student's name and his or her four test scores. It should then display each student's average test score and letter grade.

Input validation: Do not accept test scores less than zero or greater than 100.

8. Grade Book Modification

Modify the grade book application in Programming Challenge 7 so that it drops each student's lowest score when determining the test score averages and letter grades.

myCodeMate 9. Lottery Application

Write a `Lottery` class that simulates a lottery. The class should have an array of five integers named `lotteryNumbers`. The constructor should use the `Random` class (from the Java API) to generate a random number in the range of 0 through 9 for each element in the array. The class should also have a method that accepts an array of five integers that represent a person's lottery picks. The method is to compare the corresponding elements in the two arrays and return the number of digits that match. For example, the following shows the `lotteryNumbers` array and the user's array with sample numbers stored in each. There are two matching digits (elements 2 and 4).

`lotteryNumbers` array:

7	4	9	1	3

User's array:

4	2	9	7	3

In addition, the class should have a method that returns a copy of the `lotteryNumbers` array.

Demonstrate the class in a program that asks the user to enter five numbers. The program should display the number of digits that match the randomly generated lottery numbers. If all of the digits match, display a message proclaiming the user a grand prize winner.

10. Array Operations

Write a program with an array that is initialized with test data. Use any primitive data type of your choice. The program should also have the following methods:

- `getTotal`. This method should accept a one-dimensional array as its argument and return the total of the values in the array.
- `getAverage`. This method should accept a one-dimensional array as its argument and return the average of the values in the array.
- `getHighest`. This method should accept a one-dimensional array as its argument and return the highest value in the array.
- `getLowest`. This method should accept a one-dimensional array as its argument and return the lowest value in the array.

Demonstrate each of the methods in the program.

11. Number Analysis Class

Write a class with a constructor that accepts a file name as its argument. Assume the file contains a series of numbers, each written on a separate line. The class should read the contents of the file into an array, and then displays the following data:

- The lowest number in the array
- The highest number in the array
- The total of the numbers in the array
- The average of the numbers in the array

> This chapter's source code folder on the Student CD contains a text file named *Numbers.txt*. This file contains twelve random numbers. Write a program that tests the class by using this file.

12. 2D Array Operations

Write a program that creates a two-dimensional array initialized with test data. Use any primitive data type that you wish. The program should have the following methods:

- `getTotal`. This method should accept a two-dimensional array as its argument and return the total of all the values in the array.
- `getAverage`. This method should accept a two-dimensional array as its argument and return the average of all the values in the array.

- `getRowTotal`. This method should accept a two-dimensional array as its first argument and an integer as its second argument. The second argument should be the subscript of a row in the array. The method should return the total of the values in the specified row.
- `getColumnTotal`. This method should accept a two-dimensional array as its first argument and an integer as its second argument. The second argument should be the subscript of a column in the array. The method should return the total of the values in the specified column.
- `getHighestInRow`. This method should accept a two-dimensional array as its first argument and an integer as its second argument. The second argument should be the subscript of a row in the array. The method should return the highest value in the specified row of the array.
- `getLowestInRow`. This method should accept a two-dimensional array as its first argument and an integer as its second argument. The second argument should be the subscript of a row in the array. The method should return the lowest value in the specified row of the array.

Demonstrate each of the methods in this program.

13. Phone Book `ArrayList`

Write a class named `PhoneBookEntry` that has fields for a person's name and phone number. The class should have a constructor and appropriate accessor and mutator methods. Then write a program that creates at least five `PhoneBookEntry` objects and stores them in an `ArrayList`. Use a loop to display the contents of each object in the `ArrayList`.

14. Trivia Game

In this programming challenge, you will create a simple trivia game for two players. The program will work like this:

- Starting with player 1, each player gets a turn at answering 5 trivia questions. (There are 10 questions, 5 for each player.) When a question is displayed, four possible answers are also displayed. Only one of the answers is correct, and if the player selects the correct answer, he or she earns a point.
- After answers have been selected for all of the questions, the program displays the number of points earned by each player and declares the player with the highest number of points the winner.

You are to design a `Question` class to hold the data for a trivia question. The `Question` class should have `String` fields for the following data:

- A trivia question
- Possible answer 1
- Possible answer 2
- Possible answer 3
- Possible answer 4
- The number of the correct answer (1, 2, 3, or 4)

The `Question` class should have appropriate constructor(s), accessor, and mutator methods.

The program should create an array of 10 `Question` objects, one for each trivia question. (If you prefer, you can use an `ArrayList` instead of an array.) Make up your own trivia questions on the subject or subjects of your choice for the objects.

9 A Second Look at Classes and Objects

9.1 Static Class Members

CONCEPT: A static class member belongs to the class, not objects instantiated from the class.

A Quick Review of Instance Fields and Instance Methods

Recall from Chapter 6 that each instance of a class has its own set of fields, which are known as instance fields. You can create several instances of a class and store different values in each instance's fields. For example, the Rectangle class that we created in Chapter 6 has a length field and a width field. Let's say that box references an instance of the Rectangle class and we execute the following statement:

```
box.setLength(10);
```

This statement stores the value 10 in the length field that belongs to the instance that is referenced by box. You can think of instance fields as belonging to a specific instance of a class.

You will also recall that classes may have instance methods as well. When you call an instance method, it performs an operation on a specific instance of the class. For example, assuming that `box` references an instance of the `Rectangle` class, look at the following statement:

```
x = box.getLength();
```

This statement calls the `getLength` method, which returns the value of the `length` field that belongs to a specific instance of the `Rectangle` class: the one referenced by `box`. Both instance fields and instance methods are associated with a specific instance of a class, and they cannot be used until an instance of the class is created.

Static Members

It is possible to create a field or method that does not belong to any instance of a class. Such members are known as static fields and static methods. When a value is stored in a static field, it is not stored in an instance of the class. In fact, an instance of the class doesn't even have to exist in order for values to be stored in the class's static fields. Likewise, static methods do not operate on the fields that belong to any instance of the class. Instead, they can operate only on static fields. You can think of static fields and static methods as belonging to the class instead of an instance of the class. In this section, we will take a closer look at static members. First we will examine static fields.

Static Fields

When a field is declared with the key word `static`, there will be only one copy of the field in memory, regardless of the number of instances of the class that might exist. A single copy of a class's static field is shared by all instances of the class. For example, the `Countable` class shown in Code Listing 9-1 uses a static field to keep count of the number of instances of the class that are created.

Code Listing 9-1   (`Countable.java`)

```
 1  /**
 2      This class demonstrates a static field.
 3  */
 4
 5  public class Countable
 6  {
 7      private static int instanceCount = 0;
 8
 9      /**
10          The constructor increments the static
11          field instanceCount. This keeps track
12          of the number of instances of this
13          class that are created.
14      */
15
16      public Countable()
17      {
```

```
18          instanceCount++;
19      }
20
21      /**
22          The getInstanceCount method returns
23          the number of instances of this class
24          that have been created.
25          @return The value in the instanceCount field.
26      */
27
28      public int getInstanceCount()
29      {
30          return instanceCount;
31      }
32  }
```

First, notice in line 7 the declaration of the static field named instanceCount as follows:

```
private static int instanceCount = 0;
```

A static field is created by placing the key word static after the access specifier and before the field's data type. Notice that we have explicitly initialized the instanceCount field with the value 0. This initialization only takes place once, regardless of the number of instances of the class that are created.

> **NOTE:** Java automatically stores 0 in all uninitialized static member variables. The instanceCount field in this class is explicitly initialized so it is clear to anyone reading the code that the field starts with the value 0.

Next, look at the constructor in lines 16 through 19. The constructor uses the ++ operator to increment the instanceCount field. Each time an instance of the Countable class is created, the constructor will be called and the instanceCount field will be incremented. As a result, the instanceCount field will contain the number of instances of the Countable class that have been created. The getInstanceCount method, in lines 28 through 31, returns the value in instanceCount. The program in Code Listing 9-2 demonstrates this class.

Code Listing 9-2   (StaticDemo.java)

```
1  /**
2      This program demonstrates the Countable class.
3  */
4
5  public class StaticDemo
6  {
7      public static void main(String[] args)
8      {
9          int objectCount;
```

```
10
11          // Create three instances of the
12          // Countable class.
13          Countable object1 = new Countable();
14          Countable object2 = new Countable();
15          Countable object3 = new Countable();
16
17          // Get the number of instances from
18          // the class's static field.
19          objectCount = object1.getInstanceCount();
20          System.out.println(objectCount +
21                       " instances of the class " +
22                       "were created.");
23      }
24  }
```

Program Output

```
3 instances of the class were created.
```

The program creates three instances of the Countable class, referenced by the variables object1, object2, and object3. Although there are three instances of the class, there is only one copy of the static field. This is illustrated in Figure 9-1.

Figure 9-1   All instances of the class share the static field

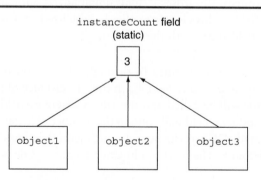

Instances of the Countable class

In line 19 the program calls the getInstanceCount method to retrieve the number of instances that have been created:

```
objectCount = object1.getInstanceCount();
```

Although the program calls the getInstanceCount method from object1, the same value would be returned from any of the objects.

Static Methods

When a class contains a static method, it isn't necessary for an instance of the class to be created in order to execute the method. The program in Code Listing 9-3 shows an example of a class with static methods.

Code Listing 9-3 (`Metric.java`)

```
1  /**
2      This class demonstrates static methods.
3  */
4
5  public class Metric
6  {
7      /**
8          The milesToKilometers method converts a
9          distance in miles to kilometers.
10         @param m The distance in miles.
11         @return The distance in kilometers.
12     */
13
14     public static double milesToKilometers(double m)
15     {
16         return m * 1.609;
17     }
18
19     /**
20         The kilometersToMiles method converts
21         a distance in kilometers to miles.
22         @param k The distance in kilometers.
23         @return The distance in miles.
24     */
25
26     public static double kilometersToMiles(double k)
27     {
28         return k / 1.609;
29     }
30 }
```

A static method is created by placing the key word `static` after the access specifier in the method header. The `Metric` class has two static methods: `milesToKilometers` and `kilometersToMiles`. Because they are declared as `static`, they belong to the class and may be called without any instances of the class being in existence. You simply write the name of the class before the dot operator in the method call. Here is an example:

```
kilometers = Metric.milesToKilometers(10.0);
```

This statement calls the `milesToKilometers` method, passing the value `10.0` as an argument. Notice that the method is not called from an instance of the class, but is called directly from the `Metric` class. Code Listing 9-4 shows a program that uses the `Metric` class. Figure 9-2 shows an example of interaction with the program.

Code Listing 9-4   (`MetricDemo.java`)

```
 1  import javax.swing.JOptionPane;
 2  import java.text.DecimalFormat;
 3
 4  /**
 5     This program demonstrates the Metric class.
 6  */
 7
 8  public class MetricDemo
 9  {
10     public static void main(String[] args)
11     {
12        String input; // To hold input
13        double miles; // A distance in miles
14        double kilos; // A distance in kilometers
15
16        // Create a DecimalFormat object.
17        DecimalFormat fmt =
18                    new DecimalFormat("0.00");
19
20        // Get a distance in miles.
21        input = JOptionPane.showInputDialog("Enter " +
22                          "a distance in miles.");
23        miles = Double.parseDouble(input);
24
25        // Convert the distance to kilometers.
26        kilos = Metric.milesToKilometers(miles);
27        JOptionPane.showMessageDialog(null,
28              fmt.format(miles) + " miles equals " +
29              fmt.format(kilos) + " kilometers.");
30
31        // Get a distance in kilometers.
32        input = JOptionPane.showInputDialog("Enter " +
33                          "a distance in kilometers:");
34        kilos = Double.parseDouble(input);
35
36        // Convert the distance to kilometers.
37        miles = Metric.kilometersToMiles(kilos);
38        JOptionPane.showMessageDialog(null,
```

```
39              fmt.format(kilos) + " kilometers equals " +
40              fmt.format(miles) + " miles.");
41
42          System.exit(0);
43      }
44 }
```

Figure 9-2   Interaction with the `MetricDemo.java` program

Static methods are convenient for many tasks because they can be called directly from the class, as needed. They are most often used to create utility classes that perform operations on data, but have no need to collect and store data. The `Metric` class is a good example. It is used as a container to hold methods that convert miles to kilometers and vice versa, but is not intended to store any data.

The only limitation that static methods have is that they cannot refer to non-static members of the class. This means that any method called from a static method must also be static. It also means that if the method uses any of the class's fields, they must be static as well.

Checkpoint

9.1   What is the difference between an instance field and a static field?

9.2   What action is possible with a static method that isn't possible with an instance method?

9.3   Describe the limitation of static methods.

9.2 Passing Objects As Arguments to Methods

CONCEPT: To pass an object as a method argument, you pass an object reference.

In Chapter 5 we discussed how primitive values, as well as references to `String` objects, can be passed as arguments to methods. You can also pass references to other types of objects as arguments to methods. For example, recall that in Chapter 6 we developed a `Rectangle` class. The program in Code Listing 9-5 creates an instance of the `Rectangle` class and then passes a reference to that object as an argument to a method.

Code Listing 9-5 (`PassObject.java`)

```java
 1  /**
 2      This program passes an object as an argument.
 3  */
 4
 5  public class PassObject
 6  {
 7     public static void main(String[] args)
 8     {
 9        // Create a Rectangle object.
10        Rectangle box = new Rectangle(12.0, 5.0);
11
12        // Pass a reference to the object to
13        // the displayRectangle method.
14        displayRectangle(box);
15     }
16
17     /**
18         The displayRectangle method displays the
19         length and width of a rectangle.
20         @param r A reference to a Rectangle
21         object.
22     */
23
24     public static void displayRectangle(Rectangle r)
25     {
26        // Display the length and width.
27        System.out.println("Length : " + r.getLength() +
28                           " Width : " + r.getWidth());
29     }
30  }
```

Program Output

```
Length : 12.0 Width : 5.0
```

In this program's main method, the box variable is a Rectangle reference variable. In line 14 its value is passed as an argument to the displayRectangle method. The displayRectangle method has a parameter variable, r, which is also a Rectangle reference variable, that receives the argument.

Recall that a reference variable holds the memory address of an object. When the displayRectangle method is called, the address that is stored in box is passed into the r parameter variable. This is illustrated in Figure 9-3. This means that when the displayRectangle method is executing, box and r both reference the same object. This is illustrated in Figure 9-4.

Figure 9-3 Passing a reference as an argument

Figure 9-4 Both box and r reference the same object

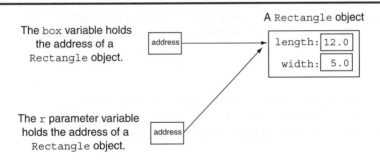

Recall from Chapter 5 that when a variable is passed as an argument to a method, it is said to be passed by value. This means that a copy of the variable's value is passed into the method's parameter. When the method changes the contents of the parameter variable, it does not affect the contents of the original variable that was passed as an argument. When a reference variable is passed as an argument to a method, however, the method has access to the object that the variable references. As you can see from Figure 9-4, the displayRectangle method has access to the same `Rectangle` object that the `box` variable references. When a method receives an object reference as an argument, it is possible for the method to modify the contents of the object referenced by the variable. This is demonstrated in Code Listing 9-6.

Code Listing 9-6   (`PassObject2.java`)

```java
 1 /**
 2     This program passes an object as an argument.
 3     The object is modified by the receiving method.
 4 */
 5
 6 public class PassObject2
 7 {
 8     public static void main(String[] args)
 9     {
10        // Create a Rectangle object.
11        Rectangle box = new Rectangle(12.0, 5.0);
12
13        // Display the object's contents.
14        System.out.println("Contents of the box object:");
15        System.out.println("Length : " + box.getLength() +
16                           " Width : " + box.getWidth());
17
18        // Pass a reference to the object to the
19        // changeRectangle method.
20        changeRectangle(box);
21
22        // Display the object's contents again.
23        System.out.println("\nNow the contents of the " +
24                           "box object are:");
25        System.out.println("Length : " + box.getLength() +
26                           " Width : " + box.getWidth());
27     }
28
29     /**
30        The changeRectangle method sets a Rectangle
31        object's length and width to 0.
32        @param r The Rectangle object to change.
33     */
34
35     public static void changeRectangle(Rectangle r)
36     {
37        r.setLength(0.0);
38        r.setWidth(0.0);
39     }
40 }
```

Program Output

```
Contents of the box object:
Length : 12.0 Width : 5.0

Now the contents of the box object are:
Length : 0.0 Width : 0.0
```

When writing a method that receives the value of a reference variable as an argument, you must take care not to accidentally modify the contents of the object that is referenced by the variable.

9.3 Returning Objects from Methods

CONCEPT: A method can return a reference to an object.

Just as methods can be written to return an int, double, float, or other primitive data type, they can also be written to return a reference to an object. For example, recall the BankAccount class that was discussed in Chapter 6. The program in Code Listing 9-7 uses a method, getAccount, which returns a reference to a BankAccount object. Figure 9-5 shows example interaction with the program.

VideoNote
Returning Objects from Methods

Code Listing 9-7   (ReturnObject.java)

```java
 1 import javax.swing.JOptionPane;
 2
 3 /**
 4    This program demonstrates how a method
 5    can return a reference to an object.
 6 */
 7
 8 public class ReturnObject
 9 {
10    public static void main(String[] args)
11    {
12       BankAccount account;
13
14       // Get a reference to a BankAccount object.
15       account = getAccount();
16
17       // Display the account's balance.
18       JOptionPane.showMessageDialog(null,
19             "The account has a balance of $" +
20             account.getBalance());
21
```

```
22              System.exit(0);
23      }
24
25      /**
26          The getAccount method creates a BankAccount
27          object with the balance specified by the
28          user.
29          @return A reference to the object.
30      */
31
32      public static BankAccount getAccount()
33      {
34          String input;          // To hold input
35          double balance;        // Account balance
36
37          // Get the balance from the user.
38          input = JOptionPane.showInputDialog("Enter " +
39                                 "the account balance.");
40          balance = Double.parseDouble(input);
41
42          // Create a BankAccount object and return
43          // a reference to it.
44          return new BankAccount(balance);
45      }
46 }
```

Figure 9-5   Interaction with the `ReturnObject.java` program

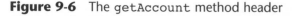

Notice that the getAccount method has a return data type of BankAccount. Figure 9-6 shows the method's return type, which is listed in the method header.

Figure 9-6   The getAccount method header

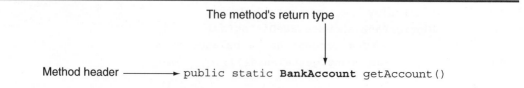

A return type of BankAccount means the method returns a reference to a BankAccount object when it terminates. The following statement, which appears in line 15, assigns the getAccount methods' return value to account:

```
account = getAccount();
```

After this statement executes, the account variable will reference the BankAccount object that was returned from the getAccount method.

Now let's look at the getAccount method. In lines 38 and 39 the method uses a JOptionPane dialog box to get the account balance from the user. In line 40 the value entered by the user is converted to a double and assigned to balance, a local variable. The last statement in the method, in line 44, is the following return statement:

```
return new BankAccount(balance);
```

This statement uses the new key word to create a BankAccount object, passing balance as an argument to the constructor. The address of the object is then returned from the method, as illustrated in Figure 9-7. Back in line 15, where the method is called, the address is assigned to account.

Figure 9-7   The getAccount method returns a reference to a BankAccount object

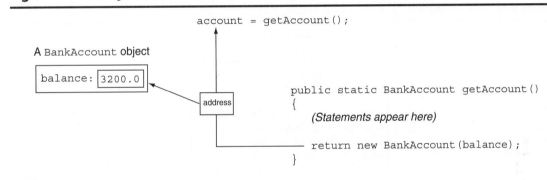

9.4 The toString Method

CONCEPT: Most classes can benefit from having a method named **toString**, which is implicitly called under certain circumstances. Typically, the method returns a string that represents the state of an object.

Quite often we need to display a message that indicates an object's state. An object's *state* is simply the data that is stored in the object's fields at any given moment. For example, recall that the BankAccount class has one field: balance. At any given moment, a BankAccount object's balance field will hold some value. The value of the balance field represents the object's state at that moment. The following might be an example of code that displays a BankAccount object's state:

```
BankAccount account = new BankAccount(1500.0);
System.out.println("The account balance is $" +
                   account.getBalance());
```

The first statement creates a BankAccount object, passing the value 1500.0 to the constructor. Recall that the BankAccount constructor stores this value in the balance field. After this statement executes, the account variable will reference the BankAccount object. In the second statement, the System.out.println method displays a string showing the value of the object's balance field. The output of this statement will look like this:

```
The account balance is $1500.0
```

Let's take a closer look at the second statement, which displays the state of the object. The argument that is passed to System.out.println is a string, which is put together from two pieces. The concatenation operator (+) joins the pieces together. The first piece is the string literal "The account balance is $". To this, the value returned from the getBalance method is concatenated. The resulting string, which is displayed on the screen, represents the current state of the object.

Creating a string that represents the state of an object is such a common task that many programmers equip their classes with a method that returns such a string. In Java, it is standard practice to name this method toString. Let's look at an example of a class that has a toString method. Figure 9-8 shows the UML diagram for the Stock class, which holds data about a company's stock.

Figure 9-8 UML diagram for the Stock class

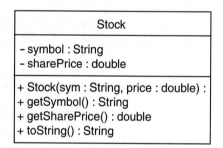

This class has two fields: symbol and sharePrice. The symbol field holds the trading symbol for the company's stock. This is a short series of characters that are used to identify the stock on the stock exchange. For example, the XYZ Company's stock might have the trading symbol XYZ. The sharePrice field holds the current price per share of the stock. Table 9-1 describes the class's methods.

Table 9-1 The Stock class methods

Method	Description
Constructor	This constructor accepts arguments that are assigned to the symbol and sharePrice fields.
getSymbol	This method returns the value in the symbol field.
getSharePrice	This method returns the value in the sharePrice field.
toString	This method returns a string representing the state of the object. The string will be appropriate for displaying on the screen.

Code Listing 9-8 shows the code for the Stock class. (This file is stored in the Student CD source code folder *Chapter 09\Stock Class Phase 1.*)

Code Listing 9-8   (Stock.java)

```java
 1 /**
 2    The Stock class holds data about a stock.
 3 */
 4
 5 public class Stock
 6 {
 7    private String symbol;        // Trading symbol of stock
 8    private double sharePrice;    // Current price per share
 9
10    /**
11       Constructor
12       @param sym The stock's trading symbol.
13       @param price The stock's share price.
14    */
15
16    public Stock(String sym, double price)
17    {
18       symbol = sym;
19       sharePrice = price;
20    }
21
22    /**
23       getSymbol method
24       @return The stock's trading symbol.
25    */
26
27    public String getSymbol()
28    {
29       return symbol;
30    }
31
32    /**
33       getSharePrice method
34       @return The stock's share price
35    */
36
37    public double getSharePrice()
38    {
39       return sharePrice;
40    }
41
42    /**
```

```
43          toString method
44          @return A string indicating the object's
45                  trading symbol and share price.
46    */
47
48    public String toString()
49    {
50        // Create a string describing the stock.
51        String str = "Trading symbol: " + symbol +
52                     "\nShare price: " + sharePrice;
53
54        // Return the string.
55        return str;
56    }
57 }
```

The `toString` method appears in lines 48 through 56. The method creates a string listing the stock's trading symbol and price per share. This string is then returned from the method. A call to the method can then be passed to `System.out.println`, as shown in the following code:

```
Stock xyzCompany = new Stock ("XYZ", 9.62);
System.out.println(xyzCompany.toString());
```

This code would produce the following output:

```
Trading symbol: XYZ
Share price: 9.62
```

In actuality, it is unnecessary to explicitly call the `toString` method in this example. If you write a `toString` method for a class, Java will automatically call the method when the object is passed as an argument to `print` or `println`. The following code would produce the same output as that previously shown:

```
Stock xyzCompany = new Stock ("XYZ", 9.62);
System.out.println(xyzCompany);
```

Java also implicitly calls an object's `toString` method any time you concatenate an object of the class with a string. For example, the following code would implicitly call the `xyzCompany` object's `toString` method:

```
Stock xyzCompany = new Stock ("XYZ", 9.62);
System.out.println("The stock data is:\n" + xyzCompany);
```

This code would produce the following output:

```
The stock data is:
Trading symbol: XYZ
Share price: 9.62
```

 Code Listing 9-9 shows a complete program demonstrating the `Stock` class's `toString` method. (This file is stored in the Student CD source code folder *Chapter 09\ Stock Class Phase 1.*)

Code Listing 9-9   (StockDemo1.java)

```
 1 /**
 2    This program demonstrates the Stock class's
 3    toString method.
 4 */
 5
 6 public class StockDemo1
 7 {
 8    public static void main(String[] args)
 9    {
10       // Create a Stock object for the XYZ Company.
11       // The trading symbol is XYZ and the current
12       // price per share is $9.62.
13       Stock xyzCompany = new Stock ("XYZ", 9.62);
14
15       // Display the object's values.
16       System.out.println(xyzCompany);
17    }
18 }
```

Program Output

```
Trading symbol: XYZ
Share price: 9.62
```

NOTE: Every class automatically has a toString method that returns a string containing the object's class name, followed by the @ symbol, followed by an integer that is usually based on the object's memory address. This method is called when necessary if you have not provided your own toString method. You will learn more about this in Chapter 11.

9.5 Writing an equals Method

CONCEPT: You cannot determine whether two objects contain the same data by comparing them with the == operator. Instead, the class must have a method such as **equals** for comparing the contents of objects.

Recall from Chapter 3 that the String class has a method named equals, which determines whether two strings are equal. You can write an equals method for any of your own classes as well.

In fact, you must write an equals method (or one that works like it) for a class in order to determine whether two objects of the class contain the same values. This is because you cannot use the == operator to compare the contents of two objects. For example, the following code might appear to compare the contents of two `Stock` objects, but in reality does not:

```
// Create two Stock objects with the same values.
Stock company1 = new Stock("XYZ", 9.62);
Stock company2 = new Stock("XYZ", 9.62);

// Use the == operator to compare the objects.
// (This is a mistake.)
if (company1 == company2)
    System.out.println("Both objects are the same.");
else
    System.out.println("The objects are different.");
```

When you use the == operator with reference variables, the operator compares the memory addresses that the variables contain, not the contents of the objects referenced by the variables. This is illustrated in Figure 9-9.

Figure 9-9   The `if` statement tests the contents of the reference variables, not the contents of the objects the variables reference

Because the two variables reference different objects in memory, they will contain different addresses. Therefore, the result of the `boolean` expression `company1 == company2` is `false` and the code reports that the objects are not the same. Instead of using the == operator to compare the two `Stock` objects, we should write an `equals` method that compares the contents of the two objects.

 In the Student CD source code folder *Chapter 09\Stock Class Phase 2* you will find a revision of the `Stock` class. This version of the class has an `equals` method. The code for the method follows (no other part of the class has changed, so only the `equals` method is shown):

```
public boolean equals(Stock object2)
{
    boolean status;

    // Determine whether this object's symbol and
    // sharePrice fields are equal to object2's
```

```
    // symbol and sharePrice fields.
    if (symbol.equals(object2.symbol) &&
        sharePrice == object2.sharePrice)
        status = true;    // Yes, the objects are equal.
    else
        status = false;   // No, the objects are not equal.


    // Return the value in status.
    return status;
}
```

The equals method accepts a Stock object as its argument. The parameter variable object2 will reference the object that was passed as an argument. The if statement performs the following comparison: If the symbol field of the calling object is equal to the symbol field of object2, *and* the sharePrice field of the calling object is equal to the sharePrice field of object2, then the two objects contain the same values. In this case, the local variable status (a boolean) is set to true. Otherwise, status is set to false. Finally, the method returns the value of the status variable.

Notice that the method can access object2's symbol and sharePrice fields directly. Because object2 references a Stock object, and the equals method is a member of the Stock class, the method is allowed to access object2's private fields.

 The program in Code Listing 9-10 demonstrates the equals method. (This file is also stored in the Student CD source code folder *Chapter 09\Stock Class Phase 2.*)

Code Listing 9-10   (StockCompare.java)

```
1    /**
2        This program uses the Stock class's equals
3        method to compare two Stock objects.
4    */
5
6    public class StockCompare
7    {
8        public static void main(String[] args)
9        {
10           // Create two Stock objects with the same values.
11           Stock company1 = new Stock("XYZ", 9.62);
12           Stock company2 = new Stock("XYZ", 9.62);
13
14           // Use the equals method to compare the objects.
15           if (company1.equals(company2))
16               System.out.println("Both objects are the same.");
17           else
18               System.out.println("The objects are different.");
19       }
20   }
```

Program Output

Both objects are the same.

If you want to be able to compare the objects of a given class, you should always write an equals method for the class.

> **NOTE:** Every class automatically has an equals method, which works the same as the == operator. This method is called when necessary if you have not provided your own equals method. You will learn more about this in Chapter 11.

9.6 Methods That Copy Objects

CONCEPT: You can simplify the process of duplicating objects by equipping a class with a method that returns a copy of an object.

You cannot make a copy of an object with a simple assignment statement, as you would with a primitive variable. For example, look at the following code:

```
Stock company1 = new Stock("XYZ", 9.62);
Stock company2 = company1;
```

The first statement creates a Stock object and assigns its address to the company1 variable. The second statement assigns company1 to company2. This does not make a copy of the object referenced by company1. Rather, it makes a copy of the address that is stored in company1 and stores that address in company2. After this statement executes, both the company1 and company2 variables will reference the same object. This is illustrated in Figure 9-10.

Figure 9-10 Both variables reference the same object

This type of assignment operation is called a *reference copy* because only the object's address is copied, not the actual object itself. To copy the object itself, you must create a new object and then set the new object's fields to the same values as the fields of the object that is being copied. This process can be simplified by equipping the class with a method that performs this operation. The method then returns a reference to the duplicate object.

In the Student CD source code folder *Chapter 09\Stock Class Phase 3* you will find a revision of the `Stock` class. This version of the class has a method named `copy`, which returns a copy of a `Stock` object. The code for the method follows (no other part of the class has changed so only the `copy` method is shown):

```java
public Stock copy()
{
   // Create a new Stock object and initialize it
   // with the same data held by the calling object.
   Stock copyObject = new Stock(symbol, sharePrice);

   // Return a reference to the new object.
   return copyObject;
}
```

The `copy` method creates a new `Stock` object and passes the calling object's `symbol` and `sharePrice` fields as arguments to the constructor. This makes the new object a copy of the calling object. The program in Code Listing 9-11 demonstrates the `copy` method. (This file is also stored in the Student CD source code folder *Chapter 09\Stock Class Phase 3*.)

Code Listing 9-11   (`ObjectCopy.java`)

```java
 1 /**
 2     This program uses the Stock class's copy method
 3     to create a copy of a Stock object.
 4 */
 5
 6 public class ObjectCopy
 7 {
 8    public static void main(String[] args)
 9    {
10       // Create a Stock object.
11       Stock company1 = new Stock("XYZ", 9.62);
12
13       // Declare a Stock variable
14       Stock company2;
15
16       // Make company2 reference a copy of the object
17       // referenced by company1.
18       company2 = company1.copy();
19
20       // Display the contents of both objects.
21       System.out.println("Company 1:\n" + company1);
22       System.out.println();
23       System.out.println("Company 2:\n" + company2);
24
25       // Confirm that we actually have two objects.
26       if (company1 == company2)
```

```
27          {
28              System.out.println("The company1 and company2 " +
29                      "variables reference the same object.");
30          }
31          else
32          {
33              System.out.println("The company1 and company2 " +
34                      "variables reference different objects.");
35          }
36      }
37 }
```

Program Output

```
Company 1:
Trading symbol: XYZ
Share price: 9.62

Company 2:
Trading symbol: XYZ
Share price: 9.62
The company1 and company2 variables reference different objects.
```

Copy Constructors

Another way to create a copy of an object is to use a copy constructor. A *copy constructor* is simply a constructor that accepts an object of the same class as an argument. It makes the object that is being created a copy of the object that was passed as an argument.

 In the Student CD source code folder *Chapter 09\Stock Class Phase 4* you will find another revision of the Stock class. This version of the class has a copy constructor. The code for the copy constructor follows (no other part of the class has changed, so only the copy constructor is shown):

```java
public Stock(Stock object2)
{
    symbol = object2.symbol;
    sharePrice = object2.sharePrice;
}
```

Notice that the constructor accepts a Stock object as an argument. The parameter variable object2 will reference the object that was passed as an argument. The constructor copies the values that are in object2's symbol and sharePrice fields to the symbol and sharePrice fields of the object that is being created.

The following code segment demonstrates the copy constructor. It creates a Stock object referenced by the variable company1. Then it creates another Stock object referenced by the variable company2. The object referenced by company2 is a copy of the object referenced by company1.

```
// Create a Stock object.
Stock company1 = new Stock("XYZ", 9.62);
// Create another Stock object that is a copy of the company1 object.
Stock company2 = new Stock(company1);
```

9.7 Aggregation

CONCEPT: Aggregation occurs when an instance of a class is a field in another class.

In real life, objects are frequently made of other objects. A house, for example, is made of door objects, window objects, wall objects, and much more. It is the combination of all these objects that makes a house object.

VideoNote
Aggregation

When designing software, it sometimes makes sense to create an object from other objects. For example, suppose you need an object to represent a course that you are taking in college. You decide to create a `Course` class, which will hold the following information:

- The course name
- The instructor's last name, first name, and office number
- The textbook's title, author, and publisher

In addition to the course name, the class will hold items related to the instructor and the textbook. You could put fields for each of these items in the `Course` class. However, a good design principle is to separate related items into their own classes. In this example, an `Instructor` class could be created to hold the instructor-related data and a `TextBook` class could be created to hold the textbook-related data. Instances of these classes could then be used as fields in the `Course` class.

Let's take a closer look at how this might be done. Figure 9-11 shows a UML diagram for the `Instructor` class. To keep things simple, the class has only the following methods:

- A constructor, which accepts arguments for the instructor's last name, first name, and office number
- A copy constructor
- A `set` method, which can be used to set all of the class's fields
- A `toString` method

Figure 9-11 UML diagram for the `Instructor` class

Instructor
– lastName : String – firstName : String – officeNumber : String

+ Instructor(lname : String, fname : String,
         office : String) :
+ Instructor(object2 : Instructor) :
+ set(lname : String, fname : String,
    office : String) : void
+ toString() : String

The code for the Instructor class is shown in Code Listing 9-12.

Code Listing 9-12 (`Instructor.java`)

```
 1 /**
 2    This class stores data about an instructor.
 3 */
 4
 5 public class Instructor
 6 {
 7    private String lastName;      // Last name
 8    private String firstName;     // First name
 9    private String officeNumber;  // Office number
10
11    /**
12       This constructor initializes the last name,
13       first name, and office number.
14       @param lname The instructor's last name.
15       @param fname The instructor's first name.
16       @param office The office number.
17    */
18
19    public Instructor(String lname, String fname,
20                      String office)
21    {
22       lastName = lname;
23       firstName = fname;
24       officeNumber = office;
25    }
26
27    /**
28       The copy constructor initializes the object
29       as a copy of another Instructor object.
30       @param object2 The object to copy.
31    */
32
33    public Instructor(Instructor object2)
34    {
35       lastName = object2.lastName;
36       firstName = object2.firstName;
37       officeNumber = object2.officeNumber;
38    }
39
40    /**
41       The set method sets a value for each field.
42       @param lname The instructor's last name.
43       @param fname The instructor's first name.
```

```
44              @param office The office number.
45         */
46
47         public void set(String lname, String fname,
48                         String office)
49         {
50             lastName = lname;
51             firstName = fname;
52             officeNumber = office;
53         }
54
55         /**
56             toString method
57             @return A string containing the instructor
58                     information.
59         */
60
61         public String toString()
62         {
63             // Create a string representing the object.
64             String str = "Last Name: " + lastName +
65                         "\nFirst Name: " + firstName +
66                         "\nOffice Number: " + officeNumber;
67
68             // Return the string.
69             return str;
70         }
71     }
```

Figure 9-12 shows a UML diagram for the TextBook class. As before, we want to keep the class simple. The only methods it has are a constructor, a copy constructor, a set method, and a toString method. The code for the TextBook class is shown in Code Listing 9-13.

Figure 9-12   UML diagram for the TextBook class

Code Listing 9-13 (TextBook.java)

```java
 1  /**
 2      This class stores data about a textbook.
 3  */
 4
 5  public class TextBook
 6  {
 7      private String title;        // Title of the book
 8      private String author;       // Author's last name
 9      private String publisher;    // Name of publisher
10
11      /**
12          This constructor initializes the title,
13          author, and publisher fields
14          @param textTitle The book's title.
15          @param auth The author's name.
16          @param pub The name of the publisher.
17      */
18
19      public TextBook(String textTitle, String auth,
20                       String pub)
21      {
22          title = textTitle;
23          author = auth;
24          publisher = pub;
25      }
26
27      /**
28          The copy constructor initializes the object
29          as a copy of another TextBook object.
30          @param object2 The object to copy.
31      */
32
33      public TextBook(TextBook object2)
34      {
35          title = object2.title;
36          author = object2.author;
37          publisher = object2.publisher;
38      }
39
40      /**
41          The set method sets a value for each field.
42          @param textTitle The book's title.
43          @param auth The author's name.
44          @param pub The name of the publisher.
45      */
```

```
46
47     public void set(String textTitle, String auth,
48                     String pub)
49     {
50        title = textTitle;
51        author = auth;
52        publisher = pub;
53     }
54
55     /**
56        toString method
57        @return A string containing the textbook
58               information.
59     */
60
61     public String toString()
62     {
63        // Create a string representing the object.
64        String str = "Title: " + title +
65                    "\nAuthor: " + author +
66                    "\nPublisher: " + publisher;
67
68        // Return the string.
69        return str;
70     }
71 }
```

Figure 9-13 shows a UML diagram for the Course class. Notice that the Course class has an Instructor object and a TextBook object as fields. Making an instance of one class a field in another class is called *object aggregation*. The word *aggregate* means "a whole which is made of constituent parts." In this example, the Course class is an aggregate class because it is made of constituent objects.

When an instance of one class is a member of another class, it is said that there is a "has a" relationship between the classes. For example, the relationships that exist among the Course, Instructor, and TextBook classes can be described as follows:

- The course *has an* instructor.
- The course *has a* textbook.

The "has a" relationship is sometimes called a *whole-part relationship* because one object is part of a greater whole. The code for the Course class is shown in Code Listing 9-14.

Figure 9-13 UML diagram for the `Course` class

```
┌─────────────────────────────────────────────┐
│                   Course                     │
├─────────────────────────────────────────────┤
│ - courseName : String                        │
│ - instructor : Instructor                    │
│ - textBook : TextBook                        │
├─────────────────────────────────────────────┤
│ + Course(name : String, instr : Instructor,  │
│              text : TextBook) :               │
│ + getName() : String                          │
│ + getInstructor() : Instructor                │
│ + getTextBook() : TextBook                    │
│ + toString() : String                         │
└─────────────────────────────────────────────┘
```

Code Listing 9-14   (`Course.java`)

```java
 1  /**
 2      This class stores data about a course.
 3  */
 4
 5  public class Course
 6  {
 7      private String courseName;      // Name of the course
 8      private Instructor instructor;  // The instructor
 9      private TextBook textBook;      // The textbook
10
11      /**
12          This constructor initializes the courseName,
13          instructor, and text fields.
14          @param name The name of the course.
15          @param instructor An Instructor object.
16          @param text A TextBook object.
17      */
18
19      public Course(String name, Instructor instr,
20                    TextBook text)
21      {
22          // Assign the courseName.
23          courseName = name;
24
25          // Create a new Instructor object, passing
26          // instr as an argument to the copy constructor.
27          instructor = new Instructor(instr);
28
29          // Create a new TextBook object, passing
30          // text as an argument to the copy constructor.
31          textBook = new TextBook(text);
32      }
```

```
33
34     /**
35        getName method
36        @return The name of the course.
37     */
38
39     public String getName()
40     {
41        return courseName;
42     }
43
44     /**
45        getInstructor method
46        @return A reference to a copy of this course's
47                Instructor object.
48     */
49
50     public Instructor getInstructor()
51     {
52        // Return a copy of the instructor object.
53        return new Instructor(instructor);
54     }
55
56     /**
57        getTextBook method
58        @return A reference to a copy of this course's
59                TextBook object.
60     */
61
62     public TextBook getTextBook()
63     {
64        // Return a copy of the textBook object.
65        return new TextBook(textBook);
66     }
67
68     /**
69        toString method
70        @return A string containing the course information.
71     */
72
73     public String toString()
74     {
75        // Create a string representing the object.
76        String str = "Course name: " + courseName +
77                     "\nInstructor Information:\n" +
78                     instructor +
79                     "\nTextbook Information:\n" +
80                     textBook;
81
```

```
82          // Return the string.
83          return str;
84     }
85 }
```

The program in Code Listing 9-15 demonstrates the Course class.

Code Listing 9-15   (CourseDemo.java)

```
 1 /**
 2     This program demonstrates the Course class.
 3 */
 4
 5 public class CourseDemo
 6 {
 7    public static void main(String[] args)
 8    {
 9       // Create an Instructor object.
10       Instructor myInstructor =
11           new Instructor("Kramer", "Shawn", "RH3010");
12
13       // Create a TextBook object.
14       TextBook myTextBook =
15           new TextBook("Starting Out with Java",
16                        "Gaddis", "Addison-Wesley");
17
18       // Create a Course object.
19       Course myCourse =
20           new Course("Intro to Java", myInstructor,
21                       myTextBook);
22
23       // Display the course information.
24       System.out.println(myCourse);
25    }
26 }
```

Program Output

```
Course name: Intro to Java
Instructor Information:
Last Name: Kramer
First Name: Shawn
Office Number: RH3010
Textbook Information:
Title: Starting Out with Java
Author: Gaddis
Publisher: Addison-Wesley
```

Aggregation in UML Diagrams

You show aggregation in a UML diagram by connecting two classes with a line that has an open diamond at one end. The diamond is closest to the class that is the aggregate. Figure 9-14 is a UML diagram that shows the relationship among the Course, Instructor, and TextBook classes. The open diamond is closest to the Course class because it is the aggregate (the whole).

Figure 9-14   UML diagram showing aggregation

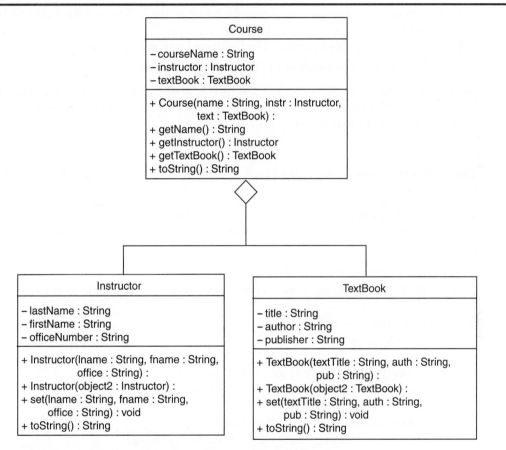

Security Issues with Aggregate Classes

When writing an aggregate class, you should be careful not to unintentionally create "security holes" that can allow code outside the class to modify private data inside the class. We will focus on the following two specific practices that can help prevent security holes in your classes:

- **Perform Deep Copies When Creating Field Objects**
  An aggregate object contains references to other objects. When you make a copy of the aggregate object, it is important that you also make copies of the objects it references. This is known as a *deep copy*. If you make a copy of an aggregate object, but only make a reference copy of the objects it references, then you have performed a *shallow copy*.

- **Return Copies of Field Objects, Not the Originals**
  When a method in the aggregate class returns a reference to a field object, return a reference to a copy of the field object.

Let's discuss each of these practices in more depth.

Perform Deep Copies When Creating Field Objects

Let's take a closer look at the Course class. First, notice the arguments that the constructor accepts in lines 19 and 20 as follows:

- A reference to a String containing the name of the course is passed into the name parameter.
- A reference to an Instructor object is passed into the instr parameter.
- A reference to a TextBook object is passed into the text parameter.

Next, notice that the constructor does not merely assign instr to the instructor field. Instead, in line 27 it creates a new Instructor object for the instructor field and passes instr to the copy constructor. Here is the statement:

```
instructor = new Instructor(instr);
```

This statement creates a copy of the object referenced by instr. The instructor field will reference the copy.

When a class has a field that is an object, it is possible that a shallow copy operation will create a security hole. For example, suppose the Course constructor had been written as follows:

```
// Bad constructor!
public Course(String name, Instructor instr, TextBook text)
{
   // Assign the courseName.
   courseName = name;

   // Assign the instructor (shallow copy)
   instructor = instr; // Causes security hole!

   // Assign the textBook (shallow copy)
   textBook = text;    // Causes security hole!
}
```

In this example, the instructor and textBook fields are merely assigned the addresses of the objects passed into the constructor. This can cause problems because there may be variables outside the Course object that also contain references to these Instructor and TextBook objects. These outside variables would provide direct access to the Course object's private data.

At this point you might be wondering why a deep copy was not also done for the courseName field. In line 23 the Course constructor performs a shallow copy, simply assigning the address of the String object referenced by name to the courseName field. This is permissible because String objects are immutable. An *immutable* object does not provide a way to change its contents. Even if variables outside the Course class reference the same object that courseName references, the object cannot be changed.

Return Copies of Field Objects, Not the Originals

When a method in an aggregate class returns a reference to a field object, it should return a reference to a copy of the field object, not the field object itself. For example, look at the getInstructor method in the Course class. The code is shown here:

```
public Instructor getInstructor()
{
   // Return a copy of the instructor object.
   return new Instructor(instructor);
}
```

Notice that the return statement uses the new key word to create a new Instructor object, passing the instructor field to the copy constructor. The object that is created is a copy of the object referenced by instructor. The address of the copy is then returned. This is preferable to simply returning a reference to the field object itself. For example, suppose the method had been written this way:

```
// Bad method
public Instructor getInstructor()
{
   // Return a reference to the instructor object.
   return instructor;   // WRONG! Causes a security hole.
}
```

This method returns the value stored in the instructor field, which is the address of an Instructor object. Any variable that receives the address can then access the Instructor object. This means that code outside the Course object can change the values held by the Instructor object. This is a security hole because the Instructor object is a private field! Only code inside the Course class should be allowed to access it.

NOTE: It is permissible to return a reference to a String object, even if the String object is a private field. This is because String objects are immutable.

Avoid Using null References

By default, a reference variable that is an instance field is initialized to the value null. This indicates that the variable does not reference an object. Because a null reference variable does not reference an object, you cannot use it to perform an operation that would require the existence of an object. For example, a null reference variable cannot be used to call a method. If you attempt to perform an operation with a null reference variable, the program will terminate. For example, look at the FullName class shown in Code Listing 9-16.

Code Listing 9-16   (`FullName.java`)

```
 1 /**
 2    This class stores a person's first, last, and middle
 3    names. The class is dangerous because it does not
 4    prevent operations on null reference fields.
 5 */
 6
 7 public class FullName
 8 {
 9    private String lastName;        // Last name
10    private String firstName;       // First name
11    private String middleName;      // Middle name
12
13    /**
14       The setLastName method sets the lastName field.
15       @param str The String to set lastName to.
16    */
17
18    public void setLastName(String str)
19    {
20       lastName = str;
21    }
22
23    /**
24       The setFirstName method sets the firstName field.
25       @param str The String to set firstName to.
26    */
27
28    public void setFirstName(String str)
29    {
30       firstName = str;
31    }
32
33    /**
34       The setMiddleName method sets the middleName field.
35       @param str The String to set middleName to.
36    */
37
38    public void setMiddleName(String str)
39    {
40       middleName = str;
41    }
42
43    /**
44       The getLength method returns the length of the
45       full name.
```

```
46          @return The length.
47     */
48
49     public int getLength()
50     {
51        return lastName.length() + firstName.length()
52                + middleName.length();
53     }
54
55     /**
56          The toString method returns the full name.
57          @return A reference to a String.
58     */
59
60     public String toString()
61     {
62        return firstName + " " + middleName + " "
63                + lastName;
64     }
65 }
```

First, notice that the class has three String reference variables as fields: lastName, firstName, and middleName. Second, notice that the class does not have a programmer-defined constructor. When an instance of this class is created, the lastName, firstName, and middleName fields will be initialized to null by the default constructor. Third, notice that the getLength method uses the lastName, firstName, and middleName variables to call the String class's length method in lines 51 and 52. Nothing is preventing the length method from being called while any or all of these reference variables are set to null. The program in Code Listing 9-17 demonstrates this.

Code Listing 9-17 (NameTester.java)

```
1  /**
2      This program creates a FullName object, and then
3      calls the object's getLength method before values
4      are established for its reference fields. As a
5      result, this program will crash.
6  */
7
8  public class NameTester
9  {
10     public static void main(String[] args)
11     {
12        int len;  // To hold the name length
13
14        // Create a FullName object.
```

```
15              FullName name = new FullName();
16
17              // Get the length of the full name.
18              len = name.getLength();
19      }
20  }
```

This program will crash when you run it because the getLength method is called before the name object's fields are made to reference String objects. One way to prevent the program from crashing is to use if statements in the getLength method to determine whether any of the fields are set to null. Here is an example:

```
public int getLength()
{
    int len = 0;

    if (lastName != null)
        len += lastName.length();

    if (firstName != null)
        len += firstName.length();

    if (middleName != null)
        len += middleName.length();

    return len;
}
```

Another way to handle this problem is to write a no-arg constructor that assigns values to the reference fields. Here is an example:

```
public FullName()
{
    lastName = "";
    firstName = "";
    middleName = "";
}
```

9.8 The this Reference Variable

CONCEPT: The **this** key word is the name of a reference variable that an object can use to refer to itself. It is available to all non-static methods.

The key word this is the name of a reference variable that an object can use to refer to itself. For example, recall the Stock class presented earlier in this chapter. The class has the following equals method that compares the calling Stock object to another Stock object that is passed as an argument:

```
public boolean equals(Stock object2)
{
   boolean status;

   // Determine whether this object's symbol and
   // sharePrice fields are equal to object2's
   // symbol and sharePrice fields.
   if (symbol.equals(object2.symbol) &&
       sharePrice == object2.sharePrice)
      status = true;    // Yes, the objects are equal.
   else
      status = false;   // No, the objects are not equal.

   // Return the value in status.
   return status;
}
```

When this method is executing, the `this` variable contains the address of the calling object. We could rewrite the `if` statement as follows, and it would perform the same operation (the changes appear in bold):

```
if (this.symbol.equals(object2.symbol) &&
    this.sharePrice == object2.sharePrice)
```

The `this` reference variable is available to all of a class's non-static methods.

Using this to Overcome Shadowing

One common use of the `this` key word is to overcome the shadowing of a field name by a parameter name. Recall from Chapter 6 that if a method's parameter has the same name as a field in the same class, then the parameter name shadows the field name. For example, look at the constructor in the `Stock` class:

```
public Stock(String sym, double price)
{
   symbol = sym;
   sharePrice = price;
}
```

This method uses the parameter `sym` to accept an argument that is assigned to the `symbol` field, and the parameter `price` to accept an argument that is assigned to the `sharePrice` field. Sometimes it is difficult (and even time-consuming) to think of a good parameter name that is different from a field name. To avoid this problem, many programmers give parameters the same names as the fields to which they correspond, and then use the `this` key word to refer to the field names. For example the `Stock` class's constructor could be written as follows:

```
public Stock(String symbol, double sharePrice)
{
   this.symbol = symbol;
   this.sharePrice = sharePrice;
}
```

Although the parameter names `symbol` and `sharePrice` shadow the field names `symbol` and `sharePrice`, the `this` key word overcomes the shadowing. Because `this` is a reference to the calling object, the expression `this.symbol` refers to the calling object's `symbol` field, and the expression `this.sharePrice` refers to the calling object's `sharePrice` field.

Using `this` to Call an Overloaded Constructor from Another Constructor

You already know that a constructor is automatically called when an object is created. You also know that you cannot call a constructor explicitly, as you do other methods. However, there is one exception to this rule: You can use the `this` keyword to call one constructor from another constructor in the same class.

To illustrate this, recall the `Stock` class that was presented earlier in this chapter. It has the following constructor:

```
public Stock(String sym, double price)
{
    symbol = sym;
    sharePrice = price;
}
```

This constructor accepts arguments that are assigned to the `symbol` and `sharePrice` fields. Let's suppose we also want a constructor that only accepts an argument for the `symbol` field, and assigns 0.0 to the `sharePrice` field. Here's one way to write the constructor:

```
public Stock(String sym)
{
    this(sym, 0.0);
}
```

This constructor simply uses the `this` variable to call the first constructor. It passes the value in `sym` as the first argument, and 0.0 as the second argument. The result is that the `symbol` field is assigned the value in `sym` and the `sharePrice` field is assigned 0.0.

Remember the following rules about using `this` to call a constructor:

- `this` can only be used to call a constructor from another constructor in the same class.
- It *must* be the first statement in the constructor that is making the call. If it is not the first statement, a compiler error will result.

Checkpoint

9.4 Look at the following code. (You might want to review the `Stock` class presented earlier in this chapter.)

```
Stock stock1 = new Stock("XYZ", 9.65);
Stock stock2 = new Stock("SUNW", 7.92);
```

While the `equals` method is executing as a result of the following statement, what object does `this` reference?

```
if (stock2.equals(stock1))
    System.out.println("The stocks are the same.");
```

9.9 Enumerated Types

CONCEPT: An enumerated data type consists of a set of predefined values. You can use the data type to create variables that can hold only the values that belong to the enumerated data type.

You've already learned the concept of data types and how they are used with primitive variables. For example, a variable of the `int` data type can hold integer values within a certain range. You cannot assign floating-point values to an `int` variable because only `int` values may be assigned to `int` variables. A data type defines the values that are legal for any variable of that data type.

Sometimes it is helpful to create your own data type that has a specific set of legal values. For example, suppose you wanted to create a data type named `Day`, and the legal values in that data type were the names of the days of the week (Sunday, Monday, and so forth). When you create a variable of the `Day` data type, you can only store the names of the days of the week in that variable. Any other values would be illegal. In Java, such a type is known as an *enumerated data type*.

You use the `enum` key word to create your own data type and specify the values that belong to that type. Here is an example of an enumerated data type declaration:

```
enum Day { SUNDAY, MONDAY, TUESDAY, WEDNESDAY,
           THURSDAY, FRIDAY, SATURDAY }
```

An enumerated data type declaration begins with the key word `enum`, followed by the name of the type, followed by a list of identifiers inside braces. The example declaration creates an enumerated data type named `Day`. The identifiers `SUNDAY`, `MONDAY`, `TUESDAY`, `WEDNESDAY`, `THURSDAY`, `FRIDAY`, and `SATURDAY`, which are listed inside the braces, are known as *enum constants*. They represent the values that belong to the `Day` data type. Here is the general format of an enumerated type declaration:

```
enum TypeName { One or more enum constants }
```

Note that the enum constants are not enclosed in quotation marks, therefore they are not strings. enum constants must be legal Java identifiers.

TIP: When making up names for enum constants, it is not required that they be written in all uppercase letters. We could have written the `Day` type's enum constants as `sunday`, `monday`, and so forth. Because they represent constant values, however, the standard convention is to write them in all uppercase letters.

Once you have created an enumerated data type in your program, you can declare variables of that type. For example, the following statement declares workDay as a variable of the Day type:

```
Day workDay;
```

Because workDay is a Day variable, the only vaues that we can legally assign to it are the enum constants Day.SUNDAY, Day.MONDAY, Day.TUESDAY, Day.WEDNESDAY, Day.THURSDAY, Day.FRIDAY, and Day.SATURDAY. If we try to assign any value other than one of the Day type's enum constants, a compiler error will result. For example, the following statement assigns the value Day.WEDNESDAY to the workDay variable:

```
Day workDay = Day.WEDNESDAY;
```

Notice that we assigned Day.WEDNESDAY instead of just WEDNESDAY. The name Day.WEDNESDAY is the *fully qualified name* of the Day type's WEDNESDAY constant. Under most circumstances you must use the fully qualified name of an enum constant.

Enumerated Types Are Specialized Classes

When you write an enumerated type declaration, you are actually creating a special kind of class. In addition, the enum constants that you list inside the braces are actually objects of the class. In the previous example, Day is a class, and the enum constants Day.SUNDAY, Day.MONDAY, Day.TUESDAY, Day.WEDNESDAY, Day.THURSDAY, Day.FRIDAY, and Day.SATURDAY are all instances of the Day class. When we assigned Day.WEDNESDAY to the workDay variable, we were assigning the address of the Day.WEDNESDAY object to the variable. This is illustrated in Figure 9-15.

Figure 9-15 The workDay variable references the Day.WEDNESDAY object

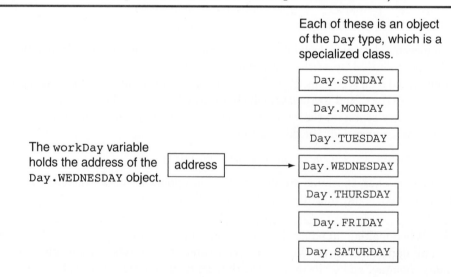

enum constants, which are actually objects, come automatically equipped with a few methods. One of them is the toString method. The toString method simply returns the name of the calling enum constant as a string. For example, assuming that the Day type has been declared as previously shown, both of the following code segments display the string WEDNESDAY (recall that the toString method is implicitly called when an object is passed to System.out.println):

```
// This code displays WEDNESDAY.
Day workDay = Day.WEDNESDAY;
System.out.println(workDay);

// This code also displays WEDNESDAY.
System.out.println(Day.WEDNESDAY);
```

enum constants also have a method named ordinal. The ordinal method returns an integer value representing the constant's ordinal value. The constant's *ordinal value* is its position in the enum declaration, with the first constant being at position 0. Figure 9-16 shows the ordinal values of each of the constants declared in the Day data type.

Figure 9-16 The Day enumerated data type and the ordinal positions of its enum constants

For example, assuming that the Day type has been declared as previously shown, look at the following code segment:

```
Day lastWorkDay = Day.FRIDAY;
System.out.println(lastWorkDay.ordinal());
System.out.println(Day.MONDAY.ordinal());
```

The ordinal value for Day.FRIDAY is 5 and the ordinal value for Day.MONDAY is 1, so this code will display:

```
5
1
```

The last enumerated data type methods that we will discuss here are equals and compareTo. The equals method accepts an object as its argument and returns true if that object is equal to the calling enum constant. For example, assuming that the Day type has been declared as previously shown, the following code segment will display "The two are the same":

```
Day myDay = Day.TUESDAY;
if (myDay.equals(Day.TUESDAY))
    System.out.println("The two are the same.");
```

The compareTo method is designed to compare enum constants of the same type. It accepts an object as its argument and returns the following:

- a negative integer value if the calling enum constant's ordinal value is less than the argument's ordinal value
- zero if the calling enum constant is the same as the argument
- a positive integer value if the calling enum constant's ordinal value is greater than the argument's ordinal value

For example, assuming that the Day type has been declared as previously shown, the following code segment will display "FRIDAY is greater than MONDAY":

```
Day myDay = Day.FRIDAY;
if (myDay.compareTo(Day.MONDAY) > 0)
    System.out.println(myDay + " is greater than "
                        + Day.MONDAY);
```

One place to declare an enumerated type is inside a class. If you declare an enumerated type inside a class, it cannot be inside a method. Code Listing 9-18 shows an example. It demonstrates the Day enumerated type.

Code Listing 9-18   (EnumDemo.java)

```
 1  /**
 2      This program demonstrates an enumerated type.
 3  */
 4
 5  public class EnumDemo
 6  {
 7      // Declare the Day enumerated type.
 8      enum Day { SUNDAY, MONDAY, TUESDAY, WEDNESDAY,
 9                 THURSDAY, FRIDAY, SATURDAY }
10
11      public static void main(String[] args)
12      {
13          // Declare a Day variable and assign it a value.
14          Day workDay = Day.WEDNESDAY;
15
16          // The following statement displays WEDNESDAY.
17          System.out.println(workDay);
18
19          // The following statement displays the ordinal
20          // value for Day.SUNDAY, which is 0.
21          System.out.println("The ordinal value for " +
22                          Day.SUNDAY + " is " +
23                          Day.SUNDAY.ordinal());
24
25          // The following statement displays the ordinal
26          // value for Day.SATURDAY, which is 6.
27          System.out.println("The ordinal value for " +
28                          Day.SATURDAY + " is " +
29                          Day.SATURDAY.ordinal());
```

```
30
31          // The following statement compares two enum constants.
32          if (Day.FRIDAY.compareTo(Day.MONDAY) > 0)
33              System.out.println(Day.FRIDAY + " is greater than " +
34                                   Day.MONDAY);
35          else
36              System.out.println(Day.FRIDAY + " is NOT greater than " +
37                                   Day.MONDAY);
38      }
39 }
```

Program Output

```
WEDNESDAY
The ordinal value for SUNDAY is 0
The ordinal value for SATURDAY is 6
FRIDAY is greater than MONDAY
```

You can also write an enumerated type declaration inside its own file. If you do, the filename must match the name of the type. For example, if we stored the Day type in its own file, we would name the file *Day.java*. This makes sense because enumerated data types are specialized classes. For example, look at Code Listing 9-19. This file, *CarType.java*, contains the declaration of an enumerated data type named CarType. When it is compiled, a byte code file named *CarType.class* will be generated.

Code Listing 9-19   (CarType.java)

```
1 /**
2     CarType enumerated data type
3 */
4
5 enum CarType { PORSCHE, FERRARI, JAGUAR }
```

Also look at Code Listing 9-20. This file, *CarColor.java*, contains the declaration of an enumerated data type named CarColor. When it is compiled, a byte code file named *CarColor.class* will be generated.

Code Listing 9-20   (CarColor.java)

```
1 /**
2     CarColor enumerated data type
3 */
4
5 enum CarColor { RED, BLACK, BLUE, SILVER }
```

Code Listing 9-21 shows the `SportsCar` class, which uses these enumerated types. Code Listing 9-22 demonstrates the class.

Code Listing 9-21 (`SportsCar.java`)

```
 1 import java.text.DecimalFormat;
 2
 3 /**
 4    SportsCar class
 5 */
 6
 7 public class SportsCar
 8 {
 9    private CarType make;     // The car's make
10    private CarColor color;   // The car's color
11    private double price;     // The car's price
12
13    /**
14       The constructor initializes the car's make,
15       color, and price.
16       @param aMake The car's make.
17       @param aColor The car's color.
18       @param aPrice The car's price.
19    */
20
21    public SportsCar(CarType aMake, CarColor aColor,
22                     double aPrice)
23    {
24       make = aMake;
25       color = aColor;
26       price = aPrice;
27    }
28
29    /**
30       getMake method
31       @return The car's make.
32    */
33
34    public CarType getMake()
35    {
36       return make;
37    }
38
39    /**
40       getColor method
41       @return The car's color.
42    */
```

```
43
44     public CarColor getColor()
45     {
46        return color;
47     }
48
49     /**
50        getPrice method
51        @return The car's price.
52     */
53
54     public double getPrice()
55     {
56        return price;
57     }
58
59     /**
60        toString method
61        @return A string indicating the car's make,
62                color, and price.
63     */
64
65     public String toString()
66     {
67        // Create a DecimalFormat object for
68        // dollar formatting.
69        DecimalFormat dollar = new DecimalFormat("#,##0.00");
70
71        // Create a string representing the object.
72        String str = "Make: " + make +
73                     "\nColor: " + color +
74                     "\nPrice: $" + dollar.format(price);
75
76        // Return the string.
77        return str;
78     }
79 }
```

Code Listing 9-22 (`SportsCarDemo.java`)

```
1 /**
2     This program demonstrates the SportsCar class.
3 */
4
5 public class SportsCarDemo
6 {
```

```
 7      public static void main(String[] args)
 8      {
 9         // Create a SportsCar object.
10         SportsCar yourNewCar = new SportsCar(CarType.PORSCHE,
11                                             CarColor.RED, 100000);
12
13         // Display the object's values.
14         System.out.println(yourNewCar);
15      }
16 }
```

Program Output

```
Make: PORSCHE
Color: RED
Price: $100,000.00
```

Switching On an Enumerated Type

Java allows you to test an enum constant with a switch statement. For example, look at the program in Code Listing 9-23. It creates a SportsCar object, and then uses a switch statement to test the object's make field.

Code Listing 9-23   (SportsCarDemo2.java)

```
 1 /**
 2    This program shows that you can switch on an
 3    enumerated type.
 4 */
 5
 6 public class SportsCarDemo2
 7 {
 8    public static void main(String[] args)
 9    {
10       // Create a SportsCar object.
11       SportsCar yourNewCar = new SportsCar(CarType.PORSCHE,
12                                          CarColor.RED, 100000);
13
14       // Get the car make and switch on it.
15       switch (yourNewCar.getMake())
16       {
17          case PORSCHE :
18             System.out.println("Your car was made in Germany.");
19             break;
20          case FERRARI :
```

```
21              System.out.println("Your car was made in Italy.");
22              break;
23           case JAGUAR :
24              System.out.println("Your car was made in England.");
25              break;
26           default:
27              System.out.println("I'm not sure where that car "
28                                 + "was made.");
29        }
30     }
31 }
```

Program Output

Your car was made in Germany.

In line 15 the switch statement tests the value returned from the yourNewCar.getMake() method. This method returns a CarType enumerated constant. Based upon the value returned from the method, the program then branches to the appropriate case statement. Notice in the case statements that the enumerated constants are not fully qualified. In other words, we had to write PORSCHE, FERRARI, and JAGUAR instead of CarType.PORSCHE, CarType.FERRARI, and CarType.JAGUAR. If you give a fully qualified enum constant name as a case expression, a compiler error will result.

> **TIP:** Notice that the switch statement in Code Listing 9-23 has a default section, even though it has a case statement for every enum constant in the CarType type. This will handle things in the event that more enum constants are added to the *CarType* file. This type of planning is an example of "defensive programming."

 Checkpoint

9.5   Look at the following statement, which declares an enumerated data type:

    enum Flower { ROSE, DAISY, PETUNIA }

a)   What is the name of the data type?

b)   What is the ordinal value for the enum constant ROSE? For DAISY? For PETUNIA?

c)   What is the fully qualifed name of the enum constant ROSE? Of DAISY? Of PETUNIA?

d)   Write a statement that declares a variable of this enumerated data type. The variable should be named flora. Initialize the variable with the PETUNIA constant.

9.6   Assume that the following enumerated data type has been declared:

    enum Creatures{ HOBBIT, ELF, DRAGON }

What will the following code display?

```
System.out.println(Creatures.HOBBIT + " "
                    + Creatures.ELF + " "
                    + Creatures.DRAGON);
```

9.7   Assume that the following enumerated data type has been declared:

```
enum Letters { Z, Y, X }
```

What will the following code display?

```
if (Letters.Z.compareTo(Letters.X) > 0)
    System.out.println("Z is greater than X.");
else
    System.out.println("Z is not greater than X.");
```

9.10 Garbage Collection

CONCEPT: The Java Virtual Machine periodically runs a process known as the garbage collector, which removes unreferenced objects from memory.

When an object is no longer needed, it should be destroyed so the memory it uses can be freed for other purposes. Fortunately, you do not have to destroy objects after you are finished using them. The Java Virtual Machine periodically performs a process known as garbage collection, which automatically removes unreferenced objects from memory. For example, look at the following code:

```
// Declare two BankAccount reference variables.
BankAccount account1, account2;

// Create an object and reference it with account1.
account1 = new BankAccount(500.0);

// Reference the same object with account2.
account2 = account1;

// Store null in account1 so it no longer
// references the object.
account1 = null;

// The object is still referenced by account2, though.
// Store null in account2 so it no longer references
// the object.
account2 = null;

// Now the object is no longer referenced, so it
// can be removed by the garbage collector.
```

This code uses two reference variables, account1 and account2. A BankAccount object is created and referenced by account1. Then, account1 is assigned to account2, which causes account2 to reference the same object as account1. This is illustrated in Figure 9-17.

Figure 9-17 Both `account1` and `account2` reference the same object

Next, the `null` value is assigned to `account1`. This removes the address of the object from the `account1` variable, causing it to no longer reference the object. Figure 9-18 illustrates this.

Figure 9-18 The object is only referenced by the `account2` variable

The object is still accessible, however, because it is referenced by the `account2` variable. The next statement assigns `null` to `account2`. This removes the object's address from `account2`, causing it to no longer reference the object. Figure 9-19 illustrates this. Because the object is no longer accessible, it will be removed from memory the next time the garbage collector process runs.

Figure 9-19 The object is no longer referenced

The `finalize` Method

If a class has a method named `finalize`, it is called automatically just before an instance of the class is destroyed by the garbage collector. If you wish to execute code just before an object is destroyed, you can create a `finalize` method in the class and place the code there. The `finalize` method accepts no arguments and has a `void` return type.

NOTE: The garbage collector runs periodically, and you cannot predict exactly when it will execute. Therefore, you cannot know exactly when an object's finalize method will execute.

9.11 Focus on Object-Oriented Design: Class Collaboration

CONCEPT: It is common for classes to interact, or collaborate, with each other to perform their operations. Part of the object-oriented design process is identifying the collaborations among classes.

In an object-oriented application it is common for objects of different classes to collaborate. This simply means that objects interact with each other. Sometimes one object will need the services of another object in order to fulfill its responsibilities. For example, let's say an object needs to read a number from the keyboard and then format the number to appear as a dollar amount. The object might use the services of a `Scanner` object to read the number from the keyboard, and then use the services of a `DecimalFormat` object to format the number. In this example, the object is collaborating with objects created from classes in the Java API. The objects that you create from your own classes can also collaborate with each other.

If one object is to collaborate with another object, then it must know something about the other object's class methods and how to call them. For example, suppose we were to write a class named `StockPurchase`, which uses an object of the `Stock` class (presented earlier in this chapter) to simulate the purchase of a stock. The `StockPurchase` class is responsible for calculating the cost of the stock purchase. To do that, it must know how to call the `Stock` class's `getSharePrice` method to get the price per share of the stock. Code Listing 9-24 shows an example of the `StockPurchase` class. (This file is stored in the Student CD source code folder *Chapter 09\StockPurchase Class*.)

Code Listing 9-24   (`StockPurchase.java`)

```
1  /**
2     The StockPurchase class represents a stock purchase.
3  */
4
5  public class StockPurchase
6  {
7     private Stock stock;  // The stock that was purchased
```

```
 8     private int shares;    // Number of shares owned
 9
10     /**
11        Constructor
12        @param stockObject The stock to purchase.
13        @param numShares The number of shares.
14     */
15
16     public StockPurchase(Stock stockObject, int numShares)
17     {
18        // Create a copy of the object referenced by
19        // stockObject.
20        stock = new Stock(stockObject);
21        shares = numShares;
22     }
23
24     /**
25        getStock method
26        @return A copy of the Stock object for the stock
27                being purchased.
28     */
29
30     public Stock getStock()
31     {
32        // Return a copy of the object referenced by stock.
33        return new Stock(stock);
34     }
35
36     /**
37        getShares method
38        @return The number of shares being purchased.
39     */
40
41     public int getShares()
42     {
43        return shares;
44     }
45
46     /**
47        getCost method
48        @return The cost of the stock purchase.
49     */
50
51     public double getCost()
52     {
53        return shares * stock.getSharePrice();
54     }
55  }
```

The constructor for this class accepts a `Stock` object representing the stock that is being purchased, and an `int` representing the number of shares to purchase. In line 20 we see the first collaboration: the `StockPurchase` constructor makes a copy of the `Stock` object by using the `Stock` class's copy constructor. The copy constructor is used again in the `getStock` method, in line 33, to return a copy of the `Stock` object.

The next collaboration takes place in the `getCost` method. This method calculates and returns the cost of the stock purchase. In line 53 it calls the `Stock` class's `getSharePrice` method to determine the stock's price per share. The program in Code Listing 9-25 demonstrates this class. (This file is also stored in the Student CD source code folder *Chapter 09\StockPurchase Class.*)

Code Listing 9-25 (`StockTrader.java`)

```java
 1 import java.util.Scanner;
 2 import java.text.DecimalFormat;
 3
 4 /**
 5    This program allows you to purchase shares of XYZ
 6    company's stock.
 7 */
 8
 9 public class StockTrader
10 {
11    public static void main(String[] args)
12    {
13       int sharesToBuy;   // Number of shares to buy.
14
15       // Create a Stock object for the company stock.
16       // The trading symbol is XYZ and the stock is
17       // currently $9.62 per share.
18       Stock xyzCompany = new Stock("XYZ", 9.62);
19
20       // Create a Scanner object for keyboard input.
21       Scanner keyboard = new Scanner(System.in);
22
23       // Create a DecimalFormat object to format numbers
24       // as dollar amounts.
25       DecimalFormat dollar = new DecimalFormat("#,##0.00");
26
27       // Display the current share price.
28       System.out.println("XYZ Company's stock is currently $"
29                  + dollar.format(xyzCompany.getSharePrice())
30                  + " per share.");
31
32       // Get the number of shares to purchase.
33       System.out.print("How many shares do you want to buy? ");
34       sharesToBuy = keyboard.nextInt();
```

```
35
36          // Create a StockPurchase object for the transaction.
37          StockPurchase buy =
38                  new StockPurchase(xyzCompany, sharesToBuy);
39
40          // Display the cost of the transaction.
41          System.out.println("Cost of the stock: $"
42                              + dollar.format(buy.getCost()));
43      }
44 }
```

Program Output with Example Input Shown in Bold

```
XYZ Company's stock is currently $9.62 per share.
How many shares do you want to buy? 100 [Enter]
Cost of the stock: $962.00
```

Determining Class Collaborations with CRC Cards

During the object-oriented design process, you can determine many of the collaborations that will be necessary among classes by examining the responsibilities of the classes. In Chapter 6, Section 6.7, we discussed the process of finding the classes and their responsibilities. Recall from that section that a class's responsibilities are as follows:

- Things that the class is responsible for knowing
- Actions that the class is responsible for doing

Often you will determine that the class must collaborate with another class in order to fulfill one or more of its responsibilities. One popular method of discovering a class's responsibilities and collaborations is by creating CRC cards. CRC stands for class, responsibilities, and collaborations.

You can use simple index cards for this procedure. Once you have gone through the process of finding the classes (which is discussed in Chapter 6, Section 6.7), set aside one index card for each class. At the top of the index card, write the name of the class. Divide the rest of the card into two columns. In the left column, write each of the class's responsibilities. As you write each responsibility, think about whether the class needs to collaborate with another class to fulfill that responsibility. Ask yourself questions such as the following:

- Will an object of this class need to get data from another object in order to fulfill this responsibility?
- Will an object of this class need to request another object to perform an operation in order to fulfill this responsibility?

If collaboration is required, write the name of the collaborating class in the right column, next to the responsibility that requires it. If no collaboration is required for a responsibility, simply write "None" in the right column, or leave it blank. Figure 9-20 shows an example CRC card for the StockPurchase class.

Figure 9-20 CRC Card

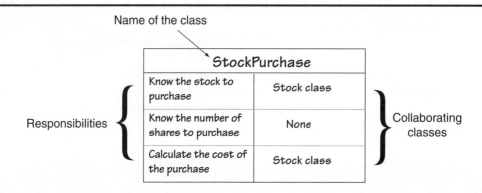

From the CRC card shown in the figure, we can see that the StockPurchase class has the following responsibilities and collaborations:

- **Responsibility:** To know the stock to purchase
  Collaboration: The Stock class
- **Responsibility:** To know the number of shares to purchase
  Collaboration: None
- **Responsibility:** To calculate the cost of the purchase
  Collaboration: The Stock class

When you have completed a CRC card for each class in the application, you will have a good idea of each class's responsibilities and how the classes must interact.

9.12 Common Errors to Avoid

The following list describes several errors that are commonly committed when learning this chapter's topics:

- **Attempting to refer to an instance field or instance method in a static method.** Static methods can refer only to other class members that are static.
- **In a method that accepts an object as an argument, writing code that accidentally modifies the object.** When a reference variable is passed as an argument to a method, the method has access to the object that the variable references. When writing a method that receives a reference variable as an argument, you must take care not to accidentally modify the contents of the object that is referenced by the variable.
- **Allowing a `null` reference to be used.** Because a `null` reference variable does not reference an object, you cannot use it to perform an operation that would require the existence of an object. For example, a `null` reference variable cannot be used to call a method. If you attempt to perform an operation with a `null` reference variable, the program will terminate. This can happen when a class has a reference variable as a field, and it is not properly initialized with the address of an object.
- **Forgetting to use the fully qualified name of an `enum` constant.** Under most circumstances you must use the fully qualified name of an enum constant. One exception to this is when the enum constant is used as a case expression in a switch statement.

Review Questions and Exercises

Multiple Choice and True/False

1. This type of method cannot access any non-static member variables in its own class.
   a. instance
   b. void
   c. static
   d. non-static

2. When an object is passed as an argument to a method, this is actually passed.
   a. a copy of the object
   b. the name of the object
   c. a reference to the object
   d. none of these; you cannot pass an object

3. If you write this method for a class, Java will automatically call it any time you concatenate an object of the class with a string.
   a. `toString`
   b. `plusString`
   c. `stringConvert`
   d. `concatString`

4. Making an instance of one class a field in another class is called _____.
   a. nesting
   b. class fielding
   c. aggregation
   d. concatenation

5. This is the name of a reference variable that is always available to an instance method and refers to the object that is calling the method.
   a. `callingObject`
   b. `this`
   c. `me`
   d. `instance`

6. This enum method returns the position of an enum constant in the declaration.
   a. `position`
   b. `location`
   c. `ordinal`
   d. `toString`

7. Assuming the following declaration exists:

   ```
   enum Seasons { SPRING, WINTER, SUMMER, FALL }
   ```
   what is the fully qualified name of the `FALL` constant?
   a. `FALL`
   b. `enum.FALL`
   c. `FALL.Seasons`
   d. `Seasons.FALL`

8. You cannot use the fully qualified name of an `enum` constant for this.

   a. a `switch` expression
   b. a `case` expression
   c. an argument to a method
   d. all of these

9. The Java Virtual Machine periodically performs this process, which automatically removes unreferenced objects from memory.

   a. memory cleansing
   b. memory deallocation
   c. garbage collection
   d. object expungement

10. If a class has this method, it is called automatically just before an instance of the class is destroyed by the Java Virtual Machine.

    a. `finalize`
    b. `destroy`
    c. `remove`
    d. `housekeeper`

11. CRC stands for

    a. Class, Return value, Composition
    b. Class, Responsibilities, Collaborations
    c. Class, Responsibilities, Composition
    d. Compare, Return, Continue

12. **True or False:** A static member method may refer to non-static member variables of the same class, but only after an instance of the class has been defined.

13. **True or False:** All static member variables are initialized to –1 by default.

14. **True or False:** When an object is passed as an argument to a method, the method can access the argument.

15. **True or False:** A method cannot return a reference to an object.

16. **True or False:** You can declare an enumerated data type inside a method.

17. **True or False:** Enumerated data types are actually special types of classes.

18. **True or False:** `enum` constants have a `toString` method.

Find the Error

The following class definition has an error. What is it?

```
1. public class MyClass
   {
        private int x;
        private double y;

        public static void setValues(int a, double b)
        {
```

```
              x = a;
              y = b;
        }
}
```

2. Assume the following declaration exists :

   ```
   enum Coffee { MEDIUM, DARK, DECAF }
   ```

   Find the error(s) in the following `switch` statement:

   ```
   // This code has errors!
   Coffee myCup = DARK;
   switch (myCup)
   {
       case Coffee.MEDIUM :
               System.out.println("Mild flavor.");
               break;
       case Coffee.DARK :
               System.out.println("Strong flavor.");
               break;
       case Coffee.DECAF :
               System.out.println("Won't keep you awake.");
               break;
       default:
               System.out.println("Never heard of it.");
   }
   ```

Algorithm Workbench

1. Consider the following class declaration:

   ```
   public class Circle
   {
       private double radius;

       public Circle(double r)
       {
          radius = r;
       }

       public double getArea()
       {
          return Math.PI * radius * radius;
       }

       public double getRadius()
       {
          return radius;
       }
   }
   ```

   a. Write a toString method for this class. The method should return a string containing the radius and area of the circle.
   b. Write an equals method for this class. The method should accept a Circle object as an argument. It should return true if the argument object contains the same data as the calling object, or false otherwise.
   c. Write a greaterThan method for this class. The method should accept a Circle object as an argument. It should return true if the argument object has an area that is greater than the area of the calling object, or false otherwise.

2. Consider the following class declaration:

```
public class Thing
{
     private int x;
     private int y;
     private static int z = 0;

     public Thing()
     {
          x = z;
          y = z;
     }
     static void putThing(int a)
     {
          z = a;
     }
}
```

Assume a program containing the class declaration defines three Thing objects with the following statements:

```
Thing one = new Thing();
Thing two = new Thing();
Thing three = new Thing();
```

   a. How many separate instances of the x member exist?
   b. How many separate instances of the y member exist?
   c. How many separate instances of the z member exist?
   d. What value will be stored in the x and y members of each object?
   e. Write a statement that will call the putThing method.

3. A pet store sells dogs, cats, birds, and hamsters. Write a declaration for an enumerated data type that can represent the types of pets the store sells.

Short Answer

1. Describe one thing you cannot do with a static method.

2. Why are static methods useful in creating utility classes?

3. Describe the difference in the way variables and class objects are passed as arguments to a method.

4. Even if you do not write an `equals` method for a class, Java provides one. Describe the behavior of the `equals` method that Java automatically provides.

5. A "has a" relationship can exist between classes. What does this mean?

6. What happens if you attempt to call a method using a reference variable that is set to `null`?

7. Is it advisable or not advisable to write a method that returns a reference to an object that is a private field? What is the exception to this?

8. What is the `this` key word?

9. Look at the following declaration:

```
enum Color { RED, ORANGE, GREEN, BLUE }
```

   a. What is the name of the data type declared by this statement?
   b. What are the `enum` constants for this type?
   c. Write a statement that defines a variable of this type and initializes it with a valid value.

10. Assuming the following `enum` declaration exists:

```
enum Dog { POODLE, BOXER, TERRIER }
```

   what will the following statements display?

```
a. System.out.println(Dog.POODLE + "\n" +
                      Dog.BOXER + "\n" +
                      Dog.TERRIER);

b. System.out.println(Dog.POODLE.ordinal() + "\n" +
                      Dog.BOXER.ordinal() + "\n" +
                      Dog.TERRIER.ordinal());

c. Dog myDog = Dog.BOXER;
   if (myDog.compareTo(Dog.TERRIER) > 0)
      System.out.println(myDog + " is greater than " +
                            Dog.TERRIER);
   else
      System.out.println(myDog + " is NOT greater than " +
                            Dog.TERRIER);
```

11. Under what circumstances does an object become a candidate for garbage collection?

Programming Challenges

1. Area Class

Write a class that has three overloaded static methods for calculating the areas of the following geometric shapes:

- circles
- rectangles
- cylinders

Here are the formulas for calculating the area of the shapes.

Area of a circle: $Area = \pi r^2$
    where π is Math.PI and r is the circle's radius

Area of a rectangle: $Area = Width \times Length$

Area of a cylinder: $Area = \pi r^2 h$
    where π is Math.PI, r is the radius of the cylinder's base, and
    h is the cylinder's height

Because the three methods are to be overloaded, they should each have the same name, but different parameter lists. Demonstrate the class in a complete program.

2. BankAccount Class Copy Constructor

VideoNote
The BankAccount Class copy Constructor Problem

Add a copy constructor to the BankAccount class. This constructor should accept a BankAccount object as an argument. It should assign to the balance field the value in the argument's balance field. As a result, the new object will be a copy of the argument object.

3. Carpet Calculator

The Westfield Carpet Company has asked you to write an application that calculates the price of carpeting for rectangular rooms. To calculate the price, you multiply the area of the floor (width times length) by the price per square foot of carpet. For example, the area of floor that is 12 feet long and 10 feet wide is 120 square feet. To cover that floor with carpet that costs $8 per square foot would cost $960. ($12 \times 10 \times 8 = 960$.)

First, you should create a class named RoomDimension that has two fields: one for the length of the room and one for the width. The RoomDimension class should have a method that returns the area of the room. (The area of the room is the room's length multiplied by the room's width.)

Next you should create a RoomCarpet class that has a RoomDimension object as a field. It should also have a field for the cost of the carpet per square foot. The RoomCarpet class should have a method that returns the total cost of the carpet.

Figure 9-21 is a UML diagram that shows possible class designs and the relationships among the classes. Once you have written these classes, use them in an application that asks the user to enter the dimensions of a room and the price per square foot of the desired carpeting. The application should display the total cost of the carpet.

4. LandTract Class

Make a LandTract class that has two fields: one for the tract's length and one for the width. The class should have a method that returns the tract's area, as well as an equals method and a toString method. Demonstrate the class in a program that asks the user to enter the dimensions for two tracts of land. The program should display the area of each tract of land and indicate whether the tracts are of equal size.

Figure 9-21   UML diagram for Programming Challenge 3

 5. Month Class

Write a class named `Month`. The class should have an `int` field named `monthNumber` that holds the number of the month. For example, January would be 1, February would be 2, and so forth. In addition, provide the following methods:

- A no-arg constructor that sets the `monthNumber` field to 1.
- A constructor that accepts the number of the month as an argument. It should set the `monthNumber` field to the value passed as the argument. If a value less than 1 or greater than 12 is passed, the constructor should set `monthNumber` to 1.
- A constructor that accepts the name of the month, such as "January" or "February" as an argument. It should set the `monthNumber` field to the correct corresponding value.
- A `setMonthNumber` method that accepts an `int` argument, which is assigned to the `monthNumber` field. If a value less than 1 or greater than 12 is passed, the method should set `monthNumber` to 1.
- A `getMonthNumber` method that returns the value in the `monthNumber` field.
- A `getMonthName` method that returns the name of the month. For example, if the `monthNumber` field contains 1, then this method should return "January".
- A `toString` method that returns the same value as the `getMonthName` method.
- An `equals` method that accepts a `Month` object as an argument. If the argument object holds the same data as the calling object, this method should return `true`. Otherwise, it should return `false`.

- A greaterThan method that accepts a Month object as an argument. If the calling object's monthNumber field is greater than the argument's monthNumber field, this method should return true. Otherwise, it should return false.
- A lessThan method that accepts a Month object as an argument. If the calling object's monthNumber field is less than the argument's monthNumber field, this method should return true. Otherwise, it should return false.

6. CashRegister Class

Write a CashRegister class that can be used with the RetailItem class that you wrote in Chapter 6's Programming Challenge 4. The CashRegister class should simulate the sale of a retail item. It should have a constructor that accepts a RetailItem object as an argument. The constructor should also accept an integer that represents the quantity of items being purchased. In addition, the class should have the following methods:

- The getSubtotal method should return the subtotal of the sale, which is the quantity multiplied by the price. This method must get the price from the RetailItem object that was passed as an argument to the constructor.
- The getTax method should return the amount of sales tax on the purchase. The sales tax rate is 6 percent of a retail sale.
- The getTotal method should return the total of the sale, which is the subtotal plus the sales tax.

Demonstrate the class in a program that asks the user for the quantity of items being purchased, and then displays the sale's subtotal, amount of sales tax, and total.

7. Sales Receipt File

Modify the program you wrote in Programming Challenge 6 to create a file containing a sales receipt. The program should ask the user for the quantity of items being purchased, and then generate a file with contents similar to the following:

```
SALES RECEIPT
Unit Price: $10.00
Quantity: 5
Subtotal: $50.00
Sales Tax: $ 3.00
Total: $53.00
```

8. Parking Ticket Simulator

For this assignment you will design a set of classes that work together to simulate a police officer issuing a parking ticket. You should design the following classes:

- The **ParkedCar** Class: This class should simulate a parked car. The class's responsibilities are as follows:
  - To know the car's make, model, color, license number, and the number of minutes that the car has been parked.
- The **ParkingMeter** Class: This class should simulate a parking meter. The class's only responsibility is as follows:
  - To know the number of minutes of parking time that has been purchased.

- **The `ParkingTicket` Class:** This class should simulate a parking ticket. The class's responsibilities are as follows:
  - To report the make, model, color, and license number of the illegally parked car
  - To report the amount of the fine, which is $25 for the first hour or part of an hour that the car is illegally parked, plus $10 for every additional hour or part of an hour that the car is illegally parked
  - To report the name and badge number of the police officer issuing the ticket
- **The `PoliceOfficer` Class:** This class should simulate a police officer inspecting parked cars. The class's responsibilities are as follows:
  - To know the police officer's name and badge number
  - To examine a `ParkedCar` object and a `ParkingMeter` object, and determine whether the car's time has expired
  - To issue a parking ticket (generate a `ParkingTicket` object) if the car's time has expired

Write a program that demonstrates how these classes collaborate.

9. Geometry Calculator

Design a `Geometry` class with the following methods:

- A static method that accepts the radius of a circle and returns the area of the circle. Use the following formula:

  $Area = \pi r^2$

  Use `Math.PI` for π and the radius of the circle for r.
- A static method that accepts the length and width of a rectangle and returns the area of the rectangle. Use the following formula:

  $Area = Length \times Width$
- A static method that accepts the length of a triangle's base and the triangle's height. The method should return the area of the triangle. Use the following formula:

  $Area = Base \times Height \times 0.5$

The methods should display an error message if negative values are used for the circle's radius, the rectangle's length or width, or the triangle's base or height.

Next, write a program to test the class, which displays the following menu and responds to the user's selection:

```
Geometry Calculator
1.  Calculate the Area of a Circle
2.  Calculate the Area of a Rectangle
3.  Calculate the Area of a Triangle
4.  Quit


Enter your choice (1-4):
```

Display an error message if the user enters a number outside the range of 1 through 4 when selecting an item from the menu.

10. Car Instrument Simulator

For this assignment, you will design a set of classes that work together to simulate a car's fuel gauge and odometer. The classes you will design are the following:

- The `FuelGauge` Class: This class will simulate a fuel gauge. Its responsibilities are as follows:

    - To know the car's current amount of fuel, in gallons.
    - To report the car's current amount of fuel, in gallons.
    - To be able to increment the amount of fuel by 1 gallon. This simulates putting fuel in the car. (The car can hold a maximum of 15 gallons.)
    - To be able to decrement the amount of fuel by 1 gallon, if the amount of fuel is greater than 0 gallons. This simulates burning fuel as the car runs.

- The `Odometer` Class: This class will simulate the car's odometer. Its responsibilities are as follows:

    - To know the car's current mileage.
    - To report the car's current mileage
    - To be able to increment the current mileage by 1 mile. The maximum mileage the odometer can store is 999,999 miles. When this amount is exceeded, the odometer resets the current mileage to 0.
    - To be able to work with a `FuelGauge` object. It should decrease the `FuelGauge` object's current amount of fuel by 1 gallon for every 24 miles traveled. (The car's fuel economy is 24 miles per gallon.)

Demonstrate the classes by creating instances of each. Simulate filling the car up with fuel, and then run a loop that increments the odometer until the car runs out of fuel. During each loop iteration, print the car's current mileage and amount of fuel.

10 Text Processing and More about Wrapper Classes

TOPICS

10.1 Introduction to Wrapper Classes

CONCEPT: Java provides wrapper classes for the primitive data types. The wrapper class for a given primitive type contains not only a value of that type, but also methods that perform operations related to the type.

Recall from Chapter 2 that the primitive data types are called "primitive" because they are not created from classes. Instead of instantiating objects, you create variables from the primitive data types, and variables do not have attributes or methods. They are designed simply to hold a single value in memory.

Java also provides wrapper classes for all of the primitive data types. A *wrapper class* is a class that is "wrapped around" a primitive data type and allows you to create objects instead of variables. In addition, these wrapper classes provide methods that perform useful operations on primitive values. For example, you have already used the wrapper class "parse" methods to convert strings to primitive values.

Although these wrapper classes can be used to create objects instead of variables, few programmers use them that way. One reason is because the wrapper classes are immutable, which means that once you create an object, you cannot change the object's value. Another reason is because they are not as easy to use as variables for simple operations. For example, to get the value stored in an object you must call a method, whereas variables can be used directly in assignment statements, mathematical operations, passed as arguments to methods, and so forth.

Although it is not normally useful to create objects from the wrapper classes, they do provide static methods that are very useful. We examine several of Java's wrapper classes in this chapter. We begin by looking at the Character class, which is the wrapper class for the char data type.

10.2 Character Testing and Conversion with the Character Class

CONCEPT: The Character class is a wrapper class for the char data type. It provides numerous methods for testing and converting character data.

The Character class is part of the java.lang package, so no import statement is necessary to use this class. The class provides several static methods for testing the value of a char variable. Some of these methods are listed in Table 10-1. Each of the methods accepts a single char argument and returns a boolean value.

Table 10-1 Some static Character class methods for testing char values

Method	Description
boolean isDigit(char *ch*)	Returns true if the argument passed into *ch* is a digit from 0 through 9. Otherwise returns false.
boolean isLetter(char *ch*)	Returns true if the argument passed into *ch* is an alphabetic letter. Otherwise returns false.
boolean isLetterOrDigit(char *ch*)	Returns true if the character passed into *ch* contains a digit (0 through 9) or an alphabetic letter. Otherwise returns false.
boolean isLowerCase(char *ch*)	Returns true if the argument passed into *ch* is a lowercase letter. Otherwise returns false.
boolean isUpperCase(char *ch*)	Returns true if the argument passed into *ch* is an uppercase letter. Otherwise returns false.
boolean isSpaceChar(char *ch*)	Returns true if the argument passed into *ch* is a space character. Otherwise returns false.
boolean isWhiteSpace(char *ch*)	Returns true if the argument passed into *ch* is a whitespace character (a space, tab, or newline character). Otherwise returns false.

The program in Code Listing 10-1 demonstrates many of these methods. Figures 10-1 and 10-2 show example interactions with the program.

Code Listing 10-1   (`CharacterTest.java`)

```java
 1 import javax.swing.JOptionPane;
 2
 3 /**
 4    This program demonstrates some of the Character
 5    class's character testing methods.
 6 */
 7
 8 public class CharacterTest
 9 {
10    public static void main(String[] args)
11    {
12       String input; // To hold the user's input
13       char ch;       // To hold a single character
14
15       // Get a character from the user and store
16       // it in the ch variable.
17       input = JOptionPane.showInputDialog("Enter " +
18                            "any single character.");
19       ch = input.charAt(0);
20
21       // Test the character.
22       if (Character.isLetter(ch))
23       {
24          JOptionPane.showMessageDialog(null,
25                        "That is a letter.");
26       }
27
28       if (Character.isDigit(ch))
29       {
30          JOptionPane.showMessageDialog(null,
31                        "That is a digit.");
32       }
33
34       if (Character.isLowerCase(ch))
35       {
36          JOptionPane.showMessageDialog(null,
37             "That is a lowercase letter.");
38       }
39
40       if (Character.isUpperCase(ch))
41       {
42          JOptionPane.showMessageDialog(null,
43             "That is an uppercase letter.");
44       }
45
```

```
46          if (Character.isSpaceChar(ch))
47          {
48              JOptionPane.showMessageDialog(null,
49                          "That is a space.");
50          }
51
52          if (Character.isWhitespace(ch))
53          {
54              JOptionPane.showMessageDialog(null,
55                "That is a whitespace character.");
56          }
57
58          System.exit(0);
59      }
60 }
```

Figure 10-1 Interaction with the `CharacterTest.java` program

Code Listing 10-2 shows a more practical application of the character testing methods. It tests a string to determine whether it is a seven-character customer number in the proper format. Figures 10-3 and 10-4 show example interactions with the program.

Figure 10-2 Interaction with the `CharacterTest.java` program

Code Listing 10-2   (CustomerNumber.java)

```java
 1 import javax.swing.JOptionPane;
 2
 3 /**
 4    This program tests a customer number to
 5    verify that it is in the proper format.
 6 */
 7
 8 public class CustomerNumber
 9 {
10    public static void main(String[] args)
11    {
12       String input;  // To hold the user's input
13
14       // Get a customer number.
15       input = JOptionPane.showInputDialog("Enter " +
16          "a customer number in the form LLLNNNN\n" +
17          "(LLL = letters and NNNN = numbers)");
18
19       // Validate the input.
20       if (isValid(input))
21       {
22          JOptionPane.showMessageDialog(null,
23                  "That's a valid customer number.");
24       }
25       else
26       {
27          JOptionPane.showMessageDialog(null,
28              "That is not the proper format of a " +
29              "customer number.\nHere is an " +
30              "example: ABC1234");
31       }
32
33       System.exit(0);
34    }
35
36    /**
37       The isValid method determines whether a
38       String is a valid customer number. If so, it
39       returns true.
40       @param custNumber The String to test.
41       @return true if valid, otherwise false.
42    */
43
44    private static boolean isValid(String custNumber)
45    {
```

```
46         boolean goodSoFar = true;    // Flag
47         int i = 0;                   // Control variable
48
49         // Test the length.
50         if (custNumber.length() != 7)
51             goodSoFar = false;
52
53         // Test the first three characters for letters.
54         while (goodSoFar && i < 3)
55         {
56             if (!Character.isLetter(custNumber.charAt(i)))
57                 goodSoFar = false;
58             i++;
59         }
60
61         // Test the last four characters for digits.
62         while (goodSoFar && i < 7)
63         {
64             if (!Character.isDigit(custNumber.charAt(i)))
65                 goodSoFar = false;
66             i++;
67         }
68
69         return goodSoFar;
70     }
71 }
```

Figure 10-3 Interaction with the **CustomerNumber.java** program

Figure 10-4 Interaction with the **CustomerNumber.java** program

In this program, the customer number is expected to be seven characters long and consist of three alphabetic letters followed by four numeric digits. The isValid method accepts a String argument, which will be tested. The method uses the following local variables, which are declared in lines 46 and 47:

```
boolean goodSoFar = true;   // Flag
int i = 0;                  // Control variable
```

The goodSoFar variable is a flag variable that is initialized with true, but will be set to false immediately when the method determines the customer number is not in a valid format. The i variable is a loop control variable.

The first test is to determine whether the string is the correct length. In line 50 the method tests the length of the custNumber argument. If the argument is not seven characters long, it is not valid and the goodSoFar variable is set to false in line 51.

Next, the method uses the following loop, in lines 54 through 59, to validate the first three characters:

```
while (goodSoFar && i < 3)
{
   if (!Character.isLetter(custNumber.charAt(i)))
      goodSoFar = false;
   i++;
}
```

Recall from Chapter 2 that the String class's charAt method returns a character at a specific position in a string (position numbering starts at 0). This code uses the Character.isLetter method to test the characters at positions 0, 1, and 2 in the custNumber string. If any of these characters are not letters, the goodSoFar variable is set to false and the loop terminates. Next, the method uses the following loop, in lines 62 through 67, to validate the last four characters:

```
while (goodSoFar && i < 7)
{
   if (!Character.isDigit(custNumber.charAt(i)))
      goodSoFar = false;
   i++;
}
```

This code uses the Character.isDigit method to test the characters at positions 3, 4, 5, and 6 in the custNumber string. If any of these characters are not digits, the goodSoFar variable is set to false and the loop terminates. Last, the method returns the value of the goodSoFar method.

Character Case Conversion

The Character class also provides the static methods listed in Table 10-2 for converting the case of a character. Each method accepts a char argument and returns a char value.

Table 10-2 Some `Character` class methods for case conversion

Method	Description
char toLowerCase(char *ch*)	Returns the lowercase equivalent of the argument passed to *ch*.
char toUpperCase(char *ch*)	Returns the uppercase equivalent of the argument passed to *ch*.

If the `toLowerCase` method's argument is an uppercase character, the method returns the lowercase equivalent. For example, the following statement will display the character a on the screen:

```
System.out.println(Character.toLowerCase('A'));
```

If the argument is already lowercase, the `toLowerCase` method returns it unchanged. The following statement also causes the lowercase character a to be displayed:

```
System.out.println(Character.toLowerCase('a'));
```

If the `toUpperCase` method's argument is a lowercase character, the method returns the uppercase equivalent. For example, the following statement will display the character A on the screen:

```
System.out.println(Character.toUpperCase('a'));
```

If the argument is already uppercase, the `toUpperCase` method returns it unchanged.

Any non-letter argument passed to `toLowerCase` or `toUpperCase` is returned as it is. Each of the following statements displays the method argument without any change:

```
System.out.println(Character.toLowerCase('*'));
System.out.println(Character.toLowerCase('$'));
System.out.println(Character.toUpperCase('&'));
System.out.println(Character.toUpperCase('%'));
```

The program in Code Listing 10-3 demonstrates the `toUpperCase` method in a loop that asks the user to enter Y or N. The program repeats as long as the user enters Y or y in response to the question.

Code Listing 10-3 (`CircleArea.java`)

```
 1 import java.util.Scanner;
 2 import java.text.DecimalFormat;
 3
 4 /**
 5    This program demonstrates the Character
 6    class's toUpperCase method.
 7 */
 8
 9 public class CircleArea
```

```
10 {
11     public static void main(String[] args)
12     {
13         double radius;       // The circle's radius
14         double area;         // The circle's area
15         String input;        // To hold a line of input
16         char choice;         // To hold a single character
17
18         // Create a Scanner object to read keyboard input.
19         Scanner keyboard = new Scanner(System.in);
20
21         // Create a DecimalFormat object.
22         DecimalFormat fmt = new DecimalFormat("0.00");
23
24         do
25         {
26             // Get the circle's radius.
27             System.out.print("Enter the circle's " +
28                             "radius: ");
29             radius = keyboard.nextDouble();
30
31             // Consume the remaining newline character.
32             keyboard.nextLine();
33
34             // Calculate and display the area.
35             area = Math.PI * radius * radius;
36             System.out.println("The area is " +
37                             fmt.format(area));
38
39             // Repeat this?
40             System.out.print("Do you want to do this " +
41                             "again? (Y or N) ");
42             input = keyboard.nextLine();
43             choice = input.charAt(0);
44
45         } while (Character.toUpperCase(choice) == 'Y');
46     }
47 }
```

Program Output with Example Input Shown in Bold

```
Enter the circle's radius: 10 [Enter]
The area is 314.16
Do you want to do this again? (Y or N) y [Enter]
Enter the circle's radius: 15 [Enter]
The area is 706.86
Do you want to do this again? (Y or N) n [Enter]
```

Checkpoint

10.1   Write a statement that converts the contents of the `char` variable `big` to lower-case. The converted value should be assigned to the variable `little`.

10.2   Write an `if` statement that displays the word "digit" if the `char` variable `ch` contains a numeric digit. Otherwise, it should display "Not a digit."

10.3   What is the output of the following statement?

```
System.out.println(Character.toUpperCase(Character.
toLowerCase('A')));
```

10.4   Write a loop that asks the user "Do you want to repeat the program or quit? (R/Q)". The loop should repeat until the user has entered an R or Q (either uppercase or lowercase).

10.5   What will the following code display?

```
char var = '$';
System.out.println(Character.toUpperCase(var));
```

10.6   Write a loop that counts the number of uppercase characters that appear in the `String` object `str`.

10.3   More String Methods

CONCEPT: The `String` class provides several methods for searching and working with `String` objects.

Searching for Substrings

The `String` class provides several methods that search for a string inside of a string. The term *substring* commonly is used to refer to a string that is part of another string. Table 10-3 summarizes some of these methods. Each of the methods in Table 10-3 returns a `boolean` value indicating whether the string was found.

Let's take a closer look at each of these methods.

The startsWith and endsWith Methods

The `startsWith` method determines whether the calling object's string begins with a specified substring. For example, the following code determines whether the string "Four score and seven years ago" begins with "Four". The method returns `true` if the string begins with the specified substring, or `false` otherwise.

```
String str = "Four score and seven years ago";
if (str.startsWith("Four"))
    System.out.println("The string starts with Four.");
else
    System.out.println("The string does not start with Four.");
```

Table 10-3 `String` methods that search for a substring

Method	Description
`boolean startsWith(String str)`	This method returns `true` if the calling string begins with the string passed into `str`.
`boolean endsWith(String str)`	This method returns `true` if the calling string ends with the string passed into `str`.
`boolean regionMatches(int start,` `    String str, int start2, int n)`	This method returns `true` if a specified region of the calling string matches a specified region of the string passed into `str`. The `start` parameter indicates the starting position of the region within the calling string. The `start2` parameter indicates the starting position of the region within `str`. The `n` parameter indicates the number of characters in both regions.

`boolean regionMatches(Boolean ignoreCase,`
`    int start, String str,`
`    int start2, int n)`
	This overloaded version of the `regionMatches` method has an additional parameter, `ignoreCase`. If `true` is passed into this parameter, the method ignores the case of the calling string and `str` when comparing the regions. If `false` is passed into the `ignoreCase` parameter, the comparison is case-sensitive.

In the code, the method call `str.startsWith("Four")` returns `true` because the string does begin with "Four". The `startsWith` method performs a case-sensitive comparison, so the method call `str.startsWith("four")` would return `false`.

The `endsWith` method determines whether the calling string ends with a specified substring. For example, the following code determines whether the string "Four score and seven years ago" ends with "ago". The method returns `true` if the string does end with the specified substring or `false` otherwise.

```
String str = "Four score and seven years ago";
if (str.endsWith("ago"))
    System.out.println("The string ends with ago.");
else
    System.out.println("The string does not end with ago.");
```

In the code, the method call `str.endsWith("ago")` returns `true` because the string does end with "ago". The `endsWith` method also performs a case-sensitive comparison, so the method call `str.endsWith("Ago")` would return `false`.

The program in Code Listing 10-4 demonstrates a search algorithm that uses the `startsWith` method. The program searches an array of strings for an element that starts with a specified string.

Code Listing 10-4 (`PersonSearch.java`)

```java
 1 import java.util.Scanner;
 2
 3 /**
 4    This program uses the startsWith method to search using
 5    a partial string.
 6 */
 7
 8 public class PersonSearch
 9 {
10    public static void main(String[] args)
11    {
12       String lookUp;  // To hold a lookup string
13
14       // Create an array of names.
15       String[] people = { "Cutshaw, Will", "Davis, George",
16                           "Davis, Jenny", "Russert, Phil",
17                           "Russell, Cindy", "Setzer, Charles",
18                           "Smathers, Holly", "Smith, Chris",
19                           "Smith, Brad", "Williams, Jean" };
20
21       // Create a Scanner object for keyboard input.
22       Scanner keyboard = new Scanner(System.in);
23
24       // Get a partial name to search for.
25       System.out.print("Enter the first few characters of " +
26                     "the last name to look up: ");
27       lookUp = keyboard.nextLine();
28
29       // Display all of the names that begin with the
30       // string entered by the user.
31       System.out.println("Here are the names that match:");
32       for (String person : people)
33       {
34          if (person.startsWith(lookUp))
35             System.out.println(person);
36       }
37    }
38 }
```

Program Output with Example Input Shown in Bold

```
Enter the first few characters of the last name to look up: Davis [Enter]
```

```
Here are the names that match:
Davis, George
Davis, Jenny
```

Program Output with Example Input Shown in Bold

Enter the first few characters of the last name to look up: **Russ [Enter]**
Here are the names that match:
Russert, Phil
Russell, Cindy

The `regionMatches` Methods

The `String` class provides overloaded versions of the `regionMatches` method, which determines whether specified regions of two strings match. The following code demonstrates:

```java
String str = "Four score and seven years ago";
String str2 = "Those seven years passed quickly";
if (str.regionMatches(15, str2, 6, 11))
    System.out.println("The regions match.");
else
    System.out.println("The regions do not match.");
```

This code will display "The regions match." The specified region of the `str` string begins at position 15, and the specified region of the `str2` string begins at position 6. Both regions consist of 11 characters. The specified region in the `str` string is "seven years" and the specified region in the `str2` string is also "seven years". Because the two regions match, the `regionMatches` method in this code returns `true`. This version of the `regionMatches` method performs a case-sensitive comparison. An overloaded version accepts an additional argument indicating whether to perform a case insensitive comparison. The following code demonstrates:

```java
String str = "Four score and seven years ago";
String str2 = "THOSE SEVEN YEARS PASSED QUICKLY";

if (str.regionMatches(true, 15, str2, 6, 11))
    System.out.println("The regions match.");
else
    System.out.println("The regions do not match.");
```

This code will also display "The regions match." The first argument passed to this version of the `regionMatches` method can be `true` or `false`, indicating whether a case-insensitive comparison should be performed. In this example, `true` is passed, so case will be ignored when the regions "seven years" and "SEVEN YEARS" are compared.

Each of these methods indicates by a `boolean` return value whether a substring appears within a string. The `String` class also provides methods that not only search for items within a string, but also report the location of those items. Table 10-4 describes overloaded versions of the `indexOf` and `lastIndexOf` methods.

Table 10-4   String methods for getting a character or substring's location

Method	Description
int indexOf(char *ch*)	Searches the calling String object for the character passed into *ch*. If the character is found, the position of its first occurrence is returned. Otherwise, −1 is returned.
int indexOf(char *ch*, int *start*)	Searches the calling String object for the character passed into *ch*, beginning at the position passed into *start* and going to the end of the string. If the character is found, the position of its first occurrence is returned. Otherwise, −1 is returned.
int indexOf(String *str*)	Searches the calling String object for the string passed into *str*. If the string is found, the beginning position of its first occurrence is returned. Otherwise, −1 is returned.
int indexOf(String *str*, int *start*)	Searches the calling String object for the string passed into *str*. The search begins at the position passed into *start* and goes to the end of the string. If the string is found, the beginning position of its first occurrence is returned. Otherwise, −1 is returned.
int lastIndexOf(char *ch*)	Searches the calling String object for the character passed into *ch*. If the character is found, the position of its last occurrence is returned. Otherwise, −1 is returned.
int lastIndexOf(char *ch*, int *start*)	Searches the calling String object for the character passed into *ch*, beginning at the position passed into *start*. The search is conducted backward through the string, to position 0. If the character is found, the position of its last occurrence is returned. Otherwise, −1 is returned.
int lastIndexOf(String *str*)	Searches the calling String object for the string passed into *str*. If the string is found, the beginning position of its last occurrence is returned. Otherwise, −1 is returned.
int lastIndexOf(String *str*, int *start*)	Searches the calling String object for the string passed into *str*, beginning at the position passed into *start*. The search is conducted backward through the string, to position 0. If the string is found, the beginning position of its last occurrence is returned. Otherwise, −1 is returned.

Finding Characters with the `indexOf` and `lastIndexOf` Methods

The `indexOf` and `lastIndexOf` methods can search for either a character or a substring within the calling string. If the item being searched for is found, its position is returned. Otherwise −1 is returned. Here is an example of code using two of the methods to search for a character:

```java
String str = "Four score and seven years ago";
int first, last;

first = str.indexOf('r');
last = str.lastIndexOf('r');

System.out.println("The letter r first appears at " +
                   "position " + first);

System.out.println("The letter r last appears at " +
                   "position " + last);
```

This code produces the following output:

```
The letter r first appears at position 3
The letter r last appears at position 24
```

The following code shows another example. It uses a loop to show the positions of each letter 'r' in the string.

```java
String str = "Four score and seven years ago";
int position;

System.out.println("The letter r appears at the " +
                   "following locations:");
position = str.indexOf('r');
while (position != -1)
{
    System.out.println(position);
    position = str.indexOf('r', position + 1);
}
```

This code will produce the following output:

```
The letter r appears at the following locations:
3
8
24
```

The following code is very similar, but it uses the `lastIndexOf` method and shows the positions in reverse order:

```java
String str = "Four score and seven years ago";
int position;

System.out.println("The letter r appears at the " +
                   "following locations.");
```

```
position = str.lastIndexOf('r');
while (position != -1)
{
   System.out.println(position);
   position = str.lastIndexOf('r', position - 1);
}
```

This code will produce the following output:

```
The letter r appears at the following locations.
24
8
3
```

Finding Substrings with the `indexOf` and `lastIndexOf` Methods

The `indexOf` and `lastIndexOf` methods can also search for substrings within a string. The following code shows an example. It displays the starting positions of each occurrence of the word "and" within a string.

```
String str = "and a one and a two and a three";
int position;
System.out.println("The word and appears at the " +
                   "following locations.");
position = str.indexOf("and");
while (position != -1)
{
   System.out.println(position);
   position = str.indexOf("and", position + 1);
}
```

This code produces the following output:

```
The word and appears at the following locations.
0
10
20
```

The following code also displays the same results, but in reverse order:

```
String str = "and a one and a two and a three";
int position;

System.out.println("The word and appears at the " +
                   "following locations.");
position = str.lastIndexOf("and");
while (position != -1)
{
   System.out.println(position);
   position = str.lastIndexOf("and", position - 1);
}
```

This code produces the following output:

```
The word and appears at the following locations.
20
10
0
```

Extracting Substrings

The String class provides several methods that allow you to retrieve a substring from a string. The methods we will examine are listed in Table 10-5.

Table 10-5 String methods for extracting substrings

Method	Description
String substring(int *start*)	This method returns a copy of the substring that begins at *start* and goes to the end of the calling object's string.
String substring(int *start*, int *end*)	This method returns a copy of a substring. The argument passed into *start* is the substring's starting position, and the argument passed into *end* is the substring's ending position. The character at the *start* position is included in the substring, but the character at the *end* position is not included.
void getChars(int *start*, int *end*, char[] *array*, int *arrayStart*)	This method extracts a substring from the calling object and stores it in a char array. The argument passed into *start* is the substring's starting position, and the argument passed into *end* is the substring's ending position. The character at the *start* position is included in the substring, but the character at the *end* position is not included. (The last character in the substring ends at *end* − 1.) The characters in the substring are stored as elements in the array that is passed into the *array* parameter. The *arrayStart* parameter specifies the starting subscript within the array where the characters are to be stored.
char[] toCharArray()	This method returns all of the characters in the calling object as a char array.

The substring Methods

The substring method returns a copy of a substring from the calling object. There are two overloaded versions of this method. The first version accepts an int argument that is the starting position of the substring. The method returns a reference to a String object containing all of the characters from the starting position to the end of the string. The character at the starting position is part of the substring. Here is an example of the method's use:

```
String fullName = "Cynthia Susan Lee";
String lastName = fullName.substring(14);
System.out.println("The full name is " + fullName);
System.out.println("The last name is " + lastName);
```

This code will produce the following output:

```
The full name is Cynthia Susan Lee
The last name is Lee
```

Keep in mind that the substring method returns a new String object that holds a copy of the substring. When this code executes, the fullName and lastName variables will reference two different String objects, as shown in Figure 10-5.

Figure 10-5 The fullName and lastName variables reference separate objects

The second version of the method accepts two int arguments. The first specifies the substring's starting position and the second specifies the substring's ending position. The character at the starting position is included in the substring, but the character at the ending position is not. Here is an example of how the method is used:

```
String fullName = "Cynthia Susan Lee";
String middleName = fullName.substring(8, 13);
System.out.println("The full name is " + fullName);
System.out.println("The middle name is " + middleName);
```

The code will produce the following output:

```
The full name is Cynthia Susan Lee
The middle name is Susan
```

The getChars and toCharArray Methods

The getChars and toCharArray methods convert the calling String object to a char array. The getChars method can be used to convert a substring, while the toCharArray method converts the entire string. Here is an example of how the getChars method might be used:

```
String fullName = "Cynthia Susan Lee";
char[] nameArray = new char[5];
```

```
        fullName.getChars(8, 13, nameArray, 0);
        System.out.println("The full name is " + fullName);
        System.out.println("The values in the array are:");
        for (int i = 0; i < nameArray.length; i++)
            System.out.print(nameArray[i] + " ");
```

This code stores the individual characters of the substring "Susan" in the elements of the nameArray array, beginning at element 0. The code will produce the following output:

```
The full name is Cynthia Susan Lee
The values in the array are:
S u s a n
```

The toCharArray method returns a reference to a char array that contains all of the characters in the calling object. Here is an example:

```
        String fullName = "Cynthia Susan Lee";
        char[] nameArray;
        nameArray = fullName.toCharArray();
        System.out.println("The full name is " + fullName);
        System.out.println("The values in the array are:");
        for (int i = 0; i < nameArray.length; i++)
            System.out.print(nameArray[i] + " ");
```

This code will produce the following output:

```
The full name is Cynthia Susan Lee
The values in the array are:
C y n t h i a   S u s a n   L e e
```

These methods can be used when you want to use an array processing algorithm on the contents of a String object. The program in Code Listing 10-5 converts a String object to an array and then uses the array to determine the number of letters, digits, and whitespace characters in the string. Figure 10-6 shows an example of interaction with the program.

Code Listing 10-5 (StringAnalyzer.java)

```java
 1  import javax.swing.JOptionPane;
 2
 3  /**
 4      This program displays the number of letters,
 5      digits, and whitespace characters in a string.
 6  */
 7
 8  public class StringAnalyzer
 9  {
10      public static void main(String [] args)
11      {
12          String input;        // To hold input
13          char[] array;        // Array for input
```

```
14          int letters = 0;     // Number of letters
15          int digits = 0;      // Number of digits
16          int whitespaces = 0; // Number of whitespaces
17
18          // Get a string from the user.
19          input = JOptionPane.showInputDialog("Enter " +
20                                              "a string:");
21
22          // Convert the string to a char array.
23          array = input.toCharArray();
24
25          // Analyze the characters.
26          for (int i = 0; i < array.length; i++)
27          {
28             if (Character.isLetter(array[i]))
29                letters++;
30             else if (Character.isDigit(array[i]))
31                digits++;
32             else if (Character.isWhitespace(array[i]))
33                whitespaces++;
34          }
35
36          // Display the results.
37          JOptionPane.showMessageDialog(null,
38                          "That string contains " +
39                          letters + " letters, " +
40                          digits + " digits, and " +
41                          whitespaces +
42                          " whitespace characters.");
43
44       System.exit(0);
45    }
46 }
```

Figure 10-6   Interaction with the `StringAnalyzer.java` program

Methods That Return a Modified `String`

The `String` class methods listed in Table 10-6 return a modified copy of a `String` object.

Table 10-6 Methods that return a modified copy of a `string` object

Method	Description
`String concat(String `*`str`*`)`	This method returns a copy of the calling `String` object with the contents of *str* concatenated to it.
`String replace(char `*`oldChar`*`,` `char `*`newChar`*`)`	This method returns a copy of the calling `String` object, in which all occurrences of the character passed into *oldChar* have been replaced by the character passed into *newChar*.
`String trim()`	This method returns a copy of the calling `String` object, in which all leading and trailing whitespace characters have been deleted.

The `concat` method performs the same operation as the + operator when used with strings. For example, look at the following code, which uses the + operator:

```
String fullName;
String firstName = "Timothy ";
String lastName = "Haynes";
fullName = firstName + lastName;
```

Equivalent code can also be written with the `concat` method. Here is an example:

```
String fullName;
String firstName = "Timothy ";
String lastName = "Haynes";
fullName = firstName.concat(lastName);
```

The `replace` method returns a copy of a `String` object, where every occurrence of a specified character has been replaced with another character. For example, look at the following code:

```
String str1 = "Tom Talbert Tried Trains";
String str2;
str2 = str1.replace('T', 'D');
System.out.println(str1);
System.out.println(str2);
```

In this code, the `replace` method will return a copy of the str1 object with every occurrence of the letter 'T' replaced with the letter 'D'. The code will produce the following output:

```
Tom Talbert Tried Trains
Dom Dalbert Dried Drains
```

Remember that the `replace` method does not modify the contents of the calling `String` object, but returns a reference to a `String` that is a modified copy of it. After the previous code executes, the `str1` and `str2` variables will reference different `String` objects.

The `trim` method returns a copy of a `String` object with all leading and trailing whitespace characters deleted. A *leading* whitespace character is one that appears at the beginning, or left side, of a string. For example, the following string has three leading whitespace characters:

```
"   Hello"
```

A *trailing* whitespace character is one that appears at the end, or right side, of a string, after the non-space characters. For example, the following string has three trailing whitespace characters:

```
"Hello   "
```

Here is an example:

```
String greeting1 = "   Hello   ";
String greeting2;
greeting2 = greeting1.trim();
System.out.println("*" + greeting1 + "*");
System.out.println("*" + greeting2 + "*");
```

In this code, the first statement assigns the string "   Hello   " (with three leading spaces and three trailing spaces) to the `greeting1` variable. The `trim` method is called, which returns a copy of the string with the leading and trailing spaces removed. The code will produce the following output:

```
*   Hello   *
*Hello*
```

One common use of the `trim` method is to remove any leading or trailing spaces that the user might have entered while inputting data.

The Static `valueOf` Methods

The `String` class has several overloaded versions of a method named `valueOf`. This method accepts a value of any primitive data type as its argument and returns a string representation of the value. Table 10-7 describes these methods.

The following code demonstrates several of these methods:

```
boolean b = true;
char [] letters = { 'a', 'b', 'c', 'd', 'e' };
double d = 2.4981567;
int i = 7;

System.out.println(String.valueOf(b));
System.out.println(String.valueOf(letters));
System.out.println(String.valueOf(letters, 1, 3));
System.out.println(String.valueOf(d));
System.out.println(String.valueOf(i));
```

Table 10-7 Some of the String class's valueOf methods

Method	Description
String valueOf(boolean *b*)	If the boolean argument passed to *b* is true, the method returns the string "true". If the argument is false, the method returns the string "false".
String valueOf(char *c*)	This method returns a String containing the character passed into *c*.
String valueOf(char[] *array*)	This method returns a String that contains all of the elements in the char array passed into *array*.

String valueOf(char[] *array*,
        int *subscript*,
        int *count*)
	This method returns a String that contains part of the elements in the char array passed into *array*. The argument passed into *subscript* is the starting subscript and the argument passed into *count* is the number of elements.

String valueOf(double *number*)	This method returns the String representation of the double argument passed into *number*.
String valueOf(float *number*)	This method returns the String representation of the float argument passed into *number*.
String valueOf(int *number*)	This method returns the String representation of the int argument passed into *number*.
String valueOf(long *number*)	This method returns the String representation of the long argument passed into *number*.

This code will produce the following output:

```
true
abcde
bcd
2.4981567
7
```

Checkpoint

10.7 Write a method that accepts a reference to a String object as an argument and returns true if the argument ends with the substring "ger". Otherwise, the method should return false.

10.8 Modify the method you wrote for Checkpoint 10.7 so it performs a case-insensitive test. The method should return true if the argument ends with "ger" in any possible combination of uppercase and lowercase letters.

10.9 Look at the following declaration:

```
String cafeName = "Broadway Cafe";
String str;
```

Which of the following methods would you use to make str reference the string "Broadway"?

```
startsWith
regionMatches
substring
indexOf
```

10.10 What is the difference between the indexOf and lastIndexOf methods?

10.11 What is the difference between the getChars and substring methods?

10.12 The + operator, when used with strings, performs the same operation as what String method?

10.13 What is the difference between the getChars and toCharArray methods?

10.14 Look at the following code:

```
String str1 = "To be, or not to be";
String str2 = str1.replace('o', 'u');
System.out.println(str1);
System.out.println(str2);
```

You hear a fellow student claim that the code will display the following:

```
Tu be ur nut tu be
Tu be ur nut tu be
```

Is your fellow student right or wrong? Why?

10.15 What will the following code display?

```
String str1 = "William ";
String str2 = " the ";
String str3 = " Conqueror";
System.out.println(str1.trim() + str2.trim() +
                   str3.trim());
```

10.16 Assume that a program has the following declarations:

```
double number = 9.47;
String str;
```

Write a statement that assigns a string representation of the number variable to str.

10.4 The StringBuilder Class

CONCEPT: The StringBuilder class is similar to the String class, except that you may change the contents of StringBuilder objects. The StringBuilder class also provides several useful methods that the String class does not have.

The StringBuilder class is similar to the String class. The main difference between the two is that you can change the contents of a StringBuilder object, but you cannot change the contents of a String object. Recall that String objects are immutable. This means that once you set the contents of a String object, you cannot change the string value that it holds. For example, look at the following code:

```
String name;
name = "George";
name = "Sally";
```

The first statement creates the name variable. The second creates a String object containing the string "George" and assigns its address to the name variable. Although we cannot change the contents of the String object, we can make the name variable reference a different String object. That's what the third statement does: It creates another String object containing the string "Sally", and assigns its address to name. This is illustrated by Figure 10-7.

Figure 10-7   The String object containing "George" is no longer referenced

Unlike String objects, StringBuilder objects have methods that allow you to modify their contents without creating a new object in memory. You can change specific characters, insert characters, delete characters, and perform other operations. The StringBuilder object will grow or shrink in size, as needed, to accommodate the changes.

The fact that String objects are immutable is rarely a problem, but you might consider using StringBuilder objects if your program needs to make a lot of changes to one or more strings. This will improve the program's efficiency by reducing the number of String objects that must be created and then removed by the garbage collector. Now let's look at the StringBuilder class's constructors and methods.

The StringBuilder Constructors

Table 10-8 lists three of the StringBuilder constructors.

Table 10-8   StringBuilder constructors

Constructor	Description
StringBuilder()	This constructor accepts no arguments. It gives the object enough storage space to hold 16 characters, but no characters are stored in it.
StringBuilder(int *length*)	This constructor gives the object enough storage space to hold *length* characters, but no characters are stored in it.
StringBuilder(String *str*)	This constructor initializes the object with the string in str. The object's initial storage space will be the length of the string plus 16.

The first two constructors create empty `StringBuilder` objects of a specified size. The first constructor makes the `StringBuilder` object large enough to hold 16 characters, and the second constructor makes the object large enough to hold *length* characters. Remember, `StringBuilder` objects automatically resize themselves, so it is not a problem if you later want to store a larger string in the object. The third constructor accepts a `String` object as its argument and assigns the object's contents to the `StringBuilder` object. Here is an example of its use:

```
StringBuilder city = new StringBuilder("Charleston");
System.out.println(city);
```

This code creates a `StringBuilder` object and assigns its address to the `city` variable. The object is initialized with the string "Charleston". As demonstrated by this code, you can pass a `StringBuilder` object to the `println` and `print` methods.

One limitation of the `StringBuilder` class is that you cannot use the assignment operator to assign strings to `StringBuilder` objects. For example, the following code will not work:

```
StringBuilder city = "Charleston";  // ERROR!!! Will not work!
```

Instead of using the assignment operator, you must use the `new` key word and a constructor, or one of the `StringBuilder` methods, to store a string in a `StringBuilder` object.

Other `StringBuilder` Methods

The `StringBuilder` class provides many of the same methods as the `String` class. Table 10-9 lists several of the `StringBuilder` methods that work exactly like their `String` class counterparts.

Table 10-9 Methods that are common to the `String` and `StringBuilder` classes

```
char charAt(int position)
void getChars(int start, int end, char[] array, int arrayStart)
int indexOf(String str)
int indexOf(String str, int start)
int lastIndexOf(String str)
int lastIndexOf(String str, int start)
int length()
String substring(int start)
String substring(int start, int end)
```

In addition, the `StringBuilder` class provides several methods that the `String` class does not have. Let's look at a few of them.

The `append` Methods

The `StringBuilder` class has several overloaded versions of a method named `append`. These methods accept an argument, which may be of any primitive data type, a `char` array, or a String object. They append a string representation of their argument to the calling object's current contents. Because there are so many overloaded versions of append, we will examine the general form of a typical call to the method as follows:

```
object.append(item);
```

After the method is called, a string representation of *item* will be appended to *object*'s contents. The following code shows some of the append methods being used:

```
StringBuilder str = new StringBuilder();

// Append values to the object.
str.append("We sold ");          // Append a String object.
str.append(12);                  // Append an int.
str.append(" doughnuts for $");  // Append another String.
str.append(15.95);               // Append a double.

// Display the object's contents.
System.out.println(str);
```

This code will produce the following output:

```
We sold 12 doughnuts for $15.95
```

The insert Methods

The StringBuilder class also has several overloaded versions of a method named insert, which inserts a value into the calling object's string. These methods accept two arguments: an int that specifies the position in the calling object's string where the insertion should begin, and the value to be inserted. The value to be inserted may be of any primitive data type, a char array, or a String object. Because there are so many overloaded versions of insert, we will examine the general form of a typical call to the method as follows:

```
object.insert(start, item);
```

In the general form, *start* is the starting position of the insertion and *item* is the item to be inserted. The following code shows some of the insert methods being used:

```
StringBuilder str = new StringBuilder("July sold cars.");
char[] array = { 'w', 'e', ' ' };

// Append values to the object.
str.insert(0, "In ");    // Insert a String.
str.insert(8, array);    // Insert a char array.
str.insert(16, 20);      // Insert an int.
str.insert(18, ' ');     // Insert a char.

// Display the object's contents.
System.out.println(str);
```

This code produces the following output:

```
In July we sold 20 cars.
```

Code Listing 10-6 shows another example of the insert method. The Telephone class has a static method named format that accepts a String containing an unformatted telephone number. The method inserts parentheses around the area code and inserts a hyphen after the prefix. The program in Code Listing 10-7 demonstrates the class.

Code Listing 10-6   (Telephone.java)

```java
 1  /**
 2      Telephone class
 3  */
 4
 5  public class Telephone
 6  {
 7     /**
 8         The format method accepts a String containing
 9         an unformatted telephone number, such as
10         9195551212. It returns a String containing a
11         formatted telephone number, such as (919)555-1212.
12         @param number The number to format.
13         @return A reference to the formatted String.
14     */
15     public static String format(String number)
16     {
17        StringBuilder str = new StringBuilder(number);
18
19        // Insert parentheses around the area code.
20        str.insert(0, '(');
21        str.insert(4, ')');
22
23        // Insert a hyphen after the prefix.
24        str.insert(8, '-');
25
26        // Return the formatted number as a string.
27        return str.toString();
28     }
29  }
```

Code Listing 10-7   (TelephoneTester.java)

```java
 1  /**
 2      This program demonstrates the Telephone
 3      class's static format method.
 4  */
```

```
 5
 6 public class TelephoneTester
 7 {
 8     public static void main(String[] args)
 9     {
10         // Create an unformatted number.
11         String phone = "9195551212";
12
13         // Get a formatted version of it.
14         String properNum = Telephone.format(phone);
15
16         // Display the formatted number.
17         System.out.println(properNum);
18     }
19 }
```

Program Output

```
(919)555-1212
```

The replace Method

The StringBuilder class has a replace method that differs slightly from the String class's replace method. While the String class's replace method replaces the occurrences of one character with another character, the StringBuilder class's replace method replaces a specified substring with a string. Here is the general form of a call to the method:

```
object.replace(start, end, str);
```

In the general form, *start* is an int that specifies the starting position of a substring in the calling object, and *end* is an int that specifies the ending position of the substring. (The starting position is included in the substring, but the ending position is not.) The *str* parameter is a String object. After the method executes, the substring will be replaced with *str*. Here is an example:

```
StringBuilder str =
    new StringBuilder("We moved from Chicago to Atlanta.");
str.replace(14, 21, "New York");
System.out.println(str);
```

The replace method in this code replaces the word "Chicago" with "New York". The code will produce the following output:

```
We moved from New York to Atlanta.
```

The delete, deleteCharAt, and setCharAt Methods

The delete and deleteCharAt methods are used to delete a substring or a character from a StringBuilder object. The setCharAt method changes a specified character to another value. Table 10-10 describes these methods.

Table 10-10 The `StringBuilder` class's `delete`, `deleteCharAt`, and `setCharAt` methods

Method	Description
`StringBuilder delete(int start, int end)`	The `start` parameter is an int that specifies the starting position of a substring in the calling object, and the `end` parameter is an int that specifies the ending position of the substring. (The starting position is included in the substring, but the ending position is not.) The method will delete the substring.
`StringBuilder deleteCharAt (int position)`	The `position` parameter specifies the location of a character that will be deleted.
`void setCharAt(int position, char ch)`	This method changes the character at `position` to the value passed into ch.

The following code demonstrates all three of these methods:

```
StringBuilder str =
    new StringBuilder("I ate 100 blueberries!");

// Display the StringBuilder object.
System.out.println(str);

// Delete the '0'.
str.deleteCharAt(8);

// Delete "blue".
str.delete(9, 13);

// Display the StringBuilder object.
System.out.println(str);

// Change the '1' to '5'
str.setCharAt(6, '5');

// Display the StringBuilder object.
System.out.println(str);
```

This code will produce the following output:

```
I ate 100 blueberries!
I ate 10 berries!
I ate 50 berries!
```

NOTE: The Java API provides a class named StringBuffer which is essentially the same as the StringBuilder class, with the same constructors and the same methods. The difference is that the methods in the StringBuffer class are *synchronized*. This means that the StringBuffer class is safe to use in a multithreaded application. Multithreaded programming is beyond the scope of this book, but in a nutshell, a *multithreaded application* is one that concurrently runs multiple threads of execution. In such an application, it is possible for more than one thread to access the same objects in memory at the same time. In multithreaded applications, it is important that the methods be synchronized, to prevent the possibility of data corruption

Because synchronization requires extra steps to be performed, the StringBuffer class is slower than the StringBuilder class. In an application where the object will not be accessed by multiple threads, you should use the StringBuilder class to get the best performance. In an application where multiple threads will be accessing the object, you should use the StringBuffer class to ensure that its data does not become corrupted.

Checkpoint

10.17 The String class is immutable. What does this mean?

10.18 In a program that makes lots of changes to strings, would it be more efficient to use String objects or StringBuilder objects? Why?

10.19 Look at the following statement:

```
String city = "Asheville";
```

Rewrite this statement so that city references a StringBuilder object instead of a String object.

10.20 You wish to add a string to the end of the existing contents of a StringBuilder object. What method do you use?

10.21 You wish to insert a string into the existing contents of a StringBuilder object. What method do you use?

10.22 You wish to delete a specific character from the existing contents of a StringBuilder object. What method do you use?

10.23 You wish to change a specific character in a StringBuilder object. What method do you use?

10.24 How does the StringBuilder class's replace method differ from the String class's replace method?

10.5 Tokenizing Strings

CONCEPT: Tokenizing a string is a process of breaking a string down into its components, which are called tokens. The `StringTokenizer` class and the `String` class's `split` method can be used to tokenize strings.

Sometimes a string will contain a series of words or other items of data separated by spaces or other characters. For example, look at the following string:

```
"peach raspberry strawberry vanilla"
```

This string contains the following four items of data: `peach`, `raspberry`, `strawberry`, and `vanilla`. In programming terms, items such as these are known as *tokens*. Notice that a space appears between the items. The character that separates tokens is known as a *delimiter*. Here is another example:

```
"17;92;81;12;46;5"
```

This string contains the following tokens: 17, 92, 81, 12, 46, and 5. Notice that a semicolon appears between each item. In this example the semicolon is used as a delimiter. Some programming problems require you to read a string that contains a list of items and then extract all of the tokens from the string for processing. For example, look at the following string that contains a date:

```
"3-22-2009"
```

The tokens in this string are 3, 22, and 2009, and the delimiter is the hyphen character. Perhaps a program needs to extract the month, day, and year from such a string. Another example is an operating system pathname, such as the following:

```
/home/rsullivan/data
```

The tokens in this string are `home`, `rsullivan`, and `data`, and the delimiter is the / character. Perhaps a program needs to extract all of the directory names from such a pathname.

The process of breaking a string into tokens is known as *tokenizing*. In this section we will discuss two of Java's tools for tokenizing strings: The `StringTokenizer` class, and the `String` class's `split` method.

The `StringTokenizer` Class

The Java API provides a class, `StringTokenizer`, which allows you to tokenize a string. The class is part of the `java.util` package, so you need the following import statement in any program that uses it:

```
import java.util.StringTokenizer;
```

When you create an instance of the `StringTokenizer` class, you pass a `String` as an argument to one of the constructors. The tokens will be extracted from this string. Table 10-11 summarizes the class's three constructors.

Table 10-11   The `StringTokenizer` constructors

Constructor	Description
`StringTokenizer(String str)`	The string to be tokenized is passed into `str`. Whitespace characters (space, tab, and newline) are used as delimiters.
`StringTokenizer(String str, String delimiters)`	The string to be tokenized is passed into `str`. The characters in `delimiters` will be used as delimiters.
`StringTokenizer(String str, String delimiters, Boolean returnDelimeters)`	The string to be tokenized is passed into `str`. The characters in `delimiters` will be used as delimiters. If the `returnDelimeters` parameter is set to `true`, the delimiters will be included as tokens. If this parameter is set to `false`, the delimiters will not be included as tokens.

The first constructor uses whitespace characters as delimiters. The following statement instantiates a `StringTokenizer` object and uses this constructor:

```
StringTokenizer strTokenizer = new StringTokenizer("2 4 6 8");
```

The second constructor accepts a second argument, which is a string containing one or more characters that are to be used as delimiters. The following statement creates an object using this constructor. It specifies that the - character is to be used as a delimiter.

```
StringTokenizer strTokenizer =
            new StringTokenizer("10-14-2009", "-");
```

The third constructor accepts a second argument, which is a string containing one or more characters that are to be used as delimiters, and a third argument, which indicates whether the delimiters should be included as tokens. The following statement creates an object using this constructor. It specifies that the - character is to be used as a delimiter and that the delimiters are to be included as tokens.

```
StringTokenizer strTokenizer =
            new StringTokenizer("10-14-2009", "-", true);
```

NOTE: The first two constructors do not include the delimiter characters as tokens.

Extracting Tokens

Once you have created a `StringTokenizer` object, you can use its methods to extract tokens from the string you passed to the constructor. Table 10-12 lists some of the `StringTokenizer` methods.

Table 10-12   Some of the `StringTokenizer` methods

Method	Description
`int countTokens()`	This method returns the number of tokens left in the string.
`boolean hasMoreTokens()`	This method returns `true` if there are more tokens left in the string. Otherwise it returns `false`.
`String nextToken()`	This method returns the next token found in the string.

The following code demonstrates how all of the tokens can be extracted from a `StringTokenizer` object. The loop executes as long as there are tokens left to extract.

```
StringTokenizer strTokenizer =
        new StringTokenizer("One Two Three");
while (strTokenizer.hasMoreTokens())
{
    System.out.println(strTokenizer.nextToken());
}
```

This code will produce the following output:

```
One
Two
Three
```

The `DateComponent` class in Code Listing 10-8 uses a `StringTokenizer` object. Its constructor accepts a string containing a date in the form MONTH/DAY/YEAR. It extracts the month, day, and year and stores these values in the `month`, `day`, and `year` fields. The methods `getMonth`, `getDay`, and `getYear` can then be used to retrieve the values. The program in Code Listing 10-9 demonstrates the class.

Code Listing 10-8   (`DateComponent.java`)

```
 1 import java.util.StringTokenizer;
 2
 3 /**
 4    The DateComponent class extracts the month,
 5    day, and year from a string containing a date.
 6 */
 7
 8 public class DateComponent
 9 {
10    private String month;    // To hold the month
11    private String day;      // To hold the day
12    private String year;     // To hold the year
13
14    /**
15        The constructor accepts a String containing a date
```

```
16          in the form MONTH/DAY/YEAR. It extracts the month,
17          day, and year from the string.
18          @param dateStr A String containing a date.
19      */
20
21      public DateComponent(String dateStr)
22      {
23          // Create a StringTokenizer object.
24          StringTokenizer strTokenizer =
25              new StringTokenizer(dateStr, "/");
26
27          // Extract the tokens.
28          month = strTokenizer.nextToken();
29          day = strTokenizer.nextToken();
30          year = strTokenizer.nextToken();
31      }
32
33      /**
34          getMonth method
35          @return The month field.
36      */
37
38      public String getMonth()
39      {
40          return month;
41      }
42
43      /**
44          getDay method
45          @return The day field.
46      */
47
48      public String getDay()
49      {
50          return day;
51      }
52
53      /**
54          getYear method
55          @return The year field.
56      */
57
58      public String getYear()
59      {
60          return year;
61      }
62 }
```

Code Listing 10-9 (`DateTester.java`)

```
1  /**
2     This program demonstrates the DateComponent class.
3  */
4
5  public class DateTester
6  {
7     public static void main(String[] args)
8     {
9        String date = "10/23/2009";
10       DateComponent dc =
11                    new DateComponent(date);
12
13       System.out.println("Here's the date: " +
14                    date);
15       System.out.println("The month is " +
16                    dc.getMonth());
17       System.out.println("The day is " +
18                    dc.getDay());
19       System.out.println("The year is " +
20                    dc.getYear());
21    }
22 }
```

Program Output

```
Here's the date: 10/23/2009
The month is 10
The day is 23
The year is 2009
```

Using Multiple Delimiters

Some situations require that you use multiple characters as delimiters in the same string. For example, look at the following email address:

joe@gaddisbooks.com

This string uses two delimiters: @ (the at symbol) and . (the period). To extract the tokens from this string we must specify both characters as delimiters to the constructor. Here is an example:

```
StringTokenizer strTokenizer =
        new StringTokenizer("joe@gaddisbooks.com", "@.");
while (strTokenizer.hasMoreTokens())
{
    System.out.println(strTokenizer.nextToken());
}
```

This code will produce the following output:

```
joe
gaddisbooks
com
```

Trimming a String before Tokenizing

When you are tokenizing a string that was entered by the user, and you are using characters other than whitespaces as delimiters, you will probably want to trim the string before tokenizing it. Otherwise, if the user enters leading whitespace characters, they will become part of the first token. Likewise, if the user enters trailing whitespace characters, they will become part of the last token. For example look at the following code:

```
// Create a string with leading and trailing whitespaces.
String str = "   one;two;three   ";
// Tokenize the string using the semicolon as a delimiter.
StringTokenizer strTokenizer = new StringTokenizer(str, ";");
// Display the tokens.
while (strTokenizer.hasMoreTokens())
{
    System.out.println("*" + strTokenizer.nextToken() + "*");
}
```

This code will produce the following output:

```
*   one*
*two*
*three   *
```

To prevent leading and/or trailing whitespace characters from being included in the first and last tokens, use the String class's trim method to remove them. Here is the same code, modified to use the trim method:

```
String str = "   one;two;three   ";
StringTokenizer strTokenizer =
                new StringTokenizer(str.trim(), ";");
while (strTokenizer.hasMoreTokens())
{
    System.out.println("*" + strTokenizer.nextToken() + "*");
}
```

This code will produce the following output:

```
*one*
*two*
*three*
```

The String Class's split Method

The String class has a method named split, which tokenizes a string and returns an array of String objects. Each element in the array is one of the tokens. The following code, which is taken from the program *SplitDemo1.java* on the Student CD, shows an example of the method's use:

```
// Create a String to tokenize.
String str = "one two three four";
// Get the tokens from the string.
String[] tokens = str.split(" ");
// Display each token.
for (String s : tokens)
    System.out.println(s);
```

The argument passed to the `split` method indicates the delimiter. In this example, a space is used as the delimiter. The code will produce the following output:

```
one
two
three
four
```

The argument that you pass to the split method is a *regular expression*. A regular expression is a string that specifies a pattern of characters. Regular expressions can be powerful tools, and are commonly used to search for patterns that exist in strings, files, or other collections of text. A complete discussion of regular expressions is outside the scope of this book. However, we will discuss some basic uses of regular expressions for the purpose of tokenizing strings.

In the previous example, we passed a string containing a single space to the `split` method. This specified that the space character was the delimiter. The `split` method also allows you to use multi-character delimiters. This means you are not limited to a single character as a delimiter. Your delimiters can be entire words, if you wish. The following code, which is taken from the program *SplitDemo2.java* on the Student CD, demonstrates:

```
// Create a string to tokenize.
String str = "one and two and three and four";
// Get the tokens, using " and " as the delimiter.
String[] tokens = str.split(" and ");
// Display the tokens.
for (String s : tokens)
    System.out.println(s);
```

This code will produce the following output:

```
one
two
three
four
```

The previous code demonstrates multi-character delimiters (delimiters containing multiple characters). You can also specify a series of characters where each individual character is a delimiter. In our discussion of the `StringTokenizer` class we used the following string as an example requiring multiple delimiters:

```
joe@gaddisbooks.com
```

This string uses two delimiters: @ (the "at" character) and . (the period). To specify that both the @ character and the . character are delimiters, we must enclose them in brackets inside our regular expression. The regular expression will look like this:

```
"[@.]"
```

Because the @ and . characters are enclosed in brackets, they will each be considered as a delimiter. The following code, which is taken from the program *SplitDemo3.java* on the Student CD, demonstrates:

```
// Create a string to tokenize.
String str = "joe@gaddisbooks.com";
// Get the tokens, using @ and . as delimiters.
String[] tokens = str.split("[@.]");
// Display the tokens.
for (String s : tokens)
   System.out.println(s);
```

This code will produce the following output:

```
joe
gaddisbooks
com
```

Checkpoint

10.25 The following string contains three tokens. What are they? What character is the delimiter?

```
"apples pears bananas"
```

10.26 Look at the following code:

```
StringTokenizer st = new StringTokenizer("one two three four");
int x = st.countTokens();
String stuff = st.nextToken();
```

What value will be stored in x? What value will the `stuff` variable reference?

10.27 Look at the following string:

```
"/home/rjones/mydata.txt"
```

a) Write the declaration of a `StringTokenizer` object that can be used to extract the following tokens from the string: `home`, `rjones`, `mydata`, and `txt`.

b) Write code using the `String` class's `split` method that can be used to extract the same tokens specified in part A.

10.28 Look at the following string:

```
"dog$cat@bird%squirrel"
```

Write code using the `String` class's `split` method that can be used to extract the following tokens from the string: `dog`, `cat`, `bird`, and `squirrel`.

Write the declaration of a `StringTokenizer` object that can be used to extract the same tokens from the string.

See the `SerialNumber` Class Case Study on the Student CD for another example using the `StringTokenizer` class.

10.6 Wrapper Classes for the Numeric Data Types

CONCEPT: The Java API provides wrapper classes for each of the numeric data types. These classes have methods that perform useful operations involving primitive numeric values.

Earlier in this chapter, we discussed the `Character` wrapper class and some of its static methods. The Java API also provides wrapper classes for all of the numeric primitive data types, as listed in Table 10-13.

You have already used many of these wrapper class's "parse" methods, which convert strings to values of the primitive types. For example, the `Integer.parseInt` method converts a string to an `int`, and the `Double.parseDouble` method converts a string to a `double`. Now we will examine other methods and uses of the wrapper classes.

Table 10-13   Wrapper classes for the numeric primitive data types

Wrapper Class	Primitive Type It Applies To
Byte	byte
Double	double
Float	float
Integer	int
Long	long
Short	short

The Static `toString` Methods

Each of the numeric wrapper classes has a static `toString` method that converts a number to a string. The method accepts the number as its argument and returns a string representation of that number. The following code demonstrates:

```
int i = 12;
double d = 14.95;
String str1 = Integer.toString(i);
String str2 = Double.toString(d);
```

The `toBinaryString`, `toHexString`, and `toOctalString` Methods

The `toBinaryString`, `toHexString`, and `toOctalString` methods are static members of the `Integer` and `Long` wrapper classes. These methods accept an integer as an argument and return a string representation of that number converted to binary, hexadecimal, or octal. The following code demonstrates these methods:

```
int number = 14;
System.out.println(Integer.toBinaryString(number));
System.out.println(Integer.toHexString(number));
System.out.println(Integer.toOctalString(number));
```

This code will produce the following output:

```
1110
e
16
```

The `MIN_VALUE` and `MAX_VALUE` Constants

The numeric wrapper classes each have a set of static `final` variables named `MIN_VALUE` and `MAX_VALUE`. These variables hold the minimum and maximum values for a particular data type. For example, `Integer.MAX_VALUE` holds the maximum value that an `int` can hold. For example, the following code displays the minimum and maximum values for an `int`:

```
System.out.println("The minimum value for an " +
                   "int is " + Integer.MIN_VALUE);
System.out.println("The maximum value for an " +
                   "int is " + Integer.MAX_VALUE);
```

Autoboxing and Unboxing

It is possible to create objects from the wrapper classes. One way is to pass an initial value to the constructor, as shown here:

```
Integer number = new Integer(7);
```

This creates an `Integer` object initialized with the value 7, referenced by the variable `number`. Another way is to simply declare a wrapper class variable, and then assign a primitive value to it. For example, look at the following code:

```
Integer number;
number = 7;
```

The first statement in this code declares an `Integer` variable named `number`. It does not create an `Integer` object, just a variable. The second statement is a simple assignment statement. It assigns the primitive value 7 to the variable. You might suspect that this will cause an error. After all, `number` is a reference variable, not a primitive variable. However, because `number` is a wrapper class variable, Java performs an autoboxing operation. *Autoboxing* is Java's process of automatically "boxing up" a value inside an object. When this assignment statement executes, Java boxes up the value 7 inside an `Integer` object, and then assigns the address of that object to the `number` variable.

Unboxing is the opposite of boxing. It is the process of converting a wrapper class object to a primitive type. The following code demonstrates an unboxing operation:

```
Integer myInt = 5;          // Autoboxes the value 5
int primitiveNumber;
primitiveNumber = myInt;    // Unboxes the object
```

The first statement in this code declares myInt as an Integer reference variable. The primitive value 5 is autoboxed, and the address of the resulting object is assigned to the myInt variable. The second statement declares primitiveNumber as an int variable. Then, the third statement assigns the myInt object to primitiveNumber. When this statement executes, Java automatically unboxes the myInt wrapper class object and stores the resulting value, which is 5, in primitiveNumber.

Although you rarely need to create an instance of a wrapper class, Java's autoboxing and unboxing features make some operations more convenient. Occasionally, you will find yourself in a situation where you want to perform an operation using a primitive variable, but the operation can only be used with an object. For example, recall the ArrayList class that we discussed in Chapter 8. An ArrayList is an array-like object that can be used to store other objects. You cannot, however, store primitive values in an ArrayList. It is intended for objects only. If you try to compile the following statement, an error will occur:

```java
ArrayList<int> list = new ArrayList<int>();   // ERROR!
```

However, you can store wrapper class objects in an ArrayList. If we need to store int values in an ArrayList, we have to specify that the ArrayList will hold Integer objects. Here is an example:

```java
ArrayList<Integer> list = new ArrayList<Integer>(); // Okay.
```

This statement declares that list references an ArrayList that can hold Integer objects. One way to store an int value in the ArrayList is to instantiate an Integer object, initialize it with the desired int value, and then pass the Integer object to the ArrayList's add method. Here is an example:

```java
ArrayList<Integer> list = new ArrayList<Integer>();
Integer myInt = 5;
list.add(myInt);
```

However, Java's autoboxing and unboxing features make it unnecessary to create the Integer object. If you add an int value to the ArrayList, Java will autobox the value. The following code works without any problems:

```java
ArrayList<Integer> list = new ArrayList<Integer>();
list.add(5);
```

When the value 5 is passed to the add method, Java boxes the value up in an Integer object. When necessary, Java also unboxes values that are retrieved from the ArrayList. The following code demonstrates this:

```java
ArrayList<Integer> list = new ArrayList<Integer>();
list.add(5);
int primitiveNumber = list.get(0);
```

The last statement in this code retrieves the item at index 0. Because the item is being assigned to an int variable, Java unboxes it and stores the primitive value in the int variable.

Checkpoint

10.29 Write a statement that converts the following integer to a string and stores it in the String object referenced by `str`:

```
int i = 99;
```

10.30 What wrapper class methods convert a number from decimal to another numbering system? What wrapper classes are these methods a member of?

10.31 What is the purpose of the MIN_VALUE and MAX_VALUE variables that are members of the numeric wrapper classes?

10.7 Focus on Problem Solving: The TestScoreReader Class

Professor Harrison keeps her students' test scores in a Microsoft Excel spreadsheet. Figure 10-8 shows a set of five test scores for five students. Each column holds a test score and each row represents the scores for one student.

Figure 10-8   Microsoft Excel spreadsheet

	A	B	C	D	E	F
1	87	79	91	82	94	
2	72	79	81	74	88	
3	94	92	81	89	96	
4	77	56	67	81	79	
5	79	82	85	81	90	
6						

In addition to manipulating the scores in Excel, Dr. Harrison wants to write a Java application that accesses them. Excel, like many commercial applications, has the ability to export data to a text file. When the data in a spreadsheet is exported, each row is written to a line, and the values in the cells are separated by commas. For example, when the data shown in Figure 10-8 is exported, it will be written to a text file in the following format:

```
87,79,91,82,94
72,79,81,74,88
94,92,81,89,96
77,56,67,81,79
79,82,85,81,90
```

This is called the *comma separated value* file format. When you save a spreadsheet in this format, Excel saves it to a file with the *.csv* extension. Dr. Harrison decides to export her spreadsheet to a *.csv* file, and then write a Java program that reads the file. The program will use the `String` class's `split` method to extract the test scores from each line, and a wrapper class to convert the tokens to numeric values. As an experiment, she writes the `TestScoreReader` class shown in Code Listing 10-10.

Code Listing 10-10 (`TestScoreReader.java`)

```java
 1 import java.io.*;
 2 import java.util.Scanner;
 3
 4 /**
 5    The TestScoreReader class reads test scores as
 6    tokens from a file and calculates the average
 7    of each line of scores.
 8 */
 9
10 public class TestScoreReader
11 {
12    private Scanner inputFile;
13    private String line;
14
15    /**
16       The constructor opens a file to read
17       the grades from.
18       @param filename The file to open.
19    */
20
21    public TestScoreReader(String filename)
22                        throws IOException
23    {
24       File file = new File(filename);
25       inputFile = new Scanner(file);
26    }
27
28    /**
29       The readNextLine method reads the next line
30       from the file.
31       @return true if the line was read, false
32       otherwise.
33    */
34
35    public boolean readNextLine() throws IOException
36    {
37       boolean lineRead; // Flag variable
38
39       // Determine whether there is more to read.
40       lineRead = inputFile.hasNext();
41
42       // If so, read the next line.
43       if (lineRead)
44          line = inputFile.nextLine();
45
```

```
46          return lineRead;
47      }
48
49      /**
50          The getAverage method calculates the average
51          of the last set of test scores read from the file.
52          @return The average.
53      */
54
55      public double getAverage()
56      {
57          int total = 0;      // Accumulator
58          double average;     // The average test score
59
60          // Tokenize the last line read from the file.
61          String[] tokens = line.split(",");
62
63          // Calculate the total of the test scores.
64          for (String str : tokens)
65          {
66              total += Integer.parseInt(str);
67          }
68
69          // Calculate the average of the scores.
70          // Use a cast to avoid integer division.
71          average = (double) total / tokens.length;
72
73          // Return the average.
74          return average;
75      }
76
77      /**
78          The close method closes the file.
79      */
80
81      public void close() throws IOException
82      {
83          inputFile.close();
84      }
85 }
```

The constructor accepts the name of a file as an argument and opens the file. The readNextLine method reads a line from the file and stores it in the line field. The method returns true if a line was successfully read from the file, or false if there are no more lines to read. The getAverage method tokenizes the last line read from the file, converts the tokens to int values, and calculates the average of the values. The average is returned. The program in Code Listing 10-11 uses the `TestScoreReader` class to open the file *Grades.csv* and get the averages of the test scores it contains.

Code Listing 10-11 (`TestAverages.java`)

```java
 1 import java.io.*;   // Needed for IOException
 2
 3 /**
 4    This program uses the TestScoreReader class
 5    to read test scores from a file and get
 6    their averages.
 7 */
 8
 9 public class TestAverages
10 {
11    public static void main(String[] args)
12                          throws IOException
13    {
14       double average;         // Test average
15       int studentNumber = 1;  // Control variable
16
17       // Create a TestScoreReader object.
18       TestScoreReader scoreReader =
19                new TestScoreReader("Grades.csv");
20
21       // Display the averages.
22       while (scoreReader.readNextLine())
23       {
24          // Get the average from the TestScoreReader.
25          average = scoreReader.getAverage();
26
27          // Display the student's average.
28          System.out.println("Average for student " +
29                           studentNumber + " is " +
30                           average);
31
32          // Increment the student number.
33          studentNumber++;
34       }
35
36       // Close the TestScoreReader.
37       scoreReader.close();
38       System.out.println("No more scores.");
39    }
40 }
```

Program Output

```
Average for student 1 is 86.6
Average for student 2 is 78.8
Average for student 3 is 90.4
Average for student 4 is 72.0
Average for student 5 is 83.4
No more scores.
```

Dr. Harrison's class works properly, and she decides that she can expand it to perform other, more complex, operations.

10.8 Common Errors to Avoid

The following list describes several errors that are commonly committed when learning this chapter's topics:

- **Using static wrapper class methods as if they were instance methods.** Many of the most useful wrapper class methods are static, and you should call them directly from the class.
- **Trying to use `String` comparison methods such as `startsWith` and `endsWith` for case-insensitive comparisons.** Most of the `String` comparison methods are case-sensitive. Only the `regionMatches` method performs a case-insensitive comparison.
- **Thinking of the first position of a string as 1.** Many of the `String` and `StringBuilder` methods accept a character position within a string as an argument. Remember, the position numbers in a string start at zero. If you think of the first position in a string as 1, you will cause an off-by-one error.
- **Thinking of the ending position of a substring as part of the substring.** Methods such as `getChars` accept the starting and ending position of a substring as arguments. The character at the *start* position is included in the substring, but the character at the *end* position is not included. (The last character in the substring ends at *end* – 1.)
- **Extracting more tokens from a `StringTokenizer` object than exist.** Trying to extract more tokens from a `StringTokenizer` object than exist will cause an error. You can use the `countTokens` method to determine the number of tokens and the `hasMoreTokens` method to determine whether there are any more unread tokens.

Review Questions and Exercises

Multiple Choice and True/False

1. The `isDigit`, `isLetter`, and `isLetterOrDigit` methods are members of this class.
   a. `String`
   b. `Char`
   c. `Character`
   d. `StringBuilder`

2. This method converts a character to uppercase.
   a. `makeUpperCase`
   b. `toUpperCase`
   c. `isUpperCase`
   d. `upperCase`

3. The `startsWith`, `endsWith`, and `regionMatches` methods are members of this class.
   a. `String`
   b. `Char`
   c. `Character`
   d. `StringTokenizer`

4. The `indexOf` and `lastIndexOf` methods are members of this class.
   a. `String`
   b. `Integer`
   c. `Character`
   d. `StringTokenizer`

5. The `substring`, `getChars`, and `toCharArray` methods are members of this class.
   a. `String`
   b. `Float`
   c. `Character`
   d. `StringTokenizer`

6. This `String` class method performs the same operation as the + operator when used on strings.
   a. `add`
   b. `join`
   c. `concat`
   d. `plus`

7. The `String` class has several overloaded versions of a method that accepts a value of any primitive data type as its argument and returns a string representation of the value. The name of the method is _____.
   a. `stringValue`
   b. `valueOf`
   c. `getString`
   d. `valToString`

8. If you do not pass an argument to the `StringBuilder` constructor, the object will have enough memory to store this many characters.
   a. 16
   b. 1
   c. 256
   d. Unlimited

9. This is one of the methods that are common to both the `String` and `StringBuilder` classes.
   a. `append`
   b. `insert`
   c. `delete`
   d. `length`

10. To change the value of a specific character in a `StringBuilder` object, use this method.
    a. `changeCharAt`
    b. `setCharAt`
    c. `setChar`
    d. `change`

11. To delete a specific character in a `StringBuilder` object, use this method.
    a. `deleteCharAt`
    b. `removeCharAt`
    c. `removeChar`
    d. `expunge`

12. The character that separates tokens in a string is known as a _____.
    a. separator
    b. tokenizer
    c. delimiter
    d. terminator

13. This `StringTokenizer` method returns `true` if there are more tokens to be extracted from a string.
    a. `moreTokens`
    b. `tokensLeft`
    c. `getToken`
    d. `hasMoreTokens`

14. These static `final` variables are members of the numeric wrapper classes and hold the minimum and maximum values for a particular data type.
    a. `MIN_VALUE` and `MAX_VALUE`
    b. `MIN` and `MAX`
    c. `MINIMUM` and `MAXIMUM`
    d. `LOWEST` and `HIGHEST`

15. **True or False:** Character testing methods, such as `isLetter`, accept strings as arguments and test each character in the string.

16. **True or False:** If the `toUpperCase` method's argument is already uppercase, it is returned as is, with no changes.

17. **True or False:** If `toLowerCase` method's argument is already lowercase, it will be inadvertently converted to uppercase.

18. **True or False:** The `startsWith` and `endsWith` methods are case-sensitive.

19. **True or False:** There are two versions of the `regionMatches` method: one that is case-sensitive and one that can be case-insensitive.

20. **True or False:** The `indexOf` and `lastIndexOf` methods can find characters, but cannot find substrings.

21. **True or False:** The `String` class's `replace` method can replace individual characters, but cannot replace substrings.

22. **True or False:** The `StringBuilder` class's `replace` method can replace individual characters, but cannot replace substrings.

23. **True or False:** You can use the = operator to assign a string to a `StringBuilder` object.

Find the Error

Find the error in each of the following code segments:

1.
```
int number = 99;
String str;
// Convert number to a string.
str.valueOf(number);
```

2.
```
// Store a name in a StringBuilder object.
StringBuilder name = "Joe Schmoe";
```

3.
```
// Change the very first character of a
// StringBuilder object to 'Z'.
str.setCharAt(1, 'Z');
```

4.
```
// Tokenize a string that is delimited
// with semicolons. The string has 3 tokens.
StringTokenizer strTokenizer =
        new StringTokenizer("One;Two;Three");
// Extract the three tokens from the string.
while (strTokenizer.hasMoreTokens())
{
    System.out.println(strTokenizer.nextToken());
}
```

Algorithm Workbench

1. The following `if` statement determines whether choice is equal to 'Y' or 'y':

   ```
   if (choice == 'Y' || choice == 'y')
   ```

   Rewrite this statement so it only makes one comparison and does not use the || operator. (*Hint: Use either the `toUpperCase` or `toLowerCase` methods.*)

2. Write a loop that counts the number of space characters that appear in the `String` object str.

3. Write a loop that counts the number of digits that appear in the `String` object `str`.

4. Write a loop that counts the number of lowercase characters that appear in the `String` object `str`.

5. Write a method that accepts a reference to a `String` object as an argument and returns `true` if the argument ends with the substring ".com". Otherwise, the method should return `false`.

6. Modify the method you wrote for Algorithm Workbench 5 so it performs a case-insensitive test. The method should return true if the argument ends with ".com" in any possible combination of uppercase and lowercase letters.

7. Write a method that accepts a `StringBuilder` object as an argument and converts all occurrences of the lowercase letter 't' in the object to uppercase.

8. Look at the following string:

   `"cookies>milk>fudge:cake:ice cream"`

   a. Write code using a `StringTokenizer` object that extracts the following tokens from the string and displays them: `cookies`, `milk`, `fudge`, `cake`, and `ice cream`.
   b. Write code using the `String` class's `split` method that extracts the same tokens as the code you wrote for part a.

9. Assume that `d` is a `double` variable. Write an `if` statement that assigns `d` to the `int` variable `i` if the value in `d` is not larger than the maximum value for an `int`.

10. Write code that displays the contents of the `int` variable `i` in binary, hexadecimal, and octal.

Short Answer

1. Why should you use `StringBuilder` objects instead of `String` objects in a program that makes lots of changes to strings?

2. A program reads a string as input from the user for the purpose of tokenizing it. Why is it a good idea to trim the string before tokenizing it?

3. Each of the numeric wrapper classes has a static `toString` method. What do these methods do?

4. How can you determine the minimum and maximum values that may be stored in a variable of a given data type?

Programming Challenges

⟨⟩ myCodeMate   ### 1. Backward String

Write a method that accepts a `String` object as an argument and displays its contents backward. For instance, if the string argument is "gravity" the method should display "ytivarg". Demonstrate the method in a program that asks the user to input a string and then passes it to the method.

2. Word Counter

Write a method that accepts a `String` object as an argument and returns the number of words it contains. For instance, if the argument is "Four score and seven years ago" the method should return the number 6. Demonstrate the method in a program that asks the user to input a string and then passes it to the method. The number of words in the string should be displayed on the screen.

3. Sentence Capitalizer

VideoNote
The Sentence
Capitalizer
Problem

Write a method that accepts a `String` object as an argument and returns a copy of the string with the first character of each sentence capitalized. For instance, if the argument is "hello. my name is Joe. what is your name?" the method should return the string "Hello. My name is Joe. What is your name?" Demonstrate the method in a program that asks the user to input a string and then passes it to the method. The modified string should be displayed on the screen.

4. Vowels and Consonants

Write a class with a constructor that accepts a `String` object as its argument. The class should have a method that returns the number of vowels in the string, and another method that returns the number of consonants in the string. Demonstrate the class in a program that performs the following steps:

1. The user is asked to enter a string.
2. The program displays the following menu:
   a. Count the number of vowels in the string
   b. Count the number of consonants in the string
   c. Count both the vowels and consonants in the string
   d. Enter another string
   e. Exit the program
3. The program performs the operation selected by the user and repeats until the user selects e, to exit the program.

5. Password Verifier

Imagine you are developing a software package for Amazon.com that requires users to enter their own passwords. Your software requires that users' passwords meet the following criteria:

- The password should be at least six characters long.
- The password should contain at least one uppercase and at least one lowercase letter.
- The password should have at least one digit.

Write a class that verifies that a password meets the stated criteria. Demonstrate the class in a program that allows the user to enter a password and then displays a message indicating whether it is valid or not.

6. Telemarketing Phone Number List

Write a program that has two parallel arrays of `String` objects. One of the arrays should hold people's names and the other should hold their phone numbers. Here are example contents of both arrays:

name Array Example Contents	phone Array Example Contents
"Harrison, Rose"	"555-2234"
"James, Jean"	"555-9098"
"Smith, William"	"555-1785"
"Smith, Brad"	"555-9224"

The program should ask the user to enter a name or the first few characters of a name to search for in the array. The program should display all of the names that match the user's input and their corresponding phone numbers. For example, if the user enters "Smith," the program should display the following names and phone numbers from the list:

```
Smith, William: 555-1785
Smith, Brad: 555-9224
```

7. Check Writer

Write a program that displays a simulated paycheck. The program should ask the user to enter the date, the payee's name, and the amount of the check. It should then display a simulated check with the dollar amount spelled out, as shown here:

	Date: 11/24/2007
Pay to the Order of: John Phillips	$1920.85
One thousand nine hundred twenty and 85 cents	

 myCodeMate

8. Sum of Numbers in a String

Write a program that asks the user to enter a series of numbers separated by commas. Here is an example of valid input:

```
7,9,10,2,18,6
```

The program should calculate and display the sum of all the numbers.

9. Sum of Digits in a String

Write a program that asks the user to enter a series of single digit numbers with nothing separating them. The program should display the sum of all the single digit numbers in the string. For example, if the user enters 2514, the method should return 12, which is the sum of 2, 5, 1, and 4. The program should also display the highest and lowest digits in the string. (*Hint: Convert the string to an array.*)

10. Word Counter

Write a program that asks the user for the name of a file. The program should display the number of words that the file contains.

11. Sales Analysis

The file *SalesData.txt* on the Student CD contains the dollar amount of sales that a retail store made each day for a number of weeks. Each line in the file contains seven numbers, which are the sales numbers for one week. The numbers are separated by a comma. The following line is an example from the file:

```
2541.36,2965.88,1965.32,1845.23,7021.11,9652.74,1469.36
```

Write a program that opens the file and processes its contents. The program should display the following:

- The total sales for each week
- The average daily sales for each week
- The total sales for all of the weeks
- The average weekly sales
- The week number that had the highest amount of sales
- The week number that had the lowest amount of sales

12. Miscellaneous String Operations

Write a class with the following static methods:

- **WordCount.** This method should accept a reference to a `String` object as an argument and return the number of words contained in the object.
- **arrayToString.** This method accepts a `char` array as an argument and converts it to a `String` object. The method should return a reference to the `String` object.
- **mostFrequent.** This method accepts a reference to a `String` object as an argument and returns the character that occurs the most frequently in the object.
- **replaceSubstring.** This method accepts three references to `String` objects as arguments. Let's call them `string1`, `string2`, and `string3`. It searches `string1` for all occurrences of `string2`. When it finds an occurrence of `string2`, it replaces it with `string3`. For example, suppose the three arguments have the following values:

      string1:   "the dog jumped over the fence"
      string2:   "the"
      string3:   "that"

With these three arguments, the method would return a reference to a `String` object with the value "that dog jumped over that fence".

Demonstrate each of these methods in a complete program.

13. Alphabetic Telephone Number Translator

Many companies use telephone numbers like 555-GET-FOOD so the number is easier for their customers to remember. On a standard telephone, the alphabetic letters are mapped to numbers in the following fashion:

      A, B, and C = 2
      D, E, and F = 3
      G, H, and I = 4
      J, K, and L = 5
      M, N, and O = 6
      P, Q, R, and S = 7
      T, U, and V = 8
      W, X, Y, and Z = 9

Write an application that asks the user to enter a 10-character telephone number in the format XXX-XXX-XXXX. The application should display the telephone number with any alphabetic characters that appeared in the original translated to their numeric equivalent. For example, if the user enters 555-GET-FOOD the application should display 555-438-3663.

14. Word Separator

Write a program that accepts as input a sentence in which all of the words are run together, but the first character of each word is uppercase. Convert the sentence to a string in which the words are separated by spaces and only the first word starts with an uppercase letter. For example, the string "StopAndSmellTheRoses." would be converted to "Stop and smell the roses."

15. Pig Latin

Write a program that reads a sentence as input and converts each word to "Pig Latin". In one version of Pig Latin, you convert a word by removing the first letter, placing that letter at the end of the word, and then appending "ay" to the word. Here is an example:

English: I SLEPT MOST OF THE NIGHT

Pig Latin: IAY LEPTSAY OSTMAY FOAY HETAY IGHTNAY

16. Morse Code Converter

Morse code is a code where each letter of the English alphabet, each digit, and various punctuation characters are represented by a series of dots and dashes. Table 10-14 shows part of the code. Write a program that asks the user to enter a string, and then converts that string to Morse code. Use hyphens for dashes and periods for dots.

Table 10-14   Morse code

Character	Code	Character	Code	Character	Code	Character	Code
space	*space*	6	-....	G	--.	Q	--.-
comma	--..--	7	--...	H	....	R	.-.
period	.-.-.-	8	---..	I	..	S	...
question mark	..--..	9	----.	J	.---	T	-
0	-----	A	.-	K	-.-	U	..-
1	.----	B	-...	L	.-..	V	...-
2	..---	C	-.-.	M	--	W	.--
3	...--	D	-..	N	-.	X	-..-
4	....-	E	.	O	---	Y	-.--
5	.....	F	..-.	P	.--.	Z	--..

11 Inheritance

CHAPTER

TOPICS

11.1 What Is Inheritance?

CONCEPT: Inheritance allows a new class to extend an existing class. The new class inherits the members of the class it extends.

Generalization and Specialization

VideoNote
Inheritance

In the real world you can find many objects that are specialized versions of other more general objects. For example, the term "insect" describes a very general type of creature with numerous characteristics. Because grasshoppers and bumblebees are insects, they have all the general characteristics of an insect. In addition, they have special characteristics of their own. For example, the grasshopper has its jumping ability, and the bumblebee has its stinger. Grasshoppers and bumblebees are specialized versions of an insect. This is illustrated in Figure 11-1.

Figure 11-1 Bumblebees and grasshoppers are specialized versions of an insect

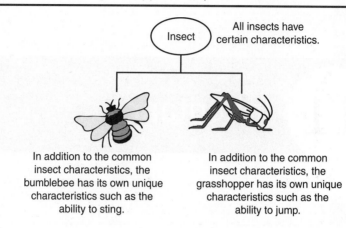

All insects have certain characteristics.

In addition to the common insect characteristics, the bumblebee has its own unique characteristics such as the ability to sting.

In addition to the common insect characteristics, the grasshopper has its own unique characteristics such as the ability to jump.

Inheritance and the "Is a" Relationship

When one object is a specialized version of another object, there is an "is a" relationship between them. For example, a grasshopper is an insect. Here are a few other examples of the "is a" relationship:

- A poodle is a dog.
- A car is a vehicle.
- A flower is a plant.
- A rectangle is a shape.
- A football player is an athlete.

When an "is a" relationship exists between objects, it means that the specialized object has all of the characteristics of the general object, plus additional characteristics that make it special. In object-oriented programming, inheritance is used to create an "is a" relationship among classes. This allows you to extend the capabilities of a class by creating another class that is a specialized version of it.

Inheritance involves a superclass and a subclass. The *superclass* is the general class and the *subclass* is the specialized class. You can think of the subclass as an extended version of the superclass. The subclass inherits fields and methods from the superclass without any of them having to be rewritten. Furthermore, new fields and methods may be added to the subclass, and that is what makes it a specialized version of the superclass.

In Chapter 7 you were introduced to the concept of inheritance and how it is used in developing a GUI application. Recall that you created classes that were extended versions of the JFrame class. In those applications, JFrame was the superclass and your specialized class was the subclass.

NOTE: At the risk of confusing you with too much terminology, it should be mentioned that superclasses are also called *base classes*, and subclasses are also called *derived classes*. Either set of terms is correct. For consistency, this text will use the terms superclass and subclass.

Let's look at an example of how inheritance can be used. Most teachers assign various graded activities for their students to complete. A graded activity can be given a numeric score such as 70, 85, 90, and so on, and a letter grade such as A, B, C, D, or F. Figure 11-2 shows a UML diagram for the GradedActivity class, which is designed to hold the numeric score of a graded activity. The setScore method sets a numeric score, and the getScore method returns the numeric score. The getGrade method returns the letter grade that corresponds to the numeric score. Notice that the class does not have a programmer-defined constructor, so Java will automatically generate a default constructor for it. This will be a point of discussion later. Code Listing 11-1 shows the code for the class.

Figure 11-2   UML diagram for the GradedActivity class

```
┌─────────────────────────────────┐
│         GradedActivity          │
├─────────────────────────────────┤
│ − score : double                │
├─────────────────────────────────┤
│ + setScore(s : double) : void   │
│ + getScore() : double           │
│ + getGrade() : char             │
└─────────────────────────────────┘
```

Code Listing 11-1   (`GradedActivity.java`)

```java
1   /**
2       A class that holds a grade for a graded activity.
3   */
4
5   public class GradedActivity
6   {
7       private double score;   // Numeric score
8
9       /**
10          The setScore method sets the score field.
11          @param s The value to store in score.
12      */
13
14      public void setScore(double s)
15      {
16          score = s;
17      }
18
19      /**
20          The getScore method returns the score.
21          @return The value stored in the score field.
22      */
23
```

```
24      public double getScore()
25      {
26         return score;
27      }
28
29      /**
30         The getGrade method returns a letter grade
31         determined from the score field.
32         @return The letter grade.
33      */
34
35      public char getGrade()
36      {
37         char letterGrade;
38
39         if (score >= 90)
40            letterGrade = 'A';
41         else if (score >= 80)
42            letterGrade = 'B';
43         else if (score >= 70)
44            letterGrade = 'C';
45         else if (score >= 60)
46            letterGrade = 'D';
47         else
48            letterGrade = 'F';
49
50         return letterGrade;
51      }
52 }
```

The program in Code Listing 11-2 demonstrates the class. Figures 11-3 and 11-4 show examples of interaction with the program.

Code Listing 11-2 (GradeDemo.java)

```
1 import javax.swing.JOptionPane;
2
3 /**
4    This program demonstrates the GradedActivity
5    class.
6 */
7
8 public class GradeDemo
9 {
10    public static void main(String[] args)
11    {
```

```
12          String input;        // To hold input
13          double testScore;    // A test score
14
15          // Create a GradedActivity object.
16          GradedActivity grade = new GradedActivity();
17
18          // Get a test score.
19          input = JOptionPane.showInputDialog("Enter " +
20                          "a numeric test score.");
21          testScore = Double.parseDouble(input);
22
23          // Store the score in the grade object.
24          grade.setScore(testScore);
25
26          // Display the letter grade for the score.
27          JOptionPane.showMessageDialog(null,
28                      "The grade for that test is " +
29                      grade.getGrade());
30
31          System.exit(0);
32      }
33 }
```

Figure 11-3 Interaction with the `GradeDemo.java` program

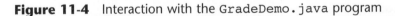

Figure 11-4 Interaction with the `GradeDemo.java` program

The `GradedActivity` class represents the general characteristics of a student's graded activity. Many different types of graded activities exist, however, such as quizzes, midterm exams, final exams, lab reports, essays, and so on. Because the numeric scores might be determined differently for each of these graded activities, we can create subclasses to handle each one. For example, we could create a `FinalExam` class that would be a subclass of the `GradedActivity` class. Figure 11-5 shows the UML diagram for such a class, and Code Listing 11-3 shows its code. It has fields for the number of questions on the exam (`numQuestions`), the number of points each question is worth (`pointsEach`), and the number of questions missed by the student (`numMissed`).

Figure 11-5 UML diagram for the `FinalExam` class

FinalExam
– numQuestions : int
– pointsEach : double
– numMissed : int
+ FinalExam(questions : int,
missed : int)
+ getPointsEach() : double
+ getNumMissed() : int

Code Listing 11-3 (`FinalExam.java`)

```
1  /**
2      This class determines the grade for a final exam.
3  */
4
5  public class FinalExam extends GradedActivity
6  {
7      private int numQuestions;       // Number of questions
8      private double pointsEach;      // Points for each question
9      private int numMissed;          // Questions missed
10
11     /**
12         The constructor sets the number of questions on the
13         exam and the number of questions missed.
14         @param questions The number of questions.
15         @param missed The number of questions missed.
16     */
17
18     public FinalExam(int questions, int missed)
19     {
20         double numericScore;        // To hold a numeric score
21
22         // Set the numQuestions and numMissed fields.
23         numQuestions = questions;
24         numMissed = missed;
25
26         // Calculate the points for each question and
```

```
27             // the numeric score for this exam.
28             pointsEach = 100.0 / questions;
29             numericScore = 100.0 - (missed * pointsEach);
30
31             // Call the inherited setScore method to
32             // set the numeric score.
33             setScore(numericScore);
34          }
35
36          /**
37             The getPointsEach method returns the number of
38             points each question is worth.
39             @return The value in the pointsEach field.
40          */
41
42          public double getPointsEach()
43          {
44             return pointsEach;
45          }
46
47          /**
48             The getNumMissed method returns the number of
49             questions missed.
50             @return The value in the numMissed field.
51          */
52
53          public int getNumMissed()
54          {
55             return numMissed;
56          }
57 }
```

Look at the header for the FinalExam class in line 5. The header uses the extends key word, which indicates that this class extends another class (a superclass). The name of the superclass is listed after the word extends. So, this line indicates that FinalExam is the name of the class being declared and GradedActivity is the name of the superclass it extends. This is illustrated in Figure 11-6.

Figure 11-6 FinalExam class header

If we want to express the relationship between the two classes, we can say that a FinalExam is a GradedActivity.

Because the FinalExam class extends the GradedActivity class, it inherits all of the public members of the GradedActivity class. Here is a list of the members of the FinalExam class.

Fields:

int numQuestions;	Declared in FinalExam
double pointsEach;	Declared in FinalExam
int numMissed;	Declared in FinalExam

Methods:

Constructor	Declared in FinalExam
getPointsEach	Declared in FinalExam
getNumMissed	Declared in FinalExam
setScore	Inherited from GradedActivity
getScore	Inherited from GradedActivity
getGrade	Inherited from GradedActivity

Notice that the GradedActivity class's score field is not listed among the members of the FinalExam class. That is because the score field is private. Private members of the superclass cannot be accessed by the subclass, so technically speaking, they are not inherited. When an object of the subclass is created, the private members of the superclass exist in memory, but only methods in the superclass can access them. They are truly private to the superclass.

You will also notice that the superclass's constructor is not listed among the members of the FinalExam class. It makes sense that superclass constructors are not inherited because their purpose is to construct objects of the superclass. In the next section we discuss in more detail how superclass constructors operate.

To see how inheritance works in this example, let's take a closer look at the FinalExam constructor in lines 18 through 34. The constructor accepts two arguments: the number of test questions on the exam, and the number of questions missed by the student. In lines 23 and 24 these values are assigned to the numQuestions and numMissed fields. Then, in lines 28 and 29, the number of points for each question and the numeric test score are calculated. In line 33, the last statement in the constructor reads as follows:

```
setScore(numericScore);
```

This is a call to the setScore method. Although no setScore method appears in the FinalExam class, the method is inherited from the GradedActivity class. The program in Code Listing 11-4 demonstrates the FinalExam class. Figure 11-7 shows an example of interaction with the program.

Code Listing 11-4 (`FinalExamDemo.java`)

```java
 1 import javax.swing.JOptionPane;
 2
 3 /**
 4    This program demonstrates the FinalExam class,
 5    which extends the GradedActivity class.
 6 */
 7
 8 public class FinalExamDemo
 9 {
10    public static void main(String[] args)
11    {
12       String input;         // To hold input
13       int questions;        // Number of questions
14       int missed;           // Number of questions missed
15
16       // Get the number of questions on the exam.
17       input = JOptionPane.showInputDialog("How many " +
18                     "questions are on the final exam?");
19       questions = Integer.parseInt(input);
20
21       // Get the number of questions the student missed.
22       input = JOptionPane.showInputDialog("How many " +
23                     "questions did the student miss?");
24       missed = Integer.parseInt(input);
25
26       // Create a FinalExam object.
27       FinalExam exam = new FinalExam(questions, missed);
28
29       // Display the test results.
30       JOptionPane.showMessageDialog(null,
31             "Each question counts " + exam.getPointsEach() +
32             " points.\nThe exam score is " +
33             exam.getScore() + "\nThe exam grade is " +
34             exam.getGrade());
35
36       System.exit(0);
37    }
38 }
```

Figure 11-7   Interaction with the `FinalExamDemo.java` program

1

Input

? How many questions are on the final exam?
20

OK   Cancel

2

Input

? How many questions did the student miss?
3

OK   Cancel

3

Message

Each question counts 5.0 points.
The exam score is 85.0
The exam grade is B

OK

In line 27 the following statement creates an instance of the `FinalExam` class and assigns its address to the `exam` variable:

```
FinalExam exam = new FinalExam(questions, missed);
```

When a `FinalExam` object is created in memory, it not only has the members declared in the `FinalExam` class, but also the non-private members declared in the `GradedActivity` class. Notice in lines 30 through 34, shown here, that two public methods of the `GradedActivity` class, `getScore` and `getGrade`, are directly called from the `exam` object:

```
JOptionPane.showMessageDialog(null,
    "Each question counts " + exam.getPointsEach() +
    " points.\nThe exam score is " +
    exam.getScore() + "\nThe exam grade is " +
    exam.getGrade());
```

When a subclass extends a superclass, the public members of the superclass become public members of the subclass. In this program the `getScore` and `getGrade` methods can be called from the `exam` object because they are public members of the object's superclass.

As mentioned before, the private members of the superclass (in this case, the `score` field) cannot be accessed by the subclass. When the `exam` object is created in memory, a `score` field exists, but only the methods defined in the superclass, `GradedActivity`, can access it. It is truly private to the superclass. Because the `FinalExam` constructor cannot directly access the `score` field, it must call the superclass's `setScore` method (which is public) to store a value in it.

Inheritance in UML Diagrams

You show inheritance in a UML diagram by connecting two classes with a line that has an open arrowhead at one end. The arrowhead points to the superclass. Figure 11-8 is a UML diagram showing the relationship between the `GradedActivity` and `FinalExam` classes.

Figure 11-8 UML diagram showing inheritance

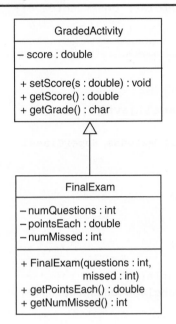

The Superclass's Constructor

You might be wondering how the constructors work together when one class inherits from another. In an inheritance relationship, the superclass constructor always executes before the subclass constructor. As was mentioned earlier, the GradedActivity class has only one constructor, which is the default constructor that Java automatically generated for it. When a FinalExam object is created, the GradedActivity class's default constructor is executed just before the FinalExam constructor is executed.

Code Listing 11-5 shows a class, SuperClass1, that has a no-arg constructor. The constructor simply displays the message "This is the superclass constructor." Code Listing 11-6 shows SubClass1, which extends SuperClass1. This class also has a no-arg constructor, which displays the message "This is the subclass constructor."

Code Listing 11-5 (SuperClass1.java)

```
1   public class SuperClass1
2   {
3       /**
4           Constructor
5       */
6
7       public SuperClass1()
8       {
```

```
 9              System.out.println("This is the " +
10                      "superclass constructor.");
11      }
12  }
```

Code Listing 11-6 (`SubClass1.java`)

```
 1  public class SubClass1 extends SuperClass1
 2  {
 3      /**
 4          Constructor
 5      */
 6
 7      public SubClass1()
 8      {
 9          System.out.println("This is the " +
10                      "subclass constructor.");
11      }
12  }
```

The program in Code Listing 11-7 creates a `SubClass1` object. As you can see from the program output, the superclass constructor executes first, followed by the subclass constructor.

Code Listing 11-7 (`ConstructorDemo1.java`)

```
 1  /**
 2      This program demonstrates the order in which
 3      superclass and subclass constructors are called.
 4  */
 5
 6  public class ConstructorDemo1
 7  {
 8      public static void main(String[] args)
 9      {
10          SubClass1 obj = new SubClass1();
11      }
12  }
```

Program Output

```
This is the superclass constructor.
This is the subclass constructor.
```

If a superclass has either (a) a default constructor or (b) a no-arg constructor that was written into the class, then that constructor will be automatically called just before a subclass constructor executes. In a moment we will discuss other situations that can arise involving superclass constructors.

Inheritance Does Not Work in Reverse

In an inheritance relationship, the subclass inherits members from the superclass, not the other way around. This means it is not possible for a superclass to call a subclass's method. For example, if we create a `GradedActivity` object, it cannot call the `getPointsEach` or the `getNumMissed` methods because they are members of the `FinalExam` class.

Checkpoint

11.1 Here is the first line of a class declaration. What is the name of the superclass? What is the name of the subclass?

```
public class Truck extends Vehicle
```

11.2 Look at the following class declarations and answer the questions that follow them:

```
public class Shape
{
    private double area;
    public void setArea(double a)
    {
        area = a;
    }
    public double getArea()
    {
        return area;
    }
}
public class Circle extends Shape
{
    private double radius;
    public void setRadius(double r)
    {
        radius = r;
        setArea(Math.PI * r * r);
    }
    public double getRadius()
    {
        return radius;
    }
}
```

a)   Which class is the superclass? Which class is the subclass?
b)   Draw a UML diagram showing the relationship between these two classes.
c)   When a `Circle` object is created, what are its public members?
d)   What members of the `Shape` class are not accessible to the `Circle` class's methods?
e)   Assume a program has the following declarations:

```
Shape s = new Shape();
Circle c = new Circle();
```

Indicate whether the following statements are legal or illegal:

```
c.setRadius(10.0);
s.setRadius(10.0);
System.out.println(c.getArea());
System.out.println(s.getArea());
```

11.3   Class B extends class A. (Class A is the superclass and class B is the subclass.) Describe the order in which the class's constructors execute when a class B object is created.

11.2 Calling the Superclass Constructor

CONCEPT: The **super** key word refers to an object's superclass. You can use the super key word to call a superclass constructor.

In the previous section you saw examples illustrating how a superclass's default constructor or no-arg constructor is automatically called just before the subclass's constructor executes. But what if the superclass does not have a default constructor or a no-arg constructor? Or, what if the superclass has multiple overloaded constructors and you want to make sure a specific one is called? In either of these situations, you use the **super** key word to call a superclass constructor explicitly. The **super** key word refers to an object's superclass and can be used to access members of the superclass.

Code Listing 11-8 shows a class, `SuperClass2`, which has a no-arg constructor and a constructor that accepts an `int` argument. Code Listing 11-9 shows `SubClass2`, which extends `SuperClass2`. This class's constructor uses the **super** key word to call the superclass's constructor and pass an argument to it.

Code Listing 11-8 (`SuperClass2.java`)

```
1   public class SuperClass2
2   {
3      /**
4          Constructor #1
5      */
6
7      public SuperClass2()
8      {
```

```
 9            System.out.println("This is the superclass " +
10                                 "no-arg constructor.");
11        }
12
13        /**
14            Constructor #2
15        */
16
17        public SuperClass2(int arg)
18        {
19            System.out.println("The following argument " +
20                                 "was passed to the superclass " +
21                                 "constructor: " + arg);
22        }
23    }
```

Code Listing 11-9 (`SubClass2.java`)

```
 1    public class SubClass2 extends SuperClass2
 2    {
 3        /**
 4            Constructor
 5        */
 6
 7        public SubClass2()
 8        {
 9            super(10);
10            System.out.println("This is the " +
11                                 "subclass constructor.");
12        }
13    }
```

The statement in line 9 of the `SubClass2` constructor calls the superclass constructor and passes the argument 10 to it. Here are three guidelines you should remember about calling a superclass constructor:

- The `super` statement that calls the superclass constructor may be written only in the subclass's constructor. You cannot call the superclass constructor from any other method.
- The `super` statement that calls the superclass constructor must be the first statement in the subclass's constructor. This is because the superclass's constructor must execute before the code in the subclass's constructor executes.
- If a subclass constructor does not explicitly call a superclass constructor, Java will automatically call the superclass's default constructor, or no-arg constructor, just

before the code in the subclass's constructor executes. This is equivalent to placing the following statement at the beginning of a subclass constructor:

```
super();
```

The program in Code Listing 11-10 demonstrates these classes.

Code Listing 11-10   (`ConstructorDemo2.java`)

```
 1  /**
 2      This program demonstrates how a superclass
 3      constructor is called with the super key word.
 4  */
 5
 6  public class ConstructorDemo2
 7  {
 8      public static void main(String[] args)
 9      {
10          SubClass2 obj = new SubClass2();
11      }
12  }
```

Program Output

```
The following argument was passed to the superclass constructor: 10
This is the subclass constructor.
```

Let's look at a more meaningful example. Recall the `Rectangle` class from Chapter 6. Figure 11-9 shows a UML diagram for the class.

Figure 11-9   UML diagram for the `Rectangle` class

```
┌──────────────────────────────────────────┐
│                 Rectangle                  │
├──────────────────────────────────────────┤
│ – length : double                          │
│ – width : double                           │
├──────────────────────────────────────────┤
│ + Rectangle(len : double, w : double)      │
│ + setLength(len : double) : void           │
│ + setWidth(w : double) : void              │
│ + getLength() : double                     │
│ + getWidth() : double                      │
│ + getArea() : double                       │
└──────────────────────────────────────────┘
```

Here is part of the class's code:

```
public class Rectangle
{
    private double length;
    private double width;
    /**
```

```
         Constructor
         @param len The length of the rectangle.
         @param w The width of the rectangle.
      */

      public Rectangle(double len, double w)
      {
         length = len;
         width = w;
      }
      (Other methods follow ...)
   }
```

Next we will design a Cube class, which extends the Rectangle class. The Cube class is designed to hold data about cubes, which not only have a length, width, and area (the area of the base), but also a height, surface area, and volume. A UML diagram showing the inheritance relationship between the Cube and Rectangle classes is shown in Figure 11-10, and the code for the Cube class is shown in Code Listing 11-11.

Figure 11-10   UML diagram for the Rectangle and Cube classes

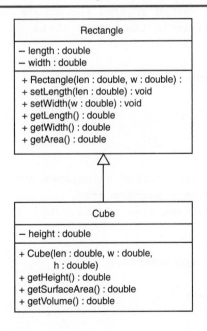

Code Listing 11-11   (Cube.java)

```
1 /**
2     This class holds data about a cube.
3 */
4
5 public class Cube extends Rectangle
6 {
```

```
 7        private double height;  // The cube's height
 8
 9        /**
10           The constructor sets the cube's length,
11           width, and height.
12           @param len The cube's length.
13           @param w The cube's width.
14           @param h The cube's height.
15        */
16
17        public Cube(double len, double w, double h)
18        {
19           // Call the superclass constructor.
20           super(len, w);
21
22           // Set the height.
23           height = h;
24        }
25
26        /**
27           The getHeight method returns the cube's height.
28           @return The value in the height field.
29        */
30
31        public double getHeight()
32        {
33           return height;
34        }
35
36        /**
37           The getSurfaceArea method calculates and
38           returns the cube's surface area.
39           @return The surface area of the cube.
40        */
41
42        public double getSurfaceArea()
43        {
44           return getArea() * 6;
45        }
46
47        /**
48           The getVolume method calculates and
49           returns the cube's volume.
50           @return The volume of the cube.
51        */
52
53        public double getVolume()
54        {
```

```
55          return getArea() * height;
56      }
57 }
```

The `Cube` constructor accepts arguments for the parameters `len`, `w`, and `h`. The values that are passed to `len` and `w` are subsequently passed as arguments to the `Rectangle` constructor in line 20:

```
super(len, w);
```

When the `Rectangle` constructor finishes, the remaining code in the `Cube` constructor is executed. The program in Code Listing 11-12 demonstrates the class.

Code Listing 11-12   (CubeDemo.java)

```
1 import java.util.Scanner;
2
3 /**
4     This program demonstrates passing arguments to a
5     superclass constructor.
6 */
7
8 public class CubeDemo
9 {
10     public static void main(String[] args)
11     {
12         double length;      // The cube's length
13         double width;       // The cube's width
14         double height;      // The cube's height
15
16         // Create a Scanner object for keyboard input.
17         Scanner keyboard = new Scanner(System.in);
18
19         // Get cube's length.
20         System.out.println("Enter the following " +
21                            "dimensions of a cube:");
22         System.out.print("Length: ");
23         length = keyboard.nextDouble();
24
25         // Get the cube's width.
26         System.out.print("Width: ");
27         width = keyboard.nextDouble();
28
29         // Get the cube's height.
30         System.out.print("Height: ");
31         height = keyboard.nextDouble();
32
```

```
33          // Create a cube object and pass the
34          // dimensions to the constructor.
35          Cube myCube =
36                  new Cube(length, width, height);
37
38          // Display the cube's properties.
39          System.out.println("Here are the cube's " +
40                              "properties.");
41          System.out.println("Length: " +
42                              myCube.getLength());
43          System.out.println("Width: " +
44                              myCube.getWidth());
45          System.out.println("Height: " +
46                              myCube.getHeight());
47          System.out.println("Base Area: " +
48                              myCube.getArea());
49          System.out.println("Surface Area: " +
50                              myCube.getSurfaceArea());
51          System.out.println("Volume: " +
52                              myCube.getVolume());
53      }
54  }
```

Program Output with Example Input Shown in Bold

```
Enter the following dimensions of a cube:
Length: 10 [Enter]
Width: 15 [Enter]
Height: 12 [Enter]
Here are the cube's properties.
Length: 10.0
Width: 15.0
Height: 12.0
Base Area: 150.0
Surface Area: 900.0
Volume: 1800.0
```

When the Superclass Has No Default or No-Arg Constructors

Recall from Chapter 6 that Java provides a default constructor for a class only when you provide no constructors for the class. This makes it possible to have a class with no default constructor. The Rectangle class we just looked at is an example. It has a constructor that accepts two arguments. Because we have provided this constructor, the Rectangle class does not have a default constructor. In addition, we have not written a no-arg constructor for the class.

If a superclass does not have a default constructor and does not have a no-arg constructor, then a class that inherits from it must call one of the constructors that the superclass does have. If it does not, an error will result when the subclass is compiled.

Summary of Constructor Issues in Inheritance

We have covered a number of important issues that you should remember about constructors in an inheritance relationship. The following list summarizes them:

- The superclass constructor always executes before the subclass constructor.
- You can write a super statement that calls a superclass constructor, but only in the subclass's constructor. You cannot call the superclass constructor from any other method.
- If a super statement that calls a superclass constructor appears in a subclass constructor, it must be the first statement.
- If a subclass constructor does not explicitly call a superclass constructor, Java will automatically call super() just before the code in the subclass's constructor executes.
- If a superclass does not have a default constructor and does not have a no-arg constructor, then a class that inherits from it must call one of the constructors that the superclass does have.

Checkpoint

11.4   Look at the following classes:

```java
public class Ground
{
    public Ground()
    {
        System.out.println("You are on the ground.");
    }
}
public class Sky extends Ground
{
    public Sky()
    {
        System.out.println("You are in the sky.");
    }
}
```

What will the following program display?

```java
public class Checkpoint
{
    public static void main(String[] args)
    {
        Sky object = new Sky();
    }
}
```

11.5 Look at the following classes:

```java
public class Ground
{
    public Ground()
    {
        System.out.println("You are on the ground.");
    }
    public Ground(String groundColor)
    {
        System.out.println("The ground is " +
                            groundColor);
    }
}
public class Sky extends Ground
{
    public Sky()
    {
        System.out.println("You are in the sky.");
    }
    public Sky(String skyColor)
    {
        super("green");
        System.out.println("The sky is " + skyColor);
    }
}
```

What will the following program display?

```java
public class Checkpoint
{
    public static void main(String[] args)
    {
        Sky object = new Sky("blue");
    }
}
```

11.3 Overriding Superclass Methods

CONCEPT: A subclass may have a method with the same signature as a superclass method. In such a case, the subclass method overrides the superclass method.

Sometimes a subclass inherits a method from its superclass, but the method is inadequate for the subclass's purpose. Because the subclass is more specialized than the superclass, it is sometimes necessary for the subclass to replace inadequate superclass methods with more suitable ones. This is known as method overriding.

For example, recall the `GradedActivity` class that was presented earlier in this chapter. This class has a `setScore` method that sets a numeric score and a `getGrade` method that returns a letter grade based on that score. But, suppose a teacher wants to curve a numeric score before the letter grade is determined. For example, Dr. Harrison determines that in order to curve the grades in her class she must multiply each student's score by a certain percentage. This gives an adjusted score that is used to determine the letter grade. To satisfy this need we can design a new class, `CurvedActivity`, which extends the `GradedActivity` class and has its own specialized version of the `setScore` method. The `setScore` method in the subclass overrides the `setScore` method in the superclass. Figure 11-11 is a UML diagram showing the relationship between the `GradedActivity` class and the `CurvedActivity` class.

Figure 11-11   The `GradedActivity` and `CurvedActivity` classes

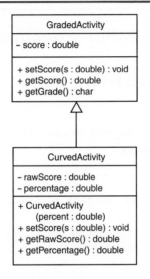

Table 11-1 summarizes the `CurvedActivity` class's fields, and Table 11-2 summarizes the class's methods.

Table 11-1   `CurvedActivity` class fields

Field	Description
rawScore	This field holds the student's unadjusted score.
percentage	This field holds the value that the unadjusted score must be multiplied by to get the curved score.

Table 11-2 CurvedActivity class methods

Method	Description
Constructor	The constructor accepts a double argument that is the curve percentage. This value is assigned to the percentage field and the rawScore field is assigned 0.0.
setScore	This method accepts a double argument that is the student's unadjusted score. The method stores the argument in the rawScore field, and then passes the result of rawScore * percentage as an argument to the superclass's setScore method.
getRawScore	This method returns the value in the rawScore field.
getPercentage	This method returns the value in the percentage field.

Code Listing 11-13 shows the code for the CurvedActivity class.

Code Listing 11-13 (CurvedActivity.java)

```
 1 /**
 2    This class computes a curved grade. It extends
 3    the GradedActivity class.
 4 */
 5
 6 public class CurvedActivity extends GradedActivity
 7 {
 8    double rawScore;      // Unadjusted score
 9    double percentage;    // Curve percentage
10
11    /**
12       The constructor sets the curve percentage.
13       @param percent The curve percentage.
14    */
15
16    public CurvedActivity(double percent)
17    {
18       percentage = percent;
19       rawScore = 0.0;
20    }
21
22    /**
23       The setScore method overrides the superclass
24       setScore method. This version accepts the
25       unadjusted score as an argument. That score is
26       multiplied by the curve percentage and the
27       result is sent as an argument to the superclass's
28       setScore method.
29       @param s The unadjusted score.
```

```
30      */
31
32      public void setScore(double s)
33      {
34         rawScore = s;
35         super.setScore(rawScore * percentage);
36      }
37
38      /**
39         The getRawScore method returns the raw score.
40         @return The value in the rawScore field.
41      */
42
43      public double getRawScore()
44      {
45         return rawScore;
46      }
47
48      /**
49         The getPercentage method returns the curve
50         percentage.
51         @return The value in the percentage field.
52      */
53
54      public double getPercentage()
55      {
56         return percentage;
57      }
58  }
```

Recall from Chapter 6 that a method's signature consists of the method's name and the data types of the method's parameters, in the order that they appear. Notice that this class's setScore method has the same signature as the setScore method in the superclass. In order for a subclass method to override a superclass method, it must have the same signature. When an object of the subclass invokes the method, it invokes the subclass's version of the method, not the superclass's.

The setScore method in the CurvedActivity class accepts an argument, which is the student's unadjusted numeric score. This value is stored in the rawScore field. Then, in line 35, the following statement is executed:

```
super.setScore(rawScore * percentage);
```

As you already know, the super key word refers to the object's superclass. This statement calls the superclass's version of the setScore method with the result of the expression rawScore * percentage passed as an argument. This is necessary because the superclass's score field is private, and the subclass cannot access it directly. In order to store a value in the superclass's score field, the subclass must call the superclass's setScore method. A subclass may call an overridden superclass method by prefixing its name with the super key word and a dot (.). The program in Code Listing 11-14 demonstrates this class.

Code Listing 11-14 (`CurvedActivityDemo.java`)

```java
 1 import java.util.Scanner;
 2
 3 /**
 4    This program demonstrates the CurvedActivity class,
 5    which inherits from the GradedActivity class.
 6 */
 7
 8 public class CurvedActivityDemo
 9 {
10    public static void main(String[] args)
11    {
12       double score;            // Raw score
13       double curvePercent;     // Curve percentage
14
15       // Create a Scanner object to read keyboard input.
16       Scanner keyboard = new Scanner(System.in);
17
18       // Get the unadjusted exam score.
19       System.out.print("Enter the student's " +
20                        "raw numeric score: ");
21       score = keyboard.nextDouble();
22
23       // Get the curve percentage.
24       System.out.print("Enter the curve percentage: ");
25       curvePercent = keyboard.nextDouble();
26
27       // Create a CurvedActivity object.
28       CurvedActivity curvedExam =
29                new CurvedActivity(curvePercent);
30
31       // Set the exam score.
32       curvedExam.setScore(score);
33
34       // Display the raw score.
35       System.out.println("The raw score is " +
36                           curvedExam.getRawScore() +
37                           " points.");
38
39       // Display the curved score.
40       System.out.println("The curved score is " +
41                           curvedExam.getScore());
```

```
42
43          // Display the exam grade.
44          System.out.println("The exam grade is " +
45                              curvedExam.getGrade());
46      }
47 }
```

Program Output with Example Input Shown in Bold

Enter the student's raw numeric score: **87 [Enter]**
Enter the curve percentage: **1.06 [Enter]**
The raw score is 87.0 points.
The curved score is 92.22
The exam grade is A

This program uses the curvedExam variable to reference a CurvedActivity object. In line 32 the following statement is used to call the setScore method:

```
curvedExam.setScore(score);
```

Because curvedExam references a CurvedActivity object, this statement calls the CurvedActivity class's setScore method, not the superclass's version.

Even though a subclass may override a method in the superclass, superclass objects still call the superclass version of the method. For example, the following code creates an object of the GradedActivity class and calls the setScore method:

```
GradedActivity regularExam = new GradedActivity();
regularExam.setScore(85);
```

Because regularExam references a GradedActivity object, this code calls the GradedActivity class's version of the setScore method.

Overloading versus Overriding

There is a distinction between overloading a method and overriding a method. Recall from Chapter 6 that overloading is when a method has the same name as one or more other methods, but a different parameter list. Although overloaded methods have the same name, they have different signatures. When a method overrides another method, however, they both have the same signature.

Both overloading and overriding can take place in an inheritance relationship. You already know that overloaded methods can appear within the same class. In addition, a method in a subclass can overload a method in the superclass. If class A is the superclass and class B is the subclass, a method in class B may overload a method in class A, or another method in class B. Overriding, on the other hand, can only take place in an inheritance relationship. If class A is the superclass and class B is the subclass, a method in class B may override a method in class A. However, a method cannot override another method in the same class. The following list summarizes the distinction between overloading and overriding:

- If two methods have the same name but different signatures, they are overloaded. This is true where the methods are in the same class or where one method is in the superclass and the other method is in the subclass.
- If a method in a subclass has the same signature as a method in the superclass, the subclass method overrides the superclass method.

The distinction between overloading and overriding is important because it can affect the accessibility of superclass methods in a subclass. When a subclass overloads a superclass method, both methods may be called with a subclass object. However, when a subclass overrides a superclass method, only the subclass's version of the method can be called with a subclass object. For example, look at the SuperClass3 class in Code Listing 11-15. It has two overloaded methods named showValue. One of the methods accepts an int argument and the other accepts a String argument.

Code Listing 11-15 (SuperClass3.java)

```
 1   public class SuperClass3
 2   {
 3      /**
 4         This method displays an int.
 5         @param arg An int.
 6      */
 7
 8      public void showValue(int arg)
 9      {
10         System.out.println("SUPERCLASS: " +
11                       "The int argument was " + arg);
12      }
13
14      /**
15         This method displays a String.
16         @param arg A String.
17      */
18
19      public void showValue(String arg)
20      {
21         System.out.println("SUPERCLASS: " +
22                       "The String argument was " + arg);
23      }
24   }
```

Now look at the SubClass3 class in Code Listing 11-16. It inherits from the SuperClass3 class.

Code Listing 11-16   (`SubClass3.java`)

```java
 1   public class SubClass3 extends SuperClass3
 2   {
 3      /**
 4          This method overrides one of the
 5          superclass methods.
 6          @param arg An int.
 7      */
 8
 9      public void showValue(int arg)
10      {
11         System.out.println("SUBCLASS: " +
12                           "The int argument was " + arg);
13      }
14
15      /**
16          This method overloads the superclass
17          methods.
18          @param arg A double.
19      */
20
21      public void showValue(double arg)
22      {
23         System.out.println("SUBCLASS: " +
24                           "The double argument was " + arg);
25      }
26   }
```

Notice that `SubClass3` also has two methods named `showValue`. The first one, in lines 9 through 13, accepts an `int` argument. This method overrides one of the superclass methods because they have the same signature. The second `showValue` method, in lines 21 through 25, accepts a `double` argument. This method overloads the other `showValue` methods because none of the others have the same signature. Although there is a total of four `showValue` methods in these classes, only three of them may be called from a `SubClass3` object. This is demonstrated in Code Listing 11-17.

Code Listing 11-17   (`ShowValueDemo.java`)

```java
 1   /**
 2       This program demonstrates the methods in the
 3       SuperClass3 and SubClass3 classes.
 4   */
 5
 6   public class ShowValueDemo
 7   {
```

```
 8        public static void main(String[] args)
 9        {
10            // Create a SubClass3 object.
11            SubClass3 myObject = new SubClass3();
12
13            myObject.showValue(10);          // Pass an int.
14            myObject.showValue(1.2);         // Pass a double.
15            myObject.showValue("Hello");     // Pass a String.
16        }
17    }
```

Program Output

```
SUBCLASS: The int argument was 10
SUBCLASS: The double argument was 1.2
SUPERCLASS: The String argument was Hello
```

When an `int` argument is passed to `showValue`, the subclass's method is called because it overrides the superclass method. In order to call the overridden superclass method, we would have to use the `super` key word in the subclass method. Here is an example:

```
public void showValue(int arg)
{
   super.showValue(arg);   // Call the superclass method.
   System.out.println("SUBCLASS: The int argument was " +
                      arg);
}
```

Preventing a Method from Being Overridden

When a method is declared with the `final` modifier, it cannot be overridden in a subclass. The following method header is an example that uses the `final` modifier:

```
public final void message()
```

If a subclass attempts to override a `final` method, the compiler generates an error. This technique can be used to make sure that a particular superclass method is used by subclasses and not a modified version of it.

Checkpoint

11.6 Under what circumstances would a subclass need to override a superclass method?

11.7 How can a subclass method call an overridden superclass method?

11.8 If a method in a subclass has the same signature as a method in the superclass, does the subclass method overload or override the superclass method?

11.9 If a method in a subclass has the same name as a method in the superclass, but uses a different parameter list, does the subclass method overload or override the superclass method?

11.10 How do you prevent a method from being overridden?

11.4 Protected Members

CONCEPT: Protected members of a class may be accessed by methods in a subclass, and by methods in the same package as the class.

Until now you have used two access specifications within a class: `private` and `public`. Java provides a third access specification, `protected`. A protected member of a class may be directly accessed by methods of the same class or methods of a subclass. In addition, protected members may be accessed by methods of any class that are in the same package as the protected member's class. A protected member is not quite private, because it may be accessed by some methods outside the class. Protected members are not quite public either because access to them is restricted to methods in the same class, subclasses, and classes in the same package as the member's class. A protected member's access is somewhere between private and public.

Let's look at a class with a protected member. Code Listing 11-18 shows the `GradedActivity2` class, which is a modification of the `GradedActivity` class presented earlier. In this class, the `score` field has been made protected instead of private.

Code Listing 11-18   (`GradedActivity2.java`)

```
 1 /**
 2     A class that holds a grade for a graded activity.
 3 */
 4
 5 public class GradedActivity2
 6 {
 7     protected double score;  // Numeric score
 8
 9     /**
10        The setScore method sets the score field.
11        @param s The value to store in score.
12     */
13
14     public void setScore(double s)
15     {
16        score = s;
17     }
18
19     /**
20        The getScore method returns the score.
21        @return The value stored in the score field.
22     */
23
24     public double getScore()
25     {
26        return score;
```

```
27      }
28
29      /**
30          The getGrade method returns a letter grade
31          determined from the score field.
32          @return The letter grade.
33      */
34
35      public char getGrade()
36      {
37          char letterGrade;
38
39          if (score >= 90)
40              letterGrade = 'A';
41          else if (score >= 80)
42              letterGrade = 'B';
43          else if (score >= 70)
44              letterGrade = 'C';
45          else if (score >= 60)
46              letterGrade = 'D';
47          else
48              letterGrade = 'F';
49
50          return letterGrade;
51      }
52 }
```

Because in line 7 the score field is declared as protected, any class that inherits from this class has direct access to it. The FinalExam2 class, shown in Code Listing 11-19 is an example. This class is a modification of the FinalExam class, which was presented earlier. This class has a new method, adjustScore, which directly accesses the superclass's score field. If the contents of score have a fractional part of .5 or greater, the method rounds up score to the next whole number. The adjustScore method is called from the constructor.

Code Listing 11-19 (FinalExam2.java)

```
 1 /**
 2     This class determines the grade for a final exam.
 3     The numeric score is rounded up to the next whole
 4     number if its fractional part is .5 or greater.
 5 */
 6
 7 public class FinalExam2 extends GradedActivity2
 8 {
 9     private int numQuestions;  // Number of questions
```

```
10      private double pointsEach;      // Points for each question
11      private int numMissed;          // Number of questions missed
12
13      /**
14         The constructor sets the number of questions on the
15         exam and the number of questions missed.
16         @param questions The number of questions.
17         @param missed The number of questions missed.
18      */
19
20      public FinalExam2(int questions, int missed)
21      {
22         double numericScore;         // To hold a numeric score
23
24         // Set the numQuestions and numMissed fields.
25         numQuestions = questions;
26         numMissed = missed;
27
28         // Calculate the points for each question and
29         // the numeric score for this exam.
30         pointsEach = 100.0 / questions;
31         numericScore = 100.0 - (missed * pointsEach);
32
33         // Call the inherited setScore method to
34         // set the numeric score.
35         setScore(numericScore);
36
37         // Adjust the score.
38         adjustScore();
39      }
40
41      /**
42         The getPointsEach method returns the number of
43         points each question is worth.
44         @return The value in the pointsEach field.
45      */
46
47      public double getPointsEach()
48      {
49         return pointsEach;
50      }
51
52      /**
53         The getNumMissed method returns the number of
54         questions missed.
55         @return The value in the numMissed field.
56      */
57
```

```
58        public int getNumMissed()
59        {
60            return numMissed;
61        }
62
63        /**
64            The adjustScore method adjusts a numeric score.
65            If score is within 0.5 points of the next whole
66            number, it rounds the score up.
67        */
68
69        private void adjustScore()
70        {
71            double fraction;
72
73            // Get the fractional part of the score.
74            fraction = score - (int) score;
75
76            // If the fractional part is .5 or greater,
77            // round the score up to the next whole number.
78            if (fraction >= 0.5)
79                score = score + (1.0 - fraction);
80        }
81 }
```

The program in Code Listing 11-20 demonstrates the class. Figure 11-12 shows an example of interaction with the program.

Code Listing 11-20 (`ProtectedDemo.java`)

```
1 import javax.swing.JOptionPane;
2
3 /**
4     This program demonstrates the FinalExam2 class,
5     which extends the GradedActivity2 class.
6 */
7
8 public class ProtectedDemo
9 {
10     public static void main(String[] args)
11     {
12         String input;          // To hold input
13         int questions;         // Number of questions
14         int missed;            // Number of questions missed
15
```

```
16          // Get the number of questions on the exam.
17          input = JOptionPane.showInputDialog("How many " +
18                          "questions are on the final exam?");
19          questions = Integer.parseInt(input);
20
21          // Get the number of questions the student missed.
22          input = JOptionPane.showInputDialog("How many " +
23                          "questions did the student miss?");
24          missed = Integer.parseInt(input);
25
26          // Create a FinalExam object.
27          FinalExam2 exam = new FinalExam2(questions, missed);
28
29          // Display the test results.
30          JOptionPane.showMessageDialog(null,
31              "Each question counts " + exam.getPointsEach() +
32              " points.\nThe exam score is " +
33              exam.getScore() + "\nThe exam grade is " +
34              exam.getGrade());
35
36          System.exit(0);
37      }
38 }
```

In the example running of the program in Figure 11-12, the student missed 5 out of 40 questions. The unadjusted numeric score would be 87.5, but the adjustScore method rounded up the score field to 88.

Figure 11-12   Interaction with the `ProtectedDemo.java` program

Protected class members may be denoted in a UML diagram with the # symbol. Figure 11-13 shows a UML diagram for the `GradedActivity2` class, with the `score` field denoted as protected.

Figure 11-13   UML diagram for the `GradedActivity2` class

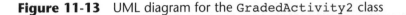

```
+-------------------------------+
|        GradedActivity2        |
+-------------------------------+
| # score : double              |
+-------------------------------+
| + setScore(s : double) : void |
| + getScore() : double         |
| + getGrade() : char           |
+-------------------------------+
```

Although making a class member protected instead of private might make some tasks easier, you should avoid this practice when possible because any class that inherits from the class, or is in the same package, has unrestricted access to the protected member. It is always better to make all fields private and then provide public methods for accessing those fields.

Package Access

If you do not provide an access specifier for a class member, the class member is given package access by default. This means that any method in the same package may access the member. Here is an example:

```
public class Circle
{
    double radius;
    int centerX, centerY;

    (Method definitions follow . . .)
}
```

In this class, the `radius`, `centerX`, and `centerY` fields were not given an access specifier, so the compiler grants them package access. Any method in the same package as the `Circle` class may directly access these members.

There is a subtle difference between protected access and package access. Protected members may be accessed by methods in the same package or in a subclass. This is true even if the subclass is in a different package. Members with package access, however, cannot be accessed by subclasses that are in a different package.

It is more likely that you will give package access to class members by accident than by design, because it is easy to forget the access specifier. Although there are circumstances under which package access can be helpful, you should normally avoid it. Be careful always to specify an access specifier for class members.

Tables 11-3 and 11-4 summarize how each of the access specifiers affect a class member's accessibility within and outside of the class's package.

Table 11-3 Accessibility from within the class's package

Access Specifier	Accessible to a subclass inside the same package?	Accessible to all other classes in the same package?
default (no modifier)	Yes	Yes
public	Yes	Yes
protected	Yes	Yes
private	No	No

Table 11-4 Accessibility from outside the class's package

Access Specifier	Accessible to a subclass outside the same package?	Accessible to all other classes outside the same package?
default (no modifier)	No	No
public	Yes	Yes
protected	Yes	No
private	No	No

 Checkpoint

11.11 When a class member is declared as protected, what code may access it?

11.12 What is the difference between private members and protected members?

11.13 Why should you avoid making class members protected when possible?

11.14 What is the difference between private access and package access?

11.15 Why is it easy to give package access to a class member by accident?

11.5 Chains of Inheritance

CONCEPT: A superclass can also inherit from another class.

Sometimes it is desirable to establish a chain of inheritance in which one class inherits from a second class, which in turn inherits from a third class, as illustrated by Figure 11-14. In some cases, this chaining of classes goes on for many layers.

In Figure 11-14, ClassC inherits ClassB's members, including the ones that ClassB inherited from ClassA. Let's look at an example of such a chain of inheritance. Consider the PassFailActivity class, shown in Code Listing 11-21, which inherits from the GradedActivity class. The class is intended to determine a letter grade of 'P' for passing, or 'F' for failing.

Figure 11-14 A chain of inheritance

(`PassFailActivity.java`)

```
1  /**
2     This class holds a numeric score and determines
3     whether the score is passing or failing.
4  */
5
6  public class PassFailActivity extends GradedActivity
7  {
8     private double minPassingScore; // Minimum passing score
9
10    /**
11       The constructor sets the minimum passing score.
12       @param mps The minimum passing score.
13    */
14
15    public PassFailActivity(double mps)
16    {
17       minPassingScore = mps;
18    }
19
20    /**
21       The getGrade method returns a letter grade
22       determined from the score field. This
23       method overrides the superclass method.
24       @return The letter grade.
25    */
26
27    public char getGrade()
28    {
29       char letterGrade;
```

```
30
31        if (super.getScore() >= minPassingScore)
32            letterGrade = 'P';
33        else
34            letterGrade = 'F';
35
36        return letterGrade;
37    }
38 }
```

The `PassFailActivity` constructor, in lines 15 through 18, accepts a double argument, which is the minimum passing grade for the activity. This value is stored in the `minPassingScore` field. The `getGrade` method, in lines 27 through 37, overrides the superclass method of the same name. This method returns a grade of `'P'` if the numeric score is greater-than or equal-to `minPassingScore`. Otherwise, the method returns a grade of `'F'`.

Suppose we wish to extend this class with another more specialized class. For example, the `PassFailExam` class, shown in Code Listing 11-22, determines a passing or failing grade for an exam. It has fields for the number of questions on the exam (`numQuestions`), the number of points each question is worth (`pointsEach`), and the number of questions missed by the student (`numMissed`).

Code Listing 11-22   (`PassFailExam.java`)

```java
 1 /**
 2     This class determines a passing or failing grade for
 3     an exam.
 4 */
 5
 6 public class PassFailExam extends PassFailActivity
 7 {
 8     private int numQuestions;      // Number of questions
 9     private double pointsEach;     // Points for each question
10     private int numMissed;         // Number of questions missed
11
12     /**
13         The constructor sets the number of questions, the
14         number of questions missed, and the minimum passing
15         score.
16         @param questions The number of questions.
17         @param missed The number of questions missed.
18         @param minPassing The minimum passing score.
19     */
20
21     public PassFailExam(int questions, int missed,
22                         double minPassing)
```

```
23    {
24        // Call the superclass constructor.
25        super(minPassing);
26
27        // Declare a local variable for the score.
28        double numericScore;
29
30        // Set the numQuestions and numMissed fields.
31        numQuestions = questions;
32        numMissed = missed;
33
34        // Calculate the points for each question and
35        // the numeric score for this exam.
36        pointsEach = 100.0 / questions;
37        numericScore = 100.0 - (missed * pointsEach);
38
39        // Call the superclass's setScore method to
40        // set the numeric score.
41        setScore(numericScore);
42    }
43
44    /**
45        The getPointsEach method returns the number of
46        points each question is worth.
47        @return The value in the pointsEach field.
48    */
49
50    public double getPointsEach()
51    {
52        return pointsEach;
53    }
54
55    /**
56        The getNumMissed method returns the number of
57        questions missed.
58        @return The value in the numMissed field.
59    */
60
61    public int getNumMissed()
62    {
63        return numMissed;
64    }
65 }
```

The PassFailExam class inherits the PassFailActivity class's members, including the ones that PassFailActivity inherited from GradedActivity. The program in Code Listing 11-23 demonstrates the class.

Code Listing 11-23 (`PassFailExamDemo.java`)

```java
 1  import java.util.Scanner;
 2
 3  /**
 4      This program demonstrates the PassFailExam class.
 5  */
 6
 7  public class PassFailExamDemo
 8  {
 9      public static void main(String[] args)
10      {
11          int questions;        // Number of questions
12          int missed;           // Number of questions missed
13          double minPassing;    // Minimum passing score
14
15          // Create a Scanner object for keyboard input.
16          Scanner keyboard = new Scanner(System.in);
17
18          // Get the number of questions on the exam.
19          System.out.print("How many questions are " +
20                           "on the exam? ");
21          questions = keyboard.nextInt();
22
23          // Get the number of questions missed.
24          System.out.print("How many questions did " +
25                           "the student miss? ");
26          missed = keyboard.nextInt();
27
28          // Get the minimum passing score.
29          System.out.print("What is the minimum " +
30                           "passing score? ");
31          minPassing = keyboard.nextDouble();
32
33          // Create a PassFailExam object.
34          PassFailExam exam =
35                new PassFailExam(questions, missed, minPassing);
36
37          // Display the points for each question.
38          System.out.println("Each question counts " +
39                           exam.getPointsEach() + " points.");
40
41          // Display the exam score.
42          System.out.println("The exam score is " +
43                           exam.getScore());
44
45          // Display the exam grade.
```

```
46            System.out.println("The exam grade is " +
47                            exam.getGrade());
48      }
49  }
```

Program Output with Example Input Shown in Bold

How many questions are on the exam? **100 [Enter]**
How many questions did the student miss? **25 [Enter]**
What is the minimum passing score? **60 [Enter]**
Each question counts 1.0 points.
The exam score is 75.0
The exam grade is P

Figure 11-15 is a UML diagram showing the inheritance relationship among the `GradedActivity`, `PassFailActivity`, and `PassFailExam` classes.

Figure 11-15 The `GradedActivity`, `PassFailActivity`, and `PassFailExam` classes

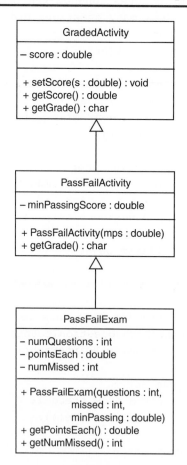

Class Hierarchies

Classes often are depicted graphically in a class hierarchy. Like a family tree, a class hierarchy shows the inheritance relationships between classes. Figure 11-16 shows a class hierarchy for the `GradedActivity`, `FinalExam`, `PassFailActivity`, and `PassFailExam` classes. The more general classes are toward the top of the tree and the more specialized classes are toward the bottom.

Figure 11-16 Class hierarchy

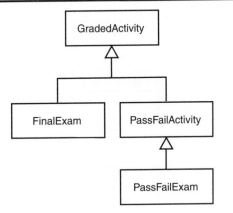

11.6 The Object Class

CONCEPT: The Java API has a class named **Object**, which all other classes directly or indirectly inherit from.

Every class in Java, including the ones in the API and the classes that you create, directly or indirectly inherits from a class named `Object`, which is part of the `java.lang` package. Here's how it happens: When a class does not use the `extends` key word to inherit from another class, Java automatically extends it from the `Object` class. For example, look at the following class declaration:

```
public class MyClass
{
    (Member Declarations . . .)
}
```

This class does not explicitly extend any other class, so Java treats it as though it were written as follows:

```
public class MyClass extends Object
{
    (Member Declarations . . .)
}
```

Ultimately, every class extends the `Object` class. Figure 11-17 shows how the `PassFailExam` class inherits from `Object`.

Figure 11-17 The line of inheritance from `Object` to `PassFailExam`

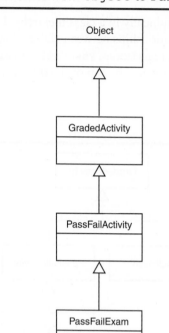

Because every class directly or indirectly extends the `Object` class, every class inherits the `Object` class's members. Two of the most useful are the `toString` and `equals` methods. In Chapter 9 you learned that every class has a `toString` and an `equals` method, and now you know why! It is because those methods are inherited from the `Object` class.

In the `Object` class, the `toString` method returns a reference to a `String` containing the object's class name, followed by the @ sign, followed by the object's hash code, which is a hexadecimal number. The `equals` method accepts a reference to an object as its argument. It returns `true` if the argument references the calling object. This is demonstrated in Code Listing 11-24.

Code Listing 11-24　(`ObjectMethods.java`)

```
 1 /**
 2     This program demonstrates the toString and equals
 3     methods that are inherited from the Object class.
 4 */
 5
 6 public class ObjectMethods
 7 {
 8     public static void main(String[] args)
 9     {
10         // Create two objects.
11         PassFailExam exam1 =
```

```
12                      new PassFailExam(0, 0, 0);
13          PassFailExam exam2 =
14                      new PassFailExam(0, 0, 0);
15
16          // Send the objects to println, which
17          // will call the toString method.
18          System.out.println(exam1);
19          System.out.println(exam2);
20
21          // Test the equals method.
22          if (exam1.equals(exam2))
23             System.out.println("They are the same.");
24          else
25             System.out.println("They are not the same.");
26      }
27 }
```

Program Output

```
PassFailExam@16f0472
PassFailExam@18d107f
They are not the same.
```

If you wish to change the behavior of either of these methods for a given class, you must override them in the class.

 Checkpoint

11.16 Look at the following class definition:

```
public class ClassD extends ClassB
{
    (Member Declarations . . .)
}
```

Because ClassD inherits from ClassB, is it true that ClassD does not inherit from the Object class? Why or why not?

11.17 When you create a class, it automatically has a toString method and an equals method. Why?

11.7 **Polymorphism**

CONCEPT: A superclass reference variable can reference objects of a subclass.

Look at the following statement that declares a reference variable named exam:

```
GradedActivity exam;
```

VideoNote
Polymorphism

This statement tells us that the exam variable's data type is GradedActivity. Therefore, we can use the exam variable to reference a GradedActivity object, as shown in the following statement:

```
exam = new GradedActivity();
```

The GradedActivity class is also used as the superclass for the FinalExam class. Because of the "is-a" relationship between a superclass and a subclass, an object of the FinalExam class is not just a FinalExam object. It is also a GradedActivity object. (A final exam is a graded activity.) Because of this relationship, we can use a GradedActivity variable to reference a FinalExam object. For example, look at the following statement:

```
GradedActivity exam = new FinalExam(50, 7);
```

This statement declares exam as a GradedActivity variable. It creates a FinalExam object and stores the object's address in the exam variable. This statement is perfectly legal and will not cause an error message because a FinalExam object is also a GradedActivity object.

This is an example of polymorphism. The term polymorphism means the ability to take many forms. In Java, a reference variable is polymorphic because it can reference objects of types different from its own, as long as those types are subclasses of its type. All of the following declarations are legal because the FinalExam, PassFailActivity, and PassFailExam classes inherit from GradedActivity:

```
GradedActivity exam1 = new FinalExam(50, 7);
GradedActivity exam2 = new PassFailActivity(70);
GradedActivity exam3 = new PassFailExam(100, 10, 70);
```

Although a GradedActivity variable can reference objects of any class that extends GradedActivity, there is a limit to what the variable can do with those objects. Recall that the GradedActivity class has three methods: setScore, getScore, and getGrade. So, a GradedActivity variable can be used to call only those three methods, regardless of the type of object the variable references. For example, look at the following code:

```
GradedActivity exam = new PassFailExam(100, 10, 70);
System.out.println(exam.getScore());      // This works.
System.out.println(exam.getGrade());      // This works.
System.out.println(exam.getPointsEach()); // ERROR! Won't work.
```

In this code, exam is declared as a GradedActivity variable and is assigned the address of a PassFailExam object. The GradedActivity class has only the setScore, getScore, and getGrade methods, so those are the only methods that the exam variable knows how to execute. The last statement in this code is a call to the getPointsEach method, which is defined in the PassFailExam class. Because the exam variable only knows about methods in the GradedActivity class, it cannot execute this method.

Polymorphism and Dynamic Binding

When a superclass variable references a subclass object, a potential problem exists. What if the subclass has overridden a method in the superclass, and the variable makes a call to that method? Does the variable call the superclass's version of the method, or the subclass's version? For example, look at the following code:

```
GradedActivity exam = new PassFailActivity(60);
exam.setScore(70);
System.out.println(exam.getGrade());
```

Recall that the PassFailActivity class extends the GradedActivity class, and it overrides the getGrade method. When the last statement calls the getGrade method, does it call the GradedActivity class's version (which returns 'A', 'B', 'C', 'D', or 'F') or does it call the PassFailActivity class's version (which returns 'P' or 'F')?

Recall from Chapter 6 that the process of matching a method call with the correct method definition is known as binding. Java performs dynamic binding or late binding when a variable contains a polymorphic reference. This means that the Java Virtual Machine determines at runtime which method to call, depending on the type of object that the variable references. So, it is the object's type that determines which method is called, not the variable's type. In this case, the exam variable references a PassFailActivity object, so the PassFailActivity class's version of the getGrade method is called. The last statement in this code will display a grade of P.

The program in Code Listing 11-25 demonstrates polymorphic behavior. It declares an array of GradedActivity variables, and then assigns the addresses of objects of various types to the elements of the array.

Code Listing 11-25 (`Polymorphic.java`)

```
 1  /**
 2      This program demonstrates polymorphic behavior.
 3  */
 4
 5  public class Polymorphic
 6  {
 7      public static void main(String[] args)
 8      {
 9          // Create an array of GradedActivity references.
10          GradedActivity[] tests = new GradedActivity[3];
11
12          // The first test is a regular exam with a
13          // numeric score of 75.
14          tests[0] = new GradedActivity();
15          tests[0].setScore(95);
16
17          // The second test is a pass/fail test. The
18          // student missed 5 out of 20 questions, and
19          // the minimum passing grade is 60.
20          tests[1] = new PassFailExam(20, 5, 60);
21
```

```
22              // The third test is the final exam. There were
23              // 50 questions and the student missed 7.
24              tests[2] = new FinalExam(50, 7);
25
26              // Display the grades.
27              for (int i = 0; i < tests.length; i++)
28              {
29                  System.out.println("Test " + (i + 1) + ": " +
30                                      "score " + tests[i].getScore() +
31                                      ", grade " + tests[i].getGrade());
32              }
33          }
34  }
```

Program Output

```
Test 1: score 95.0, grade A
Test 2: score 75.0, grade P
Test 3: score 86.0, grade B
```

You can also use parameters to accept arguments to methods polymorphically. For example, look at the following method:

```
public static void displayGrades(GradedActivity g)
{
    System.out.println("Score " + g.getScore() +
                        ", grade " + g.getGrade());
}
```

This method's parameter, g, is a GradedActivity variable. But, it can be used to accept arguments of any type that inherits from GradedActivity. For example, the following code passes objects of the FinalExam, PassFailActivity, and PassFailExam classes to the method:

```
GradedActivity exam1 = new FinalExam(50, 7);
GradedActivity exam2 = new PassFailActivity(70);
GradedActivity exam3 = new PassFailExam(100, 10, 70);
displayGrades(exam1);    // Pass a FinalExam object.
displayGrades(exam2);    // Pass a PassFailActivity object.
displayGrades(exam3);    // Pass a PassFailExam object.
```

The "Is-a" Relationship Does Not Work in Reverse

It is important to note that the "is-a" relationship does not work in reverse. Although the statement "a final exam is a graded activity" is true, the statement "a graded activity is a final exam" is not true. This is because not all graded activities are final exams. Likewise, not all GradedActivity objects are FinalExam objects. So, the following code will not work:

```
GradedActivity activity = new GradedActivity();
FinalExam exam = activity;     // ERROR!
```

You cannot assign the address of a `GradedActivity` object to a `FinalExam` variable. This makes sense because `FinalExam` objects have capabilities that go beyond those of a `GradedActivity` object. Interestingly, the Java compiler will let you make such an assignment if you use a type cast, as shown here:

```
GradedActivity activity = new GradedActivity();
FinalExam exam = (FinalExam) activity;  // Will compile but not run.
```

But, the program will crash when the assignment statement executes.

The `instanceof` Operator

There is an operator in Java named `instanceof` that you can use to determine whether an object is an instance of a particular class. Here is the general form of an expression that uses the `instanceof` operator:

> *refVar* instanceof *ClassName*

In the general form, *refVar* is a reference variable and *ClassName* is the name of a class. This is the form of a boolean expression that will return `true` if the object referenced by *refVar* is an instance of *ClassName*. Otherwise, the expression returns `false`. For example, the `if` statement in the following code determines whether the reference variable `activity` references a `GradedActivity` object:

```
GradedActivity activity = new GradedActivity();
if (activity instanceof GradedActivity)
    System.out.println("Yes, activity is a GradedActivity.");
else
    System.out.println("No, activity is not a GradedActivity.");
```

This code will display `"Yes, activity is a GradedActivity."`

The `instanceof` operator understands the "is-a" relationship that exists when a class inherits from another class. For example, look at the following code:

```
FinalExam exam = new FinalExam(20, 2);
if (exam instanceof GradedActivity)
    System.out.println("Yes, exam is a GradedActivity.");
else
    System.out.println("No, exam is not a GradedActivity.");
```

Even though the object referenced by `exam` is a `FinalExam` object, this code will display `"Yes, exam is a GradedActivity."` The `instanceof` operator returns true because `FinalExam` is a subclass of `GradedActivity`.

Checkpoint

11.18 Recall the `Rectangle` and `Cube` classes discussed earlier, as shown in Figure 11-18.

Figure 11-18 Rectangle and Cube classes

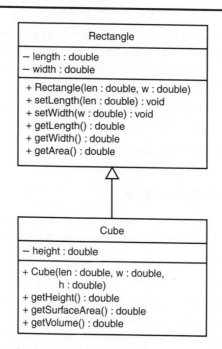

a) Is the following statement legal or illegal? If it is illegal, why?

```
Rectangle r = new Cube(10, 12, 5);
```

b) If you determined that the statement in part a is legal, are the following statements legal or illegal? (Indicate legal or illegal for each statement.)

```
System.out.println(r.getLength());
System.out.println(r.getWidth());
System.out.println(r.getHeight());
System.out.println(r.getSurfaceArea());
```

c) Is the following statement legal or illegal? If it is illegal, why?

```
Cube c = new Rectangle(10, 12);
```

11.8 Abstract Classes and Abstract Methods

CONCEPT: An abstract class is not instantiated, but other classes extend it. An abstract method has no body and must be overridden in a subclass.

An abstract method is a method that appears in a superclass, but expects to be overridden in a subclass. An abstract method has only a header and no body. Here is the general format of an abstract method header:

AccessSpecifier abstract *ReturnType MethodName(ParameterList)*;

Notice that the key word `abstract` appears in the header, and that the header ends with a semicolon. There is no body for the method. Here is an example of an abstract method header:

```
public abstract void setValue(int value);
```

When an abstract method appears in a class, the method must be overridden in a subclass. If a subclass fails to override the method, an error will result. Abstract methods are used to ensure that a subclass implements the method.

When a class contains an abstract method, you cannot create an instance of the class. Abstract methods are commonly used in abstract classes. An abstract class is not instantiated itself, but serves as a superclass for other classes. The abstract class represents the generic or abstract form of all the classes that inherit from it.

For example, consider a factory that manufactures airplanes. The factory does not make a generic airplane, but makes three specific types of airplanes: two different models of prop-driven planes and one commuter jet model. The computer software that catalogs the planes might use an abstract class named `Airplane`. That class has members representing the common characteristics of all airplanes. In addition, the software has classes for each of the three specific airplane models the factory manufactures. These classes all extend the `Airplane` class, and they have members representing the unique characteristics of each type of plane. The `Airplane` class is never instantiated, but is used as a superclass for the other classes.

A class becomes abstract when you place the `abstract` key word in the class definition. Here is the general format:

AccessSpecifier abstract class *ClassName*

An abstract class is not instantiated, but other classes extend it. An abstract method has no body and must be overridden in a subclass.

For example, look at the following abstract class `Student` shown in Code Listing 11-26. It holds data common to all students, but does not hold all the data needed for students of specific majors.

Code Listing 11-26   (`Student.java`)

```java
1   /**
2       The Student class is an abstract class that holds
3       general data about a student. Classes representing
4       specific types of students should inherit from
5       this class.
6   */
7
8   public abstract class Student
9   {
10      private String name;        // Student name
11      private String idNumber;    // Student ID
12      private int yearAdmitted;   // Year admitted
13
14      /**
15          The constructor sets the student's name,
16          ID number, and year admitted.
```

```
17          @param n The student's name.
18          @param id The student's ID number.
19          @param year The year the student was admitted.
20       */
21
22       public Student(String n, String id, int year)
23       {
24          name = n;
25          idNumber = id;
26          yearAdmitted = year;
27       }
28
29       /**
30          The toString method returns a String containing
31          the student's data.
32          @return A reference to a String.
33       */
34
35       public String toString()
36       {
37          String str;
38
39          str = "Name: " + name
40             + "\nID Number: " + idNumber
41             + "\nYear Admitted: " + yearAdmitted;
42          return str;
43       }
44
45       /**
46          The getRemainingHours method is abstract.
47          It must be overridden in a subclass.
48          @return The hours remaining for the student.
49       */
50
51       public abstract int getRemainingHours();
52    }
```

The Student class contains fields for storing a student's name, ID number, and year admitted. It also has a constructor, a toString method, and an abstract method named getRemainingHours.

This abstract method must be overridden in classes that inherit from the Student class. The idea behind this method is that it returns the number of hours remaining for a student to take in his or her major. It was made abstract because this class is intended to be the base for other classes that represent students of specific majors. For example, a CompSciStudent class might hold the data for a computer science student, and a BiologyStudent class might hold the data for a biology student. Computer science students must take courses in different disciplines than those taken by biology students. It stands to reason that the

CompSciStudent class will calculate the number of hours remaining to be taken differently than the BiologyStudent class. Let's look at an example of the CompSciStudent class, which is shown in Code Listing 11-27.

Code Listing 11-27   (CompSciStudent.java)

```java
 1 /**
 2     This class holds data for a computer science student.
 3 */
 4
 5 public class CompSciStudent extends Student
 6 {
 7     // Required hours
 8     private final int MATH_HOURS = 20;   // Math hours
 9     private final int CS_HOURS = 40;     // Comp sci hours
10     private final int GEN_ED_HOURS = 60; // Gen ed hours
11
12     // Hours taken
13     private int mathHours;  // Math hours taken
14     private int csHours;    // Comp sci hours taken
15     private int genEdHours; // General ed hours taken
16
17     /**
18         The constructor sets the student's name,
19         ID number, and the year admitted.
20         @param n The student's name.
21         @param id The student's ID number.
22         @param year The year the student was admitted.
23     */
24
25     public CompSciStudent(String n, String id, int year)
26     {
27         super(n, id, year);
28
29     }
30
31     /**
32         The setMathHours method sets the number of
33         math hours taken.
34         @param math The math hours taken.
35     */
36
37     public void setMathHours(int math)
38     {
39         mathHours = math;
40     }
41
```

```
42    /**
43        The setCsHours method sets the number of
44        computer science hours taken.
45        @param cs The computer science hours taken.
46    */
47
48    public void setCsHours(int cs)
49    {
50        csHours = cs;
51    }
52
53    /**
54        The setGenEdHours method sets the number of
55        general ed hours taken.
56        @param genEd The general ed hours taken.
57    */
58
59    public void setGenEdHours(int genEd)
60    {
61        genEdHours = genEd;
62    }
63
64    /**
65        The getRemainingHours method returns the
66        number of hours remaining to be taken.
67        @return The hours remaining for the student.
68    */
69
70    public int getRemainingHours()
71    {
72        int reqHours,        // Total required hours
73            remainingHours;  // Remaining hours
74
75        // Calculate the required hours.
76        reqHours = MATH_HOURS + CS_HOURS + GEN_ED_HOURS;
77
78        // Calculate the remaining hours.
79        remainingHours = reqHours - (mathHours + csHours
80                        + genEdHours);
81
82        return remainingHours;
83    }
84
85    /**
86        The toString method returns a string containing
87        the student's data.
88        @return A reference to a String.
89    */
```

```
 90
 91      public String toString()
 92      {
 93         String str;
 94
 95         str = super.toString() +
 96             "\nMajor: Computer Science" +
 97             "\nMath Hours Taken: " + mathHours +
 98             "\nComputer Science Hours Taken: " + csHours +
 99             "\nGeneral Ed Hours Taken: " + genEdHours;
100
101         return str;
102      }
103 }
```

The `CompSciStudent` class, which extends the `Student` class, declares the following `final` integer fields in lines 8 through 10: `MATH_HOURS`, `CS_HOURS`, and `GEN_ED_HOURS`. These fields hold the required number of math, computer science, and general education hours for a computer science student. It also declares the following fields in lines 13 through 15: `mathHours`, `csHours`, and `genEdHours`. These fields hold the number of math, computer science, and general education hours taken by the student. Mutator methods are provided to store values in these fields. In addition, the class overrides the `toString` method and the abstract `getRemainingHours` method. The program in Code Listing 11-28 demonstrates the class.

Code Listing 11-28   (`CompSciStudentDemo.java`)

```
 1  /**
 2      This program demonstrates the CompSciStudent class.
 3  */
 4
 5  public class CompSciStudentDemo
 6  {
 7      public static void main(String[] args)
 8      {
 9         // Create a CompSciStudent object.
10         CompSciStudent csStudent =
11                 new CompSciStudent("Jennifer Haynes",
12                                    "167W98337", 2004);
13
14         // Store values for math, CS, and gen ed hours.
15         csStudent.setMathHours(12);
16         csStudent.setCsHours(20);
17         csStudent.setGenEdHours(40);
18
19         // Display the student's data.
```

```
20              System.out.println(csStudent);
21
22              // Display the number of remaining hours.
23              System.out.println("Hours remaining: " +
24                              csStudent.getRemainingHours());
25      }
26   }
```

Program Output

```
Name: Jennifer Haynes
ID Number: 167W98337
Year Admitted: 2004
Major: Computer Science
Math Hours Taken: 12
Computer Science Hours Taken: 20
General Ed Hours Taken: 40
Hours remaining: 48
```

Remember the following points about abstract methods and classes:

- Abstract methods and abstract classes are defined with the `abstract` key word.
- Abstract methods have no body, and their header must end with a semicolon.
- An abstract method must be overridden in a subclass.
- When a class contains an abstract method, it cannot be instantiated. It must serve as a superclass.
- An abstract class cannot be instantiated. It must serve as a superclass.

Abstract Classes in UML

Abstract classes are drawn like regular classes in UML, except the name of the class and the names of abstract methods are shown in italics. For example, Figure 11-19 shows a UML diagram for the `Student` class.

Figure 11-19 UML Diagram for the `Student` class

Checkpoint

11.19 What is the purpose of an abstract method?

11.20 If a subclass extends a superclass with an abstract method, what must you do in the subclass?

11.21 What is the purpose of an abstract class?

11.22 If a class is defined as abstract, what can you not do with the class?

11.9 Interfaces

CONCEPT: An interface specifies behavior for a class.

In the previous section you learned that an abstract class cannot be instantiated, but is intended to serve as a superclass. You also learned that an abstract method has no body and must be overridden in a subclass. An interface is similar to an abstract class that has all abstract methods. It cannot be instantiated, and all of the methods listed in an interface must be written elsewhere. The purpose of an interface is to specify behavior for a class.

An interface looks similar to a class, except the key word `interface` is used instead of the key word `class`, and the methods that are specified in an interface have no bodies, only headers that are terminated by semicolons. Here is the general format of an interface definition:

```
public interface InterfaceName
{
    (Method headers . . .)

}
```

For example, Code Listing 11-29 shows an interface named `Relatable`, which is intended to be used with the `GradedActivity` class presented earlier. This interface has three method headers: `equals`, `isGreater`, and `isLess`. Notice that each method accepts a `GradedActivity` object as its argument. Also notice that no access specifier is used with the method headers, because all methods specified by an interface are public.

Code Listing 11-29   (`Relatable.java`)

```
 1  /**
 2      Relatable interface
 3  */
 4
 5  public interface Relatable
 6  {
 7     boolean equals(GradedActivity g);
 8     boolean isGreater(GradedActivity g);
 9     boolean isLess(GradedActivity g);
10  }
```

In order for a class to use an interface, it must implement the interface. This is accomplished with the `implements` key word. For example, suppose we have a class named `FinalExam3` that inherits from the `GradedActivity` class and implements the `Relatable` interface. The first line of its definition would look like the following:

```
public class FinalExam3 extends GradedActivity
                        implements Relatable
```

When a class implements an interface, it is agreeing to provide all of the methods that are specified by the interface. It is often said that an interface is like a "contract," and when a class implements an interface it must adhere to the contract.

A class that implements an interface must provide all of the methods that are listed in the interface, with the exact signatures specified and with the same return type. So, in the example previously shown, the `FinalExam3` class must provide an `equals` method, an `isGreater` method, and an `isLess` method, all of which accept a `GradedActivity` object as an argument and return a `boolean` value.

You might have guessed that the `Relatable` interface is named "Relatable" because it specifies methods that presumably, make relational comparisons with `GradedActivity` objects. The intent is to make any class that implements this interface "relatable" with `GradedActivity` objects by ensuring that it has an `equals`, an `isGreater`, and an `isLess` method that perform relational comparisons. But, the interface only specifies the headers for these methods, not what the methods should do. Although the programmer of a class that implements the `Relatable` interface can choose what those methods should do, he or she should provide methods that comply with this intent.

Code Listing 11-30 shows the complete code for the `FinalExam3` class, which implements the `Relatable` interface. The `equals`, `isGreater`, and `isLess` methods compare the calling object with the object passed as an argument. The program in Code Listing 11-31 demonstrates the class.

Code Listing 11-30 (FinalExam3.java)

```
 1 /**
 2     This class determines the grade for a final exam.
 3 */
 4
 5 public class FinalExam3 extends GradedActivity
 6                         implements Relatable
 7 {
 8     private int numQuestions;     // Number of questions
 9     private double pointsEach;    // Points for each question
10     private int numMissed;        // Questions missed
11
12     /**
13         The constructor sets the number of questions on the
14         exam and the number of questions missed.
15         @param questions The number of questions.
16         @param missed The number of questions missed.
```

```
17     */
18
19     public FinalExam3(int questions, int missed)
20     {
21        double numericScore;        // To hold a numeric score
22
23        // Set the numQuestions and numMissed fields.
24        numQuestions = questions;
25        numMissed = missed;
26
27        // Calculate the points for each question and
28        // the numeric score for this exam.
29        pointsEach = 100.0 / questions;
30        numericScore = 100.0 - (missed * pointsEach);
31
32        // Call the inherited setScore method to
33        // set the numeric score.
34        setScore(numericScore);
35     }
36
37     /**
38        The getPointsEach method returns the number of
39        points each question is worth.
40        @return The value in the pointsEach field.
41     */
42
43     public double getPointsEach()
44     {
45        return pointsEach;
46     }
47
48     /**
49        The getNumMissed method returns the number of
50        questions missed.
51        @return The value in the numMissed field.
52     */
53
54     public int getNumMissed()
55     {
56        return numMissed;
57     }
58
59     /**
60        The equals method compares the calling object
61        to the argument object for equality.
62        @return true if the calling
63        object's score is equal to the argument's
64        score.
```

```
65        */
66
67        public boolean equals(GradedActivity g)
68        {
69           boolean status;
70
71           if (this.getScore() == g.getScore())
72              status = true;
73           else
74              status = false;
75
76           return status;
77        }
78
79        /**
80           The isGreater method determines whether the calling
81           object is greater than the argument object.
82           @return true if the calling object's score is
83           greater than the argument object's score.
84        */
85
86        public boolean isGreater(GradedActivity g)
87        {
88           boolean status;
89
90           if (this.getScore() > g.getScore())
91              status = true;
92           else
93              status = false;
94
95           return status;
96        }
97
98        /**
99           The isLess method determines whether the calling
100          object is less than the argument object.
101          @return true if the calling object's score is
102          less than the argument object's score.
103       */
104
105       public boolean isLess(GradedActivity g)
106       {
107          boolean status;
108
109          if (this.getScore() < g.getScore())
110             status = true;
111          else
112             status = false;
```

```
113
114          return status;
115      }
116 }
```

Code Listing 11-31 (`InterfaceDemo.java`)

```
1   /**
2       This program demonstrates the FinalExam3 class, which
3       implements the Relatable interface.
4   */
5
6   public class InterfaceDemo
7   {
8       public static void main(String[] args)
9       {
10          // Exam #1 had 100 questions and the student
11          // missed 20 questions.
12          FinalExam3 exam1 = new FinalExam3(100, 20);
13
14          // Exam #2 had 100 questions and the student
15          // missed 30 questions.
16          FinalExam3 exam2 = new FinalExam3(100, 30);
17
18          // Display the exam scores.
19          System.out.println("Exam 1: " +
20                              exam1.getScore());
21          System.out.println("Exam 2: " +
22                              exam2.getScore());
23
24          // Compare the exam scores.
25          if (exam1.equals(exam2))
26              System.out.println("The exam scores " +
27                              "are equal.");
28
29          if (exam1.isGreater(exam2))
30              System.out.println("The Exam 1 score " +
31                              "is the highest.");
32
33          if (exam1.isLess(exam2))
34              System.out.println("The Exam 1 score " +
35                              "is the lowest.");
36      }
37  }
```

Fields in Interfaces

An interface can contain field declarations, but all fields in an interface are treated as `final` and `static`. Because they automatically become `final`, you must provide an initialization value. For example, look at the following interface definition:

```
public interface Doable
{
    int FIELD1 = 1;
    int FIELD2 = 2;
    (Method headers . . .)
}
```

In this interface, `FIELD1` and `FIELD2` are `final static int` variables. Any class that implements this interface has access to these variables.

Implementing Multiple Interfaces

You might be wondering why we need both abstract classes and interfaces, since they are so similar to each other. The reason is that a class can extend only one superclass, but Java allows a class to implement multiple interfaces. When a class implements multiple interfaces, it must provide the methods specified by all of them.

To specify multiple interfaces in a class definition, simply list the names of the interfaces, separated by commas, after the `implements` key word. Here is the first line of an example of a class that implements multiple interfaces:

```
public class MyClass implements Interface1,
                                 Interface2,
                                 Interface3
```

This class implements three interfaces: `Interface1`, `Interface2`, and `Interface3`.

Interfaces in UML

In a UML diagram, an interface is drawn like a class, except the interface name and the method names are italicized, and the <<interface>> tag is shown above the interface name. The relationship between a class and an interface is known as a realization relationship (the class realizes the interfaces). You show a realization relationship in a UML diagram by connecting a class and an interface with a dashed line that has an open arrowhead at one end. The arrowhead points to the interface. This depicts the realization relationship. Figure 11-20 is a UML diagram showing the relationships among the `GradedActivity` class, the `FinalExam3` class, and the `Relatable` interface.

Figure 11-20   Realization relationship in a UML diagram

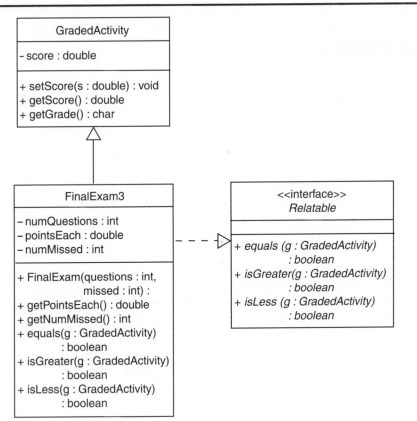

Polymorphism and Interfaces

Just as you can create reference variables of a class type, Java allows you to create reference variables of an interface type. An interface reference variable can reference any object that implements that interface, regardless of its class type. This is another example of polymorphism. For example, look at the `RetailItem` interface in Code Listing 11-32.

Code Listing 11-32   `(RetailItem.java)`

```
1  /**
2      RetailItem interface
3  */
4
5  public interface RetailItem
6  {
7      public double getRetailPrice();
8  }
```

This interface specifies only one method: `getRetailPrice`. Both the `CompactDisc` and `DvdMovie` classes, shown in Code Listings 11-33 and 11-34, implement this interface.

Code Listing 11-33   (`CompactDisc.java`)

```java
 1   /**
 2       Compact Disc class
 3   */
 4
 5   public class CompactDisc implements RetailItem
 6   {
 7      private String title;         // The CD's title
 8      private String artist;        // The CD's artist
 9      private double retailPrice;   // The CD's retail price
10
11      /**
12          Constructor
13          @param cdTitle The CD title.
14          @param cdArtist The name of the artist.
15          @param cdPrice The CD's price.
16      */
17
18      public CompactDisc(String cdTitle, String cdArtist,
19                      double cdPrice)
20      {
21         title = cdTitle;
22         artist = cdArtist;
23         retailPrice = cdPrice;
24      }
25
26      /**
27          getTitle method
28          @return The CD's title.
29      */
30
31      public String getTitle()
32      {
33         return title;
34      }
35
36      /**
37          getArtist method
38          @return The name of the artist.
39      */
40
41      public String getArtist()
42      {
```

```
43           return artist;
44       }
45
46       /**
47          getRetailPrice method (Required by the RetailItem
48          interface)
49          @return The retail price of the CD.
50       */
51
52       public double getRetailPrice()
53       {
54           return retailPrice;
55       }
56   }
```

Code Listing 11-34   (DvdMovie.java)

```
1    /**
2        DvdMovie class
3    */
4
5    public class DvdMovie implements RetailItem
6    {
7        private String title;        // The DVD's title
8        private int runningTime;      // Running time in minutes
9        private double retailPrice;   // The DVD's retail price
10
11       /**
12          Constructor
13          @param dvdTitle The DVD title.
14          @param runTime The running time in minutes.
15          @param dvdPrice The DVD's price.
16       */
17
18       public DvdMovie(String dvdTitle, int runTime,
19                                       double dvdPrice)
20       {
21           title = dvdTitle;
22           runningTime = runTime;
23           retailPrice = dvdPrice;
24       }
25
26       /**
27          getTitle method
28          @return The DVD's title.
29       */
```

```
30
31      public String getTitle()
32      {
33          return title;
34      }
35
36      /**
37         getRunningTime method
38         @return The running time in minutes.
39      */
40
41      public int getRunningTime()
42      {
43          return runningTime;
44      }
45
46      /**
47         getRetailPrice method (Required by the RetailItem
48         interface)
49         @return The retail price of the DVD.
50      */
51
52      public double getRetailPrice()
53      {
54          return retailPrice;
55      }
56  }
```

Because they implement the RetailItem interface, objects of these classes may be referenced by a RetailItem reference variable. The following code demonstrates:

```
RetailItem item1 = new CompactDisc("Songs From the Heart",
                                   "Billy Nelson",
                                   18.95);
RetailItem item2 = new DvdMovie("Planet X",
                                102,
                                22.95);
```

In this code, two RetailItem reference variables, item1 and item2, are declared. The item1 variable references a CompactDisc object and the item2 variable references a DvdMovie object. This is possible because both the CompactDisc and DvdMovie classes implement the RetailItem interface. When a class implements an interface, an inheritance relationship known as interface inheritance is established. Because of this inheritance relationship, a CompactDisc object is a RetailItem, and likewise, a DvdMovie object is a RetailItem. Therefore, we can create RetailItem reference variables and have them reference CompactDisc and DvdMovie objects.

The program in Code Listing 11-35 demonstrates how an interface reference variable can be used as a method parameter.

Code Listing 11-35   `(PolymorphicInterfaceDemo.java)`

```java
 1  import java.text.DecimalFormat;
 2
 3  /**
 4     This program demonstrates that an interface type may
 5     be used to create a polymorphic reference.
 6  */
 7
 8  public class PolymorphicInterfaceDemo
 9  {
10     public static void main(String[] args)
11     {
12        // Create a CompactDisc object.
13        CompactDisc cd =
14                new CompactDisc("Greatest Hits",
15                                "Joe Looney Band",
16                                18.95);
17        // Create a DvdMovie object.
18        DvdMovie movie =
19                new DvdMovie("Wheels of Fury",
20                             137, 12.95);
21
22        // Display the CD's title.
23        System.out.println("Item #1: " +
24                           cd.getTitle());
25
26        // Display the CD's price.
27        showPrice(cd);
28
29        // Display the DVD's title.
30        System.out.println("Item #2: " +
31                           movie.getTitle());
32
33        // Display the DVD's price.
34        showPrice(movie);
35     }
36
37     /**
38        The showPrice method displays the price
39        of a RetailItem object.
40        @param item A reference to a RetailItem object.
41     */
42
43     private static void showPrice(RetailItem item)
44     {
45        DecimalFormat dollar =
46                        new DecimalFormat("#,##.00");
```

```
47
48            System.out.println("Price: $" +
49                    dollar.format(item.getRetailPrice()));
50     }
51  }
```

Program Output

```
Item #1: Greatest Hits
Price: $18.95
Item #2: Wheels of Fury
Price: $12.95
```

There are some limitations to using interface reference variables. As previously mentioned, you cannot create an instance of an interface. In addition, when an interface variable references an object, you can use the interface variable to call only the methods that are specified in the interface. For example, look at the following code:

```
// Reference a CompactDisc object with a RetailItem variable.
RetailItem item = new CompactDisc("Greatest Hits",
                                  "Joe Looney Band",
                                  18.95);

// Call the getRetailPrice method . . .
System.out.println(item.getRetailPrice());  // OK, this works.
// Attempt to call the getTitle method . . .
System.out.println(item.getTitle());  // ERROR! Will not compile!
```

The last line of code will not compile because the RetailItem interface specifies only one method: getRetailPrice. So, we cannot use a RetailItem reference variable to call any other method.

TIP: It is possible to cast an interface reference variable to the type of the object it references, and then call methods that are members of that type. The syntax is somewhat awkward, however. The statement that causes the compiler error in the example code could be rewritten as:

```
    System.out.println(((CompactDisc)item).getTitle());
```

 Checkpoint

11.23 What is the purpose of an interface?

11.24 How is an interface similar to an abstract class?

11.25 How is an interface different from an abstract class, or any class?

11.26 If an interface has fields, how are they treated?

11.27 Write the first line of a class named Customer, which implements an interface named Relatable.

11.28 Write the first line of a class named Employee, which implements interfaces named Payable and Listable.

11.10 Common Errors to Avoid

The following list describes several errors that are commonly committed when learning this chapter's topics:

- **Attempting to access a private superclass member directly from a subclass.** Private superclass members cannot be directly accessed by a method in a subclass. The subclass must call a public or protected superclass method in order to access the superclass's private members.
- **Forgetting to call a superclass constructor explicitly when the superclass does not have a default constructor or a programmer-defined no-arg constructor.** When a superclass does not have a default constructor or a programmer-defined no-arg constructor, the subclass's constructor must explicitly call one of the constructors that the superclass does have.
- **Allowing the superclass's no-arg constructor to be implicitly called when you intend to call another superclass constructor.** If a subclass's constructor does not explicitly call a superclass constructor, Java automatically calls the superclass's no-arg constructor.
- **Forgetting to precede a call to an overridden superclass method with super.** When a subclass method calls an overridden superclass method, it must precede the method call with the key word super and a dot (.). Failing to do so results in the subclass's version of the method being called.
- **Forgetting a class member's access specifier.** When you do not give a class member an access specifier, it is granted package access by default. This means that any method in the same package may access the member.
- **Writing a body for an abstract method.** An abstract method cannot have a body. It must be overridden in a subclass.
- **Forgetting to terminate an abstract method's header with a semicolon.** An abstract method header does not have a body, and it must be terminated with a semicolon.
- **Failing to override an abstract method.** An abstract method must be overridden in a subclass.
- **Overloading an abstract method instead of overriding it.** Overloading is not the same as overriding. When a superclass has an abstract method, the subclass must have a method with the same signature as the abstract method.
- **Trying to instantiate an abstract class.** You cannot create an instance of an abstract class.
- **Implementing an interface but forgetting to provide all of the methods specified by the interface.** When a class implements an interface, all of the methods specified by the interface must be provided in the class.
- **Writing a method specified by an interface but failing to use the exact signature and return type.** When a class implements an interface, the class must have methods with the same signature and return type as the methods specified in the interface.

Review Questions and Exercises

Multiple Choice and True/False

1. In an inheritance relationship, this is the general class.
   a. subclass
   b. superclass
   c. slave class
   d. child class

2. In an inheritance relationship, this is the specialized class.
   a. superclass
   b. master class
   c. subclass
   d. parent class

3. This key word indicates that a class inherits from another class.
   a. derived
   b. specialized
   c. based
   d. extends

4. A subclass does not have access to these superclass members.
   a. public
   b. private
   c. protected
   d. all of these

5. This key word refers to an object's superclass.
   a. super
   b. base
   c. superclass
   d. this

6. In a subclass constructor, a call to the superclass constructor must _____.
   a. appear as the very first statement
   b. appear as the very last statement
   c. appear between the constructor's header and the opening brace
   d. not appear

7. The following is an explicit call to the superclass's default constructor.
   a. default();
   b. class();
   c. super();
   d. base();

8. A method in a subclass that has the same signature as a method in the superclass is an example of _____.
   a. overloading
   b. overriding

   c. composition
   d. an error

9. A method in a subclass having the same name as a method in the superclass but a different signature is an example of _____.

   a. overloading
   b. overriding
   c. composition
   d. an error

10. These superclass members are accessible to subclasses and classes in the same package.

   a. private
   b. public
   c. protected
   d. all of these

11. All classes directly or indirectly inherit from this class.

   a. `Object`
   b. `Super`
   c. `Root`
   d. `Java`

12. With this type of binding, the Java Virtual Machine determines at runtime which method to call, depending on the type of the object that a variable references.

   a. static
   b. early
   c. flexible
   d. dynamic

13. This operator can be used to determine whether a reference variable references an object of a particular class.

   a. `isclass`
   b. `typeof`
   c. `instanceof`
   d. `isinstance`

14. When a class implements an interface, it must _____.

   a. overload all of the methods listed in the interface
   b. provide all of the methods that are listed in the interface, with the exact signatures and return types specified
   c. not have a constructor
   d. be an abstract class

15. Fields in an interface are _____.

   a. `final`
   b. `static`
   c. both `final` and `static`
   d. not allowed

16. Abstract methods must be _____.
    a. overridden
    b. overloaded
    c. deleted and replaced with real methods
    d. declared as private

17. Abstract classes cannot _____.
    a. be used as superclasses
    b. have abstract methods
    c. be instantiated
    d. have fields

18. **True or False:** Constructors are not inherited.

19. **True or False:** In a subclass, a call to the superclass constructor can only be written in the subclass constructor.

20. **True or False:** If a subclass constructor does not explicitly call a superclass constructor, Java will not call any of the superclass's constructors.

21. **True or False:** An object of a superclass can access members declared in a subclass.

22. **True or False:** The superclass constructor always executes before the subclass constructor.

23. **True or False:** When a method is declared with the `final` modifier, it must be overridden in a subclass.

24. **True or False:** A superclass has a member with package access. A class that is outside the superclass's package but inherits from the superclass can access the member.

25. **True or False:** A superclass reference variable can reference an object of a subclass that extends the superclass.

26. **True or False:** A subclass reference variable can reference an object of the superclass.

27. **True or False:** When a class contains an abstract method, the class cannot be instantiated.

28. **True or False:** A class may only implement one interface.

29. **True or False:** By default all members of an interface are public.

Find the Error

Find the error in each of the following code segments:

1.
```
// Superclass
public class Vehicle
{
    (Member declarations . . . )
}
// Subclass
public class Car expands Vehicle
```

```
   {
      (Member declarations . . . )
   }

2. // Superclass
   public class Vehicle
   {
      private double cost;
      (Other methods . . . )
   }

   // Subclass
   public class Car extends Vehicle
   {
      public Car(double c)
      {
         cost = c;
      }
   }

3. // Superclass
   public class Vehicle
   {
      private double cost;
      public Vehicle(double c)
      {
         cost = c;
      }
      (Other methods . . . )
   }

   // Subclass
   public class Car extends Vehicle
   {
      private int passengers;
      public Car(int p)
      {
         passengers = c;
      }
      (Other methods . . . )
   }

4. // Superclass
   public class Vehicle
   {
      public abstract double getMilesPerGallon();
      (Other methods . . . )
   }
```

```
// Subclass
public class Car extends Vehicle
{
   private int mpg;

   public int getMilesPerGallon();
   {
      return mpg;
   }
   (Other methods . . . )
}
```

Algorithm Workbench

1. Write the first line of the definition for a `Poodle` class. The class should extend the `Dog` class.

2. Look at the following code which is the first line of a class definition:

   `public class Tiger extends Felis`

   In what order will the class constructors execute?

3. Write the declaration for class `B`. The class's members should be as follows:
   - `m`, an integer. This variable should not be accessible to code outside the class or to any class that extends class `B`.
   - `n`, an integer. This variable should be accessible only to classes that extend class `B` or in the same package as class `B`.
   - `setM`, `getM`, `setN`, and `getN`. These are the mutator and accessor methods for the member variables `m` and `n`. These methods should be accessible to code outside the class.
   - `calc`. This is a public abstract method.

   Next, write the declaration for class `D`, which extends class `B`. The class's members should be as follows:
   - `q`, a `double`. This variable should not be accessible to code outside the class.
   - `r`, a `double`. This variable should be accessible to any class that extends class `D` or in the same package.
   - `setQ`, `getQ`, `setR`, and `getR`. These are the mutator and accessor methods for the member variables `q` and `r`. These methods should be accessible to code outside the class.
   - `calc`, a public method that overrides the superclass's abstract `calc` method. This method should return the value of `q` times `r`.

4. Write the statement that calls a superclass constructor and passes the arguments `x`, `y`, and `z`.

5. A superclass has the following method:

   ```
   public void setValue(int v)
   {
      value = v;
   }
   ```

Write a statement that may appear in a subclass that calls this method, passing 10 as an argument.

6. A superclass has the following abstract method:

```
public abstract int getValue();
```

Write an example of a getValue method that can appear in a subclass.

7. Write the first line of the definition for a Stereo class. The class should extend the SoundSystem class, and it should implement the CDplayable, TunerPlayable, and CassettePlayable interfaces.

8. Write an interface named Nameable that specifies the following methods:

```
public void setName(String n)
public String getName()
```

Short Answer

1. What is an "is-a" relationship?

2. A program uses two classes: Animal and Dog. Which class is the superclass and which is the subclass?

3. What is the superclass and what is the subclass in the following line?

```
public class Pet extends Dog
```

4. What is the difference between a protected class member and a private class member?

5. Can a subclass ever directly access the private members of its superclass?

6. Which constructor is called first, that of the subclass or the superclass?

7. What is the difference between overriding a superclass method and overloading a superclass method?

8. Reference variables can be polymorphic. What does this mean?

9. When does dynamic binding take place?

10. What is an abstract method?

11. What is an abstract class?

12. What are the differences between an abstract class and an interface?

Programming Challenges

1. Employee and ProductionWorker Classes

VideoNote
The Employee and Productionworker Classes problem

Design a class named Employee. The class should keep the following information in fields:

- Employee name
- Employee number in the format XXX–L, where each X is a digit within the range 0–9 and the L is a letter within the range A–M.
- Hire date

Write one or more constructors and the appropriate accessor and mutator methods for the class.

Next, write a class named `ProductionWorker` that extends the `Employee` class. The `ProductionWorker` class should have fields to hold the following information:

- Shift (an integer)
- Hourly pay rate (a `double`)

The workday is divided into two shifts: day and night. The shift field will be an integer value representing the shift that the employee works. The day shift is shift 1 and the night shift is shift 2. Write one or more constructors and the appropriate accessor and mutator methods for the class. Demonstrate the classes by writing a program that uses a `ProductionWorker` object.

2. `ShiftSupervisor` Class

In a particular factory, a shift supervisor is a salaried employee who supervises a shift. In addition to a salary, the shift supervisor earns a yearly bonus when his or her shift meets production goals. Design a `ShiftSupervisor` class that extends the `Employee` class you created in Programming Challenge 1. The `ShiftSupervisor` class should have a field that holds the annual salary and a field that holds the annual production bonus that a shift supervisor has earned. Write one or more constructors and the appropriate accessor and mutator methods for the class. Demonstrate the class by writing a program that uses a `ShiftSupervisor` object.

3. `TeamLeader` Class

In a particular factory, a team leader is an hourly paid production worker that leads a small team. In addition to hourly pay, team leaders earn a fixed monthly bonus. Team leaders are required to attend a minimum number of hours of training per year. Design a `TeamLeader` class that extends the `ProductionWorker` class you designed in Programming Challenge 1. The `TeamLeader` class should have fields for the monthly bonus amount, the required number of training hours, and the number of training hours that the team leader has attended. Write one or more constructors and the appropriate accessor and mutator methods for the class. Demonstrate the class by writing a program that uses a `TeamLeader` object.

★ myCodeMate 4. Essay Class

Design an `Essay` class that extends the `GradedActivity` class presented in this chapter. The `Essay` class should determine the grade a student receives for an essay. The student's essay score can be up to 100 and is determined in the following manner:

Grammar: 30 points
Spelling: 20 points
Correct length: 20 points
Content: 30 points

Demonstrate the class in a simple program.

5. Course Grades

In a course, a teacher gives the following tests and assignments:

- A **lab activity** that is observed by the teacher and assigned a numeric score.
- A **pass/fail exam** that has 10 questions. The minimum passing score is 70.
- An **essay** that is assigned a numeric score.
- A **final exam** that has 50 questions.

Write a class named `CourseGrades`. The class should have a `GradedActivity` array named `grades` as a field. The array should have four elements, one for each of the assignments previously described. The class should have the following methods:

`setLab:`	This method should accept a `GradedActivity` object as its argument. This object should already hold the student's score for the lab activity. Element 0 of the `grades` field should reference this object.
`setPassFailExam:`	This method should accept a `PassFailExam` object as its argument. This object should already hold the student's score for the pass/fail exam. Element 1 of the `grades` field should reference this object.
`setEssay:`	This method should accept an `Essay` object as its argument. (See Programming Challenge 4 for the `Essay` class. If you have not completed Programming Challenge 4, use a `GradedActivity` object instead.) This object should already hold the student's score for the essay. Element 2 of the `grades` field should reference this object.
`setFinalExam:`	This method should accept a `FinalExam` object as its argument. This object should already hold the student's score for the final exam. Element 3 of the `grades` field should reference this object.
`toString:`	This method should return a string that contains the numeric scores and grades for each element in the `grades` array.

Demonstrate the class in a program.

6. `Analyzable` Interface

Modify the `CourseGrades` class you created in Programming Challenge 5 so it implements the following interface:

```
public interface Analyzable
{
    double getAverage();
    GradedActivity getHighest();
    GradedActivity getLowest();
}
```

The `getAverage` method should return the average of the numeric scores stored in the `grades` array. The `getHighest` method should return a reference to the element of the grades array that has the highest numeric score. The `getLowest` method should return a reference to the element of the grades array that has the lowest numeric score. Demonstrate the new methods in a complete program.

7. `Person` and `Customer` Classes

Design a class named `Person` with fields for holding a person's name, address, and telephone number. Write one or more constructors and the appropriate mutator and accessor methods for the class's fields.

Next, design a class named `Customer`, which extends the `Person` class. The `Customer` class should have a field for a customer number and a `boolean` field indicating whether the customer wishes to be on a mailing list. Write one or more constructors and the appropriate mutator and accessor methods for the class's fields. Demonstrate an object of the `Customer` class in a simple program.

8. `PreferredCustomer` Class

A retail store has a preferred customer plan where customers can earn discounts on all their purchases. The amount of a customer's discount is determined by the amount of the customer's cumulative purchases in the store as follows:

- When a preferred customer spends $500, he or she gets a 5 percent discount on all future purchases.
- When a preferred customer spends $1,000, he or she gets a 6 percent discount on all future purchases.
- When a preferred customer spends $1,500, he or she gets a 7 percent discount on all future purchases.
- When a preferred customer spends $2,000 or more, he or she gets a 10 percent discount on all future purchases.

Design a class named `PreferredCustomer`, which extends the `Customer` class you created in Programming Challenge 7. The `PreferredCustomer` class should have fields for the amount of the customer's purchases and the customer's discount level. Write one or more constructors and the appropriate mutator and accessor methods for the class's fields. Demonstrate the class in a simple program.

9. `BankAccount` and `SavingsAccount` Classes

Design an abstract class named `BankAccount` to hold the following data for a bank account:

- Balance
- Number of deposits this month
- Number of withdrawals
- Annual interest rate
- Monthly service charges

The class should have the following methods:

Constructor: The constructor should accept arguments for the balance and annual interest rate.

deposit:	A method that accepts an argument for the amount of the deposit. The method should add the argument to the account balance. It should also increment the variable holding the number of deposits.
withdraw:	A method that accepts an argument for the amount of the withdrawal. The method should subtract the argument from the balance. It should also increment the variable holding the number of withdrawals.
calcInterest:	A method that updates the balance by calculating the monthly interest earned by the account, and adding this interest to the balance. This is performed by the following formulas:

> Monthly Interest Rate = (Annual Interest Rate / 12)
> Monthly Interest = Balance * Monthly Interest Rate
> Balance = Balance + Monthly Interest

monthlyProcess:	A method that subtracts the monthly service charges from the balance, calls the calcInterest method, and then sets the variables that hold the number of withdrawals, number of deposits, and monthly service charges to zero.

Next, design a SavingsAccount class that extends the BankAccount class. The SavingsAccount class should have a status field to represent an active or inactive account. If the balance of a savings account falls below $25, it becomes inactive. (The status field could be a boolean variable.) No more withdrawals may be made until the balance is raised above $25, at which time the account becomes active again. The savings account class should have the following methods:

withdraw:	A method that determines whether the account is inactive before a withdrawal is made. (No withdrawal will be allowed if the account is not active.) A withdrawal is then made by calling the superclass version of the method.
deposit:	A method that determines whether the account is inactive before a deposit is made. If the account is inactive and the deposit brings the balance above $25, the account becomes active again. A deposit is then made by calling the superclass version of the method.
monthlyProcess:	Before the superclass method is called, this method checks the number of withdrawals. If the number of withdrawals for the month is more than 4, a service charge of $1 for each withdrawal above 4 is added to the superclass field that holds the monthly service charges. (Don't forget to check the account balance after the service charge is taken. If the balance falls below $25, the account becomes inactive.)

10. Ship, CruiseShip, and CargoShip Classes

Design a Ship class that the following members:

- A field for the name of the ship (a string).
- A field for the year that the ship was built (a string).

- A constructor and appropriate accessors and mutators.
- A `toString` method that displays the ship's name and the year it was built.

Design a `CruiseShip` class that extends the `Ship` class. The `CruiseShip` class should have the following members:

- A field for the maximum number of passengers (an `int`).
- A constructor and appropriate accessors and mutators.
- A `toString` method that overrides the `toString` method in the base class. The `CruiseShip` class's `toString` method should display only the ship's name and the maximum number of passengers.

Design a `CargoShip` class that extends the `Ship` class. The `CargoShip` class should have the following members:

- A field for the cargo capacity in tonnage (an `int`).
- A constructor and appropriate accessors and mutators.
- A `toString` method that overrides the `toString` method in the base class. The `CargoShip` class's `toString` method should display only the ship's name and the ship's cargo capacity.

Demonstrate the classes in a program that has a `Ship` array. Assign various `Ship`, `CruiseShip`, and `CargoShip` objects to the array elements. The program should then step through the array, calling each object's `toString` method. (See Code Listing 11-25 as an example.)

12 Exceptions and Advanced File I/O

12.1 Handling Exceptions

CONCEPT: An exception is an object that is generated as the result of an error or an unexpected event. To prevent exceptions from crashing your program, you must write code that detects and handles them.

VideoNote
Handling
Exceptions

There are many error conditions that can occur while a Java application is running that will cause it to halt execution. By now you have probably experienced this many times. For example, look at the program in Code Listing 12-1. This program attempts to read beyond the bounds of an array.

Code Listing 12-1 (`BadArray.java`)

```java
1 /**
2     This program causes an error and crashes.
3 */
4
5 public class BadArray
6 {
7     public static void main(String[] args)
8     {
```

```
 9          // Create an array with 3 elements.
10          int[] numbers = { 1, 2, 3 };
11
12          // Attempt to read beyond the bounds
13          // of the array.
14          for (int i = 0; i <= 3; i++)
15              System.out.println(numbers[i]);
16      }
17 }
```

Program Output

```
1
2
3
Exception in thread "main" java.lang.ArrayIndexOutOfBoundsException
        at BadArray.main(BadArray.java:15)
```

The `numbers` array in this program has only three elements, with the subscripts 0 though 2. The program crashes when it tries to read the element at `numbers[3]`, and displays an error message similar to that shown at the end of the program output. This message indicates that an exception occurred, and it gives some information about it. An *exception* is an object that is generated in memory as the result of an error or an unexpected event. When an exception is generated, it is said to have been "thrown." Unless an exception is detected by the application and dealt with, it causes the application to halt.

To detect that an exception has been thrown and prevent it from halting your application, Java allows you to create exception handlers. An *exception handler* is a section of code that gracefully responds to exceptions when they are thrown. The process of intercepting and responding to exceptions is called *exception handling*. If your code does not handle an exception when it is thrown, the *default exception handler* deals with it, as shown in Code Listing 12-1. The default exception handler prints an error message and crashes the program.

The error that caused the exception to be thrown in Code Listing 12-1 is easy to avoid. If the loop were written properly, it would not have tried to read outside the bounds of the array. Some errors, however, are caused by conditions that are outside the application and cannot be avoided. For example, suppose an application creates a file on the disk and the user deletes it. Later the application attempts to open the file to read from it, and because it does not exist, an error occurs. As a result, an exception is thrown.

Exception Classes

As previously mentioned, an exception is an object. Exception objects are created from classes in the Java API. The API has an extensive hierarchy of exception classes. A small part of the hierarchy is shown in Figure 12-1.

As you can see, all of the classes in the hierarchy inherit from the `Throwable` class. Just below the `Throwable` class are the classes `Error` and `Exception`. Classes that inherit from

`Error` are for exceptions that are thrown when a critical error occurs, such as an internal error in the Java Virtual Machine or running out of memory. Your applications should not try to handle these errors because they are the result of a serious condition.

All of the exceptions that you will handle are instances of classes that inherit from `Exception`. Figure 12-1 shows two of these classes: `IOException` and `RuntimeException`. These classes also serve as superclasses. `IOException` serves as a superclass for exceptions that are related to input and output operations. `RuntimeException` serves as a superclass for exceptions that result from programming errors, such as an out-of-bounds array subscript.

The chart in Figure 12-1 shows two of the classes that inherit from the `IOException` class: `EOFException` and `FileNotFoundException`. These are examples of classes that exception objects are created from. An `EOFException` object is thrown when an application attempts to read beyond the end of a file, and a `FileNotFoundException` object is thrown when an application tries to open a file that does not exist.

NOTE: The exception classes are in packages in the Java API. For example, `FileNotFoundException` is in the `java.io` package. When you handle an exception that is not in the `java.lang` package you will need the appropriate `import` statement.

Figure 12-1 Part of the exception class hierarchy

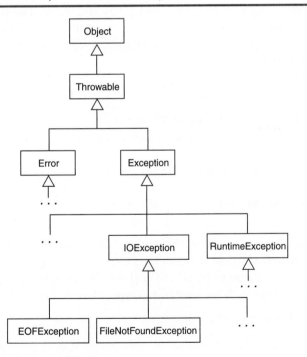

Handling an Exception

To handle an exception, you use a `try` statement. We will look at several variations of the `try` statement, beginning with the following general format:

```
try
{
    (try block statements . . .)
}
catch (ExceptionType parameterName)
{
    (catch block statements . . .)
}
```

First the key word `try` appears. Next, a block of code appears inside braces, which are required. This block of code is known as a *try block*. A *try block* is one or more statements that are executed and can potentially throw an exception. You can think of the code in the try block as being "protected" because the application will not halt if the try block throws an exception.

After the try block, a `catch` clause appears. A `catch` clause begins with the key word `catch`, followed by the code *(ExceptionType parameterName)*. This is a parameter variable declaration, where *ExceptionType* is the name of an exception class and *parameterName* is a variable name. If code in the try block throws an exception of the *ExceptionType* class, then the parameter variable will reference the exception object. In addition, the code that immediately follows the `catch` clause is executed. The code that immediately follows the `catch` clause is known as a *catch block*. Once again, the braces are required.

Let's look at an example of code that uses a `try` statement. The statement inside the following try block attempts to open the file *MyFile.txt*. If the file does not exist, the `Scanner` object throws an exception of the `FileNotFoundException` class. This code is designed to handle that exception if it is thrown.

```
try
{
    File file = new File("MyFile.txt");
    Scanner inputFile = new Scanner(file);
}
catch (FileNotFoundException e)
{
    System.out.println("File not found.");
}
```

Let's look closer. First, the code in the try block is executed. If this code throws an exception, the Java Virtual Machine searches for a `catch` clause that can deal with the exception. In order for a `catch` clause to be able to deal with an exception, its parameter must be of a type that is compatible with the exception's type. Here is this code's `catch` clause:

```
catch (FileNotFoundException e)
```

This `catch` clause declares a reference variable named e as its parameter. The e variable can reference an object of the `FileNotFoundException` class. So, this `catch` clause can deal with an exception of the `FileNotFoundException` class. If the code in the try block throws an exception of the `FileNotFoundException` class, the e variable will reference the exception object and the code in the catch block will execute. In this case, the message "File not found." will be printed. After the catch block is executed, the program will resume with the code that appears after the entire `try`/`catch` construct.

NOTE: The Java API documentation lists all of the exceptions that can be thrown from each method.

Code Listing 12-2 shows a program that asks the user to enter a file name, then attempts to open the file. If the file does not exist, an error message is printed. Figures 12-2 and 12-3 show examples of interaction with the program.

Code Listing 12-2   (OpenFile.java)

```java
 1 import java.io.*;     // For File class and FileNotFoundException
 2 import java.util.Scanner;         // For the Scanner class
 3 import javax.swing.JOptionPane;    // For the JOptionPane class
 4
 5 /**
 6     This program demonstrates how a FileNotFoundException
 7     exception can be handled.
 8 */
 9
10 public class OpenFile
11 {
12    public static void main(String[] args)
13    {
14       File file;              // For file input
15       Scanner inputFile;      // For file input
16       String fileName;        // To hold a file name
17
18       // Get a file name from the user.
19       fileName = JOptionPane.showInputDialog("Enter " +
20                           "the name of a file:");
21
22       // Attempt to open the file.
23       try
24       {
25          file = new File(fileName);
26          inputFile = new Scanner(file);
27          JOptionPane.showMessageDialog(null,
28                           "The file was found.");
29       }
30       catch (FileNotFoundException e)
31       {
32          JOptionPane.showMessageDialog(null,
33                           "File not found.");
34       }
35
36       JOptionPane.showMessageDialog(null, "Done.");
37       System.exit(0);
38    }
39 }
```

Figure 12-2   Interaction with the *OpenFile.java* program
(assume that *BadFile.txt* does not exist)

Figure 12-3   Interaction with the *OpenFile.java* program
(assume that *GoodFile.txt* does exist)

Look at the example run of the program in Figure 12-2. The user entered *BadFile.txt* as the file name. In line 25, the first statement inside the try block, a `File` object is created and this name is passed to the `File` constructor. In line 26 a reference to the `File` object is passed to the `Scanner` constructor. Because *BadFile.txt* does not exist, an exception of the `FileNotFoundException` class is thrown by the `Scanner` class constructor. When the exception is thrown, the program immediately exits the try block, skipping the remaining statement in the block (lines 27 through 28). The program jumps to the `catch` clause in line 30, which has a `FileNotFoundException` parameter, and executes the catch block that follows it. Figure 12-4 illustrates this sequence of events.

Notice that after the catch block executes, the program resumes at the statement that immediately follows the `try/catch` construct. This statement, which is in line 36, displays the message "Done."

Figure 12-4   Sequence of events with an exception

Now look at the example run of the program in Figure 12-3. In this case, the user entered *GoodFile.txt*, which is the name of a file that exists. No exception was thrown in the try block, so the program skips the catch clause and its catch block and jumps directly to the statement in line 36, which follows the `try/catch` construct. This statement displays the message "Done." Figure 12-5 illustrates this sequence of events.

Figure 12-5   Sequence of events with no exception

```
                              try
                              {
                                  file = new File(fileName);
                                  inputFile = new Scanner(file);
                                  JOptionPane.showMessageDialog(null,
                                              "The file was found.");
    If no exception is thrown in    }
    the try block, the program   catch (FileNotFoundException e)
    jumps to the statement that   {
    immediately follows the           JOptionPane.showMessageDialog(null,
    try/catch construct.                          "File not found.");
                                  }
                              JOptionPane.showMessageDialog(null, "Done.");
```

Retrieving the Default Error Message

Each exception object has a method named `getMessage` that can be used to retrieve the default error message for the exception. This is the same message that is displayed when the exception is not handled and the application halts. The program in Code Listing 12-3 demonstrates the `getMessage` method. This is a modified version of the program in Code Listing 12-2. Figure 12-6 shows the program running. In the figure, the user entered the name of a file that does not exist.

Code Listing 12-3 (`ExceptionMessage.java`)

```java
 1 import java.io.*;              // For file I/O classes
 2 import java.util.Scanner;      // For the Scanner class
 3 import javax.swing.JOptionPane;   // For the JOptionPane class
 4
 5 /**
 6    This program demonstrates how a FileNotFoundException
 7    exception can be handled.
 8 */
 9
10 public class ExceptionMessage
11 {
12    public static void main(String[] args)
13    {
14       File file;                 // For file input
15       Scanner inputFile;         // For file input
16       String fileName;           // To hold a file name
17
18       // Get a file name from the user.
19       fileName = JOptionPane.showInputDialog("Enter " +
20                                  "the name of a file:");
21
22       // Attempt to open the file.
23       try
24       {
25          file = new File(fileName);
26          inputFile = new Scanner(file);
27          JOptionPane.showMessageDialog(null,
28                        "The file was found.");
29       }
30       catch (FileNotFoundException e)
31       {
32          JOptionPane.showMessageDialog(null, e.getMessage());
33       }
34
35       JOptionPane.showMessageDialog(null, "Done.");
36       System.exit(0);
37    }
38 }
```

Code Listing 12-4 shows another example. This program forces the `parseInt` method of the `Integer` wrapper class to throw an exception.

Figure 12-6   Interaction with the *ExceptionMessage.java* program
                  (assume that *BadFile.txt* does not exist)

Code Listing 12-4   (`ParseIntError.java`)

```java
 1 /**
 2     This program demonstrates how the Integer.parseInt
 3     method throws an exception.
 4 */
 5
 6 public class ParseIntError
 7 {
 8     public static void main(String[] args)
 9     {
10         String str = "abcde";
11         int number;
12
13         try
14         {
15             number = Integer.parseInt(str);
16         }
17         catch (NumberFormatException e)
18         {
19             System.out.println("Conversion error: " +
20                                 e.getMessage());
21         }
22     }
23 }
```

Program Output

```
Conversion error: For input string: "abcde"
```

The numeric wrapper classes' "parse" methods all throw an exception of the `NumberFormatException` type if the string being converted does not contain a convertible numeric value.

Polymorphic References to Exceptions

Recall from Chapter 11 that a reference variable of a superclass type can reference subclass objects. This is called polymorphism. When handling exceptions, you can use a polymorphic reference as a parameter in the `catch` clause. For example, all of the exceptions that we have dealt with inherit from the `Exception` class. So, a `catch` clause that uses a parameter variable of the `Exception` type is capable of catching any exception that inherits from the `Exception` class. For example, the `try` statement in Code Listing 12-4 could be written as follows:

```
try
{
    number = Integer.parseInt(str);
}
catch (Exception e)
{
    System.out.println("Conversion error: " +
                        e.getMessage());
}
```

Although the `Integer` class's `parseInt` method throws a `NumberFormatException` object, this code still works because the `NumberFormatException` class inherits from the `Exception` class.

Handling Multiple Exceptions

The programs we have studied so far test only for a single type of exception. In many cases, however, the code in the try block will be capable of throwing more than one type of exception. In such a case, you need to write a `catch` clause for each type of exception that could potentially be thrown.

For example, the program in Code Listing 12-5 reads the contents of a file named *SalesData.txt*. Each line in the file contains the sales amount for one month, and the file has several lines. Here are the contents of the file:

```
24987.62
26978.97
32589.45
31978.47
22781.76
29871.44
```

The program in Code Listing 12-5 reads each number from the file and adds it to an accumulator variable. The try block contains code that can throw different types of exceptions. For example, the `Scanner` class's constructor can throw a `FileNotFoundException` if the file is not found, and the `Scanner` class's `nextDouble` method can throw an `InputMismatchException` (which is in the `java.util` package) if it reads a non-numeric value from the file. To handle these exceptions, the `try` statement has two `catch` clauses. Figure 12-7 shows the dialog box displayed by the program when no errors occur. This dialog box is displayed by the statement in lines 51 through 56. Figure 12-8 shows the dialog box displayed by the statement in lines 62 through 64 when the file cannot be found.

Figure 12-7 Dialog box displayed by the *SalesReport.java* program when no error occurs

Figure 12-8 Dialog box displayed by the *SalesReport.java* program when the file cannot be found

---

Code Listing 12-5 (`SalesReport.java`)

```
 1 import java.io.*;     // For File class and FileNotFoundException
 2 import java.util.*;   // For Scanner and InputMismatchException
 3 import java.text.DecimalFormat;   // For the DecimalFormat class
 4 import javax.swing.JOptionPane;   // For the JOptionPane class
 5
 6 /**
 7    This program demonstrates how multiple exceptions can
 8    be caught with one try statement.
 9 */
10
11 public class SalesReport
12 {
13    public static void main(String[] args)
14    {
15       String filename = "SalesData.txt"; // File name
16       int months = 0;                    // Month counter
17       double oneMonth;                   // One month's sales
18       double totalSales = 0.0;           // Total sales
19       double averageSales;               // Average sales
20
21       // Create a DecimalFormat object.
```

```
22        DecimalFormat dollar =
23                 new DecimalFormat("#,##0.00");
24
25        try
26        {
27           // Open the file.
28           File file = new File(filename);
29           Scanner inputFile = new Scanner(file);
30
31           // Process the contents of the file.
32           while (inputFile.hasNext())
33           {
34              // Get a month's sales amount.
35              oneMonth = inputFile.nextDouble();
36
37              // Accumulate the amount.
38              totalSales += oneMonth;
39
40              // Increment the month counter
41              months++;
42           }
43
44           // Close the file.
45           inputFile.close();
46
47           // Calculate the average.
48           averageSales = totalSales / months;
49
50           // Display the results.
51           JOptionPane.showMessageDialog(null,
52                          "Number of months: " + months +
53                          "\nTotal Sales: $" +
54                          dollar.format(totalSales) +
55                          "\nAverage Sales: $" +
56                          dollar.format(averageSales));
57        }
58        catch(FileNotFoundException e)
59        {
60           // Thrown by the Scanner constructor when
61           // the file is not found.
62           JOptionPane.showMessageDialog(null,
63                          "The file " + filename +
64                          " does not exist.");
65        }
66        catch(InputMismatchException e)
67        {
68           // Thrown by the Scanner class's nextDouble
69           // method when a non-numeric value is found.
```

```
70              JOptionPane.showMessageDialog(null,
71                      "Non-numeric data found " +
72                      "in the file.");
73          }
74
75          System.exit(0);
76      }
77 }
```

When an exception is thrown by code in the try block, the JVM begins searching the try statement for a catch clause that can handle it. It searches the catch clauses from top to bottom and passes control of the program to the first catch clause with a parameter that is compatible with the exception.

Using Exception Handlers to Recover from Errors

The program in Code Listing 12-5 demonstrates how a try statement can have several catch clauses in order to handle different types of exceptions. However, the program does not use the exception handlers to recover from any of the errors. Regardless of whether the file is not found or a non-numeric item is encountered in the file, this program still halts. The program in Code Listing 12-6 is a better example of effective exception handling. It attempts to recover from as many of the exceptions as possible.

Code Listing 12-6   (SalesReport2.java)

```
 1 import java.io.*;         // For File class and FileNotFoundException
 2 import java.util.*;       // For Scanner and InputMismatchException
 3 import java.text.DecimalFormat;  // For the DecimalFormat class
 4 import javax.swing.JOptionPane;  // For the JOptionPane class
 5
 6 /**
 7    This program demonstrates how exception handlers can
 8    be used to recover from errors.
 9 */
10
11 public class SalesReport2
12 {
13     public static void main(String[] args)
14     {
15         String filename = "SalesData.txt";       // File name
16         int months = 0;                          // Month counter
17         double oneMonth;                         // One month's sales
18         double totalSales = 0.0;                 // Total sales
19         double averageSales;       // Average sales
20
21         // Create a DecimalFormat object.
22         DecimalFormat dollar =
```

```
23                      new DecimalFormat("#,##0.00");
24
25          // Attempt to open the file by calling the
26          // openfile method.
27          Scanner inputFile = openFile(filename);
28
29          // If the openFile method returned null, then
30          // the file was not found. Get a new file name.
31          while (inputFile == null)
32          {
33             filename = JOptionPane.showInputDialog(
34                      "ERROR: " + filename +
35                      " does not exist.\n" +
36                      "Enter another file name: ");
37             inputFile = openFile(filename);
38          }
39
40          // Process the contents of the file.
41          while (inputFile.hasNext())
42          {
43             try
44             {
45                // Get a month's sales amount.
46                oneMonth = inputFile.nextDouble();
47
48                // Accumulate the amount.
49                totalSales += oneMonth;
50
51                // Increment the month counter.
52                months++;
53             }
54             catch(InputMismatchException e)
55             {
56                // Display an error message.
57                JOptionPane.showMessageDialog(null,
58                      "Non-numeric data found in the file.\n" +
59                      "The invalid record will be skipped.");
60
61                // Skip past the invalid data.
62                inputFile.nextLine();
63             }
64          }
65
66          // Close the file.
67          inputFile.close();
68
69          // Calculate the average.
70          averageSales = totalSales / months;
71
```

```
 72          // Display the results.
 73          JOptionPane.showMessageDialog(null,
 74                  "Number of months: " + months +
 75                  "\nTotal Sales: $" +
 76                  dollar.format(totalSales) +
 77                  "\nAverage Sales: $" +
 78                  dollar.format(averageSales));
 79          System.exit(0);
 80      }
 81
 82      /**
 83         The openFile method opens the specified file and
 84         returns a reference to a Scanner object.
 85         @param filename The name of the file to open.
 86         @return A Scanner reference, if the file exists
 87                 Otherwise, null is returned.
 88      */
 89
 90      public static Scanner openFile(String filename)
 91      {
 92          Scanner scan;
 93
 94          // Attempt to open the file.
 95          try
 96          {
 97              File file = new File(filename);
 98              scan = new Scanner(file);
 99          }
100          catch(FileNotFoundException e)
101          {
102              scan = null;
103          }
104
105          return scan;
106      }
107 }
```

Let's look at how this program recovers from a `FileNotFoundException`. The `openFile` method, in lines 90 through 106, accepts a file name as its argument. The method creates a `File` object (passing the file name to the constructor) and a `Scanner` object. If the `Scanner` class constructor throws a `FileNotFoundException`, the method returns `null`. Otherwise, it returns a reference to the `Scanner` object. In the `main` method, a loop is used in lines 31 through 38 to ask the user for a different file name in the event that the `openFile` method returns `null`.

Now let's look at how the program recovers from unexpectedly encountering a non-numeric item in the file. The statement in line 46, which calls the `Scanner` class's `nextDouble` method, is wrapped in a `try` statement that catches the `InputMismatchException`. If this exception is thrown by the `nextDouble` method, the catch block in lines 54 through 63 displays a message indicating that a non-numeric item was encountered and that the invalid record will be skipped. The invalid data is then read from the file with the `nextLine` method in line 62. Because the statement `months++` in line 52 is in the try block, it will not be executed when the exception occurs, so the number of months will still be correct. The loop continues processing with the next line in the file.

Let's look at some examples of how the program recovers from these errors. Suppose we rename *SalesData.txt* file to *SalesInfo.txt*. Figure-12-9 shows an example running of the program.

Figure 12-9   Interaction with the *SalesReport2.java* program

Now, suppose we change the name of the file back to *SalesData.txt* and edit its contents as follows:

```
24987.62
26978.97
abc
31978.47
22781.76
29871.44
```

Notice that the third item is no longer a number. Figure 12-10 shows an example running of the program.

Figure 12-10   Dialog boxes displayed by the *SalesReport2.java* program

Handle Each Exception Only Once in a `try` Statement

Not including polymorphic references, a `try` statement may have only one `catch` clause for each specific type of exception. For example, the following `try` statement will cause the compiler to issue an error message because it handles a `NumberFormatException` object with two `catch` clauses:

```
try
{
    number = Integer.parseInt(str);
}
catch (NumberFormatException e)
{
    System.out.println("Bad number format.");
}
// ERROR!!! NumberFormatException has already been caught!
catch (NumberFormatException e)
{
    System.out.println(str + " is not a number.");
}
```

Sometimes you can cause this error by using polymorphic references. For example, look at Figure 12-11, which shows an inheritance hierarchy for the `NumberFormatException` class.

Figure 12-11   Inheritance hierarchy for the `NumberFormatException` class

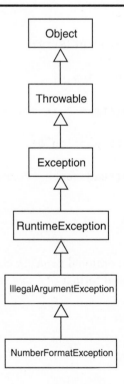

As you can see from the figure, the `NumberFormatException` class inherits from the `IllegalArgumentException` class. Now look at the following code:

```
try
{
    number = Integer.parseInt(str);
}
catch (IllegalArgumentException e)
{
    System.out.println("Bad number format.");
}
// This will also cause an error.
catch (NumberFormatException e)
{
    System.out.println(str + " is not a number.");
}
```

The compiler issues an error message regarding the second `catch` clause, reporting that `NumberFormatException` has already been caught. This is because the first `catch` clause, which catches `IllegalArgumentException` objects, will polymorphically catch `NumberFormatException` objects.

If you are handling multiple exceptions in the same `try` statement and some of the exceptions are related to each other through inheritance, then you should handle the more specialized exception classes before the more general exception classes. We can rewrite the previous code as follows, with no errors:

```
try
{
    number = Integer.parseInt(str);
}
catch (NumberFormatException e)
{
    System.out.println(str + " is not a number.");
}
catch (IllegalArgumentException e)
{
    System.out.println("Bad number format.");
}
```

The `finally` Clause

The `try` statement may have an optional `finally` clause, which must appear after all of the `catch` clauses. Here is the general format of a `try` statement with a `finally` clause:

```
try
{
    (try block statements . . .)
}
```

```
catch (ExceptionType ParameterName)
{
    (catch block statements . . .)
}
finally
{
    (finally block statements . . .)
}
```

The *finally block* is one or more statements that are always executed after the try block has executed and after any catch blocks have executed if an exception was thrown. The statements in the finally block execute whether an exception occurs or not. For example, the following code opens a file of `doubles` and reads its contents. The outer `try` statement opens the file and has a `catch` clause that catches the `FileNotFoundException`. The inner `try` statement reads values from the file and has a `catch` clause that catches the `InputMismatchException`. The finally block closes the file regardless of whether an `InputMismatchException` occurs.

```java
try
{
    // Open the file.
    File file = new File(filename);
    Scanner inputFile = new Scanner(file);

    try
    {
        // Read and display the file's contents.
        while (inputFile.hasNext())
        {
            System.out.println(inputFile.nextDouble());
        }
    }
    catch (InputMismatchException e)
    {
        System.out.println("Invalid data found.");
    }
    finally
    {
        // Close the file.
        inputFile.close();
    }
}
catch (FileNotFoundException e)
{
    System.out.println("File not found.");
}
```

The Stack Trace

Quite often, a method will call another method, which will call yet another method. For example, method A calls method B, which calls method C. The *call stack* is an internal list of all the methods that are currently executing.

When an exception is thrown by a method that is executing under several layers of method calls, it is sometimes helpful to know which methods were responsible for the method being called. A *stack trace* is a list of all the methods in the call stack. It indicates the method that was executing when an exception occurred and all of the methods that were called in order to execute that method. For example, look at the program in Code Listing 12-7. It has three methods: main, myMethod, and produceError. The main method calls myMethod, which calls produceError. The produceError method causes an exception by passing an invalid position number to the String class's charAt method. The exception is not handled by the program, but is dealt with by the default exception handler.

Code Listing 12-7 (StackTrace.java)

```
 1  /**
 2      This program demonstrates the stack trace that is
 3      produced when an exception is thrown.
 4  */
 5
 6  public class StackTrace
 7  {
 8      public static void main(String[] args)
 9      {
10          System.out.println("Calling myMethod...");
11          myMethod();
12          System.out.println("Method main is done.");
13      }
14
15      /**
16          MyMethod
17      */
18
19      public static void myMethod()
20      {
21          System.out.println("Calling produceError...");
22          produceError();
23          System.out.println("myMethod is done.");
24      }
25
26      /**
27          produceError
28      */
29
```

```
30      public static void produceError()
31      {
32          String str = "abc";
33
34          // The following statement will cause an error.
35          System.out.println(str.charAt(3));
36          System.out.println("produceError is done.");
37      }
38 }
```

Program Output

```
Calling myMethod...
Calling produceError...
Exception in thread "main" java.lang.StringIndexOutOfBoundsException:
        String index out of range: 3
            at java.lang.String.charAt(Uknown Source)
            at StackTrace.produceError(StackTrace.java:35)
            at StackTrace.myMethod(StackTrace.java:22)
            at StackTrace.main(StackTrace.java:11)
```

When the exception occurs, the error message shows a stack trace listing the methods that were called in order to produce the exception. The first method that is listed in the stack trace, charAt, is the method that is responsible for the exception. The next method, produceError, is the method that called charAt. The next method, myMethod, is the method that called produceError. The last method, main, is the method that called myMethod. The stack trace shows the chain of methods that were called when the exception was thrown.

> **NOTE:** All exception objects have a printStackTrace method, inherited from the Throwable class, which can be used to print a stack trace.

When an Exception Is Not Caught

When an exception is thrown, it cannot be ignored. It must be handled by the program, or by the default exception handler. When the code in a method throws an exception, the normal execution of that method stops and the JVM searches for a compatible exception handler inside the method. If there is no code inside the method to handle the exception, then control of the program is passed to the previous method in the call stack (that is, the method that called the offending method). If that method cannot handle the exception, then control is passed again, up the call stack, to the previous method. This continues until control reaches the main method. If the main method does not handle the exception, then the program is halted and the default exception handler handles the exception.

This was the case for the program in Code Listing 12-7. Because the produceError method did not handle the exception, control was passed back to myMethod. It didn't handle the exception either, so control was passed back to main. Because main didn't handle the exception, the program halted and the default exception handler displayed the error messages.

Checked and Unchecked Exceptions

In Java, there are two categories of exceptions: unchecked and checked. *Unchecked exceptions* are those that inherit from the `Error` class or the `RuntimeException` class. Recall that the exceptions that inherit from `Error` are thrown when a critical error occurs, such as running out of memory. You should not handle these exceptions because the conditions that cause them can rarely be dealt with in the program. Also recall that `RuntimeException` serves as a superclass for exceptions that result from programming errors, such as an out-of-bounds array subscript. It is best not to handle these exceptions either, because they can be avoided with properly written code. So, you should not handle unchecked exceptions.

All of the remaining exceptions (that is, those that do *not* inherit from `Error` or `RuntimeException`) are *checked exceptions*. These are the exceptions that you should handle in your program. If the code in a method can potentially throw a checked exception, then that method must meet one of the following requirements:

- It must handle the exception, or
- It must have a `throws` clause listed in the method header.

The `throws` clause informs the compiler of the exceptions that could get thrown from a method. For example, look at the following method:

```
// This method will not compile!
public void displayFile(String name)
{
    // Open the file.
    File file = new File(name);
    Scanner inputFile = new Scanner(file);

    // Read and display the file's contents.
    while (inputFile.hasNext())
    {
        System.out.println(inputFile.nextLine());
    }

    // Close the file.
    inputFile.close();
}
```

The code in this method is capable of throwing a `FileNotFoundException`, which is a checked exception. Because the method does not handle this exception, it must have a `throws` clause in its header or it will not compile.

The key word `throws` is written at the end of the method header, followed by a list of the types of exceptions that the method can throw. Here is the revised method header:

```
public void displayFile(String name) throws FileNotFoundException
```

The `throws` clause tells the compiler that this method can throw a `FileNotFoundException`. (If there is more than one type of exception, you separate them with commas.)

Now you know why you wrote a `throws` clause on methods that perform file operations in the previous chapters. We did not handle any of the checked exceptions that might occur, so we had to inform the compiler that our methods might pass them up the call stack.

 Checkpoint

12.1 Briefly describe what an exception is.

12.2 What does it mean to "throw" an exception?

12.3 If an exception is thrown and the program does not handle it, what happens?

12.4 Other than the `Object` class, what is the superclass for all exceptions?

12.5 What is the difference between exceptions that inherit from the `Error` class and exceptions that inherit from the `Exception` class?

12.6 What is the difference between a try block and a catch block?

12.7 After the catch block has handled the exception, where does program execution resume?

12.8 How do you retrieve an error message from an exception?

12.9 If multiple exceptions can be thrown by code in a try block, how does the JVM know which `catch` clause it should pass the control of the program to?

12.10 When does the code in a finally block execute?

12.11 What is the call stack? What is a stack trace?

12.12 A program's `main` method calls method A, which calls method B. None of these methods performs any exception handling. The code in method B throws an exception. Describe what happens.

12.13 What are the differences between a checked and an unchecked exception?

12.14 When are you required to have a `throws` clause in a method header?

12.2 Throwing Exceptions

CONCEPT: You can write code that throws one of the standard Java exceptions, or an instance of a custom exception class that you have designed.

You can use the `throw` statement to throw an exception manually. The general format of the `throw` statement is as follows:

```
throw new ExceptionType(MessageString);
```

The `throw` statement causes an exception object to be created and thrown. In this general format, *ExceptionType* is an exception class name and *MessageString* is an optional `String` argument passed to the exception object's constructor. The *MessageString* argument contains a custom error message that can be retrieved from the exception object's `getMessage` method. If you do not pass a message to the constructor, the exception will have a `null` message. Here is an example of a `throw` statement:

```
throw new Exception("Out of fuel");
```

This statement creates an object of the `Exception` class and passes the string "Out of fuel" to the object's constructor. The object is then thrown, which causes the exception-handling process to begin.

> **NOTE:** Don't confuse the `throw` statement with the `throws` clause. The `throw` statement causes an exception to be thrown. The `throws` clause informs the compiler that a method throws one or more exceptions.

Recall the `DateComponent` class from Chapter 10. Its constructor accepts a string containing a date in the form MONTH/DAY/YEAR. It uses a `Stringtokenizer` object to extract the month, day, and year from the string and stores these values in the `month`, `day`, and `year` fields. Suppose we want to prevent a `null` reference from being passed as an argument into the constructor. One way to accomplish this is to have the constructor throw an exception when such an argument is passed. Here is the modified code for the `DateComponent` constructor:

```
public DateComponent(String dateStr)
{
    // Ensure that dateStr is not null.
    if (dateStr == null)
    {
        throw new IllegalArgumentException(
                    "null reference passed to " +
                    "DateComponent constructor");
    }

    // Create a StringTokenizer object.
    StringTokenizer strTokenizer =
        new StringTokenizer(dateStr, "/");

    // Extract the tokens.
    month = strTokenizer.nextToken();
    day = strTokenizer.nextToken();
    year = strTokenizer.nextToken();
}
```

This constructor throws an `IllegalArgumentException` if the `dateStr` parameter is `null`. The message "null reference passed to `DateComponent` constructor" is passed to the exception object's constructor. When we catch this exception, we can retrieve the message by calling the object's `getMessage` method. The `IllegalArgumentException` class was chosen for this error condition because it seems like the most appropriate exception to throw in response to an illegal argument being passed to the constructor. (Note that `IllegalArgumentException` inherits from `RuntimeException`, which inherits from `Exception`.)

> **NOTE:** Because the `IllegalArgumentException` class inherits from the `RuntimeException` class, it is unchecked. If we had chosen a checked exception class, we would have to put a `throws` clause in the constructor's header.

The program in Code Listing 12-8 demonstrates how the modified constructor works.

Code Listing 12-8 (`DateComponentExceptionDemo.java`)

```
 1 /**
 2    This program demonstrates how the DateComponent
 3    class constructor throws an exception.
 4 */
 5
 6 public class DateComponentExceptionDemo
 7 {
 8    public static void main(String[] args)
 9    {
10       // Create a null String reference.
11       String str = null;
12
13       // Attempt to pass the null reference to
14       // the DateComponent constructor.
15       try
16       {
17          DateComponent dc = new DateComponent(str);
18       }
19       catch (IllegalArgumentException e)
20       {
21          System.out.println(e.getMessage());
22       }
23    }
24 }
```

Program Output

```
null reference passed to DateComponent constructor
```

Creating Your Own Exception Classes

To meet the needs of a specific class or application, you can create your own exception classes by extending the Exception class or one of its subclasses.

Let's look at an example that uses programmer-defined exceptions. Recall the BankAccount class from Chapter 6. This class holds the data for a bank account. A UML diagram for the class is shown in Figure 12-12.

There are a number of errors that could cause a BankAccount object to perform its duties incorrectly. Here are some specific examples:

- A negative starting balance is passed to the constructor.
- A negative number is passed to the deposit method.
- A negative number is passed to the withdraw method.
- The amount passed to the withdraw method exceeds the account's balance.

Figure 12-12 UML diagram for the BankAccount class

BankAccount
– balance : double
+ BankAccount() + BankAccount(startBalance : double) + BankAccount(str : String) + deposit(amount : double) : void + deposit(str : String) : void + withdraw(amount : double) : void + withdraw(str : String) : void + setBalance(b : double) : void + setBalance(str : String) : void + getBalance() : double

We can create our own exceptions that represent each of these error conditions. Then we can rewrite the class so it throws one of our custom exceptions when any of these errors occur. Let's start by creating an exception class for a negative starting balance. Code Listing 12-9 shows an exception class named NegativeStartingBalance.

Code Listing 12-9 (NegativeStartingBalance.java)

```
 1  /**
 2      NegativeStartingBalance exceptions are thrown by the
 3      BankAccount class when a negative starting balance is
 4      passed to the constructor.
 5  */
 6
 7  public class NegativeStartingBalance
 8                      extends Exception
 9  {
10      /**
11          This constructor uses a generic
12          error message.
13      */
14
15      public NegativeStartingBalance()
16      {
17          super("Error: Negative starting balance");
18      }
19
20      /**
21          This constructor specifies the bad starting
22          balance in the error message.
23          @param The bad starting balance.
24      */
25
```

```
26        public NegativeStartingBalance(double amount)
27        {
28            super("Error: Negative starting balance: " +
29                    amount);
30        }
31  }
```

Notice that this class extends the `Exception` class. It has two constructors. The no-arg constructor passes the string `"Error: Negative starting balance"` to the superclass constructor. This is the error message that is retrievable from an object's `getMessage` method. The second constructor accepts the starting balance as a `double` argument. This amount is used to pass a more detailed error message containing the starting balance amount to the superclass constructor.

The following code shows one of the `BankAccount` constructors rewritten to throw a `NegativeStartingBalance` exception when a negative value is passed as the starting balance.

```
public BankAccount(double startBalance)
                throws NegativeStartingBalance
{
    if (startBalance < 0)
        throw new NegativeStartingBalance(startBalance);

    balance = startBalance;
}
```

Note that `NegativeStartingBalance` extends the `Exception` class. This means that it is a checked exception class. Because of this, the constructor header must have a `throws` clause listing the exception type.

> You will find the modified *BankAccount.java* file on the Student CD with the rest of this chapter's code. The program in Code Listing 12-10 demonstrates the new constructor by forcing it to throw the `NegativeStartingBalance` exception.

Code Listing 12-10   (`AccountTest.java`)

```
1   /**
2       This program demonstrates how the BankAccount
3       class constructor throws custom exceptions.
4   */
5
6   public class AccountTest
7   {
8       public static void main(String [] args)
9       {
10          // Force a NegativeStartingBalance exception.
```

```
11          try
12          {
13              BankAccount account =
14                          new BankAccount(-100.0);
15          }
16          catch(NegativeStartingBalance e)
17          {
18              System.out.println(e.getMessage());
19          }
20      }
21  }
```

Program Output

Error: Negative starting balance: -100.0

Using the `@exception` Tag in Documentation Comments

When writing the documentation comments for a method, you can document the exceptions thrown by the method by using an `@exception` tag. When the `javadoc` utility sees an `@exception` tag inside a method's documentation comments, it knows that the name of an exception appears next, followed by a description of the events that cause the exception. The general format of an `@exception` tag comment is as follows:

```
@exception ExceptionName Description
```

ExceptionName is the name of an exception and *Description* is a description of the circumstances that cause the exception. Remember the following points about `@exception` tag comments:

- The `@exception` tag in a method's documentation comment must appear after the general description of the method.
- The description can span several lines. It ends at the end of the documentation comment (the `*/` symbol), or at the beginning of another tag.

When a method's documentation comments contain an `@exception` tag, the `javadoc` utility will create a Throws section in the method's documentation. This is where the descriptions of the exceptions thrown by the method will be listed. As an example, here are the documentation comments for the `BankAccount` class's constructor presented earlier:

```
/**
    This constructor sets the starting balance
    to the value passed as an argument.
    @param startBalance The starting balance.
    @exception NegativeStartingBalance When
            startBalance is negative.
*/
```

Checkpoint

12.15 What does the throw statement do?

12.16 What is the purpose of the argument that is passed to an exception object's constructor? What happens if you do not pass an argument to the constructor?

12.17 What is the difference between the throw statement and the throws clause?

12.18 If a method has a throw statement, does it always have to have a throws clause in its header? Why or why not?

12.19 If you are writing a custom exception class, how can you make sure it is checked? How can you make sure it is unchecked?

12.3 Advanced Topics: Binary Files, Random Access Files, and Object Serialization

CONCEPT: A file that contains raw binary data is known as a binary file. The content of a binary file is not formatted as text, and not meant to be opened in a text editor. A random access file is a file that allows a program to read data from any location within the file, or write data to any location within the file. Object serialization is the process of converting an object to a series of bytes and saving them to a file. Deserialization is the process of reconstructing a serialized object.

Binary Files

All the files you've been working with so far have been text files. This means that the data stored in the files has been formatted as text. Even a number, when stored in a text file with the print or println method, is converted to text. For example, consider the following program segment:

```
PrintWriter outputFile = new PrintWriter("Number.txt");
int x = 1297;
outputFile.print(x);
```

The last statement writes the contents of the variable x to the *Number.txt* file. When the number is written, however, it is stored as the characters '1', '2', '9', and '7'. This is illustrated in Figure 12-13.

Figure 12-13 The number 1297 expressed as characters

1297 expressed as characters

'1'	'2'	'9'	'7'

When a number such as 1297 is stored in the computer's memory, it isn't stored as text, however. It is formatted as a binary number. Figure 12-14 shows how the number 1297 is stored in memory, in an `int` variable, using binary. Recall that `int` variables occupy four bytes.

Figure 12-14 The number 1297 as a binary number, as it is stored in memory

1297 as a binary number

00000000	00000000	00000101	00010001

The binary representation of the number shown in Figure 12-14 is the way the raw data is stored in memory. In fact, this is sometimes called the *raw binary format*. Data can be stored in a file in its raw binary format. A file that contains binary data is often called a *binary file*.

Storing data in its binary format is more efficient than storing it as text because there are fewer conversions to take place. In addition, there are some types of data that should only be stored in their raw binary format. Images are an example. However, when data is stored in a binary file, you cannot open the file in a text editor such as Notepad. When a text editor opens a file, it assumes the file contains text.

Writing Data to a Binary File

To write data to a binary file you must create objects from the following classes:

`FileOutputStream`   This class, which is in the `java.io` package, allows you to open a file for writing binary data and establish a connection with it. It provides only basic functionality for writing bytes to the file, however.

`DataOutputStream`   This class which is in the `java.io` package, allows you to write data of any primitive type or `String` objects to a binary file. The `DataOutputStream` class by itself cannot directly access a file, however. It is used in conjunction with a `FileOutputStream` object that has a connection to a file.

You wrap a `DataOutputStream` object around a `FileOutputStream` object to write data to a binary file. The following code shows how a file named *MyInfo.dat* can be opened for binary output:

```
FileOutputStream fstream = new FileOutputStream("MyInfo.dat");
DataOutputStream outputFile = new DataOutputStream(fstream);
```

The first line creates an instance of the `FileOutputStream` class, which has the ability to open a file for binary output and establish a connection with it. You pass the name of the file that you wish open, as a string, to the constructor. The second line creates an instance of the `DataOutputStream` object that is connected to the `FileOutputStream` referenced by `fstream`. The result of this statement is that the `outputFile` variable will reference an object that is able to write binary data to the *MyInfo.dat* file.

WARNING! If the file that you are opening with the `FileOutputStream` object already exists, it will be erased and an empty file by the same name will be created.

> **NOTE:** The `FileOutputStream` constructor throws an `IOException` if an error occurs when it attempts to open the file.

If there is no reason to reference the `FileOutputStream` object, then these statements can be combined into one, as follows:

```
DataOutputStream outputFile =
       new DataOutputStream(new FileOutputStream("MyInfo.dat"));
```

Once the `DataOutputStream` object has been created, you can use it to write binary data to the file. Table 12-1 lists some of the `DataOutputStream` methods. Note that each of the methods listed in the table throws an `IOException` if an error occurs.

Table 12-1 Some of the `DataOutputStream` methods

Method	Description
void close()	Closes the file.
void writeBoolean(boolean b)	Writes the `boolean` value passed to b to the file.
void writeByte(byte b)	Writes the `byte` value passed to b to the file.
void writeChar(int c)	This method accepts an `int`, which is assumed to be a character code. The character it represents is written to the file as a two-byte Unicode character.
void writeDouble(double d)	Writes the `double` value passed to d to the file.
void writeFloat(float f)	Writes the `float` value passed to f to the file.
void writeInt(int i)	Writes the `int` value passed to i to the file.
void writeLong(long num)	Writes the `long` value passed to num to the file.
void writeShort(short s)	Writes the `short` value passed to s to the file.
void writeUTF(String str)	Writes the `String` object passed to str to the file using the Unicode Text Format.

The program in Code Listing 12-11 shows a simple demonstration. An array of `int` values is written to the file *Numbers.dat*.

Code Listing 12-11 (`WriteBinaryFile.java`)

```
 1   import java.io.*;
 2
 3   /**
 4      This program opens a binary file and writes the contents
 5      of an int array to the file.
 6   */
 7
 8   public class WriteBinaryFile
 9   {
```

```
10        public static void main(String[] args)
11                         throws IOException
12        {
13           // An array to write to the file
14           int[] numbers = { 2, 4, 6, 8, 10, 12, 14 };
15
16           // Create the binary output objects.
17           FileOutputStream fstream =
18                    new FileOutputStream("Numbers.dat");
19           DataOutputStream outputFile =
20                    new DataOutputStream(fstream);
21
22           System.out.println("Writing the numbers to the file...");
23
24           // Write the array elements to the file.
25           for (int i = 0; i < numbers.length; i++)
26              outputFile.writeInt(numbers[i]);
27
28           System.out.println("Done.");
29
30           // Close the file.
31           outputFile.close();
32        }
33  }
```

Program Output

```
Writing the numbers to the file...
Done.
```

Reading Data from a Binary File

To open a binary file for input, you use the following classes:

FileInputStream   This class which is in the java.io package, allows you to open
                   a file for reading binary data and establish a connection with it.
                   It provides only the basic functionality for reading bytes from the
                   file, however.

DataInputStream   This class which is in the java.io package, allows you to read
                   data of any primitive type, or String objects, from a binary file.
                   The DataInputStream class by itself cannot directly access a file,
                   however. It is used in conjunction with a FileInputStream object
                   that has a connection to a file.

To open a binary file for input, you wrap a DataInputStream object around a
FileInputStream object. The following code shows the file *MyInfo.dat* can be opened for
binary input:

```
FileInputStream fstream = new FileInputStream("MyInfo.dat");
DataInputStream inputFile = new DataInputStream(fstream);
```

The following code, which combines these two statements into one, can also be used:

```
DataInputStream inputFile =
        new DataInputStream(new FileInputStream("MyInfo.dat"));
```

The `FileInputStream` constructor will throw a `FileNotFoundException` if the file named by the string argument cannot be found. Once the `DataInputStream` object has been created, you can use it to read binary data from the file. Table 12-2 lists some of the `DataInputStream` methods. Note that each of the methods listed in the table throw an `EOFException` if the end of the file has already been reached.

Table 12-2   Some of the `DataInputStream` methods

Method	Description
`void close()`	Closes the file.
`boolean readBoolean()`	Reads a `boolean` value from the file and returns it.
`byte readByte()`	Reads a `byte` value from the file and returns it.
`char readChar()`	Reads a `char` value from the file and returns it. The character is expected to be stored as a two-byte Unicode character, as written by the `DataOutputStream` class's `writeChar` method.
`double readDouble()`	Reads a `double` value from the file and returns it.
`float readFloat()`	Reads a `float` value from the file and returns it.
`int readInt()`	Reads an `int` value from the file and returns it.
`long readLong()`	Reads a `long` value from the file and returns it.
`short readShort()`	Reads a `short` value from the file and returns it.
`String readUTF()`	Reads a string from the file and returns it as a `String` object. The string must have been written with the `DataOutputStream` class's `writeUTF` method.

The program in Code Listing 12-12 opens the `Numbers.dat` file that was created by the program in Code Listing 12-11. The numbers are read from the file and displayed on the screen. Notice that the program must catch the `EOFException` in order to determine when the file's end has been reached.

Code Listing 12-12   (`ReadBinaryFile.java`)

```java
 1  import java.io.*;
 2
 3  /**
 4      This program opens a binary file, reads
 5      and displays the contents.
 6  */
 7
 8  public class ReadBinaryFile
 9  {
```

```
10      public static void main(String[] args)
11                  throws IOException
12      {
13         int number;                    // A number read from the file
14         boolean endOfFile = false;     // EOF flag
15
16         // Create the binary file input objects.
17         FileInputStream fstream =
18                  new FileInputStream("Numbers.dat");
19         DataInputStream inputFile =
20                  new DataInputStream(fstream);
21
22         System.out.println("Reading numbers from the file:");
23
24         // Read the contents of the file.
25         while (!endOfFile)
26         {
27            try
28            {
29               number = inputFile.readInt();
30               System.out.print(number + " ");
31            }
32            catch (EOFException e)
33            {
34               endOfFile = true;
35            }
36         }
37
38         System.out.println("\nDone.");
39
40         // Close the file.
41         inputFile.close();
42      }
43   }
```

Program Output

```
Reading numbers from the file:
2 4 6 8 10 12 14
Done.
```

Writing and Reading Strings

To write a string to a binary file you should use the `DataOutputStream` class's `writeUTF` method. This method writes its `String` argument in a format known as *UTF-8 encoding*. Here's how the encoding works: Just before writing the string, this method writes a two-byte integer indicating the number of bytes that the string occupies. Then it writes the string's characters in Unicode. (UTF stands for Unicode Text Format.)

When the `DataInputStream` class's `readUTF` method reads from the file, it expects the first two bytes to contain the number of bytes that the string occupies. Then it reads that many bytes and returns them as a `String`.

For example, assuming that `outputFile` references a `DataOutputStream` object, the following code uses the `writeUTF` method to write a string:

```
String name = "Chloe";
outputFile.writeUTF(name);
```

Assuming that `inputFile` references a `DataInputStream` object, the following statement uses the `readUTF` method to read a UTF-8 encoded string from the file:

```
String name = inputFile.readUTF();
```

Remember that the `readUTF` method will correctly read a string only when the string is written with the `writeUTF` method.

> The Student CD contains the example programs *WriteUTF.java* and *ReadUTF.java*, which demonstrate writing and reading strings using these methods.

Appending Data to an Existing Binary File

If you pass the name of an existing file to the `FileOutputStream` constructor, it will be erased and a new empty file with the same name will be created. Sometimes, however, you want to preserve an existing file and append new data to its current contents. The `FileOutputStream` constructor takes an optional second argument, which must be a `boolean` value. If the argument is `true`, the file will not be erased if it already exists and new data will be written to the end of the file. If the argument is `false`, the file will be erased if it already exists. For example, the following code opens the file *MyInfo.dat* for output. If the file exists, it will not be deleted, and any data written to the file will be appended to the existing data.

```
FileOutputStream fstream = new FileOutputStream("MyInfo.dat", true);
DataOutputStream outputFile = new DataOutputStream(fstream);
```

Random Access Files

All of the programs that you have created to access files so far have performed *sequential file access*. With sequential access, when a file is opened for input, its read position is at the very beginning of the file. This means that the first time data is read from the file, the data will be read from its beginning. As the reading continues, the file's read position advances sequentially through the file's contents.

The problem with sequential file access is that in order to read a specific byte from the file, all the bytes that precede it must be read first. For instance, if a program needs data stored at the hundredth byte of a file, it will have to read the first 99 bytes to reach it. If you've ever listened to a cassette tape player, you understand sequential access. To listen to a song at the end of the tape, you have to listen to all the songs that are before it, or fast-forward over them. There is no way to jump immediately to that particular song.

Although sequential file access is useful in many circumstances, it can slow down a program tremendously. If the file is very large, locating data buried deep inside it can take a long time. Alternatively, Java allows a program to perform *random file access*. In random file access, a program may immediately jump to any location in the file without first reading the preceding bytes. The difference between sequential and random file access is like the difference between a cassette tape and a compact disc. When listening to a CD, there is no need to listen to or fast-forward over unwanted songs. You simply jump to the track that you want to listen to. This is illustrated in Figure 12-15.

Figure 12-15 Sequential access versus random access

Items in a sequential access file are accessed one after the other.

Items in a random access file are accessed in any order.

To create and work with random access files in Java, you use the `RandomAccessFile` class, which is in the `java.io` package. The general format of the class constructor is as follows:

```
RandomAccessFile(String filename, String mode)
```

The first argument is the name of the file. The second argument is a string indicating the mode in which you wish to use the file. The two modes are `"r"` for reading, and `"rw"` for reading and writing. When a file is opened with `"r"` as the mode, the program can only read from the file. When a file is opened with `"rw"` as the mode, the program can read from the file and write to it. Here are some examples of statements that open files using the `RandomAccessFile` class:

```
// Open a file for random reading.
RandomAccessFile randomFile =
            new RandomAccessFile("MyData.dat", "r");

// Open a file for random reading and writing.
RandomAccessFile randomFile =
            new RandomAccessFile("MyData.dat", "rw");
```

Here are some important points to remember about the two modes:

- If you open a file in `"r"` mode and the file does not exist, a `FileNotFoundException` will be thrown.
- If you open a file in `"r"` mode and try to write to it, an `IOException` will be thrown.

- If you open an existing file in "rw" mode, it will not be deleted. The file's existing contents will be preserved.
- If you open a file in "rw" mode and the file does not exist, it will be created.

Reading and Writing with the RandomAccessFile Class

A file that is opened or created with the RandomAccessFile class is treated as a binary file. In fact, the RandomAccessFile class has the same methods as the DataOutputStream class for writing data, and the same methods as the DataInputStream class for reading data. In fact, you can use the RandomAccessFile class to process a binary file sequentially. For example, the program in Code Listing 12-13 opens a file named *Letters.dat* and writes all of the letters of the alphabet to the file.

Code Listing 12-13   (WriteLetters.java)

```java
 1 import java.io.*;
 2
 3 /**
 4    This program uses a RandomAccessFile object to
 5    create the file Letters.dat. The letters of the
 6    alphabet are written to the file.
 7 */
 8
 9 public class WriteLetters
10 {
11    public static void main(String[] args)
12                      throws IOException
13    {
14    // The letters array has all 26 letters.
15    char[] letters = {
16                     'a', 'b', 'c', 'd', 'e', 'f', 'g',
17                     'h', 'i', 'j', 'k', 'l', 'm', 'n',
18                     'o', 'p', 'q', 'r', 's', 't', 'u',
19                     'v', 'w', 'x', 'y', 'z' };
20
21    System.out.println("Opening the file.");
22
23    // Open a file for reading and writing.
24    RandomAccessFile randomFile =
25            new RandomAccessFile("Letters.dat", "rw");
26
27    System.out.println("Writing data to the file...");
28
29    // Sequentially write the letters array to the file.
30    for (int i = 0; i < letters.length; i++)
31       randomFile.writeChar(letters[i]);
32
```

```
33        // Close the file.
34        randomFile.close();
35
36        System.out.println("Done.");
37    }
38 }
```

Program Output

```
Opening the file.
Writing data to the file...
Done.
```

After this program executes, the letters of the alphabet will be stored in the *Letters.dat* file. Because the `writeChar` method was used, the letters will each be stored as two-byte characters. This fact is important to know later when we want to read the characters from the file.

The File Pointer

The `RandomAccessFile` class treats a file as a stream of bytes. The bytes are numbered, with the first byte being byte 0. The last byte's number is one less than the number of bytes in the file. These byte numbers are similar to an array's subscripts, and are used to identify locations in the file.

Internally, the `RandomAccessFile` class keeps a long integer value known as the file pointer. The *file pointer* holds the byte number of a location in the file. When a file is first opened, the file pointer is set to 0. This causes it to "point" to the first byte in the file. When an item is read from the file, it is read from the byte that the file pointer points to. Reading also causes the file pointer to advance to the byte just beyond the item that was read. For example, let's say the file pointer points to byte 0 and an `int` is read from the file with the `readInt` method. An `int` is four bytes in size, so four bytes will be read from the file, starting at byte 0. After the value is read, the file pointer will be advanced to byte number 4, which is the 5th byte in the file. If another item is immediately read, the reading will begin at byte number 4. If the file pointer refers to a byte number that is beyond the end of the file, an `EOFException` is thrown when a read operation is performed.

Writing also takes place at the location pointed to by the file pointer. If the file pointer points to the end of the file when a write operation is performed, then the data will be written to the end of the file. However, if the file pointer holds the number of a byte within the file, at a location where data is already stored, then a write operation will cause data to be written over the existing data at that location.

Not only does the `RandomAccessFile` class let you read and write data, but also it allows you to move the file pointer. This means that you can immediately read data from any byte location in the file. It also means that you can write data to any location in the file, over existing data. To move the file pointer, you use the `seek` method. Here is the method's general format:

```
void seek(long position)
```

The argument is the number of the byte that you want to move the file pointer to. For example, look at the following code:

```
RandomAccessFile file =
            new RandomAccessFile("MyInfo.dat", "r");
file.seek(99);
byte b = file.readByte();
```

This code opens the file *MyInfo.dat* for reading. The `seek` method is called to move the file pointer to byte number 99 (which is the 100th byte in the file). Then, the `readByte` method is called to read byte number 99 from the file. After that statement executes, the file pointer will be advanced by one byte, so it will point to byte 100. Suppose we continue processing the same file with the following code:

```
file.seek(49);
int i = file.readInt();
```

First, the `seek` method moves the file pointer to byte number 49 (which is the 50th byte in the file). Then, the `readInt` method is called. This reads an `int` from the file. An `int` is four bytes in size, so this statement reads four bytes, beginning at byte number 49. After the statement executes the file pointer will be advanced by four bytes, so it will point to byte 53.

Although a file might contain `chars`, `ints`, `doubles`, strings, and so forth, the `RandomAccessFile` class sees it only as a stream of bytes. The class is unaware of the data types of the data stored in the file, and it cannot determine where one item of data ends and another begins. When you write a program that reads data from a random access file, it is your responsibility to know how the data is structured.

For example, recall that the program in Code Listing 12-13 wrote the letters of the alphabet to the *Letters.dat* file. Let's say the first letter is character 0, the second letter is character 1, and so forth. Suppose we want to read character 5 (the sixth letter in the file). At first, we might be tempted to try the following code:

```
// Open the file for reading.
RandomAccessFile randomFile =
            new RandomAccessFile("Letters.dat", "r");
// Move the file pointer to byte 5, which is the 6th byte.
randomFile.seek(5);
// Read the character.
char ch = randomFile.readChar();
// What will this display?
System.out.println("The sixth letter is " + ch);
```

Although this code will compile and run, you might be surprised at the result. Recall that the `writeChar` method writes a character as two bytes. Because each character occupies two bytes in the file, the sixth character begins at byte 10, not byte 5. This is illustrated in Figure 12-16. In fact, if we try to read a character starting at byte 5, we will read garbage because byte 5 is not at the beginning of a character.

Figure 12-16 Layout of the *Letters.dat* file

To determine the position of a character in the file, we must take each character's size into account. The following code will correctly read and display the sixth character. To determine the character's starting byte number, it multiplies the size of a character by the number of the character we want to locate.

```
final int CHAR_SIZE = 2;   // Each char uses two bytes
// Move the file pointer to character 5.
randomFile.seek(CHAR_SIZE * 5);
// Read the character.
char ch = randomFile.readChar();
// This will display the correct character.
System.out.println("The sixth character is " + ch);
```

The program in Code Listing 12-14 demonstrates further. It randomly reads characters 5, 10, and 3 from the file.

Code Listing 12-14 (`ReadRandomLetters.java`)

```java
 1 import java.io.*;
 2
 3 /**
 4    This program uses the RandomAccessFile class to open
 5    the file Letters.dat and randomly read letters from
 6    different locations.
 7 */
 8
 9 public class ReadRandomLetters
10 {
11    public static void main(String[] args) throws IOException
12    {
13       final int CHAR_SIZE = 2;   // 2 byte characters
14       long byteNum;              // The byte number
15       char ch;                   // A character from the file
16
17       // Open the file for reading.
18       RandomAccessFile randomFile =
19                new RandomAccessFile("Letters.dat", "r");
20
21       // Move to the character 5. This is the 6th
```

```
22        // character from the beginning of the file.
23        byteNum = CHAR_SIZE * 5;
24        randomFile.seek(byteNum);
25
26        // Read the character stored at this location
27        // and display it. Should be the letter f.
28        ch = randomFile.readChar();
29        System.out.println(ch);
30
31        // Move to character 10 (the 11th character),
32        // read the character, and display it.
33        // Should be the letter k.
34        byteNum = CHAR_SIZE * 10;
35        randomFile.seek(byteNum);
36        ch = randomFile.readChar();
37        System.out.println(ch);
38
39        // Move to character 3 (the 4th character),
40        // read the character, and display it.
41        // Should be the letter d.
42        byteNum = CHAR_SIZE * 3;
43        randomFile.seek(byteNum);
44        ch = randomFile.readChar();
45        System.out.println(ch);
46
47        // Close the file.
48        randomFile.close();
49    }
50 }
```

Program Output

```
f
k
d
```

See the Student CD for Appendix I—Working with Records and Random Access Files.

Object Serialization

In Appendix I on the Student CD, you can see how an object's fields can be retrieved and saved to a file as fields in a record. If an object contains other types of objects as fields, however, the process of saving its contents can become complicated. Fortunately, Java allows you to *serialize* objects, which is a simpler way of saving objects to a file.

When an object is serialized, it is converted into a series of bytes that contain the object's data. If the object is set up properly, even the other objects that it might contain as fields are automatically serialized. The resulting set of bytes can be saved to a file for later retrieval.

In order for an object to be serialized, its class must implement the `Serializable` interface. The `Serializable` interface, which is in the `java.io` package, has no methods or fields. It is used only to let the Java compiler know that objects of the class might be serialized. In addition, if a class contains objects of other classes as fields, those classes must also implement the `Serializable` interface, in order to be serialized.

For example, on the Student CD there is a modified version of the `BankAccount` class named `BankAccount2`. The only modification to the class is that it implements the `Serializable` interface. Here are the modified lines of code from the file:

```
import java.io.Serializable;

public class BankAccount2 implements Serializable
```

This new code tells the compiler that we want to be able to serialize objects of the `BankAccount2` class. To write a serialized object to a file, you use an `ObjectOutputStream` object. The `ObjectOutputStream` class is designed to perform the serialization process (converting an object to a series of bytes). To write the bytes to a file, you must also use an output stream object, such as `FileOutputStream`. Here is an example:

```
FileOutputStream outStream =
            new FileOutputStream("Objects.dat");
ObjectOutputStream objectOutputFile =
            new ObjectOutputStream(outStream);
```

To serialize an object and write it to the file, use the `ObjectOutputStream` class's `writeObject` method, as shown here:

```
BankAccount2 account = new BankAccount2(5000.0);
objectOutputFile.writeObject(account);
```

The `writeObject` method throws an `IOException` if an error occurs.

The process of reading a serialized object's bytes and constructing an object from them is known as *deserialization*. To deserialize an object you use an `ObjectInputStream` object, along with a `FileInputStream` object. Here is an example of how to set up the objects:

```
FileInputStream inStream =
            new FileInputStream("Objects.dat");
ObjectInputStream objectInputFile =
            new ObjectInputStream(inStream);
```

To read a serialized object from the file, use the `ObjectInputStream` class's `readObject` method. Here is an example:

```
BankAccount2 account;
account = (BankAccount2) objectInputFile.readObject();
```

The `readObject` method returns the deserialized object. Notice that you must cast the return value to the desired class type. (The `readObject` method throws a number of different exceptions if an error occurs. See the API documentation for more information.)

The following programs demonstrate how to serialize and deserialize objects. The program in Code Listing 12-15 serializes three `BankAccount2` objects, and the program in Code Listing 12-16 deserializes them.

Code Listing 12-15   `(SerializeObjects.java)`

```java
 1 import java.io.*;
 2 import java.util.Scanner;
 3
 4 /**
 5    This program serializes the objects in an array of
 6    BankAccount2 objects.
 7 */
 8
 9 public class SerializeObjects
10 {
11    public static void main(String[] args)
12                         throws IOException
13    {
14       double balance;                // An account balance
15       final int NUM_ITEMS = 3;    // Number of accounts
16
17       // Create a Scanner object for keyboard input.
18       Scanner keyboard = new Scanner(System.in);
19
20       // Create a BankAccount2 array
21       BankAccount2[] accounts =
22                      new BankAccount2[NUM_ITEMS];
23
24       // Populate the array.
25       for (int i = 0; i < accounts.length; i++)
26       {
27          // Get an account balance.
28          System.out.print("Enter the balance for " +
29                           "account " + (i + 1) + ": ");
30          balance = keyboard.nextDouble();
31
32          // Create an object in the array.
33          accounts[i] = new BankAccount2(balance);
34       }
35
36       // Create the stream objects.
37       FileOutputStream outStream =
38                new FileOutputStream("Objects.dat");
39       ObjectOutputStream objectOutputFile =
40                new ObjectOutputStream(outStream);
41
42       // Write the serialized objects to the file.
43       for (int i = 0; i < accounts.length; i++)
44       {
45          objectOutputFile.writeObject(accounts[i]);
46       }
```

```
47
48          // Close the file.
49          objectOutputFile.close();
50
51          System.out.println("The serialized objects " +
52                  "were written to the Objects.dat file.");
53      }
54 }
```

Program Output with Example Input Shown in Bold

```
Enter the balance for account 1: 5000.0 [Enter]
Enter the balance for account 2: 2500.0 [Enter]
Enter the balance for account 3: 1800.0 [Enter]
The serialized objects were written to the Objects.dat file.
```

Code Listing 12-16   (DeserializeObjects.java)

```
 1 import java.io.*;
 2
 3 /**
 4    This program deserializes the objects in the Objects.dat
 5    file and stores them in an array.
 6 */
 7
 8 public class DeserializeObjects
 9 {
10    public static void main(String[] args)
11                    throws Exception
12    {
13        double balance;              // An account balance
14        final int NUM_ITEMS = 3;     // Number of accounts
15
16        // Create the stream objects.
17        FileInputStream inStream =
18                new FileInputStream("Objects.dat");
19        ObjectInputStream objectInputFile =
20                new ObjectInputStream(inStream);
21
22        // Create a BankAccount2 array
23        BankAccount2[] accounts =
24                new BankAccount2[NUM_ITEMS];
25
26        // Read the serialized objects from the file.
27        for (int i = 0; i < accounts.length; i++)
28        {
```

```
29              accounts[i] =
30                  (BankAccount2) objectInputFile.readObject();
31          }
32
33      // Close the file.
34      objectInputFile.close();
35
36      // Display the objects.
37      for (int i = 0; i < accounts.length; i++)
38      {
39          System.out.println("Account " + (i + 1) +
40                  " $ " + accounts[i].getBalance());
41      }
42  }
43 }
```

Program Output

```
Account 1 $ 5000.0
Account 2 $ 2500.0
Account 3 $ 1800.0
```

Serializing Aggregate Objects

If a class implements the `Serializable` interface, then all of the fields in that class must be serializable. This isn't a problem for primitive variables because they are serializable just as they are. However, if the class has a reference variable as a field, then the object referenced by that variable should also be serializable. This means that the object's class should also implement the `Serializable` interface. If it doesn't, then the `transient` key word should be used in the reference variable's declaration. Here is an example:

```
private transient SomeClass refVar;
```

Because of the `transient` key word, the compiler will skip the object referenced by `refVar` during the serialization process. Fortunately, the `String` class, and most of the other classes found in the Java API, implement the `Serializable` interface.

Checkpoint

12.20 What is the difference between a text file and a binary file?

12.21 What classes do you use to write output to a binary file? What classes do you use to read from a binary file?

12.22 What is the difference between sequential and random access?

12.23 What class do you use to work with random access files?

12.24 What are the two modes that a random access file may be opened in? Explain the difference between them.

12.25 What must you do to a class in order to serialize objects of that class?

12.4 Common Errors to Avoid

- **Assuming that all statements inside a try block will execute.** When an exception is thrown, the try block is exited immediately. This means that statements appearing in the try block after the offending statement will not be executed.
- **Getting the `try`, `catch`, and `finally` clauses out of order.** In a `try` statement, the `try` clause must appear first, followed by all of the `catch` clauses, followed by the optional `finally` clause.
- **Writing two `catch` clauses that handle the same exception in the same `try` statement.** You cannot have more than one `catch` clause per exception type in the same `try` statement.
- **When catching multiple exceptions that are related to one another through inheritance, listing the more general exceptions first.** If you are handling multiple exceptions in the same `try` statement, and some of the exceptions are related to each other through inheritance, then you should handle the more specialized exception classes before the more general exception classes. Otherwise, an error will occur because the compiler thinks that you are handling the same exception more than once.
- **Forgetting to write a `throws` clause on a method that can throw a checked exception but does not handle the exception.** If a method is capable of throwing a checked exception but does not handle the exception, it must have a `throws` clause in its header that specifies the exception.
- **Calling a method but not handling an exception that it might throw.** You must either handle all of the checked exceptions that a method can throw, or list them in the calling method's `throws` clause.
- **In a custom exception class, forgetting to pass an error message to the superclass's constructor.** If you do not pass an error message to the superclass's constructor, the exception object will have a `null` error message.
- **Serializing an object with members that are not serializable.** If a class has fields that are objects of other classes, those classes must implement the `Serializable` interface in order to be serialized.

Review Questions and Exercises

Multiple Choice and True/False

1. When an exception is generated, it is said to have been _____.
   - a. built
   - b. thrown
   - c. caught
   - d. killed

2. This is a section of code that gracefully responds to exceptions.
   - a. exception generator
   - b. exception manipulator
   - c. exception handler
   - d. exception monitor

3. If your code does not handle an exception when it is thrown, it is dealt with by this.

   a. default exception handler
   b. the operating system
   c. system debugger
   d. default exception generator

4. All exception classes inherit from this class.

   a. `Error`
   b. `RuntimeException`
   c. `JavaException`
   d. `Throwable`

5. `FileNotFoundException` inherits from _____.

   a. `Error`
   b. `IOException`
   c. `JavaException`
   d. `FileException`

6. You can think of this code as being "protected" because the application will not halt if it throws an exception.

   a. try block
   b. catch block
   c. finally block
   d. protected block

7. This method can be used to retrieve the error message from an exception object.

   a. `errorMessage`
   b. `errorString`
   c. `getError`
   d. `getMessage`

8. The numeric wrapper classes' "parse" methods all throw an exception of this type.

   a. `ParseException`
   b. `NumberFormatException`
   c. `IOException`
   d. `BadNumberException`

9. This is one or more statements that are always executed after the try block has executed and after any catch blocks have executed if an exception was thrown.

   a. try block
   b. catch block
   c. finally block
   d. protected block

10. This is an internal list of all the methods that are currently executing.

   a. invocation list
   b. call stack
   c. call list
   d. list trace

11. This method may be called from any exception object, and it shows the chain of methods that were called when the exception was thrown.

    a. `printInvocationList`
    b. `printCallStack`
    c. `printStackTrace`
    d. `printCallList`

12. These are exceptions that inherit from the `Error` class or the `RuntimeException` class.

    a. unrecoverable exceptions
    b. unchecked exceptions
    c. recoverable exceptions
    d. checked exceptions

13. All exceptions that do *not* inherit from the `Error` class or the `RuntimeException` class are _____.

    a. unrecoverable exceptions
    b. unchecked exceptions
    c. recoverable exceptions
    d. checked exceptions

14. This informs the compiler of the exceptions that could get thrown from a method.

    a. `throws` clause
    b. parameter list
    c. `catch` clause
    d. method return type

15. You use this statement to throw an exception manually.

    a. `try`
    b. `generate`
    c. `throw`
    d. `System.exit(0)`

16. This is the process of converting an object to a series of bytes that represent the object's data.

    a. serialization
    b. deserialization
    c. dynamic conversion
    d. casting

17. **True or False:** You are not required to catch exceptions that inherit from the `RuntimeException` class.

18. **True or False:** When an exception is thrown by code inside a try block, all of the statements in the try block are always executed.

19. **True or False:** `IOException` serves as a superclass for exceptions that are related to programming errors, such as an out-of-bounds array subscript.

20. **True or False:** You cannot have more than one `catch` clause per `try` statement.

21. **True or False:** When an exception is thrown, the JVM searches the `try` statement's `catch` clauses from top to bottom and passes control of the program to the first `catch` clause with a parameter that is compatible with the exception.

22. **True or False:** Not including polymorphic references, a `try` statement may have only one `catch` clause for each specific type of exception.

23. **True or False:** When in the same `try` statement you are handling multiple exceptions and some of the exceptions are related to each other through inheritance, you should handle the more general exception classes before the more specialized exception classes.

24. **True or False:** The `throws` clause causes an exception to be thrown.

Find the Error

Find the error in each of the following code segments:

1.
```
catch (FileNotFoundException e)
{
    System.out.println("File not found.");
}
try
{
    File file = new File("MyFile.txt");
    Scanner inputFile = new Scanner(file);
}
```

2.
```
// Assume inputFile references a Scanner object.
try
{
    input = inputFile.nextInt();
}
finally
{
    inputFile.close();
}
catch (InputMismatchException e)
{
    System.out.println(e.getMessage());
}
```

3.
```
try
{
    number = Integer.parseInt(str);
}
catch (Exception e)
{
    System.out.println(e.getMessage());
}
```

```java
catch (IllegalArgumentException e)
{
    System.out.println("Bad number format.");
}
catch (NumberFormatException e)
{
    System.out.println(str + " is not a number.");
}
```

Algorithm Workbench

1. Look at the following program and tell what the program will output when run:

```java
public class ExceptionTest
{
    public static void main(String[] args)
    {

        int number;
        String str;

        try
        {
            str = "xyz";
            number = Integer.parseInt(str);
            System.out.println("A");
        }
        catch(NumberFormatException e)
        {
            System.out.println("B");
        }
        catch(IllegalArgumentException e)
        {
            System.out.println("C");
        }

        System.out.println("D");
    }
}
```

2. Look at the following program and tell what the program will output when run:

```java
public class ExceptionTest
{
    public static void main(String[] args)
    {
        int number;
        String str;
```

```
        try
        {
            str = "xyz";
            number = Integer.parseInt(str);
            System.out.println("A");
        }
        catch(NumberFormatException e)
        {
            System.out.println("B");
        }
        catch(IllegalArgumentException e)
        {
            System.out.println("C");
        }
        finally
        {
            System.out.println("D");
        }

        System.out.println("E");
    }
}
```

3. Write a method that searches a numeric array for a specified value. The method should return the subscript of the element containing the value if it is found in the array. If the value is not found, the method should throw an exception of the Exception class with the error message "Element not found".

4. Write a statement that throws an IllegalArgumentException with the error message "Argument cannot be negative".

5. Write an exception class that can be thrown when a negative number is passed to a method.

6. Write a statement that throws an instance of the exception class that you created in Algorithm Workbench 5.

7. The method getValueFromFile is public and returns an int. It accepts no arguments. The method is capable of throwing an IOException and a FileNotFoundException. Write the header for this method.

8. Write a try statement that calls the getValueFromFile method described in Algorithm Workbench 7. Be sure to handle all the exceptions that the method can throw.

9. Write a statement that creates an object that can be used to write binary data to the file *Configuration.dat*.

10. Write a statement that opens the file *Customers.dat* as a random access file for both reading and writing.

11. Assume that the reference variable r refers to a serializable object. Write code that serializes the object to the file *ObjectData.dat*.

Short Answer

1. What is meant when it is said that an exception is thrown?

2. What does it mean to catch an exception?

3. What happens when an exception is thrown, but the try statement does not have a catch clause that is capable of catching it?

4. What is the purpose of a finally clause?

5. Where does execution resume after an exception has been thrown and caught?

6. When multiple exceptions are caught in the same try statement and some of them are related through inheritance, does the order in which they are listed matter?

7. What types of objects can be thrown?

8. When are you required to have a throws clause in a method header?

9. What is the difference between a checked exception and an unchecked exception?

10. What is the difference between the throw statement and the throws clause?

11. What is the difference between a text file and a binary file?

12. What is the difference between a sequential access file and a random access file?

13. What happens when you serialize an object? What happens when you deserialize an object?

Programming Challenges

myCodeMate

1. TestScores **Class**

Write a class named TestScores. The class constructor should accept an array of test scores as its argument. The class should have a method that returns the average of the test scores. If any test score in the array is negative or greater than 100, the class should throw an IllegalArgumentException. Demonstrate the class in a program.

2. TestScores **Class Custom Exception**

Write an exception class named InvalidTestScore. Modify the TestScores class you wrote in Programming Challenge 1 so that it throws an InvalidTestScore exception if any of the test scores in the array are invalid.

3. RetailItem **Exceptions**

Programming Challenge 4 of Chapter 6 required you to write a RetailItem class that holds data pertaining to a retail item. Write an exception class that can be instantiated and thrown when a negative number is given for the price. Write another exception class that can be instantiated and thrown when a negative number is given for the units on hand. Demonstrate the exception classes in a program.

4. Month **Class Exceptions**

Programming Challenge 5 of Chapter 9 required you to write a Month class that holds information about the month. Write exception classes for the following error conditions:

- A number less than 1 or greater than 12 is given for the month number.
- An invalid string is given for the name of the month.

Modify the Month class so that it throws the appropriate exception when either of these errors occurs. Demonstrate the classes in a program.

5. Payroll **Class Exceptions**

Programming Challenge 5 of Chapter 6 required you to write a Payroll class that calculates an employee's payroll. Write exception classes for the following error conditions:

- An empty string is given for the employee's name.
- An invalid value is given for the employee's ID number. If you implemented this field as a string, then an empty string would be invalid. If you implemented this field as a numeric variable, then a negative number or zero would be invalid.
- An invalid number is given for the number of hours worked. This would be a negative number or a number greater than 84.
- An invalid number is given for the hourly pay rate. This would be a negative number or a number greater than 25.

Modify the Payroll class so that it throws the appropriate exception when any of these errors occurs. Demonstrate the exception classes in a program.

6. FileArray **Class**

Design a class that has a static method named writeArray. The method should take two arguments: the name of a file and a reference to an int array. The file should be opened as a binary file, the contents of the array should be written to the file, and then the file should be closed.

Write a second method in the class named readArray. The method should take two arguments: the name of a file and a reference to an int array. The file should be opened, data should be read from the file and stored in the array, and then the file should be closed. Demonstrate both methods in a program.

 ### 7. **File Encryption Filter**

File encryption is the science of writing the contents of a file in a secret code. Your encryption program should work like a filter, reading the contents of one file, modifying the data into a code, and then writing the coded contents out to a second file. The second file will be a version of the first file, but written in a secret code.

Although there are complex encryption techniques, you should come up with a simple one of your own. For example, you could read the first file one character at a time, and add 10 to the character code of each character before it is written to the second file.

(⟡) myCodeMate

8. File Decryption Filter

Write a program that decrypts the file produced by the program in Programming Challenge 7. The decryption program should read the contents of the coded file, restore the data to its original state, and write it to another file.

9. TestScores Modification for Serialization

Modify the TestScores class that you created for Programming Challenge 1 to be serializable. Write a program that creates an array of at least five TestScore objects and serializes them. Write another program that deserializes the objects from the file.

10. Exception Project

VideoNote
The Exception
Project Problem

This assignment assumes you have completed Programming Challenge 1 of Chapter 11 (Employee and ProductionWorker Classes). Modify the Employee and ProductionWorker classes so they throw exceptions when the following errors occur:

- The Employee class should throw an exception named InvalidEmployeeNumber when it receives an employee number that is less than 0 or greater than 9999.
- The ProductionWorker class should throw an exception named InvalidShift when it receives an invalid shift.
- The ProductionWorker class should throw an exception named InvalidPayRate when it receives a negative number for the hourly pay rate.

Write a test program that demonstrates how each of these exception conditions works.

13 Advanced GUI Applications

13.1 The Swing and AWT Class Hierarchy

Now that you have used some of the fundamental GUI components, let's look at how they fit into the class hierarchy. Figure 13-1 shows the parts of the Swing and AWT class hierarchy that contain the `JFrame`, `JPanel`, `JLabel`, `JTextField`, `JButton`, `JRadioButton`, and `JCheckBox` classes. Because of the inheritance relationships that exist, there are many other classes in the figure as well.

The classes that are in the unshaded top part of the figure are AWT classes and are in the `java.awt` package. The classes that are in the shaded bottom part of the figure are Swing classes and are in the `javax.swing` package. Notice that all of the components we have dealt with ultimately inherit from the `Component` class.

Figure 13-1 Part of the Swing and AWT class hierarchy

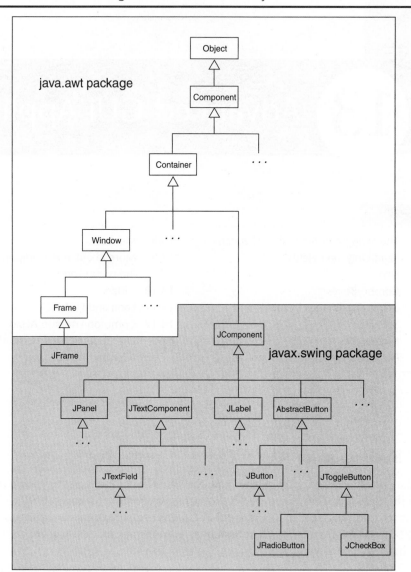

13.2 Read-Only Text Fields

CONCEPT: A read-only text field displays text that can be changed by code in the application, but cannot be edited by the user.

A read-only text field is not a new component, but a different way to use the `JTextField` component. The `JTextField` component has a method named `setEditable`, which has the following general format:

```
setEditable(boolean editable)
```

You pass a `boolean` argument to this method. By default a text field is editable, which means that the user can enter data into it. If you call the `setEditable` method and pass `false` as the argument, then the text field becomes read-only. This means it is not editable by the user. Figure 13-2 shows a window that has three read-only text fields.

Figure 13-2 A window with three read-only text fields

The following code could be used to create the read-only text fields shown in the figure:

```
// Create a read-only text field for the subtotal.
JTextField subtotalField = new JTextField(10);
subtotalField.setEditable(false);

// Create a read-only text field for the sales tax.
JTextField taxField = new JTextField(10);
taxField.setEditable(false);

// Create a read-only text field for the total.
JTextField totalField = new JTextField(10);
totalField.setEditable(false);
```

A read-only text field looks like a label with a border drawn around it. You can use the `setText` method to display data inside it. Here is an example:

```
subtotalField.setText("100.00");
taxField.setText("6.00");
totalField.setText("106.00");
```

This code causes the text fields to appear as shown in Figure 13-3.

Figure 13-3 Read-only text fields with data displayed

13.3 Lists

CONCEPT: A list component displays a list of items and allows the user to select an item from the list.

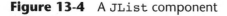

VideoNote
The JList
Component

A list is a component that displays a list of items and also allows the user to select one or more items from the list. Java provides the JList component for creating lists. Figure 13-4 shows an example. The JList component in the figure shows a list of names. At run-time, the user may select an item in the list, which causes the item to appear highlighted. In the figure, the first name is selected.

Figure 13-4   A JList component

When you create an instance of the JList class, you pass an array of objects to the constructor. Here is the general format of the constructor call:

```
JList (Object[] array)
```

The JList component uses the array to create the list of items. In this text we always pass an array of String objects to the JList constructor. For example, the list component shown in Figure 13-4 could be created with the following code:

```
String[] names = { "Bill", "Geri", "Greg", "Jean",
                    "Kirk", "Phillip", "Susan" };
JList nameList = new JList(names);
```

Selection Modes

The JList component can operate in any of the following selection modes:

- Single Selection Mode. In this mode only one item can be selected at a time. When an item is selected, any other item that is currently selected is deselected.
- Single Interval Selection Mode. In this mode multiple items can be selected, but they must be in a single interval. An interval is a set of contiguous items.
- Multiple Interval Selection Mode. In this mode multiple items may be selected with no restrictions. This is the default selection mode.

Figure 13-5 shows an example of a list in each type of selection mode.

Figure 13-5   Selection modes

| Single selection mode allows only one item to be selected at a time. | Single interval selection mode allows a single interval of contiguous items to be selected. | Multiple interval selection mode allows multiple items to be selected with no restrictions. |

The default mode is multiple interval selection. To keep our applications simple, we will use single selection mode for now. You change a `JList` component's selection mode with the `setSelectionMode` method. The method accepts an `int` argument that determines the selection mode.

The `ListSelectionModel` class, which is in the `javax.swing` package, provides the following constants that you can use as arguments to the `setSelectionMode` method:

- `ListSelectionModel.SINGLE_SELECTION`
- `ListSelectionModel.SINGLE_INTERVAL_SELECTION`
- `ListSelectionModel.MULTIPLE_INTERVAL_SELECTION`

Assuming that `nameList` references a `JList` component, the following statement sets the component to single selection mode:

```
nameList.setSelectionMode(ListSelectionModel.SINGLE_SELECTION);
```

Responding to List Events

When an item in a `JList` object is selected it generates a list selection event. You handle list selection events with a list selection listener class, which must meet the following requirements:

- It must implement the `ListSelectionListener` interface.
- It must have a method named `valueChanged`. This method must take an argument of the `ListSelectionEvent` type.

 NOTE: The `ListSelectionListener` interface is in the `javax.swing.event` package, so you must have an `import` statement for that package in your source code.

Once you have written a list selection listener class, you create an object of that class and then pass it as an argument to the `JList` component's `addListSelectionListener` method. When the `JList` component generates an event, it automatically executes the `valueChanged` method of the list selection listener object, passing the event object as an argument. You will see an example in a moment.

Retrieving the Selected Item

You may use either the `getSelectedValue` method or the `getSelectedIndex` method to determine which item in a list is currently selected. The `getSelectedValue` method returns a reference to the item that is currently selected. For example, assume that `nameList` references the `JList` component shown earlier in Figure 13-4. The following code retrieves a reference to the name that is currently selected and assigns it to the `selectedName` variable:

```
String selectedName;
selectedName = (String) nameList.getSelectedValue();
```

Note that the return value of the `getSelectedValue` method is an `Object` reference. In this code we had to cast the return value to the `String` type in order to store it in the `selectedName` variable. If no item in the list is selected, the method returns `null`.

The `getSelectedIndex` method returns the index of the selected item, or −1 if no item is selected. Internally, the items that are stored in a list are numbered. Each item's number is called its index. The first item (which is the item stored at the top of the list) has the index 0, the second item has the index 1, and so forth. You can use the index of the selected item to retrieve the item from an array. For example, assume that the following code was used to build the `nameList` component shown in Figure 13-4:

```
String[] names = { "Bill", "Geri", "Greg", "Jean",
                   "Kirk", "Phillip", "Susan" };
JList nameList = new JList(names);
```

Because the `names` array holds the values displayed in the `namesList` component, the following code could be used to determine the selected item:

```
int index;
String selectedName;
index = nameList.getSelectedIndex();
if (index != -1)
    selectedName = names[index];
```

The `ListWindow` class shown in Code Listing 13-1 demonstrates the concepts we have discussed so far. It uses a `JList` component with a list selection listener. When an item is selected from the list, it is displayed in a read-only text field. The `main` method creates an instance of the `ListWindow` class, which displays the window shown on the left in Figure 13-6. After the user selects October from the list, the window appears as that shown on the right in the figure.

Code Listing 13-1   (`ListWindow.java`)

```
1 import javax.swing.*;
2 import javax.swing.event.*;
3 import java.awt.*;
4
5 /**
6    This class demonstrates the List Component.
7 */
```

```
8
9  public class ListWindow extends JFrame
10 {
11     private JPanel monthPanel;              // To hold components
12     private JPanel selectedMonthPanel;      // To hold components
13     private JList monthList;                // The months
14     private JTextField selectedMonth;       // The selected month
15     private JLabel label;                   // A message
16
17     // The following array holds the values that will
18     // be displayed in the monthList list component.
19     private String[] months = { "January", "February",
20                          "March", "April", "May", "June", "July",
21                          "August", "September", "October", "November",
22                          "December" };
23
24     /**
25        Constructor
26     */
27
28     public ListWindow()
29     {
30        // Set the title.
31        setTitle("List Demo");
32
33        // Specify an action for the close button.
34        setDefaultCloseOperation(JFrame.EXIT_ON_CLOSE);
35
36        // Add a BorderLayout manager.
37        setLayout(new BorderLayout());
38
39        // Build the month and selectedMonth panels.
40        buildMonthPanel();
41        buildSelectedMonthPanel();
42
43        // Add the panels to the content pane.
44        add(monthPanel, BorderLayout.CENTER);
45        add(selectedMonthPanel, BorderLayout.SOUTH);
46
47        // Pack and display the window.
48        pack();
49        setVisible(true);
50     }
51
52     /**
53        The buildMonthPanel method adds a list containing
54        the names of the months to a panel.
55     */
```

```
56
57      private void buildMonthPanel()
58      {
59         // Create a panel to hold the list.
60         monthPanel = new JPanel();
61
62         // Create the list.
63         monthList = new JList(months);
64
65         // Set the selection mode to single selection.
66         monthList.setSelectionMode(
67                 ListSelectionModel.SINGLE_SELECTION);
68
69         // Register the list selection listener.
70         monthList.addListSelectionListener(
71                                 new ListListener());
72
73         // Add the list to the panel.
74         monthPanel.add(monthList);
75      }
76
77      /**
78         The buildSelectedMonthPanel method adds an
79         uneditable text field to a panel.
80      */
81
82      private void buildSelectedMonthPanel()
83      {
84         // Create a panel to hold the text field.
85         selectedMonthPanel = new JPanel();
86
87         // Create the label.
88         label = new JLabel("You selected: ");
89
90         // Create the text field.
91         selectedMonth = new JTextField(10);
92
93         // Make the text field uneditable.
94         selectedMonth.setEditable(false);
95
96         // Add the label and text field to the panel.
97         selectedMonthPanel.add(label);
98         selectedMonthPanel.add(selectedMonth);
99      }
100
101     /**
102        Private inner class that handles the event when
103        the user selects an item from the list.
```

```
104      */
105
106      private class ListListener
107                      implements ListSelectionListener
108      {
109         public void valueChanged(ListSelectionEvent e)
110         {
111            // Get the selected month.
112            String selection =
113                  (String) monthList.getSelectedValue();
114
115            // Put the selected month in the text field.
116            selectedMonth.setText(selection);
117         }
118      }
119
120      /**
121         The main method creates an instance of the
122         ListWindow class which causes it to display
123         its window.
124      */
125
126      public static void main(String[] args)
127      {
128            new ListWindow();
129      }
130 }
```

Figure 13-6 Window displayed by the `ListWindow` class

Placing a Border around a List

As with other components, you can use the `setBorder` method, which was discussed in Chapter 7, to draw a border around a `JList`. For example the following statement can be used to draw a black 1-pixel thick line border around the `monthList` component:

```
monthList.setBorder(BorderFactory.createLineBorder(Color.BLACK, 1));
```

This code will cause the list to appear as shown in Figure 13-7.

Figure 13-7 List with a line border

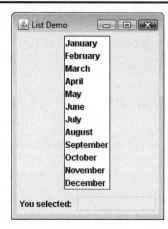

Adding a Scroll Bar to a List

By default, a list component is large enough to display all of the items it contains. Sometimes a list component contains too many items to be displayed at once, however. Most GUI applications display a scroll bar on list components that contain a large number of items. The user simply uses the scroll bar to scroll through the list of items.

List components do not automatically display a scroll bar. To display a scroll bar on a list component, you must follow the following general steps:

1. Set the number of visible rows for the list component.
2. Create a scroll pane object and add the list component to it.
3. Add the scroll pane object to any other containers, such as panels.

Let's take a closer look at how these steps can be used to apply a scroll bar to the list component created in the following code:

```
String[] names = { "Bill", "Geri", "Greg", "Jean",
                   "Kirk", "Phillip", "Susan" };
JList nameList = new JList(names);
```

First, we establish the size of the list component with the `JList` class's `setVisibleRowCount` method. The following statement sets the number of visible rows in the `nameList` component to three:

```
nameList.setVisibleRowCount(3);
```

This statement causes the `nameList` component to display only three items at a time.

Next, we create a scroll pane object and add the list component to it. A scroll pane object is a container that displays scroll bars on any component it contains. In Java we use the `JScrollPane` class to create a scroll pane object. We pass the object that we wish to add to the scroll pane as an argument to the `JScrollPane` constructor. The following statement demonstrates:

```
JScrollPane scrollPane = new JScrollPane(nameList);
```

This statement creates a `JScrollPane` object and adds the `nameList` component to it.

Next, we add the scroll pane object to any other containers that are necessary for our GUI. For example, the following code adds the scroll pane to a `JPanel`, which is then added to the `JFrame` object's content pane:

```
// Create a panel and add the scroll pane to it.
JPanel panel = new JPanel();
panel.add(scrollPane);

// Add the panel to this JFrame object's contentPane.
add(panel);
```

When the list component is displayed, it will appear as shown in Figure 13-8.

Although the list component displays three items at a time only, the user can scroll through all of the items it contains.

The `ListWindowWithScroll` class shown in Code Listing 13-2 is a modification of the `ListWindow` class. In this class, the `monthList` component shows only six items at a time, but displays a scroll bar. The code shown in bold is the new lines that are used to add the scroll bar to the list. The main method creates an instance of the class, which displays the window shown in Figure 13-9.

Figure 13-8   List component with a scroll bar

Figure 13-9   List component with scroll bars

Code Listing 13-2 (`ListWindowWithScroll.java`)

```java
 1  import javax.swing.*;
 2  import javax.swing.event.*;
 3  import java.awt.*;
 4
 5  /**
 6      This class demonstrates the List Component.
 7  */
 8
 9  public class ListWindowWithScroll extends JFrame
10  {
11      private JPanel monthPanel;            // To hold components
12      private JPanel selectedMonthPanel;    // To hold components
13      private JList monthList;              // The months
14      private JScrollPane scrollPane;       // A scroll pane
15      private JTextField selectedMonth;     // The selected month
16      private JLabel label;                 // A message
17
18      // The following array holds the values that will
19      // be displayed in the monthList list component.
20      private String[] months = { "January", "February",
21                  "March", "April", "May", "June", "July",
22                  "August", "September", "October", "November",
23                  "December" };
24
25      /**
26          Constructor
27      */
28
29      public ListWindowWithScroll()
30      {
31          // Set the title.
32          setTitle("List Demo");
33
34          // Specify an action for the close button.
35          setDefaultCloseOperation(JFrame.EXIT_ON_CLOSE);
36
37          // Add a BorderLayout manager.
38          setLayout(new BorderLayout());
39
40          // Build the month and selectedMonth panels.
41          buildMonthPanel();
42          buildSelectedMonthPanel();
43
44          // Add the panels to the content pane.
45          add(monthPanel, BorderLayout.CENTER);
```

```
46              add(selectedMonthPanel, BorderLayout.SOUTH);
47
48              // Pack and display the window.
49              pack();
50              setVisible(true);
51          }
52
53          /**
54              The buildMonthPanel method adds a list containing
55              the names of the months to a panel.
56          */
57
58          private void buildMonthPanel()
59          {
60              // Create a panel to hold the list.
61              monthPanel = new JPanel();
62
63              // Create the list.
64              monthList = new JList(months);
65
66              // Set the selection mode to single selection.
67              monthList.setSelectionMode(
68                          ListSelectionModel.SINGLE_SELECTION);
69
70              // Register the list selection listener.
71              monthList.addListSelectionListener(
72                                          new ListListener());
73
74              // Set the number of visible rows to 6.
75              monthList.setVisibleRowCount(6);
76
77              // Add the list to a scroll pane.
78              scrollPane = new JScrollPane(monthList);
79
80              // Add the scroll pane to the panel.
81              monthPanel.add(scrollPane);
82          }
83
84          /**
85              The buildSelectedMonthPanel method adds an
86              uneditable text field to a panel.
87          */
88
89          private void buildSelectedMonthPanel()
90          {
91              // Create a panel to hold the text field.
92              selectedMonthPanel = new JPanel();
```

```
 93
 94          // Create the label.
 95          label = new JLabel("You selected: ");
 96
 97          // Create the text field.
 98          selectedMonth = new JTextField(10);
 99
100          // Make the text field uneditable.
101          selectedMonth.setEditable(false);
102
103          // Add the label and text field to the panel.
104          selectedMonthPanel.add(label);
105          selectedMonthPanel.add(selectedMonth);
106       }
107
108       /**
109          Private inner class that handles the event when
110          the user selects an item from the list.
111       */
112
113       private class ListListener
114                        implements ListSelectionListener
115       {
116          public void valueChanged(ListSelectionEvent e)
117          {
118             // Get the selected month.
119             String selection =
120                     (String) monthList.getSelectedValue();
121
122             // Put the selected month in the text field.
123             selectedMonth.setText(selection);
124          }
125       }
126
127       /**
128          The main method creates an instance of the
129          ListWindowWithScroll class which causes it
130          to display its window.
131       */
132
133        public static void main(String[] args)
134        {
135           new ListWindowWithScroll();
136        }
137 }
```

NOTE: By default, when a `JList` component is added to a `JScrollPane` object, the scroll bar is only displayed when there are more items in the list than there are visible rows.

 NOTE: When a `JList` component is added to a `JScrollPane` object, a border will automatically appear around the list.

Adding Items to an Existing `JList` Component

The `JList` class's `setListData` method allows you to store items in an existing `JList` component. Here is the method's general format:

```
void setListData(Object[] data)
```

The argument passed into `data` is an array of objects that will become the items displayed in the `JList` component. Any items that are currently displayed in the component will be replaced by the new items.

In addition to replacing the existing items in a list, you can use this method to add items to an empty list. You can create an empty list by passing no argument to the `JList` constructor. Here is an example:

```
JList nameList = new JList();
```

This statement creates an empty `JList` component referenced by the `nameList` variable. You can then add items to the list, as shown here:

```
String[] names = { "Bill", "Geri", "Greg", "Jean",
                   "Kirk", "Phillip", "Susan" };
nameList.setListData(names);
```

Multiple Selection Lists

For simplicity, the previous examples used a `JList` component in single selection mode. Recall that the other two selection modes are single interval and multiple interval. Both of these modes allow the user to select multiple items. Let's take a closer look at each of these modes.

Single Interval Selection Mode

You put a `JList` component in single interval selection mode by passing the constant `ListSelectionModel.SINGLE_INTERVAL_SELECTION` to the component's `setSelectionMode` method. In single interval selection mode, single or multiple items can be selected. An interval is a set of contiguous items. (See Figure 13-5 to see an example of an interval.)

To select an interval of items, the user selects the first item in the interval by clicking on it, and then selects the last item in the interval by holding down the Shift key while clicking on it. All of the items that appear in the list from the first item through the last item are selected.

In single interval selection mode, the `getSelectedValue` method returns the first item in the selected interval. The `getSelectedIndex` method returns the index of the first item in the selected interval. To get the entire selected interval, use the `getSelectedValues` method. This method returns an array of objects. The array will hold the items in the selected interval. You can also use the `getSelectedIndices` method, which returns an array of `int` values. The values in the array will be the indices of all the selected items in the list.

Multiple Interval Selection Mode

You put a `JList` component in multiple interval selection mode by passing the constant `ListSelectionModel.MULTIPLE_INTERVAL_SELECTION` to the component's `setSelectionMode` method. In multiple interval selection mode, multiple items can be selected and the items do not have to be in the same interval. (See Figure 13-5 for an example.)

In multiple interval selection mode, the user can select single items or intervals. When the user holds down the Ctrl key while clicking on an item, it selects the item without deselecting any items that are currently selected. This allows the user to select multiple items that are not in an interval.

In multiple interval selection mode, the `getSelectedValue` method returns the first selected item. The `getSelectedIndex` method returns the index of the first selected item. The `getSelectedValues` method returns an array of objects containing the items that are selected. The `getSelectedIndices` method returns an `int` array containing the indices of all the selected items in the list.

The `MultipleIntervalSelection` class, shown in Code Listing 13-3, demonstrates a `JList` component used in multiple interval selection mode. The `main` method creates an instance of the class that displays the window shown on the left in Figure 13-10. When the user selects items from the top `JList` component and then clicks the Get Selections button, the selected items appear in the bottom `JList` component.

Code Listing 13-3 (`MultipleIntervalSelection.java`)

```
 1  import javax.swing.*;
 2  import java.awt.*;
 3  import java.awt.event.*;
 4
 5  /**
 6      This class demonstrates the List Component in
 7      multiple interval selection mode.
 8  */
 9
10  public class MultipleIntervalSelection extends JFrame
11  {
12      private JPanel monthPanel;          // To hold components
13      private JPanel selectedMonthPanel;  // To hold components
14      private JPanel buttonPanel;         // To hold the button
15
```

```
16        private JList monthList;              // To hold months
17        private JList selectedMonthList;      // Selected months
18
19        private JScrollPane scrollPane1;      // Scroll pane - first list
20        private JScrollPane scrollPane2;      // Scroll pane - second list
21
22        private JButton button;               // A button
23
24        // The following array holds the values that
25        // will be displayed in the monthList list component.
26        private String[] months = { "January", "February",
27                  "March", "April", "May", "June", "July",
28                  "August", "September", "October", "November",
29                  "December" };
30
31        /**
32           Constructor
33        */
34
35        public MultipleIntervalSelection()
36        {
37           // Set the title.
38           setTitle("List Demo");
39
40           // Specify an action for the close button.
41           setDefaultCloseOperation(JFrame.EXIT_ON_CLOSE);
42
43           // Add a BorderLayout manager.
44           setLayout(new BorderLayout());
45
46           // Build the panels.
47           buildMonthPanel();
48           buildSelectedMonthsPanel();
49           buildButtonPanel();
50
51           // Add the panels to the content pane.
52           add(monthPanel, BorderLayout.NORTH);
53           add(selectedMonthPanel,BorderLayout.CENTER);
54           add(buttonPanel, BorderLayout.SOUTH);
55
56           // Pack and display the window.
57           pack();
58           setVisible(true);
59        }
60
61        /**
62           The buildMonthPanel method adds a list containing the
63           names of the months to a panel.
```

```
64       */
65
66       private void buildMonthPanel()
67       {
68          // Create a panel to hold the list.
69          monthPanel = new JPanel();
70
71          // Create the list.
72          monthList = new JList(months);
73
74          // Set the selection mode to multiple
75          // interval selection.
76          monthList.setSelectionMode(
77            ListSelectionModel.MULTIPLE_INTERVAL_SELECTION);
78
79          // Set the number of visible rows to 6.
80          monthList.setVisibleRowCount(6);
81
82          // Add the list to a scroll pane.
83          scrollPane1 = new JScrollPane(monthList);
84
85          // Add the scroll pane to the panel.
86          monthPanel.add(scrollPane1);
87       }
88
89       /**
90          The buildSelectedMonthsPanel method adds a list
91          to a panel. This will hold the selected months.
92       */
93
94       private void buildSelectedMonthsPanel()
95       {
96          // Create a panel to hold the list.
97          selectedMonthPanel = new JPanel();
98
99          // Create the list.
100         selectedMonthList = new JList();
101
102         // Set the number of visible rows to 6.
103         selectedMonthList.setVisibleRowCount(6);
104
105         // Add the list to a scroll pane.
106         scrollPane2 =
107                 new JScrollPane(selectedMonthList);
108
109         // Add the scroll pane to the panel.
110         selectedMonthPanel.add(scrollPane2);
```

```
111      }
112
113      /**
114         The buildButtonPanel method adds a
115         button to a panel.
116      */
117
118      private void buildButtonPanel()
119      {
120         // Create a panel to hold the list.
121         buttonPanel = new JPanel();
122
123         // Create the button.
124         button = new JButton("Get Selections");
125
126         // Add an action listener to the button.
127         button.addActionListener(new ButtonListener());
128
129         // Add the button to the panel.
130         buttonPanel.add(button);
131      }
132
133      /**
134         Private inner class that handles the event when
135         the user clicks the button.
136      */
137
138      private class ButtonListener implements ActionListener
139      {
140         public void actionPerformed(ActionEvent e)
141         {
142            // Get the selected values.
143            Object[] selections =
144                           monthList.getSelectedValues();
145
146            // Store the selected items in selectedMonthList.
147            selectedMonthList.setListData(selections);
148         }
149      }
150
151      /**
152         The main method creates an instance of the
153         MultipleIntervalSelection class which causes it
154         to display its window.
155      */
156
157      public static void main(String[] args)
```

```
158     {
159         new MultipleIntervalSelection();
160     }
161 }
```

Figure 13-10   The window displayed by the `MultipleIntervalSelection` class

This is the window as it is intially displayed.

This is the window after the user has selected some items from the top list and clicked the Get Selections button.

13.4   Combo Boxes

CONCEPT: A combo box allows the user to select an item from a drop-down list.

VideoNote
The JComboBox
Component

A combo box presents a list of items that the user may select from. Unlike a list component, a combo box presents its items in a drop-down list. You use the `JComboBox` class, which is in the `javax.swing` package, to create a combo box. You pass an array of objects that are to be displayed as the items in the drop-down list to the constructor. Here is an example:

```
String[] names = { "Bill", "Geri", "Greg", "Jean",
                   "Kirk", "Phillip", "Susan" };
JComboBox nameBox = new JComboBox(names);
```

When displayed, the combo box created by this code will initially appear as the button shown on the left in Figure 13-11. The button displays the item that is currently selected. Notice that the first item in the list is automatically selected when the combo box is first displayed. When the user clicks the button, the drop-down list appears and the user may select another item.

Figure 13-11   A combo box

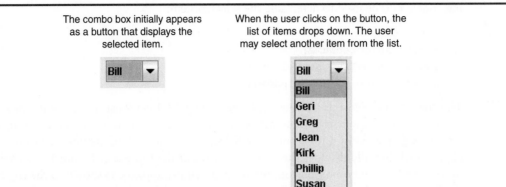

As you can see, a combo box is a combination of two components. In the case of the combo box shown in Figure 13-11, it is the combination of a button and a list. This is where the name "combo box" comes from.

Responding to Combo Box Events

When an item in a `JComboBox` object is selected, it generates an action event. As with `JButton` components, you handle action events with an action event listener class, which must have an `actionPerformed` method. When the user selects an item in a combo box, the combo box executes its action event listener's `actionPerformed` method, passing an `ActionEvent` object as an argument.

Retrieving the Selected Item

There are two methods in the `JComboBox` class that you can use to determine which item in a combo box is currently selected: `getSelectedItem` and `getSelectedIndex`. The `getSelectedItem` method returns a reference to the item that is currently selected. For example, assume that `nameBox` references the `JComboBox` component shown earlier in Figure 13-11. The following code retrieves a reference to the name that is currently selected and assigns it to the `selectedName` variable:

```
String selectedName;
selectedName = (String) nameBox.getSelectedItem();
```

Note that the return value of the `getSelectedItem` method is an `Object` reference. In this code we had to cast the return value to the `String` type in order to store it in the `selectedName` variable.

The `getSelectedIndex` method returns the index of the selected item. As with `JList` components, the items that are stored in a combo box are numbered with indices that start at 0. You can use the index of the selected item to retrieve the item from an array. For example, assume that the following code was used to build the `nameBox` component shown in Figure 13-11:

```
String[] names = { "Bill", "Geri", "Greg", "Jean",
                   "Kirk", "Phillip", "Susan" };
JComboBox nameBox = new JComboBox(names);
```

Because the `names` array holds the values displayed in the `namesBox` component, the following code could be used to determine the selected item:

```
int index;
String selectedName;
index = nameList.getSelectedIndex();
selectedName = names[index];
```

The `ComboBoxWindow` class shown in Code Listing 13-4 demonstrates a combo box. It uses a `JComboBox` component with an action listener. When an item is selected from the combo box, it is displayed in a read-only text field. The `main` method creates an instance of the class, which initially displays the window shown at the top left of Figure 13-12. When the user clicks the combo box button, the drop-down list appears as shown in the top right of the figure. After the user selects Espresso from the list, the window appears as shown at the bottom of the figure.

Figure 13-12 The window displayed by the `ComboBoxWindow` class

Code Listing 13-4 (`ComboBoxWindow.java`)

```
 1 import java.awt.*;
 2 import java.awt.event.*;
 3 import javax.swing.*;
 4
 5 /**
 6     This class demonstrates a combo box.
 7 */
 8
 9 public class ComboBoxWindow extends JFrame
10 {
```

```
11       private JPanel coffeePanel;         // To hold components
12       private JPanel selectedCoffeePanel; // To hold components
13       private JComboBox coffeeBox;         // A list of coffees
14       private JLabel label;               // Displays a message
15       private JTextField selectedCoffee;   // Selected coffee
16
17       // The following array holds the values that will
18       // be displayed in the coffeeBox combo box.
19       private String[] coffee = { "Regular Coffee",
20                                   "Dark Roast", "Cappuccino",
21                                   "Espresso", "Decaf"};
22
23       /**
24          Constructor
25       */
26
27       public ComboBoxWindow()
28       {
29          // Set the title.
30          setTitle("Combo Box Demo");
31
32          // Specify an action for the close button.
33          setDefaultCloseOperation(JFrame.EXIT_ON_CLOSE);
34
35          // Create a BorderLayout manager.
36          setLayout(new BorderLayout());
37
38          // Build the panels.
39          buildCoffeePanel();
40          buildSelectedCoffeePanel();
41
42          // Add the panels to the content pane.
43          add(coffeePanel, BorderLayout.CENTER);
44          add(selectedCoffeePanel, BorderLayout.SOUTH);
45
46          // Pack and display the window.
47          pack();
48          setVisible(true);
49       }
50
51       /**
52          The buildCoffeePanel method adds a combo box
53          with the types of coffee to a panel.
54       */
55
56       private void buildCoffeePanel()
57       {
58          // Create a panel to hold the combo box.
```

```
59          coffeePanel = new JPanel();
60
61          // Create the combo box.
62          coffeeBox = new JComboBox(coffee);
63
64          // Register an action listener.
65          coffeeBox.addActionListener(new ComboBoxListener());
66
67          // Add the combo box to the panel.
68          coffeePanel.add(coffeeBox);
69       }
70
71       /**
72          The buildSelectedCoffeePanel method adds a
73          read-only text field to a panel.
74       */
75
76       private void buildSelectedCoffeePanel()
77       {
78          // Create a panel to hold the components.
79          selectedCoffeePanel = new JPanel();
80
81          // Create the label.
82          label = new JLabel("You selected: ");
83
84          // Create the uneditable text field.
85          selectedCoffee = new JTextField(10);
86          selectedCoffee.setEditable(false);
87
88          // Add the label and text field to the panel.
89          selectedCoffeePanel.add(label);
90          selectedCoffeePanel.add(selectedCoffee);
91       }
92
93       /**
94          Private inner class that handles the event when
95          the user selects an item from the combo box.
96       */
97
98       private class ComboBoxListener
99                       implements ActionListener
100      {
101         public void actionPerformed(ActionEvent e)
102         {
103            // Get the selected coffee.
104            String selection =
105                   (String) coffeeBox.getSelectedItem();
106
```

```
107              // Display the selected coffee in the text field.
108              selectedCoffee.setText(selection);
109          }
110      }
111
112      /**
113          The main method creates an instance of the
114          ComboBoxWindow class, which causes it to display
115          its window.
116      */
117
118      public static void main(String[] args)
119      {
120          new ComboBoxWindow();
121      }
122  }
```

Editable Combo Boxes

There are two types of combo boxes: uneditable and editable. The default type of combo box is uneditable. An uneditable combo box combines a button with a list and allows the user to select items from its list only. This is the type of combo box used in the previous examples.

An editable combo box combines a text field and a list. In addition to selecting items from the list, the user may also type input into the text field. You make a combo box editable by calling the component's setEditable method, passing true as the argument. Here is an example:

```
String[] names = { "Bill", "Geri", "Greg", "Jean",
                   "Kirk", "Phillip", "Susan" };
JComboBox nameBox = new JComboBox(names);
nameBox.setEditable(true);
```

When displayed, the combo box created by this code initially appears as shown on the left of Figure 13-13. An editable combo box appears as a text field with a small button displaying an arrow joining it. The text field displays the item that is currently selected. When the user clicks the button, the drop-down list appears, as shown in the center of the figure. The user may select an item from the list. Alternatively, the user may type a value into the text field, as shown on the right of the figure. The user is not restricted to the values that appear in the list, and may type any input into the text field.

You can use the getSelectedItem method to retrieve a reference to the item that is currently selected. This method returns the item that appears in the combo box's text field, so it may or may not be an item that appears in the combo box's list.

The getSelectedIndex method returns the index of the selected item. However, if the user has entered a value in the text field that does not appear in the list, this method will return –1.

Figure 13-13   An editable combo box

The editable combo box initially
appears as a text field that
displays the selected item. A
small button with an arrow appears
next to the text field.

When the user clicks on the button,
the list of items drops down. The user
may select another item from the list.

Alternatively, the user may type input
into the text field. The user may type a
value that does not appear in the list.

Bill ▼

Bill ▼
Bill
Geri
Greg
Jean
Kirk
Phillip
Susan

Sharon ▼

Checkpoint

13.1   How do you make a text field read-only? In code, how do you store text in a text field?

13.2   What is the index of the first item stored in a JList or a JComboBox component? If one of these components holds 12 items, what is the index of the 12th item?

13.3   How do you retrieve the selected item from a JList component? How do you get the index of the selected item?

13.4   How do you cause a scroll bar to be displayed with a JList component?

13.5   How do you retrieve the selected item from a JComboBox component? How do you get the index of the selected item?

13.6   What is the difference between an uneditable and an editable combo box? Which of these is a combo box by default?

13.5 Displaying Images in Labels and Buttons

CONCEPT: Images may be displayed in labels and buttons. You use the **ImageIcon** class to get an image from a file.

In addition to displaying text in a label, you can also display an image. For example, Figure 13-14 shows a window with two labels. The top label displays a smiley face image and no text. The bottom label displays a smiley face image and text.

Figure 13-14   Labels displaying an image icon

To display an image, first you create an instance of the `ImageIcon` class, which can read the contents of an image file. The `ImageIcon` class is part of the `javax.swing` package. The constructor accepts a `String` argument that is the name of an image file. The supported file types are JPEG, GIF, and PNG. The name can also contain path information. Here is an example:

```
ImageIcon image = new ImageIcon("Smiley.gif");
```

This statement creates an `ImageIcon` object that reads the contents of the file *Smiley.gif*. Because no path was given, it is assumed that the file is in the current directory or folder. Here is an example that uses a path:

```
ImageIcon image = new ImageIcon("C:\\Chapter 12\\Images\\Smiley.gif");
```

Next, you can display the image in a label by passing the `ImageIcon` object as an argument to the `JLabel` constructor. Here is the general format of the constructor:

```
JLabel(Icon image)
```

The argument passed to the image parameter can be an `ImageIcon` object or any object that implements the `Icon` interface. Here is an example:

```
ImageIcon image = new ImageIcon("Smiley.gif");
JLabel label = new JLabel(image);
```

This creates a label with an image, but no text. You can also create a label with both an image and text. An easy way to do this is to create the label with text, as usual, and then use the `JLabel` class's `setIcon` method to add an image to the label. The `setIcon` method accepts an `ImageIcon` object as its argument. Here is an example:

```
JLabel label = new JLabel("Have a nice day!");
label.setIcon(image);
```

The text will be displayed to the right of the image. The `JLabel` class also has the following constructor:

```
JLabel(String text, Icon image, int horizontalAlignment)
```

The first argument is the text to be displayed, the second argument is the image to be displayed, and the third argument is an `int` that specifies the horizontal alignment of the label contents. You should use the constants `SwingConstants.LEFT`, `SwingConstants.CENTER`, or `SwingConstants.RIGHT` to specify the horizontal alignment. Here is an example:

```
ImageIcon image = new ImageIcon("Smiley.gif");
JLabel label = new JLabel("Have a nice day!",
                          image,
                          SwingConstants.RIGHT);
```

You can also display images in buttons, as shown in Figure 13-15.

Figure 13-15 Buttons displaying an image icon

The process of creating a button with an image is similar to that of creating a label with an image. You use an `ImageIcon` object to read the image file, then pass the `ImageIcon` object as an argument to the `JButton` constructor. To create a button with an image and no text, pass only the `ImageIcon` object to the constructor. Here is an example:

```
// Create a button with an image, but no text.
ImageIcon image = new ImageIcon("Smiley.gif");
JButton button = new JButton(image);
```

To create a button with an image and text, pass a `String` and an `ImageIcon` object to the constructor. Here is an example:

```
// Create a button with an image and text.
ImageIcon image = new ImageIcon("Smiley.gif");
JButton button = new JButton("Have a nice day!", image);
```

To add an image to an existing button, pass an `ImageIcon` object to the button's `setIcon` method. Here is an example:

```
// Create a button with an image and text.
JButton button = new JButton("Have a nice day!");
ImageIcon image = new ImageIcon("Smiley.gif");
button.setIcon(image);
```

You are not limited to small graphical icons when placing images in labels or buttons. For example, the `MyCatImage` class in Code Listing 13-5 displays a digital photograph in a label when the user clicks a button. The `main` method creates an instance of the class, which displays the window shown at the left in Figure 13-16. When the user clicks the Get Image button, the window displays the image shown at the right of the figure.

Code Listing 13-5 (`MyCatImage.java`)

```
 1 import java.awt.*;
 2 import java.awt.event.*;
 3 import javax.swing.*;
 4
 5 /**
 6    This class demonstrates how to use an ImageIcon
 7    and a JLabel to display an image.
 8 */
 9
```

```
10  public class MyCatImage extends JFrame
11  {
12      private JPanel imagePanel;     // To hold the label
13      private JPanel buttonPanel;    // To hold a button
14      private JLabel imageLabel;     // To show an image
15      private JButton button;        // To get an image
16
17
18      /**
19         Constructor
20      */
21
22      public MyCatImage()
23      {
24         // Set the title.
25         setTitle("My Cat");
26
27         // Specify an action for the close button.
28         setDefaultCloseOperation(JFrame.EXIT_ON_CLOSE);
29
30         // Create a BorderLayout manager.
31         setLayout(new BorderLayout());
32
33         // Build the panels.
34         buildImagePanel();
35         buildButtonPanel();
36
37         // Add the panels to the content pane.
38         add(imagePanel, BorderLayout.CENTER);
39         add(buttonPanel, BorderLayout.SOUTH);
40
41         // Pack and display the window.
42         pack();
43         setVisible(true);
44      }
45
46      /**
47         The buildImagePanel method adds a label to a panel.
48      */
49
50      private void buildImagePanel()
51      {
52         // Create a panel.
53         imagePanel = new JPanel();
54
55         // Create a label.
56         imageLabel = new JLabel("Click the button to " +
57                                 "see an image of my cat.");
```

```
58
59          // Add the label to the panel.
60          imagePanel.add(imageLabel);
61      }
62
63   /**
64      The buildButtonPanel method adds a button
65      to a panel.
66   */
67
68   private void buildButtonPanel()
69   {
70      ImageIcon smileyImage;
71
72      // Create a panel.
73      buttonPanel = new JPanel();
74
75      // Get the smiley face image.
76      smileyImage = new ImageIcon("Smiley.gif");
77
78      // Create a button.
79      button = new JButton("Get Image");
80      button.setIcon(smileyImage);
81
82      // Register an action listener with the button.
83      button.addActionListener(new ButtonListener());
84
85      // Add the button to the panel.
86      buttonPanel.add(button);
87   }
88
89   /**
90      Private inner class that handles the event when
91      the user clicks the button.
92   */
93
94   private class ButtonListener implements ActionListener
95   {
96      public void actionPerformed(ActionEvent e)
97      {
98         // Read the image file into an ImageIcon object.
99         ImageIcon catImage = new ImageIcon("Cat.jpg");
100
101         // Display the image in the label.
102         imageLabel.setIcon(catImage);
103
104         // Remove the text from the label.
105         imageLabel.setText(null);
```

```
106
107          // Pack the frame again to accommodate the
108          // new size of the label.
109          pack();
110       }
111    }
112
113    /**
114       The main method creates an instance of the
115       MyCatImage class, which causes it to display
116       its window.
117    */
118    public static void main(String[] args)
119    {
120       new MyCatImage();
121    }
122 }
```

Figure 13-16   Window displayed by the `MyCatImage` class

Let's take a closer look at the `MyCatImage` class. After some initial setup, the constructor calls the `buildImagePanel` method in line 34. Inside the `buildImagePanel` method, line 53 creates a `JPanel` component, referenced by the `imagePanel` variable, and then lines 56 and 57 create a `JLabel` component, referenced by the `imageLabel` variable. This is the label that will display the image when the user clicks the button. The last statement in the method, in line 60, adds the `imageLabel` component to the `imagePanel` panel.

Back in the constructor, line 35 calls the `buildButtonPanel` method, which creates the Get Image button and adds it to a panel. An instance of the `ButtonListener` inner class is also registered as the button's action listener. Let's look at the `ButtonListener` class's `actionPerformed` method. This method is executed when the user clicks the Get Image button. First, in line 99, an `ImageIcon` object is created from the file *Cat.jpg*. This file is in the same directory as the class. Next, in line 102, the image is stored in the `imageLabel` component. In line 105 the text that is currently displayed in the label is removed by passing `null` to the `imageLabel` component's `setText` method. The last statement, in line 109, calls the `JFrame` class's `pack` method. When the image was loaded into the `JLabel` component, the component resized itself to accommodate its new contents. The `JFrame` that encloses the window does not automatically resize itself, so we must call the `pack` method. This forces the `JFrame` to resize itself.

Checkpoint

13.7   How do you store an image in a JLabel component? How do you store both an image and text in a JLabel component?

13.8   How do you store an image in a JButton component? How do you store both an image and text in a JButton component?

13.9   What method do you use to store an image in an existing JLabel or JButton component?

13.6   Mnemonics and Tool Tips

CONCEPT: A mnemonic is a key that you press while holding down the Alt key to interact with a component. A tool tip is text that is displayed in a small box when the user holds the mouse cursor over a component.

Mnemonics

A mnemonic is a key on the keyboard that you press in combination with the Alt key to access a component such as a button quickly. These are sometimes referred to as shortcut keys, or hot keys. When you assign a mnemonic to a button, the user can click the button by holding down the Alt key and pressing the mnemonic key. Although users can interact with components with either the mouse or their mnemonic keys, those who are quick with the keyboard usually prefer to use mnemonic keys instead of the mouse.

You assign a mnemonic to a component through the component's `setMnemonic` method, which is inherited from the `AbstractButton` class. The method's general format is as follows:

```
void setMnemonic(int key)
```

The argument that you pass to the method is an integer code that represents the key you wish to assign as a mnemonic. The `KeyEvent` class, which is in the `java.awt.event` package, has predefined constants that you can use. These constants take the form `KeyEvent.VK_x`, where `x` is a key on the keyboard. For example, to assign the A key as a mnemonic, you would use `KeyEvent.VK_A`. (The letters VK in the constants stand for "virtual key".) Here is an example of code that creates a button with the text "Exit" and assigns the X key as the mnemonic:

```
JButton exitButton = new JButton("Exit");
exitButton.setMnemonic(KeyEvent.VK_X);
```

The user may click this button by pressing +X on the keyboard. (This means holding down the Alt key and pressing X.)

If the letter chosen as the mnemonic is in the component's text, the first occurrence of that letter will appear underlined when the component is displayed. For example, the button created with the previous code has the text "Exit". Because X was chosen as the mnemonic, the letter x will appear underlined, as shown in Figure 13-17.

Figure 13-17 Button with mnemonic X

If the mnemonic is a letter that does not appear in the component's text, then no letter will appear underlined.

NOTE: The `KeyEvent` class also has constants for symbols. For example, the constant for the ! symbol is `VK_EXCLAMATION_MARK`, and the constant for the & symbol is `VK_AMPERSAND`. See the Java API documentation for the `KeyEvent` class for a list of all the constants.

You can also assign mnemonics to radio buttons and check boxes, as shown in the following code:

```
// Create three radio buttons and assign mnemonics.
JRadioButton rb1 = new JRadioButton("Breakfast");
rb1.setMnemonic(KeyEvent.VK_B);
JRadioButton rb2 = new JRadioButton("Lunch");
rb2.setMnemonic(KeyEvent.VK_L);
JRadioButton rb3 = new JRadioButton("Dinner");
rb3.setMnemonic(KeyEvent.VK_D);

// Create three check boxes and assign mnemonics.
JCheckBox cb1 = new JCheckBox("Monday");
cb1.setMnemonic(KeyEvent.VK_M);
JCheckBox cb2 = new JCheckBox("Wednesday");
cb2.setMnemonic(KeyEvent.VK_W);
JCheckBox cb3 = new JCheckBox("Friday");
cb3.setMnemonic(KeyEvent.VK_F);
```

This code will create the components shown in Figure 13-18.

Figure 13-18   Radio buttons and check boxes with mnemonics assigned

Tool Tips

A tool tip is text that is displayed in a small box when the user holds the mouse cursor over a component. The box usually gives a short description of what the component does. Most GUI applications use tool tips as a way of providing immediate and concise help to the user. For example, Figure 13-19 shows a button with its tool tip displayed.

Figure 13-19   Button with tool tip displayed

You assign a tool tip to a component with the `setToolTipText` method, which is inherited from the `JComponent` class. Here is the method's general format:

```
void setToolTipText(String text)
```

The `String` that is passed as an argument is the text that will be displayed in the component's tool tip. For example, the following code creates the Exit button shown in Figure 13-19 and its associated tool tip:

```
JButton exitButton = new JButton("Exit");
exitButton.setToolTipText("Click here to exit.");
```

 Checkpoint

13.10 What is a mnemonic? How do you assign a mnemonic to a component?

13.11 What is a tool tip? How do you assign a tool tip to a component?

13.7 File Choosers and Color Choosers

CONCEPT: Java provides components that equip your applications with standard dialog boxes for opening files, saving files, and selecting colors.

File Choosers

A file chooser is a specialized dialog box that allows the user to browse for a file and select it. Figure 13-20 shows an example of a file chooser dialog box.

Figure 13-20   A file chooser dialog box for opening a file

You create an instance of the `JFileChooser` class, which is part of the `javax.swing` package, to display a file chooser dialog box. The class has several constructors. We will focus on two of them, which have the following general formats:

```
JFileChooser()
JFileChooser(String path)
```

The first constructor shown takes no arguments. This constructor uses the default directory as the starting point for all of its dialog boxes. If you are using Windows, this will probably be the "My Documents" folder under your account. If you are using UNIX, this will be your login directory. The second constructor takes a `String` argument containing a valid path. This path will be the starting point for the object's dialog boxes.

A `JFileChooser` object can display two types of predefined dialog boxes: An open file dialog box and a save file dialog box. Figure 13-20 shows an example of an open file dialog box. It lets the user browse for an existing file to open. A save file dialog box, as shown in Figure 13-21, is employed when the user needs to browse to a location to save a file. Both of these dialog boxes appear the same, except the open file dialog box displays "Open" in its title bar, and the save file dialog box displays "Save." Also, the open file dialog box has an Open button, and the save file dialog box has a Save button. There is no difference in the way they operate.

Displaying a File Chooser Dialog Box

To display an open file dialog box, use the `showOpenDialog` method. The method's general format is as follows:

```
int showOpenDialog(Component parent)
```

Figure 13-21   A save file dialog box

The argument can be either null or a reference to a component. If you pass null, the dialog box is normally centered in the screen. If you pass a reference to a component, such as JFrame, the dialog box is displayed over the component.

To display a save file dialog box, use the showSaveDialog method. The method's general format is as follows:

```
int showSaveDialog(Component parent)
```

Once again, the argument can be either null or a reference to a component. Both the showOpenDialog and showSaveDialog methods return an integer that indicates the action taken by the user to close the dialog box. You can compare the return value to one of the following constants:

- **JFileChooser.CANCEL_OPTION.** This return value indicates that the user clicked the Cancel button.
- **JFileChooser.APPROVE_OPTION.** This return value indicates that the user clicked the Open or Save button.
- **JFileChooser.ERROR_OPTION.** This return value indicates that an error occurred, or the user clicked the standard close button on the window to dismiss it.

If the user selected a file, you can use the getSelectedFile method to determine the file that was selected. The getSelectedFile method returns a File object, which contains data about the selected file. The File class is part of the java.io package. You can use the File object's getPath method to get the path and file name as a String. Here is an example:

```
JFileChooser fileChooser = new JFileChooser();
int status = fileChooser.showOpenDialog(null);
if (status == JFileChooser.APPROVE_OPTION)
{
    File selectedFile = fileChooser.getSelectedFile();
    String filename = selectedFile.getPath();
    JOptionPane.showMessageDialog(null, "You selected " + filename);
}
```

Color Choosers

A color chooser is a specialized dialog box that allows the user to select a color from a predefined palette of colors. Figure 13-22 shows an example of a color chooser. By clicking the HSB tab you can select a color by specifying its hue, saturation, and brightness. By clicking the RGB tab you can select a color by specifying its red, green, and blue components.

Figure 13-22   A color chooser dialog box

You use the `JColorChooser` class, which is part of the `javax.swing` package, to display a color chooser dialog box. You do not create an instance of the class, however. It has a static method named `showDialog`, with the following general format:

```
Color showDialog(Component parent, String title, Color initial)
```

The first argument can be either `null` or a reference to a component. If you pass `null`, the dialog box is normally centered in the screen. If you pass a reference to a component, such as `JFrame`, the dialog box is displayed over the component. The second argument is text that is displayed in the dialog box's title bar. The third argument indicates the color that appears initially selected in the dialog box. This method returns the color selected by the user. The following code is an example. This code allows the user to select a color, and then that color is assigned as a panel's background color.

```
JPanel panel = new JPanel();
Color selectedColor;
selectedColor = JColorChooser.showDialog(null,
                "Select a Background Color", Color.BLUE);
panel.setBackground(selectedColor);
```

13.8 Menus

CONCEPT: Java provides classes for creating systems of drop-down menus. Menus can contain menu items, checked menu items, radio button menu items, and other menus.

In the GUI applications you have studied so far, the user initiates actions by clicking components such as buttons. When an application has several operations for the user to choose from, a menu system is more commonly used than buttons. A menu system is a collection of commands organized in one or more drop-down menus. Before learning how to construct a menu system, you must learn about the basic items that are found in a typical menu system. Look at the example menu system in Figure 13-23.

Figure 13-23 Example menu system

The menu system in the figure consists of the following items:

- **Menu Bar.** At the top of the window, just below the title bar, is a menu bar. The menu bar lists the names of one or more menus. The menu bar in Figure 13-23 shows the names of two menus: File and Edit.
- **Menu.** A menu is a drop-down list of menu items. The user may activate a menu by clicking on its name on the menu bar. In the figure, the Edit menu has been activated.
- **Menu Item.** A menu item can be selected by the user. When a menu items is selected, some type of action is usually performed.
- **Check box menu item.** A check box menu item appears with a small box beside it. The item may be selected or deselected. When it is selected, a check mark appears in the box. When it is deselected, the box appears empty. Check box menu items are normally used to turn an option on or off. The user toggles the state of a check box menu item each time he or she selects it.
- **Radio button menu item.** A radio button menu item may be selected or deselected. A small circle appears beside it that is filled in when the item is selected and empty when the item is deselected. Like a check box menu item, a radio button menu item can be used to turn an option on or off. When a set of radio button menu items are grouped

with a `ButtonGroup` object, only one of them can be selected at a time. When the user selects a radio button menu item, the one that was previously selected is deselected.

- **Submenu.** A menu within a menu is called a submenu. Some of the commands on a menu are actually the names of submenus. You can tell when a command is the name of a submenu because a small right arrow appears to its right. Activating the name of a submenu causes the submenu to appear. For example, in Figure 13-23, clicking on the Sort command causes a submenu to appear.

- **Separator bar.** A separator bar is a horizontal bar that is used to separate groups of items on a menu. Separator bars are only used as a visual aid and cannot be selected by the user.

A menu system is constructed with the following classes:

- **JMenuItem.** Use this class to create a regular menu item. A `JMenuItem` component generates an action event when the user selects it.

- **JCheckBoxMenuItem.** Use this class to create a check box menu item. The class's `isSelected` method returns `true` if the item is selected, or `false` otherwise. A `JCheckBoxMenuItem` component generates an action event when the user selects it.

- **JRadioButtonMenuItem.** Use this class to create a radio button menu item. `JRadioButtonMenuItem` components can be grouped in a `ButtonGroup` object so that only one of them can be selected at a time. The class's `isSelected` method returns `true` if the item is selected, or `false` otherwise. A `JRadioButtonMenuItem` component generates an action event when the user selects it.

- **JMenu.** Use this class to create a menu. A `JMenu` component can contain `JMenuItem`, `JCheckBoxMenuItem`, and `JRadioButton` components, as well as other `JMenu` components. A submenu is a `JMenu` component that is inside another `JMenu` component.

- **JMenuBar.** Use this class to create a menu bar. A `JMenuBar` object can contain `JMenu` components.

All of these classes are in the `javax.swing` package. A menu system is a `JMenuBar` component that contains one or more `JMenu` components. Each `JMenu` component can contain `JMenuItem`, `JRadioButtonMenuItem`, and `JCheckBoxMenuItem` components, as well as other `JMenu` components. The classes contain all of the code necessary to operate the menu system.

To see an example of an application that uses a menu system, we look at the `MenuWindow` class shown in Code Listing 13-6. The class displays the window shown in Figure 13-24.

Figure 13-24 Window displayed by the `MenuWindow` class

The class demonstrates how a label appears in different colors. Notice that the window has a menu bar with two menus: File and Text. Figure 13-25 shows a sketch of the menu system. When the user opens the Text menu, he or she can select a color using the radio button menu items and the label will change to the selected color. The Text menu also contains a Visible item, which is a check box menu item. When this item is selected (checked), the label is visible. When this item is deselected (unchecked), the label is invisible.

Figure 13-25   Sketch of the `MenuWindow` class's menu system

Code Listing 13-6   (`MenuWindow.java`)

```java
 1 import javax.swing.*;
 2 import java.awt.*;
 3 import java.awt.event.*;
 4
 5 /**
 6    The MenuWindow class demonstrates a menu system.
 7 */
 8
 9 public class MenuWindow extends JFrame
10 {
11    private JLabel messageLabel;               // Displays a message
12    private final int LABEL_WIDTH = 400;       // Label's width
13    private final int LABEL_HEIGHT = 200;      // Label's height
14
15    // The following will reference menu components.
16    private JMenuBar menuBar;                   // The menu bar
17    private JMenu fileMenu;                     // The File menu
18    private JMenu textMenu;                     // The Text menu
19    private JMenuItem exitItem;                 // To exit
20    private JRadioButtonMenuItem blackItem;     // Makes text black
21    private JRadioButtonMenuItem redItem;       // Makes text red
22    private JRadioButtonMenuItem blueItem;      // Makes text blue
23    private JCheckBoxMenuItem visibleItem;      // Toggle visibility
24
25    /**
26       Constructor
27    */
28
```

```
29      public MenuWindow()
30      {
31         // Set the title.
32         setTitle("Example Menu System");
33
34         // Specify an action for the close button.
35         setDefaultCloseOperation(JFrame.EXIT_ON_CLOSE);
36
37         // Create the messageLabel label.
38         messageLabel = new JLabel("Use the Text menu to " +
39                 "change my color and make me invisible.",
40                 SwingConstants.CENTER);
41
42         // Set the label's preferred size.
43         messageLabel.setPreferredSize(
44                 new Dimension(LABEL_WIDTH, LABEL_HEIGHT));
45
46         // Set the label's foreground color.
47         messageLabel.setForeground(Color.BLACK);
48
49         // Add the label to the content pane.
50         add(messageLabel);
51
52         // Build the menu bar.
53         buildMenuBar();
54
55         // Pack and display the window.
56         pack();
57         setVisible(true);
58      }
59
60      /**
61         The buildMenuBar method builds the menu bar.
62      */
63
64      private void buildMenuBar()
65      {
66         // Create the menu bar.
67         menuBar = new JMenuBar();
68
69         // Create the file and text menus.
70         buildFileMenu();
71         buildTextMenu();
72
73         // Add the file and text menus to the menu bar.
74         menuBar.add(fileMenu);
75         menuBar.add(textMenu);
76
```

```
 77          // Set the window's menu bar.
 78          setJMenuBar(menuBar);
 79       }
 80
 81       /**
 82          The buildFileMenu method builds the File menu
 83          and returns a reference to its JMenu object.
 84       */
 85
 86       private void buildFileMenu()
 87       {
 88          // Create an Exit menu item.
 89          exitItem = new JMenuItem("Exit");
 90          exitItem.setMnemonic(KeyEvent.VK_X);
 91          exitItem.addActionListener(new ExitListener());
 92
 93          // Create a JMenu object for the File menu.
 94          fileMenu = new JMenu("File");
 95          fileMenu.setMnemonic(KeyEvent.VK_F);
 96
 97          // Add the Exit menu item to the File menu.
 98          fileMenu.add(exitItem);
 99       }
100
101       /**
102          The buildTextMenu method builds the Text menu
103          and returns a reference to its JMenu object.
104       */
105
106       private void buildTextMenu()
107       {
108          // Create the radio button menu items to change
109          // the color of the text. Add an action listener
110          // to each one.
111          blackItem = new JRadioButtonMenuItem("Black", true);
112          blackItem.setMnemonic(KeyEvent.VK_B);
113          blackItem.addActionListener(new ColorListener());
114
115          redItem = new JRadioButtonMenuItem("Red");
116          redItem.setMnemonic(KeyEvent.VK_R);
117          redItem.addActionListener(new ColorListener());
118
119          blueItem = new JRadioButtonMenuItem("Blue");
120          blueItem.setMnemonic(KeyEvent.VK_U);
121          blueItem.addActionListener(new ColorListener());
122
123          // Create a button group for the radio button items.
124          ButtonGroup group = new ButtonGroup();
```

```
125          group.add(blackItem);
126          group.add(redItem);
127          group.add(blueItem);
128
129          // Create a check box menu item to make the text
130          // visible or invisible.
131          visibleItem = new JCheckBoxMenuItem("Visible", true);
132          visibleItem.setMnemonic(KeyEvent.VK_V);
133          visibleItem.addActionListener(new VisibleListener());
134
135          // Create a JMenu object for the Text menu.
136          textMenu = new JMenu("Text");
137          textMenu.setMnemonic(KeyEvent.VK_T);
138
139          // Add the menu items to the Text menu.
140          textMenu.add(blackItem);
141          textMenu.add(redItem);
142          textMenu.add(blueItem);
143          textMenu.addSeparator();    // Add a separator bar.
144          textMenu.add(visibleItem);
145       }
146
147       /**
148          Private inner class that handles the event that
149          is generated when the user selects Exit from
150          the File menu.
151       */
152
153        private class ExitListener implements ActionListener
154        {
155           public void actionPerformed(ActionEvent e)
156           {
157              System.exit(0);
158           }
159        }
160
161       /**
162          Private inner class that handles the event that
163          is generated when the user selects a color from
164          the Text menu.
165       */
166
167        private class ColorListener implements ActionListener
168        {
169           public void actionPerformed(ActionEvent e)
170           {
171              if (blackItem.isSelected())
172                 messageLabel.setForeground(Color.BLACK);
```

```
173                else if (redItem.isSelected())
174                    messageLabel.setForeground(Color.RED);
175                else if (blueItem.isSelected())
176                    messageLabel.setForeground(Color.BLUE);
177            }
178        }
179
180    /**
181        Private inner class that handles the event that
182        is generated when the user selects Visible from
183        the Text menu.
184    */
185
186    private class VisibleListener implements ActionListener
187    {
188        public void actionPerformed(ActionEvent e)
189        {
190            if (visibleItem.isSelected())
191                messageLabel.setVisible(true);
192            else
193                messageLabel.setVisible(false);
194        }
195    }
196
197    /**
198        The main method creates an instance of the
199        MenuWindow class, which causes it to display
200        its window.
201    */
202
203    public static void main(String[] args)
204    {
205        MenuWindow mw = new MenuWindow();
206    }
207 }
```

Let's take a closer look at the MenuWindow class. Before we examine how the menu system is constructed, we should explain the code in lines 38 through 44. Lines 38 through 40 create the messageLabel component and align its text in the label's center. Then, in lines 43 and 44, the setPreferredSize method is called. The setPreferredSize method is inherited from the JComponent class, and it establishes a component's preferred size. It is called the *preferred size* because the layout manager adjusts the component's size when necessary. Normally, a label's preferred size is determined automatically, depending on its contents. We want to make this label larger, however, so the window will be larger when it is packed around the label.

The setPreferredSize method accepts a Dimension object as its argument. A Dimension object specifies a component's width and height. The first argument to the Dimension class constructor is the component's width, and the second argument is the component's height. In this class, the LABEL_WIDTH and LABEL_HEIGHT constants are defined with the values 400 and 200 respectively. So, this statement sets the label's preferred size to 400 pixels wide by 200 pixels high. (The Dimension class is part of the java.awt package.) Notice from Figure 13-24 that this code does not affect the size of the text that is displayed in the label, only the size of the label component.

To create the menu system, the constructor calls the buildMenuBar method in line 53. Inside this method, the statement in line 67 creates a JMenuBar component and assigns its address to the menuBar variable. The JMenuBar component acts as a container for JMenu components. The menu bar in this application has two menus: File and Text.

Next, the statement in line 70 calls the buildFileMenu method. The buildFileMenu method creates the File menu, which has only one item: Exit. The statement in line 89 creates a JMenuItem component for the Exit item, which is referenced by the exitItem variable. The String that is passed to the JMenuItem constructor is the text that will appear on a menu for this menu item. The statement in line 90 assigns the x key as a mnemonic to the exitItem component. Then, line 91 creates an action listener for the component (an instance of ExitListener, a private inner class), which causes the application to end.

Next, line 94 creates a JMenu object for the File menu. Notice that the name of the menu is passed as an argument to the JMenu constructor. Line 95 assigns the F key to the File menu as a mnemonic. The last statement in the buildFileMenu method, in line 98, adds exitItem to the fileMenu component.

Back in the buildMenuBar method, the statement in line 71 calls the buildTextMenu method. The buildTextMenu method builds the Text menu, which has three radio button menu items (Black, Red, and Blue), a separator bar, and a check box menu item (Visible). The code in lines 111 through 121 creates the radio button menu items, assigns mnemonic keys to them, and adds an action listener to each.

The JRadioButtonItem constructor accepts a String argument, which is the menu item's text. By default, a radio button menu item is not initially selected. The constructor can also accept an optional second argument, which is a boolean value indicating whether the item should be initially selected. Notice that in line 111, true is passed as the second argument to the JRadioButtonItem constructor. This causes the Black menu item to be initially selected.

Next, in lines 124 through 127, a button group is created and the radio button menu items are added to it. As with JRadioButton components, JRadioButtonMenuItem components may be grouped in a ButtonGroup object. As a result, only one of the grouped menu items may be selected at a time. When one is selected, any other menu item in the group is deselected.

Next, the Visible item, a check box menu item, is created in line 131. Notice that true is passed as the second argument to the constructor. This causes the item to be initially selected. A mnemonic key is assigned in line 132, and an action listener is added to the component in line 133.

Line 136 creates a JMenu component for the Text menu, and line 137 assigns a mnemonic key to it. Lines 140 through 142 add the blackItem, redItem, and blueItem radio button menu items to the Text menu. In line 143, the addSeparator method is called to add a separator bar to the menu. Because the `addSeparator` method is called just after the `blueItem` component is added and just before the `visibleItem` component is added, it will appear between the Blue and Visible items on the menu. Line 144 adds the Visible item to the Text menu.

Back in the `buildMenuBar` method, in lines 74 and 75, the File menu and Text menu are added to the menu bar. In line 78, the `setJMenuBar` method is called, passing `menuBar` as an argument. The `setJMenuBar` method is a `JFrame` method that places a menu bar in a frame. You pass a `JMenuBar` component as the argument. When the `JFrame` is displayed, the menu bar will appear at its top.

Figure 13-26 shows how the class's window appears with the File menu and the Text menu opened. Selecting a color from the Text menu causes an instance of the `ColorListener` class to execute its `actionPerformed` method, which changes the color of the text. Selecting the Visible item causes an instance of the `VisibleListener` class to execute its `actionPerformed` method, which toggles the label's visibility.

Figure 13-26   The window with the File menu and Text menu opened

The window with the File menu opened.

The window with the Text menu opened.

Checkpoint

13.12 Briefly describe each of the following menu system items:

a) Menu bar
b) Menu item
c) Check box menu item
d) Radio button menu item
e) Submenu
f) Separator bar

13.13 What class do you use to create a regular menu item? What do you pass to the class constructor?

13.14 What class do you use to create a radio button menu item? What do you pass to the class constructor? How do you cause it to be initially selected?

13.15 How do you create a relationship between radio button menu items so that only one may be selected at a time?

13.16 What class do you use to create a check box menu item? What do you pass to the class constructor? How do you cause it to be initially selected?

13.17 What class do you use to create a menu? What do you pass to the class constructor?

13.18 What class do you use to create a menu bar?

13.19 How do you place a menu bar in a JFrame?

13.20 What type of event do menu items generate when selected by the user?

13.21 How do you change the size of a component such as a JLabel after it has been created?

13.22 What arguments do you pass to the Dimension class constructor?

13.9 More about Text Components: Text Areas and Fonts

CONCEPT: A text area is a multi-line text field that can accept several lines of text input. Components that inherit from the **JComponent** class have a **setFont** method that allows you to change the font and style of the component's text.

Text Areas

In Chapter 7 you were introduced to the JTextField class, which is used to create text fields. A text field is a component that allows the user to enter a single line of text. A text area is like a text field that can accept multiple lines of input. You use the JTextArea class to create a text area. Here is the general format of two of the class's constructors:

```
JTextArea(int rows, int columns)
JTextArea(String text, int rows, int columns)
```

In both constructors, rows is the number of rows or lines of text that the text area is to display, and columns is the number of columns or characters that are to be displayed per line. In the second constructor, text is a string that the text area will initially display. For example, the following statement creates a text area with 20 rows and 40 columns:

```
JTextArea textInput = new JTextArea(20, 40);
```

The following statement creates a text area with 20 rows and 40 columns that will initially display the text stored in the String object info:

```
JTextArea textInput = new JTextArea(info, 20, 40);
```

As with the JTextField class, the JTextArea class provides the getText and setText methods for getting and setting the text contained in the component. For example, the following statement gets the text stored in the textInput text area and stores it in the String object userText:

```
String userText = textInput.getText();
```

The following statement stores the text that is in the String object info in the textInput text area:

```
textInput.setText(info);
```

JTextArea components do not automatically display scroll bars. To display scroll bars on a JTextArea component, you must add it to the scroll pane. As you already know, you create a scroll pane with the JScrollPane class. Here is an example of code that creates a text area and adds it to a scroll pane:

```
JTextArea textInput = new JTextArea(20, 40);
JScrollPane scrollPane = new JScrollPane(textInput);
```

The JScrollPane object displays both vertical and horizontal scroll bars on a text area. By default, the scroll bars are not displayed until they are needed; however, you can alter this behavior with two of the JScrollPane class's methods. The setHorizontalScrollBarPolicy method takes an int argument that specifies when a horizontal scroll bar should appear in the scroll pane. You can pass one of the following constants as an argument:

- **JScrollPane.HORIZONTAL_SCROLLBAR_AS_NEEDED.** This is the default setting. A horizontal scroll bar is displayed only when there is not enough horizontal space to display the text contained in the text area.
- **JScrollPane.HORIZONTAL_SCROLLBAR_NEVER.** This setting prevents a horizontal scroll bar from being displayed in the text area.
- **JScrollPane.HORIZONTAL_SCROLLBAR_ALWAYS.** With this setting, a horizontal scroll bar is always displayed, even when it is not needed.

The setVerticalScrollBarPolicy method also takes an int argument, which specifies when a vertical scroll bar should appear in the scroll pane. You can pass one of the following constants as an argument:

- **JScrollPane.VERTICAL_SCROLLBAR_AS_NEEDED.** This is the default setting. A vertical scroll bar is displayed only when there is not enough vertical space to display the text contained in the text area.

- **JScrollPane.VERTICAL_SCROLLBAR_NEVER.** This setting prevents a vertical scroll bar from being displayed in the text area.
- **JScrollPane.VERTICAL_SCROLLBAR_ALWAYS.** With this setting, a vertical scroll bar is always displayed, even when it is not needed.

For example, the following code specifies that a vertical scroll bar should always appear on a scroll pane's component, but a horizontal scroll bar should not appear:

```
scrollPane.setHorizontalScrollBarPolicy(
            JScrollPane.HORIZONTAL_SCROLLBAR_NEVER);
scrollPane.setVerticalScrollBarPolicy(
            JScrollPane.VERTICAL_SCROLLBAR_ALWAYS);
```

Figure 13-27 shows a text area without scroll bars, a text area with a vertical scroll bar, and a text area with both a horizontal and a vertical scroll bar.

Figure 13-27   Text areas with and without scroll bars

By default, JTextArea components do not perform line wrapping. This means that when text is entered into the component and the end of a line is reached, the text does not wrap around to the next line. If you want line wrapping, you use the JTextArea class's setLineWrap method to turn it on. The method accepts a boolean argument. If you pass true, line wrapping is turned on. If you pass false, line wrapping is turned off. Here is an example of a statement that turns a text area's line wrapping on:

```
textInput.setLineWrap(true);
```

There are two different styles of line wrapping: word wrapping and character wrapping. When word wrapping is performed, the line breaks always occur between words, never in the middle of a word. When character wrapping is performed, lines are broken between characters. This means that lines can be broken in the middle of a word. You specify the style of line wrapping that you prefer with the JTextArea class's setWrapStyleWord method. This method accepts a boolean argument. If you pass true, the text area will perform word wrapping. If you pass false, the text area will perform character wrapping. The default style is character wrapping.

Fonts

The appearance of a component's text is determined by the text's font, style, and size. The font is the name of the typeface—the style can be plain, bold, and/or italic—and the size is the size of the text in points. To change the appearance of a component's text you use the component's setFont method, which is inherited from the JComponent class. The general format of the method is as follows:

```
void setFont(Font appearance)
```

You pass a Font object as an argument to this method. The Font class constructor has the following general format:

```
Font(String fontName, int style, int size);
```

The first argument is the name of a font. Although the fonts that are available vary from system to system, Java guarantees that you will have Dialog, DialogInput, Monospaced, SansSerif, and Serif. Figure 13-28 shows an example of each of these.

Figure 13-28 Examples of fonts

The second argument to the Font constructor is an int that represents the style of the text. The Font class provides the following constants that you can use: Font.PLAIN, Font.BOLD, and Font.ITALIC. The third argument is the size of the text in points. (There are 72 points per inch, so a 72-point font has a height of one inch. Ten- and twelve-point fonts are normally used for most applications.) Here is an example of a statement that changes the text of a label to a 24-point bold serif font:

```
label.setFont(new Font("Serif", Font.BOLD, 24));
```

You can combine styles by mathematically adding them. For example, the following statement changes a label's text to a 24-point bold and italic serif font:

```
label.setFont(new Font("Serif", Font.BOLD + Font.ITALIC, 24));
```

Figure 13-29 shows an example of the serif font in plain, bold, italic, and bold plus italic styles. The following code was used to create the labels:

```
JLabel label1 = new JLabel("Serif Plain", SwingConstants.CENTER);
label1.setFont(new Font("Serif", Font.PLAIN, 24));

JLabel label2 = new JLabel("Serif Bold", SwingConstants.CENTER);
label2.setFont(new Font("Serif", Font.BOLD, 24));
```

```
JLabel label3 = new JLabel("Serif Italic", SwingConstants.CENTER);
label3.setFont(new Font("Serif", Font.ITALIC, 24));

JLabel label4 = new JLabel("Serif Bold + Italic",
                              SwingConstants.CENTER);
label4.setFont(new Font("Serif", Font.BOLD + Font.ITALIC, 24));
```

Figure 13-29 Examples of serif plain, bold, italic, and bold plus italic

✔ Checkpoint

13.23 What arguments do you pass to the `JTextArea` constructor?

13.24 How do you retrieve the text that is stored in a `JTextArea` component?

13.25 Does the `JTextArea` component automatically display scroll bars? If not, how do you accomplish this?

13.26 What is line wrapping? What are the two styles of line wrapping? How do you turn a `JTextArea` component's line wrapping on? How do you select a line wrapping style?

13.27 What type of argument does a component's `setFont` method accept?

13.28 What are the arguments that you pass to the `Font` class constructor?

 See the Simple Text Editor Application case study on the Student CD for an in-depth example that uses menus and other topics from this chapter.

13.10 Sliders

CONCEPT: A slider is a component that allows the user to adjust a number graphically within a range of values.

Sliders, which are created from the `JSlider` class, display an image of a "slider knob" that can be dragged along a track. Sliders can be horizontally or vertically oriented, as shown in Figure 13-30.

A slider is designed to represent a range of numeric values. At one end of the slider is the range's minimum value and at the other end is the range's maximum value. Both of the sliders shown in Figure 13-30 represent a range of 0 through 50. Sliders hold a numeric value in a field, and as the user moves the knob along the track, the numeric value is adjusted accordingly. Notice that the sliders in Figure 13-30 have accompanying tick marks. At every tenth value, a major tick mark is displayed along with a label indicating the value at that tick mark. Between the major tick marks are minor tick marks, which in this example are displayed at every second value. The appearance of tick marks, their spacing, and the appearance of labels can be controlled through methods in the `JSlider` class. The `JSlider` constructor has the following general format:

```
JSlider(int orientation, int minValue,
        int maxValue, int initialValue)
```

Figure 13-30 A horizontal and a vertical slider

The first argument is an `int` specifying the slider's orientation. You should use one of the constants `JSlider.HORIZONTAL` or `JSlider.VERTICAL`. The second argument is the minimum value of the slider's range and the third argument is the maximum value of the slider's range. The fourth argument is the initial value of the slider, which determines the initial position of the slider's knob. For example, the following code could be used to create the sliders shown in Figure 13-30:

```
JSlider slider1 = new JSlider(JSlider.HORIZONTAL, 0, 50, 25);
JSlider slider2 = new JSlider(JSlider.VERTICAL, 0, 50, 25);
```

You set the major and minor tick mark spacing with the methods `setMajorTickSpacing` and `setMinorTickSpacing`. Each of these methods accepts an `int` argument that specifies the intervals of the tick marks. For example, the following code sets the `slider1` object's major tick mark spacing at 10, and its minor tick mark spacing at 2:

```
slider1.setMajorTickSpacing(10);
slider1.setMinorTickSpacing(2);
```

If the `slider1` component's range is 0 through 50, then these statements would cause major tick marks to be displayed at values 0, 10, 20, 30, 40, and 50. Minor tick marks would be displayed at values 2, 4, 6, and 8, then at values 12, 14, 16, and 18, and so forth.

By default, tick marks are not displayed, and setting their spacing does not cause them to be displayed. You display tick marks by calling the `setPaintTicks` method, which accepts a `boolean` argument. If you pass `true`, then tick marks are displayed. If you pass `false`, they are not displayed. Here is an example:

```
slider1.setPaintTicks(true);
```

By default, labels are not displayed either. You display numeric labels on the slider component by calling the `setPaintLabels` method, which accepts a `boolean` argument. If you pass `true`, then numeric labels are displayed at the major tick marks. If you pass `false`, labels are not displayed. Here is an example:

```
slider1.setPaintLabels(true);
```

When the knob's position is moved, the slider component generates a change event. To handle the change event, you must write a change listener class. When you write a change listener class, it must meet the following requirements:

- It must implement the `ChangeListener` interface. This interface is in the `javax.swing.event` package.
- It must have a method named `stateChanged`. This method must take an argument of the `ChangeEvent` type.

To retrieve the current value stored in a `JSlider`, use the `getValue` method. This method returns the slider's value as an `int`. Here is an example:

```
currentValue = slider1.getValue();
```

The `TempConverter` class shown in Code Listing 13-7 demonstrates the `JSlider` component. This class displays the window shown in Figure 13-31. Two temperatures are initially shown: 32.0 degrees Fahrenheit and 0.0 degrees Celsius. A slider, which has the range of 0 through 100, allows you to adjust the Celsius temperature and immediately see the Fahrenheit conversion. The `main` method creates an instance of the class and displays the window.

Figure 13-31 Window displayed by the `TempConverterWindow` class

Code Listing 13-7 (TempConverter.java)

```java
1  import javax.swing.*;
2  import javax.swing.event.*;
3  import java.awt.*;
4  import java.text.DecimalFormat;
5
6  /**
7     This class displays a window with a slider component.
8     The user can convert the Celsius temperatures from
9     0 through 100 to Fahrenheit by moving the slider.
10 */
11
12 public class TempConverter extends JFrame
13 {
14    private JLabel label1, label2;      // Message labels
15    private JTextField fahrenheitTemp;  // Fahrenheit temp
16    private JTextField celsiusTemp;     // Celsius temp
17    private JPanel fpanel;              // Fahrenheit panel
18    private JPanel cpanel;              // Celsius panel
19    private JPanel sliderPanel;         // Slider panel
20    private JSlider slider;             // Temperature adjuster
21
22    /**
23       Constructor
24    */
25
26    public TempConverter()
27    {
28       // Set the title.
29       setTitle("Temperatures");
30
31       // Specify an action for the close button.
32       setDefaultCloseOperation(JFrame.EXIT_ON_CLOSE);
33
34       // Create the message labels.
35       label1 = new JLabel("Fahrenheit: ");
36       label2 = new JLabel("Celsius: ");
37
38       // Create the read-only text fields.
39       fahrenheitTemp = new JTextField("32.0", 10);
40       fahrenheitTemp.setEditable(false);
41       celsiusTemp = new JTextField("0.0", 10);
42       celsiusTemp.setEditable(false);
43
44       // Create the slider.
45       slider = new JSlider(JSlider.HORIZONTAL, 0, 100, 0);
```

```
46        slider.setMajorTickSpacing(20);    // Major tick every 20
47        slider.setMinorTickSpacing(5);     // Minor tick every 5
48        slider.setPaintTicks(true);        // Display tick marks
49        slider.setPaintLabels(true);       // Display numbers
50        slider.addChangeListener(new SliderListener());
51
52        // Create panels and place the components in them.
53        fpanel = new JPanel();
54        fpanel.add(label1);
55        fpanel.add(fahrenheitTemp);
56        cpanel = new JPanel();
57        cpanel.add(label2);
58        cpanel.add(celsiusTemp);
59        sliderPanel = new JPanel();
60        sliderPanel.add(slider);
61
62        // Create a GridLayout manager.
63        setLayout(new GridLayout(3, 1));
64
65        // Add the panels to the content pane.
66        add(fpanel);
67        add(cpanel);
68        add(sliderPanel);
69
70        // Pack and display the frame.
71        pack();
72        setVisible(true);
73    }
74
75    /**
76        Private inner class to handle the change events
77        that are generated when the slider is moved.
78    */
79
80    private class SliderListener implements ChangeListener
81    {
82        public void stateChanged(ChangeEvent e)
83        {
84            double fahrenheit, celsius;
85            DecimalFormat fmt = new DecimalFormat("0.0");
86
87            // Get the slider value.
88            celsius = slider.getValue();
89
90            // Convert the value to Fahernheit.
91            fahrenheit = (9.0 / 5.0) * celsius + 32.0;
92
93            // Store the Celsius temp in its display field.
```

```
 94              celsiusTemp.setText(
 95                      Double.toString(celsius));
 96
 97              // Store the Fahrenheit temp in its display field.
 98              fahrenheitTemp.setText(fmt.format(fahrenheit));
 99          }
100      }
101
102      /*
103          The main method creates an instance of the
104          class, which displays a window with a slider.
105      */
106
107      public static void main(String[] args)
108      {
109          new TempConverter();
110      }
111 }
```

 Checkpoint

13.29 What type of event does a `JSlider` generate when its slider knob is moved?

13.30 What `JSlider` methods do you use to perform each of these operations?

    a) Establish the spacing of major tick marks.
    b) Establish the spacing of minor tick marks.
    c) Cause tick marks to be displayed.
    d) Cause labels to be displayed.

13.11 Look and Feel

CONCEPT: A GUI application's appearance is determined by its look and feel. Java allows you to select an application's look and feel.

Most operating systems' GUIs have their own unique appearance and style conventions. For example, if a Windows user switches to a Macintosh, UNIX, or Linux system, the first thing he or she is likely to notice is the difference in the way the GUIs on each system appear. The appearance of a particular system's GUI is known as its look and feel.

Java allows you to select the look and feel of a GUI application. The default look and feel for Java is called *Ocean*. This is the look and feel that you have seen in all of the GUI applications that we have written in this book. Some of the other look and feel choices are Metal, Motif, and Windows. Metal was the default look and feel for previous versions of Java. Motif is similar to a UNIX look and feel. Windows is the look and feel of the Windows operating system. Figure 13-32 shows how the `TempConverterWindow` class window, presented earlier in this chapter, appears in each of these looks and feels.

NOTE: Ocean is actually a special theme of the Metal look and feel.

 NOTE: Currently the Windows look and feel is available only on computers running the Microsoft Windows operating system.

Figure 13-32 Metal, Motif, and Windows looks and feels

To change an application's look and feel, you call the `UIManager` class's static `setLookAndFeel` method. Java has a class for each look and feel, and this method takes the fully qualified class name for the desired look and feel as its argument. The class name must be passed as a string. Table 13-1 lists the fully qualified class names for the Metal, Motif, and Windows looks and feels.

Table 13-1 Look and feel class names

Class Name	Look and Feel
`"javax.swing.plaf.metal.MetalLookAndFeel"`	Metal
`"com.sun.java.swing.plaf.motif.MotifLookAndFeel"`	Motif
`"com.sun.java.swing.plaf.windows.WindowsLookAndFeel"`	Windows

When you call the `UIManager.setLookAndFeel` method, any components that have already been created need to be updated. You do this by calling the `SwingUtilities.updateComponentTreeUI` method, passing a reference to the component that you want to update as an argument.

The `UIManager.setLookAndFeel` method throws a number of exceptions. Specifically, it throws `ClassNotFoundException`, `InstantiationException`, `IllegalAccessException`, and `UnsupportedLookAndFeelException`. Unless you want to trap each of these types of exceptions, you can simply trap exceptions of type `Exception`. Here is an example of code that can be run from a `JFrame` object that changes its look and feel to Motif:

```
try
{
    UIManager.setLookAndFeel(
        "com.sun.java.swing.plaf.motif.MotifLookAndFeel");
    SwingUtilities.updateComponentTreeUI(this);
}
catch (Exception e)
{
    JOptionPane.showMessageDialog(null, "Error setting " +
                                        "the look and feel.");
    System.exit(0);
}
```

And here is an example of code that can be run from a JFrame object that changes its look and feel to Windows:

```
try
{
    UIManager.setLookAndFeel(
        "com.sun.java.swing.plaf.windows.WindowsLookAndFeel");
    SwingUtilities.updateComponentTreeUI(this);
}
catch (Exception e)
{
    JOptionPane.showMessageDialog(null, "Error setting " +
                                        "the look and feel.");
    System.exit(0);
}
```

13.12 Common Errors to Avoid

- Only retrieving the first selected item from a list component in which multiple items have been selected. If multiple items have been selected in a list component, the getSelectedValue method returns only the first selected item. Likewise, the getSelectedIndex method returns only the index of the first selected item. You should use the getSelectedValues or getSelectedIndices methods instead.
- Using 1 as the beginning index for a list or combo box. The indices for a list or combo box start at 0, not 1.
- Forgetting to add a list or text area to a scroll pane. The JList and JTextArea components do not automatically display scroll bars. You must add these components to a scroll pane object in order for them to display scroll bars.
- Using the **add** method instead of the constructor to add a component to a scroll pane. To add a component to a scroll pane, you must pass a reference to the component as an argument to the JScrollPane constructor.
- Adding a component to a scroll pane and then adding the component (not the scroll pane) to another container, such as a panel. If you add a component to a scroll pane and then intend to add that same component to a panel or other container, you must add the scroll pane instead of the component. Otherwise, the scroll bars will not appear on the component.

- Forgetting to call the **setEditable** method to give a combo box a text field. By default, a combo box is the combination of a button and a list. To make it a combination of a text field and a list, you must call the setEditable method and pass true as an argument.

- Trying to open an image file of an unsupported type. Currently, an ImageIcon object can open image files that are stored in JPEG, GIF, or PNG formats.

- Loading an image into an existing **JLabel** component and clipping part of the image. If you have not explicitly set the preferred size of a JLabel component, it resizes itself automatically when you load an image into it. The JFrame that encloses the JLabel does not automatically resize, however. You must call the JFrame object's pack method or setPreferredSize method to resize it.

- Assigning the same mnemonic to more than one component. If you assign the same mnemonic to more than one component in a window, it works only for the first component that you assigned it to.

- Forgetting to add menu items to a **JMenu** component, and **JMenu** components to a **JMenuBar** component. After you create a menu item, you must add it to a JMenu component in order for it to be displayed on the menu. Likewise, JMenu components must be added to a JMenuBar component in order to be displayed on the menu bar.

- Not calling the **JFrame** object's **setJMenuBar** method to place the menu bar. To display a menu bar, you must call the setJMenuBar method and pass it as an argument.

- Not grouping **JRadioButtonMenuItems** in a **ButtonGroup** object. Just like regular radio button components, you must group radio button menu items in a button group in order to create a mutually exclusive relationship among them.

Review Questions and Exercises

Multiple Choice and True/False

1. You can use this method to make a text field read-only.
   a. setReadOnly
   b. setChangeable
   c. setUneditable
   d. setEditable

2. A JList component generates this type of event when the user selects an item.
   a. action event
   b. item event
   c. list selection event
   d. list change event

3. To display a scroll bar with a JList component, you must _____.
   a. do nothing; the JList automatically appears with scroll bars if necessary
   b. add the JList component to a JScrollPane component
   c. call the setScrollBar method
   d. none of the above; you cannot display a scroll bar with a JList component

4. This is the `JList` component's default selection mode.
   a. single selection
   b. single interval selection
   c. multiple selection
   d. multiple interval selection

5. A list selection listener must have this method.
   a. `valueChanged`
   b. `selectionChanged`
   c. `actionPerformed`
   d. `itemSelected`

6. The `ListSelectionListener` interface is in this package.
   a. `java.awt`
   b. `java.awt.event`
   c. `javax.swing.event`
   d. `javax.event`

7. This `JList` method returns –1 if no item in the list is selected.
   a. `getSelectedValue`
   b. `getSelectedItem`
   c. `getSelectedIndex`
   d. `getSelection`

8. A `JComboBox` component generates this type of event when the user selects an item.
   a. action event
   b. item event
   c. list selection event
   d. list change event

9. You can pass an instance of this class to the `JLabel` constructor if you want to display an image in the label.
   a. `ImageFile`
   b. `ImageIcon`
   c. `JLabelImage`
   d. `JImageFile`

10. This method can be used to store an image in a `JLabel` or a `JButton` component.
    a. `setImage`
    b. `storeImage`
    c. `getIcon`
    d. `setIcon`

11. This is text that appears in a small box when the user holds the mouse cursor over a component.
    a. mnemonic
    b. instant message
    c. tool tip
    d. pop-up mnemonic

12. This is a key that activates a component just as if the user clicked it with the mouse.
    a. mnemonic
    b. key activator
    c. tool tip
    d. click simulator

13. To display an open file or save file dialog box, you use this class.
    a. JFileChooser
    b. JOpenSaveDialog
    c. JFileDialog
    d. JFileOptionPane

14. To display a dialog box that allows the user to select a color, you use this class.
    a. JColor
    b. JColorDialog
    c. JColorChooser
    d. JColorOptionPane

15. You use this class to create a menu bar.
    a. MenuBar
    b. JMenuBar
    c. JMenu
    d. JBar

16. You use this class to create a radio button menu item.
    a. JMenuItem
    b. JRadioButton
    c. JRadioButtonItem
    d. JRadioButtonMenuItem

17. You use this method to place a menu bar on a JFrame.

    a. setJMenuBar
    b. setMenuBar
    c. placeMenuBar
    d. setJMenu

18. The setPreferredSize method accepts this as its argument(s).

    a. a Size object
    b. two int values
    c. a Dimension object
    d. one int value

19. Components of this class are multi-line text fields.

    a. JMultiLineTextField
    b. JTextArea
    c. JTextField
    d. JEditField

20. This method is inherited from `JComponent` and changes the appearance of a component's text.

    a. `setAppearance`
    b. `setTextAppearance`
    c. `setFont`
    d. `setText`

21. This method sets the intervals at which major tick marks are displayed on a `JSlider` component.

    a. `setMajorTickSpacing`
    b. `setMajorTickIntervals`
    c. `setTickSpacing`
    d. `setIntervals`

22. **True or False:** You can use code to change the contents of a read-only text field.

23. **True or False:** A `JList` component automatically appears with a line border drawn around it.

24. **True or False:** In single interval selection mode, the user may select multiple items from a `JList` component.

25. **True or False:** With an editable combo box the user may only enter a value that appears in the component's list.

26. **True or False:** You can store either text or an image in a `JLabel` object, but not both.

27. **True or False:** You can store large images as well as small ones in a `JLabel` component.

28. **True or False:** Mnemonics are useful for users who are good with the keyboard.

29. **True or False:** A `JMenuBar` object acts as a container for `JMenu` components.

30. **True or False:** A `JMenu` object cannot contain other `JMenu` objects.

31. **True or False:** A `JTextArea` component does not automatically display scroll bars.

32. **True or False:** By default, a `JTextArea` component does not perform line wrapping.

33. **True or False:** A `JSlider` component generates an action event when the slider knob is moved.

34. **True or False:** By default, a `JSlider` component displays labels and tick marks.

35. **True or False:** When labels are displayed on a `JSlider` component, they are displayed on the major tick marks.

Find the Error

1.
```
// Create a read-only text field.
JTextField textField = new JTextField(10);
textField.setEditable(true);
```

2. `// Create a black 1-pixel border around list, a JList component.`
   `list.setBorder(Color.BLACK, 1);`

3. `// Create a JList and add it to a scroll pane.`
   `// Assume that array already exists.`
   `JList list = new JList(array);`
   `JScrollPane scrollPane = new JScrollPane();`
   `scrollPane.add(list);`

4. `// Assume that nameBox is a combo box and is properly set up`
   `// with a list of names to choose from.`
   `// Get value of the selected item.`
   `String selectedName = nameBox.getSelectedIndex();`

5. `JLabel label = new JLabel("Have a nice day!");`
   `label.setImage(image);`

6. `// Add a menu to the menu bar.`
   `JMenuBar menuBar = new JMenuBar(menuItem);`

7. `// Create a text area with 20 columns and 5 rows.`
   `JTextArea textArea = new JTextArea (20, 5);`

Algorithm Workbench

1. Give an example of code that creates a read-only text field.

2. Write code that creates a list with the following items: Monday, Tuesday, Wednesday, Thursday, Friday, Saturday, and Sunday.

3. Write code that adds a scroll bar to the list you created in your answer to Algorithm Workbench 2.

4. Assume that the variable `myList` references a `JList` component, and `selection` is a `String` variable. Write code that assigns the selected item in the `myList` component to the `selection` variable.

5. Assume that the variable `myComboBox` references an uneditable combo box, and `selectionIndex` is an `int` variable. Write code that assigns the index of the selected item in the `myComboBox` component to the `selectionIndex` variable.

6. Write code that stores the image in the file *dog.jpg* in a label.

7. Assume that `label` references an existing `JLabel` object. Write code that stores the image in the file *picture.gif* in the label.

8. Write code that creates a button with the text "Open File." Assign the O key as a mnemonic and assign "This button opens a file" as the component's tool tip.

9. Write code that displays a file open dialog box. If the user selects a file, the code should store the file's path and name in a `String` variable.

10. Write code that creates a text area displaying 10 rows and 15 columns. The text area should be capable of displaying scroll bars, when necessary. It should also perform word style line wrapping.

11. Write the code that creates a menu bar with one menu named File. The File menu should have the F key assigned as a mnemonic. The File menu should have three menu items: Open, Print, and Exit. Assign mnemonic keys of your choice to each of these items. Register an instance of the OpenListener class as an action listener for the Open menu item, an instance of the PrintListener class as an action listener for the Print menu item, and an instance of the ExitListener class as an action listener for the Exit menu item. Assume these classes have already been created.

12. Write code that creates a JSlider component. The component should be horizontally oriented and its range should be 0 through 1000. Labels and tick marks should be displayed. Major tick marks should appear at every 100th number, and minor tick marks should appear at every 25th number. The initial value of the slider should be set at 500.

Short Answer

1. What selection mode should you select if you want the user to select a single item only in a list?

2. You want to provide 20 items in a list for the user to select from. Which component would take up less space, a JList or a JComboBox?

3. What is the difference between an uneditable combo box and an editable combo box? Which one is a combo box by default?

4. Describe how you can store both an image and text in a JLabel component.

5. What is a mnemonic? How does the user use it?

6. What happens when the mnemonic that you assign to a component is a letter that appears in the component's text?

7. What is a tool tip? What is its purpose?

8. What do you do to a group of radio button menu items so that only one of them can be selected at a time?

9. When a checked menu item shows a check mark next to it, what happens when the user clicks on it?

10. What fonts does Java guarantee you have?

11. Why would a JSlider component be ideal when you want the user to enter a number, but you want to make sure that the number is within a range?

12. What are the standard GUI looks and feels that are available in Java?

Programming Challenges

myCodeMate **1. Scrollable Tax Calculator**

Create an application that allows you to enter the amount of a purchase and then displays the amount of sales tax on that purchase. Use a slider to adjust the tax rate between 0 percent and 10 percent.

VideoNote
The Image
Viewer Problem

2. Image Viewer

Write an application that allows the user to view image files. The application should use either a button or a menu item that displays a file chooser. When the user selects an image file, it should be loaded and displayed.

3. Dorm and Meal Plan Calculator

A university has the following dormitories:

> Allen Hall: $1,500 per semester
> Pike Hall: $1,600 per semester
> Farthing Hall: $1,200 per semester
> University Suites: $1,800 per semester
> The university also offers the following meal plans:
> 7 meals per week: $560 per semester
> 14 meals per week: $1,095 per semester
> Unlimited meals: $1,500 per semester

Create an application with two combo boxes. One should hold the names of the dormitories, and the other should hold the meal plans. The user should select a dormitory and a meal plan, and the application should show the total charges for the semester.

4. Skateboard Designer

The Skate Shop sells the skateboard products listed in Table 13-2.

Table 13-2   Skateboard products

Decks	Truck Assemblies	Wheels
The Master Thrasher $60	7.75 inch axle $35	51 mm $20
The Dictator $45	8 inch axle $40	55 mm $22
The Street King $50	8.5 inch axle $45	58 mm $24
		61 mm $28

In addition, the Skate Shop sells the following miscellaneous products and services:

> Grip tape: $10
> Bearings: $30
> Riser pads: $2
> Nuts & bolts kit: $3

Create an application that allows the user to select one deck, one truck assembly, and one wheel set from either list components or combo boxes. The application should also have a list component that allows the user to select multiple miscellaneous products. The application should display the subtotal, the amount of sales tax (at 6 percent), and the total of the order.

5. Shopping Cart System

Create an application that works like a shopping cart system for a book store. On the Student CD you will find a file named *BookPrices.txt*. This file contains the names and prices of various books, formatted in the following fashion:

> I Did It Your Way, 11.95
> The History of Scotland, 14.50
> Learn Calculus in One Day, 29.95
> Feel the Stress, 18.50

Each line in the file contains the name of a book, followed by a comma, followed by the book's retail price. When your application begins execution, it should read the contents of the file and store the book titles in a list component. The user should be able to select a title from the list and add it to a shopping cart, which is simply another list component. The application should have buttons or menu items that allow the user to remove items from the shopping cart, clear the shopping cart of all selections, and check out. When the user checks out, the application should calculate and display the subtotal of all the books in the shopping cart, the sales tax (which is 6 percent of the subtotal), and the total.

6. Cell Phone Packages

Cell Solutions, a cell phone provider, sells the following packages:

> 300 minutes per month: $45.00 per month
> 800 minutes per month: $65.00 per month
> 1500 minutes per month: $99.00 per month

The provider sells the following phones (a 6 percent sales tax applies to the sale of a phone):

> Model 100: $29.95
> Model 110: $49.95
> Model 200: $99.95

Customers may also select the following options:

> Voice mail: $5.00 per month
> Text messaging: $10.00 per month

Write an application that displays a menu system. The menu system should allow the user to select one package, one phone, and any of the options desired. As the user selects items from the menu, the application should show the prices of the items selected.

7. Shade Designer

A custom window shade designer charges a base fee of $50 per shade. In addition, charges are added for certain styles, sizes, and colors as follows:

Styles:

> Regular shades: Add $0
> Folding shades: Add $10
> Roman shades: Add $15

Sizes:

> 25 inches wide: Add $0
> 27 inches wide: Add $2
> 32 inches wide: Add $4
> 40 inches wide: Add $6

Colors:

> Natural: Add $5
> Blue: Add $0
> Teal: Add $0
> Red: Add $0
> Green: Add $0

Create an application that allows the user to select the style, size, color, and number of shades from lists or combo boxes. The total charges should be displayed.

8. Conference Registration System

Create an application that calculates the registration fees for a conference. The general conference registration fee is $895 per person, and student registration is $495 per person. There is also an optional opening night dinner with a keynote speech for $30 per person. In addition, the optional preconference workshops listed in Table 13-3 are available.

Table 13-3 Optional preconference workshops

Workshop	Fee
Introduction to E-commerce	$295
The Future of the Web	$295
Advanced Java Programming	$395
Network Security	$395

The application should allow the user to select the registration type, the optional opening night dinner and keynote speech, and as many preconference workshops as desired. The total cost should be displayed.

14 Applets and More

14.1 Introduction to Applets

CONCEPT: An applet is a Java program that is associated with a Web page and is executed in a Web browser as part of that Web page.

Recall from Chapter 1 that there are two types of programs you can create with Java: applications and applets. An *application* is a stand-alone program that runs on your computer. So far in this book we have concentrated exclusively on writing applications.

Applets are Java programs that are usually part of a Web site. If a user opens the Web site with a Java-enabled browser, the applet is executed inside the browser window. It appears to the user that the applet is part of the Web site. This is how it works: Applets are stored on a Web server along with the site's Web pages. When a user accesses a Web page on a server with his or her browser, any applets associated with the Web page are transmitted over the Internet from the server to the user's system. This is illustrated in Figure 14-1. Once the applets are transmitted, the user's system executes them.

Applets are important because they can be used to extend the capabilities of a Web page. Web pages are normally written in Hypertext Markup Language (HTML). HTML is limited, however, because it merely describes the content and layout of a Web page, and creates links to other files and Web pages. HTML does not have sophisticated abilities such as performing math calculations and interacting with the user. A programmer can write a Java applet to perform these types of operations and associate it with a Web page. When someone visits the Web page, the applet is downloaded to the visitor's browser and executed.

Figure 14-1 Applets are transmitted along with Web pages

Figure 14-2 shows an example of a Web page that has an applet. In the figure, the Web page is being viewed with Internet Explorer. This Web page briefly explains the Fahrenheit and Celsius temperature scales. The area with the text boxes and the button at the bottom of the page is generated by an applet. To see a Fahrenheit temperature converted to Celsius, the user can enter the Fahrenheit temperature into the top text box and click the Convert button. The Celsius temperature will be displayed in the read-only text box.

 An applet does not have to be on a Web server in order to be executed. The Web page shown in Figure 14-2 is in the Student CD source code folder *Chapter 14\TempConverter*. Open the *TempConverter.html* file in your Web browser to try it. Later in this chapter we will take a closer look at this Web page and its applet.

Figure 14-2 A Web page with an applet

This part of the Web page is generated by an applet.

Most Web browsers have a special version of the JVM for running applets. For security purposes, this version of the JVM greatly restricts what an applet can do. Here is a summary of the restrictions placed on applets:

- Applets cannot delete files, read the contents of files, or create files on the user's system.
- Applets cannot run any other program on the user's system.
- Applets cannot execute operating system procedures on the user's system.
- Applets cannot retrieve information about the user's system, or the user's identity.
- Applets cannot make network connections with any system except the server from which the applet was transmitted.
- If an applet displays a window, it will automatically have a message such as "Warning: Applet Window" displayed in it. This lets the user know that the window was not displayed by an application on his or her system.

These restrictions might seem severe, but they are necessary to prevent malicious code from attacking or spying on unsuspecting users. If an applet attempts to violate one of these restrictions, an exception is thrown.

Checkpoint

14.1   How is an applet that is associated with a Web page executed on a user's system?

14.2   Why do applets run in a restricted environment?

14.2 A Brief Introduction to HTML

CONCEPT: When creating a Web page, you use Hypertext Markup Language (HTML) to create a file that can be read and processed by a Web browser.

Hypertext Markup Language (HTML) is the language that Web pages are written in. Although it is beyond the scope of this book to teach you everything about HTML, this section will give you enough of the fundamentals so that you can write simple Web pages. You will need to know a little about HTML in order to run Java applets. If you are already familiar with HTML, this section is optional.

Before we continue, let's look at the meanings of the terms "hypertext" and "markup language."

Hypertext

Web pages can contain regular text and hypertext, which are both displayed in the browser window. In addition, *hypertext* can contain a link to another Web page, or perhaps another location in the same Web page. When the user clicks on the hypertext, it loads the Web page or the location that the hypertext is linked to.

Markup Language

Although HTML is called a language, it is not a programming language like Java. Instead, HTML is a *markup language*. It allows you to "mark up" a text file by inserting special instructions. These instructions tell the browser how to format the text and create any hypertext links.

To make a Web page, you create a text file that contains HTML instructions, which are known as *tags*, as well as the text that should be displayed on the Web page. The resulting file is known as an *HTML document*, and it is usually saved with the *.html* file name extension. When a Web browser reads the HTML document, the tags instruct it how to format the text, where to place images, what to do when the user clicks on a link, and more.

Most HTML tags come in pairs. The first is known as the opening tag and the second is known as the closing tag. The general format of a simple tag is as follows:

```
<tag_name>
Text
</tag_name>
```

In this general format, `tag_name` is the name of the tag. The opening tag is `<tag_name>` and the closing tag is `</tag_name>`. Both the opening and closing tags are enclosed in angle brackets (< >). Notice that in the closing tag, the tag name is preceded by a forward slash (/). The `Text` that appears between the opening and closing tags is text that is formatted or modified by the tags.

Document Structure Tags

Some of the HTML tags are used to establish the structure of an HTML document. The first of the structure tags that you should learn is the `<html></html>` tag. This tag marks the beginning and ending of an HTML document. Everything that appears between these tags, including other tags, is the content of the Web page. When you are writing an HTML document, place an `<html>` tag at the very beginning, and a `</html>` tag at the very end.

The next tag is `<head></head>`. Everything that appears between `<head>` and `</head>` is considered part of the document head. The *document head* is a section of the HTML file that contains information about the document. For example, key words that search engines use to identify a document are often placed in the document's head. The only thing that we will use the document head for is to display a title in the Web browser's title bar. You do this with the `<title></title>` tag. Any text that you place between `<title>` and `</title>` becomes the title of the page and is displayed in the browser's title bar. Code Listing 14-1 shows the contents of an HTML document with the title "My First Web Page".

Notice that the `<title></title>` tag is inside of the `<head></head>` tag. The only output displayed by this Web page is the title. Figure 14-3 shows how this Web page appears when opened in a browser.

Code Listing 14-1 `(BasicWebPage1.html)`

```html
<html>
<head>
    <title>My First Web Page</title>
</head>
</html>
```

Figure 14-3 Web page with a title only

After the document head comes the document body, which is enclosed in the `<body></body>` tag. The *document body* contains all of the tags and text that produce output in the browser window. Code Listing 14-2 shows an HTML document with text placed in its body. Figure 14-4 shows the document when opened in a browser.

Code Listing 14-2 `(BasicWebPage2.html)`

```html
<html>
<head>
    <title>Java Applications and Applets</title>
</head>
<body>
    There are two types of programs you can create with Java: applications
    and applets. An application is a stand-alone program that runs on your
    computer. Applets are Java programs that are usually part of a Web site.
    They are stored on a Web server along with the site's Web pages. When a
    remote user accesses a Web page with his or her browser, any applets
```

```
        associated with the Web page are transmitted over the Internet from the
        server to the remote user's system.
</body>
</html>
```

Figure 14-4 Web page produced by *BasicWebPage2.html*

Text Formatting Tags

The text displayed in the Web page in Figure 14-4 is unformatted, which means it appears as plain text. There are many HTML tags that you can use to change the appearance of text. For example, there are six different header tags that you can use to format text as a heading of some type. The `<h1></h1>` tag creates a level one header. A level one header appears in boldface, and is much larger than regular text. The `<h2></h2>` tag creates a level two header. A level two header also appears in boldface, but is smaller than a level one header. This pattern continues with the `<h3></h3>`, `<h4></h4>`, `<h5></h5>`, and `<h6></h6>` tags. The higher a header tag's level number is, the smaller the text that it formats appears. For example, look at the following HTML:

```
<h1>This is an h1 Header</h1>
<h2>This is an h2 Header</h2>
<h3>This is an h3 Header</h3>
<h4>This is an h4 Header</h4>
<h5>This is an h5 Header</h5>
<h6>This is an h6 Header</h6>
This is regular unformatted text.
```

When this appears in the body of an HTML document, it produces the Web page shown in Figure 14-5.

You can use the `<center></center>` tag to center a line of text in the browser window. To demonstrate, we will add the following line to the document that was previously shown in Code Listing 14-2:

```
<center><h1>Java</h1></center>
```

Figure 14-5 Header levels

This will cause the word "Java" to appear centered and as a level one header. The modified document is shown in Code Listing 14-3, and the Web page it produces is shown in Figure 14-6.

Code Listing 14-3 (`BasicWebPage3.html`)

```
<html>
<head>
    <title>Java Applications and Applets</title>
</head>
<body>
    <center>
        <h1>Java</h1>
    </center>
    There are two types of programs you can create with Java: applications
    and applets. An application is a stand-alone program that runs
    on your computer. Applets are Java programs that are usually
    part of a Web site. They are stored on a Web server along with
    the site's Web pages. When a remote user accesses a Web page
    with his or her browser, any applets associated with the Web
    page are transmitted over the Internet from the server to the
    remote user's system.
</body>
</html>
```

Figure 14-6 Web page produced by *BasicWebPage3.html*

Notice that in the HTML document, the word "Java" is enclosed in two sets of tags: the `<center>` tags and the `<h1>` tags. It doesn't matter which set of tags is used first. If we had written the line as follows, we would have gotten the same result:

```
<h1><center>Java</center></h1>
```

You can display text in boldface by using the `<b></b>` tag, and in italics by using the `<i></i>` tag. For example, the following will cause the text "Hello World" to be displayed in boldface:

```
<b>Hello World</b>
```

The following will cause "Hello World" to be displayed in italics:

```
<i>Hello World</i>
```

The following will display "Hello World" in boldface and italics:

```
<b><i>Hello World</i></b>
```

Creating Breaks in Text

We will look at three HTML tags that are used to create breaks in a document's text. These three tags are unique from the ones we previously studied because they do not occur in pairs. When you use one of these tags, you only insert an opening tag.

The `<br />` tag causes a line break to appear at the point in the text where it is inserted. It is often necessary to insert `<br />` tags in an HTML document because the browser usually ignores the newline characters that are created when you press the Enter key. For example, if the following line appears in the body of an HTML document, it will cause the output shown in Figure 14-7.

```
First line<br />Second line<br />Third line
```

Figure 14-7   Line breaks in an HTML document

First line
Second line
Third line

The `<p />` tag causes a paragraph break to appear at the point in the text where it is inserted. A paragraph break typically inserts more space into the text than a line break. For example, if the following line appears in the body of an HTML document, it will cause the output shown in Figure 14-8.

```
First paragraph<p />Second paragraph<p />Third paragraph
```

Figure 14-8   Paragraph breaks in an HTML document

First paragraph

Second paragraph

Third paragraph

The `<hr />` tag causes a horizontal rule to appear at the point in the text where it is inserted. A horizontal rule is a thin, horizontal line that is drawn across the Web page. For example, if the following text appears in the body of an HTML document, it will cause the output shown in Figure 14-9.

```
This is the first line of text.
<hr />
This is the second line of text.
<hr />
This is the third line of text.
```

Figure 14-9 Horizontal rules in a Web page

The HTML document shown in Code Listing 14-4 demonstrates each of the tags we have discussed. The Web page it produces is shown in Figure 14-10.

Code Listing 14-4 (`BasicWebPage4.html`)

```html
<html>
<head>
    <title>Java Applications and Applets</title>
</head>
<body>
    <center>
        <h1>Java</h1>
    </center>
    There are two types of programs you can create with Java: applications
    and applets.
    <p />
    <b>Applications</b>
    <br />
    An <i>application</i> is a stand-alone program that runs on
    your computer.
    <p />
    <b>Applets</b>
    <br />
    <i>Applets</i> are Java programs that are usually part of a
    Web site. They are stored on a Web server along with the site's
    Web pages. When a remote user accesses a Web page with his or
    her browser, any applets associated with the Web page are
    transmitted over the Internet from the server to the remote
    user's system.
    <hr />
</body>
</html>
```

Figure 14-10 Web page produced by *BasicWebPage4.html*

Inserting Links

As previously mentioned, a link is some element in a Web page that can be clicked on by the user. When the user clicks the link, another Web page is displayed, or some sort of action is initiated. We now look at how to insert a simple link that causes another Web page to be displayed. The tag that is used to insert a link has the following general format:

```
<a href="Address">Text</a>
```

The *Text* that appears between the opening and closing tags is the text that will be displayed in the Web page. When the user clicks on this text, the Web page that is located at *Address* will be displayed in the browser. This address is often referred to as a *uniform resource locator (URL)*. Notice that the address is enclosed in quotation marks. Here is an example:

```
<a href="http://www.gaddisbooks.com">Click here to go to
the textbook's web site.</a>
```

The HTML document shown in Code Listing 14-5 uses this link, and Figure 14-11 shows how the page appears in the browser.

Code Listing 14-5 (`LinkDemo.html`)

```html
<html>
<head>
    <title>Link Demonstration</title>
</head>
<body>
    This demonstrates a link.
    <br />
    <a href="http://www.aw.com/gaddis">Click here to go to
    the textbook's web site.</a>
</body>
</html>
```

The text that is displayed by a link is usually highlighted in some way to let the user know that it is not ordinary text. In Figure 14-11, the link text is underlined. When the user clicks on this text, the browser displays the Web page at www.aw.com/gaddis

Figure 14-11 Web page produced by *LinkDemo.html*

Checkpoint

14.3 What tag marks the beginning and end of an HTML document?

14.4 What tag marks the beginning and end of an HTML document's head section?

14.5 What statement would you use in an HTML document to display the text "My Web Page" in the browser's title bar? What section of the HTML document would this statement be written in?

14.6 What tag marks the beginning and end of an HTML document's body section?

14.7 What statement would you write in an HTML document to display the text "Student Roster" as a level one header?

14.8 What statement would you write in an HTML document to display the text "My Resume" in bold and centered on the page?

14.9 What statement would you write in an HTML document to display the text "Hello World" in bold and italic?

14.10 What tag causes a line break? What tag causes a paragraph break? What tag displays a horizontal rule?

14.11 Suppose you wanted to display the text "Click Here" as a link to the Web site http://java.sun.com. What statement would you write to create the text?

14.3 Creating Applets with Swing

CONCEPT: You extend a class from JApplet to create an applet, just as you extend a class from JFrame to create a GUI application.

By now you know almost everything necessary to create an applet. That is because applets are very similar to GUI applications. You can think of an applet as a GUI application that runs under the control of a Web browser. Instead of displaying its own window, an applet appears in the browser's window. The differences between GUI application code and applet code are summarized here:

- A GUI application class inherits from `JFrame`. An applet class inherits from `JApplet`. The `JApplet` class is part of the `javax.swing` package.

VideoNote
Creating
an Applet

- A GUI application class has a constructor that creates other components and sets up the GUI. An applet class does not normally have a constructor. Instead, it has a method named `init` that performs the same operations as a constructor. The `init` method accepts no arguments and has a `void` return type.
- The following methods, which are commonly called in a GUI application's constructor, are not called in an applet:

```
setTitle
setSize
setDefaultCloseOperation
pack
setVisible
```

The methods listed here are used in a GUI application to affect the application's window in some way. They are not usually applicable to an applet because the applet does not have a window of its own.

- There is no static `main` method needed to create an instance of the applet class. The browser creates an instance of the class automatically.

Let's look at a simple applet. Code Listing 14-6 shows an applet that displays a label.

Code Listing 14-6 (`SimpleApplet.java`)

```
 1 import javax.swing.*;
 2 import java.awt.*;
 3
 4 /**
 5    This is a simple applet.
 6 */
 7
 8 public class SimpleApplet extends JApplet
 9 {
10    /**
11       The init method sets up the applet, much
12       like a constructor.
13    */
14
15    public void init()
16    {
17       // Create a label.
18       JLabel label =
19          new JLabel("This is my very first applet.");
20
```

```
21          // Set the layout manager.
22          setLayout(new FlowLayout());
23
24          // Add the label to the content pane.
25          add(label);
26      }
27 }
```

This code is very much like a regular GUI application. Although this class extends `JApplet` instead of `JFrame`, you still add components to the content pane and use layout managers in the same way.

Running an Applet

The process of running an applet is different from that of running an application. To run an applet, you create an HTML document with an `applet` tag, which has the following general format:

```
<applet code="Filename.class" width=Wide height=High></applet>
```

In the general format, *Filename.class* is the name of the applet's *.class* file. This is the file that contains the compiled byte code. Note that you do not specify the *.java* file, which contains the Java source code. You can optionally specify a path along with the file name. If you specify only the file name, it is assumed that the file is in the same directory as the HTML document. *Wide* is the width of the applet in pixels, and *High* is the height of the applet in pixels. When a browser processes an `applet` tag, it loads specified byte code and executes it in an area that is the size specified by the *Wide* and *High* values.

The HTML document shown in Code Listing 14-7 uses an `applet` tag to load the applet shown in Code Listing 14-6. This document specifies that the applet should be displayed in an area that is 200 pixels wide by 50 pixels high. Figure 14-12 shows this document when it is displayed in a Web browser.

Code Listing 14-7   (`SimpleApplet.html`)

```
<html>
<head>
    <title>A Simple Applet</title>
</head>
<body>
    <applet code="SimpleApplet.class" width="200" height="50">
    </applet>
</body>
</html>
```

Figure 14-12 The Web page produced by *SimpleApplet.html*

 NOTE: When you load a Web page that uses an applet into your browser, you will most likely get a security warning. For example, Figure 14-13 shows the warning you get from Internet Explorer. To run the applet, click the warning message and then select Allow Blocked Content . . . from the pop-up menu that appears.

Figure 14-13 Security warning in Internet Explorer

Running an Applet with `appletviewer`

The Sun JDK comes with an applet viewer program that loads and executes an applet without the need for a Web browser. This program can be run from a command prompt with the `appletviewer` command. When you run the program, you specify the name of an HTML document as a command line argument. For example, the following command passes `SimpleApplet.html` as the command line argument:

```
appletviewer SimpleApplet.html
```

This command executes any applet that is referenced by an `applet` tag in the file *SimpleApplet.html*. The window shown in Figure 14-14 will be displayed.

Figure 14-14   Applet executed by `appletviewer`

> **NOTE:** The applet viewer does not display any output generated by text or tags in the HTML document. It only executes applets. If the applet viewer opens an HTML document with more than one `applet` tag, it will execute each applet in a separate window.

Handling Events in an Applet

In an applet, events are handled with event listeners exactly as they are in GUI applications. To demonstrate, we will examine the `TempConverter` class, which is shown in Code Listing 14-8. This class is the applet displayed in the Web page we examined at the beginning of this chapter. It has a text field where the user can enter a Fahrenheit temperature and a Convert button that converts the temperature to Celsius and displays it in a read-only text field. The temperature conversion is performed in an action listener class that handles the button's action events.

Code Listing 14-8   (`TempConverter.java`)

```
 1  import javax.swing.*;
 2  import java.awt.*;
 3  import java.awt.event.*;
 4  import java.text.DecimalFormat;
 5
 6  /**
 7     The TempConverter class is an applet that converts
 8     Fahrenheit temperatures to Celsius.
 9  */
10
11  public class TempConverter extends JApplet
12  {
13     private JPanel fPanel;              // To hold a text field
14     private JPanel cPanel;              // To hold a text field
15     private JPanel buttonPanel;         // To hold a button
16     private JTextField fahrenheit;      // Fahrenheit temperature
17     private JTextField celsius;         // Celsius temperature
18
19     /**
20        init method
21     */
22
23     public void init()
24     {
25        // Build the panels.
26        buildFpanel();
```

```
27          buildCpanel();
28          buildButtonPanel();
29
30          // Create a layout manager.
31          setLayout(new GridLayout(3, 1));
32
33          // Add the panels to the content pane.
34          add(fPanel);
35          add(cPanel);
36          add(buttonPanel);
37       }
38
39       /**
40          The buildFpanel method creates a panel with a text
41          field in which the user can enter a Fahrenheit
42          temperature.
43       */
44
45       private void buildFpanel()
46       {
47          // Create the panel.
48          fPanel = new JPanel();
49
50          // Create a label to display a message.
51          JLabel message1 =
52                  new JLabel("Fahrenheit Temperature: ");
53
54          // Create a text field for the Fahrenheit temp.
55          fahrenheit = new JTextField(10);
56
57          // Create a layout manager for the panel.
58          fPanel.setLayout(new FlowLayout(FlowLayout.RIGHT));
59
60          // Add the label and text field to the panel.
61          fPanel.add(message1);
62          fPanel.add(fahrenheit);
63       }
64
65       /**
66          The buildCpanel method creates a panel that
67          displays the Celsius temperature in a
68          read-only text field.
69       */
70
71       private void buildCpanel()
72       {
73          // Create the panel.
74          cPanel = new JPanel();
75
```

```
 76          // Create a label to display a message.
 77          JLabel message2 =
 78                  new JLabel("Celsius Temperature: ");
 79
 80          // Create a text field for the Celsius temp.
 81          celsius = new JTextField(10);
 82
 83          // Make the text field read-only.
 84          celsius.setEditable(false);
 85
 86          // Create a layout manager for the panel.
 87          cPanel.setLayout(new FlowLayout(FlowLayout.RIGHT));
 88
 89          // Add the label and text field to the panel.
 90          cPanel.add(message2);
 91          cPanel.add(celsius);
 92       }
 93
 94       /**
 95          The buildButtonPanel method creates a panel with
 96          a button that converts the Fahrenheit temperature
 97          to Celsius.
 98       */
 99
100       private void buildButtonPanel()
101       {
102          // Create the panel.
103          buttonPanel = new JPanel();
104
105          // Create a button with the text "Convert".
106          JButton convButton = new JButton("Convert");
107
108          // Add an action listener to the button.
109          convButton.addActionListener(new ButtonListener());
110
111          // Add the button to the panel.
112          buttonPanel.add(convButton);
113       }
114
115       /**
116          Private inner class that handles the action event
117          that is generated when the user clicks the convert
118          button.
119       */
120
121       private class ButtonListener implements ActionListener
122       {
123          public void actionPerformed(ActionEvent e)
```

```
124        {
125            double ftemp, ctemp;   // To hold the temperatures
126
127            // Create a DecimalFormat object to format numbers.
128            DecimalFormat formatter = new DecimalFormat("0.0");
129
130            // Get the Fahrenheit temperature and convert it
131            // to a double.
132            ftemp = Double.parseDouble(fahrenheit.getText());
133
134            // Calculate the Celsius temperature.
135            ctemp = (5.0 / 9.0) * (ftemp - 32);
136
137            // Display the Celsius temperature.
138            celsius.setText(formatter.format(ctemp));
139        }
140    }
141 }
```

Code Listing 14-9 shows the contents of `TempConverter.html`, an HTML document that uses this applet. Figure 14-15 shows the Web page produced by this document. In the figure, the user has entered a Fahrenheit temperature and converted it to Celsius.

Code Listing 14-9   `(TempConverter.html)`

```html
<html>
<head>
    <title>Fahrenheit and Celsius Temperatures</title>
</head>
<body>
    <center>
        <h1>Fahrenheit and Celsius Temperatures</h1>
    </center>
Fahrenheit and Celsius are two temperature scales in use today.
The <b>Fahrenheit</b> scale was developed by the German physicist
Daniel Gabriel Fahrenheit (1686 - 1736). In the Fahrenheit scale,
water freezes at 32 degrees and boils at 212 degrees. The
<b>Celsius</b> scale was developed by Swedish astronomer Andres Celsius
(1701 - 1744). In the Celsius scale, water freezes at 0 degrees and
boils at 100 degrees. The Celsius to Fahrenheit conversion formula
is:
<p />
<i>C</i> = (5/9) * (<i>F</i> - 32)
<p />
where <i>F</i> is the Fahrenheit temperature. You can also use
this Web page to convert Fahrenheit temperatures to Celsius.
Just enter a Fahrenheit temperature in the text box below, then
```

```
        click on the Convert button.
        <p />
        <applet code="TempConverter.class" width="300" height="150">
        </applet>
        <hr />
    </body>
</html>
```

Figure 14-15 Web page produced by *TempConverter.html*

(Browser window titled "Fahrenheit and Celsius Temperatures - Windows Internet Explorer" showing the web page)

Fahrenheit and Celsius Temperatures

Fahrenheit and Celsius are two temperature scales in use today. The **Fahrenheit** scale was developed by the German physicist Daniel Gabriel Fahrenheit (1686 - 1736). In the Fahrenheit scale, water freezes at 32 degrees and boils at 212 degrees. The **Celsius** scale was developed by Swedish astronomer Andres Celsius (1701 - 1744). In the Celsius scale, water freezes at 0 degrees and boils at 100 degrees. The Celsius to Fahrenheit conversion formula is:

$C = (5/9) * (F - 32)$

where F is the Fahrenheit temperature. You can also use this Web page to convert Fahrenheit temperatures to Celsius. Just enter a Fahrenheit temperature in the text box below, then click on the Convert button.

Fahrenheit Temperature: 45

Celsius Temperature: 7.2

Convert

Applet TempConverter started   Computer | Protected Mode: Off   100%

Checkpoint

14.12 Instead of `JFrame`, an applet class is extended from what class?

14.13 Instead of a constructor, an applet class uses what method?

14.14 Why is there no need for a static `main` method to create an instance of an applet class?

14.15 Suppose the file *MyApplet.java* contains the Java source code for an applet. What tag would you write in an HTML document to run the applet in an area that is 400 pixels wide by 200 pixels high?

14.4 Using AWT for Portability

CONCEPT: Applets that use Swing components may be incompatible with some browsers. If you want to make sure that an applet is compatible with all Java-enabled browsers, use AWT components instead of Swing.

Java provides two libraries of classes that GUI components may be created from. Recall from Chapter 7 that these libraries are AWT and Swing. AWT is the original library that has been part of Java since its earliest version. Swing is an improved library that was introduced with Java 2. All of the GUI applications in Chapters 7 and 13, as well as the applets we have studied so far in this chapter, use Swing classes for their components.

Some browsers, such as Microsoft Internet Explorer and older versions of Netscape Navigator, do not directly support the Swing classes in applets. These browsers require a *plug-in*, which is software that extends or enhances another program, in order to run applets that use Swing components. Fortunately, this plug-in is automatically installed on a computer when the Sun JDK is installed. If you have installed the JDK, you should be able to write applets that use Swing and run them with no problems.

If you are writing an applet for other people to run on their computers, however, there is no guarantee that they will have the required plug-in. If this is the case, you should use the AWT classes instead of the Swing classes for the components in your applet. Fortunately, the AWT component classes are very similar to the Swing classes, so learning to use them is simple if you already know how to use Swing.

There is a corresponding AWT class for each of the Swing classes that you have learned so far. The names of the AWT classes are the same as those of the Swing classes, except the AWT class names do not start with the letter J. For example, the AWT class to create a frame is named `Frame`, and the AWT class to create a panel is named `Panel`. Table 14-1 lists several of the AWT classes. All of these classes are in the `java.awt` package.

Table 14-1   Several AWT classes

AWT Class	Description	Corresponding Swing Class
Applet	Used as a superclass for all applets. Unlike `JApplet` objects, `Applet` objects do not have a content pane.	JApplet
Frame	Creates a frame container that may be displayed as a window. Unlike `JFrame` objects, `Frame` objects do not have a content pane.	JFrame
Panel	Creates a panel container.	JPanel
Button	Creates a button that may be clicked.	JButton
Label	Creates a label that displays text.	JLabel
TextField	Creates a single line text field, which the user may type into.	JTextField
Checkbox	Creates a check box that may be selected or deselected.	JCheckBox

The Swing classes were intentionally designed with constructors and methods that are similar to those of their AWT counterparts. In addition, events are handled in the same way for each set of classes. This makes it easy for you to use either set of classes without learning a completely different syntax for each. For example, Code Listing 14-10 shows a version of the TempConverter applet that has been rewritten to use AWT components instead of Swing components.

Code Listing 14-10   (AWTTempConverter.java)

```java
 1 import java.applet.Applet;
 2 import java.awt.*;
 3 import java.awt.event.*;
 4 import java.text.DecimalFormat;
 5
 6 /**
 7    The AWTTempConverter class is an applet that converts
 8    Fahrenheit temperatures to Celsius.
 9 */
10
11 public class AWTTempConverter extends Applet
12 {
13    private Panel fPanel;         // To hold a text field
14    private Panel cPanel;         // To hold a text field
15    private Panel buttonPanel;    // To hold a button
16    private TextField fahrenheit; // Fahrenheit temperature
17    private TextField celsius;    // Celsius temperature
18
19    /**
20       init method
21    */
22
23    public void init()
24    {
25       // Build the panels.
26       buildFpanel();
27       buildCpanel();
28       buildButtonPanel();
29
30       // Create a layout manager.
31       setLayout(new GridLayout(3, 1));
32
33       // Add the panels to the applet.
34       add(fPanel);
35       add(cPanel);
36       add(buttonPanel);
37    }
38
```

```
39    /**
40        The buildFpanel method creates a panel with a text
41        field in which the user can enter a Fahrenheit
42        temperature.
43    */
44
45    private void buildFpanel()
46    {
47        // Create the panel.
48        fPanel = new Panel();
49
50        // Create a label to display a message.
51        Label message1 =
52                 new Label("Fahrenheit Temperature: ");
53
54        // Create a text field for the Fahrenheit temp.
55        fahrenheit = new TextField(10);
56
57        // Create a layout manager for the panel.
58        fPanel.setLayout(new FlowLayout(FlowLayout.RIGHT));
59
60        // Add the label and text field to the panel.
61        fPanel.add(message1);
62        fPanel.add(fahrenheit);
63    }
64
65    /**
66        The buildCpanel method creates a panel that
67        displays the Celsius temperature in a
68        read-only text field.
69    */
70
71    private void buildCpanel()
72    {
73        // Create the panel.
74        cPanel = new Panel();
75
76        // Create a label to display a message.
77        Label message2 =
78                 new Label("Celsius Temperature: ");
79
80        // Create a text field for the Celsius temp.
81        celsius = new TextField(10);
82
83        // Make the text field read-only.
84        celsius.setEditable(false);
85
86        // Create a layout manager for the panel.
```

```
 87          cPanel.setLayout(new FlowLayout(FlowLayout.RIGHT));
 88
 89          // Add the label and text field to the panel.
 90          cPanel.add(message2);
 91          cPanel.add(celsius);
 92       }
 93
 94       /**
 95          The buildButtonPanel method creates a panel with
 96          a button that converts the Fahrenheit temperature
 97          to Celsius.
 98       */
 99
100
101       private void buildButtonPanel()
102       {
103          // Create the panel.
104          buttonPanel = new Panel();
105
106          // Create a button with the text "Convert".
107          Button convButton = new Button("Convert");
108
109          // Add an action listener to the button.
110          convButton.addActionListener(new ButtonListener());
111
112          // Add the button to the panel.
113          buttonPanel.add(convButton);
114       }
115
116       /**
117          Private inner class that handles the action event
118          that is generated when the user clicks the convert
119          button.
120       */
121
122       private class ButtonListener implements ActionListener
123       {
124          public void actionPerformed(ActionEvent e)
125          {
126             double ftemp, ctemp;  // To hold the temperatures
127
128             // Create a DecimalFormat object to format numbers.
129             DecimalFormat formatter = new DecimalFormat("0.0");
130
131             // Get the Fahrenheit temperature and convert it
132             // to a double.
133             ftemp = Double.parseDouble(fahrenheit.getText());
134
```

```
135           // Calculate the Celsius temperature.
136           ctemp = (5.0 / 9.0) * (ftemp - 32);
137
138           // Display the Celsius temperature.
139           celsius.setText(formatter.format(ctemp));
140       }
141   }
142 }
```

The only modifications that were made were as follows:

- The JApplet, JPanel, JLabel, JTextField, and JButton classes were replaced with the Applet, Panel, Label, TextField, and Button classes.
- The import javax.swing.*; statement was removed.

To run the applet in a browser, the APPLET tag in the *TempConverter.html* file must be modified to read as follows:

```
<applet code="AWTTempConverter.class" width=300 height=150>
</applet>
```

Once this change is made, the *TempConverter.html* file produces the Web page shown in Figure 14-16.

Figure 14-16 Web page running the AWTTempConverter applet

Checkpoint

14.16 To create an applet using AWT, what class do you inherit your applet class from?

14.17 In Swing, if an object's class extends JFrame or JApplet, you add components to its content pane. How do you add components to an object if its class extends Frame or Applet?

14.5 Drawing Shapes

CONCEPT: Components have an associated `Graphics` object that may be used to draw lines and shapes.

In addition to displaying standard components such as buttons and labels, Java allows you to draw lines and graphical shapes such as rectangles, ovals, and arcs. These lines and shapes are drawn directly on components. This allows a frame or a panel to become a can-vas for your drawings. Before we examine how to draw graphics on a component, however, we must discuss the *XY* coordinate system. You use the *XY* coordinate system to specify the location of your graphics.

The XY Coordinate System

The location of each pixel in a component is identified with an *X* coordinate and a *Y* coor-dinate. The coordinates are usually written in the form (*x*, *y*). The *X* coordinate identifies a pixel's horizontal location, and the *Y* coordinate identifies its vertical location. The coor-dinates of the pixel in the upper-left corner of a component are usually (0, 0). The *X* coor-dinates increase from left to right, and the *Y* coordinates increase from top to bottom. For example, Figure 14-17 illustrates a component such as a frame or a panel that is 300 pixels wide by 200 pixels high. The *X* and *Y* coordinates of the pixels in each corner, as well as the pixel in the center of the component are shown. The pixel in the center of the component has an *X* coordinate of 149 and a *Y* component of 99.

Figure 14-17   *X* and *Y* coordinates on a 300 pixel wide by 200 pixel high component

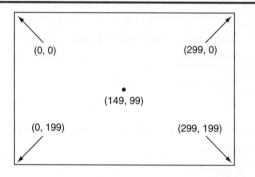

When you draw a line or shape on a component, you must indicate its position using *X* and *Y* coordinates.

Graphics Objects

Each component has an internal object that inherits from the `Graphics` class, which is part of the `java.awt` package. This object has numerous methods for drawing graphical shapes on the surface of the component. Table 14-2 lists some of these methods.

Table 14-2   Some of the `Graphics` class methods

Method	Description
`void setColor(Color c)`	Sets the drawing color for this object to that specified by the argument.
`Color getColor()`	Returns the current drawing color for this object.
`void drawLine(int x1, int y1,` `            int x2, int y2)`	Draws a line on the component starting at the coordinate (*x1*, *y1*) and ending at the coordinate (*x2*, *y2*). The line will be drawn in the current drawing color.
`void drawRect(int x, int y,` `    int width, int height)`	Draws the outline of a rectangle on the component. The upper-left corner of the rectangle will be at the coordinate (*x*, *y*). The *width* parameter specifies the rectangle's width in pixels, and *height* specifies the rectangle's height in pixels. The rectangle will be drawn in the current drawing color.
`void fillRect(int x, int y,` `    int width, int height)`	Draws a filled rectangle. The parameters are the same as those used by the `drawRect` method. The rectangle will be filled with the current drawing color.
`void drawOval(int x, int y,` `    int width, int height)`	Draws the outline of an oval on the component. The shape and size of the oval is determined by an invisible rectangle that encloses it. The upper-left corner of the rectangle will be at the coordinate (*x*, *y*). The *width* parameter specifies the rectangle's width in pixels, and *height* specifies the rectangle's height in pixels. The oval will be drawn in the current drawing color.
`void fillOval(int x, int y,` `    int width, int height)`	Draws a filled oval. The parameters are the same as those used by the `drawOval` method. The oval will be filled in the current drawing color.

`void drawArc(int x, int y,`
`    int width, int height,`
`    int startAngle,`
`    int arcAngle)`
	This method draws an arc, which is considered to be part of an oval. The shape and size of the oval are determined by an invisible rectangle that encloses it. The upper-left corner of the rectangle will be at the coordinate (*x*, *y*). The *width* parameter specifies the rectangle's width in pixels, and *height* specifies the rectangle's height in pixels. The arc begins at the angle *startAngle*, and ends at the angle *arcAngle*. The arc will be drawn in the current drawing color.

`void fillArc(int x, int y,`
`    int width, int height,`
`    int startAngle,`
`    int arcAngle)`
	This method draws a filled arc. The parameters are the same as those used by the `drawArc` method. The arc will be filled with the current drawing color.

(table continues next page)

Table 14-2 Some of the `Graphics` class methods (continued)

Method	Description
`void drawPolygon(int[] xPoints, int[] yPoints, int numPoints)`	This method draws the outline of a closed polygon on the component. The *xPoints* array contains the X-coordinates for each vertex, and the *yPoints* array contains the Y coordinates for each vertex. The argument passed into *numPoints* is the number of vertices in the polygon.
`void fillPolygon(int[] xPoints, int[] yPoints, int numPoints)`	This method draws a filled polygon. The parameters are the same as those used by the `drawPolygon` method. The polygon will be filled with the current drawing color.
`void drawString(String str, int x, int y)`	Draws the string passed into *str* using the current font. The bottom left of the string is drawn at the coordinates passed into *x* and *y*.
`void setFont(Font f)`	Sets the current font, which is used by the `drawString` method.

In order to call any of these methods, you must get a reference to a component's `Graphics` object. One way to do this is to override the `paint` method. You can override the `paint` method in any class that extends as follows:

- `JApplet`
- `JFrame`
- Any AWT class, including `Applet` and `Frame`

The `paint` method is responsible for displaying, or "painting," a component on the screen. This method is automatically called when the component is first displayed and is called again any time the component needs to be redisplayed. For example, when the component is completely or partially obscured by another window, and the obscuring window is moved, then the component's `paint` method is called to redisplay it. The header for the `paint` method is:

```
public void paint(Graphics g)
```

Notice that the method's argument is a `Graphics` object. When this method is called for a particular component, the `Graphics` object that belongs to that component is automatically passed as an argument. By overriding the `paint` method, you can use the `Graphics` object argument to draw your own graphics on the component. For example, look at the applet class in Code Listing 14-11.

This class inherits from `JApplet`, and it overrides the `paint` method. The `Graphics` object that is passed into the `paint` method's g parameter is the object that is responsible for drawing the entire applet window. Notice that in line 29 the method first calls the superclass version of the `paint` method, passing the object g as an argument. When overriding the `paint` method, you should always call the superclass's `paint` method before doing anything else. This ensures that the component will be displayed properly on the screen.

Code Listing 14-11 (`LineDemo.java`)

```
1 import javax.swing.*;
2 import java.awt.*;
3
4 /**
5    This class is an applet that demonstrates how lines
6    can be drawn.
7 */
8
9 public class LineDemo extends JApplet
10 {
11    /**
12       init method
13    */
14
15    public void init()
16    {
17       // Set the background color to white.
18       getContentPane().setBackground(Color.white);
19    }
20
21    /**
22       paint method
23       @param g The applet's Graphics object.
24    */
25
26    public void paint(Graphics g)
27    {
28       // Call the superclass paint method.
29       super.paint(g);
30
31       // Draw a red line from (20, 20) to (280, 280).
32       g.setColor(Color.red);
33       g.drawLine(20, 20, 280, 280);
34
35       // Draw a blue line from (280, 20) to (20, 280).
36       g.setColor(Color.blue);
37       g.drawLine(280, 20, 20, 280);
38    }
39 }
```

In line 32 the method sets the drawing color to red. In line 33 a line is drawn from the coordinates (20, 20) to (280, 280). This is a diagonal line drawn from the top-left area of the applet window to the bottom-right area. Next, in line 36, the drawing color is set to blue. In line 37 a line is drawn from (280, 20) to (20, 280). This is also a diagonal line. It is drawn from the top-right area of the applet window to the bottom-left area.

We can use the *LineDemo.html* file, which is on the Student CD in the same folder as the applet class, to execute the applet. The following line in the file runs the applet in an area that is 300 pixels wide by 300 pixels high:

```
<applet code="LineDemo.class" width=300 height=300>
</applet>
```

Figure 14-18 shows the applet running in the applet viewer.

Figure 14-18   `LineDemo` applet

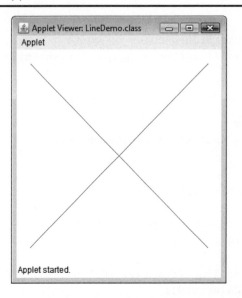

Notice that the `paint` method is not explicitly called by the applet. It is automatically called when the applet first executes. As previously mentioned, it is also called any time the applet window needs to be redisplayed.

Code Listing 14-12 shows the `RectangleDemo` class, an applet that draws two rectangles: one as a black outline and one filled with red. Each rectangle is 120 pixels wide and 120 pixels high. The file *RectangleDemo.html*, which is on the Student CD in the same folder as the applet class, executes the applet with the following tag:

```
<applet code="RectangleDemo.class" width=300 height=300>
</applet>
```

Figure 14-19 shows the applet running in the applet viewer.

Code Listing 14-12   (`RectangleDemo.java`)

```java
 1 import javax.swing.*;
 2 import java.awt.*;
 3
 4 /**
 5    This class is an applet that demonstrates how
 6    rectangles can be drawn.
 7 */
 8
 9 public class RectangleDemo extends JApplet
10 {
11    /**
12       init method
13    */
14
15    public void init()
16    {
17       // Set the background color to white.
18       getContentPane().setBackground(Color.white);
19    }
20
21    /**
22       paint method
23       @param g The applet's Graphics object.
24    */
25
26    public void paint(Graphics g)
27    {
28       // Call the superclass paint method.
29       super.paint(g);
30
31       // Draw a black unfilled rectangle.
32       g.setColor(Color.black);
33       g.drawRect(20, 20, 120, 120);
34
35       // Draw a red filled rectangle.
36       g.setColor(Color.red);
37       g.fillRect(160, 160, 120, 120);
38    }
39 }
```

Figure 14-19 `RectangleDemo` applet

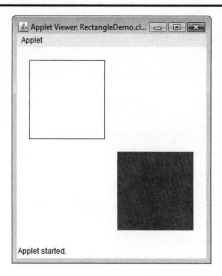

Code Listing 14-13 shows the `OvalDemo` class, an applet that draws two ovals. An oval is enclosed in an invisible rectangle that establishes the boundaries of the oval. The width and height of the enclosing rectangle defines the shape and size of the oval. This is illustrated in Figure 14-20.

When you call the `drawOval` or `fillOval` methods, you pass the *X* and *Y* coordinates of the enclosing rectangle's upper-left corner, and the width and height of the enclosing rectangle as arguments.

Code Listing 14-13   (`OvalDemo.java`)

```
 1 import javax.swing.*;
 2 import java.awt.*;
 3
 4 /**
 5    This class is an applet that demonstrates how
 6    ovals can be drawn.
 7 */
 8
 9 public class OvalDemo extends JApplet
10 {
11    /**
12       init method
13    */
14
15    public void init()
16    {
```

```
17        // Set the background color to white.
18        getContentPane().setBackground(Color.white);
19    }
20
21    /**
22       paint method
23       @param g The applet's Graphics object.
24    */
25
26    public void paint(Graphics g)
27    {
28       // Call the superclass paint method.
29       super.paint(g);
30
31       // Draw a black unfilled oval.
32       g.setColor(Color.black);
33       g.drawOval(20, 20, 120, 75);
34
35       // Draw a green filled oval.
36       g.setColor(Color.green);
37       g.fillOval(80, 160, 180, 75);
38    }
39 }
```

Figure 14-20   An oval and its enclosing rectangle

Enclosing rectangle

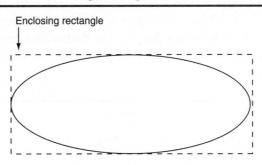

The file *OvalDemo.html*, which is on the Student CD in the same folder as the applet class, executes the applet with the following tag:

```
<applet code="OvalDemo.class" width=300 height=255>
</applet>
```

Figure 14-21 shows the applet running in the applet viewer.

Figure 14-21 `OvalDemo` applet

> **TIP:** To draw a circle, simply draw an oval with an enclosing rectangle that is square. In other words, the enclosing rectangle's width and height should be the same.

The `drawArc` method draws an arc, which is part of an oval. You pass the same arguments to `drawArc` as you do to `drawOval`, plus two additional arguments: the arc's starting angle and ending angle. The angles are measured in degrees, with 0 degrees being at the 3 o'clock position. For example, look at the following statement:

```
g.drawArc(20, 20, 100, 100, 0, 90);
```

This statement creates an enclosing rectangle with its upper-left corner at (20, 20) and with a width and height of 100 pixels each. The oval constructed from this enclosing rectangle is a circle. The arc that is drawn is the part of the oval that starts at 0 degrees and ends at 90 degrees. Figure 14-22 illustrates this arc. The dashed lines show the enclosing rectangle and the oval. The thick black line shows the arc that will be drawn.

Figure 14-22 An arc

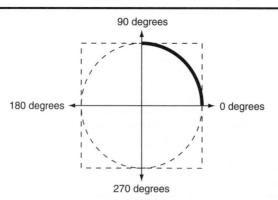

Code Listing 14-14 shows the `ArcDemo` class, which is an applet that draws four arcs: two unfilled and two filled. The filled arcs are drawn with the `fillArc` method.

The file *ArcDemo.html*, which is on the Student CD in the same folder as the applet class, executes the applet with the following tag:

```
<applet code="ArcDemo.class" width=300 height=220>
</applet>
```

Figure 14-23 shows the applet running in the applet viewer.

Code Listing 14-14   (`ArcDemo.java`)

```java
1 import javax.swing.*;
2 import java.awt.*;
3
4 /**
5    This class is an applet that demonstrates how
6    arcs can be drawn.
7 */
8
9 public class ArcDemo extends JApplet
10 {
11    /**
12       init method
13    */
14
15    public void init()
16    {
17       // Set the background color to white.
18       getContentPane().setBackground(Color.white);
19    }
20
21    /**
22       paint method
23       @param g The applet's Graphics object.
24    */
25
26    public void paint(Graphics g)
27    {
28       // Call the superclass paint method.
29       super.paint(g);
30
31       // Draw a black unfilled arc from 0 degrees
32       // to 90 degrees.
33       g.setColor(Color.black);
34       g.drawArc(0, 20, 120, 120, 0, 90);
35
36       // Draw a red filled arc from 0 degrees
37       // to 90 degrees.
```

```
38          g.setColor(Color.red);
39          g.fillArc(140, 20, 120, 120, 0, 90);
40
41          // Draw a green unfilled arc from 0 degrees
42          // to 45 degrees.
43          g.setColor(Color.green);
44          g.drawArc(0, 120, 120, 120, 0, 45);
45
46          // Draw a blue filled arc from 0 degrees
47          // to 45 degrees.
48          g.setColor(Color.blue);
49          g.fillArc(140, 120, 120, 120, 0, 45);
50      }
51 }
```

Figure 14-23   `ArcDemo` applet

The `drawPolygon` method draws an outline of a closed polygon and the `fillPolygon` method draws a closed polygon filled with the current drawing color. A polygon is constructed of multiple line segments that are connected. The point where two line segments are connected is called a *vertex*. These methods accept two `int` arrays as arguments. The first array contains the X coordinates of each vertex, and the second array contains the Y coordinates of each vertex. The third argument is an `int` that specifies the number of vertices, or connecting points.

For example, suppose we use the following arrays as arguments for the X and Y coordinates of a polygon:

```
int[] xCoords = {60, 100, 140, 140, 100, 60, 20, 20 };
int[] yCoords = {20, 20, 60, 100, 140, 140, 100, 60 };
```

The first point specified by these arrays is (60, 20), the second point is (100, 20), and so forth. There are a total of eight points specified by these arrays, and if we connect each of these points we get the octagon shown in Figure 14-24.

Figure 14-24   Points of each vertex in an octagon

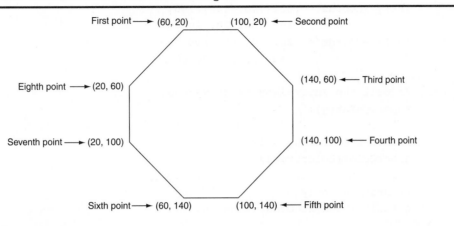

If the last point specified in the arrays is different from the first point, as in this example, then the two points are automatically connected to close the polygon. The `PolygonDemo` class in Code Listing 14-15 draws a filled polygon using these arrays as arguments.

Code Listing 14-15   (`PolygonDemo.java`)

```
1 import javax.swing.*;
2 import java.awt.*;
3
4 /**
5    This class is an applet that demonstrates how a
6    polygon can be drawn.
7 */
8
9 public class PolygonDemo extends JApplet
10 {
11    /**
12       init method
13    */
14
15    public void init()
16    {
17       // Set the background color to white.
18       getContentPane().setBackground(Color.white);
19    }
20
21    /**
22       paint method
23       @param g The applet's Graphics object.
24    */
25
26    public void paint(Graphics g)
```

```
27      {
28          int[] xCoords = {60, 100, 140, 140,
29                              100, 60, 20, 20 };
30          int[] yCoords = {20, 20, 60, 100,
31                              140, 140, 100, 60 };
32
33          // Call the superclass paint method.
34          super.paint(g);
35
36          // Set the drawing color.
37          g.setColor(Color.red);
38
39          // Draw the polygon.
40          g.fillPolygon(xCoords, yCoords, 8);
41      }
42 }
```

 The file *PolygonDemo.html*, which is on the Student CD in the same folder as the applet class, executes the applet with the following tag:

```
<applet code="PolygonDemo.class" width=160 height=160>
</applet>
```

Figure 14-25 shows the applet running in the applet viewer.

Figure 14-25 PolygonDemo applet

The drawString method draws a string as a graphic. The string is specified by its first argument, a String object. The X and Y coordinates of the lower-left point of the string are specified by the second and third arguments. For example, assuming that g references a Graphics object, the following statement draws the string "Hello World", starting at the coordinates 100, 50:

```
g.drawstring("Hello World", 100, 50);
```

You can set the font for the string with the setFont method. This method accepts a Font object as its argument. Here is an example:

```
g.setFont(new Font("Serif", Font.ITALIC, 20));
```

The Font class was covered in Chapter 13. Recall that the Font constructor's arguments are the name of a font, the font's style, and the font's size in points. You can combine font styles with the + operator, as follows:

```
g.setFont(new Font("Serif", Font.BOLD + Font.ITALIC, 24));
```

The GraphicStringDemo class in Code Listing 14-16 demonstrates the drawString method. It draws the same octagon that the PolygonDemo class drew, and then draws the string "STOP" over it to create a stop sign. The string is drawn in a bold 35-point sanserif font.

Code Listing 14-16   (GraphicStringDemo.java)

```
 1  import javax.swing.*;
 2  import java.awt.*;
 3
 4  /**
 5      This class is an applet that demonstrates how a
 6      string can be drawn.
 7  */
 8
 9  public class GraphicStringDemo extends JApplet
10  {
11      /**
12          init method
13      */
14
15      public void init()
16      {
17         // Set the background color to white.
18         getContentPane().setBackground(Color.white);
19      }
20
21      /**
22          paint method
23          @param g The applet's Graphics object.
24      */
25
26      public void paint(Graphics g)
27      {
28         int[] xCoords = {60, 100, 140, 140,
29                          100, 60, 20, 20 };
30         int[] yCoords = {20, 20, 60, 100,
31                          140, 140, 100, 60 };
32
```

```
33          // Call the superclass paint method.
34          super.paint(g);
35
36          // Set the drawing color.
37          g.setColor(Color.red);
38
39          // Draw the polygon.
40          g.fillPolygon(xCoords, yCoords, 8);
41
42          // Set the drawing color to white.
43          g.setColor(Color.white);
44
45          // Set the font and draw "STOP".
46          g.setFont(new Font("SansSerif", Font.BOLD, 35));
47          g.drawString("STOP", 35, 95);
48      }
49 }
```

 The file *GraphicStringDemo.html*, which is on the Student CD in the same folder as the applet class, executes the applet with the following tag:

```
<applet code="GraphicStringDemo.class" width=160 height=160>
</applet>
```

Figure 14-26 shows the applet running in the applet viewer.

Figure 14-26 GraphicStringDemo applet

The repaint Method

As previously mentioned, you do not call a component's paint method. It is automatically called when the component must be redisplayed. Sometimes, however, you might want to force the application or applet to call the paint method. You do this by calling the repaint method, which has the following header:

```
public void repaint()
```

The `repaint` method clears the surface of the component and then calls the `paint` method. You will see an applet that uses this method in a moment.

Drawing on Panels

Each of the preceding examples uses the entire `JApplet` window as a canvas for drawing. Sometimes, however, you might want to confine your drawing space to a smaller region within the window, such as a panel. To draw on a panel, you simply get a reference to the panel's `Graphics` object and then use that object's methods to draw. The resulting graphics are drawn only on the panel.

Getting a reference to a `JPanel` component's `Graphics` object is similar to the technique you saw in the previous examples. Instead of overriding the `JPanel` object's `paint` method, however, you should override its `paintComponent` method. This is true not only for `JPanel` objects, but also for all Swing components except `JApplet` and `JFrame`. The `paintComponent` method serves for `JPanel` and most other Swing objects the same purpose as the `paint` method: It is automatically called when the component needs to be redisplayed. When it is called, the component's `Graphics` object is passed as an argument. Here is the method's header:

```
public void paintComponent(Graphics g)
```

When you override this method, first you should call the superclass's `paintComponent` method to ensure that the component is properly displayed. Here is an example call to the superclass's version of the method:

```
super.paintComponent(g);
```

After this you can call any of the `Graphics` object's methods to draw on the component. As an example, we look at the `GraphicsWindow` class in Code Listing 14-17. When this applet is run (via the *GraphicsWindow.html* file, which is on the Student CD in the same folder as the applet class), the window shown in Figure 14-27 is displayed. A set of check boxes is displayed in a `JPanel` component on the right side of the window. The white area that occupies the majority of the window is a `DrawingPanel` object. The `DrawingPanel` class inherits from `JPanel`, and its code is shown in Code Listing-14-18. When one of the check boxes is selected, a shape appears in the `DrawingPanel` object. Figure 14-28 shows how the applet window appears when all of the check boxes are selected.

Figure 14-27   `GraphicsWindow` applet

Applet Viewer: GraphicsWindow.class
Applet

☐ Line

☐ Rectangle

☐ Filled Rectangle

☐ Oval

☐ Filled Oval

☐ Arc

☐ Filled Arc

Applet started.

Figure 14-28 `GraphicsWindow` applet with all graphics selected

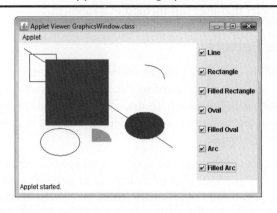

Code Listing 14-17 (`GraphicsWindow.java`)

```java
 1 import javax.swing.*;
 2 import java.awt.*;
 3 import java.awt.event.*;
 4
 5 /**
 6    This class displays a drawing panel and a set of
 7    check boxes that allow the user to select shapes.
 8    The selected shapes are drawn on the drawing panel.
 9 */
10
11 public class GraphicsWindow extends JApplet
12 {
13    // Declare an array of check box components
14    private JCheckBox[] checkBoxes;
15
16    // The following titles array contains the
17    // titles of the check boxes.
18    private String[] titles = { "Line", "Rectangle",
19                                "Filled Rectangle",
20                                "Oval", "Filled Oval",
21                                "Arc", "Filled Arc" };
22
23    // The following will reference a panel to contain
24    // the check boxes.
25    private JPanel checkBoxPanel;
26
27    // The following will reference an instance of the
28    // DrawingPanel class. This will be a panel to draw on.
29    private DrawingPanel drawingPanel;
```

```
30
31      /**
32         init method
33      */
34
35      public void init()
36      {
37         // Build the check box panel.
38         buildCheckBoxPanel();
39
40         // Create the drawing panel.
41         drawingPanel = new DrawingPanel(checkBoxes);
42
43         // Add the check box panel to the east region
44         // and the drawing panel to the center region.
45         add(checkBoxPanel, BorderLayout.EAST);
46         add(drawingPanel, BorderLayout.CENTER);
47      }
48
49      /**
50         The buildCheckBoxPanel method creates the array of
51         check box components and adds them to a panel.
52      */
53
54      private void buildCheckBoxPanel()
55      {
56         // Create the panel.
57         checkBoxPanel = new JPanel();
58         checkBoxPanel.setLayout(new GridLayout(7, 1));
59
60         // Create the check box array.
61         checkBoxes = new JCheckBox[7];
62
63         // Create the check boxes and add them to the panel.
64         for (int i = 0; i < checkBoxes.length; i++)
65         {
66            checkBoxes[i] = new JCheckBox(titles[i]);
67            checkBoxes[i].addItemListener(
68                                   new CheckBoxListener());
69            checkBoxPanel.add(checkBoxes[i]);
70         }
71      }
72
73      /**
74         A private inner class to respond to changes in the
75         state of the check boxes.
76      */
77
```

```
78     private class CheckBoxListener implements ItemListener
79     {
80        public void itemStateChanged(ItemEvent e)
81        {
82           drawingPanel.repaint();
83        }
84     }
85  }
```

Code Listing 14-18 (`DrawingPanel.java`)

```
 1 import javax.swing.*;
 2 import java.awt.*;
 3
 4 /**
 5    This class creates a panel that example shapes are
 6    drawn on.
 7 */
 8
 9 public class DrawingPanel extends JPanel
10 {
11    // Declare a check box array.
12    private JCheckBox[] checkBoxArray;
13
14    /**
15       Constructor
16    */
17
18    public DrawingPanel(JCheckBox[] cbArray)
19    {
20       // Reference the check box array.
21       checkBoxArray = cbArray;
22
23       // Set the background color to white.
24       setBackground(Color.white);
25
26       // Set the preferred size of the panel.
27       setPreferredSize(new Dimension(300, 200));
28    }
29
30    /**
31       paintComponent method
32       @param g The panel's Graphics object.
33    */
34
35    public void paintComponent(Graphics g)
```

```
36     {
37         // Call the superclass paintComponent method.
38         super.paintComponent(g);
39
40         // Draw the selected shapes.
41         if (checkBoxArray[0].isSelected())
42         {
43             g.setColor(Color.black);
44             g.drawLine(10, 10, 290, 190);
45         }
46         if (checkBoxArray[1].isSelected())
47         {
48             g.setColor(Color.black);
49             g.drawRect(20, 20, 50, 50);
50         }
51         if (checkBoxArray[2].isSelected())
52         {
53             g.setColor(Color.red);
54             g.fillRect(50, 30, 120, 120);
55         }
56         if (checkBoxArray[3].isSelected())
57         {
58             g.setColor(Color.black);
59             g.drawOval(40, 155, 75, 50);
60         }
61         if (checkBoxArray[4].isSelected())
62         {
63             g.setColor(Color.blue);
64             g.fillOval(200, 125, 75, 50);
65         }
66         if (checkBoxArray[5].isSelected())
67         {
68             g.setColor(Color.black);
69             g.drawArc(200, 40, 75, 50, 0, 90);
70         }
71         if (checkBoxArray[6].isSelected())
72         {
73             g.setColor(Color.green);
74             g.fillArc(100, 155, 75, 50, 0, 90);
75         }
76     }
77 }
```

Let's take a closer look at these classes. First, notice in lines 14 through 21 of the GraphicsWindow class that two of the class's fields are array reference variables. The checkBoxes variable references an array of JCheckBox components, and the titles variable references an array of strings. The strings in the titles array are the titles that the check boxes will display.

The first statement in the init method, line 38, is a call to the buildCheckBoxPanel method, which creates a panel for the check boxes, creates the array of check boxes, adds an item listener to each element of the array, and adds each element to the panel.

After the buildCheckBoxPanel method executes, the init method creates a DrawingPanel object with the statement in line 41. Notice that the checkBoxes variable is passed to the DrawingPanel constructor. The drawingPanel object needs a reference to the array so its paintComponent method can determine which check boxes are selected and draw the corresponding shape.

The only times that the paintComponent method is automatically called is when the component is initially displayed and when the component needs to be redisplayed. In order to display a shape immediately when the user selects a check box, we need the check box item listener to force the paintComponent method to be called. This is accomplished by the statement in line 82, in the CheckBoxListener class's itemStateChanged method. This statement calls the drawingPanel object's repaint method, which causes the drawingPanel object's surface to be cleared, and then causes the object's paintComponent method to execute. Because it is in the item listener, it is executed each time the user clicks on a check box.

Checkpoint

14.18 In an AWT component, or a class that extends JApplet or JFrame, if you want to get a reference to the Graphics object, do you override the paint or paintComponent method?

14.19 In a JPanel object, do you override the paint or paintComponent method to get a reference to the Graphics object?

14.20 When are the paint or paintComponent methods called?

14.21 In the paint or paintComponent methods, what should be done before anything else?

14.22 How do you force the paint or paintComponent methods to be called?

14.23 When using a Graphics object to draw an oval, what invisible shape is the oval enclosed in?

14.24 What values are contained in the two arrays that are passed to a Graphics object's drawPolygon method?

14.25 What Graphics class methods do you use to perform the following tasks?
   a) draw a line
   b) draw a filled rectangle
   c) draw a filled oval
   d) draw a filled arc
   e) set the drawing color
   f) draw a rectangle
   g) draw an oval
   h) draw an arc
   i) draw a string
   j) set the font

14.6 Handling Mouse Events

CONCEPT: Java allows you to create listener classes that handle events generated by the mouse.

Handling Mouse Events

The mouse generates two types of events: mouse events and mouse motion events. To handle mouse events you create a *mouse listener* class and/or a *mouse motion listener* class. A mouse listener class can respond to any of the follow events:

- The mouse button is pressed.
- The mouse button is released.
- The mouse button is clicked (pressed, then released without moving the mouse).
- The mouse cursor enters a component's screen space.
- The mouse cursor exits a component's screen space.

A mouse listener class must implement the `MouseListener` interface, which is in the `java.awt.event` package. The class must also have the methods listed in Table 14-3.

Table 14-3 Methods required by the `MouseListener` interface

Method	Description
`public void mousePressed(MouseEvent e)`	If the mouse cursor is over the component and the mouse button is pressed, this method is called.
`public void mouseClicked(MouseEvent e)`	A mouse click is defined as pressing the mouse button and releasing it without moving the mouse. If the mouse cursor is over the component and the mouse is clicked on, this method is called.
`public void mouseReleased(MouseEvent e)`	This method is called when the mouse button is released after it has been pressed. The `mousePressed` method is always called before this method.
`public void mouseEntered(MouseEvent e)`	This method is called when the mouse cursor enters the screen area belonging to the component.
`public void mouseExited(MouseEvent e)`	This method is called when the mouse cursor leaves the screen area belonging to the component.

Notice that each of the methods listed in Table 14-3 accepts a `MouseEvent` object as its argument. The `MouseEvent` object contains data about the mouse event. We will use two of the `MouseEvent` object's methods: `getX` and `getY`. These methods return the *X* and *Y* coordinates of the mouse cursor when the event occurs.

Once you create a mouse listener class, you can register it with a component using the `addMouseListener` method, which is inherited from the `Component` class. The appropriate methods in the mouse listener class are automatically called when their corresponding mouse events occur.

A mouse motion listener class can respond to the following events:

- The mouse is dragged (the button is pressed and the mouse is moved while the button is held down).
- The mouse is moved.

A mouse motion listener class must implement the `MouseMotionListener` interface, which is in the `java.awt.event` package. The class must also have the methods listed in Table 14-4. Notice that each of these methods also accepts a `MouseEvent` object as an argument.

Table 14-4 Methods required by the `MouseMotionListener` interface

Method	Description
`public void mouseDragged(MouseEvent e)`	The mouse is dragged when its button is pressed and the mouse is moved while the button is held down. This method is called when a dragging operation begins over the component. The `mousePressed` method is always called just before this method.
`public void mouseMoved(MouseEvent e)`	This method is called when the mouse cursor is over the component and it is moved.

Once you create a mouse motion listener class, you can register it with a component using the `addMouseMotionListener` method, which is inherited from the `Component` class. The appropriate methods in the mouse motion listener class are automatically called when their corresponding mouse events occur.

The `MouseEvents` class, shown in Code Listing 14-19, is an applet that demonstrates both a mouse listener and a mouse motion listener. The file *MouseEvents.html*, which is on the Student CD in the same folder as the applet class, can be used to start the applet. Figure 14-29 shows the applet running. The window displays a group of read-only text fields that represent the different mouse and mouse motion events. When an event occurs, the corresponding text field turns yellow. The last two text fields constantly display the mouse cursor's *X* and *Y* coordinates. Run this applet and experiment by clicking the mouse inside the window, dragging the mouse, moving the mouse cursor in and out of the window, and moving the mouse cursor over the text fields.

Code Listing 14-19   `(MouseEvents.java)`

```java
 1 import javax.swing.*;
 2 import java.awt.event.*;
 3 import java.awt.*;
 4
 5 /**
 6    This applet shows the mouse events as they occur.
 7 */
 8
 9 public class MouseEvents extends JApplet
10 {
11    private JTextField[] mouseStates;
12    private String[] text = {
13                 "Pressed", "Clicked", "Released",
14                 "Entered", "Exited", "Dragged",
15                 "X:", "Y:" };
16
17    /**
18       init method
19    */
20
21    public void init()
22    {
23       // Create a layout manager.
24       setLayout(new FlowLayout());
25
26       // Create the array of text fields.
27       mouseStates = new JTextField[8];
28       for (int i = 0; i < mouseStates.length; i++)
29       {
30          mouseStates[i] = new JTextField(text[i], 10);
31          mouseStates[i].setEditable(false);
32          add(mouseStates[i]);
33       }
34
35       // Add a mouse listener to this applet.
36       addMouseListener(new MyMouseListener());
37
38       // Add a mouse motion listener to this applet.
39       addMouseMotionListener(new MyMouseMotionListener());
40    }
41
42    /**
43       The clearTextFields method sets all of the text
44       backgrounds to light gray.
45    */
```

```
46
47      public void clearTextFields()
48      {
49         for (int i = 0; i < 6; i++)
50            mouseStates[i].setBackground(Color.lightGray);
51      }
52
53      /**
54         Private inner class that handles mouse events.
55         When an event occurs, the text field for that
56         event is given a yellow background.
57      */
58
59      private class MyMouseListener
60                            implements MouseListener
61      {
62         public void mousePressed(MouseEvent e)
63         {
64            clearTextFields();
65            mouseStates[0].setBackground(Color.yellow);
66         }
67
68         public void mouseClicked(MouseEvent e)
69         {
70            clearTextFields();
71            mouseStates[1].setBackground(Color.yellow);
72         }
73
74         public void mouseReleased(MouseEvent e)
75         {
76            clearTextFields();
77            mouseStates[2].setBackground(Color.yellow);
78         }
79
80         public void mouseEntered(MouseEvent e)
81         {
82            clearTextFields();
83            mouseStates[3].setBackground(Color.yellow);
84         }
85
86         public void mouseExited(MouseEvent e)
87         {
88            clearTextFields();
89            mouseStates[4].setBackground(Color.yellow);
90         }
91      }
92
```

```
93      /**
94         Private inner class to handle mouse motion events.
95      */
96
97      private class MyMouseMotionListener
98                          implements MouseMotionListener
99      {
100         public void mouseDragged(MouseEvent e)
101         {
102            clearTextFields();
103            mouseStates[5].setBackground(Color.yellow);
104         }
105
106         public void mouseMoved(MouseEvent e)
107         {
108            mouseStates[6].setText("X: " + e.getX());
109            mouseStates[7].setText("Y: " + e.getY());
110         }
111      }
112 }
```

Figure 14-29   MouseEvents applet

Using Adapter Classes

Many times when you handle mouse events, you will not be interested in handling every event that the mouse generates. This is the case with the DrawBoxes applet, which only handles mouse pressed and mouse dragged events.

This applet lets you draw rectangles by pressing the mouse button and dragging the mouse inside the applet window. When you initially press the mouse button, the position of the mouse cursor becomes the upper-left corner of a rectangle. As you drag the mouse, the lower-right corner of the rectangle follows the mouse cursor. When you release the mouse cursor, the rectangle stops following the mouse. Figure 14-30 shows an example of the applet's window. You can run the applet with the *DrawBoxes.html* file, which is on the Student CD in the same folder as the applet class. Code Listing 14-20 shows the code for the DrawBoxes class.

> **NOTE:** To draw the rectangle, you must drag the mouse cursor to the right and below the position where you initially pressed the mouse button.

Figure 14-30 DrawBoxes applet

Code Listing 14-20 (DrawBoxes.java)

```
 1 import javax.swing.*;
 2 import java.awt.event.*;
 3 import java.awt.*;
 4
 5 /**
 6    This applet demonstrates how mouse events and mouse
 7    motion events can be handled. It lets the user draw
 8    boxes by dragging the mouse.
 9 */
10
11 public class DrawBoxes extends JApplet
12 {
13    private int currentX = 0;    // Mouse cursor's X position
14    private int currentY = 0;    // Mouse cursor's Y position
15    private int width = 0;       // The rectangle's width
```

```
16      private int height = 0;    // The rectangle's height
17
18      /**
19         init method
20      */
21
22      public void init()
23      {
24         // Add a mouse listener and a mouse motion listener.
25         addMouseListener(new MyMouseListener());
26         addMouseMotionListener(new MyMouseMotionListener());
27      }
28
29      /**
30         paint method
31         @param g The applet's Graphics object.
32      */
33
34      public void paint(Graphics g)
35      {
36         // Call the superclass's paint method.
37         super.paint(g);
38
39         // Draw a rectangle.
40         g.drawRect(currentX, currentY, width, height);
41      }
42
43      /**
44         Mouse listener class
45      */
46
47      private class MyMouseListener
48                         implements MouseListener
49      {
50         public void mousePressed(MouseEvent e)
51         {
52            // Get the mouse cursor coordinates.
53            currentX = e.getX();
54            currentY = e.getY();
55         }
56
57         //
58         // The following methods are unused, but still
59         // required by the MouseListener interface.
60         //
61
62         public void mouseClicked(MouseEvent e)
63         {
```

```
64            }
65
66        public void mouseReleased(MouseEvent e)
67        {
68        }
69
70        public void mouseEntered(MouseEvent e)
71        {
72        }
73
74        public void mouseExited(MouseEvent e)
75        {
76        }
77    }
78
79    /**
80       Mouse Motion listener class
81    */
82
83    private class MyMouseMotionListener
84                    implements MouseMotionListener
85    {
86        public void mouseDragged(MouseEvent e)
87        {
88            // Calculate the size of the rectangle.
89            width = e.getX() - currentX;
90            height = e.getY() - currentY;
91
92            // Repaint the window.
93            repaint();
94        }
95
96        /**
97           The mouseMoved method is unused, but still
98           required by the MouseMotionListener interface.
99        */
100
101        public void mouseMoved(MouseEvent e)
102        {
103        }
104    }
105 }
```

Notice in the mouse listener and mouse motion listener classes that several of the methods are empty. Even though the applet handles only two mouse events, the `MyMouseListener` and `MyMouseMotionListener` classes must have all of the methods required by the interfaces they implement. If any of these methods are omitted, a compiler error results.

The Java API provides an alternative technique for creating these listener classes, which eliminates the need to define empty methods for the events you are not interested in. Instead of implementing the `MouseListener` or `MouseMotionListener` interfaces, you can extend your classes from the `MouseAdapter` or `MouseMotionAdapter` classes. These classes implement the `MouseListener` and `MouseMotionListener` interfaces and provide empty definitions for all of the required methods. When you extend a class from one of these adapter classes, it inherits the empty methods. In your extended class, you can override the methods you want and forget about the others. Both the `MouseAdapter` and `MouseMotionAdapter` classes are in the `java.awt.event` package.

The `DrawBoxes2` class shown in Code Listing 14-21 is a modification of the `DrawBoxes` class previously shown. In this version, the `MyMouseListener` class extends `MouseAdapter` and the `MyMouseMotionListener` class extends `MouseMotionAdapter`. This applet operates exactly the same as the `DrawBoxes` applet. The only difference is that this class does not have the empty methods in the listener classes.

> **NOTE:** Java provides an adapter class for all of the interfaces in the API that have more than one method.

Code Listing 14-21   (`DrawBoxes2.java`)

```
 1  import javax.swing.*;
 2  import java.awt.event.*;
 3  import java.awt.*;
 4
 5  /**
 6     This applet demonstrates how the mouse adapter
 7     classes can be used.
 8  */
 9
10  public class DrawBoxes2 extends JApplet
11  {
12     private int currentX = 0;     // Mouse cursor's X position
13     private int currentY = 0;     // Mouse cursor's Y position
14     private int width = 0;        // The rectangle's width
15     private int height = 0;       // The rectangle's height
16
17     /**
18        init method
19     */
20
21     public void init()
22     {
23        // Add a mouse listener and a mouse motion listener.
24        addMouseListener(new MyMouseListener());
25        addMouseMotionListener(new MyMouseMotionListener());
26     }
```

```
27
28    /**
29       paint method
30       @param g The applet's Graphics object.
31    */
32
33    public void paint(Graphics g)
34    {
35       // Call the superclass's paint method.
36       super.paint(g);
37
38       // Draw a rectangle.
39       g.drawRect(currentX, currentY, width, height);
40    }
41
42    /**
43       Mouse listener class
44    */
45
46    private class MyMouseListener extends MouseAdapter
47    {
48       public void mousePressed(MouseEvent e)
49       {
50          // Get the coordinates of the mouse cursor.
51          currentX = e.getX();
52          currentY = e.getY();
53       }
54    }
55
56    /**
57       Mouse Motion listener class
58    */
59
60    private class MyMouseMotionListener
61                          extends MouseMotionAdapter
62    {
63       public void mouseDragged(MouseEvent e)
64       {
65          // Calculate the size of the rectangle.
66          width = e.getX() - currentX;
67          height = e.getY() - currentY;
68
69          // Repaint the window.
70          repaint();
71       }
72    }
73 }
```

Checkpoint

14.26 What is the difference between a mouse press event and a mouse click event?

14.27 What interface would a listener class implement to handle a mouse click event? A mouse press event? A mouse dragged event? A mouse release event? A mouse move event?

14.28 What type of object do mouse listener and mouse motion listener methods accept? What methods do these types of objects provide for determining a mouse cursor's location?

14.29 If a class implements the `MouseListener` interface but does not need to use all of the methods specified by the interface, can the definitions for those methods be left out? If not, how are these methods dealt with?

14.30 What is an adapter class, and how does it make some programming tasks easier?

14.7 Timer **Objects**

CONCEPT: A `Timer` object regularly generates action events at programmer-specified time intervals.

`Timer` objects automatically generate action events at regular time intervals. This is useful when you want a program to perform an operation at certain times or after an amount of time has passed.

`Timer` objects are created from the `Timer` class, which is in the `javax.swing` package. Here is the general format of the `Timer` class's constructor:

```
Timer(int delay, ActionListener listener)
```

The argument passed into the *delay* parameter is the amount of time between action events, measured in milliseconds. A millisecond is a thousandth of a second, so a *delay* value of 1000 causes an action event to be generated every second. The argument passed into the *listener* parameter is a reference to an action listener that is to be registered with the `Timer` object. If you want to add an action listener at a later time, you can pass `null` as this argument, then use the `Timer` object's `addActionListener` method to register an action listener. Table 14-5 lists the `Timer` class's methods.

An application can use a `Timer` object to execute code automatically at regular time intervals. For example, a `Timer` object can be used to perform simple animation by moving a graphic image across the screen by a certain amount at regular time intervals. This is demonstrated in the `BouncingBall` class, shown in Code Listing 14-22. This class is an applet that displays a bouncing ball, as shown in Figure 14-31.

Table 14-5 Timer class methods

Method	Description
void addActionListener (ActionListener *listener*)	Registers the object referenced by *listener* as an action listener.
int getDelay()	Returns the current time delay in milliseconds.
Boolean isRunning()	Returns true if the Timer object is running. Otherwise, it returns false.
void setDelay(int delay)	Sets the time delay. The argument is the amount of the delay in milliseconds.
void start()	Starts the Timer object, which causes it to generate action events.
void stop()	Stops the Timer object, which causes it to stop generating action events.

Figure 14-31 BouncingBall applet

Code Listing 14-22 (`BouncingBall.java`)

```java
 1 import javax.swing.*;
 2 import java.awt.event.*;
 3 import java.awt.*;
 4
 5 /**
 6    This applet uses a Timer object to animate
 7    a bouncing ball.
 8 */
 9
10 public class BouncingBall extends JApplet
11 {
12    private final int X = 109;              // Ball's X coordinate
13    private final int WIDTH = 40;           // Ball's width
14    private final int HEIGHT = 40;          // Ball's height
15    private final int TIME_DELAY = 30;      // Time delay
16    private final int MOVE = 20;            // Pixels to move ball
17    private final int MINIMUM_Y = 50;       // Max height of ball
18    private final int MAXIMUM_Y = 400;      // Min height of ball
19    private int y = 400;                    // Ball's Y coordinate
20    private boolean goingUp = true;         // Direction indicator
21    private Timer timer;                    // Timer object
22
23
24    /**
25       init method
26    */
27
28    public void init()
29    {
30       timer = new Timer(TIME_DELAY, new TimerListener());
31       timer.start();
32    }
33
34    /**
35       paint method
36       @param g The applet's Graphics object.
37    */
38
39    public void paint(Graphics g)
40    {
41       // Call the superclass paint method.
42       super.paint(g);
43
44       // Set the drawing color to red.
45       g.setColor(Color.red);
```

```
46
47          // Draw the ball.
48          g.fillOval(X, y, WIDTH, HEIGHT);
49      }
50
51      /**
52          Private inner class that handles the Timer object's
53          action events.
54      */
55
56      private class TimerListener implements ActionListener
57      {
58          public void actionPerformed(ActionEvent e)
59          {
60              // Update the ball's Y coordinate.
61              if (goingUp)
62              {
63                  if (y > MINIMUM_Y)
64                      y -= MOVE;
65                  else
66                      goingUp = false;
67              }
68              else
69              {
70                  if (y < MAXIMUM_Y)
71                      y += MOVE;
72                  else
73                      goingUp = true;
74              }
75
76              // Force a call to the paint method.
77              repaint();
78          }
79      }
80 }
```

The BouncingBall class's init method creates a Timer object with the following statement in line 30:

```
timer = new Timer(TIME_DELAY, new TimerListener());
```

This initializes the object with a time delay of 30 milliseconds (the value of TIME_DELAY) and registers an instance of the TimerListener class as an action listener. This means that once the object is started, every 30 milliseconds it generates an action event, causing the action listener's actionPerformed method to execute. The next statement in the init method, in line 31, starts the Timer object as follows:

```
timer.start();
```

This causes the `Timer` object to commence generating action events. The `TimerListener` class's `actionPerformed` method calculates the new position of the bouncing ball and repaints the screen.

 Checkpoint

14.31 What type of events do `Timer` objects generate?

14.32 How are the time intervals between a `Timer` object's action events measured?

14.33 How do you cause a `Timer` object to begin generating action events?

14.34 How to you cause a `Timer` object to cease generating action events?

14.8 Playing Audio

CONCEPT: Sounds that have been stored in an audio file may be played from a Java program.

Java applets can play audio that is stored in a variety of popular sound file formats. The file formats directly supported are as follows:

- *.aif* or *.aiff* (Macintosh Audio File)
- *.au* (Sun Audio File)
- *.mid* or *.rmi* (MIDI File)
- *.wav* (Windows Wave File)

In order to play audio files, your computer must be equipped with a sound card and speakers. One way to play an audio file is to use the `Applet` class's `play` method. The version of the method that we will use is as follows:

```
void play(URL baseLocation, String fileName)
```

The argument passed to `baseLocation` is a `URL` object that specifies the location of the file. The argument passed to `fileName` is the name of the file. The sound that is recorded in the file is played one time.

When calling the `play` method, it is common to use either the `getDocumentBase` or `getCodeBase` methods, which are in the `Applet` class, to get a `URL` object for the first argument. The `getDocumentBase` method returns a `URL` object containing the location of the HTML file that invoked the applet. Here is an example of a call to the `play` method, using a call to `getDocumentBase` for the first argument:

```
play(getDocumentBase(), "mysound.wav");
```

This statement will load and play the *mysound.wav* sound file, stored at the same location as the HTML file that invoked the applet.

The `getCodeBase` method returns a URL object containing the location of the applet's *.class* file. Here is an example of its use:

```
play(getCodeBase(), "mysound.wav");
```

This statement will load and play the *mysound.wav* sound file, stored at the same location as the applet's *.class* file. The *AudioDemo1* folder on the Student CD contains an example applet that plays a sound file using the `play` method.

NOTE: If the sound file specified by the arguments to the play method cannot be found, no sound will be played.

Using an `AudioClip` Object

The `Applet` class's `play` method loads a sound file, plays it one time, and then releases it for garbage collection. If you need to load a sound file to be played multiple times, you should use an *AudioClip object*.

An `AudioClip` object is an object that implements the `AudioClip` interface. The `AudioClip` interface is in the `java.applet` package, and it specifies the following three methods: `play`, `loop`, and `stop`. The `play` method plays a sound one time. The `loop` method repeatedly plays a sound, and the `stop` method causes a sound to stop playing.

The `Applet` class's `getAudioClip` method can be used to create an `AudioClip` object for a given sound file as follows:

```
AudioClip getAudioClip(URL baseLocation, String fileName)
```

The argument passed to *baseLocation* is a URL object that specifies the location of a sound file, and the argument passed to *fileName* is the name of the file. The method returns an `AudioClip` object that can be used to play the sound file.

As before, we can use the `getDocumentBase` or `getCodeBase` method to get a URL object for the first argument. Here is an example of a statement that uses the `getAudioClip` method:

```
AudioClip clip = getAudioClip(getDocumentBase(), "mysound.wav");
```

This statement declares `clip` as an `AudioClip` reference variable. The object returned by the `getAudioClip` method will load the *mysound.wav* file, stored at the same location as the HTML file that invoked the applet. The address of the object will be assigned to `clip`. The following statement can then be used to play the sound file:

```
clip.play();
```

The sound file can be played repeatedly with the following statement:

```
clip.loop();
```

Any time the sound file is being played, the following statement can be used to stop it:

```
clip.stop();
```

The `AudioDemo2` class shown in Code Listing 14-23 is an applet that uses an `AudioClip` object to play a sound file. The file *AudioDemo2.html* can be used to start the applet. Figure 14-32 shows the applet running. The Play button calls the `AudioClip` object's `play` method, causing the sound file to play once. The Loop button calls the `loop` method, causing the sound file to be played repeatedly. The Stop button stops the sound file from playing. The sound file that is played is a famous NASA transmission from the Moon. NASA provides a wealth of public domain audio, video, and image files. You can find such items by going to www.nasa.gov, and then search the site using search terms such as "audio clips", "video clips", etc.

Code Listing 14-23   (`AudioDemo2.java`)

```java
 1 import java.awt.*;
 2 import java.applet.*;
 3 import java.awt.event.*;
 4 import javax.swing.*;
 5
 6 /**
 7    This applet uses the AudioClip class to play a
 8    sound. Sound source: NASA
 9 */
10
11 public class AudioDemo2 extends JApplet
12 {
13    private JLabel credit;         // Displays NASA credit
14    private JButton playButton;    // Plays the sound clip
15    private JButton loopButton;    // Loops the clip
16    private JButton stopButton;    // Stops the clip
17    private AudioClip sound;        // Holds the sound clip
18
19    /**
20       init method
21    */
22
23    public void init()
24    {
25       // Create a layout manager.
26       setLayout(new FlowLayout());
27
28       // Make the credit label and add it.
29       credit = new JLabel("Audio source: NASA");
30       add(credit);
31
32       // Make the buttons and add them.
33       makeButtons();
34
35       // Get an AudioClip object for the sound file.
36       sound = getAudioClip(getDocumentBase(), "step.wav");
37    }
38
```

```
39   /**
40       The makeButtons method creates the Play, Loop, and
41       Stop buttons, and adds them to the content pane.
42   */
43
44   private void makeButtons()
45   {
46       // Create the  Play, Loop, and Stop buttons.
47       playButton = new JButton("Play");
48       loopButton = new JButton("Loop");
49       stopButton = new JButton("Stop");
50
51       // Register an action listener with each button.
52       playButton.addActionListener(new ButtonListener());
53       loopButton.addActionListener(new ButtonListener());
54       stopButton.addActionListener(new ButtonListener());
55
56       // Add the  buttons to the content pane.
57       add(playButton);
58       add(loopButton);
59       add(stopButton);
60   }
61
62   /**
63       Private inner class that handles the action event
64       that is generated when the user clicks one of the
65       buttons.
66   */
67
68   private class ButtonListener implements ActionListener
69   {
70       public void actionPerformed(ActionEvent e)
71       {
72          // Determine which button was clicked and
73          // perform the selected action.
74          if (e.getSource() == playButton)
75             sound.play();
76          else if (e.getSource() == loopButton)
77             sound.loop();
78          else if (e.getSource() == stopButton)
79             sound.stop();
80       }
81   }
82 }
```

Figure 14-32 `AudioDemo2 applet`

Playing Audio in an Application

The previous examples show how to play an audio file in an applet. You can play audio in an application as well. The process of getting a reference to an `AudioClip` object is different, however, in a class that does not extend `JApplet`. In the *Chapter 14\AudioDemo3* folder on the Student CD you will find a Swing application named *AudioFrame.java* that demonstrates how to do it. The following code segment is from the application.

```
43        // Create a file object for the step.wav file.
44        File file = new File("step.wav");
45
46        // Get a URI object for the audio file.
47        URI uri = file.toURI();
48
49        // Get a URL for the audio file.
50        URL url = uri.toURL();
51
52        // Get an AudioClip object for the sound
53        // file using the Applet class's static
54        // newAudioClip method.
55        sound = Applet.newAudioClip(url);
```

In line 44 we create a `File` object representing the audio file. Then, in line 47 we call the File class's `toURI` method to create a `URI` object representing the audio file. The `URI` class is in the `java.net` package. (URI stands for Uniform Resource Identifier.)

Then, in line 50 we call the `URI` class's `toURL` method to create a `URL` object representing the audio file. Note that if this method cannot construct a `URL` it throws a checked exception—`MalformedURLException`. The `MalformedURLException` class is in the `java.net` package.

Last, in line 55 we call the `Applet` class's static `newAudioClip` method, passing the `URL` object as an argument. The method returns a reference to an `AudioClip` object which can be used as previously demonstrated to play the audio file.

Checkpoint

14.35 What Applet method can you use to play a sound file?

14.36 What is the difference between using the Applet method asked for in Checkpoint 14.35, and using an AudioClip object to play a sound file?

14.37 What methods do an AudioClip object have? What do they do?

14.38 What is the difference between the Applet class's getDocumentBase and getCodeBase methods?

14.9 Common Errors to Avoid

- **Forgetting a closing tag in an HTML document.** Most HTML tags have an opening tag and a closing tag. The page will not appear properly if you forget a closing tag.
- **Confusing the `<head></head>` tag with `<h1></h1>` or another header tag.** The `<head></head>` tag marks a document's head section, while the `<h1></h1>` tag marks a header, which is large bold text.
- **Using *X* and/or *Y* coordinates that are outside of the component when drawing a shape.** If you use coordinates that are outside the component to draw a shape, the shape will not appear.
- **Not calling the superclass's `paint` or `paintComponent` method.** When you override the paint or paintComponent methods, the overriding method should call the superclass's version of the method before doing anything else.
- **Overriding the `paint` method with a component extended from `JComponent`.** You should override the paint method only with AWT components, JFrame components, or JApplet components.
- **Not calling the `repaint` method to redisplay a window.** When you update the data used to draw shapes on a component, you must call the repaint method to force a call to the paint or paintComponent methods.
- **Not providing empty definitions for the unneeded methods in a mouse listener or mouse motion listener class.** When writing mouse listeners or mouse motion listeners, you must provide definitions for all the methods specified by the listener interfaces. To avoid this you can write a listener as a class that inherits from an adapter class.
- **Forgetting to start a `Timer` object.** A Timer object does not begin generating action events until it is started with a call to its start method.

Review Questions and Exercises

Multiple Choice and True/False

1. This section of an HTML document contains all of the tags and text that produce output in the browser window.
   a. head
   b. content
   c. body
   d. output

2. You place the `<title></title>` tag in this section of an HTML document.

   a. head
   b. content
   c. body
   d. output

3. Everything that appears between these tags in an HTML document is the content of the Web page.

   a. `<content></content>`
   b. `<html></html>`
   c. `<head></head>`
   d. `<page></page>`

4. To create a level one header you use this tag.

   a. `<level1></level1>`
   b. `<header1></header1>`
   c. `<h1></h1>`
   d. `<head></head>`

5. When using Swing to write an applet, you extend the applet's class from this class.

   a. `Applet`
   b. `JApplet`
   c. `JFrame`
   d. `JAppletFrame`

6. When using AWT to write an applet, you extend the applet's class from this class.

   a. `Applet`
   b. `JApplet`
   c. `JFrame`
   d. `JAppletFrame`

7. This applet method is invoked instead of a constructor.

   a. `startUp`
   b. `beginApplet`
   c. `invoke`
   d. `init`

8. The Sun JDK comes with this program, which loads and executes an applet without the need for a Web browser.

   a. `applettest`
   b. `appletload`
   c. `appletviewer`
   d. `viewapplet`

9. A class that inherits from `Applet` or `Frame` does not have one of these.

   a. an `add` method
   b. an `init` method
   c. a content pane
   d. a layout manager

10. What location on a component usually has the coordinates (0, 0)?
    a. upper-right corner
    b. upper-left corner
    c. center
    d. lower-right corner

11. In a class that extends `JApplet` or `JFrame` you override this method to get a reference to the `Graphics` object.
    a. `paint`
    b. `paintComponent`
    c. `getGraphics`
    d. `graphics`

12. In a class that extends `JPanel` you override this method to get a reference to the `Graphics` object.
    a. `paint`
    b. `paintComponent`
    c. `getGraphics`
    d. `graphics`

13. The `drawLine` method is a member of this class.
    a. `JApplet`
    b. `Applet`
    c. `JFrame`
    d. `Graphics`

14. To force the `paint` method to be called to update a component's display, you _____.
    a. call the `paint` method
    b. call the `repaint` method
    c. call the `paintAgain` method
    d. do nothing; you cannot force the `paint` method to be called

15. A class that implements this interface can handle mouse dragged events.
    a. `MouseListener`
    b. `ActionListener`
    c. `MouseMotionListener`
    d. `MouseDragListener`

16. A class that implements this interface can handle mouse click events.
    a. `MouseListener`
    b. `ActionListener`
    c. `MouseMotionListener`
    d. `MouseDragListener`

17. This `MouseEvent` method returns the X coordinate of the mouse cursor at the moment the mouse event is generated.
    a. `getXCoord`
    b. `getMouseX`

c. `getPosition`
d. `getX`

18. If a class implements a standard API interface that specifies more than one method but does not need many of the methods, this should be used instead of the interface.

    a. your own detailed versions of the needed methods
    b. an adapter class
    c. a different interface
    d. there is no other choice

19. A `Timer` object's time delay between events is specified in this unit of time.

    a. seconds
    b. microseconds
    c. milliseconds
    d. minutes

20. A `Timer` object generates this type of event.

    a. action events
    b. timer events
    c. item events
    d. interval events

21. The following `Applet` class method returns a `URL` object with the location of the HTML file that invoked the applet.

    a. `getHTMLlocation`
    b. `getDocumentBase`
    c. `getAppletBase`
    d. `getCodeBase`

22. The following `Applet` class method returns a `URL` object with the location of the applet's *.class* file.

    a. `getHTMLlocation`
    b. `getDocumentBase`
    c. `getAppletBase`
    d. `getCodeBase`

23. **True or False:** Applets cannot create files on the user's system.

24. **True or False:** Applets can read files on the user's system.

25. **True or False:** Applets cannot make network connections with any system except the server from which the applet was transmitted.

26. **True or False:** Applets can retrieve information about the user's system or the user's identity.

27. **True or False:** The `<h6>` tag produces larger text than the `<h1>` tag.

28. **True or False:** You use a static `main` method to create an instance of an applet class.

29. **True or False:** In a class that extends `JApplet`, you add components to the content pane.

30. **True or False:** In an applet, events are handled differently than in a GUI application.

31. **True or False:** An object of the `Frame` class does not have a content pane.

32. **True or False:** In an overriding `paint` method, you should never call the superclass's version of the `paint` method.

33. **True or False:** Once a `Timer` object has been started, it cannot be stopped without shutting down the program.

34. **True or False:** The `Applet` class's play method loads and plays an audio file once and then releases the memory it occupies for garbage collection.

35. **True or False:** The `loop` and `stop` methods, for use with audio files, are part of the `Applet` class.

Find the Error

Find the errors in the following code:

1. ```
   <applet code="MyApplet.java" width=100 height=50>
   </applet>
   ```

2. ```
   public void paint(Graphics g)
   {
       drawLine(0, 0, 100, 100);
   }
   ```

3. ```
   // Force a call to the paint method.
   paint();
   ```

4. ```
   public class MyPanel extends JPanel
   {
       public MyPanel()
       {
           // Constructor code...
       }

       public void paint(Graphics g)
       {
           // paint method code...
       {
   }
   ```

5. ```
   private class MyMouseListener implements MouseListener
   {
       public void mouseClicked(MouseEvent e)
       {
           mouseClicks += 1;
       }
   }
   ```
   ```

6. `private class MyMouseListener implements MouseAdapter`

```
{
    public void mouseClicked(MouseEvent e)
    {
        mouseClicks += 1;
    }
}
```

Algorithm Workbench

1. Write the text and HTML tags necessary to display "My Home Page" as a level one header, centered in the browser window.

2. You have written an applet and saved the source code in a file named `MyApplet.java`. Write the HTML tag needed to execute the applet in an area that is 300 pixels wide by 200 pixels high. Assume that the compiled applet code is stored in the same directory as the HTML document.

3. Look at the following GUI application class and indicate by line number the changes that should be made to convert this to an applet using Swing:

```
1 public class SimpleWindow extends JFrame
2 {
3     public SimpleWindow()
4     {
5         // Set the title.
6         setTitle("A Simple Window");
7
8         // Specify what happens when the close button is clicked.
9         setDefaultCloseOperation(JFrame.EXIT_ON_CLOSE);
10
11         // Add a label.
12         JLabel label = new JLabel("This is a simple window.");
13         add(label);
14
15         // Pack and display the window.
16         pack();
17         setVisible(true);
18     }
19 }
```

4. Assume that `g` references a `Graphics` object. Write code that performs the following:

   a. Draws an outline of a rectangle that is 100 pixels wide by 200 pixels high, with its upper-left corner at (50, 75).
   b. Draws a filled rectangle that is 300 pixels wide by 100 pixels high, with its upper-left corner at (10, 90).
   c. Draws a blue outline of an oval with an enclosing rectangle that is 100 pixels wide by 50 pixels high, with its upper-left corner at (10, 25).
   d. Draws a red line from (0, 5) to (150, 175).

e. Draws the string "Greetings Earthling". The lower-left point of the string should be at (80, 99). Use a bold, 20-point serif font.

f. Draws a polygon with vertices at the following points: (10, 10), (10, 25), (50, 25), and (50, 10). What shape does this code result in?

5. Rewrite the following mouse motion listener so it uses an adapter class:

```java
private class MyMouseMotionListener implements MouseMotionListener
{
    public void mouseDragged(MouseEvent e)
    {
    }

    public void mouseMoved(MouseEvent e)
    {
        mouseMovements += 1;
    }
}
```

6. Assume that a class has an inner class named `MyTimerListener` that can be used to handle the events generated by a `Timer` object. Write code that creates a `Timer` object with a time delay of one half second. Register an instance of `MyTimerListener` with the class.

Short Answer

1. When a user accesses a Web page on a remote server with his or her browser, and that Web page has an applet associated with it, is the applet executed by the server or by the user's system?

2. List at least three security restrictions imposed on applets.

3. Why are applets sometimes necessary in Web page development?

4. Why isn't it necessary to call the `setVisible` method to display an applet?

5. Why would you ever need to use the older AWT library instead of Swing to develop an applet?

6. A panel is 600 pixels wide by 400 pixels high. What are the X and Y coordinates of the pixel in the upper-left corner? The upper-right corner? The lower-left corner? The lower-right corner? The center of the panel?

7. When is a component's `paint` or `paintComponent` method called?

8. What is an adapter class? How does it make some programming tasks more convenient? Under what circumstances does the Java API provide an adapter class?

9. Under what circumstances would you want to use an `AudioClip` object to play a sound file, rather than the `Applet` class's play method?

Programming Challenges

1. FollowMe Applet

Write an applet that initially displays the word "Hello" in the center of a window. The word should follow the mouse cursor when it is moved inside the window.

VideoNote
The House
Applet Problem

2. House Applet

Write an applet that draws the house shown on the left in Figure 14-33. When the user clicks on the door or windows, they should close. The figure on the right shows the house with its door and windows closed.

3. WatchMe Applet

Write an applet that displays a drawing of two eyes in the center of its window. When the mouse cursor is not inside the window, the eyes should look ahead. When the mouse cursor is inside the window, the eyes should follow the cursor. This is illustrated in Figure 14-34.

Figure 14-33   House drawing

House with door and windows open.   House with door and windows closed.

Figure 14-34   Eyes following the mouse cursor

4. Thermometer Applet

Write an applet that displays a thermometer. The user should be able to control the temperature with a slider component. When the user moves the slider, the thermometer should show the corresponding temperature.

5. Polygon Drawer

Write an applet that lets the user click on six points. After the sixth point is clicked, the applet should draw a polygon with a vertex at each point the user clicked.

6. GridFiller Applet

Write an applet that displays a 4×4 grid. When the user clicks on a square in the grid, the applet should draw a filled circle in it. If the square already has a circle, clicking on it should cause the circle to disappear.

7. DrinkMachine Applet

Write an applet that simulates a soft drink vending machine. The simulated machine dispenses the following soft drinks: cola, lemon-lime soda, grape soda, root beer, and bottled water. These drinks cost $0.75 each to purchase.

When the applet starts, the drink machine should have a supply of 20 of each of the drinks. The applet should have a text field where the user can enter the amount of money he or she is giving the machine. The user can then click on a button to select a drink to dispense. The applet should also display the amount of change it is giving back to the user. The applet should keep track of its inventory of drinks and inform the user if he or she has selected a drink that is out of stock. Be sure to handle operator errors such as selecting a drink with no money entered and selecting a drink with an inadequate amount of money entered.

8. Stopwatch Applet

Write an applet that simulates a stopwatch. It should have a Start button and a Stop button. When the Start button is clicked the applet should count the seconds that pass. When the Stop button is clicked, the applet should stop counting seconds.

9. Slideshow Application

Write an application that displays a slideshow of images, one after the other, with a time delay between each image. The user should be able to select up to 10 images for the slide show and specify the time delay in seconds.

15.1 Introduction to Recursion

CONCEPT: A recursive method is a method that calls itself.

You have seen instances of methods calling other methods. Method A can call method B, which can then call method C. It's also possible for a method to call itself. A method that calls itself is a recursive method. Look at the message method in Code Listing 15-1.

Code Listing 15-1 (EndlessRecursion.java)

```
 1 /**
 2    This class has a recursive method.
 3 */
 4
 5 public class EndlessRecursion
 6 {
 7    public static void message()
 8    {
 9       System.out.println("This is a recursive method.");
10       message();
11    }
12 }
```

This method displays the string "This is a recursive method." and then calls itself. Each time it calls itself, the cycle is repeated. Can you see a problem with the method? There's no way to stop the recursive calls. This method is like an infinite loop because there is no code to stop it from repeating.

Like a loop, a recursive method must have some way to control the number of times it repeats. The class in Code Listing 15-2 has a modified version of the message method. It passes an integer argument, which holds the number of times the method should call itself.

Code Listing 15-2   (`Recursive.java`)

```
 1 /**
 2    This class has a recursive method, message,
 3    which displays a message n times.
 4 */
 5
 6 public class Recursive
 7 {
 8    public static void message(int n)
 9    {
10       if (n > 0)
11       {
12          System.out.println("This is a recursive method.");
13          message(n - 1);
14       }
15    }
16 }
```

This method contains an `if` statement that controls the repetition. As long as the n parameter is greater than zero, the method displays the message and calls itself again. Each time it calls itself, it passes n - 1 as the argument. For example, look at the program in Code Listing 15-3.

Code Listing 15-3   (`RecursionDemo.java`)

```
 1 /**
 2    This class demonstrates the Recursive.message method.
 3 */
 4
 5 public class RecursionDemo
 6 {
 7    public static void main(String[] args)
 8    {
 9       Recursive.message(5);
10    }
```

```
11 }
12
```

```
This is a recursive method.
This is a recursive method.
This is a recursive method.
This is a recursive method.
This is a recursive method.
```

The `main` method in this class calls the `Recursive.message` method with the argument 5, which causes the method to call itself five times. The first time the method is called, the `if` statement displays the message and then calls itself with 4 as the argument. Figure 15-1 illustrates this.

The diagram in Figure 15-1 illustrates two separate calls of the `message` method. Each time the method is called, a new instance of the n parameter is created in memory. The first time the method is called, the n parameter is set to 5. When the method calls itself, a new instance of n is created, and the value 4 is passed into it. This cycle repeats until finally, zero is passed to the method. This is illustrated in Figure 15-2.

Figure 15-1   First two calls of the method

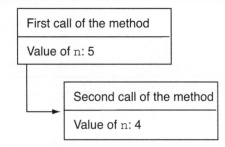

As you can see from Figure 15-2, the method is called a total of six times. The first time it is called from the `main` method of the `RecursionDemo` class, and the other five times it calls itself. The number of times that a method calls itself is known as the *depth of recursion*. In this example, the depth of recursion is five. When the method reaches its sixth call, the n parameter is set to 0. At that point, the `if` statement's conditional expression is `false`, so the method returns. Control of the program returns from the sixth instance of the method to the point in the fifth instance directly after the recursive method call. This is illustrated in Figure 15-3.

Because there are no more statements to be executed after the method call, the fifth instance of the method returns control of the program back to the fourth instance. This repeats until all instances of the method return.

Figure 15-2 Total of six calls to the **message** method

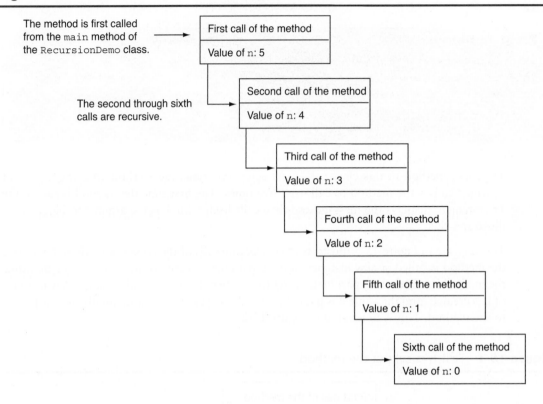

The method is first called from the main method of the RecursionDemo class.

First call of the method

Value of n: 5

The second through sixth calls are recursive.

Second call of the method

Value of n: 4

Third call of the method

Value of n: 3

Fourth call of the method

Value of n: 2

Fifth call of the method

Value of n: 1

Sixth call of the method

Value of n: 0

Figure 15-3 Control returns to the point after the recursive method call

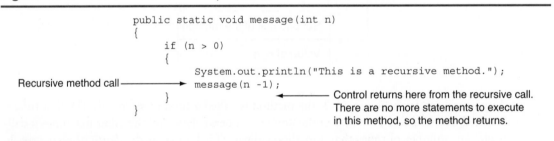

```
public static void message(int n)
{
    if (n > 0)
    {
        System.out.println("This is a recursive method.");
        message(n -1);
    }
}
```

Recursive method call ⟶ message(n -1);

Control returns here from the recursive call. There are no more statements to execute in this method, so the method returns.

15.2 Solving Problems with Recursion

CONCEPT: A problem can be solved with recursion if it can be broken down into successive smaller problems that are identical to the overall problem.

The Recursive and RecursionDemo classes shown in the previous section demonstrate the mechanics of a recursive method. Recursion can be a powerful tool for solving repetitive problems and is an important topic in upper-level computer science courses. What might not be clear to you yet is how to use recursion to solve a problem. First, it should be noted that recursion is never absolutely required to solve a problem. Any problem that can be solved recursively can also be solved iteratively, with a loop. In fact, recursive algorithms are usually less efficient than iterative algorithms. This is because a method call requires several actions to be performed by the JVM. These actions include allocating memory for parameters and local variables, and storing the address of the program location where control returns after the method terminates. These actions, which are sometimes referred to as overhead, take place with each method call. Such overhead is not necessary with a loop.

Some repetitive problems, however, are more easily solved with recursion than with iteration. Where an iterative algorithm might result in faster execution time, the programmer might be able to design a recursive algorithm faster.

In general, a recursive method works like this:

VideoNote
Reducing a
Problem with
Recursion

- If the problem can be solved now, without recursion, then the method solves it and returns.
- If the problem cannot be solved now, then the method reduces it to a smaller but similar problem and calls itself to solve the smaller problem.

In order to apply this approach, first we identify at least one case in which the problem can be solved without recursion. This is known as the *base case*. Second, we determine a way to solve the problem in all other circumstances using recursion. This is called the *recursive case*. In the recursive case, we must always reduce the problem to a smaller version of the original problem. By reducing the problem with each recursive call, the base case will eventually be reached and the recursion will stop.

Let's take an example from mathematics to examine an application of recursion. In mathematics, the notation $n!$ represents the factorial of the number n. The factorial of a nonnegative number can be defined by the following rules:

If $n = 0$ then $n! = 1$
If $n > 0$ then $n! = 1 \times 2 \times 3 \times \ldots \times n$

Let's replace the notation $n!$ with factorial(n), which looks a bit more like computer code, and rewrite these rules as follows:

If $n = 0$ then   factorial(n) = 1
If $n > 0$ then   factorial(n) = $1 \times 2 \times 3 \times \ldots \times n$

These rules state that when n is 0, its factorial is 1. When n is greater than 0, its factorial is the product of all the positive integers from 1 up to n. For instance, factorial(6) is calculated as $1 \times 2 \times 3 \times 4 \times 5 \times 6$.

When designing a recursive algorithm to calculate the factorial of any number, first we identify the base case, which is the part of the calculation that we can solve without recursion. That is the case where n is equal to 0 as follows:

If $n = 0$ then   factorial(n) = 1

This tells how to solve the problem when n is equal to 0, but what do we do when n is greater than 0? That is the recursive case, or the part of the problem that we use recursion to solve. This is how we express it:

If $n > 0$ then   factorial(n) = $n \times$ factorial($n - 1$)

This states that if *n* is greater than 0, the factorial of *n* is *n* times the factorial of *n* – 1. Notice how the recursive call works on a reduced version of the problem, *n* – 1. So, our recursive rule for calculating the factorial of a number might look like this:

If *n* = 0 then   factorial(*n*) = 1
If *n* > 0 then   factorial(*n*) = *n* × factorial(*n* – 1)

The following code shows how this might be implemented in a Java method:

```
private static int factorial(int n)
{
   if (n == 0)
      return 1;    // Base case
   else
      return n * factorial(n - 1);
}
```

The program in Code Listing 15-4 demonstrates the method. Figure 15-4 shows example interaction with the program.

Code Listing 15-4 (FactorialDemo.java)

```
 1 import javax.swing.JOptionPane;
 2
 3 /**
 4    This program demonstrates the recursive
 5    factorial method.
 6 */
 7
 8 public class FactorialDemo
 9 {
10    public static void main(String[] args)
11    {
12       String input;   // To hold user input
13       int number;     // To hold a number
14
15       // Get a number from the user.
16       input = JOptionPane.showInputDialog("Enter a " +
17                                    "nonnegative integer:");
18       number = Integer.parseInt(input);
19
20       // Display the factorial of the number.
21       JOptionPane.showMessageDialog(null,
22                   number + "! is " + factorial(number));
23
24       System.exit(0);
25    }
26
```

```
27    /**
28        The factorial method uses recursion to calculate
29        the factorial of its argument, which is assumed
30        to be a nonnegative number.
31        @param n The number to use in the calculation.
32        @return The factorial of n.
33    */
34
35    private static int factorial(int n)
36    {
37       if (n == 0)
38          return 1;   // Base case
39       else
40          return n * factorial(n - 1);
41    }
42 }
```

Figure 15-4   Interaction with the `FactorialDemo.java` program

In the example run of the program, the factorial method is called with the argument 4 passed into n. Because n is not equal to 0, the `if` statement's `else` clause executes the following statement:

```
return n * factorial(n - 1);
```

Although this is a `return` statement, it does not immediately return. Before the return value can be determined, the value of `factorial(n - 1)` must be determined. The `factorial` method is called recursively until the fifth call, in which the n parameter will be set to zero. The diagram in Figure 15-5 illustrates the value of n and the return value during each call of the method.

This diagram illustrates why a recursive algorithm must reduce the problem with each recursive call. Eventually the recursion has to stop in order for a solution to be reached. If each recursive call works on a smaller version of the problem, then the recursive calls work toward the base case. The base case does not require recursion, so it stops the chain of recursive calls.

Usually, a problem is reduced by making the value of one or more parameters smaller with each recursive call. In our `factorial` method, the value of the parameter n gets closer to 0 with each recursive call. When the parameter reaches 0, the method returns a value without making another recursive call.

Figure 15-5   Recursive calls to the factorial method

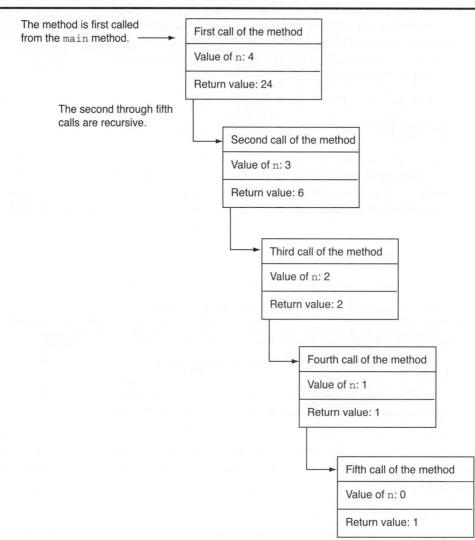

Direct and Indirect Recursion

The examples we have discussed so far show recursive methods that directly call themselves. This is known as direct recursion. There is also the possibility of creating indirect recursion in a program. This occurs when method A calls method B, which in turn calls method A. There can even be several methods involved in the recursion. For example, method A could call method B, which could call method C, which calls method A.

Checkpoint

15.1 It is said that a recursive algorithm has more overhead than an iterative algorithm. What does this mean?

15.2 What is a base case?

15.3   What is a recursive case?

15.4   What causes a recursive algorithm to stop calling itself?

15.5   What is direct recursion? What is indirect recursion?

15.3 Examples of Recursive Methods

Summing a Range of Array Elements with Recursion

In this example we look at a method, rangeSum, that uses recursion to sum a range of array elements. The method takes the following arguments: an int array that contains the range of elements to be summed, an int specifying the starting element of the range, and an int specifying the ending element of the range. Here is an example of how the method might be used:

```
int[] numbers = {1, 2, 3, 4, 5, 6, 7, 8, 9};
int sum;
sum = rangeSum(numbers, 3, 7);
```

This code specifies that rangeSum should return the sum of elements 3 through 7 in the numbers array. The return value, which in this case would be 30, is stored in sum. Here is the definition of the rangeSum method:

```
public static int rangeSum(int[] array, int start, int end)
{
   if (start > end)
      return 0;
   else
      return array[start] + rangeSum(array, start + 1, end);
}
```

This method's base case is when the start parameter is greater than the end parameter. If this is true, the method returns the value 0. Otherwise, the method executes the following statement:

```
return array[start] + rangeSum(array, start + 1, end);
```

This statement returns the sum of array[start] plus the return value of a recursive call. Notice that in the recursive call, the starting element in the range is start + 1. In essence, this statement says "return the value of the first element in the range plus the sum of the rest of the elements in the range." The program in Code Listing 15-5 demonstrates the method.

Code Listing 15-5   **(RangeSum.java)**

```
1 /**
2    This program demonstrates the recursive rangeSum method.
3 */
4
```

```
 5 public class RangeSum
 6 {
 7
 8    public static void main(String[] args)
 9    {
10       int[] numbers = { 1, 2, 3, 4, 5, 6, 7, 8, 9 };
11
12       System.out.print("The sum of elements 2 through " +
13                        "5 is "+ rangeSum(numbers, 2, 5));
14    }
15
16    /**
17       The rangeSum method calculates the sum of a specified
18       range of elements in array.
19       @param start Specifies the starting element.
20       @param end Specifies the ending element.
21       @return The sum of the range.
22    */
23
24    public static int rangeSum(int[] array, int start, int end)
25    {
26       if (start > end)
27          return 0;
28       else
29          return array[start] +
30                    rangeSum(array, start + 1, end);
31    }
32 }
```

Program Output

```
The sum of elements 2 through 5 is 18
```

Drawing Concentric Circles

In this example we look at the `Circles` applet, which uses recursion to draw concentric circles. Concentric circles are circles of different sizes, one inside another, all with a common center point. Figure 15-6 shows the applet's output. The applet code is shown in Code Listing 15-6.

Code Listing 15-6 (`Circles.java`)

```
1 import javax.swing.*;
2 import java.awt.*;
3
4 /**
5    This applet uses a recursive method to
6    draw concentric circles.
```

```
 7 */
 8
 9 public class Circles extends JApplet
10 {
11    /**
12       init method
13    */
14
15    public void init()
16    {
17       getContentPane().setBackground(Color.white);
18    }
19
20    /**
21       paint method
22       @param g The applet's Graphics object.
23    */
24
25    public void paint(Graphics g)
26    {
27       // Draw 10 concentric circles. The outermost
28       // circle's enclosing rectangle should be at
29       // (5, 5), and it should be 300 pixels wide
30       // by 300 pixels high.
31       drawCircles(g, 10, 5, 300);
32    }
33
34    /**
35       The drawCircles method draws concentric circles.
36       @param g A Graphics object.
37       @param n The number of circles to draw.
38       @param topXY The top left coordinates of the
39              outermost circle's enclosing rectangle.
40       @size The width and height of the outermost
41              circle's enclosing rectangle.
42    */
43
44    private void drawCircles(Graphics g, int n,
45                            int topXY, int size)
46    {
47       if (n > 0)
48       {
49          g.drawOval(topXY, topXY, size, size);
50          drawCircles(g, n - 1, topXY + 15, size - 30);
51       }
52    }
53 }
```

Figure 15-6   Circles applet

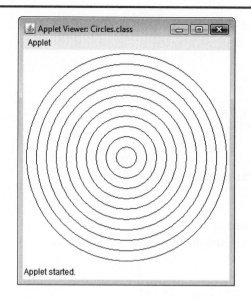

The `drawCircles` method, which is called from the applet's `paint` method, uses recursion to draw the concentric circles. The n parameter holds the number of circles to draw. When this parameter is set to 0, the method has reached its base case. Otherwise, it calls the g object's `drawOval` method to draw a circle. The `topXY` parameter holds the value to use as the X and Y coordinate of the enclosing rectangle's upper-left corner. The `size` parameter holds the value to use as the enclosing rectangle's width and height. After the circle is drawn, the `drawCircles` method is recursively called with parameter values adjusted for the next circle.

The Fibonacci Series

Some mathematical problems are designed to be solved recursively. One well-known example is the calculation of Fibonacci numbers. The Fibonacci numbers, named after the Italian mathematician Leonardo Fibonacci (born circa 1170), are the following sequence:

0, 1, 1, 2, 3, 5, 8, 13, 21, 34, 55, 89, 144, 233, . . .

Notice that after the second number, each number in the series is the sum of the two previous numbers. The Fibonacci series can be defined as follows:

If $n = 0$ then   Fib(n) = 0
If $n = 1$ then   Fib(n) = 1
If $n >= 2$ then   Fib(n) = Fib($n - 1$) + Fib($n - 2$)

A recursive Java method to calculate the nth number in the Fibonacci series is shown here:

```java
public static int fib(int n)
{
    if (n == 0)
        return 0;
```

```
        else if (n == 1)
            return 1;
        else
            return fib(n - 1) + fib(n - 2);
    }
```

Notice that this method actually has two base cases: when n is equal to 0, and when n is equal to 1. In either case, the method returns a value without making a recursive call. The program in Code Listing 15-7 demonstrates this method by displaying the first 10 numbers in the Fibonacci series.

Code Listing 15-7 (`FibNumbers.java`)

```java
 1 /**
 2     This program demonstrates the recursive fib method.
 3 */
 4
 5 public class FibNumbers
 6 {
 7    public static void main(String[] args)
 8    {
 9       System.out.println("The first 10 numbers in " +
10                          "the Fibonacci series are:");
11
12       for (int i = 0; i < 10; i++)
13          System.out.print(fib(i) + " ");
14
15       System.out.println();
16    }
17
18    /**
19       The fib method calculates the nth
20       number in the Fibonacci series.
21       @param n The nth number to calculate.
22       @return The nth number.
23    */
24
25    public static int fib(int n)
26    {
27       if (n == 0)
28          return 0;
29       else if (n == 1)
30          return 1;
31       else
32          return fib(n - 1) + fib(n - 2);
33    }
34 }
```

Program Output

Program Output

```
The first 10 numbers in the Fibonacci series are:
0 1 1 2 3 5 8 13 21 34
```

Finding the Greatest Common Divisor

Our next example of recursion is the calculation of the greatest common divisor, or GCD, of two numbers. The GCD of two positive integers, x and y, is as follows:

> if y divides x evenly, then $gcd(x, y) = y$
> Otherwise, $gcd(x, y) = gcd(y,$ remainder of $x/y)$

This definition states that the GCD of x and y is y if x/y has no remainder. This is the base case. Otherwise, the answer is the GCD of y and the remainder of x/y. The program in Code Listing 15-8 shows a recursive method for calculating the GCD.

Code Listing 15-8 (GCDdemo.java)

```java
 1 import java.util.Scanner;
 2
 3 /**
 4    This program demonstrates the recursive gcd method.
 5 */
 6
 7 public class GCDdemo
 8 {
 9    public static void main(String[] args)
10    {
11       int num1, num2; // Two numbers for GCD calculation
12
13       // Create a Scanner object for keyboard input.
14       Scanner keyboard = new Scanner(System.in);
15
16       // Get the first number from the user.
17       System.out.print("Enter an integer: ");
18       num1 = keyboard.nextInt();
19
20       // Get the second number from the user.
21       System.out.print("Enter another integer: ");
22       num2 = keyboard.nextInt();
23
24       // Display the GCD.
25       System.out.println("The greatest common divisor " +
26                          "of these two numbers is " +
27                          gcd(num1, num2));
28    }
29
30    /**
```

```
31          The gcd method calculates the greatest common
32          divisor of the arguments passed into x and y.
33          @param x A number.
34          @param y Another number.
35          @returns The greatest common divisor of x and y.
36      */
37
38      public static int gcd(int x, int y)
39      {
40          if (x % y == 0)
41              return y;
42          else
43              return gcd(y, x % y);
44      }
45 }
```

Program Output with Example Input Shown in Bold

```
Enter an integer: 49 [Enter]
Enter another integer: 28 [Enter]
The greatest common divisor of these two numbers is 7
```

15.4 A Recursive Binary Search Method

CONCEPT: The recursive binary search algorithm is more elegant and easier to understand than its iterative version.

In Chapter 8 you learned about the binary search algorithm and saw an iterative example written in Java. The binary search algorithm can also be implemented recursively. For example, the procedure can be expressed as:

If `array[middle]` *equals the search value, then the value is found.*
Else if `array[middle]` *is less than the search value, perform*
    a binary search on the upper half of the array.
Else if `array[middle]` *is greater than the search value, perform*
    a binary search on the lower half of the array.

When you compare the recursive algorithm to its iterative counterpart, it becomes evident that the recursive version is much more elegant and easier to understand. The recursive binary search algorithm is also a good example of repeatedly breaking a problem down into smaller pieces until it is solved. Here is the code for the method:

```
public static int binarySearch(int[] array, int first,
                               int last, int value)
{
    int middle;     // Mid point of search
    // Test for the base case where the
    // value is not found.
```

```
            if (first > last)
               return -1;
            // Calculate the middle position.
            middle = (first + last) / 2;
            // Search for the value.
            if (array[middle] == value)
               return middle;
            else if (array[middle] < value)
               return binarySearch(array, middle + 1,
                                       last, value);

            else
               return binarySearch(array, first,
                                       middle - 1, value);
      }
```

The first parameter, array, is the array to be searched. The next parameter, first, holds the subscript of the first element in the search range (the portion of the array to be searched). The next parameter, last, holds the subscript of the last element in the search range. The last parameter, value, holds the value to be searched for. Like the iterative version, this method returns the subscript of the value if it is found, or –1 if the value is not found. Program 15-9 demonstrates the method.

Code Listing 15-9   (RecursiveBinarySearch.java)

```java
 1 import java.util.Scanner;
 2
 3 /**
 4    This program demonstrates the recursive
 5    binary search method.
 6 */
 7
 8 public class RecursiveBinarySearch
 9 {
10    public static void main(String [] args)
11    {
12       int searchValue;  // The value to search for
13       int result;       // The search result
14       String input;     // A line of input
15       char again;       // To hold a single character
16
17       // The values in the following array are sorted
18       // in ascending order.
19       int numbers[] = {101, 142, 147, 189, 199, 207, 222,
20                        234, 289, 296, 310, 319, 388, 394,
21                        417, 429, 447, 521, 536, 600};
22
23       // Create a Scanner object for keyboard input.
24       Scanner keyboard = new Scanner(System.in);
```

```
25
26          do
27          {
28              // Get a value to search for.
29              System.out.print("Enter a value to " +
30                                  "search for: ");
31              searchValue = keyboard.nextInt();
32
33              // Search for the value
34              result = binarySearch(numbers, 0,
35                                      (numbers.length - 1),
36                                      searchValue);
37
38              // Display the results.
39              if (result == -1)
40              {
41                  System.out.println(searchValue +
42                                      " was not found.");
43              }
44              else
45              {
46                  System.out.println(searchValue +
47                                      " was found at " +
48                                      "element " + result);
49              }
50
51              // Does the user want to search again?
52              System.out.print("Do you want to search again? " +
53                                  "(Y or N): ");
54              // Consume the remaining newline.
55              keyboard.nextLine();
56              // Read a line of input.
57              input = keyboard.nextLine();
58
59          } while (input.charAt(0) == 'y' ||
60                      input.charAt(0) == 'Y');
61      }
62
63      /**
64          The binarySearch method performs a binary search
65          on an integer array.
66          @param array The array to search.
67          @param first The first element in the search range.
68          @param last The last element in the search range.
69          @param value The value to search for.
70          @return The subscript of the value if found,
71                      otherwise -1.
72      */
```

```
73
74      public static int binarySearch(int[] array, int first,
75                                     int last, int value)
76      {
77         int middle;       // Mid point of search
78
79         // Test for the base case where the
80         // value is not found.
81         if (first > last)
82            return -1;
83
84         // Calculate the middle position.
85         middle = (first + last) / 2;
86
87         // Search for the value.
88         if (array[middle] == value)
89            return middle;
90         else if (array[middle] < value)
91            return binarySearch(array, middle + 1,
92                                last, value);
93         else
94            return binarySearch(array, first,
95                                middle - 1, value);
96      }
97 }
```

Program Output with Example Input Shown in Bold

```
Enter a value to search for: 289 [Enter]
289 was found at element 8
Do you want to search again? (Y or N): y [Enter]
Enter a value to search for: 388 [Enter]
388 was found at element 12
Do you want to search again? (Y or N): y [Enter]
Enter a value to search for: 101 [Enter]
101 was found at element 0
Do you want to search again? (Y or N): y [Enter]
Enter a value to search for: 999 [Enter]
999 was not found.
Do you want to search again? (Y or N): n [Enter]
```

15.5 The Towers of Hanoi

CONCEPT: The repetitive steps involved in solving the Towers of Hanoi game can be easily implemented in a recursive algorithm.

The Towers of Hanoi is a mathematical game that is often used in computer science textbooks to illustrate the power of recursion. The game uses three pegs and a set of discs with holes through their centers. The discs are stacked on one of the pegs as shown in Figure 15-7.

Figure 15-7   The pegs and discs in the Towers of Hanoi game

Notice that the discs are stacked on the leftmost peg, in order of size with the largest disc at the bottom. The game is based on a legend where a group of monks in a temple in Hanoi have a similar set of pegs with 64 discs. The job of the monks is to move the discs from the first peg to the third peg. The middle peg can be used as a temporary holder. Furthermore, the monks must follow these rules while moving the discs:

- Only one disk may be moved at a time.
- A disk cannot be placed on top of a smaller disc.
- All discs must be stored on a peg except while being moved.

According to the legend, when the monks have moved all of the discs from the first peg to the last peg, the world will come to an end.

To play the game, you must move all of the discs from the first peg to the third peg, following the same rules as the monks. Let's look at some example solutions to this game, for different numbers of discs. If you only have one disc, the solution to the game is simple: move the disc from peg 1 to peg 3. If you have two discs, the solution requires three moves:

- Move disc 1 to peg 2.
- Move disc 2 to peg 3.
- Move disc 1 to peg 3.

Notice that this approach uses peg 2 as a temporary location. The complexity of the moves continues to increase as the number of discs increases. To move three discs requires the seven moves shown in Figure 15-8.

The following statement describes the overall solution to the problem:

Move n discs from peg 1 to peg 3 using peg 2 as a temporary peg.

The following algorithm can be used as the basis of a recursive method that simulates the solution to the game. Notice that in this algorithm we use the variables A, B, and C to hold peg numbers.

To move n discs from peg A to peg C, using peg B as a temporary peg:
If n > 0 then

Move n − 1 discs from peg A to peg B, using peg C as a temporary peg.
Move the remaining disc from peg A to peg C.
Move n − 1 discs from peg B to peg C, using peg A as a temporary peg.
End if

The base case for the algorithm is reached when there are no more discs to move. The following code is for a method that implements this algorithm. Note that the method does not actually move anything, but displays instructions indicating all of the disc moves to make.

```java
private void moveDiscs(int num, int fromPeg, int toPeg, int tempPeg)
{
    if (num > 0)
    {
        moveDiscs(num - 1, fromPeg, tempPeg, toPeg);
        System.out.println("Move a disc from peg " + fromPeg +
                           " to peg " + toPeg);
        moveDiscs(num - 1, tempPeg, toPeg, fromPeg);
    }
}
```

Figure 15-8 Steps for moving three pegs

Original setup.

First move: Move disc 1 to peg 3.

Second move: Move disc 2 to peg 2.

Third move: Move disc 1 to peg 2.

Fourth move: Move disc 3 to peg 3.

Fifth move: Move disc 1 to peg 1.

Sixth move: Move disc 2 to peg 3.

Seventh move: Move disc 1 to peg 3.

This method accepts arguments into the following four parameters:

`num`	The number of discs to move.
`fromPeg`	The peg to move the discs from.
`toPeg`	The peg to move the discs to.
`tempPeg`	The peg to use as a temporary peg.

If num is greater than 0, then there are discs to move. The first recursive call is as follows:

```
moveDiscs(num - 1, fromPeg, tempPeg, toPeg);
```

This statement is an instruction to move all but one disc from `fromPeg` to `tempPeg`, using `toPeg` as a temporary peg. The next statement is as follows:

```
System.out.println("Move a disc from peg " + fromPeg +
                    " to peg " + toPeg);
```

This simply displays a message indicating that a disc should be moved from `fromPeg` to `toPeg`. Next, another recursive call is executed as follows:

```
moveDiscs(num - 1, tempPeg, toPeg, fromPeg);
```

This statement is an instruction to move all but one disc from `tempPeg` to `toPeg`, using `fromPeg` as a temporary peg. Code Listing 15-10 shows the `Hanoi` class, which uses this method.

Code Listing 15-10 (`Hanoi.java`)

```
 1  /**
 2      This class displays a solution to the Towers of
 3      Hanoi game.
 4  */
 5
 6  public class Hanoi
 7  {
 8      private int numDiscs;    // Number of discs
 9
10      /**
11          Constructor.
12          @param n The number of discs to use.
13      */
14
15      public Hanoi(int n)
16      {
17          // Assign the number of discs.
18          numDiscs = n;
19
20          // Move the number of discs from peg 1 to peg 3
21          // using peg 2 as a temporary storage location.
22          moveDiscs(numDiscs, 1, 3, 2);
23      }
```

```
24
25     /**
26        The moveDiscs method displays a disc move.
27        @param num The number of discs to move.
28        @param fromPeg The peg to move from.
29        @param toPeg The peg to move to.
30        @param tempPeg The temporary peg.
31     */
32
33     private void moveDiscs(int num, int fromPeg,
34                           int toPeg, int tempPeg)
35     {
36        if (num > 0)
37        {
38           moveDiscs(num - 1, fromPeg, tempPeg, toPeg);
39           System.out.println("Move a disc from peg " +
40                              fromPeg + " to peg " + toPeg);
41           moveDiscs(num - 1, tempPeg, toPeg, fromPeg);
42        }
43     }
44 }
```

The class constructor accepts an argument, which is the number of discs to use in the game. It assigns this value to the numDiscs field, and then calls the moveDiscs method in line 22. In a nutshell, this statement is an instruction to move all the discs from peg 1 to peg 3, using peg 2 as a temporary peg. The program in Code Listing 15-11 demonstrates the class. It displays the instructions for moving three discs.

Code Listing 15-11 (HanoiDemo.java)

```
1 /**
2     This class demonstrates the Hanoi class, which
3     displays the steps necessary to solve the Towers
4     of Hanoi game.
5 */
6
7 public class HanoiDemo
8 {
9     static public void main(String[] args)
10    {
11        Hanoi towersOfHanoi = new Hanoi(3);
12    }
13 }
```

Program Output

```
Move a disc from peg 1 to peg 3
Move a disc from peg 1 to peg 2
Move a disc from peg 3 to peg 2
Move a disc from peg 1 to peg 3
Move a disc from peg 2 to peg 1
Move a disc from peg 2 to peg 3
Move a disc from peg 1 to peg 3
```

15.6 Common Errors to Avoid

- **Not coding a base case.** When the base case is reached, a recursive method stops calling itself. Without a base case, the method will continue to call itself infinitely.
- **Not reducing the problem with each recursive call.** Unless the problem is reduced (which usually means that the value of one or more critical parameters is reduced) with each recursive call, the method will not reach the base case. If the base case is not reached, the method will call itself infinitely.
- **Writing the recursive call in such a way that the base case is never reached.** You might have a base case and a recursive case that reduces the problem, but if the calculations are not performed in such a way that the base case is ultimately reached, the method will call itself infinitely.

Review Questions and Exercises

Multiple Choice and True/False

1. A method is called once from a program's `main` method, and then it calls itself four times. The depth of recursion is _____.
   a. one
   b. four
   c. five
   d. nine

2. This is the part of a problem that can be solved without recursion.
   a. base case
   b. solvable case
   c. known case
   d. iterative case

3. This is the part of a problem that is solved with recursion.
   a. base case
   b. iterative case
   c. unknown case
   d. recursion case

4. This is when a method explicitly calls itself.
    a. explicit recursion
    b. modal recursion
    c. direct recursion
    d. indirect recursion

5. This is when method A calls method B, which calls method A.
    a. implicit recursion
    b. modal recursion
    c. direct recursion
    d. indirect recursion

6. This refers to the actions taken internally by the JVM when a method is called.
    a. overhead
    b. set up
    c. clean up
    d. synchronization

7. **True or False:** An iterative algorithm will usually run faster than an equivalent recursive algorithm.

8. **True or False:** Some problems can be solved through recursion only.

9. **True or False:** It is not necessary to have a base case in all recursive algorithms.

10. **True or False:** In the base case, a recursive method calls itself with a smaller version of the original problem.

Find the Error

1. Find the error in the following program:

```java
public class FindTheError
{
    public static void main(String[] args)
    {
        myMethod(0);
    }
    public static void myMethod(int num)
    {
        System.out.print(num + " ");
        myMethod(num + 1);
    }
}
```

Algorithm Workbench

1. Write a method that accepts a `String` as an argument. The method should use recursion to display each individual character in the `String`.

2. Modify the method you wrote in Algorithm Workbench 1 so it displays the `String` backwards.

3. What will the following program display?

```java
public class Checkpoint
{
    public static void main(String[] args)
    {
        int num = 0;
        showMe(num);
    }
    public static void showMe(int arg)
    {
        if (arg < 10)
            showMe(arg + 1);
        else
            System.out.println(arg);
    }
}
```

4. What will the following program display?

```java
public class Checkpoint
{
    public static void main(String[] args)
    {
        int num = 0;
        showMe(num);
    }
    public static void showMe(int arg)
    {
        System.out.println(arg);
        if (arg < 10)
            showMe(arg + 1);
    }
}
```

5. What will the following program display?

```java
public class ReviewQuestion5
{
    public static void main(String[] args)
    {
        int x = 10;
        System.out.println(myMethod(x));
    }
    public static int myMethod(int num)
    {
        if (num <= 0)
            return 0;
        else
```

```
                    return myMethod(num - 1) + num;
        }
    }
```

6. Convert the following iterative method to one that uses recursion:

```
public static void sign(int n)
{
    while (n > 0)
    {
        System.out.println("No Parking");
        n--;
    }
}
```

7. Write an iterative version (using a loop instead of recursion) of the `factorial` method shown in this chapter.

Short Answer

1. What is the difference between an iterative algorithm and a recursive algorithm?

2. What is a recursive algorithm's base case? What is the recursive case?

3. What is the base case of each of the recursive methods listed in Algorithm Workbench 3, 4, and 5?

4. What type of recursive method do you think would be more difficult to debug: one that uses direct recursion or one that uses indirect recursion? Why?

5. Which repetition approach is less efficient: a loop or a recursive method? Why?

6. When recursion is used to solve a problem, why must the recursive method call itself to solve a smaller version of the original problem?

7. How is a problem usually reduced with a recursive method?

Programming Challenges

myCodeMate

1. Recursive Multiplication

Write a recursive function that accepts two arguments into the parameters x and y. The function should return the value of x times y. Remember, multiplication can be performed as repeated addition as follows:

$$7 * 4 = 4 + 4 + 4 + 4 + 4 + 4 + 4$$

2. isMember Method

Write a recursive `boolean` method named `isMember`. The method should search an array for a specified value, and return `true` if the value is found in the array, or `false` if the value is not found in the array. Demonstrate the method in a program.

3. String Reverser

Write a recursive method that accepts a string as its argument and prints the string in reverse order. Demonstrate the method in a program.

4. `maxElement` Method

Write a method named `maxElement`, which returns the largest value in an array that is passed as an argument. The method should use recursion to find the largest element. Demonstrate the method in a program.

5. Palindrome Detector

A palindrome is any word, phrase, or sentence that reads the same forward and backward. Here are some well-known palindromes:

> Able was I, ere I saw Elba
> A man, a plan, a canal, Panama
> Desserts, I stressed
> Kayak

Write a `boolean` method that uses recursion to determine if a `String` argument is a palindrome. The method should return `true` if the argument reads the same forward and backward. Demonstrate the method in a program.

6. Character Counter

Write a method that uses recursion to count the number of times a specific character occurs in an array of characters. Demonstrate the method in a program.

7. Recursive Power Method

Write a method that uses recursion to raise a number to a power. The method should accept two arguments: the number to be raised and the exponent. Assume that the exponent is a nonnegative integer. Demonstrate the method in a program.

VideoNote
The Recursive
Power Problem

8. Sum of Numbers

Write a method that accepts an integer argument and returns the sum of all the integers from 1 up to the number passed as an argument. For example, if 50 is passed as an argument, the method will return the sum of 1, 2, 3, 4, . . . 50. Use recursion to calculate the sum. Demonstrate the method in a program.

9. Ackermann's Function

Ackermann's function is a recursive mathematical algorithm that can be used to test how well a computer performs recursion. Write a method `ackermann(m, n)`, which solves Ackermann's function. Use the following logic in your method:

> If m = 0 then return n + 1
> If n = 0 then return `ackermann(m - 1, 1)`
> Otherwise, return `ackermann(m - 1, ackermann(m, n - 1))`

Test your method in a program that displays the return values of the following method calls:

```
ackermann(0, 0)   ackermann(0, 1)   ackermann(1, 1)   ackermann(1, 2)
ackermann(1, 3)   ackermann(2, 2)   ackermann(3, 2)
```

10. Recursive Population Class

In Programming Challenge 9 of Chapter 4 you wrote a population class that predicts the size of a population of organisms after a number of days. Modify the class so it uses a recursive method instead of a loop to calculate the number of organisms.

Index